Praveen K
Sharma
12/15/98

CCIE Professional Development:

Routing TCP/IP, Volume I

Jeff Doyle

CISCO SYSTEMS

CISCO PRESS

M
T | P
MACMILLAN
TECHNICAL
PUBLISHING
U·S·A

Macmillan Technical Publishing
201 West 103rd Street
Indianapolis, IN 46290 USA

CCIE Professional Development: Routing TCP/IP, Volume I

Jeff Doyle

Copyright © 1998 by Macmillan Technical Publishing

Cisco Press logo is a trademark of Cisco Systems, Inc.

Published by:
Macmillan Technical Publishing
201 West 103rd Street
Indianapolis, IN 46290 USA

Printed in the United States of America 1 2 3 4 5 6 7 8 9 0

Library of Congress Cataloging-in-Publication Number 98-84220

ISBN: 1-57870-041-8

Warning and Disclaimer

This book is designed to provide information about **TCP/IP**. Every effort has been made to make this book as complete and as accurate as possible, but no warranty or fitness is implied.

The information is provided on an "as is" basis. The author, Macmillan Technical Publishing, and Cisco Systems, Inc. shall have neither liability nor responsibility to any person or entity with respect to any loss or damages arising from the information contained in this book or from the use of the discs or programs that may accompany it.

The opinions expressed in this book belong to the author and are not necessarily those of Cisco Systems, Inc.

Feedback Information

At Cisco Press, our goal is to create in-depth technical books of the highest quality and value. Each book is crafted with care and precision, undergoing rigorous development that involves the unique expertise of members from the professional technical community.

Readers' feedback is a natural continuation of this process. If you have any comments regarding how we could improve the quality of this book, or otherwise alter it to better suit your needs, you can contact us at ciscopress@mcp.com. Please make sure to include the book title and ISBN in your message.

We greatly appreciate your assistance.

Associate Publisher	Jim LeValley
Executive Editor	Julie Fairweather
Cisco Systems Program Manager	H. Kim Lew
Managing Editor	Caroline Roop
Acquisitions Editor	Tracy Hughes
	Lynette Quinn
Development Editor	Kezia Endsley
Project Editor	Brad Herriman
Technical Editor(s)	Jennifer DeHaven Carroll
	Mike Tibodeau
Team Coordinator	Amy Lewis
Book Designer	Trina Wurst
Cover Designer	Karen Ruggles
Production Team	Argosy
Indexer	Kevin Fulcher

Trademark Acknowledgments

All terms mentioned in this book that are known to be trademarks or service marks have been appropriately capitalized. Macmillan Technical Publishing or Cisco Systems, Inc. cannot attest to the accuracy of this information. Use of a term in this book should not be regarded as affecting the validity of any trademark or service mark.

Dedications

This book would not have been possible without the concerted efforts of many dedicated people. I would like to thank the following people for their contributions:

First, thanks to Laurie McGuire, development editor, who not only improved the book but improved me as a writer.

Thanks to Jenny DeHaven Carroll and Mike Tibodeau for their careful technical editing. I would also like to thank the following people, who provided technical advice or reviews on selected sections of the book: Howard Berkowitz, Dave Katz, Burjiz Pithawala, Mikel Ravizza, Russ White, and Man-Kit Yueng.

I would like to thank the following people at Macmillan Technical Publishing: Tracy Hughes and Lynette Quinn, who managed the project, and Julie Fairweather, the Executive Editor. In addition to being highly competent, they are three of the nicest people anyone could hope to work with. Also, thanks to Jim LeValley, Associate Publisher, who first approached me about writing this book.

Thanks to Wandel & Golterman, and to Gary Archuleta, W&G's Regional Sales Manager in Denver, for arranging the use of one of their excellent protocol analyzers for the length of the project.

Finally, I want to thank my wife, Sara, and my children: Anna, Carol, James, and Katherine. Their patience, encouragement, and support were critical to the completion of this book.

About the Author

Jeff Doyle is a Senior Network Systems Consultant with International Network Services (INS) in Denver, Colorado. He is a Cisco Certified Internetwork Expert (CCIE # 1919) and a Certified Cisco Systems Instructor. He has developed and taught a variety of networking and internetworking courses.

About the Reviewers

Jennifer DeHaven Carroll is a principal consultant for International Network Services. She is CCIE number 1402. Jennifer has planned, designed and implemented many IP networks over the past 10 years, utilizing RIP version 2, IGRP, E-IGRP, OSPF and BGP. She has also developed and taught theory and Cisco implementation classes on all IP routing protocols.

Michael Tibodeau is a Systems Engineer for Cisco Systems. Over the past two years, Michael has specialized in security technologies for both his own customers and Networkers audiences. He also focuses on the Electronic Commerce and Quality of Service arenas. Michael holds a Bachelor's degree in Systems Engineering from the University of Virginia and holds a Master's degree in Systems Engineering and Management, concentrating on telecommunications.

Table of Contents

Introduction

Routing is an essential element of all but the smallest data communications networks. At one level, routing and the configuration of routers are quite simple. But as internetworks grow in size and complexity, routing issues can become at once both large and subtle. Perversely, perhaps, I am grateful for the difficult problems large-scale routing can present—as a network systems consultant, these problems are my bread and butter. Without them, the phrase "You want fries with that?" could be an unfortunate part of my daily vocabulary.

Cisco Certified Internetwork Experts are widely recognized for their ability to design, troubleshoot, and manage large internetworks. This recognition comes from the fact that you cannot become a CCIE by attending a few classes and then regurgitating some memorized facts onto a written test. A CCIE has proven his or her expertise in an intense, famously difficult hands-on lab exam.

OBJECTIVES

This book is the first in a series designed to aid you in becoming a Cisco Certified Internetwork Expert and the first of two volumes that focuses on TCP/IP routing issues. Early in the project, Kim Lew, Cisco Systems program manager, said, "Our objective is to make CCIEs, not to make people who can pass the CCIE lab." I entirely agree with that statement and have used it as a guiding principle throughout the writing of this book. Although the book includes many case studies and exercises to help you prepare for the CCIE lab, my primary objective is to increase your understanding of IP routing—both on a generic level and as it is implemented on Cisco routers.

AUDIENCE

The audience for this book is any network designer, administrator, or engineer who needs a full understanding of the interior routing protocols of TCP/IP. Although the practical aspects of the book focus on Cisco's IOS, the information is applicable to any routing platform.

The book is not only for readers who plan to become Cisco Certified Internetwork Experts, but for anyone who wishes to advance his or her knowledge of TCP/IP routing. These readers will fall into one of three categories:

- The "beginner" who has some basic networking knowledge and wishes to begin a deep study of internetworking

- The intermediate-level networking professional who has experience with routers, Cisco or otherwise, and plans to advance that experience to the expert level

- The highly experienced networking expert. This individual has extensive hands-on expertise with Cisco routers and is ready to take the CCIE lab; however, he or she wants a structured review and series of exercises for verification and validation.

CCIE Professional Development: Routing TCP/IP, Volume I focuses primarily on the intermediate-level networking professional while offering to the beginner a structured outline of fundamental information and to the expert the required challenges to hone his or her skills.

ORGANIZATION

The fourteen chapters of the book are divided into three parts.

Part I examines the basics of networks and routing. Although more advanced readers may wish to skip the first two chapters, I recommend that they at least skim Chapter 3, "Static Routing," and Chapter 4, "Dynamic Routing Protocols."

Part II covers the TCP/IP Interior Gateway Protocols. Each protocol-specific chapter begins with a discussion of the mechanics and parameters of the protocol. This general overview is followed by case studies on configuring and troubleshooting the protocol on Cisco routers in various network topologies.

The Exterior Gateway Protocols, as well as such topics as multicast routing, Quality of Service routing, router security and management, and routing IPv6 will be covered in Volume II.

Part III examines the tools available for creating and managing interoperability with multiple IP routing protocols, as well as such tools as default routes and route filtering. These chapters, like the ones in Part II, begin with concepts and conclude with case studies.

CONVENTIONS AND FEATURES

Most chapters conclude with a set of review questions, configuration exercises, and troubleshooting exercises. The review questions focus on the theoretical aspects of the chapter topic, whereas the configuration and troubleshooting exercises address Cisco-specific aspects of the chapter topic.

Also at the end of each chapter is a table with a brief description of all important Cisco IOS commands used in that chapter. The conventions used to present these commands are the same conventions used in the IOS Command Reference. The Command Reference describes these conventions as follows:

- Vertical bars (I) separate alternative, mutually exclusive, elements.

- Square brackets [] indicate optional elements.

- Braces {} indicate a required choice.

- Braces within square brackets [{}] indicate a required choice within an optional element.

- **Boldface** indicates commands and keywords that are entered literally as shown.

- *Italics* indicate arguments for which you supply values.

Important concepts are called out in margin notes for quick reference.

Figure I.1 shows the conventions used in the illustrations throughout the book.

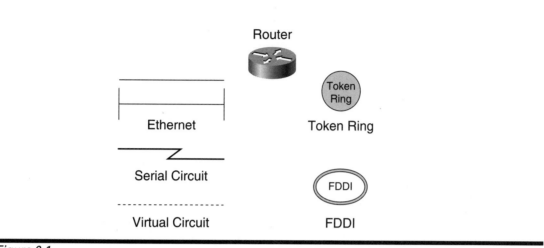

Figure 0.1
Illustration conventions used in this book.

All protocol analyzer displays shown in the book are taken from a Wandel & Goltermann DA-320 DominoLAN Internetwork Analyzer.

Foreword

In today's world of networking, mission-critical networks are being designed for data, voice, and video. Due to different traffic patterns and the quality of service required by each type of information, solid hands-on experience is imperative for managing, designing, and troubleshooting these networks.

Attaining a strong degree of hands-on experience translates into in-depth understanding of the concepts, scalability, and deployment issues of today's networks. Such experience also builds the expertise to analyze traffic patterns and the knowledge of when, where, and how to apply protocol and bandwidth features to enhance performance.

To help further your hands-on experience, Cisco Press is publishing the CCIE Professional Development series of books. Books in this series will significantly help your understanding of protocol concepts, and they provide real-world examples and case studies to strengthen the theoretical concepts examined. I highly recommend that you use these books as a hands-on learning tool by duplicating the examples and case studies using Cisco products. You can even take this further by tweaking the configuration parameters to see which changes each network goes through by using the extensive debugging features provided in each Cisco product.

In the first book of the CCIE Professional Development series, *CCIE Professional Development: Routing TCP/IP, Volume I,* Jeff Doyle does a fantastic job of building the TCP/IP concepts, from IP address classes to analyzing protocol metrics. Each chapter contains examples, network topologies with IP addresses, packet analysis, and Cisco debugging outputs. In my opinion, the best parts are the case studies, in which Jeff compares different features of the protocol by using more or less the similar topology. This generates a strong understanding of the protocol concepts and features.

I recommend *CCIE Professional Development: Routing TCP/IP, Volume I* for any networking certification, and I believe that it also makes an excellent university networking course book.

Imran Qureshi
CCIE Program Manager

PART I

Routing Basics

- Bicycles with Motors

- Data Link Addresses

- Repeaters and Bridges

- Routers

- Network Addresses

CHAPTER 1

Basic Concepts: Internetworks, Routers, and Addresses

Once upon a time, computing power and data storage were centralized. Mainframes were locked away in climate-controlled, highly secure rooms, watched over by a priesthood of IS administrators. Contact with a computer was typically accomplished by bringing a stack of Hollerith cards to the priests, who interceded on our behalf with the Big Kahuna.

The advent of the minicomputer took the computers out of the IS temple of corporations and universities and brought them to the departmental level. For a mere $100K or two, engineering and accounting and any other department with a need for data processing could have their own machines.

Following on the heels of the minicomputers were microcomputers, bringing data processing right to the desktop. Affordability and accessibility dropped from the departmental level to the individual level, making the phrase *personal computer* part of everyone's vocabulary.

Desktop computing has evolved at a mind-boggling pace, but it was certainly not an immediate alternative to centralized, mainframe-based computing. There was a ramping-up period in which both software and hardware had to be developed to a level where personal computers could be taken seriously.

BICYCLES WITH MOTORS

One of the difficulties of decentralized computing is that it isolates users from one another and from the data and applications they may need to use in common. When a file is created, how is it shared with Tom, Dick, and Harriet down the hall? The early solution to this was the storied SneakerNet: Put the file on floppy disks and hand carry them to the necessary destinations. But what happens when Tom, Dick, and Harriet modify their copies of the file? How does one ensure that all information in all versions are synchronized? What if those three coworkers are on different floors or in different buildings or cities? What if the file needs to be updated several times a day? What if there are not three coworkers, but 300 people? What if all 300 people occasionally need to print a hard copy of some modification they have made to the file?

The *local-area network*, or LAN, is a small step back to centralization. LANs are a means of pooling and sharing resources. Servers enable everyone to access a common copy of a file or a common database; no more "walkabouts" with floppies, no more worries about inconsistent information. E-mail furnishes a compromise between phone calls, which require the presence of the recipient, and physical mail service, which is called snail mail for a good reason. The sharing of printers and modem pools eliminates the need for expensive, periodically used services on every desk.

Of course, in their infancy, LANs met with more than a little derision from the mainframe manufacturers. A commonly heard jibe during the early years was, "A LAN is like a bike with a motor, and we don't make Mopeds!" What a difference a few years and a few billion dollars would make.

Physically, a LAN accomplishes resource pooling among a group of devices by connecting them to a common, shared medium, or *data link*. This medium may be twisted-pair wires (shielded or unshielded), coaxial cable, optical fiber, infrared light, or whatever. What matters is that all devices attach commonly to the data link through some sort of network interface.

Data link

A shared physical medium is not enough. Rules must govern how the data link is shared. As in any community, a set of rules is necessary to keep life orderly, to ensure that all parties behave themselves, and to guarantee that everyone gets a fair share of the available resources. For a local-area network, this set of rules, or *protocol*, is generally called a *Media Access Control* (MAC). The MAC, as the name implies, dictates how each machine will access and share a given medium.

So far, a LAN has been defined as being a community of devices such as PCs, printers, and servers coexisting on a common communications medium and following a common protocol that regulates how they access the medium. But there is one last requirement: As in any community, each individual must be uniquely identifiable.

DATA LINK ADDRESSES

In a certain community in Colorado, two individuals are named Jeff Doyle. One Jeff Doyle frequently receives telephone calls for the person with whom he shares a name—so much so that his clever wife has posted the correct number next to the phone to redirect errant callers to their desired destination. In other words, because two individuals cannot be uniquely identified, data is occasionally delivered incorrectly and a process must be implemented to correct the error.

Among family, friends, and associates, a given name is usually sufficient for accurately distinguishing individuals. However, as this example shows, most names become inaccurate over a larger population. A more unique identifier, such as a United States Social Security number, is needed to distinguish one person from every other.

Devices on a LAN must also be uniquely and individually identified or they, like humans sharing the same name, will receive data not intended for them. When data is to be delivered on a LAN, it

Frame

is encapsulated within an entity called a *frame*, a kind of binary envelope. Think of data encapsulation as being the digital equivalent of placing a letter inside an envelope, as in Figure 1.1[1]. A destination address and a return (source) address are written on the outside of the envelope. Without a destination address, the postal service would have no idea where to deliver the letter. Likewise, when a frame is placed on a data link, all devices attached to the link "see" the frame; therefore, some mechanism must indicate which device should pick up the frame and read the enclosed data.

Figure 1.2 shows the format of most common LAN frames. Notice that every case includes a destination address and a source address. The format of the address depends on the particular MAC protocol, but all the addresses serve the same purpose: to uniquely identify the machine for which the frame is destined and the device from which it was sent.

The three most common data links currently used in LANs are Ethernet, Token Ring, and FDDI. Although each link is drastically different from the others, they share a common format for addressing devices on the network. This format, originally standardized by Xerox's Palo Alto Research Center (PARC)[2] and now administered by the Institute of Electrical and Electronics Engineers

---

[1]   As will be seen later, creating a data link layer frame is really more like putting an envelope inside a larger envelope.

[2]   The full name, as reading any modern text on networking will tell you, is The Now Famous Xerox PARC.

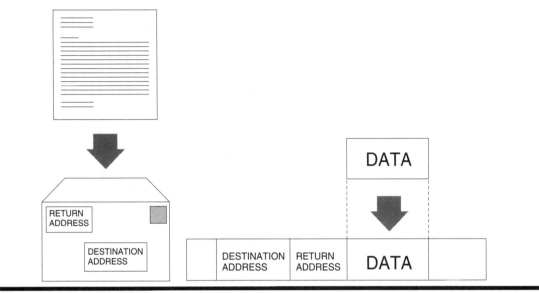

Figure 1.1
Encapsulation means putting data into a frame—a kind of digital "envelope" for delivery.

(IEEE), is variously called the burned-in address,[3] the physical address, the machine address, or most commonly, the MAC address.

The MAC address is a 48-bit number, which, as Figure 1.3 shows, is designed so that every device anywhere on the planet should be uniquely identifiable. Most everyone has heard the legends of large batches of network interface cards being turned out with identical burned-in addresses by unscrupulous "cloning" companies or as the result of "stuck" programming code. Although most of those stories are nothing more than legends, one can imagine what would happen if all devices on a LAN had the same MAC address: Imagine a town in which every resident is named Wessvick Smackley. Men, women, children, dogs, and cats all named

---

[3] *The address is usually permanently programmed, or burned in, to a ROM on the network interface.*

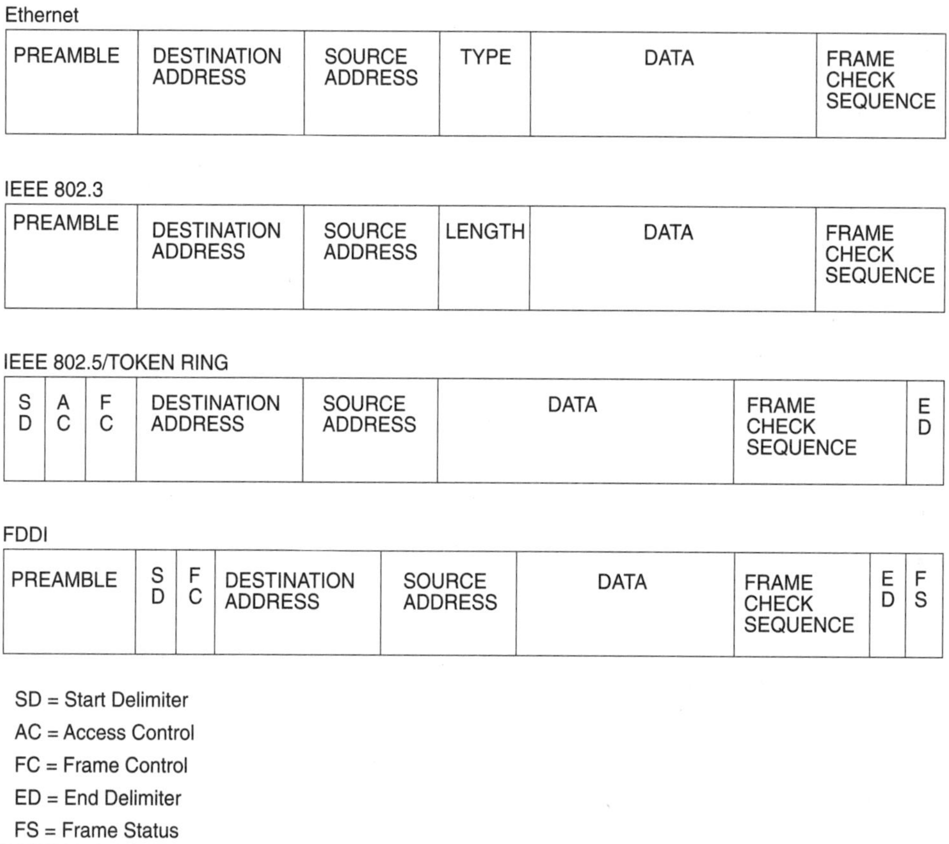

Ethernet

PREAMBLE	DESTINATION ADDRESS	SOURCE ADDRESS	TYPE	DATA	FRAME CHECK SEQUENCE

IEEE 802.3

PREAMBLE	DESTINATION ADDRESS	SOURCE ADDRESS	LENGTH	DATA	FRAME CHECK SEQUENCE

IEEE 802.5/TOKEN RING

S D	A C	F C	DESTINATION ADDRESS	SOURCE ADDRESS	DATA	FRAME CHECK SEQUENCE	E D

FDDI

PREAMBLE	S D	F C	DESTINATION ADDRESS	SOURCE ADDRESS	DATA	FRAME CHECK SEQUENCE	E D	F S

SD = Start Delimiter

AC = Access Control

FC = Frame Control

ED = End Delimiter

FS = Frame Status

Figure 1.2

The frame format of a few common LAN data link frames.

Wessvick Smackley. Everyday communication, not to mention the career of the town gossip, would be unimaginably difficult.[4]

Although the MAC addresses are by convention referred to as "addresses," they are really names. Think about it: Because the

---

[4] In real life, duplicate MAC addresses on a network are most likely to occur as the result of network administrators using locally administered addresses. This occurrence is common enough on Token Ring networks that one step of the Token Ring insertion process is a duplicate address check.

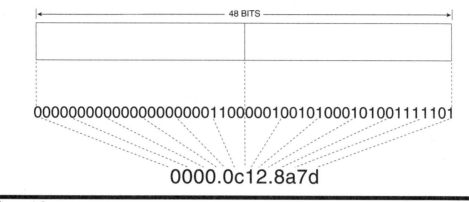

Figure 1.3
A MAC address.

identifier is burned in, or permanently assigned, to a device, it is a part of that device and goes wherever the device goes.[5]

Most adults have several street addresses through their lives, but few have more than one given name. A name identifies an entity—whether a person or a PC. An address describes where that person or PC is located.

In the interest of clarity, this book uses the term *data link identifier* or *MAC identifier* instead of MAC address. The reason for making such a distinction will soon be clear.

REPEATERS AND BRIDGES

The information presented so far may be distilled into a few brief statements:

- A data communication network is a group of two or more devices connected by a common, shared medium.

---

[5]   *Although some data link addresses may be or must be administratively configured, the point is that they are identifiers, unique within a network.*

- These devices have an agreed-upon set of rules, usually called the Media Access Control, or MAC, that govern how the media is shared.

- Each and every device has an identifier, and each identifier is unique to only one device.

- Using these identifiers, the devices communicate by encapsulating the data they need to send within a virtual envelope called a *frame*.

So here's this wonderful resource-sharing tool called a LAN. It's so wonderful, in fact, that everyone wants to be connected to it. And herein is the rub. As a LAN grows, new problems present themselves.

The first problem is one of physical distance. Figure 1.4 shows that three factors can influence an electrical signal. These factors may decrease or eliminate any intelligence the signal represents:

- Attenuation

- Interference

- Distortion

As the distance the signal must travel down the wire increases, so do the degrading effects of these three factors. Photonic pulses traveling along an optical fiber are much less susceptible to interference but will still succumb to attenuation and distortion.

Repeaters are added to the wire at certain intervals to alleviate the difficulties associated with excessive distance. A repeater is placed on the media some distance from the signal source but still near enough to be able to correctly interpret the signal (see Figure 1.5). It then repeats the signal by producing a new, clean copy of the old degraded signal. Hence, the name *repeater*.

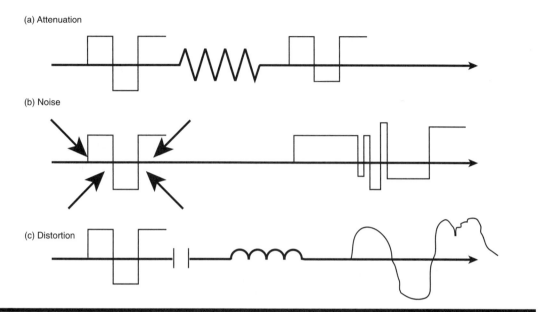

Figure 1.4

Attenuation, interference, and distortion prevent a signal from arriving in the same shape it was in when it left. Attenuation (a) is a function of the resistance of the wire. A certain amount of signal energy must be spent "pushing past" the resistance. Interference (b) is a function of outside influences—noise—which adds characteristics to the signal that should not be there. Distortion (c) is a function of the wire impeding different frequency components of the signal in different ways.

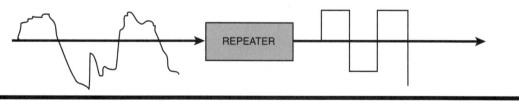

Figure 1.5

By placing a repeater in the link at a distance where the original signal can still be recognized, despite the effects of attenuation, interference, and distortion, a fresh signal can be generated and the length of the wire extended.

A repeater may be thought of as part of the physical medium. It has no real intelligence, but merely regenerates a signal; a digital repeater is sometimes facetiously called a "bit spitter" for this reason.

The second problem associated with growing LANs is congestion. Repeaters are added to extend the distance of the wire and to add devices; however, the fundamental reason for having a LAN is to share resources. When a too-large population tries to share limited resources, the rules of polite behavior begin to be violated and conflicts erupt. Among humans, poverty, crime, and warfare may result. On Ethernet networks, collisions deplete the available bandwidth. On Token Ring and FDDI networks, the token rotation time and timing jitter may become prohibitively high.

Drawing boundaries between populations of LAN devices is a solution to overcrowding. This task is accomplished by the use of *bridges*.[6]

Figure 1.6 shows the most common type of bridge: a *transparent bridge*. It performs three simple functions: learning, forwarding, and filtering. It is transparent in that end stations have no knowledge of the bridge.

The bridge learns by listening *promiscuously* on all its ports. That is, every time a station transmits a frame, the bridge examines the source identifier of the frame. It then records the identifier in a *bridging table*, along with the port on which it was heard. The bridge therefore learns which stations are out port 1, which are out port 2, and so on.

In Figure 1.6, the bridge uses the information in its bridging table to forward frames when a member of one population—say, a sta-

---

[6]   *If you cut through the marketing hype surrounding modern Ethernet and Token Ring switches, you'll find that these very useful tools are merely high-performance bridges.*

tion out port 1—wants to send a frame to a member of another population: a station out port 2.

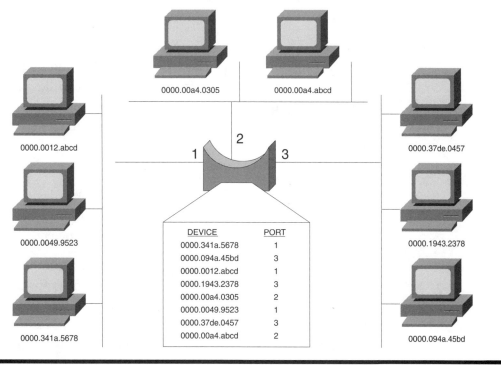

Figure 1.6

The transparent bridge segments network devices into manageable populations. A bridging table tracks the members of each population and manages communication between the populations.

A bridge that only learns and forwards would have no use. The real utility of a bridge is in the third function, filtering. Figure 1.6 shows that if a station out port 2 sends a frame to another station out port 2, the bridge will examine the frame. The bridge consults its bridging table and sees that the destination device is out the same port on which the frame was received and will not forward the frame. The frame is filtered.

Bridges enable the addition of far more devices to a network than would be possible if all the devices were in a single population, contending for the same bandwidth. *Filtering* means that only frames that need to be forwarded to another population will be, and resources are conserved. Ethernet networks are divided into collision domains; Token Ring and FDDI networks are divided into multiple rings.

Figure 1.7 illustrates two perspectives of a transparent bridge. It is transparent because the end stations have no knowledge of it. At the same time, a transparent bridge has no real knowledge of the topology of a network; the bridge only knows which identifiers are heard on each of its ports.

Some other types of bridges are source-route bridges, source-route/transparent bridges, translating bridges, and encapsulating bridges. For a complete discussion of bridge issues and functionality, see Perlman [1992], cited in the recommended reading list at the end of this chapter.

The third problem posed by LAN growth is one of locality. Repeaters allow the distance of a LAN to be extended, but only within certain geographic limitations. Extending a LAN across the city or across the continent presents prohibitive costs in physical materials, engineering and construction, and legal issues such as rights-of-way. Such distances require the use of a *wide-area network*, or WAN.[7] Table 1.1 compares and contrasts LANs and WANs.

A fourth problem is one of scalability. Bridges allow a network to be segregated into smaller populations of stations; in this way station-to-station traffic is localized. Certain types of frames cannot be localized, though. Some applications require data to be

---

7   *A third term, which is falling into general disuse, is metropolitan-area network, or MAN. It is just as well that this term is dying off; it grays the distinction between a LAN and a WAN. Is a MAN a big LAN or a small WAN? Dying also is a truly bad pun, which is that bridges ensure that no MAN is an island.*

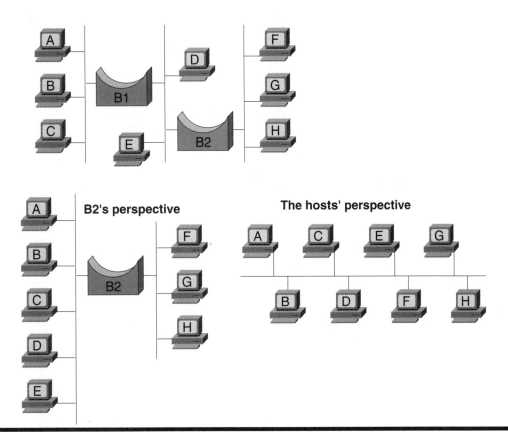

Figure 1.7
Two perspectives of a transparent bridge.

broadcast—that is, the data must be delivered to all stations on a network. Ethernet, Token Ring, and FDDI networks use a reserved destination identifier of all ones (0XFFFF.FFFF.FFFF) for broadcasting. Bridges must forward a broadcast frame out all ports to ensure that all stations receive a copy. As a bridged network becomes larger and larger, more and more stations will be originating broadcast traffic; soon, broadcasted frames cause the network to become congested again.

Table 1.1   *Fundamental differences between LANs and WANs.*

LAN	WAN
Limited geographic area	Citywide to worldwide geographic area
Privately owned and controlled media	Media leased from a service provider
Plentiful, cheap bandwidth	Limited, expensive bandwidth

To manage broadcast traffic and other scaling challenges, another kind of boundary is necessary. Bridges allow the network to be divided into populations of stations, but a way to create populations of networks within a larger network is also needed. This network of networks is better known as an *internetwork*. The device that makes internetworks possible is a router.

Internetwork

ROUTERS

Routers have been known by several names. Back in ancient times when what is now the Internet was called the ARPANET, routers were called IMPs, for *internet message processors*.[8] More recently, routers were called *gateways*; remnants of this nomenclature can still be found in terms such as Border *Gateway* Protocol (BGP) and Interior *Gateway* Routing Protocol (IGRP).[9] In the Open System Interconnection (OSI) world, routers are known as *Intermediate Systems* (IS).

---

[8]   *The parent of modern packet-switched networks was the AlohaNet, created at the University of Hawaii in the late 1960s by Norman Abramson. Because routers at that time were called IMPs, Dr. Abramson rather impishly named his router Menehune: a Hawaiian elf.*

[9]   *The term gateway is now generally accepted to mean an application gateway, as opposed to a router, which would be a network gateway.*

All of these aliases are descriptive of some aspect of what a router does. As *internet message processor* implies, a router switches data messages, or packets, from one network to another. As *gateway* implies, a router is a gateway through which data can be sent to reach another network. And as *Intermediate System* implies, a router is an intermediary for the End System–to–End System delivery of internetwork data.

Router, as a name, is probably the most descriptive of what the modern versions of these devices do. A router sends information along a route—a path—between two networks. This path may traverse a single router or many routers. Furthermore, in internetworks that have multiple paths to the same destination, modern routers use a set of procedures to determine and use the best route. Should that route become less than optimal or entirely unusable, the router selects the next-best path. The procedures used by the router to determine and select the best route and to share information about network reachability and status with other routers are referred to collectively as a *routing protocol*.

Router

Routing protocol

Just as a data link may directly connect two devices, a router also creates a connection between two devices. The difference is that, as Figure 1.8 shows, whereas the communication path between two devices sharing a common data link is a physical path, the communication path provided by routers between two devices on different networks is a higher-level, logical path.

This concept is vitally important for understanding a router's function. Notice that the logical path, or route, between the devices in Figure 1.8 traverses several types of data links: an Ethernet, an FDDI ring, a serial link, and a Token Ring. As noted earlier, to be delivered on the physical path of a data link, data must be encapsulated within a frame, a sort of digital envelope. Likewise,

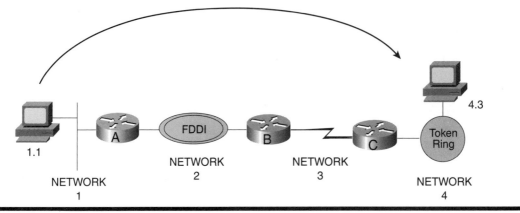

Figure 1.8

A router creates a logical path between networks.

_____

Packet

_____

to be delivered across the logical path of a routed internetwork, data must also be encapsulated; the digital envelope used by routers is a *packet*.

As noted earlier, each type of data link has its own unique frame format. The internetwork route depicted in Figure 1.8 crosses several data links, but the packet remains the same from end to end.

How is this possible? Figure 1.9 shows how the packet is actually delivered across the route:

1. The originating host encapsulates the data to be delivered within a packet. The packet must then be delivered across the host's data link to the local router—that host's *default gateway*—so the host encapsulates the packet within a frame. This operation is the same as placing an envelope inside of a larger envelope, for example, inserting an envelope containing a letter into a Federal Express envelope.

The destination data link identifier of the frame is the identifier of the interface of the local router,[10] and the source data link identifier is the host's.

2. That router (router A in Figure 1.9) removes the packet from the Ethernet frame; router A knows that the next-hop router on the path is router B, out its FDDI interface, so router A encapsulates the packet in an FDDI frame. Now the destination identifier in the frame is the FDDI interface of router B, and the source identifier is the FDDI interface of router A.

3. Router B removes the packet from the FDDI frame, knows that the next-hop router on the path is router C across the serial link, and sends the packet to C encapsulated in the proper frame for the serial link.

4. Router C removes the packet and recognizes that the station for which the packet is destined is on its directly connected Token Ring network; C encapsulates the packet in a Token Ring frame with the destination identifier of the destination station and the source identifier of its Token Ring interface. The packet has been delivered.

The key to understanding this entire process is to notice that the frames and their related data link identifiers, which have relevance only for each individual network, change for each network the packet traverses. The packet remains the same from end to end.

---

[10] *Although the purpose of a router is to create pathways between data links (networks), the router must also obey the protocols of the networks to which it is attached. So a router interface connected to an Ethernet will have a MAC identifier and must obey the CSMA/CD rules, a Token Ring interface must obey Token Ring rules, and so forth. In other words, a router is not only a router, but also a station on each of its attached networks.*

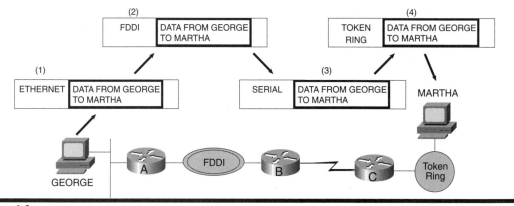

Figure 1.9

The frame changes from data link to data link, but the packet remains the same across the entire logical path.

But how did the originating host know that the packet needed to be delivered to its default gateway for routing? And how did the routers know where to send the packet?

NETWORK ADDRESSES

Each member network in a routed internetwork requires a unique identifier.

For devices to correctly communicate on a LAN, they must be uniquely identified by means of a data link identifier. If a routed *internetwork*—a network of networks—is to be created, then each member network must likewise be uniquely identifiable.

The most fundamental criterion for a routed internetwork is that for a router to correctly deliver packets to their proper destination, each and every network, or data link, must be uniquely identified. Providing this unique identification is the purpose of a *network address*.

Network address

Figure 1.10 suggests a type of network address. Notice that every network has its own unique address. Notice also that the point-to-point serial link has an address. A common mistake that beginners make is to forget that serial links are also networks and therefore require their own addresses for routing to work.

Now one of the two questions posed at the end of the last section can be answered: The routers can deliver the packet because the originating host put a destination address in the packet. From the perspective of the router, the destination address is all that is needed. As a rule, all routers really care about is the location of each network. Individual devices are not relevant to the router; the router only needs to deliver the packet to the correct destination network. When the packet arrives at the network, the data link identifier can be used to deliver the data to the individual device on the network.

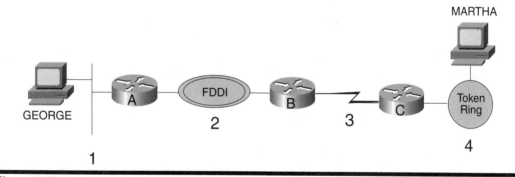

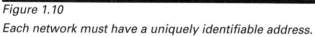

Figure 1.10

Each network must have a uniquely identifiable address.

How routers handle destination addresses is critically important and bears repeating. The purpose of a router is to deliver packets to the proper destination networks. As such, the only individual devices routers typically care about are other routers. When a router sees that the destination address of a packet is one of its directly connected networks, it acts as a station on that network and uses the data link identifier of the destination device to deliver the packet (encapsulated in a frame) on the network.[11]

The fundamental purpose and function of a router

With this understanding of the relationship between routers and network addresses, a question arises: When the router sees that the destination address of a packet is one of its directly connected networks, how does the router know where to deliver the packet? After all, Figure 1.10 showed that there is no reference by the originating station to the destination station's data link identifier.

A related question was asked at the end of the last section: How did the originating host know that the packet needed to be delivered to its default gateway for routing?

The answer to both of these questions is that the network addresses shown in Figure 1.10 are not sufficient. Each device on a network must be again identified uniquely, this time as a member of that particular network. The network address must have both a network identifier and a host identifier (Figure 1.11). The originating host must be able to recognize its own and others' network addresses, to say in effect: "I need to deliver this packet to device 4.3. My network address is 1.2; therefore, I know that the destination is on a different network than mine, and I'll need to send the packet to my local router for delivery."

The two parts of a network address

Likewise router C must be able to recognize, "I've received a packet with a destination address of 4.3. Because my Token Ring interface has an address of 4.1, I know that network 4 is one of my directly connected networks. As a member of that network myself, I know that station 4.3 has a MAC identifier of 0000.2354.AC6B; I'll just pop this packet into a Token Ring frame and deliver it."

---

[11] It should be pointed out that there are such things as host routes, a route to a specific device. These will be seen later in this book. However, at this point, host routes just confuse the issue.

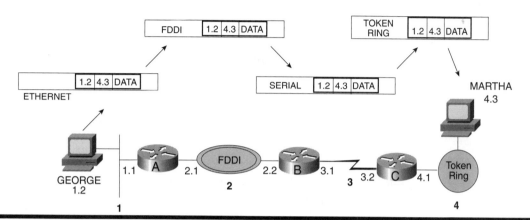

Figure 1.11

Each network must have a uniquely identifiable address.

LOOKING AHEAD

This chapter has established that a network address must have both a network portion and a host portion and that some mechanism must exist for mapping a network address to a data link identifier. Chapter 2, "TCP/IP Review," shows how IP meets these requirements. It examines the IP address format, the method by which IP does network-to-data link mappings, and a few other mechanisms important to the IP routing process.

RECOMMENDED READING

Perlman, R. *Interconnections: Bridges and Routers*. Reading, Massachusetts: Addison-Wesley; 1992. Radia Perlman is one of the giants in the field of internetworking, and this book is a classic. Not only is it a good basic text, but Perlman's sarcasm when she discusses the politics around standards bodies should not be missed.

REVIEW QUESTIONS

1. What is the primary purpose of a LAN?
2. What is a protocol?
3. What is the purpose of a MAC protocol?
4. What is a frame?
5. What feature is common to all frame types?
6. What is a MAC address or MAC identifier?
7. Why is a MAC address not a true address?
8. What are the three sources of signal degradation on a data link?
9. What is the purpose of a repeater?
10. What is the purpose of a bridge?
11. What makes a transparent bridge transparent?
12. Name three fundamental differences between LANs and WANs.
13. What is the purpose of a broadcast MAC identifier? What is the broadcast MAC identifier, in hex and in binary?
14. What is the primary similarity between a bridge and a router? What is the primary difference between a bridge and a router?
15. What is a packet? What is the primary similarity between a frame and a packet? What is the primary difference between a frame and a packet?
16. As a packet progresses across an internetwork, does the source address change?
17. What is a network address? What is the purpose of each part of a network address?
18. What is the primary difference between a network address and a data link identifier?

- The TCP/IP Protocol Layers

- The IP Packet Header

- IP Addresses

- ARP

- ICMP

- The Host-to-Host Layer

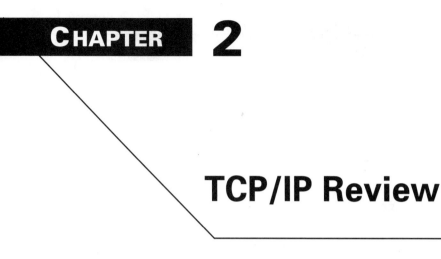

2

TCP/IP Review

The purpose of this chapter is to examine the details of the protocols that enable, control, or contribute to the routing of TCP/IP, not to do an in-depth study of the TCP/IP protocol suite. Several books on the recommended reading list at the end of the chapter cover the subject in depth. Read at least one.

Conceived in the early 1970s by Vint Cerf and Bob Kahn, TCP/IP and its layered protocol architecture predates the ISO's OSI reference model. A brief review of TCP/IP's layers will be useful in understanding how the various functions and services examined in this chapter interrelate.

THE TCP/IP PROTOCOL LAYERS

Figure 2.1 shows the TCP/IP protocol suite in relationship to the OSI reference model. The network interface layer, which corresponds to the OSI physical and data link layers, is not really part of the specification. However, it has become a de facto layer either as shown in Figure 2.1 or as separate physical and data link layers. It is described in this section in terms of the OSI physical and data link layers.

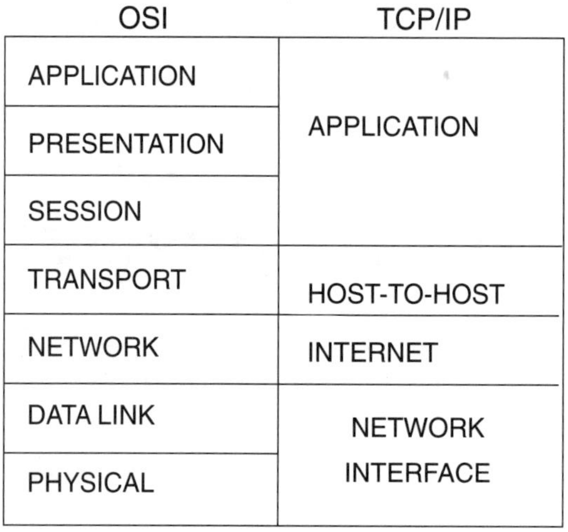

OSI	TCP/IP
APPLICATION	APPLICATION
PRESENTATION	
SESSION	
TRANSPORT	HOST-TO-HOST
NETWORK	INTERNET
DATA LINK	NETWORK INTERFACE
PHYSICAL	

Figure 2.1

The TCP/IP protocol suite.

The *physical layer* contains the protocols relating to the physical medium on which TCP/IP will be communicating. Officially, the protocols of this layer fall within four categories that together describe all aspects of physical media:

- *Electrical/optical* protocols describe signal characteristics such as voltage or photonic levels, bit timing, encoding, and signal shape.

- *Mechanical* protocols are specifications such as the dimensions of a connector or the metallic makeup of a wire.

- *Functional* protocols describe *what* something does. For example, "Request to Send" is the functional description of pin 4 of an EIA-232-D connector.

- *Procedural* protocols describe *how* something is done. For example, a binary 1 is represented on an EIA-232-D lead as a voltage more negative than −3 volts.

The *data link layer* was described in Chapter 1, "Basic Concepts: Internetworks, Routers, and Addresses." This layer contains the protocols that control the physical layer: how the medium is accessed and shared, how devices on the medium are identified, and how data is framed before being transmitted on the medium. Examples of data link protocols are IEEE 802.3/Ethernet, IEEE 802.5/Token Ring, and FDDI.

The *internet layer*, corresponding to the OSI network layer, is primarily responsible for enabling the routing of data across logical internetwork paths, such as in Figure 1.9, by defining a packet format and an addressing format. This layer is, of course, the one with which this book is most concerned.

The *host-to-host layer*, corresponding to the OSI transport layer, specifies the protocols that control the internet layer, much as the data link layer controls the physical layer. Both the host-to-host and data link layers can define such mechanisms as flow and error control. The difference is that while data link protocols control traffic on the data link—the physical medium connecting two devices—the transport layer controls traffic on the logical link—the end-to-end connection of two devices whose logical connection traverses a series of data links.

The *application layer* corresponds to the OSI session, presentation, and application layers. Although some routing protocols such as BGP and RIP reside at this layer, the most common services of the application layer provide the interfaces by which user applications access the network.

A function common to the protocol suite of Figure 2.1 and any other protocol suites is multiplexing between layers. Many applications may use a service at the host-to-host layer, and many services at the host-to-host layer may use the internet layer. Multiple protocol suites (IP, IPX, AppleTalk, for example) may share a physical link via common data link protocols.

THE IP PACKET HEADER

Figure 2.2 shows the format of the IP packet header, specified in RFC 791. Most fields in this packet have some importance to routing.

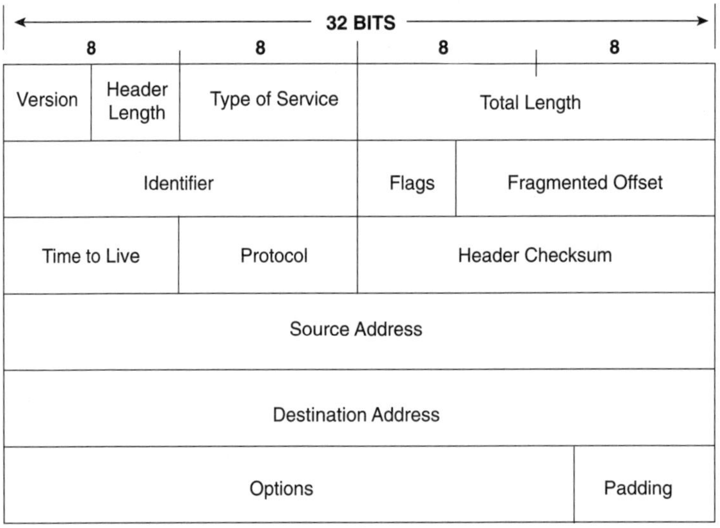

←	32 BITS		→
8	8	8	8
Version / Header Length	Type of Service	Total Length	
Identifier		Flags	Fragmented Offset
Time to Live	Protocol	Header Checksum	
Source Address			
Destination Address			
Options			Padding

Figure 2.2
The IP packet protocol.

Version identifies the IP version to which the packet belongs. This four-bit field is usually set to binary 0100; version 4 (IPv4) is in current, common use. A newer version of the protocol, not yet in widespread deployment, is version 6 (IPv6), sometimes referred to as "next-generation IP"(IPng). All currently assigned version numbers can be seen in Table 2.1, along with a few of the relevant RFCs. All versions other than 4 and 6 (built on an earlier proposal called Simple Internet Protocol, or SIP, which also carried a version number of 6) now exist only as "culture," and it will be left to the curious to read their cited RFCs.

Header Length is a four-bit field that tells, as the name implies, the length of the IP header. The reason this field is included is that the Options field (described later in this section) can vary in size. The minimum length of the IP header is 20 octets, and the options may increase this size up to a maximum of 24 octets. This field describes the length of the header in terms of 32-bit words—five for the minimum 160-bit size and six for the maximum.

Table 2.1   *IP version numbers.*

Number	Version	RFC
0	Reserved	
1–3	Unassigned	
4	Internet Protocol (IP)	791
5	ST Datagram Mode	1190
6	Simple Internet Protocol (SIP)	
6	IPng	1883
7	TP/IX	1475
8	P Internet Protocol (PIP)	1621
9	TCP and UDP over Bigger Addresses (TUBA)	1347
10–14	Unassigned	
15	Reserved	

Type of Service (TOS) is an eight-bit field that can be used for specifying special handling of the packet. This field actually can be broken down into two subfields: Precedence and TOS. Precedence sets a priority for the packet, the way a package might be sent overnight, 2-day delivery, or general post. TOS allows the selection of a delivery service in terms of throughput, delay, reliability, and monetary cost. Although this field is not commonly used (all the bits will usually be set to zero), early specifications of the Open Shortest Path First (OSPF) protocol called for TOS routing. Also, the Precedence bits are occasionally used in Quality of Service (QoS) applications. Figure 2.3 summarizes the eight TOS bits; for more information, see RFC 1340 and RFC 1349.

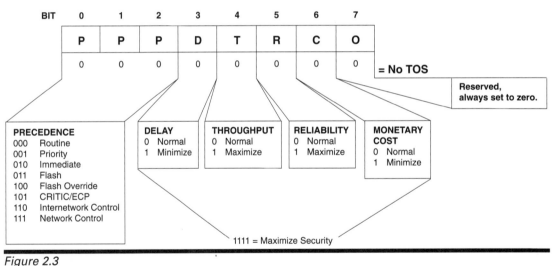

Figure 2.3

The Type of Service field.

Total Length is a 16-bit field specifying the total length of the packet, including the header, in octets. By subtracting the header length, a receiver may determine the size of the packet's data payload. Because the largest decimal number that can be described with 16 bits is 65,535, the maximum possible size of an IP packet is 65,535 octets.

Identifier is a 16-bit field used in conjunction with the *Flags* and *Fragment Offset* fields for fragmentation of a packet. Packets must be fragmented into smaller packets if the original length exceeds the Maximum Transmission Unit (MTU) of a data link through which they pass. For example, consider a 5,000-byte packet traveling through an internetwork. It encounters a data link whose MTU is 1,500 bytes—that is, the frame can contain a maximum packet size of 1,500 bytes. The router that places the packet onto this data link must first fragment the packet into chunks of no more than 1,500 octets each. The router then marks each fragment with the same number in the Identifier field so that a receiving device can identify the fragments that go together.[1]

Flags is a three-bit field in which the first bit is unused. The second is the Don't Fragment (DF) bit. When the DF bit is set to one, a router cannot fragment the packet. If the packet cannot be forwarded without fragmenting, the router drops the packet and sends an error message to the source. This function enables the testing of MTUs in an internetwork. The DF bit can be set using the Extended Ping utility on Cisco routers, as shown in Figure 2.4.

The DF bit can be used in troubleshooting to determine a path's MTU.

The third bit is the More Fragments (MF) bit. When a router fragments a packet, it sets the MF bit to one in all but the last fragment so that the receiver knows to keep expecting fragments until it encounters a fragment with MF = 0.

Fragment Offset is a 13-bit field that specifies the offset, in units of eight octets, from the beginning of the header to the beginning of the fragment.[2] Because fragments may not always arrive in

---

[1] *A fragmented packet is not reassembled at the other end of the data link; the packet stays fragmented until it reaches its final destination.*

[2] *Units of eight octets are used so that a maximum-size packet of 65,535 bytes may be described with 13 bits.*

sequence, the Fragment Offset field allows the pieces to be reassembled in the correct order.

Note that if a single fragment is lost during a transmission, the entire packet must be resent and refragmented at the same point in the internetwork. Therefore, error-prone data links could cause a disproportionate delay. And if a fragment is lost because of congestion, the retransmission of the entire series of fragments may increase the congestion.

Time to Live (TTL) is an eight-bit field that will be set with a certain number when the packet is first generated. As the packet is passed from router to router, each router will decrement this number. If the number reaches zero, the packet will be discarded and an error message will be sent to the source. This process prevents "lost" packets from wandering endlessly through an internetwork.

As originally conceived, the TTL was specified in seconds; if a packet was delayed more than a second in a router, the router would adjust the TTL accordingly. However, this approach is difficult to implement and is rarely supported. Most routers simply decrement the TTL by one, no matter what the actual delay, so the TTL is really a hop count. The recommended default TTL is 64, although values such as 15 and 32 are not uncommon.

Using **trace** to learn the route to a destination

Some trace utilities, such as Cisco's **trace** command, make use of the TTL field. If the router is told to trace the route to a host address such as 10.11.12.13, the router will send three packets with the TTL set to one; the first router will decrement it to zero, drop the packets, and send back error messages to the source. By reading the source address of the error messages, the first router on the path is now known. The next three packets will be sent with a TTL of two. The first router decrements to one, the second to zero, and an error message is received from the second router. The third set has a TTL of three, and so forth, until the destination is found. All routers along the internetwork path will have identified themselves. Figure 2.5 shows the output from a trace on a Cisco router.

```
Handy#ping
Protocol [ip]:
Target IP address: 172.16.113.17
Repeat count [5]: 1
Datagram size [100]:
Timeout in seconds [2]:
Extended commands [n]: y
Source address:
Type of service [0]:
Set DF bit in IP header? [no]: y
Validate reply data? [no]:
Data pattern [0xABCD]:
Loose, Strict, Record, Timestamp, Verbose[none]: r
Number of hops [ 9 ]:
Loose, Strict, Record, Timestamp, Verbose[RV]:
Sweep range of sizes [n]: y
Sweep min size [76]: 500
Sweep max size [18024]: 2000
Sweep interval [1]: 500
Type escape sequence to abort.
Sending 4, [500..2000]-byte ICMP Echos to 172.16.113.17, timeout is 2 seconds:
Packet has IP options:  Total option bytes= 39, padded length=40
   Record route: <*> 0.0.0.0 0.0.0.0 0.0.0.0 0.0.0.0
               0.0.0.0 0.0.0.0 0.0.0.0 0.0.0.0

Reply to request 0 (16 ms) (size 500).  Received packet has options
   Total option bytes= 40, padded length=40
   Record route: 172.16.192.5 172.16.113.18 172.16.113.17 172.16.113.17
         172.16.192.6 172.16.192.5 <*> 0.0.0.0 0.0.0.0 0.0.0.0
   End of list

Reply to request 1 (24 ms) (size 1000).  Received packet has options
 , Total option bytes= 40, padded length=40
   Record route: 172.16.192.5 172.16.113.18 172.16.113.17 172.16.113.17
         172.16.192.6 172.16.192.5 <*> 0.0.0.0 0.0.0.0 0.0.0.0
   End of list

Reply to request 2 (28 ms) (size 1500).  Received packet has options
   Total option bytes= 40, padded length=40
   Record route: 172.16.192.5 172.16.113.18 172.16.113.17 172.16.113.17
         172.16.192.6 172.16.192.5 <*> 0.0.0.0 0.0.0.0 0.0.0.0
   End of list

Unreachable from 172.16.192.6, maximum MTU 1478 (size 2000).
   Received packet has options
   Total option bytes= 39, padded length=40
   Record route: <*> 0.0.0.0 0.0.0.0 0.0.0.0 0.0.0.0
         0.0.0.0 0.0.0.0 0.0.0.0 0.0.0.0 0.0.0.0

Success rate is 75 percent (3/4), round-trip min/avg/max = 16/22/28 ms
Handy#
```

Figure 2.4

The Cisco Extended Ping utility allows the setting of the DF bit to test MTUs across an internetwork. In the figure, the largest MTU of the path to destination 172.16.113.17 is 1,478 octets.

```
Elvis#trace www.cisco.com

Type escape sequence to abort.
Tracing the route to cio-sys.Cisco.COM (192.31.7.130)

  1 172.18.197.17 4 msec 4 msec
  2 ltlrichard-s1-13.hwy51.com (172.18.197.1) 36 msec 44msec 2536 msec
  3 cperkins-rtf-fr2.hwy51.com(10.168.204.3) 104 msec 60 msec *
  4 cberry.hwy51.com (10.168.193.1) 92 msec *
  5 jllewis-inner.hwy51.com (10.168.207.59) 44 msec * 44 msec
  6 bholly-fw-outer-rt.hwy51.com (10.168.207.94) 44 msec * 48 msec
  7 sl-stk-14-S10/0:6-512k.sprintlink.net (144.228.214.107) 92 msec *
  8 sl-stk-2-F1/0/0.sprintlink.net (144.228.40.2) 52 msec 1156 msec *
  9 sl-mae-w-H1/0-T3.sprintlink.net (144.228.10.46) 100 msec 124 msec 2340 msec
 10 sanjose1-br1.bbnplanet.net (198.32.136.19) 2264 msec 164 msec *
 11 paloalto-br2.bbnplanet.net (4.0.1.10) 64 msec 60 msec *
 12 su-pr2.bbnplanet.net (131.119.0.218) 76 msec 76 msec 76 msec
 13 cisco.bbnplanet.net (131.119.26.10) 2560 msec 76 msec 936 msec
 14 sty.cisco.com (192.31.7.39) 84 msec 72 msec *
 15 cio-sys.Cisco.COM (192.31.7.130) 60 Msec * 64 msec
ELVIS#
```

Figure 2.5

The trace utility uses the TTL field to identify routers along a route. Asterisks indicate timed-out packets.

Protocol is an eight-bit field that gives the "address," or protocol number, of the host-to-host or transport layer protocol for which the information in the packet is destined. Table 2.2 shows a few of the more common of the 100 different protocol numbers currently assigned.

Table 2.2   *A few well-known protocol numbers .*

Protocol Number	Host-to-Host Layer Protocol
1	Internet Control Message Protocol (ICMP)
2	Internet Group Management Protocol (IGMP)
3	Gateway to Gateway Protocol (GGP)
4	IP in IP
6	Transmission Control Protocol (TCP)
8	Exterior Gateway Protocol (EGP)
17	User Datagram Protocol (UDP)
35	Inter-Domain Policy Routing Protocol (IDPR)
45	Inter-Domain Routing Protocol (IDRP)

Table 2.2   *A few well-known protocol numbers, continued.*

Protocol Number	Host-to-Host Layer Protocol
46	Resource Reservation Protocol (RSVP)
47	Generic Routing Encapsulation (GRE)
54	NBMA Next Hop Resolution Protocol (NHRP)
88	Cisco Internet Gateway Routing Protocol (IGRP)
89	Open Shortest Path First (OSPF)

Header Checksum is the error correction field for the IP header. The checksum is not calculated for the encapsulated data; UDP, TCP, and ICMP have their own checksums for doing this. The field contains a 16-bit one's complement checksum, calculated by the originator of the packet. The receiver will again calculate a 16-bit one's complement sum, including the original checksum. If no errors have occurred during the packet's travels, the resulting checksum will be all ones. Remember that each router decrements the TTL; therefore, the checksum must be recalculated at each router. RFC 1141 discusses some strategies for simplifying this calculation.

Source and *Destination Addresses* are the 32-bit IP addresses of the originator of the packet and the destination of the packet. The format of IP addresses is covered in the next section, "IP Addresses."

Options is a variable-length field and, as the name implies, is optional. Space is added to the packet header to contain either source-generated information or for other routers to enter information; the options are used primarily for testing. The most frequently used options follow.

Using the Options field to test routers and paths

- *Loose source routing*, in which a series of IP addresses for router interfaces is listed. The packet must pass through each of these addresses, although multiple hops may be taken between the addresses.

- *Strict source routing*, where again a series of router addresses is listed. Unlike loose source routing, the packet must follow the route exactly. If the next hop is not the next address on the list, an error occurs.

- *Record route* provides room for each router to enter the address of its outgoing interface as the packet transits so that a record is kept of all routers the packet encounters. Record route provides a function similar to *trace* except that the outgoing interfaces both on the path to the destination and on the return path are recorded.

- *Timestamp* is an option similar to record route except each router also enters a timestamp—the packet not only keeps track of where it has been but also records when it was there.

All these options may be invoked by using the Extended Ping on Cisco routers. Record route is used in Figure 2.4, loose source routing and timestamp are used in Figure 2.6, and strict source routing is used in Figure 2.7.

Padding ensures that the header ends on a 32-bit boundary by adding zeros after the option field until a multiple of 32 is reached.

A protocol analyzer capture of an IP header is shown in Figure 2.8. Compare the information shown with Figure 2.2.

IP ADDRESSES

IP addresses are 32 bits long; like all network-level addresses, they have a network portion and a host portion. The network portion uniquely identifies the data link (that is, the network) and is common to all devices attached to the network. The host portion uniquely identifies a particular device attached to the network.

```
Handy#ping
Protocol [ip]:
Target IP address: 172.16.113.9
Repeat count [5]:
Datagram size [100]:
Timeout in seconds [2]:
Extended commands [n]: y
Source address:
Type of service [0]:
Set DF bit in IP header? [no]:
Validate reply data? [no]:
Data pattern [0xABCD]:
Loose, Strict, Record, Timestamp, Verbose[none]: l
Source route: 172.16.113.14 172.16.113.10
Loose, Strict, Record, Timestamp, Verbose[LV]: t
Number of timestamps [ 6 ]: 2
Loose, Strict, Record, Timestamp, Verbose[LTV]:
Sweep range of sizes [n]:
Type escape sequence to abort.
Sending 5, 100-byte ICMP Echos to 172.16.113.9, timeout is 2 seconds:
Packet has IP options:  Total option bytes= 23, padded length=24
   Loose source route: <*> 172.16.113.14 172.16.113.10
   Timestamp: Type 0.  Overflows: 0 length 12, ptr 5
     >>Current pointer<<
     Time= 0
     Time= 0

Request 0 timed out
Reply to request 1 (76 ms).  Received packet has options
   Total option bytes= 24, padded length=24
   Loose source route: 172.16.113.13 172.16.192.6 <*>
   Timestamp: Type 0.  Overflows: 6 length 12, ptr 13
     Time= 80FF4798
     Time= 80FF4750
     >>Current pointer<<
   End of list

Request 2 timed out
Reply to request 3 (76 ms).  Received packet has options
   Total option bytes= 24, padded length=24
   Loose source route: 172.16.113.13 172.16.192.6 <*>
   Timestamp: Type 0.  Overflows: 6 length 12, ptr 13
   Time= 80FF4FC0
   Time= 80FF4F78
   >>Current pointer<<
End of list

Request 4 timed out
Success rate is 40 percent (2/5), round-trip min/avg/max = 76/76/76 ms
Handy#
```

Figure 2.6

The Cisco Extended Ping may be used to set parameters in the Options field of the IP header. In this example, loose source routing and timestamp are used.

```
Handy#ping
Protocol [ip]:
Target IP address: 172.16.113.10
Repeat count [5]: 2
Datagram size [100]:
Timeout in seconds [2]:
Extended commands [n]: y
Source address:
Type of service [0]:
Set DF bit in IP header? [no]:
Validate reply data? [no]:
Data pattern [0xABCD]:
Loose, Strict, Record, Timestamp, Verbose[none]: s
Source route: 172.16.192.6 172.16.113.17 172.16.113.10
Loose, Strict, Record, Timestamp, Verbose[SV]:
Sweep range of sizes [n]:
Type escape sequence to abort.
Sending 2, 100-byte ICMP Echos to 172.16.113.10, timeout is 2 seconds:
Packet has IP options:  Total option bytes= 15, padded length=16
  Strict source route: <*> 172.16.192.6 172.16.113.17 172.16.113.10

Reply to request 0 (80 ms).  Received packet has options
  Total option bytes= 16, padded length=16
  Strict source route: 172.16.113.10 172.16.113.17 172.16.192.6 <*>
  End of list

Reply to request 1 (76 ms).  Received packet has options
  Total option bytes= 16, padded length=16
  Strict source route: 172.16.113.10 172.16.113.17 172.16.192.6 <*>
  End of list

Success rate is 100 percent (2/2), round-trip min/avg/max = 76/78/80 ms
Handy#
```

Figure 2.7

Extended Ping is used here to set strict source routing in the ping packets.

There are several ways to represent the 32 bits of an IP address. For instance, the 32-bit IP address

00001010110101100101011110000011

could be represented in decimal as

181,819,267.

The binary format is cumbersome, and the decimal format is time-consuming to calculate. A better format is shown in Figure

2.9. The 32 bits of the address comprise four octets, each of which can be represented with a decimal number between 0 and 255, with dots between the decimal representations. In the figure, the 32-bit address is mapped into a dotted-decimal representation.

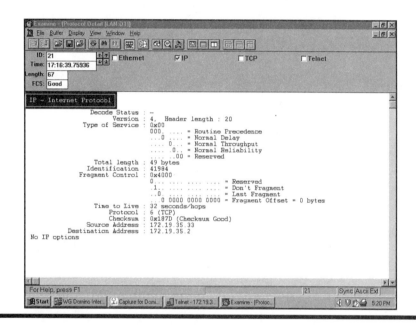

Figure 2.8

You can see the fields of an IP packet's header and the values contained in each field in this protocol analyzer display.

An important distinction to remember when working with IP addresses is that dotted decimal is just an easy way for humans to read and write IP addresses. Always remember that the router is not reading an address in terms of four octets; rather, the router sees a 32-bit binary string. Many pitfalls can be avoided by keeping this fact firmly in mind.

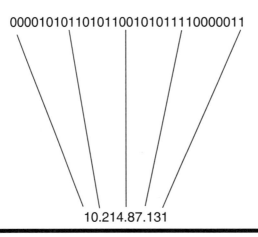

Figure 2.9

The dotted-decimal format is a convenient way to write IP addresses, but it should not be confused with what the router (or host) sees—a 32-bit string.

Probably the most distinctive characteristic of IP addresses is that unlike other network-level addresses, the network and host portions can vary in size within the 32-bit boundaries. That is, the network portion might take up most of the 32 bits or the host portion might or they might divide the bits equally. Protocols, such as NetWare and AppleTalk, were designed for use in relatively small internetworks,[3] and as a result their network-level addresses have fixed-length network and host portions. This arrangement certainly makes life easier; a receiving device knows to read a certain number of bits into the address to find the network part, and the rest is host address.

TCP/IP, however, was designed from the first to be flexible enough to be used in any internetwork, from the tiny to the colossal. This flexibility makes IP addresses more difficult to manage. The basics

---

[3] *However, their popularity has caused them to be used on a much larger scale than the original designers had envisioned; as a result, interesting difficulties and challenges arise in large Novell and Apple internetworks.*

of administering IP addresses are presented in this section, and then some more advanced techniques are introduced in Chapter 7, "Routing Information Protocol Version 2."

The First Octet Rule

Without putting too fine a point on it, it can be said that there are three sizes of internetworks as measured by the number of hosts: big, medium, and small.

- Big internetworks, by definition, have a huge number of hosts. Relatively few big internetworks exist.

- Small internetworks are just the opposite. Each one is small because it has a small number of hosts; a huge number of small internetworks exist.

- Medium internetworks are just that: a medium number of them (in relation to big and small ones) and a medium number of hosts in each one.

This high level of addressing focus requires three types—*classes*—of network address for the three sizes of internetworks. Addresses for big internetworks need to be capable of addressing many hosts, but because so few big internetworks exist, only a few big-network addresses are required.

The situation is reversed for small internetworks. Because there are many small internetworks, a large number of small-network addresses are needed. But because a small internetwork has a small number of hosts, each of the many network addresses only requires a few host addresses.

For medium-sized internetworks, a medium number of network addresses and a medium number of host addresses will be available for each network address.

Figure 2.10 shows how the network and host portions of IP addresses are divvied up for these three classes.

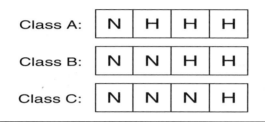

Figure 2.10

Class A, B, and C IP address formats.

The big, medium, and small networks described thus far map to address classes as follows:

- *Class A* IP addresses are for big internetworks. The first octet is the network portion, and the last three octets are the host portion. Only 256 numbers are available in the eight-bit network part, but 2^{24} or 16,777,216 numbers are available in the host part of each of those network addresses.

- *Class B* addresses are for medium-size internetworks. The first two octets are the network portion, and the last two octets are the host portion. There are 2^{16} or 65,536 available numbers in the network part and an equal number in the host part.

- *Class C* addresses are just the opposite of class A. The first three octets are the network portion, and the last octet is the host portion.

Because all IP addresses are 32-bit binary strings, a way of distinguishing the class to which a particular address belongs is necessary. The *first octet rule*, illustrated in Figure 2.11, provides the means to make such a distinction and can be described as follows:

- For class A addresses, the first bit of the first octet—that is, the left-most bit of the entire 32-bit string—is always set to zero. Therefore, we can find the minimum and maximum numbers in the class A range by setting all the remaining bits in the first octet to zero (for the minimum) and one (for the maximum). This action results in the decimal numbers 0 and 127 with a few exceptions: 0 is reserved as part of the default address (Chapter 12, "Default Routes and On-Demand Routing"), and 127 is reserved for internal loopback addresses.[4] That leaves 1 through 126; any IP address whose first octet is between 1 and 126 inclusive is a class A address.

- Class B addresses always have their left-most bit set to one and the second bit set to zero. Again finding the minimum and maximum number of the first octet by setting all remaining bits to zero and then to one, we see in Figure 2.9 that any address whose first octet is in the decimal range 128 through 191 is a class B address.

- In class C addresses, the first two bits are set to one, and the third bit is set to zero. The result is a first octet range of 192 through 223.[5]

---

[4] *UNIX machines use an internal loopback address (typically 127.0.0.1) to send traffic to themselves. Data may be sent to this address and returned to the transmitting process without ever leaving the device.*

[5] *Notice that 223 does not exhaust all available numbers in the first octet. See Configuration Exercise 1 at the end of this chapter.*

RULE	MINIMUMS AND MAXIMUMS	DECIMAL RANGE
Class A: First bit is always 0.	**0**0000000 = 0 **0**1111111 = 127	1 - 126* *0 and 127 are reserved.
Class B: First two bits are always 10.	**10**000000 = 128 **10**111111 = 191	128 - 191
Class C: First three bits are always 110.	**110**00000 = 192 **110**11111 = 223	192 - 223

Figure 2.11

The first octet rule.

So far IP addressing doesn't seem so difficult. A router or host could easily determine the network part of an IP address by using the first octet rule. If the first bit is 0, then read the first eight bits to find the network address. If the first two bits are 10, then read the first 16 bits; and if the first three bits are 110, then read 24 bits in to get the network address. Unfortunately, things are not that easy.

Address Masks

The address for an entire data link—a non-host-specific network address—is represented by the network portion of an IP address, with all host bits set to zero. For instance, the InterNIC, the body that administers IP addresses, might assign to an applicant an address of 172.21.0.0.[6] This address is a class B address because 172 is between 128 and 191, so the last two octets make up the host bits. Notice that they are all set to zero. The first 16 bits (172.21.) are assigned, but address owners are free to do whatever they please with the host bits.

Each device or interface will be assigned a unique, host-specific address such as 172.21.35.17. The device, whether a host or a router, obviously needs to know its own address, but it also needs to be able to determine the network to which it belongs—in this case, 172.21.0.0.

This task is accomplished by means of an *address mask*. The address mask is a 32-bit string, one bit for each bit of the IP address. As a 32-bit string, the mask can be represented in dotted-decimal format just like an IP address. This representation tends to be a stumbling block for some beginners: Although the address mask can be written in dotted decimal, it is not an address. Table 2.3 shows the standard address masks for the three classes of IP address.

Table 2.3   *Address masks for class A, B, and C network addresses.*

Class	Mask	Dotted Decimal
A	11111111000000000000000000000000	255.0.0.0
B	11111111111111110000000000000000	255.255.0.0
C	11111111111111111111111100000000	255.255.255.0

---

[6]   *Actually, this address would never be assigned. It is from a group of addresses reserved for private use; most of the addresses used in this book are from this reserved pool, described in RFC 1918. Reserved addresses are: 10.0.0.0–10.255.255.255, 172.16.0.0–172.31.255.255, and 192.168.0.0–192.168.255.255.*

For each bit of the IP address, the device performs a Boolean (logical) AND function with the corresponding bit of the address mask. The AND function can be stated as follows:

> Compare two bits and derive a result. The result will be one if and only if both bits are one. If either or both bits are zero, the result will be zero.

Figure 2.12 shows how, for a given IP address, the address mask is used to determine the network address. The mask has a one in every bit position corresponding to a network bit of the address and a zero in every bit position corresponding to a host bit. Because 172.21.35.17 is a class B address, the mask must have the first two octets set to all ones and the last two octets, the host part, set to all zeros. As Table 2.3 shows, this mask can be represented in dotted decimal as 255.255.0.0.

Truth Table for Boolean AND:

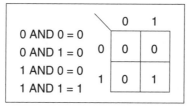

```
            0 AND 0 = 0           0   1
            0 AND 1 = 0    0 │ 0 │ 0 │
            1 AND 0 = 0    1 │ 0 │ 1 │
            1 AND 1 = 1
```

```
        │ 10101100000101010010001100010001 = 172.21.35.17
  AND   │ 11111111111111110000000000000000 = 255.255.0.0
        ▼ 10101100000101010000000000000000 = 172.21.0.0
```

Figure 2.12

Each bit of this class B address is ANDed with the corresponding bit of the address mask to derive the network address.

A logical AND is performed on the IP address and its mask for every bit position; the result is shown in Figure 2.12. In the result, every network bit is repeated, and all the host bits become zeros. So by assigning an address of 172.21.35.17 and a mask of 255.255.0.0 to an interface, the device will know that the interface belongs to network 172.21.0.0. Applying the AND operator to an IP address and its address mask always reveals the network address.

An address and mask are assigned to an interface of a Cisco router (in this example, the E0 interface) by means of the following commands:

```
Smokey(config)# interface ethernet 0
Smokey(config-if)# ip address 172.21.35.17 255.255.0.0
```

But why use address masks at all? So far, using the first octet rule seems much simpler.

Subnets and Subnet Masks

Never lose sight of why network-level addresses are necessary in the first place. For routing to be accomplished, each and every data link (network) must have a unique address; in addition, each and every host on that data link must have an address that both identifies it as a member of the network and distinguishes it from any other host on that network.

The need for network-level addressing

As defined so far, a single class A, B, or C address can be used only on a single data link. To build an internetwork, separate addresses must be used for each data link so that those networks are uniquely identifiable. If a separate class A, B, or C address were assigned to each data link, less than 17 million data links could be addressed before all IP addresses were depleted. This approach is obviously impractical,[7] as is the fact that to make full use of the host address space in the previous example, more than 65,000 devices would have to reside on data link 172.21.0.0!

The only way to make class A, B, or C addresses practical is by dividing each major address, such as 172.21.0.0, into subnetwork addresses. Recall two facts:

1. The host portion of an address can be used as desired.
2. The network portion of an IP address is determined by the address mask assigned to that interface.

Figure 2.13 shows an internetwork to which the major class B address 172.21.0.0 has been assigned. Five data links are interconnecting the routers, each one of which requires a network address. As it stands, 172.21.0.0 would have to be assigned to a single data link, and then four more addresses would have to be requested for the other four data links.

Notice what was done in Figure 2.13. The address mask is not a standard 16-bit mask for class B addresses; the mask has been extended another eight bits so that the first 24 bits of the IP address are interpreted as network bits. In other words, the routers and hosts have been given a mask that causes them to read the first eight host bits as part of the network address. The result is that the major network address applies to the entire internetwork, and each data link has become a subnetwork, or subnet. A *subnet* is a subset of a major class A, B, or C address space.

Subnet

The IP address now has three parts: the network part, the subnet part, and the host part. The address mask is now a *subnet mask*, or a mask that is longer than the standard address mask. The first

Subnet mask

---

[7]   *Seventeen million data links may seem like a lot until you consider that even a single moderate-size business may have dozens or hundreds of data links.*

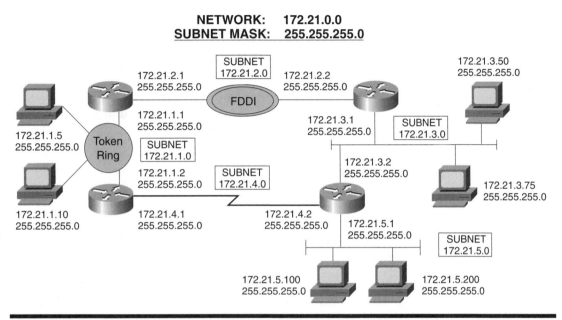

NETWORK: 172.21.0.0
SUBNET MASK: 255.255.255.0

Figure 2.13

Subnet masks allow a single network address to be used on multiple data links by "borrowing" some of the host bits for use as subnet bits.

two octets of the address will always be 172.21, but the third octet—whose bits are now subnet bits instead of host bits—may range from 0 to 255. The internetwork in Figure 2.12 has subnets 1, 2, 3, 4, and 5 (172.21.*1*.0 through 172.21.*5*.0). Up to 256 subnets may be assigned under the single class B address, using the mask shown.

Two words of caution are in order. First, not all routing protocols can support subnet addresses in which the subnet bits are all zeros or all ones. The reason is that these protocols, called *classful* protocols, cannot differentiate between an all-zero subnet and the major network number. For instance, subnet 0 in Figure 2.13 would be 172.21.0.0; the major IP address is also 172.21.0.0. The two cannot be distinguished without further information.

Classful protocols

Likewise, classful routing protocols cannot differentiate a broad-cast on the all-ones subnet from an all-subnets broadcast address.[8] For example, the all-ones subnet in Figure 2.13 would be 172.21.255.0. For that subnet, the all-hosts broadcast address would be 172.21.255.255, but that is also the broadcast for all hosts on all subnets of major network 172.21.0.0. Again, the two addresses cannot be distinguished without further information. RIP version 1 and IGRP are both classful routing protocols; Chapter 7 introduces *classless* routing protocols, which can indeed use the all-zeros and all-ones subnets.

The second caution has to do with the verbal description of sub-nets and their masks. Subnetting the third octet of a class B address, as is done is Figure 2.13, is very common; also common is hearing people describe such a subnet design as "using a class C mask with a class B address," or "subnetting a class B address into a class C." Both descriptions are wrong! Such descriptions fre-quently lead to misunderstandings about the subnet design or to a poor understanding of subnetting itself. The proper way to describe the subnetting scheme of Figure 2.12 is either as "a class B address with 8 bits of subnetting," or as "a class B address with a 24-bit mask."

The subnet mask may be represented in any of three for-mats—dotted decimal, bitcount, and hexadecimal—as shown in Figure 2.14. Dotted decimal is still the most common format, although the bitcount format is becoming increasingly popular. Compared to dotted decimal, the bitcount format is easier to write (the address is followed by a forward slash and the number of bits that are masked for the network part). In addition, the bitcount

---

[8]   *The all-hosts IP broadcast address is all ones: 255.255.255.255. An all-hosts broad-cast for a particular subnet would set all host bits to one; for instance, an all hosts broadcast for subnet 172.21.1.0 would be 172.21.1.255. Finally, a broadcast for all hosts on all subnets sets the subnet bits and the host bits to all ones: 172.21.255.255.*

format is more descriptive of what the mask is really doing and therefore avoids the type of semantic misunderstandings described in the previous paragraph. Many UNIX systems use the hexadecimal format.

DOTTED DECIMAL
255.255.255.0

BITCOUNT
172.21.0.0/24

HEXADECIMAL
0xFFFFFF00

Figure 2.14

The subnet mask in Figure 2.13 may be represented in three different formats.

Although the address mask must be specified to Cisco routers in dotted decimal, using the command shown previously, the mask may be displayed by various **show** commands in any of the three formats by using the command **ip netmask-format [dec|hex|bit]** in line configuration mode. For example, to configure a router to display its masks in bitcount format, use:

```
Gladys(config)# line vty 0 4
Gladys(config-line)# ip netmask-format bit
```

Designing Subnets

As established in the previous section, subnet bits cannot be all zeros or all ones in classful environments. Likewise, an IP host address cannot have all its host bits set to zero—this setting is reserved for the address router's use to represent the network or subnet itself. And the host bits cannot be set to all ones, as this setting is the broadcast address. These restrictions apply to the host bits with no exceptions and are starting points for designing subnets. Beyond these starting points, network designers need to choose the most appropriate subnetting scheme in terms of matching the address space to the particulars of an internetwork.

When designing subnets and their masks, the number of available subnets under a major network address and the number of available hosts on each subnet are both calculated with the same formula: $2^n - 2$, where n is the number of bits in the subnet or host space and 2 is subtracted to account for the unavailable all-zeros and all-ones addresses. For example, given a class A address of 10.0.0.0, a subnet mask of 10.0.0.0/16 (255.255.0.0) means that the 8-bit subnet space will yield $2^8 - 2 = 254$ available subnets and $2^{16} - 2 = 65,534$ host addresses available on each of those subnets. On the other hand, a mask of 10.0.0.0/24 (255.255.255.0) means that a 16-bit subnet space is yielding 65,534 subnets and an 8-bit host space is yielding 254 host addresses for each subnet.

A stepwise method for designing subnets

The following steps are used to subnet an IP address:

1. Determine how many subnets are required and how many hosts per subnet are required.
2. Use the $2^n - 2$ formula to determine the number of subnet bits and the number of host bits that will satisfy the requirements established in step 1. If multiple subnet masks can satisfy the requirements, choose the one that will best scale to future needs. For example, if the internetwork is most likely to grow by adding subnets, choose more subnet bits; if the internetwork is most likely to grow by adding hosts to existing subnets, choose more host bits. Avoid choosing a scheme in which either all subnets or all host addresses within the subnets will be used up immediately, leaving no room for future growth.

3. Working in binary, determine all available bit combinations in the subnet space; in each instance, set all the host bits to zero. Convert the resulting subnet addresses to dotted decimal. These are the subnet addresses.

4. For each subnet address, again working in binary, write all possible bit combinations for the host space without changing the subnet bits. Convert the results to dotted decimal; these are the host addresses available for each subnet.

The importance of doing the last two steps in binary cannot be overemphasized. *The single greatest source of mistakes when working with subnets is trying to work with them in dotted decimal without understanding what is happening at the binary level.* Again, dotted decimal is for convenience in reading and writing IP addresses. Routers and hosts see the addresses as 32-bit binary strings; to successfully work with IP addresses, they must be seen the way the routers and hosts see them.

> When configuring subnets, always work in binary instead of dotted decimal.

The last paragraph may seem a bit overzealous in light of the examples given so far; the patterns of subnet and host addresses have been quite apparent without having to see the addresses and masks in binary. The next section uses the four design steps to derive a subnet design in which the dotted-decimal representations are not so obvious.

Breaking the Octet Boundary

In the examples given so far, the subnet spaces have fallen on octet boundaries. This arrangement is not always the most practical or efficient choice. What if, for instance, you need to subnet a class B address across 500 data links, each with a maximum of 100 hosts? This requirement is easily met, but only by using nine bits in the subnet field: $2^9 - 2 = 510$ available subnets, leaving seven bits for the host field, and $2^7 - 2 = 126$ available hosts per subnet. No other bit combination will satisfy this requirement.

Notice, also, that there is no way to subnet a class C address on an octet boundary—doing so would use up all of the last byte, leaving no room for host bits. The subnet bits and host bits must share the last octet, as the following example shows.

Step 1: Figure 2.15 shows the internetwork of Figure 2.13 but with a class C address of 192.168.100.0 assigned. There are five data links; therefore, the address must be subnetted to provide for at least five subnet addresses. The illustration also indicates the number of hosts (including router interfaces) that need to be addressed on each subnet. The maximum host address requirement is 25 for the two ethernets. Therefore, the full subnetting requirements are at least five subnets and at least 25 host addresses per subnet.

Step 2: Applying the $2^n - 2$ formula, three subnet bits and five host bits will satisfy the requirements: $2^3 - 2 = 6$ and $2^5 - 2 = 30$. A class C mask with three bits of subnetting is represented as 255.255.255.224 in dotted decimal.

Step 3: Figure 2.16 shows the derivation of the subnet bits. The subnet mask derived in step 2 is written in binary, and the IP address is written below it. Vertical lines are drawn as markers for the subnet space, and within this space all possible bit combinations are written by counting up from zero in binary.

In Figure 2.17, the unchanged network bits are filled in to the left of the subnet space and the host bits, which are all zeros in the subnet addresses, are filled in to the right of the subnet space. The results are converted to dotted decimal, and these are the six subnet addresses (remembering that the first and last addresses, which have 000 and 111 in the subnet space, cannot be used).

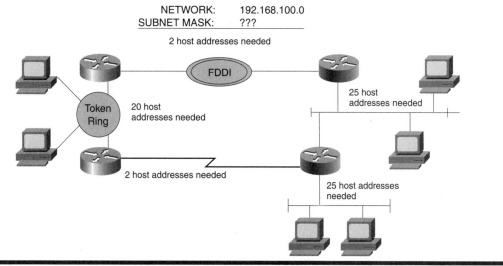

Figure 2.15

The network from Figure 2.13 but with a class C mask assigned. Subnetting an entire octet will not work here; there would be no space left for host bits.

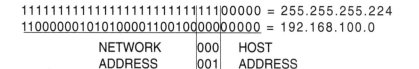

```
11111111111111111111111|111|00000 = 255.255.255.224
11000000101010000110010|000|00000 = 192.168.100.0
```

NETWORK	000	HOST
ADDRESS	001	ADDRESS
SPACE	010	SPACE
	011	
	100	
	101	◀ SUBNET
	110	ADDRESS
	111	SPACE

Figure 2.16

The subnet bits are derived by marking the masked subnet bit space and then writing all possible bit combinations in the space by counting up from zero in binary.

```
11111111111111111111111111|111|00000 = 255.255.255.224
11000000101010000110010000|00000 = 192.168.100.0
11000000101010000110010000|00000 = 192.168.100.0
11000000101010000110010000|01|00000 = 192.168.100.32
11000000101010000110010001|0|00000 = 192.168.100.64
11000000101010000110010001|1|00000 = 192.168.100.96
11000000101010000110010010|0|00000 = 192.168.100.128
11000000101010000110000010|1|00000 = 192.168.100.160
11000000101010000110000011|0|00000 = 192.168.100.192
11000000101010000110000011|1|00000 = 192.168.100.224
```

Figure 2.17

The subnet addresses are derived by filling in the network address to the left of the subnet space, setting all host bits to zero to the right of the subnet space, and converting the results to dotted decimal.

Step 4: The last step is to calculate the host addresses available to each subnet. This step is done by choosing a subnet and, keeping the network and subnet bits unchanged, writing all bit combinations in the host space by counting up from zero in binary.

Figure 2.18 shows this step for subnet 192.168.100.32. Notice the patterns in the results: The first address, in which the host bits are all zero, is the subnet address. The last address, in which the host bits are all one, is the broadcast address for subnet 192.168.100.32. The host addresses count up from the subnet address to the broadcast address, and if the sequence were to continue, the next address would be the second subnet, 192.168.100.64.

The importance of understanding subnetting at the binary level should now be clear. Presented with an address such as 192.168.100.160, you cannot be sure whether it is a host address, a subnet address, or a broadcast address. Even when the subnet mask is known, things are not always readily apparent.

Readers are encouraged to calculate all host addresses for all the remaining subnets in the example and to carefully observe the patterns that result in the addresses. Understanding these patterns will help in situations such as the one presented in the next section.

```
                NETWORK                HOST
                BITS                   BITS
11000000101010000110010000100000 = 192.168.100.32 ← SUBNET
11000000101010000110010000100001 = 192.168.100.33
11000000101010000110010000100010 = 192.168.100.34
11000000101010000110010000100011 = 192.168.100.35
11000000101010000110010000100100 = 192.168.100.36
11000000101010000110010000100101 = 192.168.100.37
11000000101010000110010000100110 = 192.168.100.38
11000000101010000110010000100111 = 192.168.100.39
11000000101010000110010000101000 = 192.168.100.40
11000000101010000110010000101001 = 192.168.100.41
11000000101010000110010000101010 = 192.168.100.42
11000000101010000110010000101011 = 192.168.100.43
11000000101010000110010000101100 = 192.168.100.44
11000000101010000110010000101101 = 192.168.100.45
11000000101010000110010000101110 = 192.168.100.46
11000000101010000110010000101111 = 192.168.100.47
11000000101010000110010000110000 = 192.168.100.48
11000000101010000110010000110001 = 192.168.100.49
11000000101010000110010000110010 = 192.168.100.50
11000000101010000110010000110011 = 192.168.100.51    VALID
11000000101010000110010000110100 = 192.168.100.52    HOST
11000000101010000110010000110101 = 192.168.100.53    ADDRESSES
11000000101010000110010000110110 = 192.168.100.54
11000000101010000110010000110111 = 192.168.100.55
11000000101010000110010000111000 = 192.168.100.56
11000000101010000110010000111001 = 192.168.100.57
11000000101010000110010000111010 = 192.168.100.58
11000000101010000110010000111011 = 192.168.100.59
11000000101010000110010000111100 = 192.168.100.60
11000000101010000110010000111101 = 192.168.100.61
11000000101010000110010000111110 = 192.168.100.62
11000000101010000110010000111111 = 192.168.100.63 ← BROADCAST
```

Figure 2.18

The host addresses for a subnet are derived by writing all possible bit combinations in the host space. These are the host bits for subnet 192.168.100.32.

Troubleshooting a Subnet Mask

The necessity frequently arises to "dissect" a given host address and mask, usually to identify the subnet to which it belongs. For instance, if an address is to be configured on an interface, a good practice is to first verify that the address is valid for the subnet to which the subnet is connected.

Use the following steps to reverse-engineer an IP address:

1. Write the given subnet mask in binary.
2. Write the IP host address in binary.
3. Knowing the class of the host address, the subnet bits of the mask should be apparent. Using the mask bits as a guide, draw a line between the last network bit and the first subnet bit of the address. Draw another line between the last subnet bit and the first host bit.
4. Write the network and subnet bits of the address, setting all host bits to zero. The result is the address of the subnet to which the host address belongs.
5. Again write the network and subnet bits of the address, this time setting all host bits to one. The result is the broadcast address of the subnet.
6. Knowing that the subnet address is the first address in the sequence and that the broadcast address is the last address in the sequence, you also know that all addresses between these two are valid host addresses.

A stepwise method for finding the subnet and broadcast address of a host address

Figure 2.19 shows these steps applied to 172.30.0.141/25. The address is a class B, so it is known that the first 16 bits are the network bits; therefore, the last nine bits of the 25-bit mask mark the subnet space. The subnet address is found to be 172.30.0.128, and the broadcast address is 172.30.0.255. Knowing that the valid host addresses for the subnet are bounded by these two addresses, it is determined that the host addresses for subnet 172.30.0.128 are 172.30.0.129 through 172.30.0.254.

Several things about this example tend to bother folks who are new to subnetting. Some are bothered by the third octet of the address, which is all zeros. Some are bothered by the single subnet bit in the last octet. Some think that the broadcast address looks suspiciously invalid. All of these uneasy feelings arise from reading the addresses in dotted decimal. When the addresses and the mask are seen in binary, these suspicions are assuaged and everything is seen to be legitimate; the mask sets a nine-bit subnet space—all of the third octet, and the first bit of the fourth octet. The moral of the story is that if everything is known to be correct in binary, don't worry if the dotted-decimal representation looks funny.

```
                                    172.30.0.141/25

(1) Write subnet mask:   11111111111111111111111110000000 = 255.255.255.128
(2) Write IP address:    10101100000111100000000010001101 = 172.30.0.141


(3) Mark the subnet      11111111111111111 11111111 0000000 = 255.255.255.128
    space.               10101100000111100 00000001 0001101 = 172.30.0.141


Derive the...            11111111111111111 11111111 0000000 = 255.255.255.128
                         10101100000111100 00000001 0001101 = 172.30.0.141
(4) subnet address:      10101100000111100 00000001 0000000 = 172.30.0.128
(5) broadcast address:   10101100000111100 00000001 1111111 = 172.30.0.255
```

(6) Valid host addresses for this subnet are 172.30.0.129 – 172.30.0.254.

Figure 2.19
Given an IP address and a subnet mask, follow these steps to find the subnet, the broadcast, and the host addresses.

ARP

Chapter 1 explained that routers pass packets across a logical path, composed of multiple data links, by reading and acting on the network addresses in the packets. The packets are passed across the individual data links by encapsulating the packets in frames, which use data link identifiers (MAC addresses, for example) to get the frame from source to destination on the link. One of the major topics of this book concerns the mechanisms by which routers discover and share information about network addresses so that routing may take place. Similarly, devices on a data link need a way to discover their neighbors' data link identifiers so that frames may be transmitted to the correct destination.

Several mechanisms can provide this information;[9] IP uses the Address Resolution Protocol (ARP), described in RFC 826. Figure 2.20 shows how ARP works. A device needing to discover the data link identifier of another device will create an ARP Request packet. This request will contain the IP address of the device in question (the target) and the source IP address and data link identifier (MAC address) of the device making the request (the sender). The ARP Request packet is then encapsulated in a frame with the sender's MAC address as the source and a broadcast address for the destination (Figure 2.21).[10]

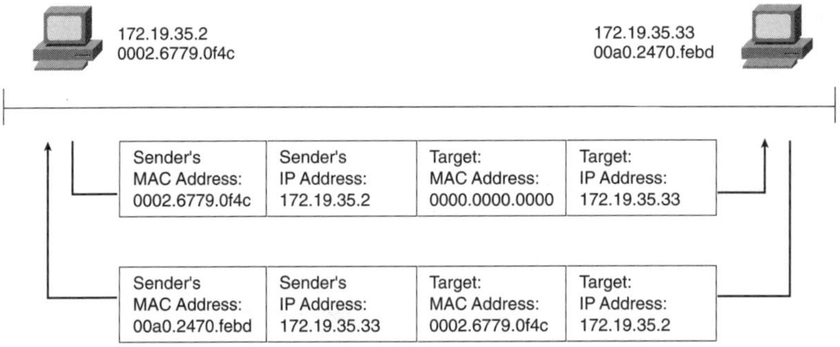

Figure 2.20

ARP is used to map a device's data link identifier to its IP address.

The broadcast address means that all devices on the data link will receive the frame and examine the encapsulated packet. All devices except the target will recognize that the packet is not for

---

[9] *NetWare, for example, makes the MAC address of the device the host portion of the network-level address—a very sensible thing to do.*

[10] *Like an IP broadcast, the MAC broadcast is an address of all ones: ffff.ffff.ffff.*

them and will drop the packet. The target will send an ARP Reply to the source address, supplying its MAC address (Figure 2.22).

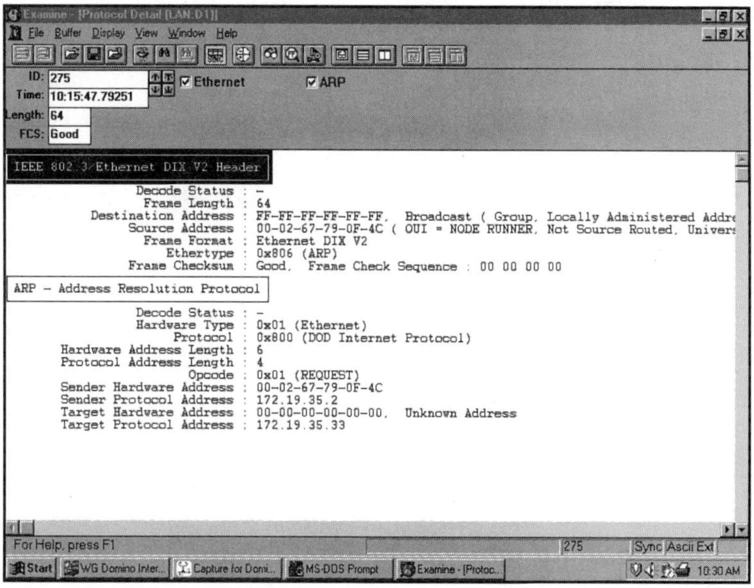

Figure 2.21

An analyzer capture of the ARP Request depicted in Figure 2.20, with its encapsulating frame.

Cisco routers will display ARP activity when the debug function **debug arp** is invoked, as shown in Figure 2.23.

Figure 2.24 shows the ARP packet format. As the fields are described, compare them with the ARP packets in Figures 2.21 and 2.22.

Hardware Type specifies the type of hardware, as described in RFC 1700.[11] Examples of some of the more common type numbers are shown in Table 2.4.

---

[11] *J. Postel and J. Reynolds. "Assigned Numbers." RFC 1700, October 1994. This RFC specifies all numbers in use in various fields throughout the TCP/IP protocol suite. This large document (230 pages) is a valuable reference, and a copy should be kept accessible.*

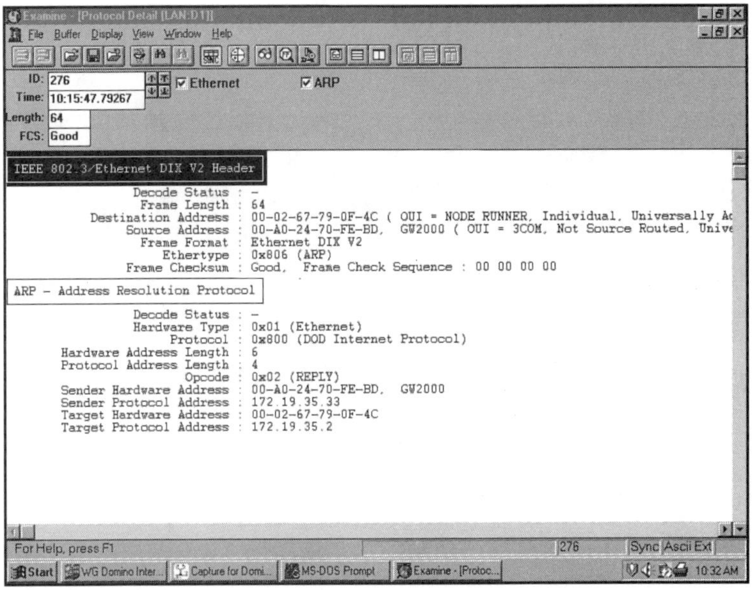

Figure 2.22

An analyzer capture of the ARP Reply depicted in Figure 2.20.

```
Aretha#debug arp
IP ARP: rcvd req src 172.19.35.2 0002.6779.0f4c, dst 172.21.5.1 Ethernet0
IP ARP: sent rep src 172.21.5.1 0000.0c0a.2aa9,
        dst 172.19.35.2 0002.6779.0f4c Ethernet0

Aretha#
```

Figure 2.23

Router Aretha (172.21.5.1) responds to an ARP request from host 172.19.35.2.

Protocol Type specifies the type of network-level protocol the sender is mapping to the data link identifier; IP is 0x0800.

Hardware Address Length specifies the length, in octets, of the data link identifiers. MAC addresses would be 6.

Protocol Address Length specifies the length, in octets, of the network-level address. IP would be 4.

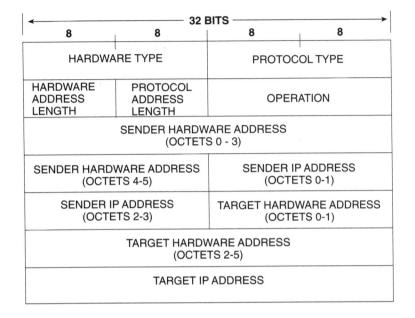

Figure 2.24

The ARP packet format.

Table 2.4 *Common hardware type codes.*

Number	Hardware Type
1	Ethernet
3	X.25
4	Proteon ProNET Token Ring
6	IEEE 802 Networks
7	ARCnet
11	Apple LocalTalk
14	SMDS
15	Frame Relay

Table 2.4 *Common hardware type codes, continued.*

Number	Hardware Type
16	ATM
17	HDLC
18	Fibre Channel
19	ATM
20	Serial Link

Operation specifies whether the packet is an ARP Request (1) or an ARP Reply (2). Other values may also be found here, indicating other uses for the ARP packet. Examples are Reverse ARP Request (4), Reverse ARP Reply (5), Inverse ARP Request (8), and Inverse ARP Reply (9).

The final 20 octets are the fields for the sender's and target's data link identifiers and IP addresses.

In the top screen in Figure 2.25, the command **show arp** is used to examine the ARP table in a Cisco router. Notice the Age column. As this column would indicate, ARP information is removed from the table after a certain time to prevent the table from becoming congested with old information. Cisco routers hold ARP entries for four hours (14,400 seconds); this default can be changed. The following example changes the ARP timeout to 30 minutes (1,800 seconds):

```
Martha(config)# interface ethernet 0
Martha(config-if)# arp timeout 1800
```

The middle screen of Figure 2.25 shows the ARP table of a Windows 95 PC, and the bottom shows the ARP table from a Linux machine. Although the format is different from the Cisco display, the essential information is the same in all three tables.

```
Martha#show arp

Protocol    Address        Age (min)   Hardware    Addr   Type   Interface
Internet    10.158.43.34        2      0002 . 6779 . 0f4c  ARPA   Ethernet0
Internet    10.158.43.1         -      0000 . 0c0a . 2aa9  ARPA   Ethernet0
Internet    10.158.43.25       18      00a0 . 24a8 . a1a5  ARPA   Ethernet0
Internet    10.158.43.100       6      0000 . 0c0a . 2c51  ARPA   Ethernet0
Martha#
```

```
C:\WINDOWS>arp -a
Interface: 148.158.43.25

    Internet Address        Physical Address        Type
    10.158.43.1             00-00-0c-0a-2a-a9        dynamic
    10.158.43.34            00-02-67-79-0f-4c        dynamic
    10.158.43.100           00-00-0c-0a-2c-51        dynamic
```

```
Linux:~# arp -a

Address          HW type          HW address              Flags   Mask
10.158.43.1      10Mbps Ethernet  00:00:0C:0A:2A:A9        C       *
10.158.43.100    10Mbps Ethernet  00:00:0C:0A:2C:51        C       *
10.158.43.25     10Mbps Ethernet  00:A0:24:A8:A1:A5        C       *
Linux:~#
```

Figure 2.25

The ARP table for three devices connected to the same network: a Cisco router, a Windows 95 host, and a Linux host.

ARP entries may also be permanently placed in the table. To statically map 172.21.5.131 to hardware address 0000.00a4.b74c, with a SNAP encapsulation type, use the following:

```
Martha(config)# arp 172.21.5.131 0000.00a4.b74c snap
```

The command **clear arp-cache** forces a deletion of all dynamic entries from the ARP table. It also clears the fast-switching cache and the IP route cache.

Several variations of ARP exist; at least one, proxy ARP, is important to routing.

Proxy ARP

Sometimes called *promiscuous ARP* and described in RFCs 925 and 1027, proxy ARP is a method by which routers may make themselves available to hosts. For example, a host 192.168.12.5/24 needs to send a packet to 192.168.20.101/24, but it is not configured with default gateway information and therefore does not know how to reach a router. It may issue an ARP Request for 192.168.20.101; the local router, receiving the request and knowing how to reach network 192.168.20.0, will issue an ARP Reply with its own data link identifier in the hardware address field. In effect, the router has tricked the local host into thinking that the router's interface is the interface of 192.168.20.101. All packets destined for that address will be sent to the router.

Figure 2.26 shows another use for proxy ARP. Of particular interest here are the address masks. The router is configured with a 28-bit mask (four bits of subnetting for the class C address), but the hosts are all configured with 24-bit, default class C mask. As a result, the hosts will not be aware that subnets exist. Host 192.168.20.66, wanting to send a packet to 192.168.20.25, will issue an ARP Request. The router, recognizing that the target address is on another subnet, will respond with its own hardware address. Proxy ARP makes the subnetted network topology transparent to the hosts.

The ARP cache in Figure 2.27 gives a hint that proxy ARP is in use. Notice that multiple IP addresses are mapped to a single MAC identifier; the addresses are for hosts, but the hardware MAC identifier belongs to the router interface.

Proxy ARP is enabled by default on Cisco routers and may be disabled on a per interface basis with the command **no ip proxy-arp**.

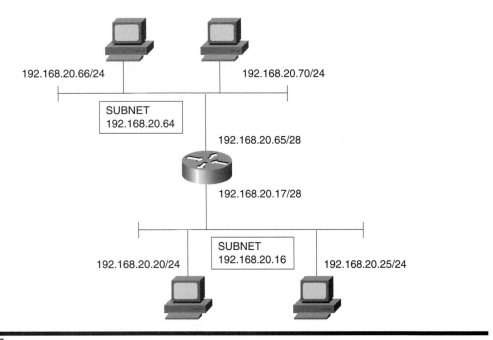

Figure 2.26

Proxy ARP enables the use of transparent subnets.

```
C:\WINDOWS>arp -a

Interface: 192.168.20.66
  Internet Address      Physical Address       Type
  192.168.20.17         00-00-0c-0a-2a-a9      dynamic
  192.168.20.20         00-00-0c-0a-2a-a9      dynamic
  192.168.20.25         00-00-0c-0a-2a-a9      dynamic
  192.168.20.65         00-00-0c-0a-2c-51      dynamic
  192.168.20.70         00-02-67-79-0f-4c      dynamic
```

Figure 2.27

This ARP table from host 192.168.20.66 in Figure 2.26 shows multiple IP addresses mapped to one MAC identifier, indicating that proxy ARP is in use.

Gratuitous ARP

A host may occasionally issue an ARP Request with its own IP address as the target address. These ARP Requests, known as *gratuitous ARPs,* have two uses:

- A gratuitous ARP may be used for duplicate address checks. A device that issues an ARP Request with its own IP address as the target and receives an ARP Reply from another device will know that the address is a duplicate.

- A gratuitous ARP may be used to advertise a new data link identifier. This use takes advantage of the fact that when a device receives an ARP Request for an IP address that is already in its ARP cache, the cache will be updated with the sender's new hardware address.

Many IP implementations do not use gratuitous ARP, but you should be aware of its existence.

Reverse ARP

Instead of mapping a hardware address to a known IP address, Reverse ARP (RARP) maps an IP address to a known hardware address. Some devices, such as diskless workstations, may not know their IP address at startup. RARP may be programmed into firmware on these devices, allowing them to issue an ARP Request that has their burned-in hardware address. The reply from a RARP server will supply the appropriate IP address.

RARP is being largely supplanted by Bootstrap Protocol (BOOTP) and its extension Dynamic Host Configuration Protocol (DHCP), both of which can provide more information than the IP address, and which, unlike RARP, can be routed off the local data link.

ICMP

The Internet Control Message Protocol, or ICMP, described in RFC 792, specifies a variety of messages whose common purpose is to manage the internetwork. ICMP messages may be classified as either error messages or queries and responses. Figure 2.28 shows the general ICMP packet format. The packets are identified by type; many of the packet types have more specific types, and these are identified by the code field. Table 2.5 lists the various ICMP packet types and their codes, as described in RFC 1700.

Table 2.5   *ICMP packet types and code fields.*

Type	Code	Name
0	0	ECHO REPLY
3		DESTINATION UNREACHABLE
	0	Network Unreachable
	1	Host Unreachable
	2	Protocol Unreachable
	3	Port Unreachable
	4	Fragmentation Needed and Don't Fragment Flag Set
	5	Source Route Failed
	6	Destination Network Unknown
	7	Destination Host Unknown
	8	Source Host Isolated
	9	Destination Network Administratively Prohibited
	10	Destination Host Administratively Prohibited
	11	Destination Network Unreachable for Type of Service

Table 2.5 *ICMP packet types and code fields, continued.*

Type	Code	Name
	12	Destination Host Unreachable for Type of Service
4	0	SOURCE QUENCH
5		REDIRECT
	0	Redirect Datagram for the Network (or Subnet)
	1	Redirect Datagram for the Host
	2	Redirect Datagram for the Network and Type of Service
	3	Redirect Datagram for the Host and Type of Service
6	0	ALTERNATE HOST ADDRESS
8	0	ECHO
9	0	ROUTER ADVERTISEMENT
10	0	ROUTER SELECTION
11		TIME EXCEEDED
	0	Time to Live Exceeded in Transit
	1	Fragment Reassembly Time Exceeded
12		PARAMETER PROBLEM
	0	Pointer Indicates the Error
	1	Missing a Required Option
	2	Bad Length
13	0	TIMESTAMP
14	0	TIMESTAMP REPLY
15	0	INFORMATION REQUEST (Obsolete)
16	0	INFORMATION REPLY (Obsolete)
17	0	ADDRESS MASK REQUEST

Table 2.5 *ICMP packet types and code fields, continued.*

Type	Code	Name
18	0	ADDRESS MASK REPLY
30		TRACEROUTE
31		DATAGRAM CONVERSION ERROR
32		MOBILE HOST REDIRECT
33		IPv6 WHERE-ARE-YOU
34		IPv6 I-AM-HERE
35		MOBILE REGISTRATION REQUEST
36		MOBILE REGISTRATION REPLY

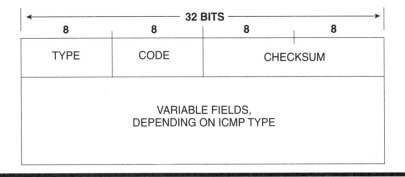

Figure 2.28

The ICMP packet header includes a type field, a code field that further identifies some types, and a checksum. The rest of the fields depend on the type and code.

Figures 2.29 and 2.30 show analyzer captures of two of the most well-known ICMP messages—Echo Request and Echo Reply, which are used by the ping function.

Although most ICMP types have some bearing on routing functionality, three types are of particular importance.

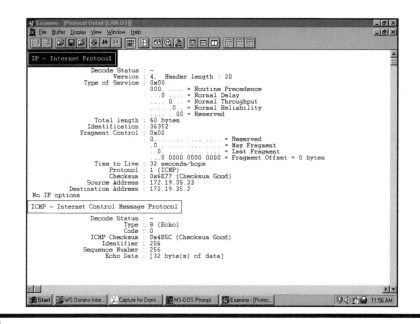

Figure 2.29

An ICMP Echo message, shown with its IP header.

Router Advertisement and *Router Selection*, types 9 and 10, respectively, are used by the ICMP Router Discovery Protocol (IRDP).

Redirect, ICMP type 5, is used by routers to notify hosts of another router on the data link that should be used for a particular destination. Suppose two routers, router A and router B, are connected to the same Ethernet. Host X, also on the Ethernet, is configured to use router A as its default gateway; the host sends a packet to router A, and A sees that the destination address of the packet is reachable via router B (that is, router A must forward the packet out the same interface on which it was received). Router A forwards the packet to B but also sends an ICMP redirect to host X informing it that in the future, to reach that particular destination, X should forward the packet to router B. Figure 2.31 shows a router sending a redirect.

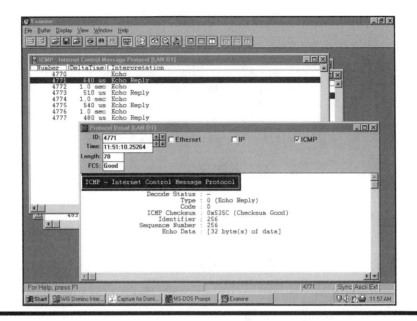

Figure 2.30
An ICMP Echo Reply without the IP header displayed. The packet summary window in the background shows four Echo/Echo Reply pairs, which make up four Pings.

```
Pip#debug  ip icmp
ICMP packet debugging is on
ICMP: redirect sent to 10.158.43.25 for dest  10.158.40.1, use gw
10.158.43.10
0
Pip#
```

Figure 2.31
*Using the debugging function **debug ip icmp**, this router can be seen sending a redirect to host 10.158.43.25, informing it that the correct router for reaching destination 10.158.40.1 is reachable via gateway (gw) 10.158.43.10.*

A frequently used trick to avoid redirects on data links with multiple attached gateways is to set each host's default gateway as its own IP address. The hosts will then ARP for any address, and if the address is not on the data link, the correct router should respond via proxy ARP. The benefits of using this tactic merely to avoid redirects are debatable; redirects are decreased or eliminated but at the expense of increased ARP traffic.

Redirects are enabled by default on Cisco routers and may be disabled on a per interface basis with the command **no ip redirects**.

THE HOST-TO-HOST LAYER

The host-to-host layer of the TCP/IP protocol is aptly named. Whereas the internet layer is responsible for the logical paths between networks, the host-to-host layer is responsible for the full logical path between two hosts on disparate networks.[12] From another viewpoint, the host-to-host layer is an interface to the lower layers of the protocol suite, freeing applications from any concern about how their data is actually being delivered.

An analogy to this service is a corporate mailroom. A package may be given to the mailroom with requirements stated for its delivery (general delivery, overnight). The person making the delivery request does not need to know, and is probably not interested in, the actual mechanics of delivering the package. The mailroom people will arrange for the proper service (postal, FedEx, cross-town bicycle courier) to fulfill the delivery requirements.

The two primary services offered by the host-to-host layer are TCP and UDP.

TCP

The Transmission Control Protocol, or TCP, described in RFC 793, provides applications with a reliable, connection-oriented service. In other words, TCP provides the appearance of a point-to-point connection.

---

[12] *Similarly, it can be said that the equivalent functions of the OSI session layer, residing above the transport layer, provide a logical, end-to-end path between two applications across an internetwork.*

Point-to-point connections have two characteristics:

- They have only one path to the destination. A packet entering one end of the connection cannot become lost, because the only place to go is the other end.

- Packets arrive in the same order in which they are sent.

TCP provides the appearance of a point-to-point connection, although in reality there is no such connection. The internet layer TCP is utilizing is a connectionless, best-effort packet delivery service. The analog of this is the postal service. If a stack of letters is given to the mail carrier for delivery, there is no guarantee that the letters will arrive stacked in the same order, that they will all arrive on the same day, or indeed that they will arrive at all. The postal service merely commits to making its best effort to deliver the letters.

Likewise, the internet layer does not guarantee that all packets will take the same route, and therefore there is no guarantee that they will arrive in the same sequence and time intervals as they were sent, or that they will arrive at all.

On the other hand, a telephone call is connection-oriented service. Data must arrive sequentially and reliably, or it is useless. Like a telephone call, TCP must first establish a connection, then transfer data, and then perform a disconnect when the data transfer is complete.

TCP uses three fundamental mechanisms to accomplish a connection-oriented service on top of a connectionless service:

- Packets are labeled with sequence numbers so that the receiving TCP service can put out-of-sequence packets into the correct sequence before delivering them to the destination application.

- TCP uses a system of acknowledgments, checksums, and timers to provide reliability. A receiver may notify a sender when it recognizes that a packet in a sequence has failed to arrive or has errors, or a sender may assume that a packet has not arrived if the receiver does not send an acknowledgment within a certain amount of time after transmission. In both cases, the sender will resend the packet in question.

- TCP uses a mechanism called *windowing* to regulate the flow of packets; windowing decreases the chances of packets being dropped because of full buffers in the receiver.

TCP attaches a header to the application layer data; the header contains fields for the sequence numbers and other information necessary for these mechanisms as well as fields for addresses called port numbers, which identify the source and destination applications of the data. The application data with its attached TCP header is then encapsulated within an IP packet for delivery. Figure 2.32 shows the fields of the TCP header, and Figure 2.33 shows an analyzer capture of a TCP header.

Source and *Destination Port* are 16-bit fields that specify the source and destination applications for the encapsulated data. Like other numbers used by TCP/IP, RFC 1700 describes all port numbers in common and not-so-common use. A port number for an application, when coupled with the IP address of the host the application resides on, is called a *socket*. A socket uniquely identifies every application in an internetwork.

Sequence Number is a 32-bit number that identifies where the encapsulated data fits within a data stream from the sender. For example, if the sequence number of a segment is 1343 and the seg-

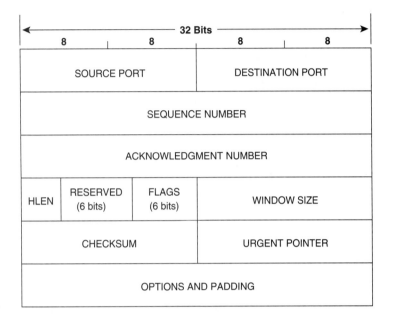

Figure 2.32
The TCP header format.

ment contains 512 octets of data, the next segment should have a sequence number of 1343 + 512 + 1 = 1856.

Acknowledgment Number is a 32-bit field that identifies the sequence number the source next expects to receive from the destination. If a host receives an acknowledgment number that does not match the next sequence number it intends to send (or has sent), it knows not only that packets have been lost but also which packets have been lost.

Header Length, sometimes called *Data Offset*, is a four-bit field indicating the length of the header in 32-bit words. This field is necessary to identify the beginning of the data because the length of the Options field is variable.

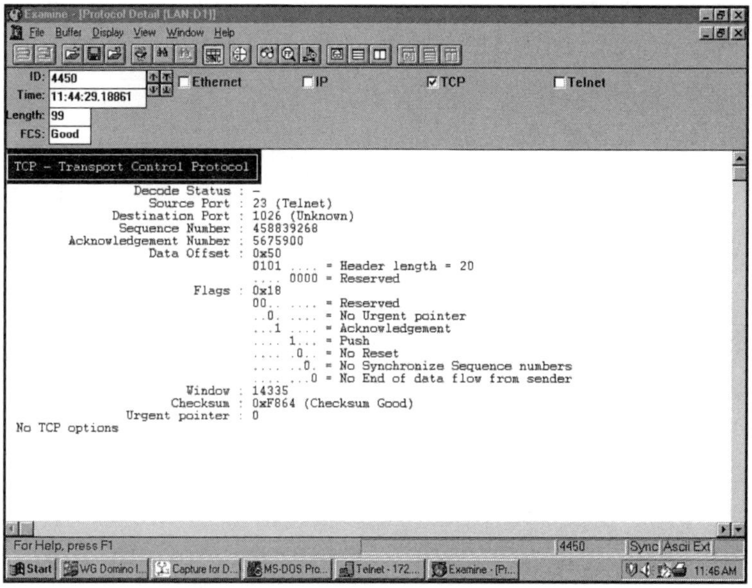

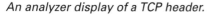

Figure 2.33
An analyzer display of a TCP header.

The *Reserved* field is six bits, which are always set to zero.

Flags are six 1-bit flags that are used for data flow and connection control. The flags are Urgent (URG), Acknowledgment (ACK), Push (PSH), Reset (RST), Synchronize (SYN), and Final (FIN).

Window Size is a 16-bit field used for flow control. It specifies the number of octets, starting with the octet indicated by the Acknowledgment Number, that the sender of the segment will accept from its peer at the other end of the connection before the peer must stop transmitting and wait for an acknowledgment.

Checksum is 16 bits, covering both the header and the encapsulated data, allowing error detection.

Urgent Pointer is used only when the URG flag is set. The 16-bit number is added to the Sequence Number to indicate the end of the urgent data.

Options, as the name implies, specifies options required by the sender's TCP process. The most commonly used option is Maximum Segment Size, which informs the receiver of the largest segment the sender is willing to accept. The remainder of the field is padded with zeros to ensure that the header length is a multiple of 32 octets.

UDP

User Datagram Protocol, or UDP, described in RFC 768, provides a connectionless, best-effort packet delivery service. At first take, it may seem questionable that any application would prefer an unreliable delivery over the connection-oriented TCP. The advantage of UDP, however, is that no time is spent setting up a connection—the data is just sent. Applications that send short bursts of data will realize a performance advantage by using UDP instead of TCP.

Figure 2.34 shows another advantage of UDP: a much smaller header than TCP. The Source and Destination Port fields are the same as they are in the TCP header; the UDP length indicates the length of the entire segment in octets. The checksum covers the entire segment, but unlike TCP, the checksum here is optional; when no checksum is used, the field is set to all zeros. Figure 2.35 shows an analyzer capture of a UDP header.

Figure 2.34
The UDP header format.

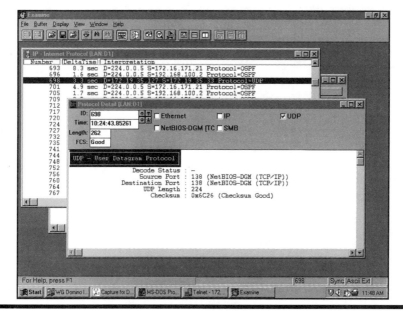

Figure 2.35

An analyzer display of a UDP header.

LOOKING AHEAD

The focus of this chapter has largely been on the mechanisms by which a device's internet layer (or OSI network layer) identifies itself and how it maps to the network interface (or OSI data link) layer. Internet layer functions that are important to routing were also examined. The following chapter examines the routing function and the information a router requires to perform that function.

SUMMARY TABLE: CHAPTER 2
COMMAND REVIEW

Command	Description
arp *ip-address hardware-address*	Statically maps an IP address type [*alias*]to a hardware address
arp timeout *seconds*	Sets the amount of time a Cisco router holds ARP entries
clear arp-cache	Forces the deletion of all dynamic entries from the ARP table
debug ip icmp	Displays ICMP events as they occur on the router.
ip address *ip-address mask*	Assigns an IP address and [*secondary*] mask to an interface
ip netmask-format{bitcount|decimal| hexadecimal}	Configures a router to display IP (address, mask) pairs in bitcount, dotted-decimal, or hexadecimal format
ip proxy-arp	Enables proxy ARP
ip redirects	Enables ICMP redirects

RECOMMENDED READING

Baker, F., ed. "Requirements for IP Version 4 Routers," RFC 1812, June 1995. This paper documents both requirements and recommendations for routers that will run IP.

Braden, R., ed. "Requirements for Internet Hosts—Communication Layers," RFC 1122, October 1989. The host-centric companion paper to RFC 1812.

Comer, D. E. *Internetworking with TCP/IP*, Vol. 1. Englewood Cliffs, New Jersey: Prentice-Hall; 1991. This book, like Perlman's, is a classic. Although you don't need to read both Comer and Stevens, doing so certainly couldn't hurt.

Stevens, W. R. *TCP/IP Illustrated*, Vol. 1. Reading, Massachusetts: Addison-Wesley; 1994. An excellent book on TCP/IP. Along with an in-depth introduction to the protocols, Stevens offers a wealth of captures from a live network that is diagrammed inside the front cover.

REVIEW QUESTIONS

1. What are the five layers of the TCP/IP protocol suite? What is the purpose of each layer?

2. What is the most common IP version presently in use?

3. What is fragmentation? What fields of the IP header are used for fragmentation?

4. What is the purpose of the TTL field in the IP header? How does the TTL process work?

5. What is the first octet rule?

6. How are class A, B, and C IP addresses recognized in dotted decimal? How are they recognized in binary?

7. What is an address mask, and how does it work?

8. What is a subnet? Why are subnets used in IP environments?

9. Why can't a subnet of all zeros or all ones be used in a classful routing environment?

10. What is ARP?

11. What is proxy ARP?

12. What is a redirect?

13. What is the essential difference between TCP and UDP?

14. What mechanisms does TCP use to provide connection-oriented service?

15. Instead of ARP, Novell NetWare uses a network address that includes a device's MAC address as the host portion. Why can't IP do this?

16. NetWare has a transport layer service similar to TCP called Sequenced Packet Exchange (SPX), but no service similar to UDP. Applications requiring connectionless

service directly access the connectionless IPX at the network layer. What purpose does UDP serve by providing a connectionless service on top of what is already a connectionless service?

CONFIGURATION EXERCISES

1. The first octet rule says that the highest class C address is 223, but it is known that for eight bits the highest decimal number is 255. There are two more classes: Class D addresses are for multicast, and class E addresses are for experimental usage. Class D addresses have, as their first four bits, 1110. What is the decimal range of the first octet of class D addresses?

2. Select a subnet mask for 10.0.0.0 so that there will be at least 16,000 subnets with at least 700 host addresses available on each subnet. Select a subnet mask for 172.27.0.0 so that there are at least 500 subnets with at least 100 host addresses available on each subnet.

3. How many subnets are available if a class C address has six bits of subnetting? How many host addresses are available per subnet? Is there a practical use for such a subnetting scheme?

4. Use a 28-bit mask to derive the available subnets of 192.168.147.0. Derive the available host addresses of each subnet.

5. Use a 29-bit mask to derive the available subnets of 192.168.147.0. Derive the available host addresses of each subnet.

6. Use a 20-bit mask to derive the available subnets of 172.16.0.0. Write the range (that is, the numerically lowest to the numerically highest address) of available host addresses for each subnet.

TROUBLESHOOTING EXERCISES

1. For the following host addresses and subnet masks, find what subnet each address belongs to, the broadcast address of that subnet, and the range of host addresses for that subnet:

   10.14.87.60/19

   172.25.0.235/27

   172.25.16.37/25

2. You have been told to configure 192.168.13.175 on an interface with a mask of 255.255.255.240. Is there a problem? If so, what is it?

CHAPTER 3

Static Routing

An important observation from Chapter 2, "TCP/IP Review," is that the data link/physical layers and the transport/network layers, as defined by the OSI model, perform very similar duties: They provide the means for conveying data from a source to a destination across some path. The difference is that the data link/physical layers provide communications across a physical path, whereas the transport/network layers provide communications across a logical or virtual path made up of a series of data links.

Further, Chapter 2 showed that for communications to take place across a physical path, certain information about data link identifiers and encapsulations must be acquired and stored in a database such as the ARP cache. Similarly, information that the transport/network layers require to do their job must also be acquired and stored. This information is stored in the *route table*, also known as the *forwarding database*.

This chapter examines what sort of information is required to route a packet, how that information is stored in the route table, how to enter the information into the database, and some techniques for building a routed internetwork by entering the proper information into the proper routers' route tables.

THE ROUTE TABLE

To understand the kind of information that exists in the route table, it is useful to begin with an examination of what happens when a framed packet arrives at one of a router's interfaces. The data-link identifier in the frame's destination address field is examined. If it contains either the identifier of the router's interface or a broadcast identifier, the router strips off the frame and passes the enclosed packet to the network layer. At the network layer, the destination address of the packet is examined. If the destination address is either the IP address of the router's interface or an all-hosts broadcast address, the protocol field of the packet is examined and the enclosed data is sent to the appropriate internal process.[1]

Any other destination address calls for routing. The address may be for a host on another network to which the router is attached (including the router interface attached to that network) or for a host on a network not directly connected to the router. The address may also be a directed broadcast, in which there is a distinct network or subnet address, and the remaining host bits are all ones. These addresses are also routable.

If the packet is to be routed, the router will do a route table lookup to acquire the correct route. At a minimum, each route entry in the database must contain two items:

- A destination address. This is the address of the network the router can reach. As this chapter explains, the router may have more than one route to the same address and/or a group of subnets of the same or of varying lengths grouped under the same major IP network address.

---

[1] *There is also the special case of a multicast address, which is destined for a group of devices, but not for all devices. An example of a multicast address is the class D address 224.0.0.5, reserved for all OSPF-speaking routers.*

- A pointer to the destination. This pointer either will indicate that the destination network is directly connected to the router or it will indicate the address of another router on a directly connected network. That router, which will be one router hop closer to the destination, is a *next-hop router.*

The router will match the most specific address it can.[2] In descending order of specificity, the address may be one of the following:

- A host address (a *host route*)

- A subnet

- A group of subnets (a *summary route*)

- A major network number

- A group of major network numbers (a *supernet*)

- A default address

This chapter provides examples of the first four types. Supernets are covered in Chapter 7, "Routing Information Protocol Version 2." A default address is considered a least-specific address and is matched only if no other match can be found. Default addressing is the topic of Chapter 12, "Default Routes and On-Demand Routing."

If the destination address of the packet cannot be matched to any route table entry, the packet is dropped and a Destination Unreachable ICMP message is sent to the source address.

Figure 3.1 shows a simple internetwork and the route table entries required by each router. Of primary importance here is the "big picture," seeing how the route tables work as a whole to

---

[2] *There are two basic procedures for finding the best match, depending upon whether the router is behaving* classfully *or* classlessly. *Classful table lookups are explained in more detail in Chapter 5, "Routing Information Protocol (RIP), and classless table lookups are explained in Chapter 7, "Routing Information Protocol Version 2."*

transport packets correctly and efficiently. The destination addresses that the router can reach are listed in the Network column of the route tables. The pointers to the destinations are in the Next Hop column.

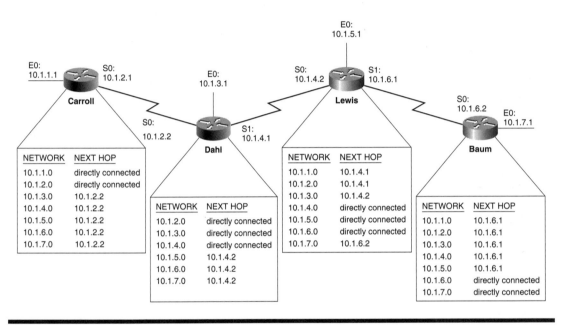

Figure 3.1

The minimum information needed for each route table entry consists of the destination networks and the pointers to those networks.

If router Carroll in Figure 3.1 receives a packet with a source address of 10.1.1.97 and a destination address of 10.1.7.35, a route table lookup determines that the best match for the destination address is subnet 10.1.7.0, reachable via next-hop address

10.1.2.2, on interface S0. The packet is sent to that next router (Dahl), which does a lookup in its own table and sees that network 10.1.7.0 is reachable via next-hop address 10.1.4.2, out interface S1. The process continues until the packet reaches router Baum. That router, receiving the packet on its interface S0, does a lookup, and sees that the destination is on one of its directly connected networks, out E0. Routing is completed, and the packet is delivered to host 10.1.7.35 on the Ethernet link.

The routing process, as explained, assumes that the router can match its listed next-hop addresses to its interfaces. For example, router Dahl must know that Lewis's address 10.1.4.2 is reachable via interface S1. Dahl will know from the IP address and subnet mask assigned to S1 that S1 is directly connected to subnet 10.1.4.0. It then knows that 10.1.4.2, a member of the same subnet, must be connected to the same network.

Notice that every router must have consistent and accurate information for correct packet switching to occur. For example, in Figure 3.1 an entry for network 10.1.1.0 is missing from Dahl's route table. A packet from 10.1.1.97 to 10.1.7.35 will be delivered, but when a reply is sent from 10.1.7.35 to 10.1.1.97, the packet is passed from Baum to Lewis to Dahl. Dahl does a lookup and finds that it has no entry for subnet 10.1.1.0, so the packet is dropped, and an ICMP Destination Unreachable message is sent to host 10.1.7.35.

Figure 3.2 shows the actual Cisco route table from router Lewis of Figure 3.1. The command for examining the IP route table of a Cisco router is **show ip route**.

```
Lewis#show ip route
Codes: C - connected, S - static, I - IGRP, R - RIP, M - mobile, B - BGP,
       D - EIGRP, EX - EIGRP external, O - OSPF, IA - OSPF inter area,
       N1 - OSPF NSSA external type 1, N2 - OSPF NSSA external type 2,
       E1 - OSPF external type 1, E2 - OSPF external type 2, E - EGP,
       i - IS-IS, L1 - IS-IS level-1, L2 - IS-IS level-2, * - candidate default,
       U - per-user static route, o - ODR

Gateway of last resort is not set

     10.0.0.0/24 is subnetted, 7 subnets
S       10.1.3.0 [1/0] via 10.1.4.1
S       10.1.2.0 [1/0] via 10.1.4.1
S       10.1.1.0 [1/0] via 10.1.4.1
S       10.1.7.0 [1/0] via 10.1.6.2
C       10.1.6.0 is directly connected, Serial1
C       10.1.5.0 is directly connected, Ethernet0
C       10.1.4.0 is directly connected, Serial0
Lewis#
```

Figure 3.2

The Cisco route table for router Lewis of Figure 3.1.

Examine the contents of this database and compare it with the generic table shown for Lewis in Figure 3.1. A key at the top of the table explains the letters down the left side of the table. These letters indicate how each route entry was learned; in Figure 3.2 all routes are tagged with either a C for "directly connected," or an S for "static entry." The statement "gateway of last resort is not set" refers to a default route.

At the top of the table is a statement indicating that the route table knows of seven subnets of the major network address 10.0.0.0, subnetted with a 24-bit mask. For each of the seven route entries, the destination subnet is shown; for the entries that are not directly connected—routes for which the packet must be forwarded to a next-hop router—a bracketed tuple indicates [administrative distance/metric] for that route. Administrative distances are introduced later in this chapter and are covered in detail in Chapter 11, "Route Redistribution."

Metrics, discussed in greater detail in Chapter 4, "Dynamic Routing Protocols," are a way for routes to be rated by preference—the lower the metric, the "shorter" the path. Notice that the static routes shown in Figure 3.2 have a metric of 0. Finally, either the address of the directly connected interface of the next-hop router or the interface to which the destination is connected is shown.

CONFIGURING STATIC ROUTES

The route table acquires information in two ways. The information may be entered manually, by means of a static route entry, or automatically by one of several systems of automatic information discovery and sharing known as *dynamic routing protocols*. The bulk of this book concerns dynamic IP routing protocols, but this discussion of static route configuration will prepare you to understand the subsequent chapters.

More to the point, static routing is preferred over dynamic routing in certain circumstances. As with any process, the more automatic it is, the less control we have over it. Although dynamic (automatic) routing requires much less human intervention, static routing allows very precise control over the routing behavior of an internetwork. The price to be paid for this precision is the necessity of manual reconfiguration any time the topology of the network changes.

Case Study: Simple Static Routes

Figure 3.3 shows an internetwork with four routers and six networks. Notice that the subnets of network 10.0.0.0 are *discontiguous*—there is a different major network subnet (192.168.1.192, in the Tigger-to-Piglet link) separating 10.1.0.0 from the other 10.0.0.0 subnets. The subnets of 10.0.0.0 are also *variably subnetted*—the subnet masks are not consistent

Discontiguous networks

Variable subnetting

throughout the internetwork. Finally, the subnet address of Pooh's Ethernet link is an all-zero subnet. Later chapters demonstrate that an addressing scheme with these characteristics causes problems for simpler, classful routing protocols such as RIP and IGRP; static routes work fine here.

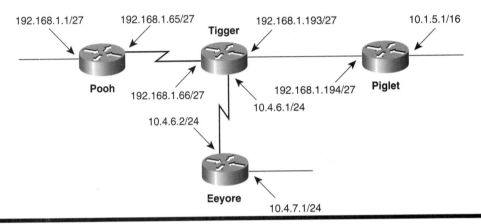

Figure 3.3
Routing protocols such as RIP and IGRP cannot easily route this discontiguous, variably subnetted internetwork, but static routing will work.

The procedure for statically routing an internetwork has three steps:

The steps for creating simple static route configurations

1. For each data link within the internetwork, identify all addresses (subnet or network).
2. For each router, identify all data links not directly connected to that router.
3. For each router, write a route statement for each data link not directly connected to it.

Writing route statements for a router's directly connected data links is unnecessary, because the addresses and masks configured on the router's interfaces cause those networks to be recorded in its route table.

For example, the internetwork in Figure 3.3 has six subnets:

- 10.1.0.0/16

- 10.4.6.0/24

- 10.4.7.0/24

- 192.168.1.192/27

- 192.168.1.64/27

- 192.168.1.0/27

To configure static routes for Piglet, the subnets that are not directly connected are identified as follows:

- 10.4.6.0/24

- 10.4.7.0/24

- 192.168.1.64/27

- 192.168.1.0/27

These are the subnets for which static routes must be written. The commands for entering Piglet's static routes are as follows:[3]

```
Piglet(config)# ip route 192.168.1.0 255.255.255.224 192.168.1.193
Piglet(config)# ip route 192.168.1.64 255.255.255.224 192.168.1.193
Piglet(config)# ip route 10.4.6.0 255.255.255.0 192.168.1.193
Piglet(config)# ip route 10.4.7.0 255.255.255.0 192.168.1.193
```

---

[3] *For the static routes in this example and the subsequent examples in this chapter to work properly, two global commands must be added to the routers:* **ip classless** *and* **ip subnet-zero**. *These commands are introduced in Chapter 7 and are mentioned here for readers who wish to try the configuration examples in a lab.*

Following the same steps, the route entries for the other three routers are:

```
Pooh(config)# ip route 192.168.1.192 255.255.255.224 192.168.1.66
Pooh(config)# ip route 10.1.0.0 255.255.0.0 192.168.1.66
Pooh(config)# ip route 10.4.6.0 255.255.255.0 192.168.1.66
Pooh(config)# ip route 10.4.7.0 255.255.255.0 192.168.1.66

Tigger(config)# ip route 192.168.1.0 255.255.255.224 192.168.1.65
Tigger(config)# ip route 10.1.0.0 255.255.0.0 192.168.1.194
Tigger(config)# ip route 10.4.7.0 255.255.255.0 10.4.6.2

Eeyore(config)# ip route 192.168.1.0 255.255.255.224 10.4.6.1
Eeyore(config)# ip route 192.168.1.64 255.255.255.224 10.4.6.1
Eeyore(config)# ip route 192.168.1.192 255.255.255.224 10.4.6.1
Eeyore(config)# ip route 10.1.0.0 255.255.0.0 10.4.6.1
```

The routing commands themselves are easily read if the reader remembers that each command describes a route table entry. The command is **ip route**, followed by the address to be entered into the table, a mask for determining the network portion of the address, and the address of the directly connected interface of the next-hop router.

An alternative configuration command for static routes specifies the interface out of which a network is reached instead of the address of the next-hop router. For example, the route entries for Tigger could be as follows:

```
Tigger(config)# ip route 192.168.1.0 255.255.255.224 S0
Tigger(config)# ip route 10.1.0.0 255.255.0.0 E0
Tigger(config)# ip route 10.4.7.0 255.255.255.0 S1
```

Figure 3.4 compares the route table resulting from this configuration with the route table resulting from entries pointing to a next-hop router. Notice that a certain inaccuracy is introduced; all networks specified with a static route referring to an exit interface are entered into the table as if they are directly connected to that interface. The implications for route redistribution are discussed in Chapter 11.

A point of interest in Figure 3.4 is that the header for the 10.0.0.0 subnets indicates the variable subnet masks used in the internetwork. Variable Length Subnet Masking (VLSM) can be a useful tool and is discussed at length in Chapter 7.

```
Tigger#show ip route

Gateway of last resort is not set

     10.0.0.0 is variably subnetted, 3 subnets, 2 masks
C       10.4.6.0 255.255.255.0 is directly connected, Serial1
S       10.4.7.0 255.255.255.0 [1/0] via 10.4.6.2
S       10.1.0.0 255.255.0.0 [1/0] via 192.168.1.194
     192.168.1.0 255.255.255.224 is subnetted, 3 subnets
C       192.168.1.64 is directly connected, Serial0
S       192.168.1.0 [1/0] via 192.168.1.65
C       192.168.1.192 is directly connected, Ethernet0
Tigger#
```

```
Tigger#show ip route

Gateway of last resort is not set

     10.0.0.0 is variably subnetted, 3 subnets, 2 masks
C       10.4.6.0 255.255.255.0 is directly connected, Serial1
S       10.4.7.0 255.255.255.0 is directly connected, Serial1
S       10.1.0.0 255.255.0.0 is directly connected, Ethernet0
     192.168.1.0 255.255.255.224 is subnetted, 3 subnets
C       192.168.1.64 is directly connected, Serial0
S       192.168.1.0 is directly connected, Serial0
C       192.168.1.192 is directly connected, Ethernet0
Tigger#
```

Figure 3.4
The top route table is the result of static route entries pointing to the next-hop router. The bottom route table is the result of static routes that point to the interface a packet must exit to reach the destination network.[4]

Case Study: Summary Routes

A *summary route* is an address that encompasses several more specific addresses in a route table. It is the address mask used with a route entry that makes static routes as flexible as they are; by using an appropriate address mask, it is sometimes possible to create a single summary route for several destination addresses.

[4]   *The key normally seen at the top of the route table (as in Figure 3.2) has been removed for clarity.*

For example, the preceding case study uses a separate entry for each data link. The mask of each entry corresponds to the address mask used on the device interfaces connected to that data link. Looking again at Figure 3.3, you can see that subnets 10.4.6.0/24 and 10.4.7.0/24 could be specified to Piglet with a single entry of 10.4.0.0/16, reachable via Tigger. Likewise, subnets 192.168.1.0/27 and 192.168.1.64/27 could be accounted for in its route table with a single entry pointing to 192.168.1.0/24, also reachable via Tigger. These two route entries, 10.4.0.0/16 and 192.16.1.0/24, are summary routes.

Using summary routes, Piglet's static route entries are:

```
Piglet(config)# ip route 192.168.1.0 255.255.255.0 192.168.1.193
Piglet(config)# ip route 10.4.0.0 255.255.0.0 192.168.1.193
```

All subnets of network 10.0.0.0 are reachable from Pooh via Tigger, so a single entry to that major network address and a corresponding mask is all that is needed:

```
Pooh(config)# ip route 192.168.1.192 255.255.255.224 192.168.1.66
Pooh(config)# ip route 10.0.0.0 255.0.0.0 192.168.1.66
```

From Eeyore, all destination addresses beginning with 192 are reachable via Tigger. The single route entry does not even have to specify all of the class C address bits:[5]

```
Eeyore(config)# ip route 192.0.0.0 255.0.0.0 10.4.6.1
Eeyore(config)# ip route 10.1.0.0 255.255.0.0 10.4.6.1
```

By summarizing a group of subnets or even major networks, the number of static route entries may be reduced drastically—in this example, by more than one-third. However, caution must be used when summarizing addresses; when done incorrectly, unexpected routing behavior may occur (see "Case Study: Tracing a Failed Route," later in this chapter). Summarization and the problems

---

[5] *This method of summarizing a group of major network addresses with a mask shorter than the default address mask for that class is known as supernetting and is introduced in Chapter 7.*

that can develop from incorrect summarization are examined in more depth in Chapters 8, "Enhanced Interior Gateway Routing Protocol (EIGRP)," and 9, "Open Shortest Path First."

Case Study: Alternative Routes

In Figure 3.5, a new link has been added between Pooh and Eeyore. All packets from Pooh to the 10.0.0.0 networks will take this new path with the exception of packets destined for the host 10.4.7.25; a policy is in place stating that traffic to this host must go through Tigger. The static route commands at Pooh will be:

```
Pooh(config)# ip route 192.168.1.192 255.255.255.224 192.168.1.66
Pooh(config)# ip route 10.0.0.0 255.0.0.0 192.168.1.34
Pooh(config)# ip route 10.4.7.25 255.255.255.255 192.168.1.66
```

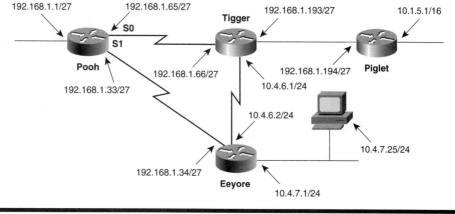

Figure 3.5

A more direct path from Pooh to the 10.4.0.0 subnets is added to the internetwork.

The first two route entries are the same as before except that the second path now points to the new interface 192.168.1.34 at Eeyore. The third entry is a *host route*, pointing to the single host 10.4.7.25 and made possible by setting the address mask to all ones. Notice that unlike the entry for the other 10.0.0.0 subnets, this host route points to Tigger's interface 192.168.1.66.

The debugging function **debug ip packet** is turned on in Pooh (Figure 3.6) to observe the paths packets take from the router as a result of the new route entries. A packet is sent from a host 192.168.1.15 to host 10.4.7.25. The first two debug trap messages show that the packet is routed from interface E0 to the next-hop router 192.168.1.66 (Tigger) out interface S0, as required, and that the reply packet was received on S0 and routed to the host 192.168.1.15 out E0.

```
Pooh#debug ip packet
IP packet debugging is on
Pooh#
IP: s=192.168.1.15 (Ethernet0), d=10.4.7.25 (Serial0), g=192.168.1.66, forward
IP: s=10.4.7.25 (Serial0), d=192.168.1.15 (Ethernet0), g=192.168.1.15, forward
Pooh#
IP: s=192.168.1.15 (Ethernet0), d=10.4.7.100 (Serial1), g=192.168.1.34, forward
IP: s=10.4.7.100 (Serial0), d=192.168.1.15 (Ethernet0), g=192.168.1.15, forward
Pooh#
```

Figure 3.6

Debugging verifies that the new route entries at Pooh are working correctly.

Next a packet is sent from host 192.168.1.15 to host 10.4.7.100. Packets destined for any host on 10.0.0.0 subnets, other than host 10.4.7.25, should be routed across the new link to Eeyore's interface 192.186.1.34. The third debug message verifies that this is indeed happening. However, the fourth message shows something that may initially be surprising. The response from 10.4.7.100 to 192.168.1.15 arrived on Pooh's interface S0 from Tigger.

Remember that the route entries in the other routers have not changed from the original example. This result may or may not be desired, but it does illustrate two characteristics of static routes. First, if the internetwork topology changes, the routers that are required to know about those changes must be reconfigured; and second, static routes can be used to create very specific routing behavior. In this example, perhaps it is desirable to have traffic taking one path in one direction and another path in the opposite direction.

A final observation about this example is that packets routed from Pooh to subnet 10.1.5.0 take a less-than-optimal route, from Pooh to Eeyore to Tigger instead of directly from Pooh to Tigger. A more efficient configuration is:

```
Pooh(config)# ip route 192.168.1.192 255.255.255.224 192.168.1.66
Pooh(config)# ip route 10.0.0.0 255.0.0.0 192.168.1.34
Pooh(config)# ip route 10.1.0.0 255.255.0.0 192.168.1.66
Pooh(config)# ip route 10.4.7.25 255.255.255.255 192.168.1.66
```

The third entry will now send all packets for subnet 10.1.5.0 directly to Tigger.

Case Study: Floating Static Routes

Unlike other static routes, a floating static route is not permanently entered in the route table; it appears only under the special circumstance of the failure of a more-preferred route.

In Figure 3.7, a new router (Rabbit) is connected to Piglet via their respective Serial 0 interfaces, but a new connection has been added between the two Serial 1 interfaces. This second link has been added for redundancy: If the primary link 10.1.10.0 fails, floating static routes will direct traffic across the backup link 10.1.20.0.

Additionally, the mask on Piglet's Ethernet interface has changed from 10.1.5.1/16 to 10.1.5.1/24. This change allows the single route entry at Tigger

```
ip route 10.1.0.0 255.255.0.0 192.168.1.194
```

to point not only to 10.1.5.0 but also to all of the new subnets used in association with the new router.

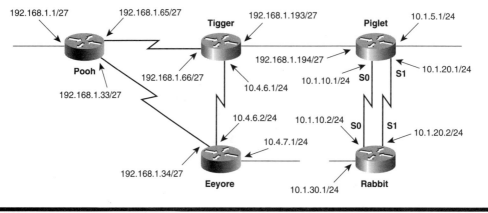

Figure 3.7

A new router has been connected to Piglet. Two serial links are used—one for the primary link and one for the backup link.

To create the floating static route, Piglet's route entries are as follows:

```
ip route 192.168.1.0 255.255.255.0 192.168.1.193
ip route 10.4.0.0 255.255.0.0 192.168.1.193
ip route 10.1.30.0 255.255.255.0 10.1.10.1
ip route 10.1.30.0 255.255.255.0 10.1.20.1 50
```

And Rabbit's route entries are:

```
ip route 10.4.0.0 255.255.0.0 10.1.10.1
ip route 10.4.0.0 255.255.0.0 10.1.20.1 50
ip route 10.1.5.0 255.255.255.0 10.1.10.1
ip route 10.1.5.0 255.255.255.0 10.1.20.1 50
ip route 192.168.0.0 255.255.0.0 10.1.10.1
ip route 192.168.0.0 255.255.0.0 10.1.20.1 50
```

Two entries at Piglet point to Rabbit's network 10.1.30.0; one specifies a next-hop address of Rabbit's S0 interface, and the other specifies a next-hop address of Rabbit's S1 interface. Rabbit has similar double entries for every route.

Notice that all static routes using subnet 10.1.20.0 are followed by a 50. This number specifies an *administrative distance*, which is a measure of preferability; when duplicate paths to the same net-

Administrative distance

work are known, the router will prefer the path with the lower administrative distance. At first this idea sounds like a metric; however, a metric specifies the preferability of a route, whereas an administrative distance specifies the preferability of the means by which the route was discovered.

For example, static routes pointing to a next-hop address have an administrative distance of 1, and static routes referencing an exit interface have an administrative distance of 0. If two static routes point to the same destination, but one references a next-hop address and one references an exit interface, the latter—with the lower administrative distance—will be preferred.

By increasing the administrative distances of the static routes traversing subnet 10.1.20.0 to 50, they become less preferred than the routes traversing subnet 10.1.10.0. Figure 3.8 shows three iterations of Rabbit's route table. In the first table, all routes to nonconnected networks use a next-hop address of 10.1.10.1. The bracketed numbers associated with each route indicate an administrative distance of 1 and a metric of 0 (because no metrics are associated with static routes).

Next, trap messages announce that the state of the primary link connected to Serial 0 has changed to "down," indicating a failure. A look at the second iteration of the route table shows that all nonconnected routes now point to a next-hop address of 10.1.20.1. Because the more-preferred entry is no longer available, the router has switched to the less-preferred backup link, with the administrative distance of 50 indicated in the brackets. And because subnet 10.1.10.0 has failed, it no longer shows up in the route table as a directly connected network.

Before the third iteration of the route table, trap messages indicate that the state of the primary link has changed to "up." The route table then shows that subnet 10.1.10.0 is again in the table, and the router is again using the next-hop address of 10.1.10.1.

```
Rabbit#show ip route
     10.0.0.0 is variably subnetted, 5 subnets, 2 masks
C       10.1.10.0 255.255.255.0 is directly connected, Serial0
S       10.4.0.0 255.255.0.0 [1/0] via 10.1.10.1
S       10.1.5.0 255.255.255.0 [1/0] via 10.1.10.1
C       10.1.30.0 255.255.255.0 is directly connected, Ethernet0
C       10.1.20.0 255.255.255.0 is directly connected, Serial1
S    192.168.0.0 255.255.0.0 [1/0] via 10.1.10.1
Rabbit#

%LINEPROTO-5-UPDOWN: Line protocol on Interface Serial0, changed state to down
%LINK-3-UPDOWN: Interface Serial0, changed state to down


Rabbit#show ip route

     10.0.0.0 is variably subnetted, 4 subnets, 2 masks
S       10.4.0.0 255.255.0.0 [50/0] via 10.1.20.0
S       10.1.5.0 255.255.255.0 [50/0] via 10.1.20.1
C       10.1.30.0 255.255.255.0 is directly connected, Ethernet0
C       10.1.20.0 255.255.255.0 is directly connected, Serial1
S    192.168.0.0 255.255.0.0 [50/0] via 10.1.20.1
Rabbit#

%LINK-3-UPDOWN: Interface Serial0, changed state to up
%LINEPROTO-5-UPDOWN: Line protocol on Interface Serial0, changed state to up


Rabbit#show ip route
10.0.0.0 is variably subnetted, 5 subnets, 2 masks
C    10.1.10.0 255.255.255.0 is directly connected, Serial0
S    10.4.0.0 255.255.0.0 [1/0] via 10.1.10.1
S    10.1.5.0 255.255.255.0 [1/0] via 10.1.10.1
C    10.1.30.0 255.255.255.0 is directly connected, Ethernet0
C    10.1.20.0 255.255.255.0 is directly connected, Serial1
S 192.168.0.0 255.255.0.0 [1/0] via 10.1.10.1
Rabbit#
```

Figure 3.8

When the primary link 10.1.10.0 fails, the backup link 10.1.20.0 is used. When the primary link is restored, it is again the preferred path.

Chapter 11 discusses the administrative distances associated with the various dynamic routing protocols, but it can be said here that the administrative distances of all dynamic routing protocols are substantially higher than 1. Therefore, by default a static route to a network will always be preferred over a dynamically discovered route to the same network.

Case Study: Load Sharing

The problem with the configuration used in the previous section is that under normal circumstances the second link is never utilized. The bandwidth available on the link is wasted. *Load sharing*, also known as *load balancing*, allows routers to take advantage of multiple paths to the same destination by sending packets over all the available routes.

Load sharing can be equal cost or unequal cost, where *cost* is a generic term referring to whatever metric (if any) is associated with the route.

- *Equal-cost* load sharing distributes traffic equally among multiple paths with equal metrics.

- *Unequal-cost* load sharing distributes packets among multiple paths with different metrics. The traffic is distributed inversely proportional to the cost of the routes. That is, paths with lower costs are assigned more traffic, and paths with higher costs are assigned less traffic.

Some routing protocols support both equal-cost and unequal-cost load sharing, whereas others support only equal cost. Static routes, which have no metric, support only equal-cost load sharing.

To configure the parallel links in Figure 3.7 for load sharing using static routes, Piglet's route entries are:

```
ip route 192.168.1.0 255.255.255.0 192.168.1.193
ip route 10.4.0.0 255.255.0.0 192.168.1.193
ip route 10.1.30.0 255.255.255.0 10.1.10.1
ip route 10.1.30.0 255.255.255.0 10.1.20.1
```

and Rabbit's route entries are:

```
ip route 10.4.0.0 255.255.0.0 10.1.10.1
```

```
ip route 10.4.0.0 255.255.0.0 10.1.20.1
ip route 10.1.5.0 255.255.255.0 10.1.10.1
ip route 10.1.5.0 255.255.255.0 10.1.20.1
ip route 192.168.0.0 255.255.0.0 10.1.10.1
ip route 192.168.0.0 255.255.0.0 10.1.20.1
```

These entries were also used in the preceding section for floating static routes, except both links now use the default administrative distance of 1. Rabbit's route table, shown in Figure 3.9, now has two routes to each destination.

```
Rabbit#show ip route
Codes: C - connected, S - static, I - IGRP, R - RIP, M - mobile, B - BGP
       D - EIGRP, EX - EIGRP external, O - OSPF, IA - OSPF inter area
       E1 - OSPF external type 1, E2 - OSPF external type 2, E - EGP
       i - IS-IS, L1 - IS-IS level-1, L2 - IS-IS level-2, * - candidate default,
       U - per-user static route

Gateway of last resort is not set

     10.0.0.0/8 is variably subnetted, 4 subnets, 2 masks
C        10.1.10.0/24 is directly connected, Serial0
S        10.1.5.0/24 [1/0] via 10.1.10.1
                     [1/0] via 10.1.20.1
S        10.4.0.0/16 [1/0] via 10.1.10.1
                     [1/0] via 10.1.20.1
C        10.1.20.0/24 is directly connected, Serial1
S     192.168.0.0/16 [1/0] via 10.1.10.1
                     [1/0] via 10.1.20.1
Rabbit#
```

Figure 3.9

This route table indicates that there are two paths to the same destination networks. The router will balance the load across these multiple paths.

Load sharing is also either per destination or per packet.

Per Destination Load Sharing and Fast Switching

Per destination load balancing distributes the load according to destination address. Given two paths to the same network, all packets for one destination on the network may travel over the first path, all packets for a second destination on the same network may travel over the second path, all packets for a third destination may again be sent over the first path, and so on. This type of load balancing occurs in Cisco routers when they are *fast switching*, the default Cisco switching mode.

Fast switching works as follows: When a router switches the first packet to a particular destination, a route table lookup is performed and an exit interface is selected. The necessary data-link information to frame the packet for the selected interface is then retrieved (from the ARP cache, for instance), and the packet is encapsulated and transmitted. The retrieved route and data-link information is then entered into a fast switching cache, and as subsequent packets to the same destination enter the router, the information in the fast cache allows the router to immediately switch the packet without performing another route table and ARP cache lookup.

While switching time and processor utilization are decreased, fast switching means that all packets to a specific destination are routed out the same interface. When a packet addressed to a different host on the same network enters the router and an alternate route exists, the router may send all packets for that destination on the alternate route. Therefore, the best the router can do is balance traffic on a per destination basis.

Per Packet Load Sharing and Process Switching

Per packet load sharing means that one packet to a destination is sent over one link, the next packet to the same destination is sent over the next link, and so on, given equal-cost paths. If the paths are unequal cost, the load balancing may be one packet over the higher-cost link for every three packets over the lower-cost link, or some other proportion depending upon the ratio of costs. Cisco routers will do per packet load balancing when they are *process switching*.

Process switching simply means that for every packet, the router performs a route table lookup, selects an interface, and then looks up the data link information. Because each routing decision is independent for each packet, all packets to the same destination are not forced to use the same interface. To enable process switching on an interface, use the command **no ip route-cache**.

In Figure 3.10, host 192.168.1.15 has sent six pings to host 10.1.30.25. Using **debug ip packet,** the ICMP echo request and echo reply packets are observed at Piglet. Looking at the exit interfaces and the forwarding addresses, it can be observed that both Piglet and Rabbit are using S0 and S1 alternately. Note that the command **debug ip packet** allows only process switched packets to be observed. Fast switched packets are not displayed.

```
Piglet#debug ip packet
IP packet debugging is on
Piglet#
IP:  s=192.168.1.15 (Ethernet0), d=10.1.30.25 (Serial0), g=10.1.10.2, forward
IP:  s=10.1.30.25 (Serial0), d=192.168.1.15 (Ethernet0), g=192.168.1.193, forward
IP:  s=192.168.1.15 (Ethernet0), d=10.1.30.25 (Serial1), g=10.1.20.2, forward
IP:  s=10.1.30.25 (Serial1), d=192.168.1.15 (Ethernet0), g=192.168.1.193, forward
IP:  s=192.168.1.15 (Ethernet0), d=10.1.30.25 (Serial0), g=10.1.10.2, forward
IP:  s=10.1.30.25 (Serial0), d=192.168.1.15 (Ethernet0), g=192.168.1.193, forward
IP:  s=192.168.1.15 (Ethernet0), d=10.1.30.25 (Serial1), g=10.1.20.2, forward
IP:  s=10.1.30.25 (Serial1), d=192.168.1.15 (Ethernet0), g=192.168.1.193, forward
IP:  s=192.168.1.15 (Ethernet0), d=10.1.30.25 (Serial0), g=10.1.10.2, forward
IP:  s=10.1.30.25 (Serial0), d=192.168.1.15 (Ethernet0), g=192.168.1.193, forward
IP:  s=192.168.1.15 (Ethernet0), d=10.1.30.25 (Serial1), g=10.1.20.2, forward
IP:  s=10.1.30.25 (Serial1), d=192.168.1.15 (Ethernet0), g=192.168.1.193, forward
Piglet#
```

Figure 3.10

This router is alternating between S0 and S1 to send packets to the same destination. Notice that the router on the other end of the two links is doing the same thing with the reply packets.

Like many design choices, per packet load balancing has a price. The traffic may be distributed more evenly among the various links than with per destination load balancing, but the lower switching time and processor utilization of fast switching are lost.

Case Study: Recursive Table Lookups

All route entries do not necessarily need to point to the next-hop router. Figure 3.11 shows a simplified version of the internetwork of Figure 3.7. In this internetwork, Pooh is configured with:

```
ip route 10.1.30.0 255.255.255.0 10.1.10.2
ip route 10.1.10.0 255.255.255.0 192.168.1.194
ip route 192.168.1.192 255.255.255.224 192.168.1.66
```

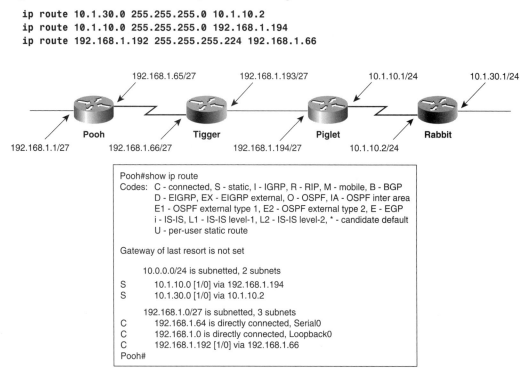

Figure 3.11

To reach network 10.1.30.0, Pooh must perform three route table lookups.

If Pooh needs to send a packet to host 10.1.30.25, it will look into its route table and find that the subnet is reachable via 10.1.10.2. Because that address is not on a directly connected network, Pooh must again consult the table to find that network 10.1.10.0 is reachable via 192.168.1.194. That subnet is also not directly connected, so a third table lookup is called for. Pooh will find that

192.168.1.192 is reachable via 192.168.1.66, which is on a directly connected subnet. The packet can now be forwarded.

Because each table lookup costs processor time, under normal circumstances forcing a router to perform multiple lookups is a poor design decision. Fast switching significantly reduces these adverse effects by limiting the recursive lookups to the first packet to each destination, but a justification should still be identified before using such a design.

Figure 3.12 shows an example of an instance in which recursive lookups may be useful. Here, Sanderz reaches all networks via Heffalump. However, the network administrator plans to eliminate Heffalump and repoint all of Sanderz's routes through Woozle. The first 12 entries point not to Heffalump, but to the appropriate router attached to the 10.87.14.0 subnet. The last entry specifies that the 10.87.14.0 subnet is reached via Heffalump.

With this configuration, all of Sanderz's entries can be repointed through Woozle simply by changing the last static entry:

```
Sanderz(config)# ip route 10.87.14.0 255.255.255.0 10.23.5.95
Sanderz(config)# no ip route 10.87.14.0 255.255.255.0 10.23.5.20
```

Had all the static routes referenced 10.23.5.20 as the next-hop address, it would have been necessary to delete all 13 lines and type 13 new lines. Nevertheless, the effort saved in retyping static routes must be weighed carefully against the extra processing burden that recursive lookups put on the router.

TROUBLESHOOTING STATIC ROUTES

Followers of the assorted American political scandals of the past 30 or so years will have heard a congressional investigator ask the question, "What did he know and when did he know it?" The same question serves an internetworking investigator well. When troubleshooting routing problems, the first step should almost always be to examine the route table. What does the router know?

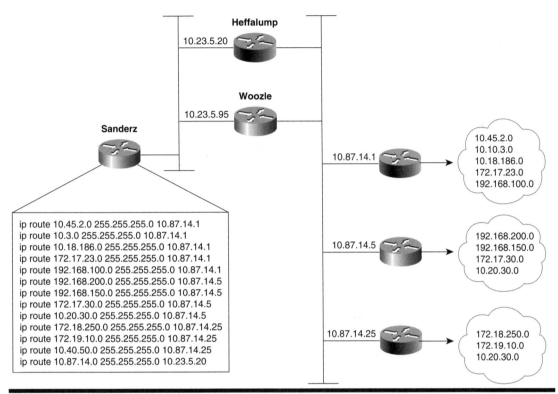

Figure 3.12

Configuring Sanderz for recursive lookups enables the network administrator to redirect all of that router's exit traffic from Heffalump to Woozle by changing one route entry.

Does the router know how to reach the destination in question? Is the information in the route table accurate? Knowing how to trace a route is essential to successfully troubleshooting an internetwork.

Case Study: Tracing a Failed Route

Figure 3.13 shows a previously configured internetwork, with each router's associated static routes. A problem has been discovered. Devices on subnet 192.168.1.0/27, connected to Pooh's Ethernet interface, can communicate with devices on subnet 10.1.0.0/16 just fine. However, when a ping is sent from Pooh itself to subnet 10.1.0.0/16, the ping fails (Figure 3.14). This seems strange. If packets being routed by Pooh successfully reach their destinations, why do packets originated by the same router fail?

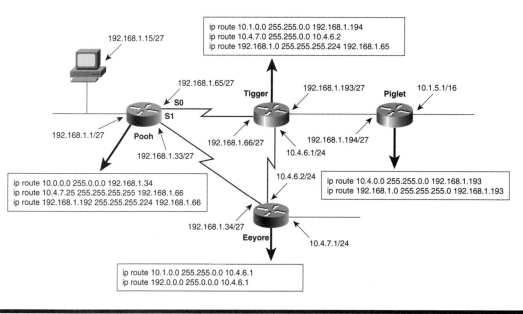

Figure 3.13

Packets from subnet 192.168.1.0/27 to subnet 10.1.0.0/16 are routed correctly, but Pooh itself cannot ping any device on 10.1.0.0/16.

Addressing this problem requires tracing the route of the ping. First, Pooh's route table is examined (Figure 3.15). The destination address of 10.1.5.1 matches the route entry for 10.0.0.0/8, which (according to the table) is reached via the next-hop address 192.168.1.34—one of Eeyore's interfaces.

Next the route table for Eeyore must be examined (Figure 3.16). The destination address 10.1.5.1 matches the entry 10.1.0.0/16, with a next-hop address of 10.4.6.1. This address is one of Tigger's interfaces.

```
C:\WINDOWS>ping 10.1.5.1

Pinging 10.1.5.1 with 32 bytes of data:

Reply from 10.1.5.1:  bytes=32 time=22ms TTL=253
Reply from 10.1.5.1:  bytes=32 time=22ms TTL=253
Reply from 10.1.5.1:  bytes=32 time=22ms TTL=253
Reply from 10.1.5.1:  bytes=32 time=22ms TTL=253
```

```
Pooh#ping 10.1.5.1
Type escape sequence to abort.
Sending 5, 100-byte ICMP Echoechoes to 10.1.5.1, timeout is 2 seconds:
.....
Success rate is 0 percent (0/5)
Pooh#
```

Figure 3.14

A device on subnet 192.168.1.0/27 successfully pings Piglet's Ethernet interface, but pings from Pooh fail.

```
Pooh#show ip route
Codes:  C - connected, S - static, I - IGRP, R - RIP, M - mobile, B - BGP
        D - EIGRP, EX - EIGRP external, O - OSPF, IA - OSPF inter area
        E1 - OSPF external type 1, E2 - OSPF external type 2, E - EGP
        i - IS-IS, L1 - IS-IS level-1, L2 - IS-IS level-2, * - candidate default

Gateway of last resort is not set

     10.0.0.0 is variably subnetted, 2 subnets, 2 masks
S       10.0.0.0 255.0.0.0 [1/0] via 192.168.1.34
S       10.4.7.25 255.255.255.255 [1/0] via 192.168.1.66
     192.168.1.0 255.255.255.224 is subnetted, 4 subnets
C       192.168.1.64 is directly connected, Serial0
C       192.168.1.32 is directly connected, Serial1
C       192.168.1.0 is directly connected, Ethernet0
S       192.168.1.192 [1/0] via 192.168.1.66
Pooh#
```

Figure 3.15

A packet with a destination address of 10.1.5.1 matches the route entry for 10.0.0.0/8 and will be forwarded to the next-hop router at 192.168.1.34.

Figure 3.17 shows Tigger's route table. The destination address matches the entry for 10.1.0.0/16 and will be forwarded to 192.168.1.194, which is at Piglet.

```
Eeyore#show ip route
Codes: C - connected, S - static, I - IGRP, R - RIP, M - mobile, B - BGP
       D - EIGRP, EX - EIGRP external, O - OSPF, IA - OSPF inter area
       E1 - OSPF external type 1, E2 - OSPF external type 2, E - EGP
       i - IS-IS, L1 - IS-IS level-1, L2 - IS-IS level-2, * - candidate default

Gateway of last resort is not set

     10.0.0.0 is variably subnetted, 3 subnets, 2 masks
C       10.4.6.0 255.255.255.0 is directly connected, Serial1
C       10.4.7.0 255.255.255.0 is directly connected, Ethernet0
S       10.1.0.0 255.255.0.0 [1/0] via 10.4.6.1
     192.168.1.0 255.255.255.224 is subnetted, 1 subnets
C       192.168.1.32 is directly connected, Serial0
S     192.0.0.0 255.0.0.0 [1/0] via 10.4.6.1
Eeyore#
```

Figure 3.16

10.1.5.1 matches the entry for 10.1.0.0/16 and will be forwarded to 10.4.6.1.

```
Tigger#show ip route
Codes: C - connected, S - static, I - IGRP, R - RIP, M - mobile, B - BGP
       D - EIGRP, EX - EIGRP external, O - OSPF, IA - OSPF inter area
       E1 - OSPF external type 1, E2 - OSPF external type 2, E - EGP
       i - IS-IS, L1 - IS-IS level-1, L2 - IS-IS level-2, * - candidate default

Gateway of last resort is not set

     10.0.0.0 is variably subnetted, 3 subnets, 2 masks
C       10.4.6.0 255.255.255.0 is directly connected, Serial1
S       10.4.7.0 255.255.255.0 [1/0] via 10.4.6.2
S       10.1.0.0 255.255.0.0 [1/0] via 192.168.1.194
     192.168.1.0 255.255.255.224 is subnetted, 3 subnets
C       192.168.1.64 is directly connected, Serial0
S       192.168.1.0 [1/0] via 192.168.1.65
C       192.168.1.192 is directly connected, Ethernet0
Tigger#
```

Figure 3.17

10.1.5.1 matches the entry for 10.1.0.0/16 and will be forwarded to 192.168.1.194.

Piglet's route table (Figure 3.18) reveals that the target network, 10.1.0.0, is directly connected. In other words, the packet has arrived. The target address 10.1.5.1 is Piglet's own interface to that network. Because the path to the address has just been verified as good, we can assume that the ICMP echo packets from Pooh are reaching the destination.

```
Piglet#show ip route
Codes: C - connected, S - static, I - IGRP, R - RIP, M - mobile, B - BGP
       D - EIGRP, EX - EIGRP external, O - OSPF, IA - OSPF inter area
       E1 - OSPF external type 1, E2 - OSPF external type 2, E - EGP
       i - IS-IS, L1 - IS-IS level-1, L2 - IS-IS level-2, * - candidate default
Gateway of last resort is not set
     10.0.0.0 255.255.0.0 is subnetted, 2 subnets
C       10.1.0.0 is directly connected, Ethernet1
S       10.4.0.0 [1/0] via 192.168.1.193
     192.168.1.0 is variably subnetted, 2 subnets, 2 masks
S       192.168.1.0 255.255.255.0 [1/0] via 192.168.1.193
C       192.168.1.192 255.255.255.224 is directly connected, Ethernet0
Piglet#
```

Figure 3.18
The destination network, 10.1.0.0, is directly connected to Piglet.

The next step is to trace the path of the responding ICMP echo reply packets. To trace this path, you need to know the source address of the echo packet—that address will be the destination address of the echo reply packet. The source address of a packet that is originated from a router is the address of the interface from which the packet was transmitted.[6] In this example, Pooh originally forwarded the echo packet to 192.168.1.34. Figure 3.13 shows that the source address of that packet is 192.168.1.33. So this address is the destination address to which Piglet will send the echo reply.

Referring again to Piglet's route table in Figure 3.18, 192.168.1.33 will match the entry for 192.168.1.0/24 and be forwarded to 192.168.1.193, which is another of Tigger's interfaces. A reexam-

---

[6]   *Unless the Extended Ping utility is used to set the source address to something different.*

ination of Tigger's route table in Figure 3.17 at first suggests that there is an entry for 192.168.1.0. However, care must be taken to correctly interpret the information that is actually there.

Compare the entries in Tigger's route table for the 10.0.0.0 subnets to those of the 192.168.1.0 subnets. The heading for the former says that 10.0.0.0 is variably subnetted; in other words, Tigger's static route to subnet 10.4.7.0 uses a 24-bit mask, and the static route to subnet 10.1.0.0 uses a 16-bit mask. The table records the correct mask at each subnet.

The heading for 192.168.1.0 is different. This heading states that Tigger knows of three subnets of 192.168.1.0 and that they all have a mask of 255.255.255.224. This mask will be used on the destination address of 192.168.1.33 to derive a destination network of 192.168.1.32/27. The route table has entries for 192.168.1.64/27, 192.168.1.0/27, and 192.168.1.192/27. There is no entry for 192.168.1.32/27, so the router does not know how to reach this subnet.

The problem, then, is that the ICMP echo reply packet is being dropped at Tigger. One solution is to create another static route entry for network 192.168.1.32, with a mask of 255.255.255.224 and pointing to a next hop of either 192.168.1.65 or 10.4.6.2. Another solution would be to change the mask in the existing static route entry for 192.168.1.0 from 255.255.255.224 to 255.255.255.0.

The moral of this story is that when you are tracing a route, you must consider the complete communication process. Verify not only that the path to a destination is good but also that the return path is good.

Check both the destination and return path when a route fails.

Case Study: A Protocol Conflict

Figure 3.19 shows two routers connected by two Ethernet networks, one of which includes a bridge. This bridge handles traffic for several other links not shown and occasionally becomes congested. The host Milne is a mission-critical server; the network administrator is worried about traffic to Milne being delayed by the bridge, so a static host route has been added in Roo that will direct packets destined for Milne across the top Ethernet, avoiding the bridge.

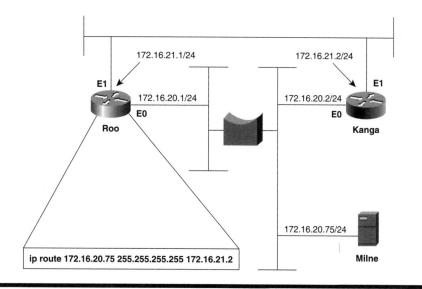

Figure 3.19

A host route directs packets from Roo to Milne across the top Ethernet, avoiding the occasionally congested bridge.

This solution seems to be logical, but it isn't working. After the static route was added, packets routed through Roo no longer reach the server. Not only that, but packets routed through Kanga no longer reach the server, although no changes were made to that router.

The first step, as always, is to check the route table. Roo's route table (Figure 3.20) indicates that packets with a destination address of 172.16.20.75 will in fact be forwarded to Kanga's E1 interface, as desired. Kanga is directly connected to the destination network, so no more routing should be occurring; a quick check verifies that the Ethernet interfaces are functioning at both Kanga and at Milne.

```
Roo#show ip route
Codes: C - connected, S - static, I - IGRP, R - RIP, M - mobile, B - BGP
       D - EIGRP, EX - EIGRP external, O - OSPF, IA - OSPF inter area
       E1 - OSPF external type 1, E2 - OSPF external type 2, E - EGP
       i - IS-IS, L1 - IS-IS level-1, L2 - IS-IS level-2, * - candidate  default,
       U - per-user static route

Gateway of last resort is not set

     172.16.0.0/16 is variably subnetted, 3 subnets, 2 masks
C        172.16.20.0/24 is directly connected, Ethernet0
C        172.16.21.0/24 is directly connected, Ethernet1
S        172.16.20.75/32 [1/0] via 172.16.21.2
Roo#
```

Figure 3.20

Roo's route table, showing the static host route to Milne via Kanga's E1 interface.

In Figure 3.21, a trace is performed from Roo to Milne, and a symptom is found. Instead of delivering the packets to Milne, Kanga is forwarding them to Roo's E0 interface. Roo forwards the packets to Kanga's E1 interface, and Kanga sends the packets right back to Roo. A routing loop seems to have occurred, but why?

Check a router's ARP cache when packets do not go to the correct destination on a data link.

The suspicious aspect of all of this is that Kanga should not be routing the packet, which appears to be the case. Kanga should recognize that the destination address of the packet is for its directly connected network 172.16.20.0 and should be using the data link to deliver the packet to the host. Therefore, suspicion should fall on the data link. Just as the route table should be examined to see whether the router has the correct information for reaching a network across a logical path, the ARP cache should be examined to see whether the router has the correct information for reaching a host across a physical path.

```
Roo#trace 172.16.20.75

Type escape sequence to abort.
Tracing the route to 172.16.20.75
   1   172.16.21.2   0   msec   0   msec   0   msec
   2   172.16.20.1   4   msec   0   msec   0   msec
   3   172.16.21.2   4   msec   0   msec   0   msec
   4   172.16.20.1   0   msec   0   msec   4   msec
   5   172.16.21.2   0   msec   0   msec   4   msec
   6   172.16.20.1   0   msec   0   msec   4   msec
   7   172.16.21.2   0   msec   0   msec   4   msec
   8   172.16.20.1   0   msec   0   msec   4   msec
   9   172.16.21.2   4   msec   0   msec   4   msec
  10   172.16.20.1   4   msec   0   msec   4   msec
  11   172.16.21.2   4   msec
Roo#
```

Figure 3.21

A trace from Roo to Milne reveals that Kanga is forwarding the packets back to Roo instead of delivering them to the correct destination.

Figure 3.22 shows the ARP cache for Kanga. The IP address for Milne is in Kanga's cache as expected, with a MAC identifier of 00e0.1e58.dc39. When Milne's interface is checked, though, it shows that it has a MAC identifier of 0002.6779.0f4c; Kanga has somehow acquired incorrect information.

```
Kanga#show arp
Protocol  Address        Age (min)   Hardware Addr   Type   Interface
Internet  172.16.21.1         2      00e0.1e58.dc3c  ARPA   Ethernet1
Internet  172.16.20.2         -      00e0.1e58.dcb1  ARPA   Ethernet0
Internet  172.16.21.2         -      00e0.1e58.dcb4  ARPA   Ethernet1
Internet  172.16.20.75        2      00e0.1e58.dc39  ARPA   Ethernet0
Kanga#
```

Figure 3.22

Kanga's ARP cache has an entry for Milne, but the associated data link identifier is wrong.

Another look at Kanga's ARP table reveals that the MAC identifier associated with Milne is suspiciously similar to the MAC identifier of Kanga's own Cisco interfaces (the MAC addresses with no ages associated with them are for the router's interfaces). Because Milne is not a Cisco product, the first three octets of its MAC identifier should be different from the first three octets of Kanga's MAC identifier. The only other Cisco product in the internetwork is Roo, so its ARP cache is examined (Figure 3.23); 00e0.1e58.dc39 is the MAC identifier of Roo's E0 interface.

```
Roo#show arp
Protocol  Address       Age (min)    Hardware Addr    Type    Interface
Internet  172.16.21.1        -        00e0.1e58.dc3c   ARPA    Ethernet0
Internet  172.16.20.1        -        00e0.1e58.dc39   ARPA    Ethernet0
Internet  172.16.20.2        7        00e0.1e58.dcb1   ARPA    Ethernet0
Internet  172.16.21.2        7        00e0.1e58.dcb4   ARPA    Ethernet1
Roo#
```

Figure 3.23

Roo's ARP cache shows that the MAC identifier that Kanga has for Milne is actually Roo's E0 interface.

So Kanga mistakenly believes that the E0 interface of Roo is Milne. It frames packets destined for Milne with a destination identifier of 00e0.1e58.dc39; Roo accepts the frame, reads the destination address of the enclosed packet, and routes the packet back to Kanga.

But how did Kanga get the wrong information? The answer is proxy ARP. When Kanga first receives a packet for Milne, it will ARP for that device's data link identifier. Milne responds, but Roo also hears the ARP Request on its E0 interface. Because Roo has a route to Milne on a different network from the one on which it received the ARP Request, it issues a proxy ARP in reply. Kanga receives Milne's ARP reply and enters it into the ARP cache. The proxy ARP reply from Roo arrives later because of the delay of the bridge. The original ARP cache entry is overwritten by what Kanga thinks is new information.

There are two solutions to the problem. The first is to turn off proxy ARP at Roo's E0 with the command:

```
Roo(config)#interface e0
Roo(config-if)#no ip proxy-arp
```

The second solution is to configure a static ARP entry for Milne at Kanga with the command:

```
Kanga(config)#arp 172.16.20.75 0002.6779.0f4c arpa
```

This entry will not be overwritten by any ARP reply. Figure 3.24 shows the static ARP entry being entered and the resulting ARP cache at Kanga. Note that because the entry is static, no age is associated with it.

```
Kanga(config)#arp 172.16.20.75 00a0.24a8.a1a5 arpa
Kanga(config)#^Z
Kanga#
%SYS-5-CONFIG_I: Configured from console by console
Kanga#sh arp
Protocol  Address        Age (min)   Hardware Addr   Type   Interface
Internet  172.16.21.1           10   00e0.1e58.dc3c  ARPA   Ethernet1
Internet  172.16.20.2            -   00e0.1e58.dcb1  ARPA   Ethernet0
Internet  172.16.21.2            -   00e0.1e58.dcb4  ARPA   Ethernet1
Internet  172.16.20.75           -   0002.6779.0f4c  ARPA
Kanga#
```

Figure 3.24

A static ARP entry corrects the problem caused by proxy ARP.

The circumstances of the network should help determine which of the two solutions is best. A static ARP entry means that if the network interface at Milne is ever replaced, someone must remember to change the ARP entry to reflect the new MAC identifier. On the other hand, turning off proxy ARP is a good solution only if no hosts make use of it.

LOOKING AHEAD

For precise control over routing behavior in an internetwork, static routing is a powerful tool. However, if topology changes are prevalent, the demands of manual reconfiguration may make static routing administratively unfeasible. Dynamic routing protocols enable an internetwork to respond quickly and automatically to topology changes. Before examining the details of specific IP routing protocols, the general issues surrounding all dynamic protocols must be examined. The next chapter introduces dynamic routing protocols.

SUMMARY TABLE: CHAPTER 3 COMMAND REVIEW

Command	Description
arp *ip-address hardware-address*	Statically maps an IP *type* [*alias*] address to a hardware address.
debug ip packet	Displays information on IP packets received, generated, and forwarded. Information on fast-switched packets will not be displayed.
ip proxy-arp	Enables proxy ARP.
ip route *prefix mask{address\interface} [distance]*[permanent]	Statically adds a route entry to the route table.
ip route-cache	Configures the type of switching cache an interface will use.

REVIEW QUESTIONS

1. What information must be stored in the route table?
2. What does it mean when a route table says that an address is variably subnetted?
3. What are discontiguous subnets?
4. What command is used to examine the route table in a Cisco router?
5. What are the two bracketed numbers associated with the non-directly connected routes in the route table?
6. When static routes are configured to reference an exit interface instead of a next-hop address, in what way will the route table be different?
7. What is a summary route? In the context of static routing, how are summary routes useful?
8. What is an administrative distance?
9. What is a floating static route?
10. What is the difference between equal-cost and unequal-cost load sharing?
11. How does the switching mode at an interface affect load sharing?
12. What is a recursive table lookup?

CONFIGURATION EXERCISES

1. Configure static routes for each router of the internetwork shown in Figure 3.25. Write the routes so that every subnet of the internet has an individual entry.

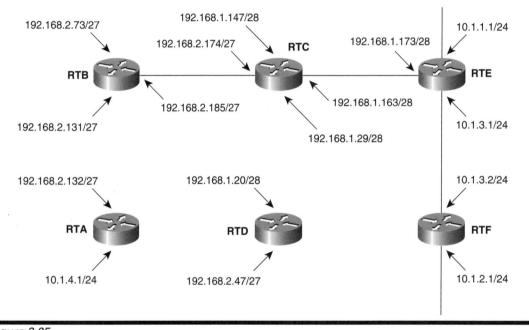

192.168.2.73/27

192.168.1.147/28

192.168.2.174/27   **RTC**

192.168.1.173/28   10.1.1.1/24

RTB

192.168.1.163/28

192.168.2.185/27

192.168.2.131/27

192.168.1.29/28

10.1.3.1/24

192.168.2.132/27   192.168.1.20/28   10.1.3.2/24

RTA   **RTD**   **RTF**

RTE

10.1.4.1/24   192.168.2.47/27   10.1.2.1/24

Figure 3.25
The internetwork for Configuration Exercises 1 and 2.

2. Rewrite the static routes created in Configuration Exercise 1 to use the minimum possible route entries.[7] (Hint: RTA will have only two static route entries.)

---

[7] *If this exercise is being implemented in a lab, be sure to add the command* **ip classless** *to all six routers.*

3. For the internetwork shown in Figure 3.26, write static routes for each router. Assume that all links are identical media. Use load balancing and floating static routes for maximum efficiency and redundancy.

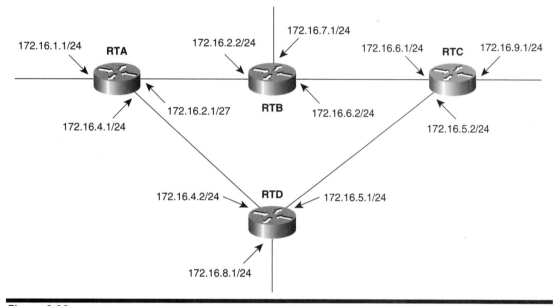

Figure 3.26

The internetwork for Configuration Exercise 3.

TROUBLESHOOTING EXERCISES

1. In the internetwork of Figure 3.3 and the associated configurations, the route entries for Piglet are changed from

```
Piglet(config)# ip route 192.168.1.0 255.255.255.0 192.168.1.193
Piglet(config)# ip route 10.4.0.0 255.255.0.0 192.168.1.193
```

to

```
Piglet(config)# ip route 192.168.1.0 255.255.255.224 192.168.1.193
Piglet(config)# ip route 10.0.0.0 255.255.0.0 192.168.1.193
```

What is the result?

2. The static route configurations for the routers in Figure 3.27 are as follows:

```
RTA
ip route 172.20.96.0 255.255.240.0 172.20.20.1
ip route 172.20.82.0 255.255.240.0 172.20.20.1
ip route 172.20.64.0 255.255.240.0 172.20.20.1
ip route 172.20.160.0 255.255.240.0 172.20.30.255
ip route 172.20.144.0 255.255.240.0 172.20.30.255
ip route 172.20.128.0 255.255.240.0 172.20.30.255
RTB
ip route 172.20.192.0 255.255.240.0 172.20.16.50
ip route 172.20.224.0 255.255.240.0 172.20.16.50
ip route 172.20.128.0 255.255.240.0 172.20.16.50
ip route 172.20.160.0 255.255.240.0 172.20.30.255
ip route 172.20.144.0 255.255.240.0 172.20.30.255
ip route 172.20.128.0 255.255.240.0 172.20.30.255
RTC
ip route 172.20.192.0 255.255.240.0 172.20.16.50
ip route 172.20.208.0 255.255.255.0 172.20.16.50
ip route 172.20.224.0 255.255.240.0 172.20.16.50
ip route 172.20.96.0 255.255.240.0 172.20.20.1
ip route 172.20.82.0 255.255.240.0 172.20.20.1
ip route 172.20.64.0 255.255.240.0 172.20.20.1
```

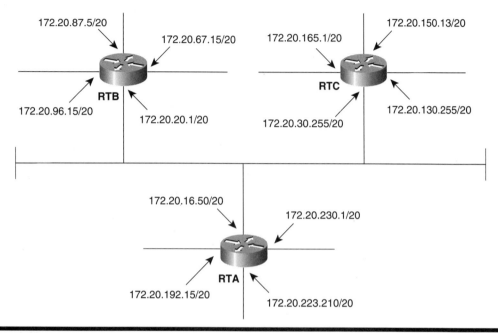

Figure 3.27
The internetwork for Troubleshooting Exercise 2.

Users are complaining of several connectivity problems in this internet. Find the mistakes in the static route configurations.

3. Figure 3.28 shows another internetwork in which users are complaining of connectivity problems. Figures 3.29 through 3.32 show the route tables of the four routers. Find the mistakes in the static route configurations

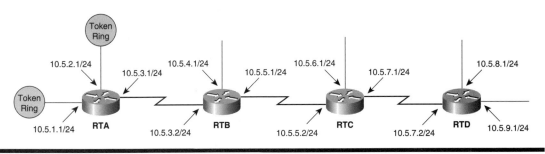

Figure 3.28

The internetwork for Troubleshooting Exercise 3.

```
RTA#show ip route
Codes:  C - connected, S - static, I - IGRP, R - RIP, M - mobile, B - BGP
        D - EIGRP, EX - EIGRP external, O - OSPF, IA - OSPF inter area
        E1 - OSPF external type 1, E2 - OSPF external type 2, E - EGP
        i - IS-IS, L1 - IS-IS level-1, L2 - IS-IS level-2, * - candidate default,
        U - per-user static route

Gateway of last resort is not set

     10.0.0.0/8 is subnetted, 9 subnets
S       10.5.9.0 [1/0] via 10.5.3.2
S       10.5.8.0 [1/0] via 10.5.3.2
S       10.5.7.0 [1/0] via 10.5.3.2
S       10.5.6.0 [1/0] via 10.5.3.2
S       10.5.5.0 [1/0] via 10.5.3.2
S       10.5.4.0 [1/0] via 10.5.3.2
C       10.5.3.0 is directly connected, Serial0
C       10.5.2.0 is directly connected, TokenRing1
C       10.5.1.0 is directly connected, TokenRing0
RTA#
```

Figure 3.29

The route table of RTA, Figure 3.28.

```
RTB#show ip route
Codes: C - connected, S - static, I - IGRP, R - RIP, M - mobile, B - BGP
       D - EIGRP, EX - EIGRP external, O - OSPF, IA - OSPF inter area
       E1 - OSPF external type 1, E2 - OSPF external type 2, E - EGP
       i - IS-IS, L1 - IS-IS level-1, L2 - IS-IS level-2, * - candidate default,
       U - per-user static route

Gateway of last resort is not set

     10.0.0.0/8 is subnetted, 9 subnets
S       10.5.9.0 [1/0] via 10.5.5.2
S       10.5.8.0 [1/0] via 10.5.5.2
S       10.5.7.0 [1/0] via 10.5.5.2
S       10.5.6.0 [1/0] via 10.5.5.2
C       10.5.5.0 is directly connected, Serial1
C       10.5.4.0 is directly connected, TokenRing0
C       10.5.3.0 is directly connected, Serial0
S       10.5.2.0 [1/0] via 10.5.3.1
S       10.5.1.0 [1/0] via 10.5.3.1
RTB#
```

Figure 3.30

The route table of RTB, Figure 3.28.

```
RTC#show ip route
Codes: C - connected, S - static, I - IGRP, R - RIP, M - mobile, B - BGP
       D - EIGRP, EX - EIGRP external, O - OSPF, IA - OSPF inter area
       N1 - OSPF NSSA external type 1, N2 - OSPF NSSA external type 2
       E1 - OSPF external type 1, E2 - OSPF external type 2, E - EGP
       i - IS-IS, L1 - IS-IS level-1, L2 - IS-IS level-2, * - candidate default,
       U - per-user static route, o - ODR

Gateway of last resort is not set

     10.0.0.0/24 is subnetted, 8 subnets
S       10.5.9.0 [1/0] via 10.5.7.2
S       10.5.8.0 [1/0] via 10.5.5.1
C       10.5.7.0 is directly connected, Serial1
C       10.5.6.0 is directly connected, Ethernet0
S       10.1.1.0 [1/0] via 10.5.5.1
C       10.5.5.0 is directly connected, Serial0
S       10.5.3.0 [1/0] via 10.5.5.1
S       10.5.2.0 [1/0] via 10.5.5.1
RTC#
```

Figure 3.31

The route table of RTC, Figure 3.28.

```
RTD#show ip route
Codes: C - connected, S - static, I - IGRP, R - RIP, M - mobile, B - BGP
       D - EIGRP, EX - EIGRP external, O - OSPF, IA - OSPF inter area
       N1 - OSPF NSSA external type 1, N2 - OSPF NSSA external type 2
       E1 - OSPF external type 1, E2 - OSPF external type 2, E - EGP
       i - IS-IS, L1 - IS-IS level-1, L2 - IS-IS level-2, * - candidate default,
       U - per-user static route, o - ODR

Gateway of last resort is not set

     10.0.0.0/24 is subnetted, 9 subnets
C       10.5.9.0 is directly connected, Ethernet1
C       10.5.8.0 is directly connected, Ethernet0
C       10.5.7.0 is directly connected, Serial0
S       10.5.6.0 [1/0] via 10.5.7.1
S       10.5.5.0 [1/0] via 10.5.7.1
S       10.4.5.0 [1/0] via 10.5.7.1
S       10.5.3.0 [1/0] via 10.5.7.1
S       10.5.2.0 [1/0] via 10.5.7.1
S       10.5.1.0 [1/0] via 10.5.7.1
RTD#
```

Figure 3.32

The route table of RTD, Figure 3.28.

- Routing Protocol Basics

- Distance Vector Routing Protocols

- Link State Routing Protocols

- Interior and Exterior Gateway Protocols

- Static or Dynamic Routing?

CHAPTER 4

Dynamic Routing Protocols

The last chapter explained what a router needs to know to correctly switch packets to their respective destinations and how that information is put into the route table manually. This chapter shows how routers can discover this information automatically and share that information with other routers via dynamic routing protocols. A *routing protocol* is the language a router speaks with other routers in order to share information about the reachability and status of networks.

Dynamic routing protocols not only perform these path determination and route table update functions but also determine the next-best path if the best path to a destination becomes unusable. The capability to compensate for topology changes is the most important advantage dynamic routing offers over static routing.

Obviously, for communications to occur the communicators must speak the same language. There are eight major IP routing protocols from which to choose; if one router speaks RIP and another speaks OSPF, they cannot share routing information because they are not speaking the same language. Subsequent chapters examine all the IP routing protocols in current use, and even consider how to make a router "bilingual," but first it is necessary to explore some characteristics and issues common to all routing protocols—IP or otherwise.

ROUTING PROTOCOL BASICS

All dynamic routing protocols are built around an algorithm. Generally, an *algorithm* is a step-by-step procedure for solving a problem. A routing algorithm must, at a minimum, specify the following:

- A procedure for passing reachability information about networks to other routers

- A procedure for receiving reachability information from other routers

- A procedure for determining optimal routes based on the reachability information it has and for recording this information in a route table

- A procedure for reacting to, compensating for, and advertising topology changes in an internetwork

A few issues common to any routing protocol are path determination, metrics, convergence, and load balancing.

Path Determination

All networks within an internetwork must be connected to a router, and wherever a router has an interface on a network that interface must have an address on the network. This address is the originating point for reachability information.

Figure 4.1 shows a simple three-router internetwork. Router A knows about networks 192.168.1.0, 192.168.2.0, and 192.168.3.0 because it has interfaces on those networks with corresponding addresses and appropriate address masks. Likewise, router B knows about 192.168.3.0, 192.168.4.0, 192.168.5.0, and 192.186.6.0; router C knows about 192.168.6.0, 192.168.7.0, and 198.168.1.0. Each interface implements the data link and physical protocols of the network to which it is attached, so the router also knows the state of the network (up or down).

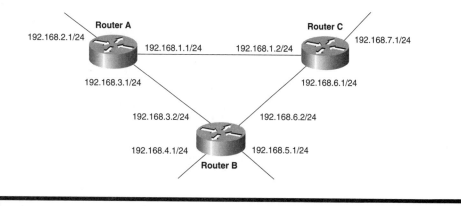

Figure 4.1

Each router knows about its directly connected networks from its assigned addresses and masks.

At first glance, the information-sharing procedure seems simple. Look at router A:

1. Router A examines its IP addresses and associated masks and deduces that it is attached to networks 192.168.1.0, 192.186.2.0, and 192.168.3.0.

2. Router A enters these networks into its route table, along with some sort of flag indicating that the networks are directly connected.

3. Router A places the information into a packet: "My directly connected networks are 192.168.1.0, 192.186.2.0, and 192.168.3.0."

4. Router A transmits copies of these route information packets, or *routing updates*, to routers B and C.

5. Routers B and C, having performed the same steps, have sent updates with their directly connected networks to A. Router A enters the received information into its route table, along with the source address of the router that sent the update packet. Router A now knows about all the networks, and it knows the addresses of the routers to which they are attached.

This procedure does seem quite simple. So why are routing protocols so much more complicated than this? Look again at Figure 4.1.

- What should router A do with the updates from B and C after it has recorded the information in the route table? Should it, for instance, pass B's routing information packet to C and pass C's packet to B?

- If router A does not forward the updates, information sharing may not be complete. For instance, if the link between B and C does not exist, those two routers would not know about each other's networks. Router A must forward the update information, but this step opens a whole new set of problems.

- If router A hears about network 192.168.4.0 from both router B and router C, which router should be used to reach that network? Are they both valid? Which one is the best path?

- What mechanism will be used to ensure that all routers receive all routing information while preventing update packets from circulating endlessly through the internetwork?

- The routers share certain directly connected networks (192.168.1.0, 192.168.3.0, and 192.168.6.0). Should the routers still advertise these networks?

These questions are almost as simplistic as the preceding prelimi-nary explanation of routing protocols, but they should give you a feel for some of the issues that contribute to the complexity of the protocols. Each routing protocol addresses these questions one way or another, as will become clear in following sections and chapters.

Metrics

When there are multiple routes to the same destination, a router must have a mechanism for calculating the best path. A *metric* is a variable assigned to routes as a means of ranking them from best to worst or from most preferred to least preferred. Consider the following example of why metrics are needed.

Assuming that information sharing has properly occurred in the internetwork of Figure 4.1, router A might have a route table that looks like Table 4.1.

Table 4.1 *A rudimentary route table for router A of Figure 4.1.*

Network	Next-Hop Router
192.168.1.0	Directly connected
192.168.2.0	Directly connected
192.168.3.0	Directly connected
192.168.4.0	B, C
192.168.5.0	B, C
192.168.6.0	B, C
192.168.7.0	B, C

This route table says that the first three networks are directly con-nected and that no routing is needed from router A to reach them, which is correct. The last four networks, according to this table, can be reached via router B or router C. This information is also correct. But if network 192.168.7.0 can be reached via either router B or router C, which path is the preferable path? Metrics are needed to rank the alternatives.

The "best" or "shortest" route is the most preferred route according to a particular protocol's metric.

Different routing protocols use different, and sometimes multiple, metrics. For example, RIP defines the "best" route as the one with the least number of router hops; IGRP defines the "best" route based on a combination of the lowest bandwidth along the route and the total delay of the route. The following sections provide basic definitions of these and other commonly used metrics. Further complexities—such as how some routing protocols use multiple metrics and deal with routes that have identical metric values—are covered later, in the protocol-specific chapters of this book.

Hop Count

A hop count metric simply counts router hops. For instance, from router A it is 1 hop to network 192.168.5.0 if packets are sent out interface 192.168.3.1 (through router B) and 2 hops if packets are sent out 192.168.1.1 (through routers C and B). Assuming hop count is the only metric being applied, the best route is the one with the fewest hops, in this case, A-B.

But is the A-B link really the best path? If the A-B link is a DS-0 link and the A-C and C-B links are T-1 links, the 2-hop route may actually be best because bandwidth plays a role in how efficiently traffic travels through the network.

Bandwidth

A bandwidth metric would choose a higher-bandwidth path over a lower-bandwidth link. However, bandwidth by itself still may not be a good metric. What if one or both of the T1 links are heavily loaded with other traffic and the 56K link is lightly loaded? Or what if the higher-bandwidth link also has a higher delay?

Load

This metric reflects the amount of traffic utilizing the links along the path. The best path is the one with the lowest load.

Unlike hop count and bandwidth, the load on a route changes, and therefore the metric will change. Care must be taken here. If the metric changes too frequently, *route flapping*—the frequent change of preferred routes—may occur. Route flaps can have adverse effects on the router's CPU, the bandwidth of the data links, and the overall stability of the network.

Route flapping

Delay

Delay is a measure of the time a packet takes to traverse a route. A routing protocol using delay as a metric would choose the path with the least delay as the best path. There may be many ways to measure delay. Delay may take into account not only the delay of the links along the route but also such factors as router latency and queuing delay. On the other hand, the delay of a route may be not measured at all; it may be a sum of static quantities defined for each interface along the path. Each individual delay quantity would be an estimate based on the type of link to which the interface is connected.

Reliability

Reliability measures the likelihood that the link will fail in some way and can be either variable or fixed. Examples of variable-reliability metrics are the number of times a link has failed or the number of errors it has received within a certain time period. Fixed-reliability metrics are based on known qualities of a link as determined by the network administrator. The path with highest reliability would be selected as best.

Cost

This metric is configured by a network administrator to reflect more- or less-preferred routes. Cost may be defined by any policy or link characteristic or may reflect the arbitrary judgment of the network administrator.

The term *cost* is often used as a generic term when speaking of route choices. For example, "RIP chooses the lowest-cost path based on hop count." Another generic term is *shortest,* as in "RIP chooses the shortest path based on hop count." When used in this context, either *lowest-cost* (or *highest-cost*) and *shortest* (or *longest*) merely refer to a routing protocol's view of paths based on its specific metrics.

Convergence

A dynamic routing protocol must include a set of procedures for a router to inform other routers about its directly connected networks, to receive and process the same information from other routers, and to pass along the information it receives from other routers. Further, a routing protocol must define a metric by which best paths may be determined.

A further criteria for routing protocols is that the reachability information in the route tables of all routers in the internetwork must be consistent. If router A in Figure 4.1 determines that the best path to network 192.168.5.0 is via router C and if router C determines that the best path to the same network is through router A, router A will send packets destined for 192.168.5.0 to C, C will send them back to A, A will again send them to C, and so on. This continuous circling of traffic between two or more destinations is referred to as a *routing loop*.

Routing loop

The process of bringing all route tables to a state of consistency is called *convergence*. The time it takes to share information across an internetwork and for all routers to calculate best paths is the *convergence time*.

Figure 4.2 shows an internetwork that was converged, but now a topology change has occurred. The link between the two left-most routers has failed; both routers, being directly connected, know about the failure from the data link protocol and proceed to inform their neighbors of the unavailable link. The neighbors update their route tables accordingly and inform their neighbors, and the process continues until all routers know about the change.

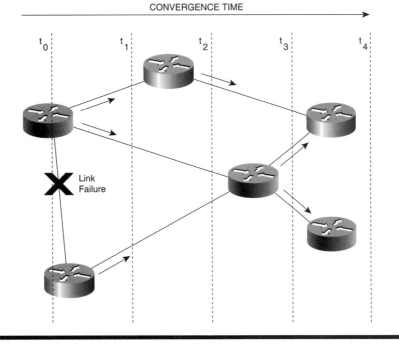

Figure 4.2

Reconvergence after a topology change takes time. While the internetwork is in an unconverged state, routers are susceptible to bad routing information.

Notice that at time t_2 the three left-most routers know about the topology change but the three right-most routers have not yet heard the news. Those three have old information and will continue to switch packets accordingly. It is during this intermediate time, when the internetwork is in an unconverged state, that routing errors may occur. Therefore convergence time is an important factor in any routing protocol. The faster a network can reconverge after a topology change, the better.

Load Balancing

Recall from Chapter 3, "Static Routing," that load balancing is the practice of distributing traffic among multiple paths to the same destination in order to use bandwidth efficiently. As an example of the usefulness of load balancing, consider Figure 4.1 again. All the networks in Figure 4.1 are reachable from two paths. If a device on 192.168.2.0 sends a stream of packets to a device on 192.168.6.0, router A may send them all via router B or router C. In both cases, the network is 1 hop away. However, sending all packets on a single route probably is not the most efficient use of available bandwidth. Instead, load balancing should be implemented to alternate traffic between the two paths. As noted in Chapter 3, load balancing can be equal cost or unequal cost and per packet or per destination.

DISTANCE VECTOR ROUTING PROTOCOLS

Most routing protocols fall into one of two classes: *distance vector* or *link state*. The basics of distance vector routing protocols are examined here; the next section covers link state routing protocols. Distance vector algorithms are based on the work done of R.

E. Bellman,[1] L. R. Ford, and D. R. Fulkerson[2] and for this reason occasionally are referred to as *Bellman-Ford* or *Ford-Fulkerson* algorithms.

The name distance vector is derived from the fact that routes are advertised as vectors of (distance, direction), where distance is defined in terms of a metric and direction is defined in terms of the next-hop router. For example, "Destination A is a distance of 5 hops away, in the direction of next-hop router X." As that statement implies, each router learns routes from its neighboring routers' perspectives and then advertises the routes from its own perspective. Because each router depends on its neighbors for information, which the neighbors in turn may have learned from their neighbors, and so on, distance vector routing is sometimes facetiously referred to as "routing by rumor."

Distance vector routing protocols include the following:

- Routing Information Protocol (RIP) for IP

- Xerox Networking System's XNS RIP

- Novell's IPX RIP

- Cisco's Internet Gateway Routing Protocol (IGRP)

- DEC's DNA Phase IV

- AppleTalk's Routing Table Maintenance Protocol (RTMP)

---

[1] *R. E. Bellman.* Dynamic Programming. *Princeton, New Jersey: Princeton University Press; 1957.*

[2] *L. R. Ford Jr. and D. R. Fulkerson.* Flows in Networks. *Princeton, New Jersey: Princeton University Press; 1962.*

Common Characteristics

A typical distance vector routing protocol uses a routing algorithm in which routers periodically send routing updates to all neighbors by broadcasting their entire route tables.[3]

The preceding statement contains a lot of information. Following sections consider it in more detail.

Periodic Updates

Periodic updates means that at the end of a certain time period, updates will be transmitted. This period typically ranges from 10 seconds for AppleTalk's RTMP to 90 seconds for Cisco's IGRP. At issue here is the fact that if updates are sent too frequently, congestion may occur; if updates are sent too infrequently, convergence time may be unacceptably high.

Neighbors

In the context of routers, *neighbors* always means routers sharing a common data link. A distance vector routing protocol sends its updates to neighboring routers[4] and depends on them to pass the update information along to their neighbors. For this reason, distance vector routing is said to use hop-by-hop updates.

Broadcast Updates

When a router first becomes active on a network, how does it find other routers and how does it announce its own presence? Several methods are available. The simplest is to send the updates to the broadcast address (in the case of IP, 255.255.255.255). Neighbor-

---

[3] *A notable exception to this convention is Cisco's Enhanced IGRP. EIGRP is a distance vector protocol, but its updates are not periodic, are not broadcasted, and do not contain the full route table. EIGRP is covered in Chapter 8, "Enhanced Interior Gateway Routing Protocol (EIGRP)."*

[4] *This statement is not entirely true. Hosts also can listen to routing updates in some implementations; but all that is important for this discussion is how routers work.*

ing routers speaking the same routing protocol will hear the broadcasts and take appropriate action. Hosts and other devices uninterested in the routing updates will simply drop the packets.

Full Routing Table Updates

Most distance vector routing protocols take the very simple approach of telling their neighbors everything they know by broadcasting their entire route table, with some exceptions that are covered in following sections. Neighbors receiving these updates glean the information they need and discard everything else.

Routing by Rumor

Figure 4.3 shows a distance vector algorithm in action. In this example, the metric is hop count. At time t_0, routers A through D have just become active. Looking at the route tables across the top row, at t_0 the only information any of the four routers has is its own directly connected networks. The tables identify these networks and indicate that they are directly connected by having no next-hop router and by having a hop count of 0. Each of the four routers will broadcast this information on all links.

At time t_1, the first updates have been received and processed by the routers. Look at router A's table at t_1. Router B's update to router A said that router B can reach networks 10.1.2.0 and 10.1.3.0, both 0 hops away. If the networks are 0 hops from B, they must be 1 hop from A. Router A incremented the hop count by 1 and then examined its route table. It already knew about 10.1.2.0, and the hop count (0) was less than the hop count B advertised, (1), so A disregarded that information.

Network 10.1.3.0 was new information, however, so A entered this in the route table. The source address of the update packet was router B's interface (10.1.2.2) so that information is entered along with the calculated hop count.

Top diagram: networks 10.1.1.0, 10.1.2.0, 10.1.3.0, 10.1.4.0, 10.1.5.0 with interface addresses .1 / .1, .2 / .1, .2 / .1, .2 / .1 across Routers A, B, C, D.

t_0

Router A NET	VIA	HOPS	Router B NET	VIA	HOPS	Router C NET	VIA	HOPS	Router D NET	VIA	HOPS
10.1.1.0	--	0	10.1.2.0	--	0	10.1.3.0	--	0	10.1.4.0	--	0
10.1.2.0	--	0	10.1.3.0	--	0	10.1.4.0	--	0	10.1.5.0	--	0

t_1

Router A NET	VIA	HOPS	Router B NET	VIA	HOPS	Router C NET	VIA	HOPS	Router D NET	VIA	HOPS
10.1.1.0	--	0	10.1.2.0	--	0	10.1.3.0	--	0	10.1.4.0	--	0
10.1.2.0	--	0	10.1.3.0	--	0	10.1.4.0	--	0	10.1.5.0	--	0
10.1.3.0	10.1.2.2	1	10.1.1.0	10.1.2.1	1	10.1.2.0	10.1.3.1	1	10.1.3.0	10.1.4.1	1
			10.1.4.0	10.1.3.2	1	10.1.5.0	10.1.4.2	1			

t_2

Router A NET	VIA	HOPS	Router B NET	VIA	HOPS	Router C NET	VIA	HOPS	Router D NET	VIA	HOPS
10.1.1.0	--	0	10.1.2.0	--	0	10.1.3.0	--	0	10.1.4.0	--	0
10.1.2.0	--	0	10.1.3.0	--	0	10.1.4.0	--	0	10.1.5.0	--	0
10.1.3.0	10.1.2.2	1	10.1.1.0	10.1.2.1	1	10.1.2.0	10.1.3.1	1	10.1.3.0	10.1.4.1	1
10.1.4.0	10.1.2.2	2	10.1.4.0	10.1.3.2	1	10.1.5.0	10.1.4.2	1	10.1.2.0	10.1.4.1	2
			10.1.5.0	10.1.3.2	2	10.1.1.0	10.1.3.1	2			

t_3

Router A NET	VIA	HOPS	Router B NET	VIA	HOPS	Router C NET	VIA	HOPS	Router D NET	VIA	HOPS
10.1.1.0	--	0	10.1.2.0	--	0	10.1.3.0	--	0	10.1.4.0	--	0
10.1.2.0	--	0	10.1.3.0	--	0	10.1.4.0	--	0	10.1.5.0	--	0
10.1.3.0	10.1.2.2	1	10.1.1.0	10.1.2.1	1	10.1.2.0	10.1.3.1	1	10.1.3.0	10.1.4.1	1
10.1.4.0	10.1.2.2	2	10.1.4.0	10.1.3.2	1	10.1.5.0	10.1.4.2	1	10.1.2.0	10.1.4.1	2
10.1.5.0	10.1.2.2	3	10.1.5.0	10.1.3.2	2	10.1.1.0	10.1.3.1	2	10.1.1.0	10.1.4.1	3

Figure 4.3

Distance vector protocols converge hop-by-hop.

Notice that the other routers performed similar operations at the same time t_1. Router C, for instance, disregarded the information about 10.1.3.0 from B and 10.1.4.0 from C but entered information about 10.1.2.0, reachable via B's interface address 10.1.3.1, and 10.1.5.0, reachable via C's interface 10.1.4.2. Both networks were calculated as 1 hop away.

At time t_2, the update period has again expired and another set of updates has been broadcast. Router B sent its latest table; router A again incremented B's advertised hop counts by 1 and compared. The information about 10.1.2.0 is again discarded for the same reason as before. 10.1.3.0 is already known, and the hop count hasn't changed, so that information is also discarded. 10.1.4.0 is new information and is entered into the route table.

The network is converged at time t_3. Every router knows about every network, the address of the next-hop router for every network, and the distance in hops to every network.

Time for an analogy. You are wandering in the Sangre de Cristo mountains of northern New Mexico—a wonderful place to wander if you aren't lost. But you are lost. You come upon a fork in the trail and a sign pointing west, reading "Taos, 15 miles." You have no choice but to trust the sign. You have no clue what the terrain is like over that 15 miles; you don't know whether there is a better route or even whether the sign is correct. Someone could have turned it around, in which case you will travel deeper into the forest instead of to safety!

Distance vector algorithms provide road signs to networks.[5] They provide the direction and the distance, but no details about what lies along the route. And like the sign at the fork in the trail, they are vulnerable to accidental or intentional misdirection. Following are some of the difficulties and refinements associated with distance vector algorithms.

Route Invalidation Timers

Now that the internetwork in Figure 4.3 is fully converged, how will it handle reconvergence when some part of the topology changes? If network 10.1.5.0 goes down, the answer is simple enough—router D, in its next scheduled update, flags the network as unreachable and passes the information along.

---

[5] *The road sign analogy is commonly used. You can find a good presentation in Radia Perlman's* Interconnections, *pp. 205–210.*

But what if, instead of 10.1.5.0 going down, router D fails? Routers A, B, and C still have entries in their route tables about 10.1.5.0; the information is no longer valid, but there's no router to inform them of this fact. They will unknowingly forward packets to an unreachable destination—a black hole has opened in the internetwork.

This problem is handled by setting a route invalidation timer for each entry in the route table. For example, when router C first hears about 10.1.5.0 and enters the information into its route table, C sets a timer for that route. At every regularly scheduled update from router D, C discards the update's already-known information about 10.1.5.0 as described in "Routing by Rumor." But as C does so, it resets the timer on that route.

If router D goes down, C will no longer hear updates about 10.1.5.0. The timer will expire, C will flag the route as unreachable and will pass the information along in the next update.

Typical periods for route timeouts range from three to six update periods. A router would not want to invalidate a route after a single update has been missed, because this event may be the result of a corrupted or lost packet or some sort of network delay. At the same time, if the period is too long, reconvergence will be excessively slow.

Split Horizon

According to the distance vector algorithm as it has been described so far, at every update period each router broadcasts its entire route table to every neighbor. But is this really necessary? Every network known by router A in Figure 4.3, with a hop count higher than 0, has been learned from router B. Common sense suggests that for router A to broadcast the networks it has learned from router B back to router B is a waste of resources. Obviously, B already knows about those networks.

A route pointing back to the router from which packets were received is called a *reverse route*. *Split horizon* is a technique for preventing reverse routes between two routers.

Besides not wasting resources, there is a more important reason for not sending reachability information back to the router from which the information was learned. The most important function of a dynamic routing protocol is to detect and compensate for topology changes—if the best path to a network becomes unreachable, the protocol must look for a next-best path.

Look yet again at the converged internetwork of Figure 4.3 and suppose that network 10.1.5.0 goes down. Router D will detect the failure, flag the network as unreachable, and pass the information along to router C at the next update interval. However, before D's update timer triggers an update, something unexpected happens. C's update arrives, claiming that it can reach 10.1.5.0, one hop away! Remember the road sign analogy? Router D has no way of knowing that C is not advertising a legitimate next-best path. It will increment the hop count and make an entry into its route table indicating that 10.1.5.0 is reachable via router C's interface 10.1.4.1, just 2 hops away.

Now a packet with a destination address of 10.1.5.3 arrives at router C. C consults its route table and forwards the packet to D. D consults its route table and forwards the packet to C, C forwards it back to D, *ad infinitum*. A routing loop has occurred.

Implementing split horizon prevents the possibility of such a routing loop. There are two categories of split horizon: simple split horizon and split horizon with poisoned reverse.

Simple split horizon

The rule for simple split horizon is, When sending updates out a particular interface, do not include networks that were learned from updates received on that interface.

The routers in Figure 4.4 implement simple split horizon. Router C sends an update to router D for networks 10.1.1.0, 10.1.2.0, and 10.1.3.0. Networks 10.1.4.0 and 10.1.5.0 are not included because they were learned from router D. Likewise, updates to router B include 10.1.4.0 and 10.1.5.0 with no mention of 10.1.1.0, 10.1.2.0, and 10.1.3.0.

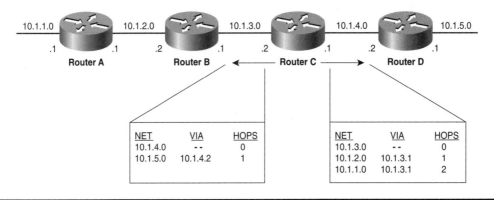

Figure 4.4
Simple split horizon does not advertise routes back to the neighbors from whom the routes were learned.

Simple split horizon works by suppressing information. Split horizon with poisoned reverse is a modification that provides more positive information.

Split horizon with poisoned reverse

The rule for split horizon with poisoned reverse is, When sending updates out a particular interface, designate any networks that were learned from updates received on that interface as unreachable.

In the scenario of Figure 4.4, router C would in fact advertise 10.1.4.0 and 10.1.5.0 to router D, but the network would be marked as unreachable. Figure 4.5 shows what the route tables from C to B and D would look like. Notice that a route is marked as unreachable by setting the metric to infinity; in other words, the network is an infinite distance away. Coverage of a routing protocol's concept of infinity continues in the next section.

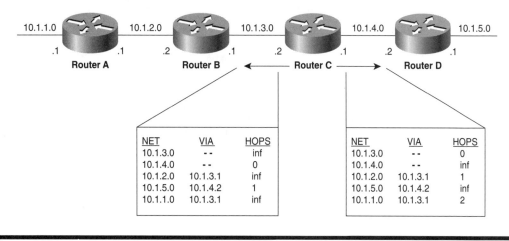

Figure 4.5

Split horizon with poisoned reverse advertises reverse routes but with an unreachable (infinite) metric.

Split horizon with poisoned reverse is considered safer and stronger than simple split horizon—a sort of "bad news is better than no news at all" approach. For example, suppose that router B in Figure 4.5 receives corrupted information causing it to believe that subnet 10.1.1.0 is reachable via router C. Simple split horizon would do nothing to correct this misperception, whereas a poisoned reverse update from router C would immediately stop the potential loop. For this reason, most modern distance vector implementations use split horizon with poisoned reverse. The trade-off is that routing update packets are larger, which may exacerbate any congestion problems on a link.

Counting to Infinity

Split horizon will break loops between neighbors, but it will not stop loops in a network such as the one in Figure 4.6. Again, 10.1.5.0 has failed. Router D sends the appropriate updates to its neighbors router C (the dashed arrows) and router B (the solid arrows). Router B marks the route via D as unreachable, but router A is advertising a next-best path to 10.1.5.0, which is 3 hops away. B posts that route in its route table.

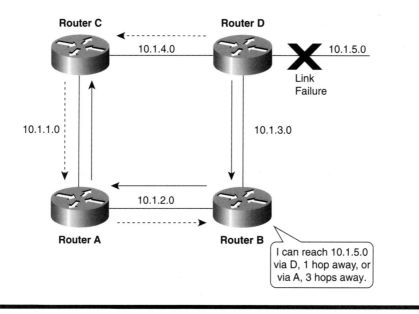

Figure 4.6

Split horizon will not prevent routing loops here.

B now informs D that it has an alternative route to 10.1.5.0. D posts this information and updates C, saying that it has a 4-hop route to the network. C tells A that 10.1.5.0 is 5 hops away. A tells B that the network is now 6 hops away.

"Ah," router B thinks, "router A's path to 10.1.5.0 has increased in length. Nonetheless, it's the only route I've got, so I'll use it!"

B changes the hop count to 7, updates D, and around it goes again. This situation is the *counting-to-infinity* problem because the hop count to 10.1.5.0 will continue to increase to infinity. All routers are implementing split horizon, but it doesn't help.

The way to alleviate the effects of counting to infinity is to define infinity. Most distance vector protocols define infinity to be 16 hops. As the updates continue to loop among the routers in Figure 4.6, the hop count to 10.1.5.0 in all routers will eventually increment to 16. At that time, the network will be considered unreachable.

Defining infinity

This method is also how routers advertise a network as unreachable. Whether it is a poisoned reverse route, a network that has failed, or a network beyond the maximum network diameter of 15 hops, a router will recognize any 16-hop route as unreachable.

Setting a maximum hop count of 15 helps solve the counting-to-infinity problem, but convergence will still be very slow. Given an update period of 30 seconds, a network could take up to 7.5 minutes to reconverge and is susceptible to routing errors during this time. The two methods for speeding up reconvergence are triggered updates and holddown timers.

Triggered Updates

Triggered updates, also known as *flash updates*, are very simple: If a metric changes for better or for worse, a router will immediately send out an update without waiting for its update timer to expire. Reconvergence will occur far more quickly than if every router had to wait for regularly scheduled updates, and the problem of counting to infinity is greatly reduced, although not completely eliminated. Regular updates may still occur along with triggered updates. Thus a router might receive bad information about a route from a not-yet-reconverged router after having received correct information from a triggered update. Such a situation shows that confusion and routing errors may still occur while an inter-network is reconverging, but triggered updates will help to iron things out more quickly.

A further refinement is to include in the update only the networks that actually triggered it, rather than the entire route table. This technique reduces the processing time and the impact on network bandwidth.

Holddown Timers

Triggered updates add responsiveness to a reconverging internet-work. *Holddown timers* introduce a certain amount of skepticism to reduce the acceptance of bad routing information.

If the distance to a destination increases (for example, the hop count increases from 2 to 4), the router sets a holddown timer for that route. Until the timer expires, the router will not accept any new updates for the route.

Obviously, a trade-off is involved here. The likelihood of bad rout-ing information getting into a table is reduced but at the expense of the reconvergence time. Like other timers, holddown timers must be set with care. If the holddown period is too short, it will be ineffective, and if it is too long, normal routing will be adversely affected.

Asynchronous Updates

Figure 4.7 shows a group of routers connected to an Ethernet backbone. The routers should not broadcast their updates at the same time; if they do, the update packets will collide. Yet this sit-uation is exactly what can happen when a several routers share a broadcast network. System delays related to the processing of updates in the routers tend to cause the update timers to become synchronized. As a few routers become synchronized, collisions will begin to occur, further contributing to system delays, and eventually all routers sharing the broadcast network may become synchronized.

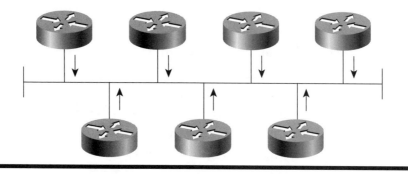

Figure 4.7

If update timers become synchronized, collisions may occur.

Asynchronous updates may be maintained by one of two methods:

- Each router's update timer is independent of the routing process and is, therefore, not affected by processing loads on the router.

- A small random time, or *timing jitter*, is added to each update period as an offset.

If routers implement the method of rigid, system-independent timers, then all routers sharing a broadcast network must be brought online in a random fashion. Rebooting the entire group of routers simultaneously could result in all the timers attempting to update at the same time.

Adding randomness to the update period is effective if the variable is large enough in proportion to the number of routers sharing the broadcast network. Sally Floyd and Van Jacobson[6] have calculated that a too-small randomization will be overcome by a large enough network of routers and that to be effective the update timer should range as much as 50% of the median update period.

LINK STATE ROUTING PROTOCOLS

The information available to a distance vector router has been compared to the information available from a road sign. Link state routing protocols are like a road map. A link state router cannot be fooled as easily into making bad routing decisions, because it has a complete picture of the network. The reason is that unlike the routing-by-rumor approach of distance vector, link state routers have firsthand information from all their peer[7] routers. Each router originates information about itself, its directly connected links, and the state of those links (hence the name). This information is passed around from router to router, each router making a copy of it, but never changing it. The ultimate objective is that every router has identical information about the internetwork, and each router will independently calculate its own best paths.

Link state protocols, sometimes called *shortest path first* or *distributed database* protocols, are built around a well-known algorithm from graph theory, E. W. Dijkstra'a shortest path algorithm. Examples of link state routing protocols are:

- Open Shortest Path First (OSPF) for IP

- The ISO's Intermediate System to Intermediate System (IS-IS) for CLNS and IP

- DEC's DNA Phase V

- Novell's NetWare Link Services Protocol (NLSP)

---

[6] *S. Floyd and V. Jacobson. "The Synchronisation of Periodic Routing Messages." ACM Sigcomm '93 Symposium, September 1993.*

[7] *That is, all routers speaking the same routing protocol.*

Although link state protocols are rightly considered more complex than distance vector protocols, the basic functionality is not complex at all:

1. Each router establishes a relationship—an adjacency—with each of its neighbors.

2. Each router sends *link state advertisements* (LSAs), sometimes called *link state packets* (LSPs), to each neighbor. One LSA is generated for each of the router's links, identifying the link, the state of the link, the metric cost of the router's interface to the link, and any neighbors that may be connected to the link. Each neighbor receiving an advertisement in turn forwards (*floods*) the advertisement to its own neighbors.

   Link state advertisement

3. Each router stores a copy of all the LSAs it has seen in a database. If all works well, the databases in all routers should be identical.

4. The completed *topological database*, also called the *link state database*, describes a graph of the internetwork. Using the Dijkstra algorithm, each router calculates the shortest path to each network and enters this information into the route table.

Neighbors

Neighbor discovery is the first step in getting a link state environment up and running. In keeping with the friendly neighbor terminology, a Hello protocol is used for this step. The protocol will define a Hello packet format and a procedure for exchanging the packets and processing the information the packets contain.

At a minimum, the Hello packet will contain a *router ID* and the address of the network on which the packet is being sent. The router ID is be something by which the router originating the packet can be uniquely distinguished from all other routers; for

Router ID

instance, an IP address from one of the router's interfaces. Other fields of the packet may carry a subnet mask, Hello intervals, a specified maximum period the router will wait to hear a Hello before declaring the neighbor "dead," a descriptor of the circuit type, and flags to help in bringing up adjacencies.

Adjacent neighbors

When two routers have discovered each other as neighbors, they go through a process of synchronizing their databases in which they exchange and verify database information until their databases are identical. The details of database synchronization are described in Chapters 9, "Open Shortest Path First," and 10, "Integrated IS-IS." To perform this database synchronization, the neighbors must be *adjacent*—that is, they must agree on certain protocol-specific parameters such as timers and support of optional capabilities. By using Hello packets to build adjacencies, link state protocols can exchange information in a controlled fashion. Contrast this approach with distance vector, which simply broadcasts updates out any interface configured for that routing protocol.

Beyond building adjacencies, Hello packets serve as keepalives to monitor the adjacency. If Hellos are not heard from an adjacent neighbor within a certain established time, the neighbor is considered unreachable and the adjacency is broken. A typical interval for the exchange of hello packets is 10 seconds, and a typical dead period is four times that.

Link State Flooding

After the adjacencies are established, the routers may begin sending out LSAs. As the term *flooding* implies, the advertisements are sent to every neighbor. In turn, each received LSA is copied and forwarded to every neighbor except the one that sent the LSA. This process is the source of one of link state's advantages over distance vector. LSAs are forwarded almost immediately, whereas distance vector must run its algorithm and update its route table before routing updates, even the triggered ones, can be forwarded. As a result, link state protocols converge much faster than distance vector protocols converge when the topology changes.

The flooding process is the most complex piece of a link state protocol. There are several ways to make flooding more efficient and more reliable, such as using unicast and multicast addresses, checksums, and positive acknowledgments. These topics are examined in the protocol-specific chapters, but two procedures are vitally important to the flooding process: sequencing and aging.

Sequence Numbers

A difficulty with flooding, as described so far, is that when all routers have received all LSAs, the flooding must stop. A time-to-live value in the packets could simply be relied on to expire, but it is hardly efficient to permit LSAs to wander the internetwork until they expire. Take the internetwork in Figure 4.8. Subnet 172.22.4.0 at router A has failed, and A has flooded an LSA to its neighbors B and D, advertising the new state of the link. B and D dutifully flood to their neighbors, and so on.

Look next at what happens at router C. An LSA arrives from router B at time t_1, is entered into C's topological database, and is forwarded to router F. At some later time t_3, another copy of the same LSA arrives from the longer A-D-E-F-C route. Router C sees that it already has the LSA in its database; the question is, should C forward this LSA to router B? The answer is no because B has already received the advertisement. Router C knows this because the sequence number of the LSA it received from router F is the same as the sequence number of the LSA it received earlier from router B.

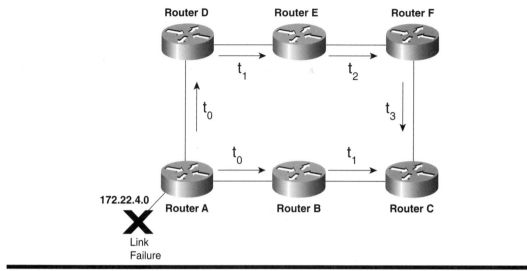

Figure 4.8
When a topology change occurs, LSAs advertising the change will be flooded throughout the internetwork.

When router A sent out the LSA, it included an identical sequence number in each copy. This sequence number is recorded in the routers' topological databases along with the rest of the LSA; when a router receives an LSA that is already in the database and its sequence number is the same, the received information is discarded. If the information is the same but the sequence number is greater, the received information and new sequence number are entered into the database and the LSA is flooded. In this way, flooding is abated when all routers have seen a copy of the most recent LSA.

As described so far, it seems that routers could merely verify that their link state databases contain the same LSA as the newly received LSA and make a flood/discard decision based on that information, without needing a sequence number. But imagine that immediately after Figure 4.8's network 172.22.4.0 failed, it came back up. Router A might send out an LSA advertising the network as down, with a sequence number of 166; then it sends out a new LSA announcing the same network as up, with a sequence number of 167. Router C receives the down LSA and then the up LSA from the A-B-C path, but then it receives a delayed down LSA from the A-D-E-F-C path. Without the sequence numbers, C would not know whether or not to believe the delayed down LSA. With sequence numbers, C's database will indicate that the information from router A has a sequence number of 167; the late LSA has a sequence number of 166 and is therefore recognized as old information and discarded.

Because the sequence numbers are carried in a set field within the LSAs, the numbers must have some upper bound. What happens when this maximum sequence number is reached?

Linear Sequence Number Spaces

One approach is to use a linear sequence number space so large that it is unlikely the upper limit will ever be reached. If, for instance, a 32-bit field is used, there are $2^{32} = 4,294,967,296$ available sequence numbers starting with zero. Even if a router was creating a new link state packet every 10 seconds, it would take some 1361 years to exhaust the sequence number supply; few routers are expected to last so long.

In this imperfect world, unfortunately, malfunctions occur. If a link state routing process somehow runs out of sequence numbers, it must shut itself down and stay down long enough for its LSAs to age out of all databases before starting over at the lowest sequence number (see the section "Aging," later in this chapter).

A more common difficulty presents itself during router restarts. If router A restarts, it probably will have no way of remembering the sequence number it last used and must begin again at, say, one. But if its neighbors still have router A's previous sequence numbers in their databases, the lower sequence numbers will be interpreted as older sequence numbers and will be ignored. Again, the routing process must stay down until all old LSAs are aged out of the internetwork. Given that a maximum age might be an hour or more, this solution is not very attractive.

A better solution is to add a new rule to the flooding behavior described thus far: If a restarted router issues to a neighbor an LSA with a sequence number that appears to be older than the neighbor's stored sequence number, the neighbor will send its own stored LSA and sequence number back to the router. The router will thus learn the sequence number it was using before it restarted and may adjust accordingly.

Care must be taken, however, that the last-used sequence number was not close to the maximum; otherwise, the restarting router will simply have to restart again. A rule must be set limiting the "jump" the router may make in sequence numbers—for instance, a rule might say that the sequence numbers cannot make a single increase more than one-half the total sequence number space. (The actual formulas are more complex than this example, taking into account age constraints.)

IS-IS uses a 32-bit linear sequence number space.

Circular Sequence Number Spaces

Another approach is to use a circular sequence number space, where the numbers "wrap"—that is, in a 32-bit space the number following 4,294,967,295 is 0. Malfunctions can cause interesting dilemmas here, too. A restarting router may encounter the same believability problem as discussed for linear sequence numbers.

Circular sequence numbering creates a curious bit of illogic. If x is any number between 1 and 4,294,967,295 inclusive, then $0 < x < 0$. This situation can be managed in well-behaved internetworks by asserting two rules for determining when a sequence number is greater than or less than another sequence number. Given a sequence number space n and two sequence numbers a and b, a is considered more recent (of larger magnitude) in either of the following situations:

- $a > b$, and $(a - b) \le n/2$

- $a < b$, and $(b - a) > n/2$

For the sake of simplicity, take a sequence number space of six bits, shown in Figure 4.9:

$$n = 2^6 = 64, \quad \text{so } n/2 = 32.$$

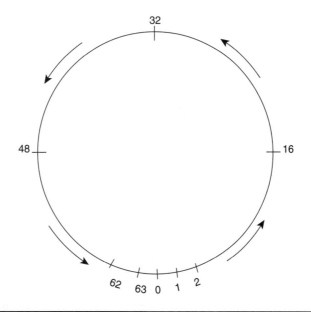

Figure 4.9

A six-bit circular address space.

Given two sequence numbers 48 and 18, 48 is more recent because by rule (1):

$$48 > 18 \quad \text{and} \quad (48 - 18) = 30, \quad \text{and} \quad 30 < 32.$$

Given two sequence numbers 3 and 48, 3 is more recent because by rule (2):

$$3 < 48 \quad \text{and} \quad (48 - 3) = 45, \quad \text{and} \quad 45 > 32.$$

Given two sequence numbers 3 and 18, 18 is more recent because by rule (1):

$$18 > 3 \quad \text{and} \quad (18 - 3) = 15, \quad \text{and} \quad 15 < 32.$$

So the rules seem to enforce circularity.

But what about a not-so-well-behaved internetwork? Imagine an internetwork running a six-bit sequence number space. Now imagine that one of the routers on the internetwork decides to go belly-up, but as it does so, it blurts out three identical LSAs with a sequence number of 44 (101100). Unfortunately, a neighboring router is also malfunctioning—it is dropping bits. The neighbor drops a bit in the sequence number field of the second LSA, drops yet another bit in the third LSA, and floods all three. The result is three identical LSAs with three different sequence numbers:

44	(101100)
40	(101000)
8	(001000)

Applying the circularity rules reveals that 44 is more recent than 40, which is more recent than 8, which is more recent than 44! The result is that every LSA will be continuously flooded, and databases will be continually overwritten with the "latest" LSA, until finally buffers become clogged with LSAs, CPUs become overloaded, and the whole internetwork comes crashing down.

This chain of events sounds pretty far-fetched. It is, however, factual. The ARPANET, the precursor of the modern Internet, ran an early link state protocol with a six-bit circular sequence number space; on October 27, 1980, two routers experiencing the malfunctions just described brought the entire ARPANET to a standstill.[8]

Lollipop-Shaped Sequence Number Spaces

This whimsically-named construct was proposed by Dr. Radia Perlman.[9] Lollipop-shaped sequence number spaces are a hybrid of linear and circular sequence number spaces; if you think about it, a lollipop has a linear component and a circular component. The problem with circular spaces is that there is no number less than all other numbers. The problem with linear spaces is that they are—well—not circular. That is, their set of sequence numbers is finite.

When router A restarts, it would be nice to begin with a number *a* that is less than all other numbers. Neighbors will recognize this number for what it is, and if they have a pre-restart number *b* in their databases from router A, they can send that number to router A and router A will jump to that sequence number. Router A might be able to send more than one LSA before hearing about the sequence number it had been using before restarting. Therefore, it is important to have enough restart numbers so that A cannot use them all before neighbors either inform it of a previously used number or the previously used number ages out of all databases.

---

[8] E. C. Rosen. *"Vulnerabilities of Network Control Protocols: An Example."* Computer Communication Review, *July 1981.*

[9] R. Perlman. *"Fault-Tolerant Broadcasting of Routing Information."* Computer Networks, *Vol. 7, December 1983, pp. 395–405.*

These linear restart numbers form the stick of the lollipop. When they have been used up, or after a neighbor has provided a sequence number to which A can jump, A enters a circular number space, the candy part of the lollipop.

One way of designing a lollipop address space is to use signed sequence numbers, where $-k < 0 < k$. The negative numbers counting up from $-k$ to 1 form the stick, and the positive numbers from 0 to k are the circular space. Perlman's rules for the sequence numbers are as follows. Given two numbers a and b and a sequence number space n, b is more recent than a if and only if:

1. $a < 0$ and $a < b$, or
2. $a > 0, a < b$, and $(b - a) < n/2$, or
3. $a > 0, b > 0, a > b$, and $(a - b) > n/2$.

Figure 4.10 shows an implementation of the lollipop-shaped sequence number space. A 32-bit signed number space N is used, yielding 2^{31} positive numbers and 2^{31} negative numbers. $-N$ (-2^{31}, or 0x80000000) and $N - 1$ ($2^{31} - 1$, or 0x7FFFFFFF) are not used. A router coming online will begin its sequence numbers at $-N + 1$ (0x80000001) and increment up to zero, at which time it has entered the circular number space. When the sequence reaches N $- 2$ (0x7FFFFFFE), the sequence wraps back to zero (again, N–1 is unused).

Next, suppose the router restarts. The sequence number of the last LSA sent before the restart is 0x00005de3 (part of the circular sequence space). As it synchronizes its database with its neighbor after the restart, the router sends an LSA with a sequence number of 0x80000001 ($-N + 1$). The neighbor looks into its own database and finds the pre-restart LSA with a sequence number of 0x00005de3. The neighbor sends this LSA to the restarted router, essentially saying, "This is where you left off." The restarted

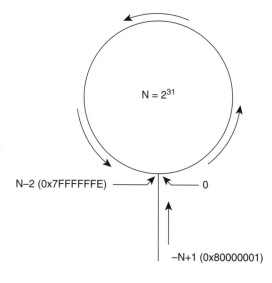

Figure 4.10
A lollipop-shaped sequence number space.

router then records the LSA with the positive sequence number. If it needs to send a new copy of the LSA at some future time, the new sequence number will be 0x00005de6.

Lollipop sequence spaces were used with the original version of OSPF, OSPFv1 (RFC 1131). Although the use of signed numbers was an improvement over the linear number space, the circular part was found to be vulnerable to the same ambiguities as a purely circular space. The deployment of OSPFv1 never progressed beyond the experimental stage. The current version of OSPF, OSPFv2 (originally specified in RFC 1247) adopts the best features of linear and lollipop sequence number spaces. It uses a signed number space like lollipop sequence numbers, beginning with 0x80000001. However, when the sequence number goes positive, the sequence space continues to be linear until it reaches the maximum of 0x7FFFFFFF. At that point the OSPF process must flush the LSA from all link state databases before restarting.

Aging

The LSA format should include a field for the age of the advertisement. When an LSA is created, the router sets this field to zero. As the packet is flooded, each router increments the age of the advertisement.[10]

Maximum age difference

This process of aging adds another layer of reliability to the flooding process. The protocol defines a maximum age difference (MaxAgeDiff) value for the internetwork. A router may receive multiple copies of the same LSA with identical sequence numbers but different ages. If the difference in the ages is lower than the MaxAgeDiff, it is assumed that the age difference was the result of normal network latencies; the original LSA in the database is retained, and the newer LSA (with the greater age) is not flooded. If the difference is greater than the MaxAgeDiff value, it is assumed that an anomaly has occurred in the internetwork in which a new LSA was sent without incrementing the sequence number. In this case, the newer LSA will be recorded, and the packet will be flooded. A typical MaxAgeDiff value is 15 minutes (used by OSPF).

Maximum age

The age of an LSA continues to be incremented as it resides in a link state database. If the age for a link state record is incremented up to some maximum age (MaxAge)—again defined by the specific routing protocol—the LSA, with age field set to the MaxAge value, is flooded to all neighbors and the record is deleted from the databases.

---

[10] *Of course, another option would be to start with some maximum age and decrement. OSPF increments; IS-IS decrements.*

If the LSA is to be flushed from all databases when MaxAge is reached, there must be a mechanism to periodically validate the LSA and reset its timer before MaxAge is reached. A link state refresh time (LSRefeshTime)[11] is established; when this time expires, a router floods a new LSA to all its neighbors, who will reset the age of the sending router's records to the new received age. OSPF defines a MaxAge of 1 hour and an LSRefreshTime of 30 minutes.

Link state refresh time

The Link State Database

In addition to flooding LSAs and discovering neighbors, a third major task of the link state routing protocol is establishing the link state database. The link state or topological database stores the LSAs as a series of records. Although a sequence number and age and possibly other information are included in the LSA, these variables exist mainly to manage the flooding process. The important information for the shortest path determination process is the advertising router's ID, its attached networks and neighboring routers, and the cost associated with those networks or neighbors. As the previous sentence implies, LSAs may include two types of generic information:[12]

- *Router link information* advertises a router's adjacent neighbors with a triple of (Router ID, Neighbor ID, Cost), where cost is the cost of the link to the neighbor.

- *Stub network information* advertises a router's directly connected stub networks (networks with no neighbors) with a triple of (Router ID, Network ID, Cost).

---

[11] *LSRefreshTime, MaxAge, and MaxAgeDiff are OSPF architectural constants.*
[12] *Actually, there can be more than two types of information and multiple types of link state packets. They are covered in the chapters on specific protocols.*

The shortest path first (SPF) algorithm is run once for the router link information to establish shortest paths to each router, and then stub network information is used to add these networks to the routers. Figure 4.11 shows an internetwork of routers and the links between them; stub networks are not shown for the sake of simplicity. Notice that several links have different costs associated with them at each end. A cost is associated with the outgoing direction of an interface. For instance, the link from RB to RC has a cost of 1, but the same link has a cost of 5 in the RC to RB direction.

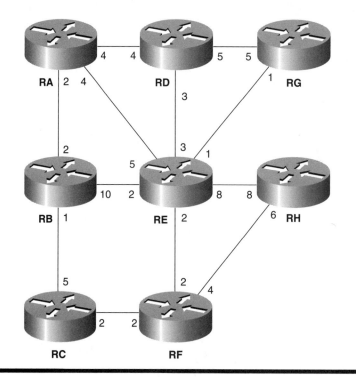

Figure 4.11

Link costs are calculated for the outgoing direction from an interface and do not necessarily have to be the same at all interfaces on a network.

Table 4.2 shows a generic link state database for the internetwork of Figure 4.11, a copy of which is stored in every router. As you read through this database, you will see that it completely describes the internetwork. Now it is possible to compute a tree that describes the shortest path to each router by running the SPF algorithm.

Table 4.2 *The topological database for the internetwork in Figure 4.11 .*

Router ID	Neighbor	Cost
RA	RB	2
RA	RD	4
RA	RE	4
RB	RA	2
RB	RC	1
RB	RE	10
RC	RB	5
RC	RF	2
RD	RA	4
RD	RE	3
RD	RG	5
RE	RA	5
RE	RB	2
RE	RD	3
RE	RF	2
RE	RG	1
RE	RH	8
RF	RC	2
RF	RE	2

Table 4.2   *The topological database for the internetwork in Figure 4.11, continued.*

Router ID	Neighbor	Cost
RF	RH	4
RG	RD	5
RG	RE	1
RH	RE	8
RH	RF	6

The SPF Algorithm

It is unfortunate that Dijkstra's algorithm is so commonly referred to in the routing world as the shortest path first algorithm. After all, the objective of every routing protocol is to calculate shortest paths. It is also unfortunate that Dijkstra's algorithm is often made to appear more esoteric than it really is; many writers just can't resist putting it in set theory notation. The clearest description of the algorithm comes E. W. Dijkstra's original paper. Here it is in his own words, followed by a "translation" for the link state routing protocol:

Construct [a] tree of minimum total length between the *n* nodes. (The tree is a graph with one and only one path between every two nodes.)

In the course of the construction that we present here, the branches are divided into three sets:

I. the branches definitely assigned to the tree under construction (they will be in a subtree);

II. the branches from which the next branch to be added to set I, will be selected;

III. the remaining branches (rejected or not considered).

The nodes are divided into two sets:

A. the nodes connected by the branches of set I,

B. the remaining nodes (one and only one branch of set II will lead to each of these nodes).

We start the construction by choosing an arbitrary node as the only member of set A, and by placing all branches that end in this node in set II. To start with, set I is empty. From then onwards we perform the following two steps repeatedly.

Step 1: The shortest branch of set II is removed from this set and added to set I. As a result, one node is transferred from set B to set A.

Step 2: Consider the branches leading from the node, that has just been transferred to set A, to the nodes that are still in set B. If the branch under construction is longer than the corresponding branch in set II, it is rejected; if it is shorter, it replaces the corresponding branch in set II, and the latter is rejected.

We then return to step 1 and repeat the process until sets II and B are empty. The branches in set I form the tree required.[13]

Adapting the algorithm for routers, first note that Dijkstra describes three sets of branches: I, II, and III. In the router, three databases represent the three sets:

- *The Tree Database.* This database represents set I. Links (branches) are added to the shortest path tree by adding them here. When the algorithm is finished, this database will describe the shortest path tree.

- *The Candidate Database.* This database corresponds to set II. Links are copied from the link state database to this list

13 E. W. Dijkstra. *"A Note on Two Problems in Connexion with Graphs."* Numerische Mathematik, *Vol. 1, 1959, pp. 269–271.*

in a prescribed order, where they become candidates to be added to the tree.

- *The Link State Database.* The repository of all links, as has been previously described. This topological database corresponds to set III.

Dijkstra also specifies two sets of nodes, set A and set B. Here the nodes are routers. Specifically, they are the routers represented by Neighbor ID in the Router Links triples (Router ID, Neighbor ID, Cost). Set A comprises the routers connected by the links in the Tree database. Set B is all other routers. Since the whole point is to find a shortest path to every router, set B should be empty when the algorithm is finished.

Here's a version of Dijkstra's algorithm adapted for routers:

1. A router initializes the Tree database by adding itself as the root. This entry shows the router as its own neighbor, with a cost of 0.
2. All triples in the link state database describing links to the root router's neighbors are added to the Candidate database.
3. The cost from the root to each link in the Candidate database is calculated. The link in the Candidate database with the lowest cost is moved to the Tree database. If two or more links are an equally low cost from the root, choose one.
4. The Neighbor ID of the link just added to the Tree database is examined. With the exception of any triples whose Neighbor ID is already in the Tree database, triples in the link state database describing that router's neighbors are added to the Candidate database.

5. If entries remain in the Candidate database, return to step 3. If the Candidate database is empty, then terminate the algorithm. At termination, a single Neighbor ID entry in the Tree database should represent every router, and the shortest path tree is complete.

Table 4.3 summarizes the process and results of applying Dijkstra's algorithm to build a shortest path tree for the network in Figure 4.11. Router RA from Figure 4.11 is running the algorithm, using the link state database of Table 4.2. Figure 4.12 shows the shortest path tree constructed for router RA by this algorithm. After each router calculates its own tree, it can examine the other routers' network link information and add the stub networks to the tree fairly easily tasks. From this information, entries may be made into the routing table.

Table 4.3 *Dijkstra's algorithm applied to the database of Table 4.1.*

Candidate	Cost to Root	Tree	Description
		RA,RA,0	Router A adds itself to the tree as root.
RA,RB,2 RA,RD,4 RA,RE,4	2 4 4	RA,RA,0	The links to all of RA's neighbors are added to the candidate list
RA,RD,4 RA,RE,4 RB,RC,1 ~~RB,RE,10~~	4 4 3	RA,RA,0 RA,RB,2	(RA,RB,2) is the lowest-cost link on the candidate list, so it is added to the tree. All of RB's neighbors except those already in the tree are added to the candidate list. (RA,RE,4) is a lower-cost link to RE than (RB,RE,10), so the latter is dropped from the candidate list.
RA,RD,4 RA,RE,4 RC,RF,2	4 4 5	RA,RA,0 RA,RB,2 RB,RC,1	(RB,RC,1) is the lowest-cost link on the candidate list, so it is added to the tree. All of RC's neighbors except those already on the tree become candidates.

Table 4.3 *Dijkstra's algorithm applied to the database of Table 4.1, continued.*

Candidate	Cost to Root	Tree	Description
RA,RE,4 RC,RF,2 RD,RE,3 RD,RG,5	4 5 7 9	RA,RA,0 RA,RB,2 RB,RC,1 RA,RD,4	(RA,RD,4) and (RA,RE,4) are both a cost of 4 from RA; (RC,RF,2) is a cost of 5. (RA,RD,4) is added to the tree and its neighbors become candidates. Two paths to RE are on the candidate list; (RD,RE,3)is a higher cost from RA and is dropped.
RC,RF,2 ~~RD,RG,5~~ RE,RF,2 RE,RG,1 RE,RH,8	5 9 6 5 12	RA,RA,0 RA,RB,2 RB,RC,1 RA,RD,4 RA,RE,4	(RF,RE,1) is added to the tree. All of RE's neighbors not already on the tree are added to the candidate list. The higher-cost link to RG is dropped.
RE,RF,2 RE,RG,1 ~~RE,RH,8~~ RF,RH,4	6 5 12 9	RA,RA,0 RA,RB,2 RB,RC,1 RA,RD,4 RA,RE,4 RC,RF,2	(RC,RF,2) is added to the tree, and its neighbors are added to the candidate list. (RE,RG,1) could have been selected instead because it has the same cost (5) from RA. The higher-cost path to RH is dropped.
RF,RH,4		RA,RA,0 RA,RB,2 RB,RC,1 RA,RD,4 RA,RE,4 RC,RF,2 RE,RG,1	(RE,RG,1) is added to the tree. RG has no neighbors that are not already on the tree, so nothing is added to the candidate list.
		RA,RA,0 RA,RB,2 RB,RC,1 RA,RD,4 RA,RE,4 RC,RF,2 RE,RG,1 RF,RH,4	(RF,RH,4) is the lowest-cost link on the candidate list, so it is added to the tree. No candidates remain on the list, so the algorithm is terminated. The shortest path tree is complete.

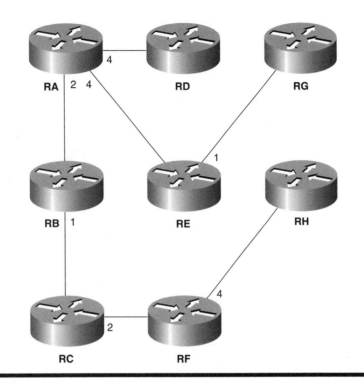

Figure 4.12
The shortest path tree derived by the algorithm in Table 4.3.

Areas

An *area* is a subset of the routers that make up an internetwork. Dividing an internetwork into areas is a response to three concerns commonly expressed about link state protocols:

Potential shortcomings of link state routing

- The necessary databases require more memory than a distance vector protocol requires.

- The complex algorithm requires more CPU time than a distance vector protocol requires.

- The flooding of link state packets adversely affects available bandwidth, particularly in unstable internetworks.

Modern link state protocols and the routers that run them are designed to reduce these effects, but cannot eliminate them. The last section examined what the link state database might look like, and how an SPF algorithm might work, for a small eight-router internetwork. Remember that the stub networks that would be connected to those eight routers and that would form the leaves of the SPF tree were not even taken into consideration. Now imagine an 8000-router internetwork, and you can understand the concern about the impact on memory, CPU, and bandwidth.

This impact can be greatly reduced by the use of areas, as in Figure 4.13. When an internetwork is subdivided into areas, the routers within an area need to flood LSAs only within that area and therefore need to maintain a link state database only for that area. The smaller database means less required memory in each router and fewer CPU cycles to run the SPF algorithm on that database. If frequent topology changes occur, the resulting flooding will be confined to the area of the instability.

Area Border Routers

The routers connecting two areas (*Area Border Routers*, in OSPF terminology) belong to both areas and must maintain separate topological databases for each. Just as a host on one network that wants to send a packet to another network only needs to know how to find its local router, a router in one area that wants to send a packet to another area only needs to know how to find its local Area Border Router. In other words, the intra-area router/inter-area router relationship is the same as the host/router relationship but at a higher hierarchical level.

Distance vector protocols, such as RIP and IGRP, do not use areas. Given that these protocols have no recourse but to see a large

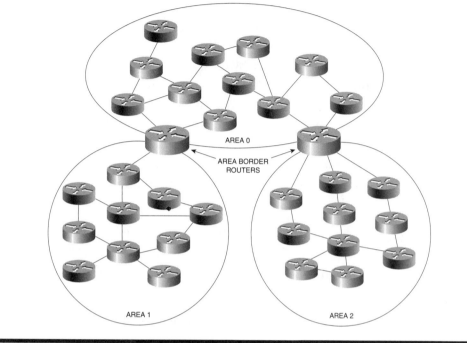

Figure 4.13
The use of areas reduces link state's demand for system resources.

internetwork as a single entity, must calculate a route to every network, and must broadcast the resulting huge route table every 30 or 90 seconds, it becomes clear that link state protocols utilizing areas can actually save system resources.

INTERIOR AND EXTERIOR GATEWAY PROTOCOLS

Areas introduce a hierarchy to the internetwork architecture. Another layer is added to this hierarchical structure by grouping areas into larger areas. These higher-level areas are called *autonomous systems* in the IP world and *routing domains* in the ISO world.

An autonomous system was once defined as a group of routers under a common administrative domain running a common routing protocol. Given the fluidity of modern internetworking life, the latter part of the definition is no longer very accurate. Departments, divisions, and even entire companies frequently merge, and internetworks that were designed with different routing protocols merge along with them. The result is that many internetworks nowadays combine multiple routing protocols with multiple degrees of inelegance, all under common administrations. So a contemporary definition of an autonomous system is an internetwork under a common administration.

Autonomous system

The routing protocols that run within an autonomous system are referred to as *Interior Gateway Protocols* (IGPs). All the protocols given in this chapter as examples of distance vector or link state protocols are IGPs.

Routing protocols that route between autonomous systems or routing domains are referred to as *Exterior Gateway Protocols* (EGPs). Whereas IGPs discover paths between networks, EGPs discover paths between autonomous systems. Examples of EGPs include the following:

- Border Gateway Protocol (BGP) for IP

- Exterior Gateway Protocol (EGP) for IP (yes, an EGP named EGP)

- The ISO's InterDomain Routing Protocol (IDRP)

Novell also incorporates an EGP functionality, called Level 3 Routing, into NLSP.

Having given these definitions, it must be said that the common usage of the term *autonomous system* is not so absolute. Various standards documents, literature, and people tend to give various meanings to the term. As a result, it is important to understand the context in which one is reading or hearing the term.

This book uses *autonomous system* in one of two contexts:

- Autonomous system may refer to a routing domain, as defined at the beginning of this section. In this context, an autonomous system is a system of one or more IGPs that is autonomous from other systems of IGPs. An EGP is used to route between these autonomous systems.

- Autonomous system may also refer to a *process domain*, or a single IGP process that is autonomous from other IGP processes. For example, a system of OSPF-speaking routers may be referred to as an OSPF autonomous system. The chapters on IGRP and EIGRP also use autonomous system in this context. Redistribution is used to route between these autonomous systems.

The context will indicate which form of autonomous system is under discussion at different points throughout this book.

STATIC OR DYNAMIC ROUTING?

When reading (or being lectured about) all the glorious details of dynamic routing protocols, it's hard not to come away with the impression that dynamic routing is always better than static routing. It's important to keep in mind that the primary duty of a dynamic routing protocol is to automatically detect and adapt to topological changes in the internetwork. The price of this "automation" is paid in bandwidth and maybe queue space, in memory, and in processing time.

A frequent objection to static routing is that it is hard to administer. This criticism may be true of medium to large topologies with many alternative routes, but it is certainly not true of small internetworks with few or no alternative routes.

The internetwork in Figure 4.14 has a hub-and-spoke topology popular in smaller internetworks. If a spoke to any router breaks, is there another route for a dynamic routing protocol to choose? This internetwork is an ideal candidate for static routing. Configure one static route in the hub router for each spoke router and a single default route in each spoke router pointing to the hub, and the internetwork is ready to go. (Default routes are covered in Chapter 12, "Default Routes and On-Demand Routing.")

When designing an internetwork, the simplest solution is almost always the best solution. It is good practice to choose a dynamic routing protocol only after determining that static routing is not a practical solution for the design at hand.

LOOKING AHEAD

Now that the basics of dynamic routing protocols have been examined, it is time to examine specific routing protocols. The following chapter looks at RIP, the oldest and simplest of the dynamic routing protocols.

RECOMMENDED READING

Perlman, R. *Interconnections: Bridges and Routers*. Reading, Massachusetts: Addison-Wesley; 1992. This book was already plugged in Chapter 1, "Basic Concepts: Internetworks, Routers, and Addresses"; if you haven't read it yet, you really should.

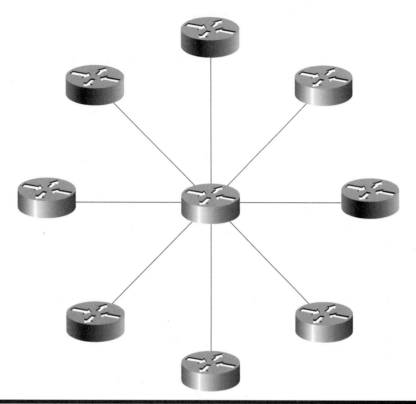

Figure 4.14
This hub-and-spoke internetwork is ideal for static routing.

REVIEW QUESTIONS

1. What is a routing protocol?
2. What basic procedures should a routing algorithm perform?
3. Why do routing protocols use metrics?
4. What is convergence time?
5. What is load balancing? Name four different types of load balancing.
6. What is a distance vector routing protocol?
7. Name several problems associated with distance vector protocols.
8. What are neighbors?
9. What is the purpose of route invalidation timers?
10. Explain the difference between simple split horizon and split horizon with poisoned reverse.
11. What is the counting-to-infinity problem, and how can it be controlled?
12. What are holddown timers, and how do they work?
13. What are the differences between distance vector and link state routing protocols?
14. What is the purpose of a topological database?
15. Explain the basic steps involved in converging a link state internetwork.
16. Why are sequence numbers important in link state protocols?
17. What purpose does aging serve in a link state protocol?
18. Explain how an SPF algorithm works.
19. How do areas benefit a link state internetwork?
20. What is an autonomous system?
21. What is the difference between an IGP and an EGP?

PART II

Interior Routing Protocols

- **Operation of RIP**

  RIP Timers and Stability Features

  RIP Message Format

  Request Message Types

  Classful Routing

- **Configuring RIP**

  Case Study: A Basic RIP Configuration

  Case Study: Passive Interfaces

  Configuring Unicast Updates

  Case Study: Discontiguous Subnets

  Case Study: Manipulating RIP Metrics

- **Troubleshooting RIP**

CHAPTER 5

Routing Information Protocol (RIP)

The oldest of the distance vector IP routing protocols still in widespread use, RIP currently exists in two versions. This chapter deals with version 1 of RIP. Chapter 7, "Routing Information Protocol Version 2," covers version 2, which adds several enhancements to RIPv1. Most notably, RIPv1 is a classful routing protocol, whereas RIPv2 is classless. This chapter introduces classful routing, and Chapter 7 introduces classless routing.

Distance vector protocols, based on the algorithms developed by Bellman,[1] Ford, and Fulkerson,[2] were implemented as early as 1969 in networks such as ARPANET and CYCLADES. In the mid-1970s Xerox developed a protocol called PARC[3] Universal Protocol, or PUP, to run on its 3Mbps experimental predecessor to modern Ethernet. PUP was routed by the Gateway Information Protocol (GWINFO). PUP evolved into the Xerox Network Systems (XNS) protocol suite; concurrently, the Gateway Information Protocol became the XNS Routing Information Protocol. In turn, XNS RIP has become the precursor of such common routing protocols as Novell's IPX RIP, AppleTalk's Routing Table Maintenance Protocol (RTMP), and, of course, IP RIP.

---

[1] R. E. Bellman. Dynamic Programming. *Princeton, New Jersey: Princeton University Press; 1957.*

[2] L. R. Ford Jr. and D. R. Fulkerson. Flows in Networks. *Princeton, New Jersey: Princeton University Press; 1962.*

[3] *Palo Alto Research Center.*

The 4.2 Berkeley Software Distribution of UNIX, released in 1982, implemented RIP in a daemon called *routed*; many more recent versions of UNIX are based on the popular 4.2BSD and implement RIP in either *routed* or *gated*.[4] Oddly enough, a standard for RIP was not released until 1988, after the protocol was in extensive deployment. That was RFC 1058, written by Charles Hedrick, and it remains the only formal standard of RIPv1.

Depending on the literature one reads, RIP is either unjustly maligned or undeservedly popular. Although it does not have the capabilities of many of its successors, its simplicity and widespread use mean that compatibility problems between implementations are rare. RIP was designed for smaller internetworks in which the data links are fairly homogeneous. Within these constraints, and especially within many UNIX environments, RIP will continue to be a popular routing protocol.

OPERATION OF RIP

The RIP process operates from UDP port 520; all RIP messages are encapsulated in a UDP segment with both the Source and Destination Port fields set to that value. RIP defines two message types: *Request messages* and *Response messages*. A Request message is used to ask neighboring routers to send an update. A Response message carries the update. The metric used by RIP is hop count, with 1 signifying a directly connected network of the advertising router and 16 signifying an unreachable network.

The metric for RIP is hop count.

On startup, RIP broadcasts a packet carrying a Request message out each RIP-enabled interface. The RIP process then enters a loop, listening for RIP Request or Response messages from other routers. Neighbors receiving the Request send a Response containing their routing table.

---

[4] Pronounced "route-dee" and "gate-dee."

When the requesting router receives the Response messages, it processes the enclosed information. If a particular route entry included in the update is new, it is entered into the routing table along with the address of the advertising router, which is read from the source address field of the update packet. If the route is for a network that is already in the table, the existing entry will be replaced only if the new route has a lower hop count. If the advertised hop count is higher than the recorded hop count and the update was originated by the recorded next-hop router, the route will be marked as unreachable for a specified holddown period. If at the end of that time the same neighbor is still advertising the higher hop count, the new metric will be accepted.[5]

RIP Timers and Stability Features

After startup, the router gratuitously sends a Response message out every RIP-enabled interface every 30 seconds, on average. The Response message, or update, contains the router's full routing table with the exception of entries suppressed by the split horizon rule. The update timer initiating this periodic update includes a random variable to prevent table synchronization.[6] As a result, the time between individual updates from a typical RIP process may be from 25 to 35 seconds. The specific random variable used by Cisco IOS, RIP_JITTER, subtracts up to 15% (4.5 seconds) from the update time. Therefore, updates from Cisco routers vary between 25.5 and 30 seconds (Figure 5.1). The destination address of the update is the all-hosts broadcast 255.255.255.255.[7]

Several other timers are employed by RIP. Recall from Chapter 4, "Dynamic Routing Protocols," the invalidation timer, which dis-

---

[5] *Holddowns are used by Cisco IOS, but are not part of the stability features specified in RFC 1058.*

[6] *Synchronization of routing tables is discussed in Chapter 4, "Dynamic Routing Protocols."*

[7] *Some implementations of RIP may broadcast only on broadcast media and send updates to the directly connected neighbor on point-to-point links. Cisco's RIP will broadcast on any link type unless configured to do otherwise.*

tance vector protocols use to limit the amount of time a route can stay in a routing table without being updated. RIP calls this timer the *expiration* timer, or *timeout*. Cisco's IOS calls it the *invalid* timer. The expiration timer is initialized to 180 seconds whenever a new route is established and is reset to the initial value whenever an update is heard for that route. If an update for a route is not heard within that 180 seconds (six update periods), the hop count for the route is changed to 16, marking the route as unreachable.

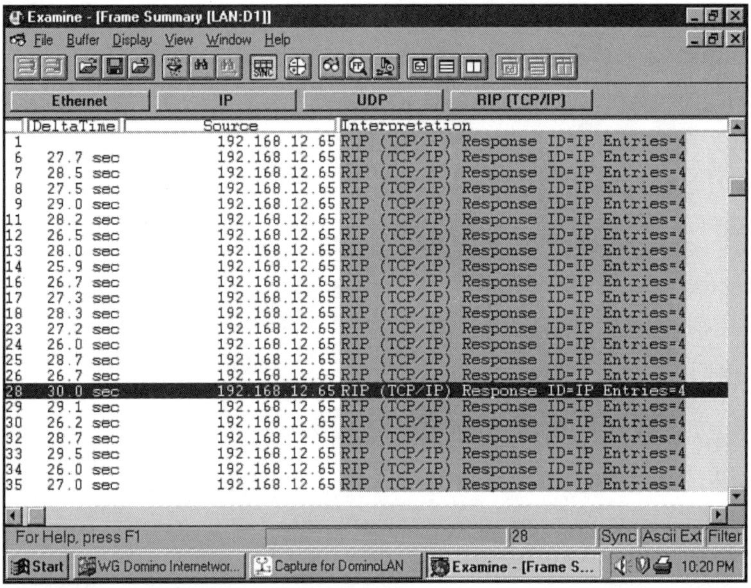

Figure 5.1

RIP adds a small random variable to the update timer at each reset to help avoid routing table synchronization. The RIP updates from Cisco routers vary from 25.5 to 30 seconds, as shown in the delta times of these updates.

Another timer, the *garbage collection* or *flush* timer, is set to 240 seconds–60 seconds longer than the expiration time.[8] The route will be advertised with the unreachable metric until the garbage collection timer expires, at which time the route is removed from the routing table. Figure 5.2 shows a routing table in which a route has been marked as unreachable, but has not yet been flushed.

```
Mayberry#show ip route
Codes: C - connected, S - static, I - IGRP, R - RIP, M - mobile, B - BGP
       D - EIGRP, EX - EIGRP external, O - OSPF, IA - OSPF inter area
       E1 - OSPF external type 1, E2 - OSPF external type 2, E - EGP
       i - IS-IS, L1 - IS-IS level-1, L2 - IS-IS level-2, * - candidate  default

Gateway of last resort is not set

     10.0.0.0 255.255.0.0 is subnetted, 4 subnets
C       10.2.0.0 is directly connected, Serial0
R       10.3.0.0 255.255.0.0 is possibly down,
          routing via 10.1.1.1, Ethernet0
C       10.1.0.0 is directly connected, Ethernet0
R       10.4.0.0 [120/1] via 10.2.2.2, 00:00:00, Serial0
Mayberry#
```

Figure 5.2
This router has not heard an update for subnet 10.3.0.0 for more than six update periods. The route has been marked unreachable, but has not yet been flushed from the routing table.

The third timer is the holddown timer. Although RFC 1058 does not call for the use of holddowns, Cisco's implementation of RIP does use them. An update with a hop count higher than the metric recorded in the routing table will cause the route to go into hold-down for 180 seconds (again, three update periods).

These four timers can be manipulated with the command:

timers basic *update invalid holddown flush*

---

[8]   *Cisco routers use a 60-second garbage collection timer, although RFC 1058 prescribes 120 seconds.*

This command applies to the entire RIP process. If the timing of one router is changed, the timing of all the routers in the RIP domain must be changed. Therefore, these timers should not be changed from their default values without a specific, carefully considered reason.

RIP employs split horizon with poison reverse and triggered updates. A triggered update occurs whenever the metric for a route is changed and, unlike regularly scheduled updates, may include only the entry or entries that changed. Also unlike regular updates, a triggered update does not cause the receiving router to reset its update timer; if it did, a topology change could cause many routers to reset at the same time and thus cause the periodic updates to become synchronized. To avoid a "storm" of triggered updates after a topology change, another timer is employed. When a triggered update is transmitted, this timer is randomly set between 1 and 5 seconds; subsequent triggered updates cannot be sent until the timer expires.

Silent hosts

Some hosts may employ RIP in a "silent" mode. These so-called *silent hosts* do not generate RIP updates, but listen for them and update their internal routing tables accordingly. As an example, using *routed* with the *-q* option enables RIP in silent mode on a UNIX host.

RIP Message Format

The RIP message format is shown in Figure 5.3. Each message contains a command and a version number and can contain entries for up to 25 routes. Each route entry includes an address family identifier, the IP address reachable by the route, and the hop count for the route. If a router must send an update with more than 25 entries, multiple RIP messages must be produced. Note that the initial portion of the message is four octets, and each route entry is 20 octets. Therefore the maximum message size is 4 + (25 X 20) = 504 octets. Including an eight-byte UDP header will make the maximum RIP datagram size (not including the IP header) 512 octets.

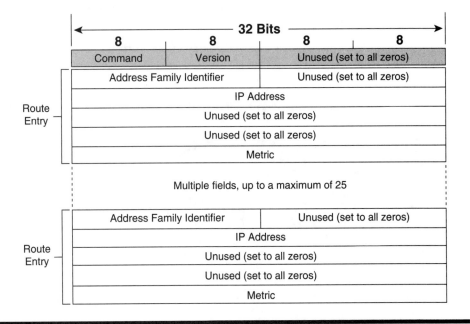

Figure 5.3
The RIP message format.

Command will always be set to either one, signifying a Request message, or two, signifying a Response message. There are other commands, but they are all either obsolete or reserved for private use.

Version will be set to one for RIPv1.

Address Family Identifier is set to two for IP. The only exception to this is a request for a router's (or host's) full routing table, as discussed in the following section.

IP Address is the address of the destination of the route. This entry may be a major network address, a subnet, or a host route. The section titled "Classful Route Lookups" examines how RIP distinguishes among these three types of entries.

Metric is, as previously mentioned, a hop count between 1 and 16.

An analyzer decode of a RIP message is shown in Figure 5.4.

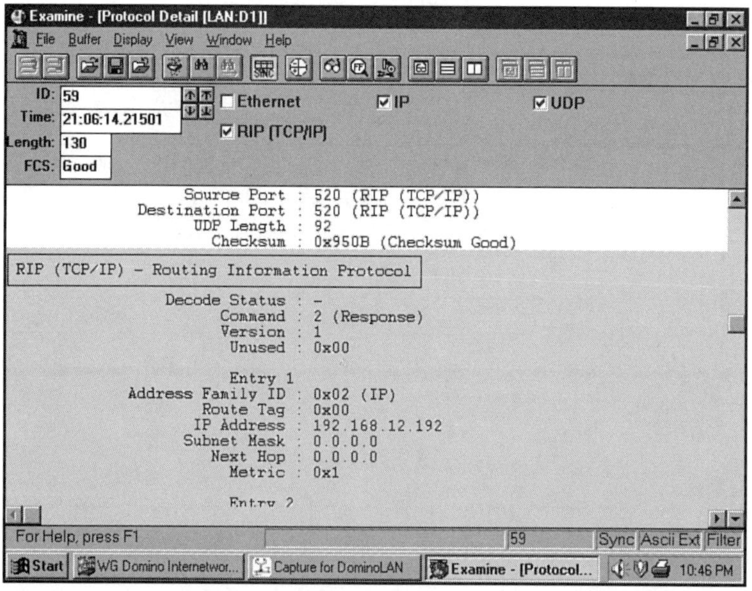

Figure 5.4

The protocol analyzer labels the fields that RIPv1 does not use as Subnet Mask and Next Hop. These fields are used by RIPv2 and are described in Chapter 7.

Several historical influences contributed to the inelegant format of the RIP message in which far more bit spaces are unused than are used. These influences range from RIP's original development as an XNS protocol and the developer's intentions for it to adapt to a large set of address families to the influence of BSD, and its use of socket addresses to the need for fields to fall on 32-bit word boundaries.

Request Message Types

A RIP Request message may request either a full routing table or information on specific routes only. In the former case, the Request message will have a single route entry in which the address family identifier is set to zero, the address is all zeros (0.0.0.0), and the metric is 16. A device receiving such a request responds by unicasting its full routing table to the requesting address, honoring such rules as split horizon and boundary summarization (discussed in "Classful Routing: A Summarization at Boundary Routers," later in this chapter).

Some diagnostic processes may need to know information about a specific route or routes. In this case, a Request message may be sent with entries specifying the addresses in question. A device receiving this request will process the entries one-by-one, building a Response message from the Request message. If the device has an entry in its routing table corresponding to an address in the request, it will enter the metric of its own route entry into the metric field. If not, the metric field will be set to 16. The response will tell exactly what the router knows, with no consideration given to split horizon or boundary summarization.

As noted previously, hosts may run RIP in silent mode. This approach allows them to keep their routing tables up-to-date by listening to RIP updates from routers without having to send RIP

Response messages uselessly on the network. However, diagnostic processes may need to examine the routing table of these silent hosts. Therefore, RFC 1058 specifies that if a silent host receives a request from a UDP port other than the standard RIP port of 520, the host must send a response.

Classful Routing

The routing table in Figure 5.5 contains RIP-derived routes, which are recognized from the key to the left of each entry. Of significance in these entries are the bracketed tuples; as discussed in Chapter 3, "Static Routing," the first number is the administrative distance, and the second number is the metric. It is readily seen that RIP has an administrative distance of 120, and as already stated, the metric for RIP is hop count. Therefore, network 10.8.0.0 is 2 hops away, via either E0 or S1. If more than one route exists to the same destination with equal hop counts, equal-cost load balancing will be performed. The routing table of Figure 5.5 contains several multiple, equal-cost routes.

RIPv1 can perform equal-cost load balancing.

When a packet enters a RIP-speaking router and a route table lookup is performed, the various choices in the table are pruned until a single path remains. First, the network portion of the destination address is read and the routing table is consulted for a match. It is this first step of reading the major class A, B, or C network number that defines a classful routing table lookup. If there is no match for the major network, the packet is dropped and an ICMP Destination Unreachable message is sent to the packet's source. If there is a match for the network portion, the subnets listed for that network are examined. If a match can be found, the packet is routed. If a match cannot be made, the packet is dropped and a Destination Unreachable message is sent.

Definition of a classful route lookup

```
MtPilate#show ip route
Codes:  C - connected, S - static, I - IGRP, R - RIP, M - mobile, B - BGP
        D - EIGRP, EX - EIGRP external, O - OSPF, IA - OSPF inter area
        E1 - OSPF external type 1, E2 - OSPF external type 2, E - EGP
        i - IS-IS, L1 - IS-IS level-1, L2 - IS-IS level-2, * - candidate default

Gateway of last resort is not set

     10.0.0.0 255.255.0.0 is subnetted, 9 subnets
R       10.10.0.0  [120/3] via 10.5.5.1, 00:00:20, Serial1
                   [120/3] via 10.1.1.1, 00:00:21, Ethernet0
R       10.11.0.0  [120/3] via 10.5.5.1, 00:00:21, Serial1
                   [120/3] via 10.1.1.1, 00:00:21, Ethernet0
R       10.8.0.0   [120/2] via 10.1.1.1, 00:00:21, Ethernet0
                   [120/2] via 10.5.5.1, 00:00:21, Serial1
R       10.9.0.0   [120/2] via 10.5.5.1, 00:00:21, Serial1
                   [120/2] via 10.1.1.1, 00:00:21, Ethernet0
R       10.3.0.0   [120/1] via 10.1.1.1, 00:00:21, Ethernet0
                   [120/1] via 10.5.5.1, 00:00:21, Serial1
C       10.1.0.0 is directly connected, Ethernet0
R       10.6.0.0   [120/1] via 10.1.1.1, 00:00:21, Ethernet0
                   [120/1] via 10.5.5.1, 00:00:22, Serial1
R       10.7.0.0   [120/2] via 10.1.1.1, 00:00:22, Ethernet0
                   [120/2] via 10.5.5.1, 00:00:22, Serial1
C       10.5.0.0 is directly connected, Serial1
     172.25.0.0 255.255.255.0 is subnetted, 3 subnets
R       172.25.153.0 [120/1] via 172.25.15.2, 00:00:03, Serial0
R       172.25.131.0 [120/1] via 172.25.15.2, 00:00:03, Serial0
C       172.25.15.0 is directly connected, Serial0
```

Figure 5.5

This routing table contains subnets of networks 10.0.0.0 and 172.25.0.0. All networks not directly connected were derived by RIP.

Classful Routing: Directly Connected Subnets

Classful route lookups can be illustrated with three examples (referring to Figure 5.5):

1. If a packet with a destination address of 192.168.35.3 enters this router, no match for network 192.168.35.0 is found in the routing table and the packet is dropped.

2. If a packet with a destination address of 172.25.33.89 enters the router, a match is made to class B network 172.25.0.0/24. The subnets listed for this network are then examined; no match can be made for subnet 172.25.33.0, so that packet, too, is dropped.

3. Finally, a packet destined for 172.25.153.220 enters the router. This time 172.25.0.0/24 is matched, then subnet 172.25.153.0 is matched, and the packet is forwarded to next-hop address 172.25.15.2.

Another look at Figure 5.3 reveals that there is no provision for RIP to advertise a subnet mask along with each route entry. And accordingly, no masks are associated with the individual subnets in the routing table. Therefore, if the router whose forwarding database is depicted in Figure 5.5 receives a packet with a destination address of 172.25.131.23, there is no positive way to determine where the subnet bits end and the host bits begin, or even if the address is subnetted at all.

The router's only recourse is to assume that the mask configured on one of its interfaces attached to 172.25.0.0 is used consistently throughout the internetwork. It will use its own mask for 172.25.0.0 to derive the subnet of the destination address. As the routing tables throughout this chapter illustrate, a router that is directly connected to a network will list the network in a heading along with the subnet mask of the connecting interface and will then list all the known subnets of the network. If the network is not directly connected, there is a listing only for the major-class network and no associated mask.

Because the destination addresses of packets being routed by a classful routing protocol are interpreted according to the subnet masks locally configured on the router's interfaces, all subnet masks within a major, class-level network must be consistent.

Classful Routing: Summarization at Boundary Routers

A question arises from the preceding discussion: How does a RIP process interpret the subnet of a major network if it has no interfaces attached to that network? Without an interface on the class A, B, or C network of the destination, the router has no way of knowing the correct subnet mask to use and therefore no way of correctly identifying the subnet.

The solution is simple: If a router has no direct attachments to the network, then it needs only a single route entry pointing toward a router that is directly attached.

Figure 5.6 shows a router that is attached at the boundary of two major networks, the class A network 10.0.0.0 and the class C network 192.168.115.0. This *boundary router* does not send details of the subnets of one major network into the other major network. As the illustration shows, it automatically performs summarization, or *subnet hiding*. It advertises only the address 10.0.0.0 into network 192.168.115.0 and advertises only the address 192.168.115.0 into network 10.0.0.0.

> Boundary routers perform route summarization, also known as subnet hiding.

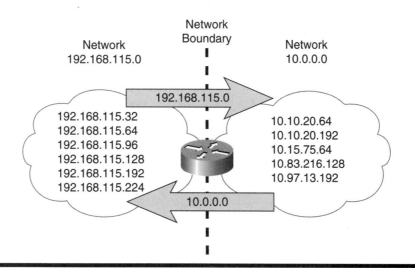

Figure 5.6

This router, at the boundary of two major networks, does not advertise the subnets of one network to routers within the other network.

In this way, the routing tables for routers within network 192.168.115.0 have only a single entry that directs packets for 10.0.0.0 toward the boundary router. The boundary router has an interface directly on network 10.0.0.0 and therefore has a subnet mask with which to derive the subnet for routing a packet within that network's "cloud." Figure 5.7 shows what the routing table of a router within 192.168.115.0 would look like with a single, subnetless entry for 10.0.0.0.

```
Raleigh#show ip route
Codes: C - connected, S - static, I - IGRP, R - RIP, M - mobile, B - BGP
       D - EIGRP, EX - EIGRP external, O - OSPF, IA - OSPF inter area
       E1 - OSPF external type 1, E2 - OSPF external type 2, E - EGP
       i - IS-IS, L1 - IS-IS level-1, L2 - IS-IS level-2, * - candidate default

Gateway of last resort is not set

R    10.0.0.0 [120/1] via 192.168.115.40, 00:00:10, Ethernet1
     192.168.115.0 255.255.255.240 is subnetted, 6 subnets
C        192.168.115.32 is directly connected, Ethernet1
R        192.168.115.64 [120/1] via 192.168.115.99, 00:00:13, Ethernet0
C        192.168.115.96 is directly connected, Ethernet0
C        192.168.115.128 is directly connected, Serial0
R        192.168.115.192 [120/1] via 192.168.115.99, 00:00:13, Ethernet0
R        192.168.115.224 [120/1] via 192.168.115.130, 00:00:25, Serial0
Raleigh#
```

Figure 5.7

This router has a single entry pointing toward network 10.0.0.0. The next-hop address is the boundary router, since the network is recorded as being one hop away.

Chapter 3's brief discussion of discontiguous subnets—subnets of a major network address separated by a different major network—notes that they present a problem for classful routing protocols such as RIP and IGRP. The problem occurs when discontiguous subnets are automatically summarized at network boundaries. A case study in the configuration section of this chapter demonstrates the problem and a solution.

Classful Routing: Summary

The defining characteristic of a classful routing protocol is that it does not advertise an address mask along with the advertised destination address. Therefore, a classful routing protocol must first match the major class A, B, or C network portion of a destination address. For every packet passing through the router:

1. If the destination address is a member of a directly connected major network, the subnet mask configured on the interface attached to that network will be used to determine the subnet of the destination address. Therefore, the same subnet mask must be used consistently throughout that major network.
2. If the destination address is not a member of a directly connected major network, the router will try to match only the major class A, B, or C portion of the destination address.

CONFIGURING RIP

In keeping with the simple nature of RIP, configuration is an easy task. There is one command to enable the RIP process and one command for each network on which RIP is to run. Beyond that, RIP has few configuration options.

Case Study: A Basic RIP Configuration

Only two steps are necessary to configure RIP:

1. Enable RIP with the command **router rip.**
2. Specify each major network on which to run RIP with the **network** command.

Figure 5.8 shows a four-router internetwork, with four major network numbers. Router Goober is attached to two subnets of network 172.17.0.0. The commands necessary to enable RIP are:

```
Goober(config)#router rip
Goober(config-router)#network 172.17.0.0
```

Similarly, Opie has two subnets of the same network and will configure with the following commands:

```
Opie(config)#router rip
Opie(config-router)#network 172.17.0.0
```

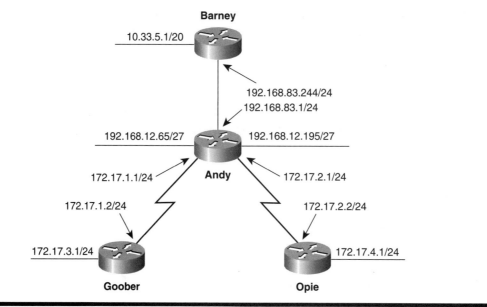

Figure 5.8

Both Andy and Barney are border routers between class-level networks.

Executing any **router** command puts the router into **config-router** mode, indicated in the prompt. The classful nature of RIP and the subnet hiding at network boundaries mean that no subnets can be specified with the **network** command—only major class A, B, or C network addresses. RIP can run on any interface configured with any address belonging to the network specified with the **network** command.

Barney is attached to two networks—10.0.0.0 and 192.168.83.0. Therefore, both networks must be specified:

```
Barney(config)#router rip
Barney(config-router)#network 10.0.0.0
Barney(config-router)#network 192.168.83.0
```

Andy has one attachment to network 192.168.83.0, attachments to two subnets of 192.168.12.0, and attachments to two subnets of 172.17.0.0. Its configuration is:

```
Andy(config)#router rip
Andy(config-router)#network 172.17.0.0
Andy(config-router)#network 192.168.12.0
Andy(config-router)#network 192.168.83.0
```

In Figure 5.9, the command **debug ip rip** has been turned on in Andy. Of particular interest here is the subnet hiding that the router is performing. The subnets 192.168.12.64 and 192.168.12.192 are advertised between interfaces E0 and E2, which are both attached to network 192.168.12.0, but the network is summarized out E1, S0, and S1, which are all attached to different networks. Likewise, networks 192.168.83.0 and 172.17.0.0 are being summarized across classful boundaries. Notice also that Andy is receiving a summary route for network 10.0.0.0 from Barney. Finally, split horizon can be observed here. For example, the advertisement to Barney out E1 contains no entries for 10.0.0.0 or 192.168.83.0.

Case Study: Passive Interfaces

The router Floyd has been added to the internetwork (Figure 5.10). It is desired that no RIP advertisements be exchanged between Floyd and Andy. This is easy enough at Floyd:

```
Floyd(config)#router rip
Floyd(config-router)#network 192.168.100.0
```

```
Andy#debug ip rip
RIP protocol debugging is on
Andy#
RIP: sending update to 255.255.255.255 via Ethernet0 (192.168.12.65)
        subnet 192.168.12.192, metric 1
        network 10.0.0.0, metric 2
        network 192.168.83.0, metric 1
        network 172.17.0.0, metric 1
RIP: sending update to 255.255.255.255 via Ethernet1 (192.168.83.1)
        network 192.168.12.0, metric 1
        network 172.17.0.0, metric 1
RIP: sending update to 255.255.255.255 via Ethernet2 (192.168.12.195)
        subnet 192.168.12.64, metric 1
        network 10.0.0.0, metric 2
        network 192.168.83.0, metric 1
        network 172.17.0.0, metric 1
RIP: sending update to 255.255.255.255 via Serial0 (172.17.1.1)
        subnet 172.17.4.0, metric 2
        subnet 172.17.2.0, metric 1
        network 10.0.0.0, metric 2
        network 192.168.83.0, metric 1
        network 192.168.12.0, metric 1
RIP: sending update to 255.255.255.255 via Serial1 (172.17.2.1)
        subnet 172.17.1.0, metric 1
        subnet 172.17.3.0, metric 2
        network 10.0.0.0, metric 2
        network 192.168.83.0, metric 1
        network 192.168.12.0, metric 1
RIP: received update from 172.17.1.2 on Serial0
        172.17.3.0 in 1 hops
RIP: received update from 192.168.83.244 on Ethernet1
        10.0.0.0 in 1 hops
RIP: received update from 172.17.2.2 on Serial1
        172.17.4.0 in 1 hops
```

Figure 5.9

These debug messages show the RIP updates received and sent by router Andy. The results of both network summarization and split horizon can be observed in the update entries.

By not including a network statement for 172.17.0.0, Floyd will not advertise on interface 172.17.12.66. Andy, however, has two interfaces attached to 172.17.0.0; the network must be included under RIP. To block RIP broadcasts on an interface connected to a subnet of a RIP-enabled network, add the **passive-interface** command to the RIP process. Andy's RIP configuration is:

```
router rip
 passive-interface Ethernet0
 network 172.17.0.0
 network 192.168.12.0
 network 192.168.83.0
```

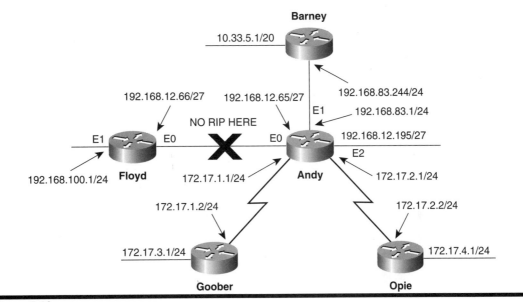

Figure 5.10
Network policy calls for no RIP exchanges between Andy and Floyd.

Passive-interface is not a RIP-specific command; it may be configured under any IP routing protocol. Using the **passive-interface** command essentially makes a router a silent host on the data link specified. Like other silent hosts, it still listens to RIP broadcasts on the link and updates its routing table accordingly. If the desired result is to prevent the router from learning routes on the link, it must be achieved by more intricate control of routing updates, namely by filtering out updates. (Route filters are discussed in Chapter 13, "Route Filtering.") Unlike a silent host, the router does not respond to a RIP Request received on a passive interface.

Case Study: Configuring Unicast Updates

Next, router Bea is added to the Ethernet link that Andy and Floyd share (Figure 5.11). The no-RIP policy between Andy and Floyd remains in place, but now Bea and Andy, as well as Bea and Floyd, must exchange RIP advertisements.

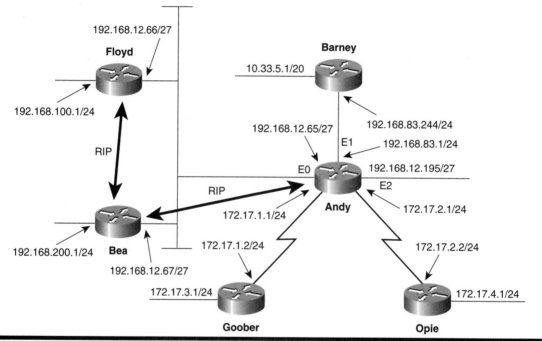

Figure 5.11

No RIP updates should be exchanged between Andy and Floyd, but both should exchange updates with Bea.

The configuration of Bea is straightforward:

```
router rip
  network 192.168.12.0
  network 192.168.200.0
```

The addition of a **neighbor** command under the RIP processes of Andy enables RIP to send a unicast advertisement to Bea's interface while the **passive-interface** command continues to prevent broadcast updates on the link.[9]

Andy's configuration is:

```
router rip
  passive-interface Ethernet0
  network 172.17.0.0
  network 192.168.12.0
  network 192.168.83.0
  neighbor 192.168.12.67
```

Because Floyd must now send advertisements to Bea, a network command for 192.168.12.0 must be added. **Passive-interface** is also added to prevent broadcast updates, and a **neighbor** command is added to enable unicast updates to Bea:

```
router rip
  passive-interface Ethernet0
  network 192.168.12.0
  network 192.168.100.0
  neighbor 192.168.12.67
```

By enabling **debug ip rip events** at Andy, the results of the new configuration can be verified (Figure 5.12). Andy is receiving updates from Bea, but not from Floyd, and is sending updates directly to Bea's interface, but is not broadcasting on its E0.

---

[9]   *Another use of* **neighbor** *is to enable unicast updates on nonbroadcast media such as Frame Relay.*

```
Andy#debug ip rip events
RIP event debugging is on
Andy#
RIP:  received update from 192.168.12.67 on Ethernet0
RIP:  Update contains 1 routes
RIP:  sending update to 255.255.255.255 via Ethernet1 (192.168.83.1)
RIP:  Update contains 4 routes
RIP:  sending update to 255.255.255.255 via Ethernet2 (192.168.12.195)
RIP:  Update contains 6 routes
RIP:  sending update to 255.255.255.255 via Serial0 (172.17.1.1)
RIP:  Update contains 7 routes
RIP:  sending update to 255.255.255.255 via Serial1 (172.17.2.1)
RIP:  Update contains 7 routes
RIP:  sending update to 192.168.12.67 via Ethernet0 (192.168.12.65)
RIP:  Update contains 4 routes
RIP:  received update from 172.17.1.2 on Serial0
RIP:  Update contains 1 routes
RIP:  received update from 172.17.2.2 on Serial1
RIP:  Update contains 1 routes
RIP:  received update from 192.168.12.67 on Ethernet0
RIP:  Update contains 1 routes
```

Figure 5.12

The only updates Andy is sending out interface E0 are unicasts to Bea. Updates are being received from Bea, but not from Floyd.

Although Bea has learned routes from both Andy and from Floyd, and is broadcasting updates on the shared Ethernet, the policy still works because split horizon prevents Bea from advertising the routes learned from those two routers back onto the Ethernet.

Case Study: Discontiguous Subnets

In Figure 5.13, another router has been added to the internetwork with a subnet 10.33.32.0/20 on its E1 interface. The problem is that the other subnet of network 10.0.0.0, 10.33.0.0/20, is connected to Barney, and the only route between the subnets is via 192.168.83.0 and 192.168.12.0—two entirely different networks. As a result, network 10.0.0.0 is discontiguous.

Barney will consider itself a border router between network 10.0.0.0 and network 192.168.83.0; likewise, Ernest_T will consider itself a border router between 10.0.0.0 and 192.168.12.0. Both will advertise a summary route of 10.0.0.0, and as a result Andy will be fooled into thinking that it has two equal-cost paths to the same network. Andy will load share on the links to Barney and Ernest_T, and there is now only a 50-50 chance that packets to network 10.0.0.0 will reach the correct subnet.

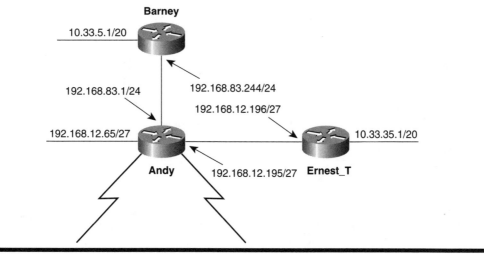

Figure 5.13
Classful protocols such as RIP and IGRP cannot route a topology in which the subnets of network 10.0.0.0 are separated by different networks.

The solution is to configure subnets of network 10.0.0.0 on the same links on which 192.168.83.0/24 and 192.168.12.192/27 reside. This is accomplished with secondary IP addresses, as follows:

```
Barney(config)#interface e0
Barney(config-if)#ip address 10.33.55.1 255.255.240.0 secondary

Andy(config)#interface e1
Andy(config-if)#ip address 10.33.55.2 255.255.240.0 secondary
Andy(config-if)#interface e2
Andy(config-if)#ip address 10.33.75.1 255.255.240.0 secondary
Andy(config-if)#router rip
Andy(config-router)#network 10.0.0.0
```

```
Ernest_T(config)#interface e0
Ernest_T(config-if)#ip address 10.33.75.2 255.255.240.0 secondary
```

Because Andy did not previously have an interface on network 10.0.0.0, a network statement is added to the RIP process. The result of the configuration can be seen in Figure 5.14. The existing logical network structure remains in place, and a contiguous network 10.0.0.0 is "overlaid" onto it.

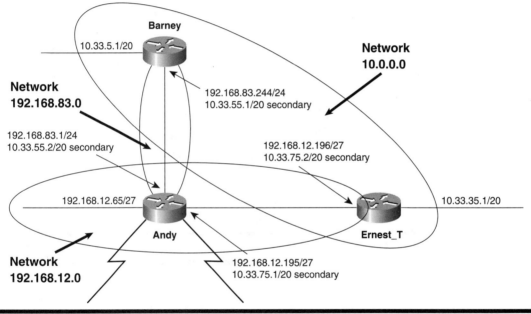

Figure 5.14

Secondary addresses are used to connect the subnets of network 10.0.0.0 across the same links on which other network addresses exist.

Figure 5.15 shows Ernest_T's routing table. Of interest here are the dual, equal-cost routes associated with next-hop addresses 10.33.75.1 and 192.168.12.195.

```
Ernest_T#show ip route
Codes:  C - connected, S - static, I - IGRP, R - RIP, M - mobile, B - BGP
        D - EIGRP, EX - EIGRP external, O - OSPF, IA - OSPF inter area
        E1 - OSPF external type 1, E2 - OSPF external type 2, E - EGP
        i - IS-IS, L1 - IS-IS level-1, L2 - IS-IS level-2, * - candidate default

Gateway of last resort is not set

     10.0.0.0 255.255.240.0 is subnetted, 4 subnets
C       10.33.32.0 is directly connected, Ethernet1
R       10.33.48.0   [120/1] via 10.33.75.1, 00:00:05, Ethernet0
R       10.33.0.0    [120/2] via 10.33.75.1, 00:00:05, Ethernet0
C       10.33.64.0 is directly connected, Ethernet0
R     192.168.83.0   [120/1] via 192.168.12.195, 00:00:05, Ethernet0
                     [120/1] via 10.33.75.1, 00:00:05, Ethernet0
     192.168.12.0 255.255.255.224 is subnetted, 2 subnets
R       192.168.12.64 [120/1] via 192.168.12.195, 00:00:05, Ethernet0
C       192.168.12.192 is directly connected, Ethernet0
R     192.168.200.0   [120/2] via 192.168.12.195, 00:00:05, Ethernet0
                      [120/2] via 10.33.75.1, 00:00:05, Ethernet0
R     172.17.0.0     [120/1] via 192.168.12.195, 00:00:06, Ethernet0
                     [120/1] via 10.33.75.1, 00:00:06, Ethernet0
Ernest_T#
```

Figure 5.15

The routing process in this router sees the subnets 192.168.12.192/27 and 10.33.64.0/20 as separate links, although they reside on the same physical interface.

Because the routing process sees secondary addresses as separate data links, caution should be used when planning them on RIP or IGRP networks. A separate RIP update will be broadcast on each subnet; if the updates are large and the bandwidth of the physical link is limited (such as on serial links), the multiple updates can cause congestion. Multiple updates on a link configured with secondary addresses can be observed in Figure 5.17, later in this chapter.

The use of secondary addresses can contribute to congestion on the network.

Type cautiously when entering secondary addresses. If you omit the keyword "secondary," the router will assume that the primary address is to be replaced with the new address. Making this mistake on an in-service interface will have serious consequences.

Case Study: Manipulating RIP Metrics

A serial link, to be used as a backup, has been added between Ernest_T and Barney (Figure 5.16). This link should be used only if the route via Andy fails. The problem is that the path between Barney's 10.33.0.0 subnet and Ernest_T's 10.33.32.0 subnet is 1 hop via the serial link and 2 hops via the preferred Ethernet links. Under normal circumstances, RIP will choose the serial link.

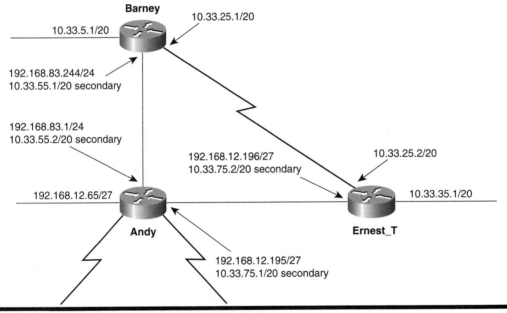

Figure 5.16

RIP metrics must be manipulated so that the 2-hop Ethernet route between Barney and Ernest_T will be preferred over the 1-hop serial route.

The route metrics can be manipulated with the **offset-list** command. The command specifies a number to add to the metric of a route entry and references an access list[10] to determine which route entries to modify. The syntax of the command is:

---

[10] *See Appendix B for a tutorial on access lists.*

offset-list {*access-list-number* | *name*} {**in** | **out**} *offset* [*type number*]

The configuration of Ernest_T is:

```
Ernest_T(config)#access-list 1 permit 10.33.0.0 0.0.0.0
Ernest_T(config)#router rip
Ernest_T(config-router)#network 192.168.12.0
Ernest_T(config-router)#network 10.0.0.0
Ernest_T(config-router)#offset-list 1 in 2 Serial0
```

An access list is written that identifies the route to subnet 10.33.0.0. The syntax of the offset list says, "Examine RIP advertisements incoming from interface S0. For route entries matching the addresses specified in access list 1, add 2 hops to the metric."

After Barney is configured, it will have the following entries in its configuration file:

```
router rip
  offset-list 5 in 2 Serial0
  network 10.0.0.0
  network 192.168.83.0
!
access-list 5 permit 10.33.32.0 0.0.0.0
```

Figure 5.17 shows the results of the configuration at Ernest_T.

Alternatively, instead of having the two routers modify incoming routes, the routers can be configured to modify their outgoing routes. The following configurations will have the same effects as the previous configurations:

ERNEST_T:

```
router rip
  offset-list 3 out 2 Serial0
  network 192.168.12.0
  network 10.0.0.0
!
access-list 3 permit 10.33.32.0 0.0.0.0
```

BARNEY:

```
router rip
  offset-list 7 out 2 Serial0
  network 10.0.0.0
  network 192.168.83.0
!
access-list 7 permit 10.33.0.0 0.0.0.0
```

```
Ernest_T#debug ip rip
RIP protocol debugging is on
Ernest_T#
RIP: received update from 192.168.12.195 on Ethernet0
        192.168.12.64 in 1 hops
        10.0.0.0 in 1 hops
        192.168.83.0 in 1 hops
        192.168.200.0 in 2 hops
        172.17.0.0 in 1 hops
RIP: received update from 10.33.75.1 on Ethernet0
        10.33.48.0 in 1 hops
        10.33.0.0 in 2 hops
        192.168.83.0 in 1 hops
        192.168.12.0 in 1 hops
        192.168.200.0 in 2 hops
        172.17.0.0 in 1 hops
RIP: received update from 10.33.25.1 on Serial0
        10.33.32.0 in 3 hops
        10.33.48.0 in 1 hops
        10.33.0.0 in 3 hops
        192.168.83.0 in 1 hops
        192.168.200.0 in 3 hops
        172.17.0.0 in 2 hops
RIP: sending update to 255.255.255.255 via Ethernet0 (192.168.12.196)
        network 10.0.0.0, metric 1
RIP: sending update to 255.255.255.255 via Ethernet0 (10.33.75.2)
        subnet 10.33.32.0, metric 1
        subnet 10.33.16.0, metric 1
RIP: sending update to 255.255.255.255 via Ethernet1 (10.33.35.1)
        subnet 10.33.48.0, metric 2
        subnet 10.33.0.0, metric 3
        subnet 10.33.16.0, metric 1
        subnet 10.33.64.0, metric 1
        network 192.168.83.0, metric 2
        network 192.168.12.0, metric 1
        network 192.168.200.0, metric 3
        network 172.17.0.0, metric 2
RIP: sending update to 255.255.255.255 via Serial0 (10.33.25.2)
        subnet 10.33.32.0, metric 3
        subnet 10.33.0.0, metric 3
        subnet 10.33.64.0, metric 1
        network 192.168.12.0, metric 1
        network 192.168.200.0, metric 3
        network 172.17.0.0, metric 2
```

Figure 5.17

The addition of the hops specified in the offset list changes the hop count to subnet 10.33.0.0/20 via S0 from 1 to 3. Now the 2-hop route via E0 is used.

Several other options are available for configuring offset lists. If no interface is identified, the list will modify all incoming or outgoing updates specified by the access list on any interface. If no access list is called (by using a zero as the access list number), the offset list will modify all incoming or outgoing updates.

Caution should be applied when choosing whether to use offset lists on incoming or outgoing advertisements. If more than two routers are attached to a broadcast network, consideration must be given to whether a single router should broadcast a modified advertisement to all its neighbors or whether a single router should modify a received advertisement.

Offset lists: incoming versus outgoing

Care must also be exercised when implementing offset lists on routes that are in use. When an offset list causes a next-hop router to advertise a higher metric than it had been advertising, the route will be marked unreachable until the holddown timer expires.

TROUBLESHOOTING RIP

Troubleshooting RIP is relatively simple. Most difficulties with classful protocols such as RIP involve either misconfigured subnet masks or discontiguous subnets. If a routing table contains inaccurate or missing routes, check all subnets for contiguity and all subnet masks for consistency.

A final command may be useful when a high-speed router is sending multiple RIP messages to a low-speed router. In such a case, the low-speed router may not be able to process updates as fast as they are received, and routing information may be lost. **Output-delay** *delay* may be used under the RIP command to set an interpacket gap of between 8 and 50 milliseconds (the default is 0 milliseconds).

LOOKING AHEAD

The simplicity, maturity, and widespread acceptance of RIP ensure that it will be in service for many years to come. However, the very simplicity of RIP limits it to small, homogeneous internetworks. The next chapter takes up IGRP, Cisco's answer to some of the limitations of RIP.

SUMMARY TABLE: CHAPTER 5 COMMAND REVIEW

Command	Description
debug ip rip [events]	Summarizes RIP traffic to and from the router
ip address *ip-address mask* secondary	Configures an interface with the indicated ip address as a secondary address
neighbor *ip-address*	Establishes the link indicated by the ip address as a neighbor of the interface
network *network-number*	Specifies the indicated network as one that will run RIP
offset-list {*access-list-number* | *name*} {in | out} *offset* [*type number*]	Stipulates that a route entry belonging to the indicated access list will have the indicated offset number added to its metric
output-delay *delay*	Sets an interpacket gap of the indicated delay length to accommodate processing delays between high-speed and low-speed routers
passive-interface *type number*	Blocks RIP broadcasts on the interface indicated by type and number
router rip	Enables RIP
timers basic *update invalid holddown flush*	Manipulates the value of the indicated timer

RECOMMENDED READING

Hedrick, C. "Routing Information Protocol." RFC 1058, June 1988.

REVIEW QUESTIONS

1. What port does RIP use?
2. What metric does RIP use? How is the metric used to indicate an unreachable network?
3. What is the update period for RIP?
4. How many updates must be missed before a route entry will be marked as unreachable?
5. What is the purpose of the garbage collection timer?
6. Why is a random timer associated with triggered updates? What is the range of this timer?
7. What is the difference between a RIP Request message and a RIP Response message?
8. Which two types of Request messages does RIP use?
9. Under what circumstances will a RIP response be sent?
10. Why does RIP hide subnets at major network boundaries?

CONFIGURATION EXERCISES

1. Write configurations for the six routers in Figure 5.18 to route to all subnets via RIP.
2. Change the configurations of Configuration Exercise 1 so that RIP updates are unicast between RTC and RTD, instead of broadcast.
3. The bandwidth of the serial link between RTC and RTD in Figure 5.18 is very limited. Configure RIP to send updates across this link every two minutes. Carefully consider what timers must be changed and on what routers the timers must be changed.

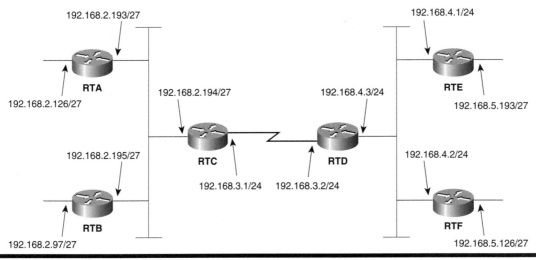

192.168.2.193/27

192.168.4.1/24

RTA

192.168.2.194/27   192.168.4.3/24

RTE

192.168.2.126/27

192.168.5.193/27

192.168.2.195/27   RTC   RTD   192.168.4.2/24

192.168.3.1/24   192.168.3.2/24

RTB

RTF

192.168.2.97/27

192.168.5.126/27

Figure 5.18

The internetwork for Configuration Exercises 1 through 4.

4. A policy has been established that dictates that network 192.168.4.0 should be unreachable from RTA and that network 192.168.5.0 should be unreachable from RTB. Use one or more offset lists to implement this policy.

5. According to the section, "Classful Routing: Directly Connected Subnets," subnet masks within a major, class-level network must be consistent. The section does not, however, say that subnet masks within a major, class-level network must be identical. The RIP configuration for both routers in Figure 5.19 follows.

```
router rip
  network 192.168.20.0
```

Will packets be routed correctly in this small internetwork? Explain why or why not.

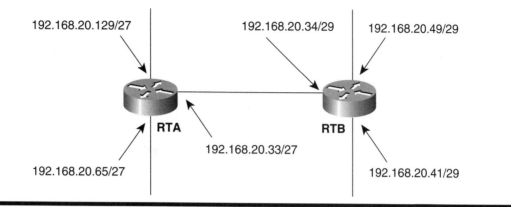

Figure 5.19

The internetwork for Configuration Exercise 5.

TROUBLESHOOTING EXERCISES

1. In the first offset list example, the access list in Barney is changed from

```
access-list 5 permit 10.33.32.0 0.0.0.0
```

to

```
access-list 5 deny 10.33.32.0 0.0.0.0
access-list 5 permit any
```

What is the result?

2. Figure 5.20 shows an internetwork in which the IP address masks on one router have been misconfigured. Figures 5.21 through 5.23 show the routing tables of RTA, RTB, and RTC, respectively. Based on what you know about the way RIP advertises and receives updates, explain each entry in RTB's routing table. Explain why RTB's entry for subnet 172.16.26.0 indicates a 32-bit mask. If any entries are missing in any of the routing tables, explain why.

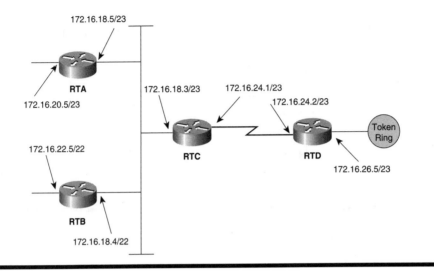

Figure 5.20

The internetwork for Troubleshooting Exercises 2 and 3.

```
RTA#show ip route
Codes: C - connected, S - static, I - IGRP, R - RIP, M - mobile, B - BGP
       D - EIGRP, EX - EIGRP external, O - OSPF, IA - OSPF inter area
       E1 - OSPF external type 1, E2 - OSPF external type 2, E - EGP
       i - IS-IS, L1 - IS-IS level-1, L2 - IS-IS level-2, * - candidate default,
       U - per-user static route

Gateway of last resort is not set

     172.16.0.0/16 is subnetted, 4 subnets
R       172.16.24.0 [120/1] via 172.16.18.3, 00:00:01, Ethernet0
R       172.16.26.0 [120/2] via 172.16.18.3, 00:00:01, Ethernet0
C       172.16.20.0 is directly connected, Ethernet1
C       172.16.18.0 is directly connected, Ethernet0
RTA#
```

Figure 5.21

The routing table of RTA in Figure 5.20.

```
RTB#show ip route
Codes: C - connected, S - static, I - IGRP, R - RIP, M - mobile, B - BGP
       D - EIGRP, EX - EIGRP external, O - OSPF, IA - OSPF inter area
       N1 - OSPF NSSA external type 1, N2 - OSPF NSSA external type 2
       E1 - OSPF external type 1, E2 - OSPF external type 2, E - EGP
       i - IS-IS, L1 - IS-IS level-1, L2 - IS-IS level-2, * - candidate default,
       U - per-user static route, o - ODR

Gateway of last resort is not set

     172.16.0.0/16 is variably subnetted, 4 subnets, 2 masks
R       172.16.24.0/22 [120/1] via 172.16.18.3, 00:00:20, Ethernet0
R       172.16.26.0/32 [120/2] via 172.16.18.3, 00:00:20, Ethernet0
C       172.16.20.0/22 is directly connected, Ethernet1
C       172.16.16.0/22 is directly connected, Ethernet0
RTB#
```

Figure 5.22

The routing table of RTB in Figure 5.20.

```
RTC#show ip route
Codes: C - connected, S - static, I - IGRP, R - RIP, M - mobile, B - BGP
       D - EIGRP, EX - EIGRP external, O - OSPF, IA - OSPF inter area
       N1 - OSPF NSSA external type 1, N2 - OSPF NSSA external type 2
       E1 - OSPF external type 1, E2 - OSPF external type 2, E - EGP
       i - IS-IS, L1 - IS-IS level-1, L2 - IS-IS level-2, * - candidate default,
       U - per-user static route, o - ODR

Gateway of last resort is not set

     172.16.0.0/23 is subnetted, 4 subnets
C       172.16.24.0 is directly connected, Serial0
R       172.16.26.0 [120/1] via 172.16.24.2, 00:00:09, Serial0
R       172.16.20.0 [120/1] via 172.16.18.5, 00:00:25, Ethernet0
C       172.16.18.0 is directly connected, Ethernet0
RTC#
```

Figure 5.23

The routing table of RTC in Figure 5.20.

3. Users on subnet 172.16.18.0/23 in Figure 5.20 are complaining that connectivity to subnet 172.16.26.0/23 is intermittent—sometimes it can be reached, sometimes it can't. (The bad subnet masks of RTB have been corrected.) A first examination of the routing tables of RTC and

RTD (Figure 5.24) seems to show no problems. All subnets are in both tables. Yet a minute or so later, RTC shows subnet 172.16.26.0/23 to be unreachable (Figure 5.25), whereas RTD still shows all subnets. A few minutes after that, the subnet is back in RTC's routing table (Figure 5.26). In each of the three figures, the routing table of RTD shows no change. A careful examination of the routing tables in Figures 5.24 through 5.26 will reveal the problem. What is it?

```
RTC#show ip route
Codes:  C - connected, S - static, I - IGRP, R - RIP, M - mobile, B - BGP
        D - EIGRP, EX - EIGRP external, O - OSPF, IA - OSPF inter area
        N1 - OSPF NSSA external type 1, N2 - OSPF NSSA external type 2
        E1 - OSPF external type 1, E2 - OSPF external type 2, E - EGP
        i - IS-IS, L1 - IS-IS level-1, L2 - IS-IS level-2, * - candidate default,
        U - per-user static route, o - ODR

Gateway of last resort is not set

     172.16.0.0/23 is subnetted, 5 subnets
C        172.16.24.0 is directly connected, Serial0
R        172.16.26.0 [120/1] via 172.16.24.2, 00:02:42, Serial0
R        172.16.20.0 [120/1] via 172.16.18.5, 00:00:22, Ethernet0
R        172.16.22.0 [120/1] via 172.16.18.4, 00:00:05, Ethernet0
C        172.16.18.0 is directly connected, Ethernet0
```

```
RTD#show ip route
Codes:  C - connected, S - static, I - IGRP, R - RIP, M - mobile, B - BGP
        D - EIGRP, EX - EIGRP external, O - OSPF, IA - OSPF inter area
        E1 - OSPF external type 1, E2 - OSPF external type 2, E - EGP
        i - IS-IS, L1 - IS-IS level-1, L2 - IS-IS level-2, * - candidate default,
        U - per-user static route

Gateway of last resort is not set

     172.16.0.0/16 is subnetted, 5 subnets
C        172.16.24.0 is directly connected, Serial0
C        172.16.26.0 is directly connected, TokenRing0
R        172.16.20.0 [120/2] via 172.16.24.1, 00:00:00, Serial0
R        172.16.22.0 [120/2] via 172.16.24.1, 00:00:00, Serial0
R        172.16.18.0 [120/1] via 172.16.24.1, 00:00:00, Serial0
```

Figure 5.24

The routing tables of RTC and RTD in Figure 5.20.

```
RTC#show ip route
Codes:  C - connected, S - static, I - IGRP, R - RIP, M - mobile, B - BGP
        D - EIGRP, EX - EIGRP external, O - OSPF, IA - OSPF inter area
        N1 - OSPF NSSA external type 1, N2 - OSPF NSSA external type 2
        E1 - OSPF external type 1, E2 - OSPF external type 2, E - EGP
        i - IS-IS, L1 - IS-IS level-1, L2 - IS-IS level-2, * - candidate default,
        U - per-user static route, o - ODR

Gateway of last resort is not set

        172.16.0.0/23 is subnetted, 5 subnets
C          172.16.24.0 is directly connected, Serial0
R          172.16.26.0/23 is possibly down,
              routing via 172.16.24.2, Serial0
R          172.16.20.0 [120/1] via 172.16.18.5, 00:00:19, Ethernet0
R          172.16.22.0 [120/1] via 172.16.18.4, 00:00:24, Ethernet0
C          172.16.18.0 is directly connected, Ethernet0
```

```
RTD#show ip route
Codes:  C - connected, S - static, I - IGRP, R - RIP, M - mobile, B - BGP
        D - EIGRP, EX - EIGRP external, O - OSPF, IA - OSPF inter area
        E1 - OSPF external type 1, E2 - OSPF external type 2, E - EGP
        i - IS-IS, L1 - IS-IS level-1, L2 - IS-IS level-2, * - candidate default,
        U - per-user static route

Gateway of last resort is not set

        172.16.0.0/16 is subnetted, 5 subnets
C          172.16.24.0 is directly connected, Serial0
C          172.16.26.0 is directly connected, TokenRing0
R          172.16.20.0 [120/2] via 172.16.24.1, 00:00:15, Serial0
R          172.16.22.0 [120/2] via 172.16.24.1, 00:00:15, Serial0
R          172.16.18.0 [120/1] via 172.16.24.1, 00:00:15, Serial0
```

Figure 5.25

The routing tables of RTC and RTD, examined approximately 60 seconds after Figure 5.24.

```
RTC#show ip route
Codes:  C - connected, S - static, I - IGRP, R - RIP, M - mobile, B - BGP
        D - EIGRP, EX - EIGRP external, O - OSPF, IA - OSPF inter area
        N1 - OSPF NSSA external type 1, N2 - OSPF NSSA external type 2
        E1 - OSPF external type 1, E2 - OSPF external type 2, E - EGP
        i - IS-IS, L1 - IS-IS level-1, L2 - IS-IS level-2, * - candidate default,
        U - per-user static route, o - ODR

Gateway of last resort is not set

     172.16.0.0/23 is subnetted, 5 subnets
C       172.16.24.0 is directly connected, Serial0
R       172.16.26.0 [120/1] via 172.16.24.2, 00:00:09, Serial0
R       172.16.20.0 [120/1] via 172.16.18.5, 00:00:11, Ethernet0
R       172.16.22.0 [120/1] via 172.16.18.4, 00:00:18, Ethernet0
C       172.16.18.0 is directly connected, Ethernet0
```

```
RTC#
RTD#show ip route
Codes:  C - connected, S - static, I - IGRP, R - RIP, M - mobile, B - BGP
        D - EIGRP, EX - EIGRP external, O - OSPF, IA - OSPF inter area
        E1 - OSPF external type 1, E2 - OSPF external type 2, E - EGP
        i - IS-IS, L1 - IS-IS level-1, L2 - IS-IS level-2, * - candidate default,
        U - per-user static route

Gateway of last resort is not set

     172.16.0.0/16 is subnetted, 5 subnets
C       172.16.24.0 is directly connected, Serial0
C       172.16.26.0 is directly connected, TokenRing0
R       172.16.20.0 [120/2] via 172.16.24.1, 00:00:19, Serial0
R       172.16.22.0 [120/2] via 172.16.24.1, 00:00:19, Serial0
R       172.16.18.0 [120/1] via 172.16.24.1, 00:00:19, Serial0
```

Figure 5.26

The routing tables of RTC and RTD, examined approximately 120 seconds after Figure 5.25.

CHAPTER 6

Interior Gateway Routing Protocol (IGRP)

Cisco developed IGRP in the mid-1980s as an answer to the limitations of RIP, the most important of which are the hop count metric and the 15-hop internetwork size. IGRP calculates a composite metric from a variety of route variables and provides "knobs" for weighting the variables to reflect the specific characteristics and needs of the internetwork. Although hop count is not one of these variables, IGRP does track hop count and can be implemented on internets of up to 255 hops in diameter.

IGRP's other advantages over RIP are unequal-cost load sharing, an update period three times longer than RIP's, and a more efficient update packet format. The chief disadvantage of IGRP is that it is proprietary to Cisco and therefore limited to Cisco products, whereas RIP is a part of any IP routing process on any platform.

Cisco's objective when developing IGRP was to create a versatile, robust protocol capable of being adapted to a variety of routed protocol suites. Although it has proven to be a very popular routing protocol for IP, IGRP has been adapted to only one other routed protocol, the ISO Connectionless Network Protocol (CLNP). See the Cisco configuration manuals for more information on routing CLNS with IGRP.

OPERATION OF IGRP

From a high-altitude view, IGRP shares many operational characteristics with RIP. It is a classful distance vector protocol that periodically broadcasts its entire routing table—with the exception of routes suppressed by split horizon—to all its neighbors. Like RIP, IGRP broadcasts a request packet out all IGRP-enabled interfaces upon startup and performs a sanity check on received updates to verify that the source address of the packet belongs to the same subnet on which the update was received.[1] New update entries with reachable metrics are placed in the routing table, and an entry replaces an older entry to the same destination only if the metric is smaller. Split horizon with poisoned reverse, triggered updates, and holddown timers are used for stability; IGRP summarizes addresses at network boundaries.

Unlike RIP, which is accessed via UDP, the IGRP process is accessed directly from the IP layer as protocol 9.

IGRP also utilizes the concept of autonomous systems. Recall from Chapter 4, "Dynamic Routing Protocols," that an autonomous system can be defined either as a routing domain or as a process domain. An IGRP autonomous system is an IGRP process domain—a set of routers whose common routing protocol is an IGRP process.

By defining and tracking multiple autonomous systems, IGRP allows the establishment of multiple process domains within an IGP environment, isolating the communications within one domain from the communications within another domain. Traffic between the domains can then be closely regulated by redistribution (Chapter 11, "Route Redistribution") and route filtering (Chapter 13, "Route Filtering").

---

[1] *This sanity check can be disabled with the command* no validate-update-source.

Figure 6.1 illustrates the contrast between process domains and routing domains. Here two autonomous systems (ASs) are defined: AS 10 and AS 40. These systems are routing domains–a set of routers running one or more IGPs under a common administration. They communicate via an Exterior Gateway Protocol (in this case, Border Gateway Protocol, or BGP).

Within AS 10 are two IGRP process domains: IGRP 20 and IGRP 30. Under IGRP, the 20 and 30 are defined as autonomous system numbers. In this context the numbers serve to distinguish two routing processes within the same routing domain. IGRP 20 and IGRP 30 communicate via the single router connected to both domains. This router runs both IGRP processes and redistributes between them. The configuration section of this chapter includes a case study demonstrating the configuration of multiple IGRP process domains.

Within its updates, IGRP classifies route entries into one of three categories: interior routes, system routes, and exterior routes.

An *interior* route is a path to a subnet of the network address of the data link on which the update is being broadcast. In other words, a subnet advertised as an interior route is "local" to the major network to which the advertising router and the receiving router are commonly connected.

A *system* route is a path to a network address, which has been summarized by a network boundary router.

An *exterior* route is a path to a network that has been flagged as a *default network*. A default network is an address to which a router will send any packet that cannot be matched to a more specific destination.[2] Default networks and their configuration are covered in Chapter 12, "Default Routes and On-Demand Routing."

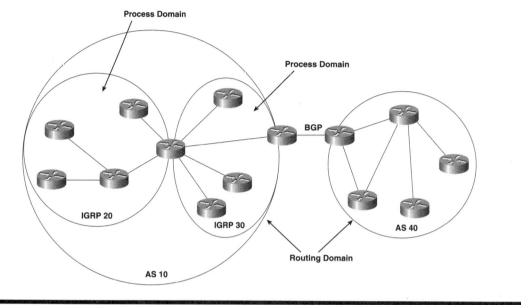

Figure 6.1

An autonomous system number may specify a routing domain, which is a group of routers running one or more IGP processes under a single administrative domain. An autonomous system number may also specify a process domain, which is a group of routers sharing routing information by means of a single routing process.

Figure 6.2 shows how IGRP uses these three categories. The routers LeHand and Tully are connected to subnet 192.168.2.64/26, so major network 192.168.2.0 is considered the "local" network shared by those two routers. LeHand is also attached to 192.168.2.192/26, which is another subnet of the network connecting the two routers. Therefore, LeHand advertises that subnet to Tully as an internal route.

However, the local network for LeHand and Thompson is 192.168.3.0. LeHand is the boundary router between major net-

---

2 *Classifying a default network as an external route is unique to IGRP and EIGRP. Open protocols such as RIP and OSPF advertise default networks with the address 0.0.0.0.*

works 192.168.2.0 and 192.168.3.0, so 192.168.2.0 will be advertised to Thompson as a system route. Likewise, 192.168.3.0 is advertised to Tully as a system route.

192.168.1.0 is a network in another autonomous system, and LeHand has been configured to advertise that network address as a default route. 192.168.1.0 will therefore be advertised to both Thompson and Tully as an external route.

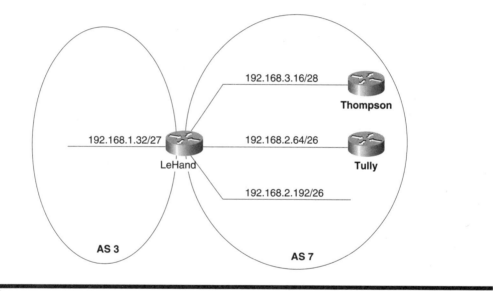

Figure 6.2

LeHand advertises subnet 192.168.2.192/26 to Tully as an internal route. Network 192.168.3.0 is advertised to Tully as a system route, and 192.168.1.0 is advertised as an external route.

IGRP Timers and Stability Features

The IGRP update period is 90 seconds. A random jitter variable of up to 20% is subtracted from each update time to prevent update timer synchronization, so the time elapsed between individual updates will vary from 72 to 90 seconds.

When a route is first learned, the invalid timer for that route is set for 270 seconds, or three times the update period. The flush timer is set for 630 seconds—seven times the update period. Each time an update is received for the route, these timers are reinitialized. If the invalid timer expires before an update is heard, the route is marked as unreachable. It will be held in the routing table and advertised as unreachable until the flush timer expires, at which time the route will be deleted from the table.

The 90-second timer used by IGRP, in comparison to the 30-second timer used by RIP, means that, compared to RIP, IGRP uses less bandwidth for periodic updates. However, the trade-off is that in some cases IGRP may be slower to converge than RIP. For example, if a router goes offline, IGRP takes three times as long as RIP to detect the dead neighbor.

If a destination becomes unreachable or if the next-hop router increases the metric of a destination enough to cause a triggered update, the route will be placed in holddown for 280 seconds (three update periods plus 10 seconds). Until the holddown timer expires, no new information will be accepted about this destination. IGRP holddown may be disabled with the command **no metric holddown**. In loop-free topologies, where holddown has no real benefit, disabling the function can reduce reconvergence time.

The default timers can be changed with the following command:

```
timers basic update invalid holddown flush [sleeptime]
```

This command is also used to manipulate RIP timers with the exception of the **sleeptime** option. Sleeptime is a timer used to specify a period, in milliseconds, to delay a regular routing update after receiving a triggered update.

The default timers should be changed only in response to an observable problem and only after careful consideration of the consequences. For example, the periods might be reduced to speed up reconvergence in an unstable topology. The price to be paid is increased update traffic—which might contribute to congestion on low-bandwidth links—and an increased number of router CPU cycles to handle the updates. Care must be taken to ensure that the timers are adjusted equally throughout an autonomous system, and configuration management must ensure that any routers added to the autonomous system in the future also are configured with the modified timers.

IGRP Metrics

The link characteristics from which IGRP calculates its composite metric are bandwidth, delay, load, and reliability. By default, IGRP chooses a route based on bandwidth and delay. If a data link is thought of as a pipe, then bandwidth is the width of the pipe and delay is the length of the pipe. In other words, bandwidth is a measure of the carrying capacity, and delay is a measure of the end-to-end travel time. Load and reliability are taken into consideration only if the router is configured to do so. IGRP also tracks the smallest Maximum Transmission Unit (MTU) along each route, although the MTU is not used in the composite metric calculation. The quantities associated with IGRP's composite metric on a specific interface can be observed with the **show interfaces** command (Figure 6.3).

Bandwidth is expressed in units of kilobits. It is a static number used for metric calculation only and does not necessarily reflect the actual bandwidth of the link—that is, bandwidth is not measured dynamically. For example, the default bandwidth of a serial interface is 1544, whether the interface is attached to a T1 or a 56K line. This bandwidth number may be changed from the default with the **bandwidth** command.

Bandwidth

```
Newfoundland#show interface fddi0
Fddi0 is administratively down, line protocol is down
   Hardware is DAS FDDI, address is 00e0.1e8e.d1d9 (bia 00e0.1e8e.d1d9)
   Internet address is 172.20.50.1/24
   MTU 4470 bytes, BW 100000 Kbit, DLY 100 usec, rely 255/255, load 1/255
   Encapsulation SNAP, loopback not set, keepalive not set
   ARP type: SNAP, ARP Timeout 04:00:00
   Phy-A state is off, neighbor is Unknown, status no signal
   Phy-B state is off, neighbor is Unknown, status no signal
   ECM is out, CFM is isolated, RMT is isolated
   Requested token rotation 5000 usec, negotiated 5017 usec
   Configured tvx is 3400 usec, using 5242.90 usec, ring not operational
   0 SMT frames processed, 0 dropped, 20 SMT buffers
   Upstream neighbor 0000.f800.0000, downstream neighbor 0000.f800.0000
   Last input never, output never, output hang never
   Last clearing of "show interface" counters never
   Queuing strategy: fifo
   Output queue 0/40, 0 drops; input queue 0/75, 0 drops
   5 minute input rate 0 bits/sec, 0 packets/sec
   5 minute output rate 0 bits/sec, 0 packets/sec
      0 packets input, 0 bytes, 0 no buffer
      Received 0 broadcasts, 0 runts, 0 giants
      0 input errors, 0 CRC, 0 frame, 0 overrun, 0 ignored, 0 abort
      0 packets output, 0 bytes, 0 underruns
      0 output errors, 0 collisions, 2 interface resets
      0 output buffer failures, 0 output buffers swapped out
      2 transitions, 0 traces
Newfoundland#
```

Figure 6.3

*The output of every **show interface** command includes metric statistics for the interface. This FDDI interface shows MTU = 4470 bytes, bandwidth = 100 megabits per second, delay = 100 microseconds, reliability = 100%, and load = .39% (minimum load).*

IGRP updates use a three-octet number, referred to in this book as BW_{IGRP}, which is the inverse of the bandwidth scaled by a factor of 10^7. So if the bandwidth of an interface is 1544, then

$$BW_{IGRP} = 10^7/1544 = 6476, \text{ or } 0x00194C.$$

Delay   Delay, like bandwidth, is a static figure and is not measured dynamically. It is displayed by the **show interface** command as DLY, in units of microseconds. The default delay of an interface may be changed with the **delay** command, which specifies the delay in tens of microseconds. Figure 6.4 shows the **bandwidth** and **delay** commands used to change the defaults of the interface of Figure 6.3.

When carried in an IGRP update, delay is a three-octet number expressed in the same 10-microsecond units as specified by the **delay** command. To avoid confusion, this number will be referred to as DLY_{IGRP}, to differentiate it from DLY, in microseconds, observed with **show interface**. For example, if DLY is 50, then

$$DLY_{IGRP} = DLY/10 = 50/10 = 5, \text{ or } 0x000005.$$

IGRP also uses delay to indicate an unreachable route by setting $DLY_{IGRP} = 0xFFFFFF$. This number translates to approximately 167.8 seconds, so the maximum end-to-end delay of an IGRP route is 167 seconds.

Because IGRP uses bandwidth and delay as its default metrics, these quantities must be configured correctly and consistently on all interfaces of all IGRP routers. Changing the bandwidth or delay of an interface should be done only for good reasons and only with a full understanding of the results of those changes. In most cases, it is best to leave the default values unchanged. A notable exception is serial interfaces. As noted earlier in this section, serial interfaces on Cisco routers have a default bandwidth of 1544 no matter what the bandwidth is of the connected link. The **bandwidth** command should be used to set the interface to the actual bandwidth of the serial link.

Changing default values for bandwidth and delay

It is also important to note that OSPF also uses the bandwidth statement to calculate its metric. Therefore, if IGRP metrics must to be manipulated in an internet where both IGRP and OSPF are running, use the **delay** to influence IGRP. Changing the bandwidth will affect both IGRP and OSPF.

```
Newfoundland(config)#interface fddi0
Newfoundland(config-if)#bandwidth 75000
Newfoundland(config-if)#delay 5
Newfoundland(config-if)#^Z
Newfoundland#
%SYS-5-CONFIG_I: Configured from console by console
Newfoundland#show interface fddi0
Fddi0 is administratively down, line protocol is down
  Hardware is DAS FDDI, address is 00e0.1e8e.d1d9 (bia 00e0.1e8e.d1d9)
  Internet address is 172.20.50.1/24
  MTU 4470 bytes, BW 75000 Kbit, DLY 50 usec, rely 255/255, load 1/255
  Encapsulation SNAP, loopback not set, keepalive not set
  ARP type: SNAP, ARP Timeout 04:00:00
  Phy-A state is off, neighbor is Unknown, status no signal
  Phy-B state is off, neighbor is Unknown, status no signal
  ECM is out, CFM is isolated, RMT is isolated
  Requested token rotation 5000 usec, negotiated 5017 usec
  Configured tvx is 3400 usec, using 5242.90 usec, ring not operational
  0 SMT frames processed, 0 dropped, 20 SMT buffers
  Upstream neighbor 0000.f800.0000, downstream neighbor 0000.f800.0000
  Last input never, output never, output hang never
  Last clearing of "show interface" counters never
  Queuing strategy: fifo
  Output queue 0/40, 0 drops; input queue 0/75, 0 drops
  5 minute input rate 0 bits/sec, 0 packets/sec
  5 minute output rate 0 bits/sec, 0 packets/sec
     0 packets input, 0 bytes, 0 no buffer
     Received 0 broadcasts, 0 runts, 0 giants
     0 input errors, 0 CRC, 0 frame, 0 overrun, 0 ignored, 0 abort
     0 packets output, 0 bytes, 0 underruns
     0 output errors, 0 collisions, 2 interface resets
     0 output buffer failures, 0 output buffers swapped out
     2 transitions, 0 traces
```

Figure 6.4

*The **bandwidth** and **delay** commands are used to change the metric defaults of the fddi0 interface. The new quantities can be seen in the output of the **show interface** command.*

Table 6.1 lists the bandwidths and delays for a few common interfaces. (The default bandwidth of a serial interface is always 1544; Table 6.1 shows the figures that would result from using the **bandwidth** command to reflect the actual connected bandwidth.)

Table 6.1 *Common BW$_{IGRP}$ and DLY$_{IGRP}$ quantities.*

Media	Bandwidth	BW$_{IGRP}$	Delay	DLY$_{IGRP}$
100M ATM	100000K	100	100μS	10
Fast Ethernet	100000K	100	100μS	10
FDDI	100000K	100	100μS	10
HSSI	45045K	222	20000μS	2000
16M Token Ring	16000K	625	630μS	63
Ethernet	10000K	1000	1000μS	100
T1	1544K	6476	20000μS	2000
DS0	64K	156250	20000μS	2000
56K	56K	178571	20000μS	2000
Tunnel	9K	1111111	500000μS	50000

Reliability is measured dynamically and is expressed as an eight-bit number, where 255 is a 100% reliable link and 1 is a minimally reliable link. In the output of **show interface**, reliability is shown as a fraction of 255, for example, 234/255 (Figure 6.5).

Reliability

Load, in an IGRP update, is an eight-bit number. Load is represented in the output of **show interface** as a fraction of 255, such as 40/255 (Figure 6.6); 1 is a minimally loaded link, and 255 is a 100% loaded link.

Load

If reliability or load is to be used as a metric or as part of a composite metric, the algorithm for calculating the metric must not allow sudden changes in the error rate or channel occupancy to destabilize the internetwork. As an example, if a "raw," or instantaneous, measure of load is used, a burst of heavy traffic could cause a route to go into holddown and an abrupt drop in traffic could trigger an update. To prevent frequent metric changes, reliability and load are calculated based on an exponentially weighted

```
Casablanca#show interface ethernet0
Ethernet0 is up, line protocol is up
  Hardware is Lance, address is 0000.0c76.5b7c (bia 0000.0c76.5b7c)
  Internet address is 172.20.1.1 255.255.255.0
  MTU 1500 bytes, BW 10000 Kbit, DLY 1000 usec, rely 234/255, load 1/255
  Encapsulation ARPA, loopback not set, keepalive set (10 sec)
  ARP type: ARPA, ARP Timeout 4:00:00
  Last input 0:00:28, output 0:00:06, output hang never
  Last clearing of "show interface" counters 0:06:05
  Output queue 0/40, 0 drops; input queue 0/75, 0 drops
  5 minute input rate 0 bits/sec, 0 packets/sec
  5 minute output rate 0 bits/sec, 0 packets/sec
     22 packets input, 3758 bytes, 0 no buffer
     Received 21 broadcasts, 0 runts, 0 giants
     0 input errors, 0 CRC, 0 frame, 0 overrun, 0 ignored, 0 abort
     0 input packets with dribble condition detected
     125 packets output, 11254 bytes, 0 underruns
     39 output errors, 694 collisions, 0 interface resets, 0 restarts
     0 output buffer failures, 0 output buffers swapped out
Casablanca#
```

Figure 6.5

This interface shows a reliability of 234/255, or 91.8%.

```
Yalta#show interface serial 1
Serial1 is up, line protocol is up
  Hardware is HD64570
  Internet address is 172.20.20.2 255.255.255.0
  MTU 1500 bytes, BW 56 Kbit, DLY 20000 usec, rely 255/255, load 40/255
  Encapsulation HDLC, loopback not set, keepalive set (10 sec)
  Last input 0:00:08, output 0:00:00, output hang never
  Last clearing of "show interface" counters 0:05:05
  Output queue 0/40, 0 drops; input queue 0/75, 0 drops
  5 minute input rate 10000 bits/sec, 1 packet/sec
  5 minute output rate 9000 bits/sec, 1 packet/sec
     456 packets input, 397463 bytes, 0 no buffer
     Received 70 broadcasts, 0 runts, 0 giants
     0 input errors, 0 CRC, 0 frame, 0 overrun, 0 ignored, 0 abort
     428 packets output, 395862 bytes, 0 underruns
     0 output errors, 0 collisions, 0 interface resets, 0 restarts
     0 output buffer failures, 0 output buffers swapped out
     0 carrier transitions
     DCD=up DSR=up DTR=up RTS=up CTS=up
```

Figure 6.6

This interface shows a load of 40/255, or 15.7%.

average with a 5-minute time constant, which is updated every 5 seconds.

The composite metric for each IGRP route is calculated as

$$\text{metric} = [k1*BW_{IGRP(min)} + (k2*BW_{IGRP(min)})/(256-LOAD) + k3*DLY_{IGRP(sum)}] * [k5/(RELIABILITY+k4)],$$

where $BW_{IGRP(min)}$ is the minimum BW_{IGRP} of all the outgoing interfaces along the route to the destination and $DLY_{IGRP(sum)}$ is the total DLY_{IGRP} of the route.

The values k1 through k5 are configurable weights; their default values are k1=k3=1 and k2=k4=k5=0. These defaults can be changed with the command:

metric weights tos k1 k2 k3 k4 k5[3]

If k5 is set to zero, the [k5/(RELIABILITY+k4)] term is not used.

Given the default values for k1 through k5, the composite metric calculation used by IGRP reduces to the default metric:

$$\text{metric} = BW_{IGRP(min)} + DLY_{IGRP(sum)}$$

The network example in Figure 6.7 shows the bandwidths and delays configured on each interface and a forwarding database from one of the routers with the derived IGRP metrics.[4]

The routing table itself shows only the derived metric, but the actual variables recorded by IGRP for each route can be seen by using the command **show ip route** *address*, as in Figure 6.8. Here the minimum bandwidth on the route from Casablanca to subnet

---

[3]   tos *is a relic of Cisco's original intention to have IGRP do type of service routing; this plan was never adopted, and tos in this command is always set to zero.*
[4]   *Also notice the administrative distance, which is 100 for IGRP.*

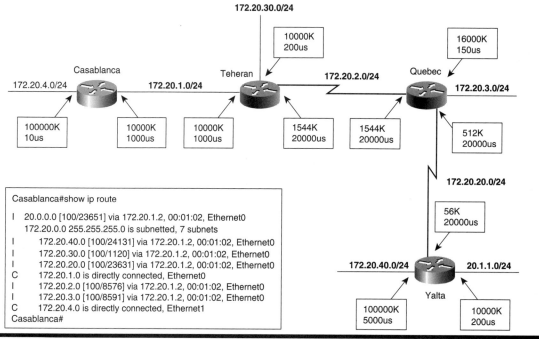

Figure 6.7

By default, the total delay is added to the minimum bandwidth to derive the IGRP metric.

172.20.40.0/24 is 512K, at Quebec. The total delay of the route is $(1000 + 20000 + 20000 + 5000) = 46000$ microseconds.

$$BW_{IGRP(min)} = 10^7/512 = 19531$$

$$DLY_{IGRP(sum)} = 46000/10 = 4600$$

$$\text{metric} = BW_{IGRP(min)} + DLY_{IGRP(sum)} = 19531 + 4600 = 24131$$

Figure 6.8 shows that IGRP also records the smallest MTU along the route as well as the hop count. MTU is not used in the metric calculation. Hop count is the hop count reported by the next-hop router and is used only to limit the diameter of the network. By default, the maximum hop count is 100 and can be configured from 1 to 255 with the command **metric maximum-hops**. If the

```
Casablanca#show ip route 172.20.40.0
Routing entry for 172.20.40.0 255.255.255.0
  Known via "igrp 1", distance 100, metric 24131
  Redistributing via igrp 1
  Advertised by igrp 1 (self originated)
  Last update from 172.20.1.2 on Ethernet0, 00:00:54 ago
  Routing Descriptor Blocks:
  * 172.20.1.2, from 172.20.1.2, 00:00:54 ago, via Ethernet0
      Route metric is 24131, traffic share count is 1
      Total delay is 46000 microseconds, minimum bandwidth is 512 Kbit
      Reliability 255/255, minimum MTU 1500 bytes
      Loading 1/255, Hops 2
```

Figure 6.8

The metric for the route from Casablanca to subnet 172.20.40.0 is calculated from the minimum bandwidth of 512K and the total delay of 46000 microseconds.

maximum hop count is exceeded, the route will be marked unreachable by setting the delay to 0xFFFFFF.

Note that all metrics are calculated from the outgoing interfaces along the route. For example, the metric for the route from Yalta to subnet 172.20.4.0/24 is different from the metric for the route from Casablanca to subnet 172.20.40.0/24. This is due to the differences in the configured bandwidth on the link between Yalta and Quebec and to the differences in the delay on the outgoing interfaces to the two destination subnets.

IGRP Packet Format

The IGRP packet format is shown in Figure 6.9. The efficient design, in comparison to the RIP format of Figure 5.3, is readily apparent. At the same time, IGRP updates provide much more information than RIP, which sends little more than a snapshot of the sender's routing table. No field is unused, and after the 12-octet header the individual route entries appear one after the other. In contrast to RIP, IGRP does not use padding to force each entry to end on a 32-bit word boundary. Each update packet can carry a maximum of 104 fourteen-octet entries, so with the 12-octet header the maximum IGRP packet size is 12 + (104 X 14) = 1468 octets. Adding a 32-octet IP header brings the maximum IGRP packet size to 1500 bytes.

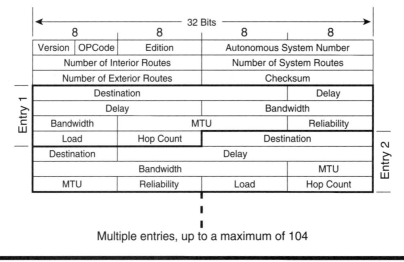

Multiple entries, up to a maximum of 104

Figure 6.9
The IGRP packet format.

Version will always be set to one.

Opcode will be one for an IGRP Request packet and two for an IGRP Update packet. A Request packet consists of a header with no entries.

Edition is incremented by the sender of an update whenever there is a change of routing information. The edition number helps the router avoid accepting an old update that arrives after the newer update.

Autonomous System Number is, more accurately, the ID number of the IGRP process. This tag allows multiple IGRP processes to exchange information over a common data link.

Number of Interior Routes is the number of entries in the update that are subnets of a directly connected network. If none of the directly connected networks is subnetted, this field will be zero. Interior route entries always appear first in the update. This field, along with the subsequent fields for number of system routes and number of exterior routes, tell an IGRP process how many 14-octet entries are contained in the packet and hence the packet length.

Number of System Routes tells the number of routes to networks that are not directly connected—in other words, routes that have been summarized by a network border router. The entries numbered in this field, if any, follow the interior route entries.

Number of Exterior Routes is the number of routes to networks that have been identified as default networks. The entries numbered in this field, if any, appear last in the update.

Checksum is calculated on the IGRP header and all entries. To calculate the checksum, the field is set to zero and the 16-bit one's complement sum of the packet (not including the IP header) is calculated. The 16-bit one's complement of that sum is then stored in the checksum field. Upon receipt, the 16-bit one's complement of the packet is again calculated, this time including the transmitted checksum field. When performed on an error-free packet, the result will be all ones (0xFFFF).

Destination is the first field of each route entry. It may seem odd at first glance that the field is only three octets long, given that IP addresses are four octets. As it turns out, a destination can be made recognizable in three octets because of IGRP's route categorization. If the entry is an interior route, at least the first octet of the IP address will always be known from the address of the interface on which the update was received. Therefore, the destination fields of interior route entries will contain only the last three octets of the address. Similarly, if the entry is a system or external route, the route will have been summarized and at least the last octet will be all zeros. Therefore the destination fields of system and external route entries will contain only the first three octets of the address.

For example, if an interior route of 20.40.0 is received on interface 172.20.1.1/24, it is recognized as subnet 172.20.40.0/24. Similarly, if system routes 192.168.14 and 20.0.0 are received, IGRP will understand these destinations as major network addresses 192.168.14.0 and 20.0.0.0.

Delay is the 24-bit $DLY_{IGRP(sum)}$ previously explained—the sum of the configured delays expressed in units of 10 microseconds.

Bandwidth is the 24-bit $BW_{IGRP(min)}$ previously explained—10,000,000 divided by the lowest configured bandwidth of any interface along the route.

MTU is the smallest Maximum Transmission Unit of any link along the route to the destination. Although an included parameter, it has never been used in the calculation of metrics.

Reliability is a number between 0x01 and 0xFF that reflects the total outgoing error rates of the interfaces along the route, calculated on a five-minute exponentially weighted average.

Load is also a number between 0x01 and 0xFF, reflecting the total outgoing load of the interfaces along the route, calculated on a five-minute exponentially weighted average.

Hop Count is a number between 0x01 and 0xFF indicating the number of hops to the destination. A router will advertise a directly connected network with a hop count of 0; subsequent routers will record and advertise the route relative to the next-hop router. For example, in Figure 6.8 Casablanca shows subnet 172.20.40.0 to be two hops away. Figure 6.7 shows the meaning of the hop count: 172.20.40.0 is two hops from the next-hop router, Teheran.

An analyzer decode of a portion of an IGRP update packet is shown in Figure 6.10.

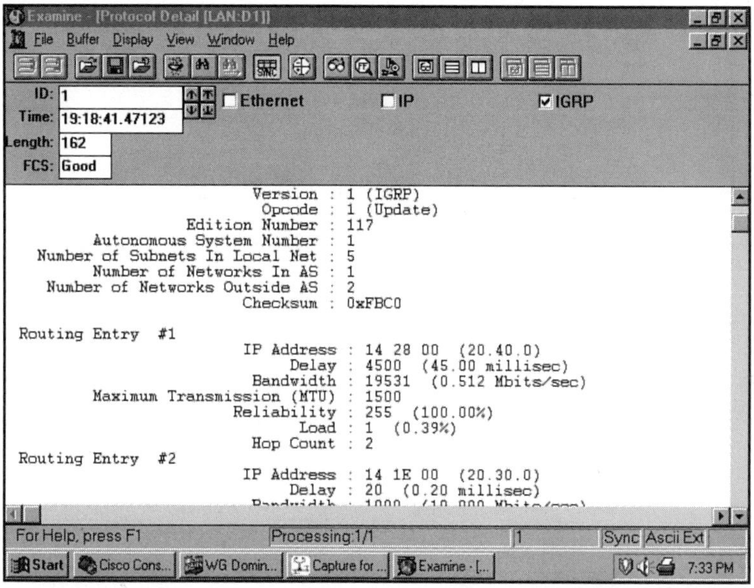

Figure 6.10
The header and the first entry of an IGRP update can be seen in this analyzer decode.

CONFIGURING IGRP

Although a few more configuration options are available to IGRP than to RIP, the basic configuration is every bit as simple: The **router** command is used to establish the routing process, and the **network** command is used to specify each network on which IGRP is to run. As with RIP, only major network numbers can be specified because IGRP is also a classful protocol.

The commands **neighbor,** for sending unicast updates, and **passive-interface,** for preventing updates from being broadcast on selected subnets, were introduced in Chapter 5, "Routing Information Protocol (RIP)." They can be used with IGRP just as with RIP.

Offset-list was also introduced in Chapter 5. When used with IGRP, the offset variable is *delay* instead of *hops*.

A significant difference from RIP is that each IGRP has a process ID, which allows multiple processes to be run on the same router.

Case Study: A Basic IGRP Configuration

Only two steps are necessary to configure IGRP:

1. Enable IGRP with the command **router igrp** *process-id*.
2. Specify each major network on which to run IGRP with the **network** command.

The process ID is carried in the 16-bit autonomous system field of the update packet. The selection of a process ID is arbitrary—any number between 1 and 65,535 (0 is not allowed) can be used, as long as it is used consistently on all routers that must share information via that particular IGRP process. Figure 6.11 shows a simple internetwork; the configurations for the three routers are as follows:

```
McCloy(config)#router igrp 10
McCloy(config-router)#network 192.168.1.0
McCloy(config-router)#network 192.168.2.0

Acheson(config)#router igrp 10
Acheson(config-router)#network 192.168.2.0
Acheson(config-router)#network 172.16.0.0

Kennan(config)#router igrp 10
Kennan(config-router)#network 172.16.0.0
Kennan(config-router)#network 10.0.0.0
```

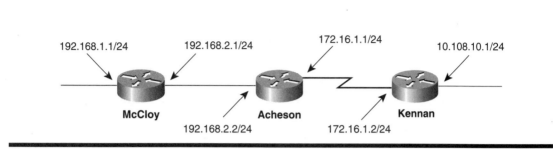

Figure 6.11

IGRP will perform address summarization at these three network boundary routers.

IGRP will perform subnet hiding, or summarization, at network boundaries. In the case of Figure 6.11, all three routers are network boundary routers.

Case Study: Unequal-Cost Load Balancing

Given up to six parallel routes of equal cost,[5] IGRP will do equal-cost load balancing under the same fast/process switching constraints as RIP. Unlike RIP, IGRP can also perform unequal-cost load balancing. An additional serial link has been added between Acheson and Kennan in Figure 6.12, with a configured bandwidth of 256K. The goal is to have Acheson perform unequal-cost load balancing across these two links–spreading the traffic load inversely proportional to the metrics of the link.

Examining the route from Acheson's S0 interface to network 10.0.0.0, the minimum bandwidth is 1544K (assuming Kennan's Ethernet interface is using the default 10000K bandwidth). Referring to Table 6.1, $DLY_{IGRP(sum)}$ for the serial interface and the Ethernet interface is $2000 + 100 = 2100$. $BW_{IGRP(min)}$ is $10^7/1544 = 6476$, so the composite metric of the route is $6476 + 2100 = 8576$.

---

[5] *The default is four paths. See the case study on setting maximum paths for further details.*

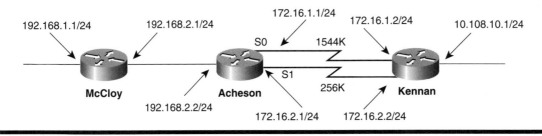

Figure 6.12

IGRP can be configured to perform unequal-cost load balancing across links such as the two between Acheson and Kennan.

The minimum bandwidth on the route via Acheson's S1 to 10.0.0.0 is 256K; $DLY_{IGRP(sum)}$ is the same as on the first route. Therefore, the composite metric for this route is $10^7/256 + 2100$ = 41162. Without further configuration, IGRP will simply select the path with the lowest metric cost. Figure 6.13 shows that Acheson is using only the path with a metric of 8576.

```
Acheson#show ip route
Codes: C - connected, S - static, I - IGRP, R - RIP, M - mobile, B - BGP
       D - EIGRP, EX - EIGRP external, O - OSPF, IA - OSPF inter area
       E1 - OSPF external type 1, E2 - OSPF external type 2, E - EGP
       i - IS-IS, L1 - IS-IS level-1, L2 - IS-IS level-2, * - candidate default

Gateway of last resort is not set

I    10.0.0.0 [100/8576] via 172.16.1.2, 00:00:06, Serial0
I    192.168.1.0 [100/1600] via 192.168.2.1, 00:00:06, Ethernet0
C    192.168.2.0 is directly connected, Ethernet0
     172.16.0.0 255.255.255.0 is subnetted, 2 subnets
C       172.16.1.0 is directly connected, Serial0
C       172.16.2.0 is directly connected, Serial1
Acheson#
```

Figure 6.13

Acheson is using only the lowest-cost link to network 10.0.0.0. Additional configuration is needed to enable unequal-cost load balancing.

The **variance** command is used to determine which routes are feasible for unequal-cost load sharing. Variance defines a multiplier by which a metric may differ, or vary, from the metric of the lowest-cost route. Any route whose metric exceeds the metric of the lowest-cost route, multiplied by the variance, will not be considered a feasible route.

Variance

The default variance is one, meaning that the metrics of multiple routes must be equal in order to load balance. Variance must be specified in whole numbers.

The metric of Acheson's route through S1 is $41162/8576 = 4.8$ times larger than the metric of the S0 route. So to conduct unequal-cost load balancing over Acheson, the variance at Acheson should be five. The IGRP configuration is:

```
router igrp 10
  network 172.16.0.0
  network 192.168.2.0
  variance 5
```

After specifying a variance of five at Acheson, its routing table will include the second, higher cost route (Figure 6.14). The following three conditions must be met for a route to be included in unequal-cost load sharing:

1. The maximum-paths limit must not be exceeded as a result of adding the route to a load-sharing "group."
2. The next-hop router must be metrically closer to the destination. That is, its metric for the route must be smaller than the local router's metric. A next-hop router, being closer to the destination, is often referred to as the *downstream* router.
3. The metric of the lowest-cost route, when multiplied by the variance, must be greater than the metric of the route to be added.

```
Acheson(config)#router igrp 10
Acheson(config-router)#variance 5
Acheson(config-router)#^Z
Acheson#
%SYS-5-CONFIG_I: Configured from console by console
Acheson#clear ip route *
Acheson#show ip route
Codes: C - connected, S - static, I - IGRP, R - RIP, M - mobile, B - BGP
       D - EIGRP, EX - EIGRP external, O - OSPF, IA - OSPF inter area
       E1 - OSPF external type 1, E2 - OSPF external type 2, E - EGP
       i - IS-IS, L1 - IS-IS level-1, L2 - IS-IS level-2, * - candidate default

Gateway of last resort is not set

I  10.0.0.0 [100/8576] via 172.16.1.2, 00:00:07, Serial0
        [100/41162] via 172.16.2.2, 00:00:07, Serial1
I  192.168.1.0 [100/1600] via 192.168.2.1, 00:00:07, Ethernet0
C  192.168.2.0 is directly connected, Ethernet0
   172.16.0.0 255.255.255.0 is subnetted, 2 subnets
C     172.16.1.0 is directly connected, Serial0
C     172.16.2.0 is directly connected, Serial1
Acheson#
```

Figure 6.14

The composite metric of the second path to 10.0.0.0 is 41162, or 4.8 times the metric of the lowest-cost route. IGRP will enter the second path into the routing table if the variance is set to at least five.

The rules concerning per destination versus per packet load sharing, discussed in Chapter 3, "Static Routing," apply here as well. Load sharing is per destination if the packet is fast switched and per packet if process switching is used. Figure 6.15 shows a debug output resulting from 20 ping packets being sent through Acheson; fast switching has been turned off with **no ip route-cache,** and the router is performing unequal-cost, per packet load balancing. For every five packets sent over the 1544K link (to next hop 172.16.1.2), one packet is sent over the 256K link (to next hop 172.16.2.2). This corresponds to the approximately five-to-one variance of the metrics of these two paths.

If variance is set at one, IGRP enters only the lowest-cost route to a destination into the routing table. In some situations, however—for example, to decrease reconvergence time or aid in troubleshooting—all feasible routes should be entered into the table, even though no load balancing should occur. All packets should use the lowest-cost route and switch to the next-best path only if the primary fails. There is an implicit default command (that is, it exists, but is not observed in the configuration file) of **traffic-share balanced**. To configure the router to only use the minimum-cost path even when multiple paths are shown in the routing table, change this default to **traffic-share min**. If there are multiple minimum-cost paths and **traffic-share min** is configured, IGRP will perform equal-cost load balancing.

```
Acheson#debug ip packet
IP packet debugging is on
Acheson#
IP: s=192.168.2.1 (Ethernet0), d=10.108.10.1 (Serial0), g=172.16.1.2, forward
IP: s=192.168.2.1 (Ethernet0), d=10.108.10.1 (Serial0), g=172.16.1.2, forward
IP: s=192.168.2.1 (Ethernet0), d=10.108.10.1 (Serial0), g=172.16.1.2, forward
IP: s=192.168.2.1 (Ethernet0), d=10.108.10.1 (Serial0), g=172.16.1.2, forward
IP: s=192.168.2.1 (Ethernet0), d=10.108.10.1 (Serial0), g=172.16.1.2, forward
IP: s=192.168.2.1 (Ethernet0), d=10.108.10.1 (Serial1), g=172.16.2.2, forward
IP: s=192.168.2.1 (Ethernet0), d=10.108.10.1 (Serial0), g=172.16.1.2, forward
IP: s=192.168.2.1 (Ethernet0), d=10.108.10.1 (Serial0), g=172.16.1.2, forward
IP: s=192.168.2.1 (Ethernet0), d=10.108.10.1 (Serial0), g=172.16.1.2, forward
IP: s=192.168.2.1 (Ethernet0), d=10.108.10.1 (Serial0), g=172.16.1.2, forward
IP: s=192.168.2.1 (Ethernet0), d=10.108.10.1 (Serial0), g=172.16.1.2, forward
IP: s=192.168.2.1 (Ethernet0), d=10.108.10.1 (Serial1), g=172.16.2.2, forward
IP: s=192.168.2.1 (Ethernet0), d=10.108.10.1 (Serial0), g=172.16.1.2, forward
IP: s=192.168.2.1 (Ethernet0), d=10.108.10.1 (Serial0), g=172.16.1.2, forward
IP: s=192.168.2.1 (Ethernet0), d=10.108.10.1 (Serial0), g=172.16.1.2, forward
IP: s=192.168.2.1 (Ethernet0), d=10.108.10.1 (Serial0), g=172.16.1.2, forward
IP: s=192.168.2.1 (Ethernet0), d=10.108.10.1 (Serial0), g=172.16.1.2, forward
IP: s=192.168.2.1 (Ethernet0), d=10.108.10.1 (Serial1), g=172.16.2.2, forward
IP: s=192.168.2.1 (Ethernet0), d=10.108.10.1 (Serial0), g=172.16.1.2, forward
IP: s=192.168.2.1 (Ethernet0), d=10.108.10.1 (Serial0), g=172.16.1.2, forward
Acheson#
```

Figure 6.15

Per packet load sharing is being performed, with one packet being sent over the high-cost link for every five packets sent over the low-cost link.

Case Study: Setting Maximum Paths

The maximum number of routes over which IGRP can load balance is set with the **maximum-paths** *paths* command. *Paths* may be any number from one to six in IOS 11.0 and later and any number from one to four in earlier versions. The default for all versions is four.

Figure 6.16 shows three parallel paths of varying costs from McCloy to network 172.18.0.0. The network administrator wants to load balance over a maximum of only two of these routes while ensuring that if either of these paths should fail, the third route will replace it.

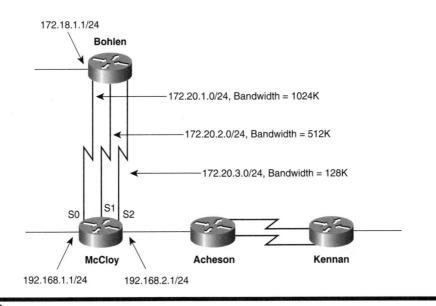

Figure 6.16

*The **maximum-paths** and **variance** commands can be used together to configure load balancing over only two of the three links between McCloy and Bohlen. If either link fails, the third will take its place.*

The metrics from McCloy are:

Via S0: 9765 + (2000 + 100) = 11865

Via S1: 19531 + (2000 + 100) = 21631

Via S2: 78125 + (2000 + 100) = 80225

The metric of the S2 route is 6.76 times as large as the lowest-cost metric, so the variance is seven. McCloy's IGRP configuration is

```
router igrp 10
  variance 7
  network 172.20.0.0
  network 192.168.1.0
  network 192.168.2.0
  maximum-paths 2
```

The **variance** command ensures that any of the three routes to 172.18.0.0 is feasible; the **maximum-paths** command limits the load-sharing group to only the two best routes. The results of this configuration can be seen in Figure 6.17. The first routing table shows that McCloy was load balancing over the two links with the lowest of the three metrics, S0 and S1. After a failure of the S1 link, the second routing table shows that the router is now load balancing over the S0 and S2 links. In each instance, the router will load balance inversely proportional to the metrics of the two paths.

Case Study: Multiple IGRP Processes

Two new routers, Lovett and Harriman, have been added to the internetwork (Figure 6.18). A decision has been made to create two IGRP autonomous system "domains" in the internetwork with no communications between the two. Figure 6.19 shows the two autonomous systems and the related links for each.

```
McCloy#show ip route
Codes: C - connected, S - static, I - IGRP, R - RIP, M - mobile, B - BGP
       D - EIGRP, EX - EIGRP external, O - OSPF, IA - OSPF inter area
       E1 - OSPF external type 1, E2 - OSPF external type 2, E - EGP
       i - IS-IS, L1 - IS-IS level-1, L2 - IS-IS level-2, * - candidate default

Gateway of last resort is not set

I    10.0.0.0 [100/8676] via 192.168.2.2, 00:00:02, Ethernet1
C    192.168.1.0 is directly connected, Ethernet0
C    192.168.2.0 is directly connected, Ethernet1
     172.20.0.0 255.255.255.0 is subnetted, 3 subnets
C       172.20.1.0 is directly connected, Serial0
C       172.20.2.0 is directly connected, Serial1
C       172.20.3.0 is directly connected, Serial2
I    172.18.0.0 [100/11865] via 172.20.1.2, 00:00:17, Serial0
              [100/21631] via 172.20.2.2, 00:00:17, Serial1
McCloy#
%LINEPROTO-5-UPDOWN: Line protocol on Interface Serial1, changed state to down
%LINK-3-UPDOWN: Interface Serial1, changed state to down
McCloy#show ip route
Codes: C - connected, S - static, I - IGRP, R - RIP, M - mobile, B - BGP
       D - EIGRP, EX - EIGRP external, O - OSPF, IA - OSPF inter area
       E1 - OSPF external type 1, E2 - OSPF external type 2, E - EGP
       i - IS-IS, L1 - IS-IS level-1, L2 - IS-IS level-2, * - candidate default

Gateway of last resort is not set

I    10.0.0.0 [100/8676] via 192.168.2.2, 00:00:02, Ethernet1
C    192.168.1.0 is directly connected, Ethernet0
C    192.168.2.0 is directly connected, Ethernet1
     172.20.0.0 255.255.255.0 is subnetted, 2 subnets
C       172.20.1.0 is directly connected, Serial0
C       172.20.3.0 is directly connected, Serial2
I    172.18.0.0 [100/11865] via 172.20.1.2, 00:00:08, Serial0
              [100/80225] via 172.20.3.2, 00:00:08, Serial2
McCloy#
```

Figure 6.17

*The routing table for McCloy, before and after the failure of one of three links, shows the results of using the **variance** and **maximum-paths** commands to configure load sharing to 172.18.0.0.*

The configurations for Bohlen, Lovett, McCloy, and Kennan are straightforward: Bohlen, Lovett, and McCloy will run IGRP 10,

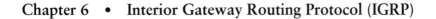

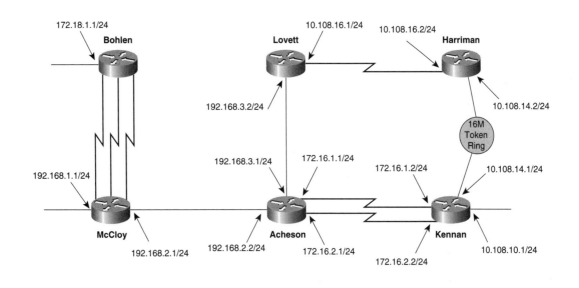

Figure 6.18
Separate routing domains are to be created in this internetwork.

and Kennan will run IGRP 15. At Acheson, the configuration will be:

```
router igrp 10
  network 192.168.2.0
  network 192.168.3.0
!
router igrp 15
  network 172.16.0.0
```

Each process will run only on the interfaces of the networks specified. At Harriman, both interfaces belong to network 10.0.0.0:

```
router igrp 10
  passive-interface TokenRing0
  network 10.0.0.0
!
router igrp 15
  passive-interface Serial0
  network 10.0.0.0
```

Using the **passive-interface** command prevents IGRP updates from being broadcast on data links where they don't belong.

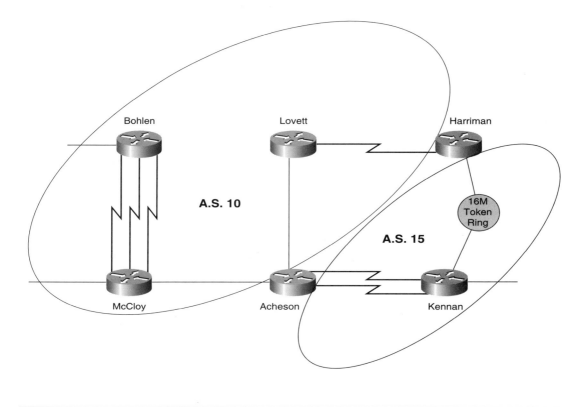

Figure 6.19
The routers Harriman and Acheson will each run multiple IGRP processes to facilitate the creation of separate autonomous systems (AS 10 and AS 15) within this IGP.

TROUBLESHOOTING IGRP

Like RIP, troubleshooting IGRP is usually an easy task. In most cases, it is a matter of following a route through the internetwork and examining the routing tables at each hop until the source of the trouble is discovered. The trouble is usually related to a mis-configured address or mask or to discontiguous addressing.

When the timers and other variables of the IGRP process are changed from their defaults, the likelihood of causing problems increases. This is especially true if these values are changed without fully understanding the effects the changes will have. The first case study demonstrates this situation; IGRP is doing what it should, but the trouble is due to "cockpit error." The second case study demonstrates that a discontiguous range of addresses does not always result from a configuration error.

Case Study: Unequal-Cost Load Balancing, Again

The entire internetwork of Figure 6.20 is routed with a single IGRP process, and the bandwidths for the serial links are configured to the numbers shown. Default delays are used. Notice that the addresses of the link between Lovett and Harriman are different from the previous examples. Because network 10.0.0.0 can be reached from Acheson not only by the two serial links but also via the Ethernet to Lovett, the network administrator wants to distribute the traffic proportionately among all three routes:.

The access points to network 10.0.0.0 are:

- Kennnan's Token Ring interface

- Kennan's Ethernet interface

- Harriman's Token Ring interface

Of Kennan's two interfaces to network 10.0.0.0, the lowest delay will be advertised, which is on the Token Ring interface. The minimum bandwidths of all three routes are the bandwidths of the serial interfaces. The metrics of the three routes from Acheson are:

Via S0: 6476 + (2000 + 63) = 8539

Via S1: 39062 + (2000 + 63) = 41125

Via E1: 6476 + (100 + 2000 + 63) = 8639

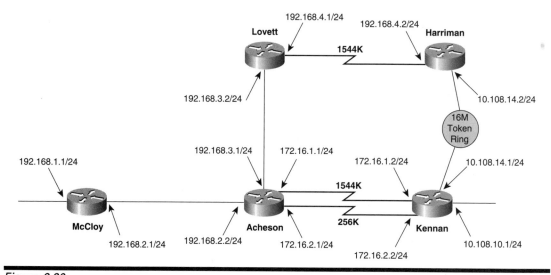

Figure 6.20

This internetwork has three paths from Acheson to network 10.0.0.0.

The highest metric is 4.8 times the lowest metric, so variance will be five.

The variance is configured, but the administrator finds that load balancing is not working as expected (Figure 6.21). The routing table shows only the two routes via Kennan; the route via Lovett is between the highest and lowest metrics, but is not included.

Recall the three rules for including a route in a load sharing "group," as noted in the configuration case study on unequal-cost load balancing. In this example, the second rule, which says that the next-hop router must be metrically closer to the destination than the local best route, is being violated. At Lovett, the metric to 10.0.0.0 is 6476 + (2000 + 63) = 8539. This is equal to, but not better than, Acheson's best route.

The metric at Lovett can be made lower than 8539 by slightly increasing the bandwidth or slightly decreasing the delay on the serial interface. In this case, the delay is decreased by 10 microseconds:

```
Lovett(config)#interface serial 0
Lovett(config-if)#delay 1999
```

The resulting routing table is shown in Figure 6.22.

```
Acheson#show ip route
Codes:  C - connected, S - static, I - IGRP, R - RIP, M - mobile, B - BGP
        D - EIGRP, EX - EIGRP external, O - OSPF, IA - OSPF inter area
        E1 - OSPF external type 1, E2 - OSPF external type 2, E - EGP
        i - IS-IS, L1 - IS-IS level-1, L2 - IS-IS level-2, * - candidate default

Gateway of last resort is not set
I    10.0.0.0 [100/8539] via 172.16.1.2, 00:00:11, Serial0
             [100/41125] via 172.16.2.2, 00:00:11, Serial1
I    192.168.1.0 [100/1600] via 192.168.2.1, 00:00:11, Ethernet0
C    192.168.2.0 is directly connected, Ethernet0
C    192.168.3.0 is directly connected, Ethernet1
I    192.168.4.0 [100/8576] via 192.168.3.2, 00:00:11, Ethernet1
     172.16.0.0 255.255.255.0 is subnetted, 2 subnets
C       172.16.1.0 is directly connected, Serial0
C       172.16.2.0 is directly connected, Serial1
Acheson#
```

Figure 6.21

The route to 10.0.0.0 via Lovett is not included in the table for load sharing.

When manipulating metrics, pay close attention to the results. If the cost of a path does not reasonably reflect its actual capacity, the traffic load may be distorted—a low-bandwidth link may be overloaded, or a high-bandwidth link may be underutilized.

Case Study: A Segmented Network

Some time after the internetwork of Figure 6.20 has been up and running, with load sharing working properly, users begin to complain that traffic to subnet 10.108.14.0 through Acheson is

```
Acheson#show ip route
Codes:  C - connected, S - static, I - IGRP, R - RIP, M - mobile, B - BGP
        D - EIGRP, EX - EIGRP external, O - OSPF, IA - OSPF inter area
        E1 - OSPF external type 1, E2 - OSPF external type 2, E - EGP
        i - IS-IS, L1 - IS-IS level-1, L2 - IS-IS level-2, * - candidate default

Gateway of last resort is not set

I     10.0.0.0 [100/8539] via 172.16.1.2, 00:00:14, Serial0
               [100/41125] via 172.16.2.2, 00:00:14, Serial1
               [100/8638] via 192.168.3.2, 00:00:14, Ethernet1
I     192.168.1.0 [100/1600] via 192.168.2.1, 00:01:02, Ethernet0
C     192.168.2.0 is directly connected, Ethernet0
C     192.168.3.0 is directly connected, Ethernet1
I     192.168.4.0 [100/8575] via 192.168.3.2, 00:00:14, Ethernet1
      172.16.0.0 255.255.255.0 is subnetted, 2 subnets
C        172.16.1.0 is directly connected, Serial0
C        172.16.2.0 is directly connected, Serial1
Acheson#
```

Figure 6.22

After the delay on Lovett's serial interface is decreased by 10µS, Acheson will accept Lovett's route to 10.0.0.0.

intermittent. When the network administrator sends 100 pings to an address on this network, they confirm that traffic is indeed intermittent (Figure 6.23).

```
Acheson#ping
Protocol [ip]:
Target IP address: 10.108.14.83
Repeat count [5]: 100
Datagram size [100]:
Timeout in seconds [2]:
Extended commands [n]:
Sweep range of sizes [n]:
Type escape sequence to abort.
Sending 100, 100-byte ICMP Echoes to 10.108.14.83, timeout is 2 seconds:
!!!!!.....!!!!!.....!!!!!.....!!!!!.....!!!!!.....!!!!!.....!!!!!
.....!!!!!.....!!!!!.....!
Success rate is 46% (46/100), round-trip min/avg/max = 32/34/40 ms
Acheson#
```

Figure 6.23

The intermittent behavior of traffic to subnet 10.108.14.0 can be observed with these pings. Only 45% are successful.

There is a nonrandom pattern to the ping results: five successful pings alternating with six timeouts. Enabling packet debugging and sending more pings reveals what is happening (Figure 6.24). Acheson is load balancing as it should, with a pattern of 5/5/1 (five packets via E1, five packets via S0, one packet via S1). The packets sent via E1 are successful, but all packets sent across the serial links fail.

```
Acheson#debug ip packet
IP packet debugging is on
Acheson#ping
Protocol [ip]:
Target IP address: 10.108.14.83
Repeat count [5]: 15
Datagram size [100]:
Timeout in seconds [2]:
Extended commands [n]:
Sweep range of sizes [n]:
Type escape sequence to abort.
Sending 15, 100-byte ICMP Echoes to 10.108.14.83, timeout is 2 seconds:
IP: s=172.16.1.1 (local), d=10.108.14.83 (Serial0), len 100, sending.
IP: s=172.16.1.1 (local), d=10.108.14.83 (Serial0), len 100, sending.
IP: s=172.16.1.1 (local), d=10.108.14.83 (Serial0), len 100, sending.
IP: s=172.16.2.1 (local), d=10.108.14.83 (Serial1), len 100, sending.!!!!!
IP: s=192.168.3.1 (local), d=10.108.14.83 (Ethernet1), len 100, sending
IP: s=10.108.14.83 (Ethernet1), d=192.168.3.1 (Ethernet1), len 114, rcvd 3
IP: s=192.168.3.1 (local), d=10.108.14.83 (Ethernet1), len 100, sending
IP: s=10.108.14.83 (Ethernet1), d=192.168.3.1 (Ethernet1), len 114, rcvd 3
IP: s=192.168.3.1 (local), d=10.108.14.83 (Ethernet1), len 100, sending
IP: s=10.108.14.83 (Ethernet1), d=192.168.3.1 (Ethernet1), len 114, rcvd 3
IP: s=192.168.3.1 (local), d=10.108.14.83 (Ethernet1), len 100, sending
IP: s=10.108.14.83 (Ethernet1), d=192.168.3.1 (Ethernet1), len 114, rcvd 3
IP: s=192.168.3.1 (local), d=10.108.14.83 (Ethernet1), len 100, sending
IP: s=10.108.14.83 (Ethernet1), d=192.168.3.1 (Ethernet1), len 114, rcvd 3
IP: s=192.168.3.1 (local), d=10.108.14.83 (Serial0), len 100, sending.
IP: s=172.16.1.1 (local), d=10.108.14.83 (Serial0), len 100, sending.
IP: s=172.16.1.1 (local), d=10.108.14.83 (Serial0), len 100, sending.
IP: s=172.16.1.1 (local), d=10.108.14.83 (Serial0), len 100, sending.
IP: s=172.16.1.1 (local), d=10.108.14.83 (Serial0), len 100, sending.
IP: s=172.16.2.1 (local), d=10.108.14.83 (Serial1), len 100, sending.
Success rate is 33% (5/15), round-trip min/avg/max = 36/36/40 ms
Acheson#
```

Figure 6.24

Sending 15 pings with packet debugging turned on reveals a large clue. Packets taking the route via Lovett successfully reach their destination, whereas all packets through Kennan fail.

Further investigation uncovers a disconnected lobe cable at Kennan's Token Ring interface, and the problem is repaired. The question remains: Why did the routes via the serial interfaces stay up? They were not marked unreachable, because Kennan's ethernet interface was still good. The router is summarizing network 10.0.0.0 to network 172.16.0.0, so there is no way for it to communicate the failed subnet.

LOOKING AHEAD

The final case study, and other examples, demonstrates some of the limitations and vulnerabilities of classful routing protocols. Chapter 7, "Routing Information Protocol Version 2," presents RIPv2, the first of the classless protocols. More important, Chapter 7 discusses how classless protocols overcome such problems as discontiguous subnets and segmented networks and how their support of variable-length subnet masking allows more efficient address space design.

SUMMARY TABLE: CHAPTER 6
COMMAND REVIEW

Command	Description
bandwidth *kilobits*	Specifies the bandwidth parameter, in kilobits per second, on an interface. Used by some routing protocols to calculate metrics; has no influence on the actual bandwidth of the data link.
delay *tens-of-microseconds*	Specifies the delay parameter, in tens of microseconds, on an interface. Used by some routing protocols to calculate metrics; has no influence on the actual delay of the data link.
ip address *ip-address mask* [secondary]	Specifies the ip address and address mask of an interface.
maximum-paths *maximum*	Specifies the maximum number of parallel routes an IP routing protocol can support, from one to six, with a default of four.
metric holddown	Toggles the IGRP holddown on or off.
metric maximum-hops *hops*	Specifies the maximum number of hops IGRP can advertise before a route is marked unreachable, with a maximum of 255 and a default of 100.
metric weights *tos k1 k2 k3 k4 k5*	Specifies how much weight the bandwidth, load, delay, and reliability parameters should be given in the IGRP and EIGRP metric calculations.
neighbor *ip-address*	Defines a unicast address to which a RIP, IGRP, or EGP routing update should be send.
network *network-number*	Specifies the network address of one or more directly connected interfaces on which IGRP, EIGRP, or RIP processes should be enabled.
offset-list {access-list-number | name}{in | out} *offset* [*type number*]	Specifies a number of hops (for RIP) or additional delay (for IGRP) to be added to the metrics of incoming or outgoing route advertisements.
passive-interface *type number*	Disables the transmission of routing updates on an interface.
router igrp *autonomous-system*	Enables the indicated IGRP routing process on a router.
show interface [*type number*]	Displays the configured and monitored characteristics of an interface.

Command	Description
show ip route [*address* [*mask*]][*protocol* [*process-ID*]]	Displays the current routing table as a whole or by entry.
timers basic *update invalid holddown flush* [*sleeptime*]	Adjusts EGP, RIP, or IGRP process timers.
traffic-share {balanced | min}	Specifies whether an IGRP or EIGRP routing process should use unequal-cost load balancing or equal cost only.
validate-update-source	Toggles the source address validation function of RIP and IGRP routing processes.
variance *multiplier*	Specifies a multiplier by which a route metric can vary from the lowest-cost metric and still be included in an unequal-cost load balancing group.

RECOMMENDED READING

Hedrick, C. L. "An Introduction to IGRP." Rutgers University, August 1991. This paper can be downloaded from the following site: http://cco.cisco.com/warp/public/103/5.html. Although dated, it remains the best publicly available paper on the technical operation of IGRP.

REVIEW QUESTIONS

1. Which UDP port number is used to access IGRP?
2. What is the maximum IGRP internetwork diameter, in hops?
3. What is the default update period for IGRP?
4. Why does IGRP specify an autonomous system number?
5. Referring to Figure 6.11, will the router McCloy advertise 192.168.1.0 as an interior, system, or external route? Similarly, as what type of route will Acheson advertise 172.16.0.0?

6. What is the default IGRP holddown time?

7. Which variables can IGRP use to calculate its composite metric?

8. How many entries can be carried within a single IGRP update packet?

CONFIGURATION EXERCISES

1. Write configurations for the six routers in Figure 6.25 to route to all subnets via IGRP. Use autonomous system number 50.

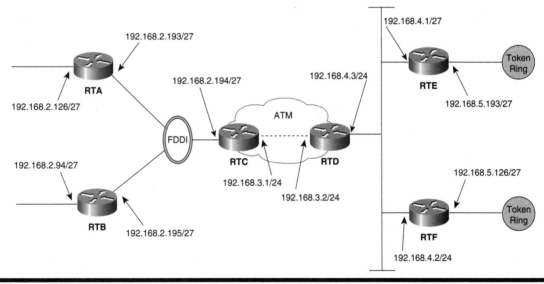

Figure 6.25

The internetwork for Configuration Exercises 1 through 3.

2. Figures 6.26 through 6.29 show the outgoing interfaces for the route from subnet 192.168.2.96/27 to subnet 192.168.5.96/27. Assuming that IGRP is using the default bandwidth and delay metrics, calculate the composite metric of this route.

```
RTA#show interface fddi0
Fddi0 is up, line protocol is up
  Hardware is DAS FDDI, address is 00e0.1e8e.d1d9 (bia 00e0.1e8e.d1d9)
  Internet address is 192.168.2.193/27
  MTU 4470 bytes, BW 100000 Kbit, DLY 100 usec, rely 255/255, load 1/255
  Encapsulation SNAP, loopback not set, keepalive not set
  ARP type: SNAP, ARP Timeout 04:00:00
  Phy-A state is off, neighbor is Unknown, status no signal
  Phy-B state is off, neighbor is Unknown, status no signal
  ECM is out, CFM is isolated, RMT is isolated
  Requested token rotation 5000 usec, negotiated 5017 usec
  Configured tvx is 3400 usec, using 5242.90 usec, ring not operational
  0 SMT frames processed, 0 dropped, 20 SMT buffers
  Upstream neighbor 0000.f800.0000, downstream neighbor 0000.f800.0000
  Last input never, output never, output hang never
  Last clearing of "show interface" counters never
  Queuing strategy: fifo
  Output queue 0/40, 0 drops; input queue 0/75, 0 drops
  5 minute input rate 0 bits/sec, 0 packets/sec
  5 minute output rate 0 bits/sec, 0 packets/sec
    0 packets input, 0 bytes, 0 no buffer
    Received 0 broadcasts, 0 runts, 0 giants
    0 input errors, 0 CRC, 0 frame, 0 overrun, 0 ignored, 0 abort
    0 packets output, 0 bytes, 0 underruns
    0 output errors, 0 collisions, 2 interface resets
    0 output buffer failures, 0 output buffers swapped out
    2 transitions, 0 traces
RTA#
```

Figure 6.26

The FDDI interface of RTA in Figure 6.25..

```
RTC# show interfaces atm 3/1
ATM3/1 is up, line protocol is up
  Hardware is cxBus ATM
  Internet address is 192.168.3.1, subnet mask is 255.255.255.0
  MTU 4470 bytes, BW 155000 Kbit, DLY 70 usec, rely 255/255, load 1/255
  Encapsulation ATM, loopback not set, keepalive set (10 sec)
  Encapsulation(s): AAL5, PVC mode
  256 TX buffers, 256 RX buffers, 1024 Maximum VCs, 1 Current VCs
  Signalling vc = 1, vpi = 0, vci = 5
  ATM NSAP address: 14.84D3.01.6A3A23.8340.DEAC.F021.8357.2192.A78E.13
  Last input 0:00:05, output 0:00:05, output hang never
  Last clearing of "show interface" counters never
  Output queue 0/40, 0 drops; input queue 0/75, 0 drops
  Five minute input rate 0 bits/sec, 0 packets/sec
  Five minute output rate 0 bits/sec, 0 packets/sec
     144 packets input, 3148 bytes, 0 no buffer
     Received 0 broadcasts, 0 runts, 0 giants
     0 input errors, 0 CRC, 0 frame, 0 overrun, 0 ignored, 0 abort
     154 packets output, 4228 bytes, 0 underruns
     0 output errors, 0 collisions, 1 interface resets, 0 restarts
```

Figure 6.27

The ATM interface of RTC in Figure 6.25.

```
RTD#show interface ethernet1/2
Ethernet1/2 is up, line protocol is up
  Hardware is Lance, address is 0000.0c0a.2c51 (bia 0000.0c0a.2c51)
  Internet address is 192.168.4.3/24
  MTU 1500 bytes, BW 10000 Kbit, DLY 1000 usec, rely 255/255, load 1/255
  Encapsulation ARPA, loopback not set, keepalive set (10 sec)
  ARP type: ARPA, ARP Timeout 04:00:00
  Last input 00:00:00, output 00:00:06, output hang never
  Last clearing of "show interface" counters never
  Queueing strategy: fifo
  Output queue 0/40, 0 drops; input queue 0/75, 0 drops
  5 minute input rate 0 bits/sec, 0 packets/sec
  5 minute output rate 0 bits/sec, 0 packets/sec
     85496 packets input, 8284044 bytes, 0 no buffer
     Received 85421 broadcasts, 0 runts, 0 giants, 0 throttles
     0 input errors, 0 CRC, 0 frame, 0 overrun, 0 ignored, 0 abort
     0 input packets with dribble condition detected
     38594 packets output, 3478807 bytes, 0 underruns
     0 output errors, 1 collisions, 5 interface resets
     0 babbles, 0 late collision, 15 deferred
     0 lost carrier, 0 no carrier
     0 output buffer failures, 0 output buffers swapped out
RTD#
```

Figure 6.28

The Ethernet interface of RTD in Figure 6.25.

```
RTF#show interface tokenring0
TokenRing0 is up, line protocol is up
  Hardware is TMS380, address is 0000.3090.c7df (bia 0000.3090.c7df)
  Internet address is 192.168.5.126/27
  MTU 4464 bytes, BW 16000 Kbit, DLY 630 usec, rely 255/255, load 1/255
  Encapsulation SNAP, loopback not set, keepalive set (10 sec)
  ARP type: SNAP, ARP Timeout 04:00:00
  Ring speed: 16Mbps
  Single ring node, Transparent Bridge capable
  Group Address: 0x00000000, Functional Address: 0x08000000
  Ethernet Transit OUI: 0x000000
  Last input 00:00:03, output 00:00:03, output hang never
  Last clearing of "show interface" counters never
  Output queue 0/40, 0 drops; input queue 0/75, 0 drops
  5 minute input rate 0 bits/sec, 0 packets/sec
  5 minute output rate 0 bits/sec, 0 packets/sec
     29245 packets input, 1934430 bytes, 0 no buffer
     Received 75700 broadcasts, 0 runts, 0 giants
     0 input errors, 0 CRC, 0 frame, 0 overrun, 0 ignored, 0 abort
     31612 packets output, 2220089 bytes, 0 underruns
     0 output errors, 0 collisions, 2 interface resets
     0 output buffer failures, 0 output buffers swapped out
     5 transitions
RTF#
```

Figure 6.29

The Token Ring interface for RTF in Figure 6.25.

3. The command **metric weights 0 1 1 0 1 1** has been added to the IGRP configurations of the six routers in Figure 6.25. Recalculate the composite metric for the route from subnet 192.168.2.96/27 to subnet 192.168.5.96/27.

4. The two routers in Figure 6.30 are running IGRP. The bandwidths and delays shown are configured on the interfaces at both ends of their respective links. What commands must be added to the routers to enable unequal-cost load balancing across all links?

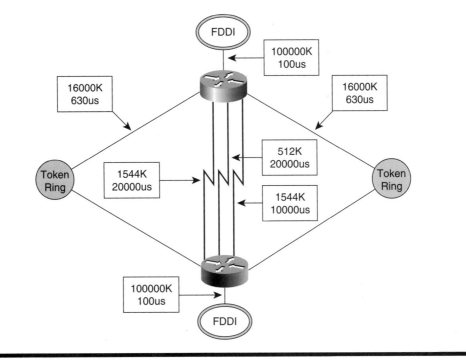

Figure 6.30
The internetwork for Configuration Exercise 4.

TROUBLESHOOTING EXERCISES

1. Figure 6.31 shows the routing table of RTA in Figure 6.32. Although there are no reachability problems in this internetwork, RTA's routing table contains an unexpected entry: Network 192.168.3.0 is reachable via the less-desirable serial links. In Figures 6.33 through 6.36, debugging is used to observe the IGRP updates on the four routers. Although the cause of the problem cannot be determined from these debug messages, the router from which the problem originates can be discovered. Based on the information given, create a hypothesis that explains the most likely cause of the problem.

```
RTA#show ip route
Codes:  C - connected, S - static, I - IGRP, R - RIP, M - mobile, B - BGP
        D - EIGRP, EX - EIGRP external, O - OSPF, IA - OSPF inter area
        N1 - OSPF NSSA external type 1, N2 - OSPF NSSA external type 2
        E1 - OSPF external type 1, E2 - OSPF external type 2, E - EGP
        i - IS-IS, L1 - IS-IS level-1, L2 - IS-IS level-2, * - candidate default,
        U - per-user static route, o - ODR

Gateway of last resort is not set

     10.0.0.0/24 is subnetted, 1 subnets
C       10.1.1.0 is directly connected, Serial1
I  192.168.1.0/24 [100/8676] via 172.17.16.56, 00:00:38, Ethernet0
I  192.168.2.0/24 [100/1200] via 172.17.16.56, 00:00:38, Ethernet0
I  192.168.3.0/24 [100/12476] via 172.16.17.9, 00:00:19, Serial0
     172.16.0.0/30 is subnetted, 1 subnets
C       172.16.17.8 is directly connected, Serial0
     172.17.0.0/28 is subnetted, 1 subnets
C       172.17.16.48 is directly connected, Ethernet0
RTA#
```

Figure 6.31

The routing table of RTA in Figure 6.32.

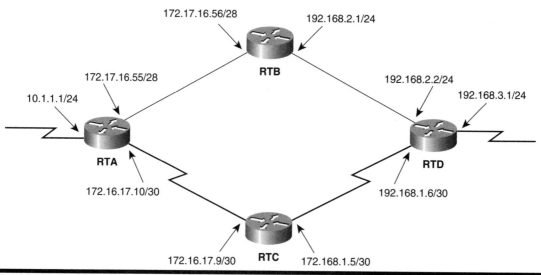

Figure 6.32

The internetwork for Troubleshooting Exercise 1.

```
RTA#debug ip igrp transactions
IGRP protocol debugging is on
RTA#
IGRP:   received update from 172.17.16.56 on Ethernet0
        network 192.168.1.0, metric 8676 (neighbor 8576)
        network 192.168.2.0, metric 1200 (neighbor 1100)
IGRP:   sending update to 255.255.255.255 via Ethernet0 (172.17.16.55)
        network 10.0.0.0, metric=8476
        network 192.168.3.0, metric=12476
        network 172.16.0.0, metric=8476
IGRP:   sending update to 255.255.255.255 via Serial0 (172.16.17.10)
        network 10.0.0.0, metric=8476
        network 192.168.1.0, metric=8676
        network 192.168.2.0, metric=1200
        network 172.17.0.0, metric=1100
IGRP:   sending update to 255.255.255.255 via Serial1 (10.1.1.1)
        network 192.168.1.0, metric=8676
        network 192.168.2.0, metric=1200
        network 192.168.3.0, metric=12476
        network 172.16.0.0, metric=8476
        network 172.17.0.0, metric=1100
IGRP:   received update from 172.16.17.9 on Serial0
        network 192.168.1.0, metric 10476 (neighbor 8476)
        network 192.168.2.0, metric 10576 (neighbor 8576)
        network 192.168.3.0, metric 12476 (neighbor 10476)
```

Figure 6.33

The IGRP updates sent and received by RTA in Figure 6.32.

```
RTB#debug ip igrp transactions
IGRP protocol debugging is on
RTB#
IGRP:   received update from 172.17.16.55 on Ethernet0
        network 10.0.0.0, metric 8576 (neighbor 8476)
        network 192.168.3.0, metric 12576 (neighbor 12476)
        network 172.16.0.0, metric 8576 (neighbor 8476)
IGRP:   sending update to 255.255.255.255 via Ethernet0 (172.17.16.56)
        network 192.168.1.0, metric=8576
        network 192.168.2.0, metric=1100
IGRP:   sending update to 255.255.255.255 via Ethernet1 (192.168.2.1)
        network 10.0.0.0, metric=8576
        network 172.16.0.0, metric=8576
        network 172.17.0.0, metric=1100
IGRP:   received update from 192.168.2.2 on Ethernet1
        network 192.168.1.0, metric 8576 (neighbor 8476)
        network 192.168.3.0, metric 8576 (neighbor 8476)
```

Figure 6.34

The IGRP updates sent and received by RTB in Figure 6.32.

```
RTC#debug ip igrp transactions
IGRP protocol debugging is on
RTC#
IGRP:   sending update to 255.255.255.255 via Serial0 (172.16.17.9)
        network 192.168.1.0, metric=8476
        network 192.168.2.0, metric=8576
        network 192.168.3.0, metric=10476
IGRP:   sending update to 255.255.255.255 via Serial1 (192.168.1.5)
        network 10.0.0.0, metric=10476
        network 172.16.0.0, metric=8476
        network 172.17.0.0, metric=8576
IGRP:   received update from 172.16.17.10 on Serial0
        network 10.0.0.0, metric 10476 (neighbor 8476)
        network 192.168.1.0, metric 10676 (neighbor 8676)
        network 192.168.2.0, metric 8676 (neighbor 1200)
        network 172.17.0.0, metric 8576 (neighbor 1100)
IGRP:   received update from 192.168.1.6 on Serial1
        network 10.0.0.0, metric 10676 (neighbor 8676)
        network 192.168.2.0, metric 8576 (neighbor 1100)
        network 192.168.3.0, metric 10476 (neighbor 8476)
        network 172.16.0.0, metric 10676 (neighbor 8676)
        network 172.17.0.0, metric 8676 (neighbor 1200)
```

Figure 6.35

The IGRP updates sent and received by RTC in Figure 6.32.

2. Users on subnets 172.16.1.8/29 and 172.16.2.16/29 in Figure 6.37 are reporting that they cannot connect to servers on subnet 172.17.1.8/29. Figures 6.38 through 6.41 show analyzer captures of the IGRP updates on the two Ethernet links. Part of the IP header is also shown in each screen. Determine which router originated each update and then find the problem.

```
RTD#debug ip igrp transactions
IGRP protocol debugging is on
RTD#
IGRP: received update from 192.168.2.1 on Ethernet0·
      network 10.0.0.0, metric 8676 (neighbor 8576)
      network 172.16.0.0, metric 8676 (neighbor 8576)
      network 172.17.0.0, metric 1200 (neighbor 1100)
IGRP: sending update to 255.255.255.255 via Ethernet0 (192.168.2.2)
      network 192.168.1.0, metric=8476
      network 192.168.3.0, metric=8476
IGRP: sending update to 255.255.255.255 via Serial0 (192.168.1.6)
      network 10.0.0.0, metric=8676
      network 192.168.2.0, metric=1100
      network 192.168.3.0, metric=8476
      network 172.16.0.0, metric=8676
      network 172.17.0.0, metric=1200
IGRP: sending update to 255.255.255.255 via Serial1 (192.168.3.1)
      network 10.0.0.0, metric=8676
      network 192.168.1.0, metric=8476
      network 192.168.2.0, metric=1100
      network 172.16.0.0, metric=8676
      network 172.17.0.0, metric=1200
IGRP: received update from 192.168.1.5 on Serial0
      network 10.0.0.0, metric 12476 (neighbor 10476)
      network 172.16.0.0, metric 10476 (neighbor 8476)
      network 172.17.0.0, metric 10576 (neighbor 8576)
```

Figure 6.36

The IGRP updates sent and received by RTD in Figure 6.32.

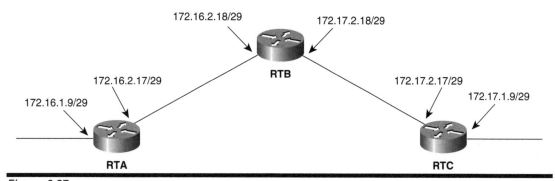

Figure 6.37

The internetwork for Troubleshooting Exercise 2.

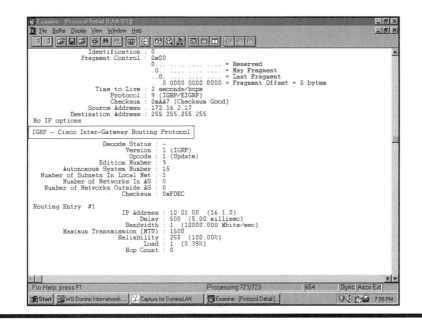

Figure 6.38

An analyzer capture of an IGRP update from the internetwork in Figure 6.37.

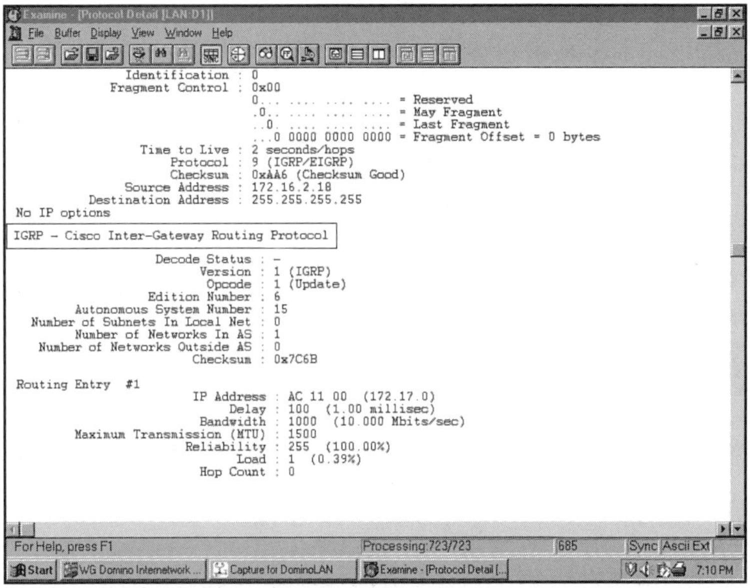

Figure 6.39

An analyzer capture of an IGRP update from the internetwork in Figure 6.37.

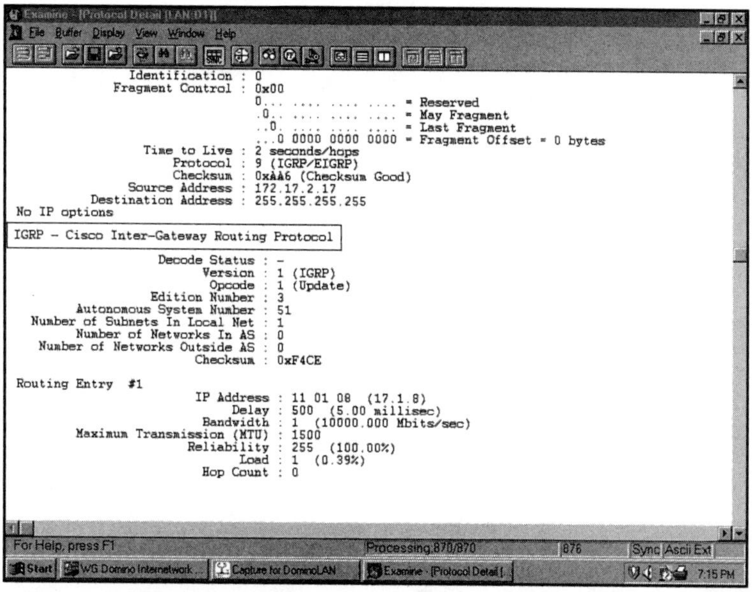

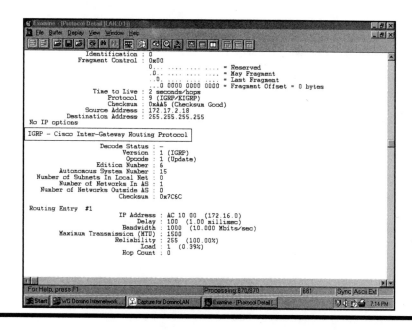

Figure 6.40

An analyzer capture of an IGRP update from the internetwork in Figure 6.37.

Figure 6.41

An analyzer capture of an IGRP update from the internetwork in Figure 6.37.

Routing Information Protocol Version 2

RIPv2 is defined in RFC 1723[1] and is supported in IOS versions 11.1 and later. RIPv2 is not a new protocol; rather, it is RIPv1 with some extensions to bring it more up-to-date with modern routing environments. These extensions are:

- Subnet masks carried with each route entry

- Authentication of routing updates

- Next-hop addresses carried with each route entry

- External route tags

- Multicast route updates

The most important of these extensions is the addition of a Subnet Mask field to the routing update entries, enabling the use of variable-length subnet masks and qualifying RIPv2 as a classless routing protocol.

RIPv2 is the first of the classless routing protocols discussed in this book. As such, this chapter serves as an introduction to classless routing, as well as to RIPv2.

---

[1] *Supplemental to this RFC are RFC 1721, "RIP Version 2 Protocol Analysis," and RFC 1722, "RIP Version 2 Protocol Applicability Statement."*

OPERATION OF RIPv2

All of the operational procedures, timers, and stability functions of RIPv1 remain the same in version 2, with the exception of the broadcast updates. RIPv2 multicasts updates to other RIPv2-speaking routers, using the reserved class D address 224.0.0.9. The advantage of multicasting is that devices on the local network that are not concerned with RIP routing do not have to spend time "unwrapping" broadcast packets from the router. The multicast updates are examined further in the section, "Compatibility with RIPv1."

After a look at how the RIP message format accommodates the version 2 extensions, this section focuses on the operation and benefits of these additional features.

RIPv2 Message Format

The RIPv2 message format is shown in Figure 7.1; the basic structure is the same as for RIPv1. All the extensions to the original protocol are carried within what were unused fields. Like version 1, RIPv2 updates can contain entries for up to 25 routes. Also like version 1, RIPv2 operates from UDP port 520 and has a maximum datagram size (with an eight-byte UDP header) of 512 octets.

Command will always be set to either one, signifying a request message, or two, signifying a response message.

Version will be set to two for RIPv2. If it is set to zero, or if it is set to one but the message is not a valid RIPv1 format, the message will be discarded. RIPv2 will process valid RIPv1 messages.

Address Family Identifier is set to two for IP. The only exception is a request for a router's (or host's) full routing table, in which case it will be set to zero.

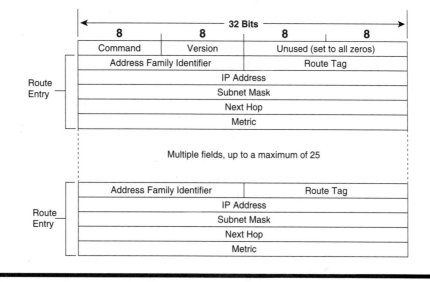

Figure 7.1

RIPv2 takes advantage of the unused fields of the version 1 message so that the extensions do not change the basic format.

Route Tag provides a field for tagging external routes or routes that have been redistributed into the RIPv2 process. One suggested use of this 16-bit field is to carry the autonomous system number of routes that have been imported from an external routing protocol. Although RIP itself does not use this field, external routing protocols connected to a RIP domain in multiple locations may use the route tag field to exchange information across the RIP domain. The field may also be used to group certain external routes for easier control within the RIP domain. The use of route tags is discussed further in Chapter 14, "Route Maps."

IP Address is the address of the destination of the route. It may be a major network address, a subnet, or a host route.

Subnet Mask is 32-bit mask that identifies the network and subnet portion of the IP address. The significance of this field is discussed in the section "Variable-Length Subnet Masking."

Next Hop identifies a better next-hop address, if one exists, than the address of the advertising router. That is, it indicates a next-hop address, on the same subnet, that is metrically closer to the destination than the advertising router is. If the field is set to all zeros (0.0.0.0), the address of the advertising router is the best next-hop address. An example of where this field would be useful is given at the end of this section.

Metric is a hop count between 1 and 16.

Figure 7.2 shows four routers connected to an Ethernet link.[2] Jicarilla, Mescalero, and Chiricahua are all in autonomous system number 65501 and are speaking RIPv2. Chiricahua is a border router between autonomous system 65501 and autonomous system 65502; in the second autonomous system, it speaks BGP to Lipan.

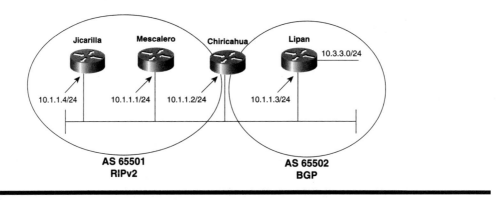

Figure 7.2
Although they share a common data link, Jicarilla and Mescalero speak only RIPv2; Lipan speaks only BGP. Chiricahua is responsible for informing the first two routers of any routes learned from the latter.

---

[2]   *This figure is an adaptation of an example presented by Gary Malkin in RFC 1722.*

Here, Chiricahua is advertising routes it learns from BGP to the RIP-speaking routers (Figure 7.3).[3] In its RIPv2 advertisements, Chiricahua will use the Route Tag field to indicate that subnet 10.3.3.0, with a mask of 255.255.255.0, is in autonomous system 65502 (0xFFDE). Chiricahua will also use the Next Hop field to inform Jicarilla and Mescalero that the best next-hop address to 10.3.3.0 is Lipan's interface, 10.1.1.3, rather than its own interface. Note that because Lipan does not run RIP, and Jicarilla and Mescalero do not run BGP, Jicarilla and Mescalero have no way of knowing directly that Lipan is the best next-hop router, even though it is reachable on the same subnet.

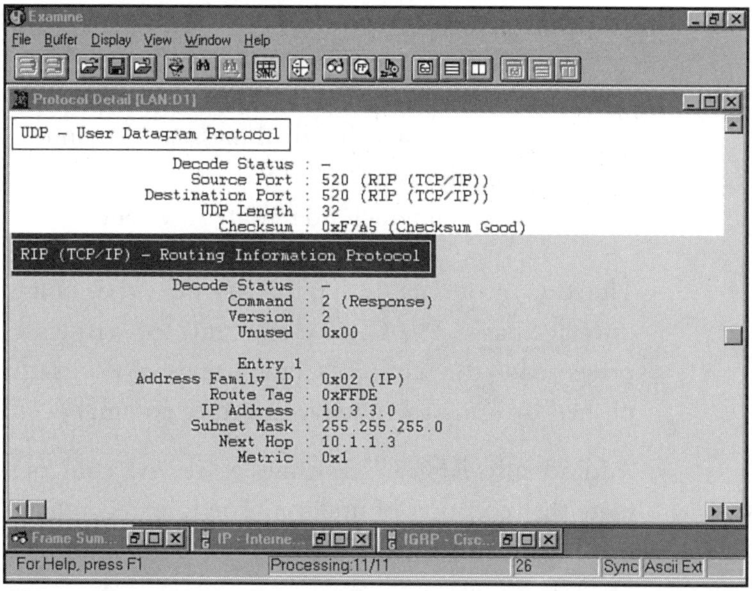

Figure 7.3

This protocol capture of a RIPv2 update from Chiricahua shows the Route Tag, Subnet Mask, and Next Hop fields being used to advertise subnet 10.3.3.0.

---

[3]   *Redistribution refers to the practice of advertising routes learned from one protocol to another protocol; it is discussed in detail in Chapter 11, "Route Redistribution."*

Compatibility with RIPv1

RIPv1 handles updates in a flexible manner. If the Version field indicates version 1 but any bits of any unused fields are set to one, the update is discarded. If the version is greater than 1, the fields defined as unused in version 1 are ignored and the message is processed. As a result, newer editions of the protocol, like RIPv2, can be backward compatible with RIPv1.

Compatibility settings
for RIPv1 and RIPv2

RFC 1723 defines a "compatibility switch" with four settings, which allows versions 1 and 2 to interoperate:

1. *RIP-1,* in which only RIPv1 messages are transmitted
2. *RIP-1 Compatibility,* which causes RIPv2 to broadcast its messages instead of multicast them so that RIPv1 may receive them
3. *RIP-2,* in which RIPv2 messages are multicast to destination address 224.0.0.9
4. *None,* in which no updates are sent

The RFC recommends that these switches be configurable on a per interface basis. The Cisco commands for settings 1 through 3 are presented in the section "Configuring RIPv2;" setting 4 is accomplished by using the **passive-interface** command.

Settings for controlling
reception of updates

Additionally, RFC 1723 defines a "receive control switch" to regulate the reception of updates. The four recommended settings of this switch are:

1. RIP-1 Only
2. RIP-2 Only
3. Both
4. None

This switch should also be configurable on a per interface basis. The Cisco commands for settings 1 through 3 are also presented in the configuration section of this chapter. Setting 4 can be accomplished by using an access list to filter UDP source port 520, by not including a network statement for the interface,[4] or by configuring a route filter as discussed in Chapter 13, "Route Filtering."

Classless Route Lookups

Chapter 5, "Routing Information Protocol (RIP)," explains classful route lookups, in which a destination address is first matched to its major network address in the routing table and is then matched to a subnet of the major network. If no match is found at either of these steps, the packet is dropped.

This default behavior can be changed, even for classful routing protocols such as RIPv1 and IGRP, by entering the global command **ip classless**. When a router performs classless route lookups, it does not pay attention to the class of the destination address. Instead, it performs a bit-by-bit best match between the destination address and all its known routes. This capability can be very useful when working with default routes, as demonstrated in Chapter 12, "Default Routes and On-Demand Routing." When coupled with the other features of classless routing protocols, classless route lookups can be very powerful.

Classless Routing Protocols

The true defining characteristic of classless routing protocols is the capability to carry subnet masks in their route advertisements.

Classless routing protocols carry subnet masks in their routing updates.

---

[4] *This method would work only if no other interface on the router on which RIP should run is attached to the same major network.*

One benefit of having a mask associated with each route is that the all-zeros and all-ones subnets are now available for use. Chapter 2, "TCP/IP Review," explained that classful routing protocols cannot distinguish between an all-zeros subnet (172.16.0.0, for example) and the major network number (172.16.0.0). Likewise, they cannot distinguish between a broadcast on the all-ones subnet (172.16.255.255) and an all-subnets broadcast (172.16.255.255).

If the subnet masks are included, this difficulty disappears. You can readily see that 172.16.0.0/16 is the major network number and that 172.16.0.0/24 is an all-zeros subnet. 172.168.255.255/16 and 172.16.255.255/24 are just as distinguishable.

By default, the Cisco IOS rejects an attempt to configure an all-zeros subnet as an invalid address/mask combination even if a classless routing protocol is running. To override this default behavior, enter the global command **ip subnet-zero**.

Classless routing protocols enable the use of variable-length subnet masking.

A much greater benefit of having a subnet mask associated with each route is being able to use variable-length subnet masking (VLSM) and to summarize a group of major network addresses with a single aggregate address. Variable-length subnet masks are examined in the following section, and address aggregation (or supernetting) is introduced in Chapter 8, "Enhanced Interior Gateway Routing Protocol (EIGRP)."

Variable-Length Subnet Masking

If a subnet mask can be individually associated with each destination address advertised throughout an internetwork, there is no reason why all the masks must be of equal length. That fact is the basis for VLSM.

A simple application of VLSM is shown in Figure 7.4. Each data link of the internetwork shown must have a uniquely identifiable subnet address, and each subnet address must contain enough host addresses to accommodate the devices attached to the data link.

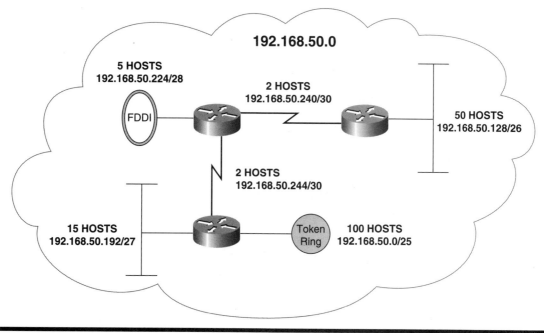

Figure 7.4

Using VLSM, the class C address shown can be subnetted to accommodate this internetwork and the hosts on each of its data links.

Given the class C network address assigned to this internet, subnetting cannot be accomplished at all without VLSM. The token ring, with its need for 100 host addresses, requires a 25-bit mask (1 bit of subnetting); a mask any longer would not leave enough host bits. But if all masks must be of equal length, only one more subnet can be created from the class C address.[5] There would not be enough subnets to go around.

With VLSM the widely varying host address requirements of the internetwork of Figure 7.4 can be met using a class C network address. Table 7.1 shows the subnets and the address ranges available within each.

Table 7.1 *The subnets of Figure 7.4 .*

Subnet/Mask	Address Range	Broadcast Address
192.168.50.0/25	192.168.50.1–192.168.50.126	192.168.50.127
192.168.50.128/26	192.168.50.129–192.168.50.190	192.168.50.191
192.168.50.192/27	192.168.50.193–192.168.50.222	192.168.50.223
192.168.50.224/28	192.168.50.225–192.168.50.238	192.168.50.239
192.168.50.240/30	192.168.50.241–192.168.50.242	192.168.50.243
192.168.50.244/30	192.168.50.245–192.168.50.246	192.168.50.247

Many people, including many who work with VLSM, make the technique more complicated than it is. The complete key to VLSM is this: After a network address is subnetted in the standard fashion, those subnets can themselves be subnetted. In fact, one will occasionally hear VLSM referred to as "sub-subnetting."

VLSM can be thought of as sub-subnetting.

A close examination of the addresses in Table 7.1 (in binary, as always) will reveal how VLSM works.[6] First, a 25-bit mask is used to divide the network address into two subnets: 192.168.50.0/25 and 192.168.50.128/25. The first subnet provides 126 host addresses to meet the needs of the token ring in Figure 7.4.

---

[5]   *This statement assumes that the all-zeros and all-ones subnets—the only subnets available with a single bit of subnetting—can be routed.*

[6]   *The reader is strongly encouraged to work through this entire example in binary.*

From Chapter 2, you know that subnetting involves expanding the default network mask so that some host bits are interpreted as network bits. This same procedure is applied to the remaining subnet 192.168.50.128/25. One of the Ethernets requires 50 host addresses, so the mask of the remaining subnet is expanded to 26 bits. This step provides two sub-subnets, 192.168.50.128/26 and 192.168.192/26, each with 62 available host addresses. The first sub-subnet is taken for the larger Ethernet, leaving the second to again be subnetted for the other data links.

This procedure is repeated twice more to provide the necessary subnets of the necessary size for the smaller Ethernet and the FDDI ring. A subnet of 192.168.50.240/28 remains, as do two serial links requiring subnets. Any point-to-point link will, by its very nature, require only two host addresses—one at each end. Thirty-bit masks are used to create the two serial link subnets, each with just two available host addresses.

Point-to-point links, requiring a subnet address but only two host addresses per subnet, are one justification for using VLSM. For example, Figure 7.5 shows a typical WAN topology with remote routers connected via Frame Relay PVCs to a hub router. Modern practice usually calls for each of these PVCs to be configured on a point-to-point subinterface.[7] Without VLSM, equal-size subnets would be necessary; the size would be dictated by the subnet with the largest number of host devices.

Suppose a class B address is used for the network in Figure 7.5 and each router is attached to several LANs, each of which may have up to 175 attached devices. A 24-bit mask would be necessary for each subnet, including each PVC. Consequently, for every PVC in the internetwork, 252 addresses are wasted. With VLSM, a single

---

[7] *Subinterfaces are outside the scope of this book. Readers who are not already familiar with these useful tools are referred to the* Cisco Configuration Guide.

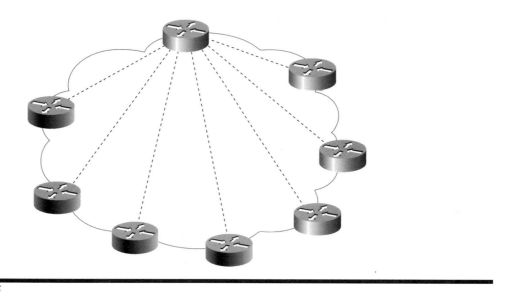

Figure 7.5

VLSM allows each of these PVCs to be configured as a separate subnet without wasting host addresses.

subnet can be selected and sub-subnetted with a 30-bit mask; enough subnets will be created for up to 64 point-to-point links (Figure 7.6).

Examples of VLSM address designs appear in this and subsequent chapters. Chapter 8 introduces another major justification for using VLSM, hierarchical addressing, as well as address aggregation.

Authentication

A security concern with any routing protocol is the possibility of a router accepting invalid routing updates. The source of invalid updates may be an attacker trying to maliciously disrupt the inter-network or trying to capture packets by tricking the router into sending them to the wrong destination. A more mundane source of invalid updates may be a malfunctioning router. RIPv2 includes

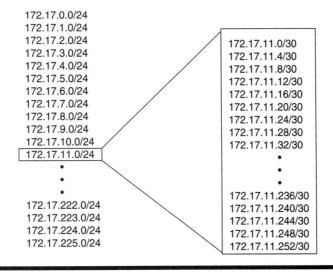

Figure 7.6
This class B address has been subnetted with a 24-bit mask. 172.17.11.0 has been sub-subnetted with a 30-bit mask; the resulting 64 subnets can be assigned to point-to-point links.

the capability to authenticate the source of a routing update by including a password.

Authentication is supported by modifying what would normally be the first route entry of the RIP message, as shown in Figure 7.7. With authentication the maximum number of entries a single update can carry is reduced to 24. The presence of authentication is indicated by setting the Address Family Identifier field to all ones (0xFFFF). The Authentication Type for simple password authentication is two (0x0002), and the remaining 16 octets carry an alphanumeric password of up to 16 characters. The password is left justified in the field, and if the password is less than 16 octets, the unused bits of the field are set to zero.

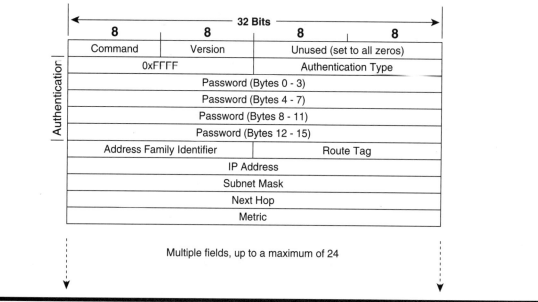

Figure 7.7

The RIPv2 authentication information, when configured, is carried in the first route entry space.

| | Simple password authentication for RIPv2 is in plain text. |

Figure 7.8 shows an analyzer capture of a RIPv2 message with authentication. The figure also shows a difficulty with the default RIP authentication: The password is transmitted in plain text. Anyone who can capture a packet containing a RIPv2 update message can read the authentication password.

Although RFC 1723 describes only simple password authentication, foresight is shown by including the Authentication Type field. Cisco IOS takes advantage of this feature and provides the option of using MD5 authentication instead of simple password authentication.[8] Cisco uses the first and last route entry spaces for MD5 authentication purposes.

The Cisco IOS supports MD5 authentication for RIPv2.

---
8   *MD5 is described in RFC 1321. A good discussion of MD5 can also be found in the following book: Charlie Kaufman, Radia Perlman, and Mike Spencer.* Network Security: Private Communication in a Public World. *Prentice Hall, 1995, pp. 120–122.*

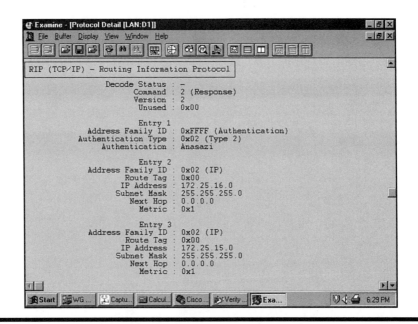

Figure 7.8

When simple password authentication is used, the password is carried in plain text and can be read by anyone who can "sniff" the packet carrying the update.

MD5 is a one-way *message digest* or *secure hash* function, produced by RSA Data Security, Inc. It is also occasionally referred to as a *cryptographic checksum* because it works in somewhat the same way as an arithmetic checksum. MD5 computes a 128-bit hash value from a plain text message of arbitrary length (a RIPv2 update, for instance) and a password. This "fingerprint" is transmitted along with the message. The receiver, knowing the same password, calculates its own hash value. If nothing in the message has changed, the receiver's hash value should match the sender's value transmitted with the message.

Figure 7.9 shows an update from the same router of Figure 7.8, but with MD5 authentication. The authentication type is three, and no password can be seen. Notice that Cisco is using both the first and the last route entry space for authentication information. Because this usage is not part of the open RIPv2 standard, the analyzer indicates "Authentication out of Place."

```
Examine - [Protocol Detail [LAN:D1]]                                    _ 8 X
File  Buffer  Display  View  Window  Help                               _ 8 X
                       Command : 2 (Response)
                       Version : 2
                        Unused : 0x00

                       Entry 1
            Address Family ID : 0xFFFF (Authentication)
            Authentication Type : 0x03 (Unknown Type)
                 Authentication :

                       Entry 2
            Address Family ID : 0x02 (IP)
                     Route Tag : 0x00
                    IP Address : 172.25.16.0
                   Subnet Mask : 255.255.255.0
                      Next Hop : 0.0.0.0
                        Metric : 0x1

                       Entry 3
            Address Family ID : 0x02 (IP)
                     Route Tag : 0x00
                    IP Address : 172.25.15.0
                   Subnet Mask : 255.255.255.0
                      Next Hop : 0.0.0.0
                        Metric : 0x1

Authentication out of Place
                       Entry 4
            Address Family ID : 0xFFFF (Authentication)
            Authentication Type : 0x01 (Unknown Type)
                 Authentication : D.*...\...>..Y..

Start   Exploring -   WG Domin...   Capture for ...   Examine - [.          7:43 PM
```

Figure 7.9

This update was originated from the same router as the update in Figure 7.8, but MD5 authentication is being used.

CONFIGURING RIPv2

Because RIPv2 is merely an enhancement of RIPv1 and not a separate protocol, the commands introduced in Chapter 5 for manipulating timers and metrics and for configuring unicast updates or no updates at all are used in exactly the same way. After a brief look at configuring a RIPv2 process, the rest of this section concentrates on configuring the new extensions.

Case Study: A Basic RIPv2 Configuration

By default, a RIP process configured on a Cisco router sends only RIPv1 messages but listens to both RIPv1 and RIPv2. This default is changed with the **version** command, as in the following example:

```
router rip
  version 2
  network 172.25.0.0
  network 192.168.50.0
```

In this mode, the router sends and receives only RIPv2 messages. Likewise, the router can be configured to send and receive only RIPv1 messages:

```
router rip
  version 1
  network 172.25.0.0
  network 192.168.50.0
```

The default behavior can be restored by entering the command **no version** in config-router mode.

Case Study: Compatibility with RIPv1

The interface-level "compatibility switches" recommended by RFC 1723 are implemented in Cisco IOS with the commands **ip rip send version** and **ip rip receive version**.

The internetwork in Figure 7.10 contains routers speaking both RIPv1 and RIPv2. Additionally, Pojoaque is a Linux host running *routed*, which understands only RIPv1. The configuration of Taos is:

```
interface Ethernet0
  ip address 192.168.50.129 255.255.255.192
  ip rip send version 1
  ip rip receive version 1
!
interface Ethernet1
  ip address 172.25.150.193 255.255.255.240
  ip rip send version 1 2
!
interface Ethernet2
```

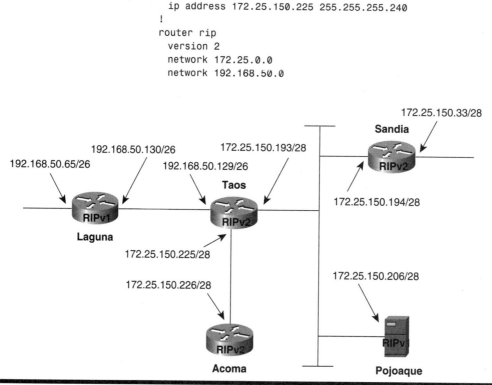

Figure 7.10

Taos is running RIPv2 but must also speak version 1 to some devices.

Because router Laguna is a RIPv1 speaker, E0 of Taos is configured to send and receive RIPv1 updates. E1 is configured to send both version 1 and 2 updates, to accommodate the RIPv1 at Pojoaque and the RIPv2 at Sandia. E2 has no special configuration; it sends and receives version 2 by default.

In Figure 7.11, **debug ip rip** is used to observe the messages sent and received by Taos. There are several points of interest here. First, notice the difference between the traps for RIPv1 and RIPv2 messages. The address mask and the Next Hop and Route Tag fields (both set to all zeros, in this case) of the RIPv2 updates can be observed. Second, it can be observed that interface E1 is broadcasting RIPv1 updates and multicasting RIPv2 updates. Third, because Taos has not been configured to receive RIPv1, the updates from Pojoaque (172.25.150.206) are being ignored. (Pojoaque has been misconfigured and is broadcasting its routing table.)[9]

```
Taos#debug ip rip
RIP protocol debugging is on
Taos#
RIP:  received v2 update from 172.25.150.194 on Ethernet1
      172.25.150.32/28 - 0.0.0.0 in 1 hops
RIP:  ignored v1 packet from 172.25.150.206 (illegal version)
RIP:  sending v1 update to 255.255.255.255 via Ethernet0 (192.168.50.129)
      network 172.25.0.0, metric 1
RIP:  sending v1 update to 255.255.255.255 via Ethernet1 (172.25.150.193)
      subnet 172.25.150.224, metric 1
      network 192.168.50.0, metric 1
RIP:  sending v2 update to 224.0.0.9 via Ethernet1 (172.25.150.193)
      172.25.150.224/28 - 0.0.0.0, metric 1, tag 0
      192.168.50.0/24 - 0.0.0.0, metric 1, tag 0
RIP:  sending v2 update to 224.0.0.9 via Ethernet2 (172.25.150.225)
      172.25.150.32/28 - 0.0.0.0, metric 2, tag 0
      172.25.150.192/28 - 0.0.0.0, metric 1, tag 0
      192.168.50.0/24 - 0.0.0.0, metric 1, tag 0
RIP:  received v1 update from 192.168.50.130 on Ethernet0
      192.168.50.64 in 1 hops
RIP:  received v2 update from 172.25.150.194 on Ethernet1
      172.25.150.32/28 - 0.0.0.0 in 1 hops
```

Figure 7.11
Using debugging, the RIP versions sent and received by Taos can be observed.

Perhaps the most important observation to be made from Figure 7.11 concerns the update being broadcast to Pojoaque: It does not include subnet 172.25.150.32. Taos knows this subnet, having learned it via multicast RIPv2 updates from Sandia. But Pojoaque

---

[9] *Intentionally misconfigured for this example actually, with the* routed -s *option.*

cannot receive those multicasts because it speaks only RIPv1. Moreover, although Taos knows the subnet, the split horizon rule prevents Taos from advertising it out the same interface on which it was learned.

So, Pojoaque does not know about subnet 172.25.150.32. Two remedies are available: First, Sandia could be configured to send both RIP versions. Second, split horizon can be turned off at Taos's E1 interface with the following configuration:

```
interface Ethernet1
  ip address 172.25.150.193 255.255.255.240
  ip rip send version 1 2
  no ip split-horizon
```

Figure 7.12 shows the results. Taos is now including subnet 172.25.150.32 in its updates. Some forethought must be given to the possible consequences of disabling split horizon; Taos is now not only advertising 172.25.150.32 to Pojoaque but also advertising it back to Sandia.

Case Study: Using VLSM

Referring again to Figure 7.10, the subnet 172.25.150.0/24 has been assigned to the internet shown. That subnet has been further subnetted to fit the various data links by expanding the mask to 28 bits; the available sub-subnets, in binary and dotted decimal, are shown in Figure 7.13. Each of the subnets[10] will have, according to the $2^n - 2$ formula, 14 host addresses. Out of these, 172.25.150.32, 172.25.150.192, and 172.25.150.224 have been used.

---

[10] *Now that the concept should be firmly in place, from here on the single term subnet will be used for a subnet, a sub-subnet, a sub-sub-subnet, or whatever.*

```
Taos#debug ip rip
RIP protocol debugging is on
Taos#
RIP:   ignored v1 packet from 172.25.150.206 (illegal version)
RIP:   received v2 update from 172.25.150.194 on Ethernet1
       172.25.150.32/28 -> 0.0.0.0 in 1 hops
RIP:   sending v1 update to 255.255.255.255 via Ethernet0 (192.168.50.129)
       network 172.25.0.0, metric 1
RIP:   sending v1 update to 255.255.255.255 via Ethernet1 (172.25.150.193)
       subnet 172.25.150.32, metric 2
       subnet 172.25.150.224, metric 1
       subnet 172.25.150.192, metric 1
       network 192.168.50.0, metric 1
RIP:   sending v2 update to 224.0.0.9 via Ethernet1 (172.25.150.193)
       172.25.150.32/28 -> 172.25.150.194, metric 2, tag 0
       172.25.150.224/28 -> 0.0.0.0, metric 1, tag 0
       172.25.150.192/28 -> 0.0.0.0, metric 1, tag 0
       192.168.50.0/24 -> 0.0.0.0, metric 1, tag 0
```

Figure 7.12

With split horizon disabled on E1, Taos now includes subnet 172.25.150.32 in its updates to Pojoaque.

```
11111111111111111111111111110000  =  255.255.255.240
10101100000011001100101100000000  =  172.25.150.0/28
10101100000011001100101100010000  =  172.25.150.16/28
10101100000011001100101100100000  =  172.25.150.32/28
10101100000011001100101100110000  =  172.25.150.48/28
10101100000011001100101101000000  =  172.25.150.64/28
10101100000011001100101101010000  =  172.25.150.80/28
10101100000011001100101101100000  =  172.25.150.96/28
10101100000011001100101101110000  =  172.25.150.112/28
10101100000011001100101110000000  =  172.25.150.128/28
10101100000011001100101110010000  =  172.25.150.144/28
10101100000011001100101110100000  =  172.25.150.160/28
10101100000011001100101110110000  =  172.25.150.176/28
10101100000011001100101111000000  =  172.25.150.192/28
10101100000011001100101111010000  =  172.25.150.208/28
10101100000011001100101111100000  =  172.25.150.224/28
10101100000011001100101111110000  =  172.25.150.240/28
```

Figure 7.13

VLSM is applied to subnet 172.25.150.0/24.

In Figure 7.14, a token ring has been added to Taos, with 60 hosts. A subnet with at least six host bits is required to accommodate this data link. A classful routing protocol would require that five of the subnets from Figure 7.13 be assigned to the token ring [5 × (2^4 − 2) = 70], using secondary addresses. With classless protocols and VLSM, four of the subnets from Figure 7.13 can be combined into a single subnet with a 26-bit mask. This step will provide six host bits (62 host addresses), and no secondary addressing is necessary. Four subnets, 172.25.150.64/28 to 172.25.150.112/28, are combined under one 26-bit mask: 172.25.150.64/26. Notice that the four subnets are not selected at random; the first 26 masked bits are identical and are unique within the group of 16 subnets.[11]

Also, in Figure 7.14, four serial links and four routers have been added to the internetwork. Without VLSM, four of the subnets from Figure 7.13 would have to be used for the four serial links. With VLSM, a single subnet from Figure 7.13 can be used for all four serial links. 172.25.150.240 is selected, and a 30-bit mask is used to create the subnets in Figure 7.15. Each of the resulting four subnets contains two host addresses.

The fundamental objective of subnetting is always the same: A router must be able to identify every data link with a unique address, distinct from any other address in the internetwork. That is the common goal in the preceding two examples. In the first example, multiple addresses were combined into a single address by reducing the size of the mask until only the bits common to all of the addresses remain. Note that this result also happens when subnets are summarized by the major network address. In the second example, multiple subnets were created from a single subnet by expanding the subnet mask.

---

[11] *The technique used here to combine several addresses into one address serves as an introduction to address aggregation, covered in Chapter 8.*

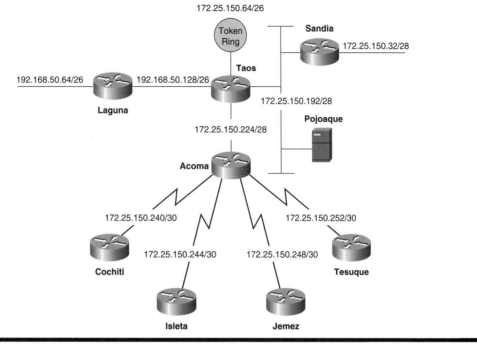

Figure 7.14
VLSM can be used to adapt addresses to the requirements of individual data links.

```
1111111111111111111111111111100  =  255.255.255.252
10101100000011001100101101111000  =  172.25.150.240/30
10101100000011001100101101111010100  =  172.25.150.244/30
10101100000011001100101101111111000  =  172.25.150.248/30
10101100000011001100101101111111100  =  172.25.150.252/30
```

Figure 7.15
A 30-bit mask is applied to subnet 172.25.150.240.

Case Study: Discontiguous Subnets and Classless Routing

Figure 7.16 shows that two Ethernets are connected to each of the four new routers. At each site, one Ethernet is a member of subnet

172.25.150.0/24 and will have no more than 12 hosts. This is easy enough. Four unused subnets are chosen from Figure 7.13 and assigned.

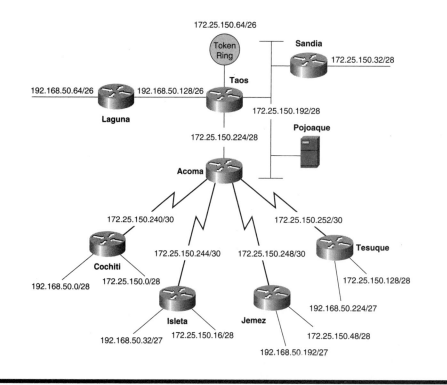

Figure 7.16

Cochiti, Isleta, Jemez, and Tesuque are each attached to two Ethernets. One Ethernet at each router is a member of subnet 172.25.150.0/24, and the other is a member of network 192.168.50.0/24.

The other Ethernet at each site is a member of network 192.168.50.0 and will have no more than 25 hosts. Subnets 192.168.50.64/26 and 192.168.50.128/26 are being used, which leaves 192.168.50.0/26 and 192.168.50.192/26. By increasing the mask to 27 bits, these two subnets can be divided into four, each with five host bits—enough for 30 host addresses per subnet. Figure 7.17 shows the four subnets in binary.

```
11111111111111111111111111100000  =  255.255.255.224
11000000101010001100100000000000  =  192.169.50.0/27
11000000101010001100100000100000  =  192.168.50.32/27
11000000101010001100100011000000  =  192.168.50.192/27
11000000101010001100100011100000  =  192.168.50.224/27
```

Figure 7.17

Subnet 192.169.50.0/26 is further subnetted with a 27-bit mask.

Having assigned all subnet addresses, the next concern is the fact that the subnets of 192.168.50.0 are discontiguous. Chapter 5 presents a case study on discontiguous subnets and demonstrates how to use secondary interfaces to connect them. Classless routing protocols have no such difficulties with discontiguous subnets. Because each route update includes a mask, subnets of one major network can be advertised into another major network.

The default behavior of RIPv2, however, is to summarize at network boundaries the same as RIPv1. To turn off summarization and allow subnets to be advertised across network boundaries, use the command **no auto-summary** with the RIP process. The configuration for Cochiti is:

```
interface Ethernet0
  ip address 192.168.50.1 255.255.255.224
!
interface Ethernet1
  ip address 172.25.150.1 255.255.255.240
!
interface Serial0
  ip address 172.25.150.242 255.255.255.252
!
router rip
  version 2
  network 172.25.0.0
  network 192.168.50.0
  no auto-summary
```

Isleta, Jemez, and Tesuque will have similar configurations. Summarization must also be turned off at Taos and at Acoma. Recall from Figure 7.10 that Laguna was running RIPv1. For this configuration to work, it must be changed to version 2.

Careful consideration should be given to what effect the variable masks will have on Pojoaque, where RIPv1 continues to run. The debug messages in Figure 7.18 show the version 1 and version 2 updates sent from Taos onto subnet 172.25.150.192/28. The version 1 updates will include only those subnets whose masks are 28 bits, the same as the subnet on which the updates are being broadcast. Although Pojoaque will not receive advertisements for 172.25.150.64/26 or any of the serial link subnets, an analysis of those subnet addresses shows that Pojoaque will, in this case, correctly interpret the addresses as being different from its own subnet. Packets destined for these subnets will be sent to Taos for routing.

Case Study: Authentication

Cisco's implementation of RIPv2 message authentication includes the choice of simple password or MD5 authentication, and the option of defining multiple keys, or passwords, on a "key chain." The router may then be configured to use different keys at different times.

The steps for setting up RIPv2 authentication follow.

1. Define a key chain with a name.
2. Define the key or keys on the key chain.
3. Enable authentication on an interface and specify the key chain to be used.
4. Specify whether the interface will use clear text or MD5 authentication.
5. Optionally configure key management.

```
Taos#debug ip rip
RIP protocol debugging is on
RIP: sending v1 update to 255.255.255.255 via Ethernet0 (172.25.150.193)
     subnet 172.25.150.0, metric 3
     subnet 172.25.150.16, metric 3
     subnet 172.25.150.32, metric 2
     subnet 172.25.150.48, metric 3
     subnet 172.25.150.128, metric 3
     subnet 172.25.150.192, metric 1
     subnet 172.25.150.224, metric 1
     network 192.168.50.0, metric 1
RIP: sending v2 update to 224.0.0.9 via Ethernet0 (172.25.150.193)
     172.25.150.0/28 -> 0.0.0.0, metric 3, tag 0
     172.25.150.16/28 -> 0.0.0.0, metric 3, tag 0
     172.25.150.32/28 -> 0.0.0.0, metric 2, tag 0
     172.25.150.48/28 -> 0.0.0.0, metric 3, tag 0
     172.25.150.64/26 -> 0.0.0.0, metric 1, tag 0
     172.25.150.128/28 -> 0.0.0.0, metric 3, tag 0
     172.25.150.192/28 -> 0.0.0.0, metric 1, tag 0
     172.25.150.224/28 -> 0.0.0.0, metric 1, tag 0
     172.25.150.240/30 -> 0.0.0.0, metric 2, tag 0
     172.25.150.244/30 -> 0.0.0.0, metric 2, tag 0
     172.25.150.248/30 -> 0.0.0.0, metric 2, tag 0
     172.25.150.252/30 -> 0.0.0.0, metric 2, tag 0
     192.168.50.0/27 -> 0.0.0.0, metric 3, tag 0
     192.168.50.32/27 -> 0.0.0.0, metric 3, tag 0
     192.168.50.64/26 -> 0.0.0.0, metric 2, tag 0
     192.168.50.128/26 -> 0.0.0.0, metric 1, tag 0
     192.168.50.192/27 -> 0.0.0.0, metric 3, tag 0
     192.168.50.224/27 -> 0.0.0.0, metric 3, tag 0
```

Figure 7.18

Although the RIPv2 update from Taos includes all subnets in the internetwork, the RIPv1 update includes only a summary route to network 192.168.50.0 and only those subnets of 172.25.150.0 whose masks are the same as the interface on which the update is being sent.

In the following example, a key chain named Tewa is configured at Taos. Key 1, the only key on the chain, has a password of Kachina; interface E0 then uses the key, with MD5 authentication, to validate updates from Laguna.

```
Taos(config)#key chain Tewa
Taos(config-keychain)#key 1
Taos(config-keychain-key)#key-string Kachina
Taos(config-keychain-key)#interface ethernet 0
Taos(config-if)#ip rip authentication key-chain Tewa
Taos(config-if)#ip rip authentication mode md5
```

A key chain must be configured, even if there is only one key on it. Although any routers that will exchange authenticated updates must have the same password, the name of the key chain has significance only on the local router. Laguna, for instance, might have a key chain named Keres, but the key string must be Kachina to speak to Taos.

If the command **ip rip authentication mode md5** is not added, the interface will use the default clear text authentication. Although clear text authentication may be necessary to communicate with some RIPv2 implementations, it is almost always wise to use the far more secure MD5 authentication whenever possible.

Key management is used to migrate from one authentication key to another. In the following example, Laguna is configured to begin using the first key at 4:30 p.m. on November 28, 1997, for 12 hours (43200 seconds). The second key becomes valid at 4:00 a.m. on November 29, 1997, and will be used until 1:00 p.m. on April 15, 1998. The third key becomes valid at 12:30 p.m. on April 15, 1998, and will remain valid permanently after that.

```
key chain Keres
  key 1
   key-string Kachina
   accept-lifetime 16:30:00 Nov 28 1997 duration 43200
   send-lifetime 16:30:00 Nov 28 1997 duration 43200
  key 2
   key-string Kiva
   accept-lifetime 04:00:00 Nov 29 1997 13:00:00 Apr 15 1998
   send-lifetime 04:00:00 Nov 29 1997 13:00:00 Apr 15 1998
  key 3
   key-string Koshare
   accept-lifetime 12:30:00 Apr 15 1998 infinite
   send-lifetime 12:30:00 Apr 15 1998 infinite
 !
interface Ethernet0
  ip address 198.168.50.130 255.255.255.192
  ip rip authentication key-chain Keres
  ip rip authentication mode md5
```

As the configuration shows, the password that is accepted from other routers and the password that is used with transmitted messages are managed separately. Both the **accept-lifetime** and the **send-lifetime** commands must have a specified start time and may have either a specified duration or end time or the keyword *infinite*. The key numbers are examined from the lowest to the highest, and the first valid key is used.

Although this configuration uses a 30-minute overlap to compensate for differences in system times, it is highly recommended that a time synchronization protocol such as Network Time Protocol (NTP) be used with key management.[12]

TROUBLESHOOTING RIPv2

Two configuration problems common to RIPv2 are mismatched versions and misconfigured authentication. Both difficulties are easy to discover with debugging, as Figure 7.19 shows.

```
Jemez#debug ip rip events
RIP event debugging is on
Jemez#
RIP: ignored v1 packet from 172.25.150.249 (illegal version)
RIP: ignored v2 packet from 172.25.150.249 (invalid authentication)
Jemez#
```

Figure 7.19

Debugging reveals mismatched versions and misconfigured authentication.

A more likely source of trouble with RIPv2, or any classless routing protocol, is a misconfigured variable-length subnet mask. VLSM is not difficult, but if a VLSM scheme is not designed and managed carefully it can cause some unusual routing difficulties.

---

[12] *NTP is outside the scope of this book. Refer to the* Cisco Configuration Guide *for more information.*

Case Study: Misconfigured VLSM

Host C in Figure 7.20 cannot communicate across the internetwork, and it cannot even ping the other hosts or routers on the local data link. Hosts A and B have no communications problems with each other or with any other host across the internetwork, but they cannot communicate with C. All hosts are configured to use 172.19.35.1 as the default gateway address.

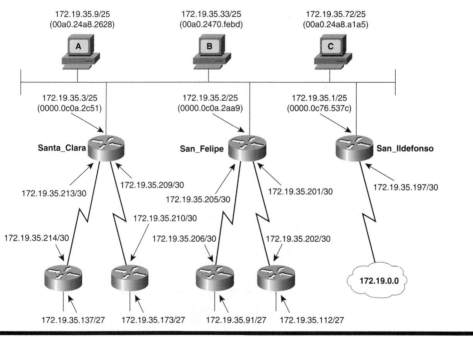

Figure 7.20

Hosts A and B can communicate across the internetwork, but host C cannot.

When an attempt is made to ping host C from host A or B, the first ping is successful and subsequent pings fail (Figure 7.21). The fact that at least one ICMP Echo Request packet reached C and at least one Echo Reply packet was returned indicates that the problem is not related to the hardware or data link.

The strange ping behavior leads to the hypothesis that after the first successful packet, subsequent packets—either the Echo Requests from B or the Echo Replies from C—are somehow being misdirected. Because this behavior is happening on the local data link, the Address Resolution Protocol (ARP) caches should be examined.

Figures 7.22 and 7.23 show the ARP caches for C and B, respectively. The suspicions about ARP are confirmed here. C's cache contains the correct MAC address for B (00a0.2470.febd), but B's cache has a MAC address of 0000.0c0a.2aa9 associated with C. A closer look at both caches shows that 0000.0c0a.2aa9 is the MAC address of San_Felipe's locally attached interface. This information can be deduced from the fact that the same MAC address is mapped to IP address 172.19.35.2 and to the IP addresses reachable via that router.

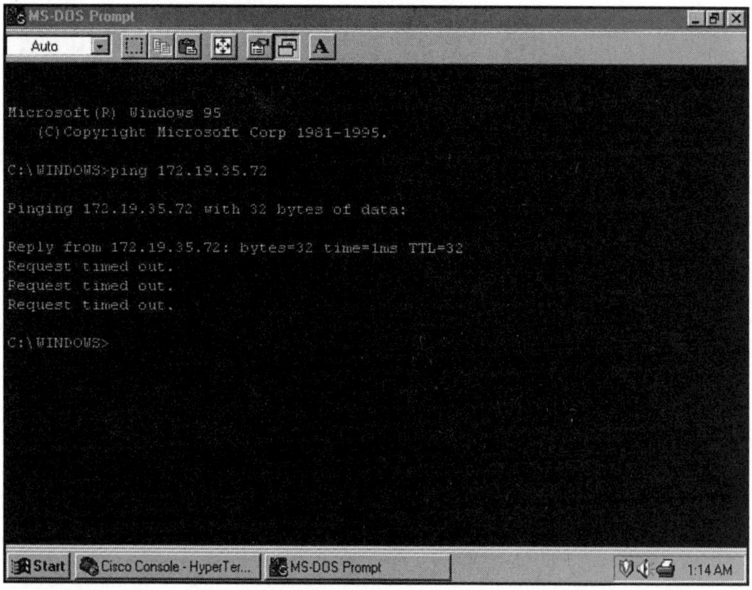

Figure 7.21

When host B pings host C, the first ping is successful and subsequent pings fail.

```
Linux 1.2.13 (Zuni.pueblo.com) (ttyp0)



Zuni login: root
Password:
Last login: Sat Nov 29 11:21:57 on tty1
Linux 1.2.13.
You have mail.
Zuni:~# arp -a
Address              HW type            HW address         Flags   Mask
172.19.35.112        10Mbps Ethernet    00:00:0C:0A:2A:A9  C       *
172.19.35.1          10Mbps Ethernet    00:00:0C:76:5B:7C  C       *
172.19.35.33         10Mbps Ethernet    00:A0:24:70:FE:BD  C       *
172.19.35.2          10Mbps Ethernet    00:00:0C:0A:2A:A9  C       *
172.19.35.3          10Mbps Ethernet    00:00:0C:0A:2C:51  C       *
172.19.35.9          10Mbps Ethernet    00:A0:24:A8:26:28  C       *
172.19.35.91         10Mbps Ethernet    00:00:0C:0A:2A:A9  C       *
Zuni:~#
```

Figure 7.22

Host C's ARP cache shows the correct MAC address associated with all addresses.

The ping results begin to make sense. B broadcasts an ARP Request for 172.19.35.72. C sends an ARP Reply, and B sends its first ping correctly. In the meantime, San_Felipe has received the ARP Request and apparently believes that it has a route to 172.19.35.72. It responds with a proxy ARP (later than C because it has to perform a route lookup first), which causes B to overwrite C's MAC address. Subsequent Echo Request packets are sent to San_Felipe, where they are routed off the local data link and lost. A protocol analyzer attached to the Ethernet proves the point (Figure 7.24).

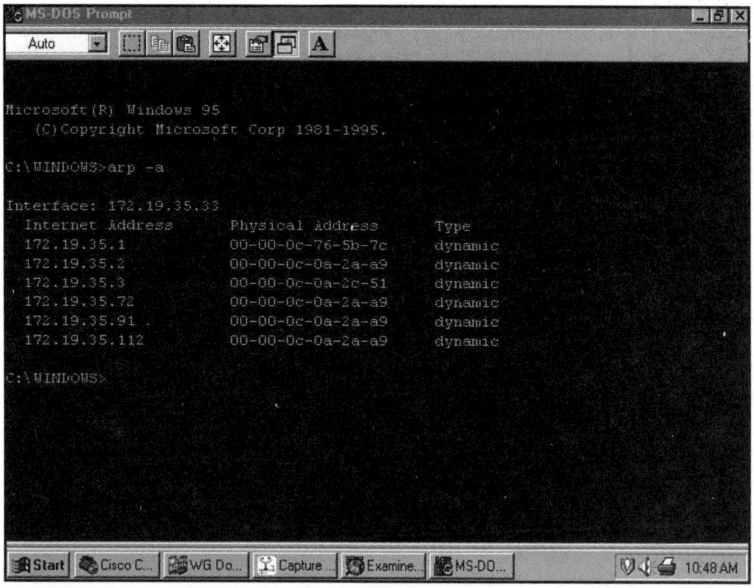

Figure 7.23

Host B's ARP cache shows that C's IP address is mapped to the MAC address of San_Felipe's interface 172.19.35.2.

If you know that the trouble is a routing problem, it remains only to find the cause. First, the subnet addresses for each data link should be determined (Figure 7.25). Next, C's IP address should be compared with all the subnets reachable via San_Felipe, in binary, to find any conflicts. Figure 7.26 shows the addresses with the subnet bits of the last octet in bold.

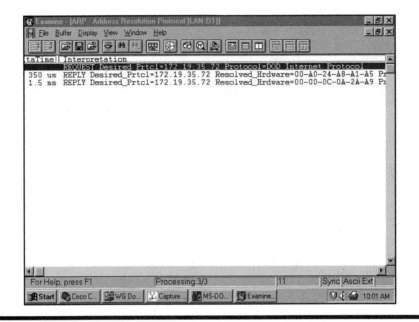

Figure 7.24

A protocol analyzer, filtering for ARP packets, shows B's ARP request to C and replies from both host C (00a0.24a8.a1a5) and router San_Felipe (0000.0c0a.2aa9).

A comparison shows that the first three bits of 172.19.35.72/25 match subnet 172.19.35.64/27. San Felipe has routes to both 172.19.35.0/25 and to 172.19.35.64/27 (Figure 7.27). When it receives a packet destined for host C, it will be able to match one bit to subnet 172.19.35.0/25 but three bits to 172.19.35.64/27. As a result, the router will choose the more specific subnet and route the packet off the local data link and into oblivion.

The solution to this trouble is to readdress either host C or subnet 172.19.35.64. This step sounds easy on paper. In real life, it may involve some difficult decisions, as it did for the client on whose internetwork this case study is based.

Figure 7.28 shows all the subnets of 172.19.35.0, based on a 27-bit mask. The intention was to combine the first four subnets into a single subnet with a 25-bit mask to accommodate up to 85

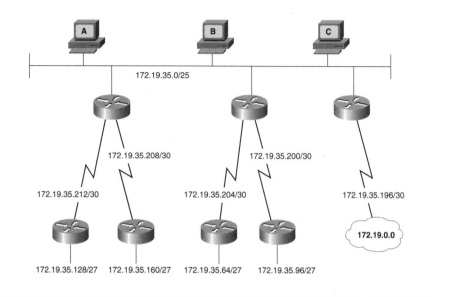

Figure 7.25

When analyzing any addressing scheme, and especially a VLSM design, the subnets for every data link should be determined so that conflicts and overlaps may be discovered.

```
10101100000010011001000110100100 0   =   172.19.35.72/25
10101100000010011001000110000000 0   =   172.19.35.0/25
10101100000010011001000110100000 0   =   172.19.35.64/27
10101100000010011001000110110000 0   =   172.19.35.96/27
10101100000010011001000111100100 0   =   172.19.35.200/30
10101100000010011001000111100110 0   =   172.19.35.204/30
```

Figure 7.26

C's IP addresses with subnet bits of the last octet highlighted.

hosts on the "backbone" Ethernet. This decision is valid because the grouping will use all the subnets whose first bit is zero; no other address can cause a conflict. Next, 172.19.35.192/27 is subnetted with a 30-bit mask to be used on the serial links. Again, this design decision is valid. Subnets 172.19.35.128/27 and 172.19.35.160 are used as is. The error occurred when subnets 172.19.35.64/27 and 172.19.35.96/27 were selected to be used on two "remote" networks. These subnets had already been spoken for.

```
San_Felipe#show ip route
Codes:  C - connected, S - static, I - IGRP, R - RIP, M - mobile, B - BGP
        D - EIGRP, EX - EIGRP external, O - OSPF, IA - OSPF inter area
        E1 - OSPF external type 1, E2 - OSPF external type 2, E - EGP
        i - IS-IS, L1 - IS-IS level-1, L2 - IS-IS level-2, * - candidate default,
        U - per-user static route

Gateway of last resort is 172.19.35.1 to network 0.0.0.0

     172.19.0.0/16 is variably subnetted, 10 subnets, 3 masks
R       172.19.35.128/27 [120/1] via 172.19.35.3, 00:00:07, Ethernet0
R       172.19.35.160/27 [120/1] via 172.19.35.3, 00:00:08, Ethernet0
R       172.19.35.212/30 [120/1] via 172.19.35.3, 00:00:08, Ethernet0
R       172.19.35.208/30 [120/1] via 172.19.35.3, 00:00:08, Ethernet0
C       172.19.35.204/30 is directly connected, Serial0
C       172.19.35.200/30 is directly connected, Serial1
R       172.19.35.196/30 [120/1] via 172.19.35.1, 00:00:17, Ethernet0
C       172.19.35.0/25 is directly connected, Ethernet0
R       172.19.35.64/27 [120/1] via 172.19.35.206, 00:00:11, Serial0
R       172.19.35.96/27 [120/1] via 172.19.35.202, 00:00:23, Serial1
R* 0.0.0.0/0 [120/1] via 172.19.35.1, 00:00:18, Ethernet0
San_Felipe#
```

Figure 7.27

San_Felipe has routes to both 172.19.35.0/25 and to 172.19.35.64/27; the second route is a better match of host C's address than is the first route.

```
11111111111111111111111111111111  =  255.255.255.224
10101100000010011001000110000000  =  172.19.35.0/27
10101100000010011001000110010000  =  172.19.35.32/27
10101100000010011001000110100000  =  172.19.35.64/27
10101100000010011001000110110000  =  172.19.35.96/27
10101100000010011001000111000000  =  172.19.35.128/27
10101100000010011001000111010000  =  172.19.35.160/27
10101100000010011001000111100000  =  172.19.35.192/27
10101100000010011001000111110000  =  172.19.35.224/27
```

Figure 7.28

A 27-bit subnet mask is applied to subnet 172.19.35.0.

The difficult decision is in deciding whether to re-address the backbone, giving up some address space there, or to re-address the two remote subnets and give up address space on each of them. The second option was chosen, using a 28-bit mask to divide 172.19.35.224/27 into two subnets for the remote sites.

LOOKING AHEAD

Although RIPv2 presents some decided improvements over RIPv1, it is still limited to a maximum of 15 hops and, therefore, to small internetworks. Chapters 8, "Enhanced Interior Gateway Routing Protocol (EIGRP)," 9, "Open Shortest Path First," and 10, "Integrated IS-IS," examine three protocols that can be used in much larger internetworks and with which design strategies such as VLSM become very powerful tools for controlling them.

SUMMARY TABLE: CHAPTER 7 COMMAND REVIEW

Command	Description
accept-lifetime *start-time*{**infinite**|*end-time*| **duration** *seconds*}	Specifies the time period during which the authentication key on a key chain is received as valid
auto-summary	Toggles the automatic summarization of routes on network boundaries
debug ip rip [events]	Enables the display of messages on RIP transactions
ip classless	Enables the forwarding of packets on the route for which the router can find the best match without consideration of the class of the destination address
ip rip authentication key-chain *name-of-chain*	Enables RIPv2 authentication on an interface and specifies the name of the key chain to be used
ip rip authentication mode{text|md5}	Specifies whether an interface will use clear text or md5 authentication
ip rip receive version [1] [2]	Specifies the version or versions of RIP messages that an interface will accept
ip rip send version [1] [2]	Specifies the version or versions of RIP messages that an interface will send
ip split-horizon	Toggles the split horizon function on an interface
ip subnet-zero	Allows the use of all-zeros subnets for interface addresses and routing updates

Command	Description
key *number*	Specifies a key on a key chain
key chain *name-of-chain*	Specifies a group of keys
key-string *text*	Specifies the authentication string, or password, used by a key
network *network-number*	Specifies the network address of one or more directly connected interfaces on which IGRP, EIGRP, or RIP processes should be enabled
passive-interface *type number*	Disables the transmission of routing updates on an interface
router rip	Enables the RIP routing process on a router
send-lifetime *start-time*{**infinite**|*end-time*| **duration** *seconds*}	Specifies the time period during which the authentication key on a key chain may be sent
show ip route [*address* [*mask*]][*protocol*[*process-ID*]]	Displays the current routing table as a whole or by entry
version	Specifies the version of the RIP routing process

RECOMMENDED READING

Malkin, G. S. "RIP Version 2: Carrying Additional Information." RFC 1723, November 1994.

REVIEW QUESTIONS

1. Which three fields are new to the RIPv2 message format?
2. Besides the extensions defined by the three fields of question 1, what are the other two major changes from RIPv1?
3. What is the multicast address used by RIPv2? What is the advantage of multicasting messages over broadcasting them?
4. What is the purpose of the Route Tag field in the RIPv2 message?
5. What is the purpose of the Next Hop field?

6. What is the UDP port number used by RIPv2?

7. Which one feature must a routing protocol have to be a classless routing protocol?

8. Which one feature must a routing protocol have to use VLSM?

9. Which two types of authentication are available with Cisco's RIPv2? Are they both defined in RFC 1723?

CONFIGURATION EXERCISES

1. In the example of Figure 7.10, router Taos was configured to send both version 1 and version 2 updates so that the *routed* process in the Linux host Pojoaque would understand the updates from Taos. Is there another way to configure Taos besides using the **ip rip send version** command?

2. An internetwork has been assigned the address 192.168.100.0. Subnet this address to meet the following requirements:

   ○ One subnet with 50 hosts

   ○ Five subnets with 10 hosts

   ○ One subnet with 25 hosts

   ○ Four subnets with 5 hosts

   ○ Ten serial links

3. Configure the four routers in Figure 7.29 to run RIP. RTC is running IOS 10.3 and for corporate policy reasons cannot be upgraded.

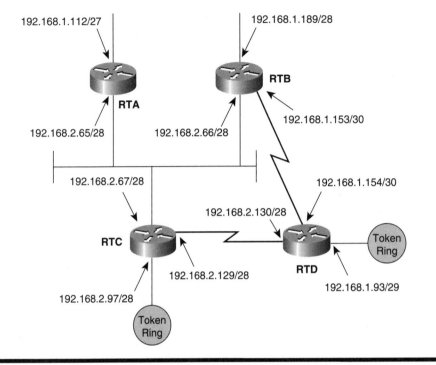

Figure 7.29

The internetwork for Configuration Exercises 3 through 5.

4. Configure RTB and RTD in Figure 7.29 to authenticate the RIP updates being exchanged over the serial link.

5. Configure RTB and RTD in Figure 7.29 to change to a new authentication key 3 days from the time the key in Configuration Exercise 4 went into effect. Have the new key stay in effect for 10 hours and then have the routers change to yet another key.

TROUBLESHOOTING EXERCISES

1. Figures 7.31 through 7.33 show the configurations for the three routers in Figure 7.30. Which subnets are in the routing tables of each router? From each router, which subnets are reachable and which subnets (if any) are unreachable?

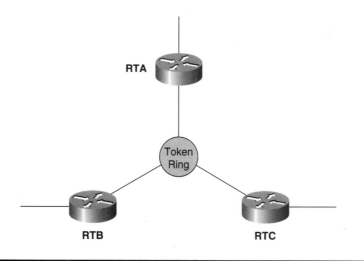

Figure 7.30
The internetwork for Troubleshooting Exercises 1 and 2.

2. The configurations of RTA and RTB in Figure 7.30 is changed as follows:

```
interface TokenRing0
  ip address 192.168.13.35 255.255.255.224
  ip rip receive version 1 2
  ring-speed 16
```

Will any subnets be added to any routing tables as a result of this change? Explain why or why not.

```
RTA#show running-config
Building configuration...

Current configuration:
!
version 11.2
no service udp-small-servers
no service tcp-small-servers
!
hostname RTA
!
!
!
interface Ethernet0
  ip address 192.168.13.86 255.255.255.248
!
interface Serial0
  no ip address
  shutdown
!
interface Serial1
  no ip address
  shutdown
!
interface TokenRing0
  ip address 192.168.13.34 255.255.255.224
  ring-speed 16
!
router rip
  version 2
  network 192.168.13.0
!
no ip classless
!
!
line con 0
line aux 0
line vty 0 4
  login
!
end

RTA#
```

Figure 7.31

The configuration of RTA in Figure 7.30.

```
RTB#show running-config
Building configuration...

Current configuration:
!
version 11.2
no service udp-small-servers
no service tcp-small-servers
!
hostname RTB
!
!
!
interface Ethernet0
 ip address 192.168.13.90 255.255.255.240
!
interface Serial0
 no ip address
 shutdown
!
interface Serial1
 no ip address
 shutdown
!
interface TokenRing0
 ip address 192.168.13.35 255.255.255.224
 ring-speed 16
!
router rip
 version 2
 network 192.168.13.0
!
no ip classless
!
!
line con 0
line aux 0
line vty 0 4
 login
!
end

RTB#
```

Figure 7.32

The configuration of RTB in Figure 7.30.

```
RTC#show running-config
Building configuration...

Current configuration:
!
version 11.1
service udp-small-servers
service tcp-small-servers
!
hostname RTC
!
!
!
interface Ethernet0
  ip address 192.168.13.75 255.255.255.224
!
interface Serial0
 no ip address
 shutdown
!
interface Serial1
 no ip address
 shutdown
!
interface TokenRing0
  ip address 192.168.13.33 255.255.255.224
  ring-speed 16
!
router rip
  network 192.168.13.0
!
no ip classless
!
line con 0
line 1 8
line aux 0
line vty 0 4
  login
!
end

RTC#
```

Figure 7.33

The configuration of RTC in Figure 7.30.

- **Operation of EIGRP**

  Protocol-Dependent Modules

  Reliable Transport Protocol

  Neighbor Discovery and Recovery

  The Diffusing Update Algorithm

  EIGRP Packet Formats

  Address Aggregation

- **Configuring EIGRP**

  Case Study: A Basic EIGRP Configuration

  Case Study: Redistribution with IGRP

  Case Study: Disabling Automatic Summarization

  Case Study: Address Aggregation

  Authentication

- **Troubleshooting EIGRP**

  Case Study: A Missing Neighbor

  Stuck-in-Active Neighbors

CHAPTER 8

Enhanced Interior Gateway Routing Protocol (EIGRP)

First released in IOS 9.21, Enhanced Interior Gateway Routing protocol (EIGRP) is, as the name says, an enhancement of IGRP. The name is apt because unlike RIPv2, EIGRP is far more than the same protocol with some added extensions. EIGRP remains a distance vector protocol and uses the same composite metrics as IGRP uses. Beyond that, there are few similarities.

EIGRP is occasionally described as a distance vector protocol that acts like a link state protocol. To recap the extensive discussion in Chapter 4, a distance vector protocol shares everything it knows but only with directly connected neighbors. Link state protocols announce information only about their directly connected links, but they share the information with all routers in their routing domain or area.

All the distance vector protocols discussed so far run some variant of the Bellman-Ford (or Ford-Fulkerson) algorithm. These protocols are prone to routing loops and counting to infinity. As a result, they must implement loop-avoidance measures such as split horizon, route poisoning, and hold-down timers. Because each router must run the routing algorithm on received routes before passing those routes along to its neighbors, larger internetworks may be slow to converge. More important, distance vector protocols advertise routes; the change of a critical link may mean the advertisement of many changed routes.

Compared to distance vector protocols, link state protocols are far less susceptible to routing loops and bad routing information. The forwarding of link state packets is not dependent on performing the route calculations first, so large internetworks may converge faster. And only links and their states are advertised, not routes, which means the change of a link will not cause the advertisement of all routes using that link. However, compared to distance vector algorithms, the complex Dijkstra algorithms and the associated databases place a higher demand on CPU and memory.

Regardless of whether other routing protocols perform route calculations before sending distance vector updates to neighbors or after building a topological database, their common denominator is that they perform the calculations individually. In contrast, EIGRP uses a system of *diffusing computations*—route calculations that are performed in a coordinated fashion among multiple routers—to attain fast convergence while remaining loop free at every instant.

Diffusing computations

EIGRP updates are nonperiodic, partial, and bounded.

Although EIGRP updates are still vectors of distances transmitted to directly connected neighbors, they are nonperiodic, partial, and bounded. *Nonperiodic* means that updates are not sent at regular intervals; rather, updates are sent only when a metric or topology change occurs. *Partial* means that the updates will include only routes that have changed, not every entry in the route table. *Bounded* means that the updates are sent only to affected routers. These characteristics mean that EIGRP uses much less bandwidth than typical distance vector protocols use. This feature can be especially important on low-bandwidth, high-cost WAN links.

Another concern when routing over low-bandwidth WAN links is the maximum amount of bandwidth used during periods of convergence, when routing traffic is high. By default, EIGRP uses no more than 50% of the bandwidth of a link. Later IOS releases allow this percentage to be changed with the command **ip band-width-percent eigrp.**

EIGRP is a classless protocol (that is, each route entry in an update includes a subnet mask). Variable-length subnet masks may be used with EIGRP not only for sub-subnetting as described in Chapter 7, "Routing Information Protocol Version 2," but also for address aggregation—the summarization of a group of major network addresses.

Beginning with IOS 11.3, EIGRP packets can be authenticated using an MD5 cryptographic checksum. The basics of authentication and MD5 are covered in Chapter 7; an example of configuring EIGRP authentication is included in this chapter.

Finally, a major feature of EIGRP is that it can route not only IP but also IPX and AppleTalk.

OPERATION OF EIGRP[1]

EIGRP uses the same formula as IGRP uses to calculate its composite metric. However, EIGRP scales the metric components by 256 to achieve a finer metric granularity. So if the minimum configured bandwidth on the path to a destination is 512K and the total configured delay is 46000 microseconds, IGRP would calculate a composite metric of 24131. (See Chapter 6, "Interior Gateway Routing Protocol (IGRP)," for a detailed discussion of IGRP metric calculations.) EIGRP, however, will multiply the bandwidth and delay components by 256 for a metric of 256 x 24131 = 6177536.

---

[1]   *A major software revision of EIGRP was released in IOS 10.3(11), 11.0(8), and 11.1(3). The performance and stability improvements of the later version make it highly preferable over the older version.*

EIGRP has four components (Figure 8.1):

- Protocol-Dependent Modules

- Reliable Transport Protocol (RTP)

- Neighbor Discovery/ Recovery

- Diffusing Update Algorithm (DUAL)

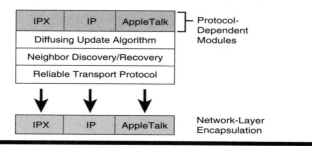

Figure 8.1

The four major components of EIGRP. RTP and neighbor discovery are lower-level protocols that enable the correct operation of DUAL. DUAL can perform route computations for multiple routed protocols.

This section examines each EIGRP component, with particular emphasis on DUAL, and ends with a discussion of address aggregation.

Protocol-Dependent Modules

EIGRP implements modules for IP, IPX, and AppleTalk, which are responsible for the protocol-specific routing tasks. For example, the IPX EIGRP module is responsible for exchanging route information about IPX networks with other IPX EIGRP processes and for passing the information to the DUAL. Additionally, the IPX module will send and receive SAP information.

As Figure 8.1 shows, the traffic for the individual modules is encapsulated within their respective network layer protocols. EIGRP for IPX, for example, is carried in IPX packets.

EIGRP will automatically redistribute with other protocols in many cases:

- IPX EIGRP will automatically redistribute with IPX RIP and NLSP.

- AppleTalk EIGRP will automatically redistribute with AppleTalk RTMP.

- IP EIGRP will automatically redistribute routes with IGRP if the IGRP process is in the same autonomous system.

The configuration section includes an example of redistributing between IGRP and EIGRP. (Redistribution with other IP routing protocols is the subject of Chapter 11, "Route Redistribution.")

Configuration of EIGRP for IPX and AppleTalk is outside the scope of this book. Refer to the *Cisco Configuration Guide* for more information.

Reliable Transport Protocol

The Reliable Transport Protocol (RTP) manages the delivery and reception of EIGRP packets. *Reliable delivery* means that delivery is guaranteed and that packets will be delivered in order.

Guaranteed delivery is accomplished by means of a Cisco-proprietary algorithm known as *reliable multicast*, using the reserved class D address 224.0.0.10. Each neighbor receiving a reliably multicast packet will unicast an acknowledgment.

Ordered delivery is ensured by including two sequence numbers in the packet. Each packet includes a sequence number assigned by the sending router. This sequence number is incremented by one each time the router sends a new packet. In addition, the sending router places in the packet the sequence number of the last packet received from the destination router.

In some cases, RTP may use *unreliable delivery*. No acknowledgment is required, and no sequence number will be included for unreliably delivered EIGRP packets.

EIGRP uses multiple packet types, all of which are identified by protocol number 88 in the IP header.

- *Hellos* are used by the neighbor discovery and recovery process. Hello packets are multicast and use unreliable delivery.

- *Acknowledgments* (ACKs) are Hello packets with no data in them. ACKs are always unicast and use unreliable delivery.

- *Updates* convey route information. Unlike RIP and IGRP updates, these packets are transmitted only when necessary, contain only necessary information, and are sent only to routers that require the information. When updates are required by a specific router, they are unicast. When updates are required by multiple routers, such as upon a metric or topology change, they are multicast. Updates always use reliable delivery.

- *Queries* and *Replies* are used by the DUAL finite state machine to manage its diffusing computations. Queries can be multicast or unicast, and replies are always unicast. Both queries and replies use reliable delivery.

- *Requests* were a type of packet originally intended for use in route servers. This application was never implemented, and request packets are noted here only because they are mentioned in some older EIGRP documentation.

If any packet is reliably multicast and an ACK is not received from a neighbor, the packet will be retransmitted as a unicast to that unresponding neighbor. If an ACK is not received after 16 of these unicast retransmissions, the neighbor will be declared dead.

The time to wait for an ACK before switching from multicast to unicast is specified by the *multicast flow timer*. The time between the subsequent unicasts is specified by the *retransmission timeout* (RTO). Both the multicast flow timer and the RTO are calculated for each neighbor from the *smooth round-trip time* (SRTT). The SRTT is the average elapsed time, measured in milliseconds, between the transmission of a packet to the neighbor and the receipt of an acknowledgment. The formulas for calculating the exact values of the SRTT, the RTO, and the multicast flow timer are proprietary.

The following two subsections discuss the EIGRP components that use the various packet types.

Neighbor Discovery/Recovery

Because EIGRP updates are nonperiodic, it is especially important to have a process whereby neighbors—EIGRP-speaking routers on directly connected networks—are discovered and tracked. On most networks, Hellos are multicast every 5 seconds, minus a small random time to prevent synchronization. On multipoint X.25, Frame Relay, and ATM interfaces, with access link speeds of T1 or slower, Hellos are unicast every 60 seconds.[2] This longer Hello interval is also the default for ATM SVCs and for ISDN PRI

---

[2]   *Point-to-point subinterfaces send Hellos every 5 seconds.*

interfaces. In all cases, the Hellos are unacknowledged. The default Hello interval can be changed on a per interface basis with the command **ip hello-interval eigrp**.

When a router receives a Hello packet from a neighbor, the packet will include a *hold time*. The hold time tells the router the maximum time it should wait to receive subsequent Hellos. If the hold timer expires before a Hello is received, the neighbor is declared unreachable and DUAL is informed of the loss of a neighbor. By default, the hold time is three times the Hello interval—180 seconds for low-speed non-broadcast multi-access (NBMA) networks and 15 seconds for all other networks. The default can be changed on a per interface basis with the command **ip hold-time eigrp**. The capability to detect a lost neighbor within 15 seconds, as opposed to 180 seconds for RIP and 270 seconds for IGRP, is one factor contributing to EIGRP's fast reconvergence.

Information about each neighbor is recorded in a neighbor table. As Figure 8.2 shows, the *neighbor table* records the IP address of the neighbor and the interface on which the neighbor's Hellos are received. The hold time advertised by the neighbor is recorded, as is the SRTT and the *uptime*—the time since the neighbor was added to the table. The RTO is the time, in milliseconds, that the router will wait for an acknowledgment of a unicast packet sent after a multicast has failed. If an EIGRP update, query, or reply is sent, a copy of the packet will be queued. If the RTO expires before an ACK is received, another copy of the queued packet is sent. The Q Count indicates the number of enqueued packets. The sequence number of the last update, query, or reply packet received from the neighbor is also recorded in the neighbor table. The RTP tracks these sequence numbers to ensure that packets from the neighbor are not received out of order. Finally, the H column records the order in which the neighbors were learned.

```
Wright#show ip eigrp neighbors
IP-EIGRP neighbors for process 1
H   Address   Interface  Hold Uptime    SRTT   RTO    Q     Seq
                         (sec)          (ms)          Cnt   Num
3   10.1.1.2  Et0          10 09:01:27    12   200    0     5
2   10.1.4.2  Se1          13 09:02:11    23   200    0     11
1   10.1.2.2  Et1          14 09:02:12     8   200    0     15
0   10.1.3.2  Se0          12 09:02:12    21   200    0     13
Wright#
```

Figure 8.2

The command **show ip eigrp neighbors** is used to observe the IP EIGRP neighbor table.

The Diffusing Update Algorithm

The design philosophy behind DUAL is that even temporary routing loops are detrimental to the performance of an internetwork. DUAL uses diffusing computations, first proposed by E. W. Dijkstra and C. S. Scholten,[3] to perform distributed shortest-path routing while maintaining freedom from loops at every instant. Although many researchers have contributed to the development of DUAL, the most prominent work is that of J. J. Garcia-Luna-Aceves.[4]

DUAL: Preliminary Concepts

For DUAL to operate correctly, a lower-level protocol must assure that the following conditions are met:[5]

---

[3] *Edsger W. Dijkstra and C. S. Scholten. "Termination Detection for Diffusing Computations."* Information Processing Letters, *Vol. 11, No. 1, pp. 1–4: 29 August 1980.*

[4] *J. J. Garcia-Luna-Aceves. "A Unified Approach for Loop-Free Routing Using Link States or Distance Vectors,"* ACM SIGCOMM Computer Communications Review, *Vol. 19, No. 4, pp. 212–223: September 1989. J. J. Garcia-Luna-Aceves. "Loop-Free Routing Using Diffusing Computations,"* IEEE/ACM Transactions on Networking, *Vol. 1, No. 1, February 1993.*

[5] *J. J. Garcia-Luna-Aceves. "Area-Based, Loop-Free Internet Routing."* Proceedings of IEEE INFOCOMM 94. *Toronto, Ontario, Canada, June 1994.*

- A node detects within a finite time the existence of a new neighbor or the loss of connectivity with a neighbor.

- All messages transmitted over an operational link are received correctly and in the proper sequence within a finite time.

- All messages, changes in the cost of a link, link failures, and new-neighbor notifications are processed one at a time within a finite time and in the order in which they are detected.

Cisco's EIGRP uses Neighbor Discovery/Recovery and RTP to establish these preconditions.

Before the operation of DUAL can be examined, a few terms and concepts must be described.

Adjacency

Upon startup, a router uses Hellos to discover neighbors and to identify itself to neighbors. When a neighbor is discovered, EIGRP will attempt to form an adjacency with that neighbor. An *adjacency* is a virtual link between two neighbors over which route information is exchanged. When adjacencies have been established, the router will receive updates from its neighbors. The updates will contain all routes known by the sending routers and the metrics of those routes. For each route, the router will calculate a distance based on the distance advertised by the neighbor and the cost of the link to that neighbor.

Feasible distance

The lowest calculated metric to each destination will become the *feasible distance* (FD) of that destination. For example, a router may be informed of three different routes to subnet 172.16.5.0 and may calculate metrics of 380672, 12381440, and 660868 for the three routes. 380672 will become the FD because it is the lowest calculated distance.

The *feasibility condition* (FC) is a condition that is met if a neighbor's advertised distance to a destination is lower than the router's FD to that same destination.

Feasibility condition

If a neighbor's advertised distance to a destination meets the FC, the neighbor becomes a *feasible successor*[6] for that destination. For example, if the FD to subnet 172.16.5.0 is 380672 and a neighbor advertises a route to that subnet with a distance of 355072, the neighbor will become a feasible successor; if the neighbor advertises a distance of 380928, it will not satisfy the FC and will not become a feasible successor.

Feasible successor

The concepts of feasible successors and the FC are central to loop avoidance. Because feasible successors are always "downstream" (that is, a shorter metric distance to the destination than the FD), a router will never choose a path that will lead back through itself. Such a path would have a distance larger than the FD.

Every destination for which one or more feasible successors exist will be recorded in a *topological table*, along with the following items:

- The destination's FD

- All feasible successors

- Each feasible successor's advertised distance to the destination

- The locally calculated distance to the destination via each feasible successor, based on the feasible successor's advertised distance and the cost of the link to that successor

---

[6] Successor *simply means a router that is one hop closer to a destination—in other words, a next-hop router.*

- The interface connected to the network on which each feasible successor is found[7]

Successor

For every destination listed in the topological table, the route with the lowest metric is chosen and placed into the route table. The neighbor advertising that route becomes the *successor*, or the next-hop router to which packets for that destination are sent.

An example will help clarify these terms, but first a brief discussion of the internetwork used in the examples in this section is necessary. Figure 8.3 shows the EIGRP-based internetwork that is used throughout this and the next three subsections.[8] The command **metric weights 0 0 0 1 0 0** has been added to the EIGRP process so that only delay is used in the metric calculations. The **delay** command has been used with the numbers shown at each link; for example, the interfaces of routers Wright and Langley, connected to subnet 10.1.3.0, have been configured with a delay of 2. These steps have been taken to simplify the examples that follow.

It should be pointed out that although the delay parameters used here sacrifice realism for simplicity, the way the metrics are manipulated is realistic. Many parameters are calculated from an interface's **bandwidth** specification; some, such as the **ip bandwidth-percent eigrp**, apply directly to EIGRP. Others, such as OSPF cost, do not. As a result, changes of the configured bandwidth should be avoided except to set serial links to their actual bandwidth. If interface metrics need to be manipulated to influ-

---

[7]   *Actually, the interface is not explicitly recorded in the route table. Rather, it is an attribute of the neighbor itself. This convention implies that the same router, seen across multiple parallel links, will be viewed by EIGRP as multiple neighbors.*

[8]   *Several of the illustrations in this and the following section, and in the network example used throughout, are adapted from Dr. Garcia-Luna's "Loop-Free Routing Using Diffusing Computations," with his permission.*

ence EIGRP (or IGRP) routing, use **delay**. Many unexpected headaches can be avoided.

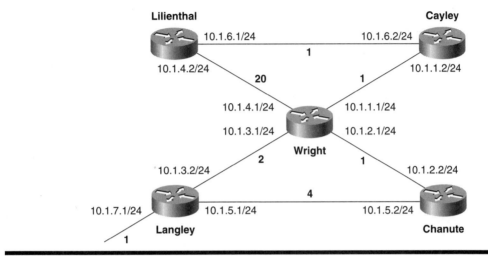

Figure 8.3
The examples and illustrations of this and the next two subsections are based on this EIGRP network.

In Figure 8.4, the command **show ip eigrp topology** is used to observe the topology table of router Langley. Each of the seven subnets shown in Figure 8.3 is listed, along with the feasible successors for the subnets. For example, the feasible successors for subnet 10.1.6.0 are 10.1.3.1 (Wright) and 10.1.5.2 (Chanute), via interfaces S0 and S1, respectively.

Two metrics in parentheses are also associated with each feasible successor. The first number is the locally calculated metric from Langley to the destination. The second number is the metric advertised by the neighbor. For example, in Figure 8.3 the metric from Langley to subnet 10.1.6.0 via Wright is 256 x (2 + 1 + 1) = 1024, and the metric advertised by Wright for that destination is 256 x (1 + 1) = 512. The two metrics for the same destination via Chanute are 256 x (4 + 1 + 1 + 1) = 1792 and 256 x (1 + 1 + 1) = 768.

```
Langley#show ip eigrp topology
IP-EIGRP Topology Table for process 1

Codes: P - Passive, A - Active, U - Update, Q - Query, R - Reply,
       r - Reply status

P 10.1.3.0/24, 1 successors, FD is 512
         via Connected, Serial0
P 10.1.2.0/24, 1 successors, FD is 768
         via 10.1.3.1 (768/256), Serial0
         via 10.1.5.2 (1280/256), Serial1
P 10.1.1.0/24, 1 successors, FD is 768
         via 10.1.3.1 (768/256), Serial0
         via 10.1.5.2 (1536/512), Serial1
P 10.1.7.0/24, 1 successors, FD is 256
         via Connected, Ethernet0
P 10.1.6.0/24, 1 successors, FD is 1024
         via 10.1.3.1 (1024/512), Serial0
         via 10.1.5.2 (1792/768), Serial1
P 10.1.5.0/24, 1 successors, FD is 1024
         via Connected, Serial1
P 10.1.4.0/24, 1 successors, FD is 5632
         via 10.1.3.1 (5632/5120), Serial0
         via 10.1.5.2 (6400/5376), Serial1
Langley#
```

Figure 8.4

The topology table of router Langley.

The lowest metric from Langley to subnet 10.1.6.0 is 1024, so that is the feasible distance (FD). Figure 8.5 shows Langley's route table, with the chosen successors.

Langley has only one successor for every route. The topology table of Cayley (Figure 8.6) shows that there are two successors for 10.1.4.0 because the locally calculated metric for both routes matches the FD. Both routes are entered into the route table (Figure 8.7), and Cayley will perform equal-cost load balancing.

```
Langley#show ip route
Codes: C - connected, S - static, I - IGRP, R - RIP, M - mobile, B - BGP
       D - EIGRP, EX - EIGRP external, O - OSPF, IA - OSPF inter area
       E1 - OSPF external type 1, E2 - OSPF external type 2, E - EGP
       i - IS-IS, L1 - IS-IS level-1, L2 - IS-IS level-2, * - candidate default
       U - per-user static route

Gateway of last resort is not set

     10.0.0.0/8 is subnetted, 7 subnets
C       10.1.3.0 is directly connected, Serial0
D       10.1.2.0 [90/768] via 10.1.3.1, 00:32:06, Serial0
D       10.1.1.0 [90/768] via 10.1.3.1, 00:32:07, Serial0
C       10.1.7.0 is directly connected, Ethernet0
D       10.1.6.0 [90/1024] via 10.1.3.1, 00:32:07, Serial0
C       10.1.5.0 is directly connected, Serial1
D       10.1.4.0 [90/5632] via 10.1.3.1, 00:32:07, Serial0
Langley#
```

Figure 8.5

Langley's route table shows that a single successor has been chosen for each known destination, based on the lowest metric distance.

```
Cayley#show ip eigrp topology
IP-EIGRP Topology Table for process 1

Codes: P - Passive, A - Active, U - Update, Q - Query, R - Reply,
       r - Reply status

P 10.1.3.0/24, 1 successors, FD is 768
        via 10.1.1.1 (768/512), Ethernet0
P 10.1.2.0/24, 1 successors, FD is 512
        via 10.1.1.1 (512/256), Ethernet0
P 10.1.1.0/24, 1 successors, FD is 256
        via Connected, Ethernet0
P 10.1.7.0/24, 1 successors, FD is 1024
        via 10.1.1.1 (1024/768), Ethernet0
P 10.1.6.0/24, 1 successors, FD is 256
        via Connected, Serial0
P 10.1.5.0/24, 1 successors, FD is 1536
        via 10.1.1.1 (1536/1280), Ethernet0
P 10.1.4.0/24, 2 successors, FD is 5376
        via 10.1.6.1 (5376/5120), Serial0
        via 10.1.1.1 (5376/5120), Ethernet0
Cayley#
```

Figure 8.6

The topology table of Cayley, showing two successors to subnet 10.1.4.0.

```
Cayley#show ip route
Codes: C - connected, S - static, I - IGRP, R - RIP, M - mobile, B - BGP
       D - EIGRP, EX - EIGRP external, O - OSPF, IA - OSPF inter area
       N1 - OSPF NSSA external type 1, N2 - OSPF NSSA external type 2
       E1 - OSPF external type 1, E2 - OSPF external type 2, E - EGP
       i - IS-IS, L1 - IS-IS level-1, L2 - IS-IS level-2, * - candidate default
       U - per-user static route, o - ODR

Gateway of last resort is not set

     10.0.0.0/24 is subnetted, 7 subnets
D       10.1.3.0 [90/768] via 10.1.1.1, 00:01:19, Ethernet0
D       10.1.2.0 [90/512] via 10.1.1.1, 00:01:19, Ethernet0
C       10.1.1.0 is directly connected, Ethernet0
D       10.1.7.0 [90/1024] via 10.1.1.1, 00:01:19, Ethernet0
C       10.1.6.0 is directly connected, Serial0
D       10.1.5.0 [90/1536] via 10.1.1.1, 00:01:19, Ethernet0
D       10.1.4.0 [90/5376] via 10.1.1.1, 00:01:19, Ethernet0
                 [90/5376] via 10.1.6.1, 00:01:19, Serial0
Cayley#
```

Figure 8.7

Equal-cost load sharing will be performed between the two successors to 10.1.4.

```
Chanute#show ip eigrp topology
IP-EIGRP Topology Table for process 1

Codes: P - Passive, A - Active, U - Update, Q - Query, R - Reply,
       r - Reply status

P 10.1.3.0/24, 1 successors, FD is 768
        via 10.1.2.1 (768/512), Ethernet0
        via 10.1.5.1 (1536/512), Serial0
P 10.1.2.0/24, 1 successors, FD is 256
        via Connected, Ethernet0
P 10.1.1.0/24, 1 successors, FD is 512
        via 10.1.2.1 (512/256), Ethernet0
P 10.1.7.0/24, 1 successors, FD is 1024
        via 10.1.2.1 (1024/768), Ethernet0
        via 10.1.5.1 (1280/256), Serial0
P 10.1.6.0/24, 1 successors, FD is 768
        via 10.1.2.1 (768/512), Ethernet0
P 10.1.5.0/24, 1 successors, FD is 1024
        via Connected, Serial0
P 10.1.4.0/24, 1 successors, FD is 5376
        via 10.1.2.1 (5376/5120), Ethernet0
Chanute#
```

Figure 8.8

Several of the subnets reachable from Chanute have only one feasible successor.

The topology table of Chanute (Figure 8.8) shows several routes for which there is only one feasible successor. For example, the route to 10.1.6.0 has an FD of 768, and Wright (10.1.2.1) is the only feasible successor. Langley has a route to 10.1.6.0, but its metric is 256 x (2 + 1 + 1) = 1024, which is greater than the FD. Therefore, Langley's route to 10.1.6.0 does not satisfy the FC, and Langley does not qualify as a feasible successor.

If a feasible successor advertises a route for which the locally calculated metric is lower than the metric via the present successor, the feasible successor will become the successor. The following conditions can cause this situation to occur:

- A newly discovered route

- The cost of a successor's route increasing beyond that of a feasible successor

- The cost of a feasible successor's route decreasing to below the cost of the successor's route

For example, Figure 8.9 shows that Lilienthal's successor to subnet 10.1.3.0 is Cayley (10.1.6.2). Suppose the cost of the link between Lilienthal and Wright is decreased to one. Wright (10.1.4.1) is advertising a distance of 512 to subnet 10.1.3.0; with the new cost of the link to Wright, Lilienthal's locally calculated metric to the subnet via that router is now 768. Wright will replace Cayley as the successor to subnet 10.1.3.0.

Next, suppose Lilienthal discovers a new neighbor that is advertising a distance of 256 to subnet 10.1.3.0. This distance is lower than the FD, so the new neighbor will become a feasible successor. Suppose further that the cost of the link to the new neighbor is 256. Lilienthal's locally calculated metric to 10.1.3.0 via the new neighbor will be 512. This metric is lower than the distance via Wright, so the new neighbor will become the successor to 10.1.3.0.

```
Lilienthal#show ip eigrp topology
IP-EIGRP Topology Table for process 1

Codes: P - Passive, A - Active, U - Update, Q - Query, R - Reply,
       r - Reply status

P 10.1.3.0/24, 1 successors, FD is 1024
         via 10.1.6.2 (1024/768), Serial0
         via 10.1.4.1 (5632/512), Serial1
P 10.1.2.0/24, 1 successors, FD is 768
         via 10.1.6.2 (768/512), Serial0
         via 10.1.4.1 (5376/256), Serial1
P 10.1.1.0/24, 1 successors, FD is 512
         via 10.1.6.2 (512/256), Serial0
         via 10.1.4.1 (5376/256), Serial1
P 10.1.7.0/24, 1 successors, FD is 1280
         via 10.1.6.2 (1280/1024), Serial0
         via 10.1.4.1 (5888/768), Serial1
P 10.1.6.0/24, 1 successors, FD is 256
         via Connected, Serial0
P 10.1.5.0/24, 1 successors, FD is 1792
         via 10.1.6.2 (1792/1536), Serial0
         via 10.1.4.1 (6400/1280), Serial1
P 10.1.4.0/24, 1 successors, FD is 5120
         via Connected, Serial1
Lilienthal#
```

Figure 8.9

The topology table for Lilienthal.

Feasible successors are important because they reduce the number of diffusing computations and therefore increase performance. Feasible successors also contribute to lower reconvergence times. If a link to a successor fails or if the cost of the link increases beyond the FD, the router will first look into its topology table for a feasible successor. If one is found, it will become the successor. The router will only begin a diffusing computation if a feasible successor cannot be found.

The following section gives a more formal set of rules for when and how a router will search for feasible successors. This set of rules is called the *DUAL finite state machine*.

The DUAL Finite State Machine

When an EIGRP router is performing no diffusing computations, each route is in the *passive state*. Referring to any of the topology tables in the previous section, a key to the left of each route indicates a passive state.

A router will reassess its list of feasible successors for a route, as described in the last section, any time an *input event* occurs. An input event can be:

- A change in the cost of a directly connected link

- A change in the state (up or down) of a directly connected link

- The reception of an update packet

- The reception of a query packet

- The reception of a reply packet

The first step in its reassessment is a *local computation* in which the distance to the destination is recalculated for all feasible successors. The possible results are:

- If the feasible successor with the lowest distance is different from the existing successor, the feasible successor will become the successor.

- If the new distance is lower than the FD, the FD will be updated.

- If the new distance is different from the existing distance, updates will be sent to all neighbors.

While the router is performing a local computation, the route remains in the passive state. If a feasible successor is found, an update is sent to all neighbors and no state change occurs.

If a feasible successor cannot be found in the topology table, the router will begin a diffusing computation and the route will change to the *active state*. Until the diffusing computation is completed and the route transitions back to the passive state, the router cannot:

- Change the route's successor

- Change the distance it is advertising for the route

- Change the route's FD

- Begin another diffusing computation for the route

A router begins a diffusing computation by sending queries to all of its neighbors (Figure 8.10). The query will contain the new locally calculated distance to the destination. Each neighbor, upon receipt of the query, will perform its own local computation:

- If the neighbor has one or more feasible successors for the destination, it will send a reply to the originating router. The reply will contain that neighbor's minimum locally calculated distance to the destination.

- If the neighbor does not have a feasible successor, it too will change the route to the active state and will begin a diffusing computation.

For each neighbor to which a query is sent, the router will set a *reply status flag* (r) to keep track of all outstanding queries. The diffusing computation is complete when the router has received a reply to every query sent to every neighbor.

In some cases, a router does not receive a reply to every query sent. For example, this may happen in large networks with many low-bandwidth or low-quality links. At the beginning of the diffusing computation, an Active timer is set for 3 minutes.[9] If all expected replies are not received before the Active time expires, the route is declared *stuck-in-active* (SIA). The neighbor or neighbors that did not reply will be removed from the neighbor table, and the diffusing computation will consider the neighbor to have responded with an infinite metric.

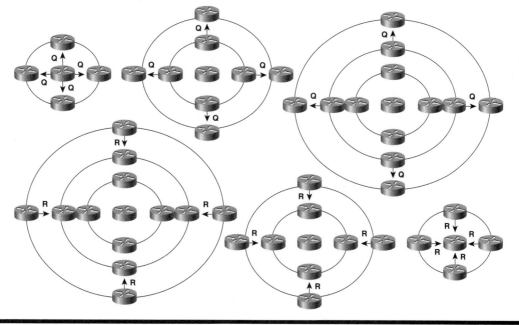

Figure 8.10

A diffusing computation grows as queries are sent and shrinks as replies are received.

The default 3-minute Active time can be changed or disabled with the command **timers active-time**. The deletion of a neighbor because of a lost query obviously can have disruptive results, and SIAs should never occur in a stable, well-designed internetwork. The troubleshooting section of this chapter discusses SIAs in more detail.

At the completion of the diffusing computation, the originating router will set FD to infinity to ensure that any neighbor replying with a finite distance to the destination will meet the FC and

---

[9] *The default Active timer is 1 minute in some earlier IOS versions.*

become a feasible successor. For each of these replies, a metric is calculated based on the distance advertised in the reply plus the cost of the link to the neighbor who sent the reply. A successor is selected based on the lowest metric, and FD is set to this metric. Any feasible successors that do not satisfy the FC for this new FD will be removed from the topology table. Note that a successor is not chosen until all replies have been received.

Since there are multiple types of input events can cause a route to change state, some of which may occur while a route is active, DUAL defines multiple active states. A *query origin flag* (O) is used to indicate the current state. Figure 8.11 and Table 8.1 show the complete DUAL finite state machine.

Table 8.1   *Input events for the DUAL finite state machine.*

Input Event	Description
IE1	Any input event for which FC is satisfied or the destination is unreachable
IE2	Query received from the successor; FC not satisfied
IE3	Input event other than a query from the successor; FC not satisfied
IE4	Input event other than last reply or a query from the successor
IE5	Input event other than last reply, a query from the successor, or an increase in distance to destination
IE6	Input event other than last reply
IE7	Input event other than last reply or increase in distance to destination
IE8	Increase in distance to destination
IE9	Last reply received; FC not met with current FD
IE10	Query received from the successor
IE11	Last reply received; FC met with current FD
IE12	Last reply received; set FD to infinity

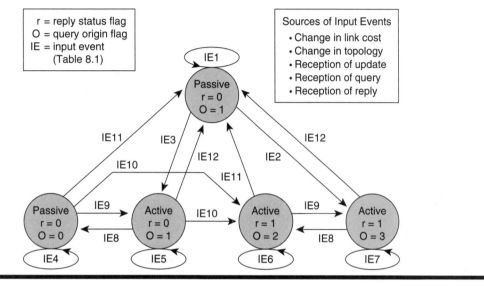

Figure 8.11

The DUAL finite state machine. The query origin flag (O) marks the current state of the diffusing calculation. See Table 8.1 for a description of each input event (IE).

Two examples will help clarify the DUAL process. Figure 8.12 shows the example network, focusing only on each router's path to subnet 10.1.7.0; refer to Figure 8.3 for specific addresses. On the data links, an arrow indicates the successor each router is using to reach 10.1.7.0. In parentheses are each router's locally calculated distance to the subnet, the router's FD, the reply status flag (r), and the query origin flag (O), respectively. Active routers are indicated with a circle.

Diffusing Computation: Example 1

This example focuses only on Cayley and its route to subnet 10.1.7.0. In Figure 8.13, the link between Cayley and Wright (10.1.1.1) has failed. EIGRP interprets the failure as a link with an infinite distance.[10] Cayley checks its topology table for a feasible successor to 10.1.7.0 and finds none (refer to Figure 8.6).

---

[10] *An infinite distance is indicated by a delay of 0xFFFFFFFF, or 4294967295.*

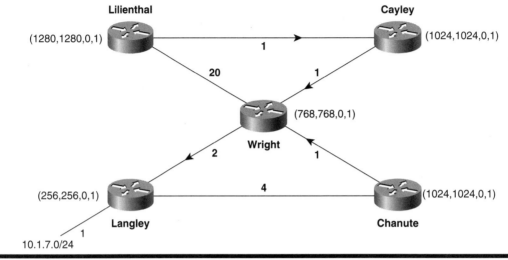

Figure 8.12
All routes to subnet 10.1.7.0 are in the passive state, indicated by r = 0 and O = 1.

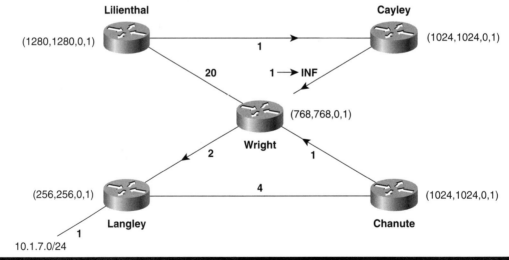

Figure 8.13
The link between Wright and Cayley has failed, and Cayley does not have a feasible successor to subnet 10.1.7.0.

Cayley's route becomes active (Figure 8.14). The distance and the FD of the route are changed to unreachable, and a query containing the new distance is sent to Cayley's neighbor, Lilienthal. Cayley's reply status flag for Lilienthal is set to one, indicating that a reply is expected. Because the input event was not the reception of a query (IE3), O=1.

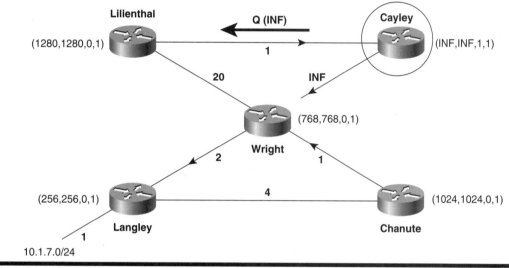

Figure 8.14

Cayley's route to 10.1.7.0 transitions to active, and Lilienthal is queried for a feasible successor.

Upon receipt of the query, Lilienthal performs a local computation (Figure 8.15). Because Lilienthal has a feasible successor for 10.1.7.0 (see Figure 8.9), the route does not become active. Wright becomes the new successor, and a reply is sent with Lilienthal's distance to 10.1.7.0 via Wright. Because the distance to 10.1.7.0 has increased and the route did not become active, the FD is unchanged at Lilienthal.

Upon receipt of the reply from Lilienthal, Cayley sets r=0 and the route becomes passive (Figure 8.16). Lilienthal becomes the new successor, and the FD is set to the new distance. Finally, an update is sent to Lilienthal with Cayley's locally calculated metric. Lilienthal will also send an update advertising its new metric.

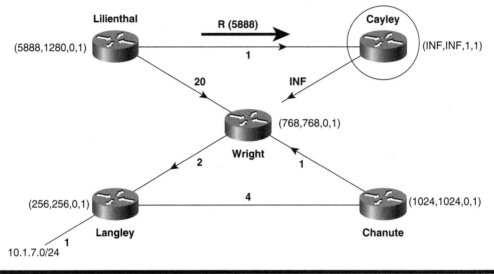

Figure 8.15
Lilienthal has a feasible successor to 10.1.7.0. A local computation is performed, a reply is sent to Cayley with the distance via Wright, and an update is sent to Wright.

EIGRP packet activity can be observed with the debug command **debug eigrp packets**. By default, all EIGRP packets are displayed. Because Hellos and ACKs can make the debug output hard to follow, the command allows the use of optional keywords so that only specified packet types are displayed. In Figure 8.17, **debug eigrp packets query reply update** is used to observe the packet activity at Cayley for the events described in this example.

Flags, in the debug messages, indicate the state of the flags in the EIGRP packet header (see the section "The EIGRP Packet Header" later in this chapter). 0x0 indicates that no flags are set. 0x1 indicates that the *initialization* bit is set. This flag is set when the enclosed route entries are the first in a new neighbor relationship.

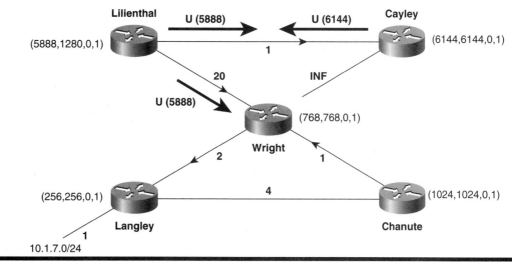

Figure 8.16

Cayley's route to 10.1.7.0 becomes passive, and an update is sent to Lilienthal.

```
Cayley#debug eigrp packet update query reply
EIGRP Packets debugging is on
    (UPDATE, QUERY, REPLY)
B#
%LINEPROTO-5-UPDOWN: Line protocol on Interface Ethernet0, changed state to down
EIGRP: Enqueueing QUERY on Serial0 iidbQ un/rely 0/1 serno 45-49
EIGRP: Enqueueing QUERY on Serial0 nbr 10.1.6.1 iidbQ un/rely 0/0 peerQ un/rely
0/0 serno 45-49
EIGRP: Sending QUERY on Serial0 nbr 10.1.6.1
  AS 1, Flags 0x0, Seq 45/64 idbQ 0/0 iidbQ un/rely 0/0 peerQ un/rely 0/1 serno
45-49
EIGRP: Received REPLY on Serial0 nbr 10.1.6.1
  AS 1, Flags 0x0, Seq 65/45 idbQ 0/0 iidbQ un/rely 0/0 peerQ un/rely 0/0
EIGRP: Enqueueing UPDATE on Serial0 iidbQ un/rely 0/1 serno 50-54
EIGRP: Enqueueing UPDATE on Serial0 nbr 10.1.6.1 iidbQ un/rely 0/0 peerQ un/rely
 0/0 serno 50-54
EIGRP: Sending UPDATE on Serial0 nbr 10.1.6.1
  AS 1, Flags 0x0, Seq 46/66 idbQ 0/0 iidbQ un/rely 0/0 peerQ un/rely 0/1 serno
50-54
EIGRP: Received UPDATE on Serial0 nbr 10.1.6.1
  AS 1, Flags 0x0, Seq 67/46 idbQ 0/0 iidbQ un/rely 0/0 peerQ un/rely 0/1
```

Figure 8.17

The EIGRP packet events described in this example can be observed in these debug messages.

0x2 indicates that the *conditional receive* bit is set. This flag is used
in the proprietary Reliable Multicasting algorithm.

Seq is the Packet Sequence Number/Acknowledged Sequence Number.

idbq indicates packets in the input queue/packets in the output queue of the interface.

iidbq indicates unreliable multicast packets awaiting transmission/reliable multicast packets awaiting transmission on the interface.

peerQ indicates unreliable unicast packets awaiting transmission/reliable unicast packets awaiting transmission on the interface.

serno is a pointer to a doubly linked serial number for the route. This is used by an internal (and proprietary) mechanism for tracking the correct route information in a rapidly changing topology.

Diffusing Computation: Example 2

This example focuses on Wright and its route to subnet 10.1.7.0. Although the combination of input events portrayed here (the delay of a link changing twice during a diffusing computation) is unlikely to occur in real life, the example shows how DUAL handles multiple metric changes.

In Figure 8.18, the cost of the link between Wright and Langley changes from 2 to 10. The distance to 10.1.7.0 via Langley now exceeds Wright's FD, causing that router to begin a local computation. The metric is updated, and Wright sends updates to all its neighbors except the neighbor on the link whose cost changed (Figure 8.19).

Note that Langley was the only feasible successor to subnet 10.1.7.0 because Chanute's locally calculated metric is higher than Wright's FD (1024 > 768). The metric increase on the Wright-Langley link causes Wright to look in its topology table for a new successor. Because the only feasible successor that Wright

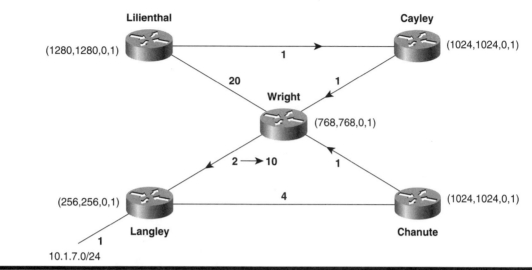

Figure 8.18

Cayley's route to 10.1.7.0 becomes passive, and an update is sent to Lilienthal.

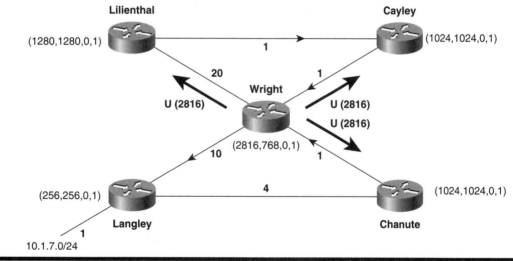

Figure 8.19

Wright sends updates containing the new metric to all neighbors except Langley.

can find in its topology table is Langley, the route becomes active. Queries are sent to the neighbors (Figure 8.20).

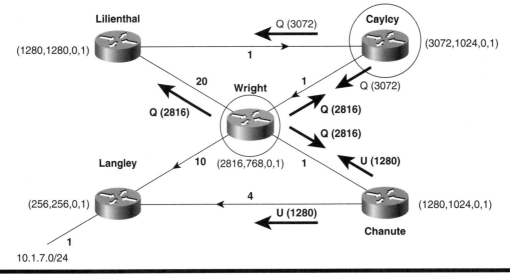

Figure 8.20
Wright's route to 10.1.7.0 becomes active, and it queries its neighbors for a feasible successor. In response to the earlier update from Wright, Cayley makes its route active and queries its neighbors; also, Chanute changes its metric and sends updates.

At the same time, the updates sent by Wright in Figure 8.19 cause Cayley, Lilienthal, and Chanute to perform a local calculation.

At Cayley, the route via Wright now exceeds Cayley's FD (2816 > 1024). The route goes active and queries are sent to the neighbors.

Lilienthal is using Cayley as a successor and in Figure 8.20 has not yet received the query from Cayley. Therefore, Lilienthal merely recalculates the metric of the path via Wright, finds that it no longer meets the FC, and drops the path from the topology table.

At Chanute, Wright is the successor. Because Wright's advertised distance no longer meets the FC at Chanute (2816 > 1024) and because Chanute does have a feasible successor (refer to Figure

8.8), Wright is deleted from Chanute's topology table. Langley becomes the successor at Chanute; the metric is updated, and Chanute sends updates to its neighbors (refer to Figure 8.20). The route at Chanute never becomes active.

Cayley, Lilienthal, and Chanute each respond differently to the queries from Wright (Figure 8.21).

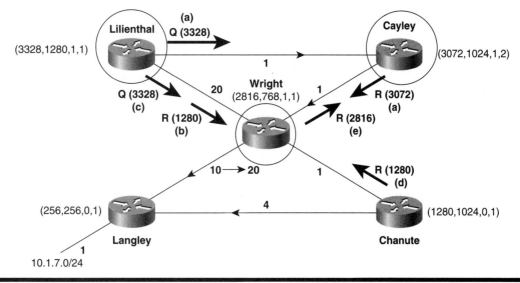

Figure 8.21

Cayley (a) replies to Wright's query. Lilienthal (b) replies to Wright's query and (c) goes active for the route, sending queries in response to Cayley's query. Chanute (d) replies to Wright's query. Wright (e) replies to Cayley's query.

Cayley is already active. Because the input event is a query from the successor, the query origin flag will be 2 (O=2) (refer to Figure 8.11 and Table 8.1).

Lilienthal, upon the receipt of Wright's query, sends a response with its distance via Cayley. However, just after the reply is sent, Lilienthal receives the query from Cayley. The FD is exceeded, the metric is updated, and the route goes active. Lilienthal queries its neighbors.

Chanute, which has already switched to Langley as its successor, merely sends a reply.

While all this is going on, Figure 8.21 shows that the cost of the link between Wright and Langley again increases, from 10 to 20. Wright will recalculate the metric to 10.1.7.0 based on this new cost, but because the route is active, neither the FD nor the distance it advertises will change until the route becomes passive.

According to Figure 8.11 and Table 8.1, an increase in the distance to the destination while the route is active will cause O=0 (Figure 8.22). Wright responds to the query from Lilienthal. The distance it reports is the distance it had when the route first became active (remember, the advertised distance cannot change while the route is active). Cayley also sends a reply to Lilienthal's query.

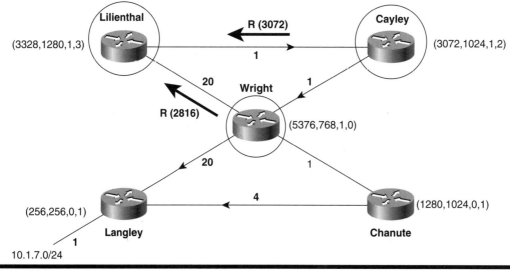

Figure 8.22

Wright cannot change the metric it advertises until the route becomes passive.

Lilienthal, having received replies to all its queries, will transition the route to passive (Figure 8.23). A new FD is set for the route. Cayley remains the successor because its advertised route is lower than the FD at Lilienthal. Lilienthal also sends a reply to Cayley's query.

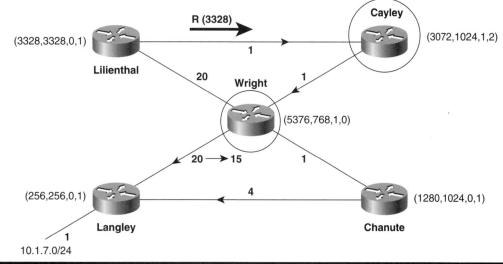

Figure 8.23

Having received the last expected reply, Lilienthal changes its route to the passive state (r=0, O=1).

Figure 8.23 also shows that the distance has changed again, from 20 to 15. Wright recalculates its local distance for the route again, to 4096 (Figure 8.24). If it were to receive a query before going passive, the route would still be advertised with a distance of 2816—the distance when the route went active.

When Cayley receives the reply to its query, its route to 10.1.7.0 also becomes passive (Figure 8.24) and a new FD is set. Although Wright's locally calculated metric is 4096, the last metric it advertised was 2816. Therefore, Wright meets the FC at Cayley and becomes the successor to 10.1.7.0. A reply is sent to Wright.

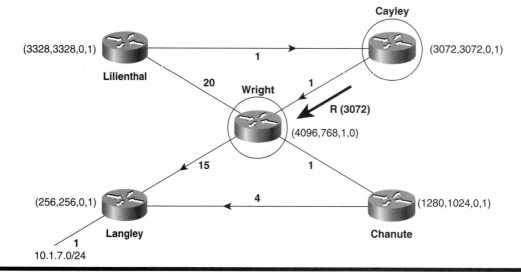

Figure 8.24

Having received its last expected reply, Cayley changes its route to the passive state.

In Figure 8.25, Wright has received a reply to every query it sent, and its route becomes passive. It chooses Chanute as its new successor and changes the FD to the sum of Chanute's advertised distance and the cost of the link to that neighbor. Wright sends an update to all its neighbors, advertising the new locally calculated metric.

Cayley is already using Wright as the successor. When it receives the update from Wright with a lower cost, it changes its locally calculated metric and FD accordingly and updates its neighbors (Figure 8.26).

The update from Cayley has no effect at Wright because it does not satisfy the FC there. At Lilienthal the update causes a local computation. Lilienthal lowers the metric, lowers the FD, and updates its neighbors (Figure 8.27).

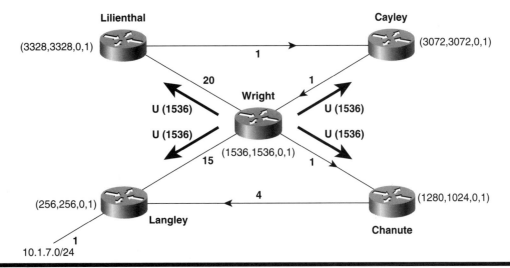

Figure 8.25

Wright transitions to passive, chooses Chanute as the successor, changes the FD, and updates all neighbors.

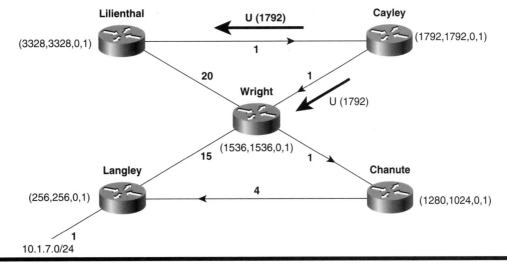

Figure 8.26

Cayley recalculates its metric, changes the FD based on the lower cost advertised by Wright, and updates its neighbors.

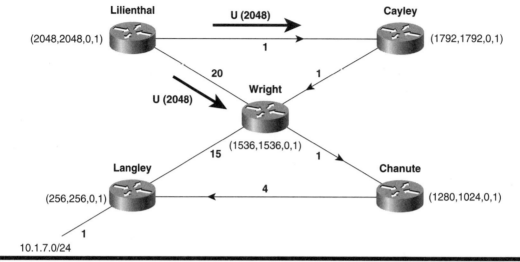

Figure 8.27

Lilienthal recalculates its metric, changes the FD based on the update from Cayley, and updates its neighbors.

Although they are rather elaborate and may take several readings to fully understand, this and the previous example contain the important core behavior of diffusing computations:

- Any time an input event occurs, perform a local calculation.

- If one or more feasible successors are found in the topology table, make the one(s) with the lowest metric cost the successor(s).

- If no feasible successor can be found, make the route active and query the neighbors for a feasible successor.

- Keep the route active until all queries are answered by a reply or by the expiration of the active timer.

- If the diffusing calculation does not result in the discovery of a feasible successor, declare the destination unreachable.

EIGRP Packet Formats

The IP header of an EIGRP packet specifies protocol number 88, and the maximum length of the packet will be the IP maximum transmission unit (MTU)—usually 1500 octets. Following the IP header is an EIGRP header followed by various *Type/Length/Value* (TLV) triplets. These TLVs will not only carry the route entries but also may provide fields for the management of the DUAL process, multicast sequencing, and IOS software versions.

The EIGRP Packet Header

Figure 8.28 shows the EIGRP header, which begins every EIGRP packet.

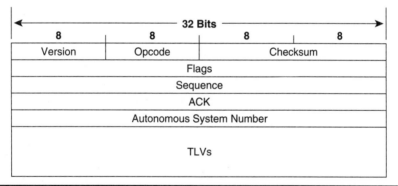

Figure 8.28
The EIGRP packet header.

Version specifies the particular version of the originating EIGRP process. Although two software releases of EIGRP are currently available,[11] the version of the EIGRP process itself has not changed since its release.

---

[11] *Because of the improvements to its stability beginning with IOS 10.3(11), 11.0(8), and 11.1(3) use of the later version of EIGRP is highly recommended.*

Opcode specifies the EIGRP packet type, as shown in Table 8.2. Although the IPX SAP packet type is included in the table, a discussion of IPX EIGRP is outside the scope of this book.

Table 8.2   *EIGRP packet types.*

OPcode	Type
1	Update
3	Query
4	Reply
5	Hello
6	IPX SAP

Checksum is a standard IP checksum. It is calculated for the entire EIGRP packet, excluding the IP header.

Flags currently include just two flags. The right-most bit is *Init*, which when set (0x00000001) indicates that the enclosed route entries are the first in a new neighbor relationship. The second bit (0x00000002) is the Conditional Receive bit, used in the proprietary Reliable Multicasting algorithm.

Sequence is the 32-bit sequence number used by the RTP.

ACK is the 32-bit sequence number last heard from the neighbor to which the packet is being sent. A Hello packet with a nonzero ACK field will be treated as an ACK packet rather than as a Hello. Note that an ACK field will only be nonzero if the packet itself is unicast because acknowledgments are never multicast.

Autonomous System Number is the identification number of the EIGRP domain.

Following the header are the TLVs, whose various types are listed in Table 8.3. IPX and AppleTalk types are included, although they are not discussed in this book. Each TLV includes one of the two-octet type numbers listed in Table 8.3, a two-octet field specifying the length of the TLV, and a variable field whose format is determined by the type.

Table 8.3 *Type/length/value (TLV) types.*

Number	TLV Type
General TLV Types	
0x0001	EIGRP Parameters
0x0003	Sequence
0x0004	Software Version[12]
0x0005	Next Multicast Sequence
IP-Specific TLV Types	
0x0102	IP Internal Routes
0x0103	IP External Routes
AppleTalk-Specific TLV Types	
0x0202	AppleTalk Internal Routes
0X0203	AppleTalk External Routes
0x0204	AppleTalk Cable Configuration
IPX-Specific TLV Types	
0x0302	IPX Internal Routes
0x0303	IPX External Routes

General TLV Fields

These TLVs carry EIGRP management information and are not specific to any one routed protocol. The Parameters TLV, which is

---

[12] *This packet indicates whether the older software release is running (software version 0) or the newer release, as of IOS 10.3(11), 11.0(8), and 11.1(3), is running (version 1).*

used to convey metric weights and the hold time, is shown in Figure 8.29. The Sequence, Software Version, and Next Multicast Sequence TLVs are used by Cisco's proprietary Reliable Multicast algorithm and are beyond the scope of this book.

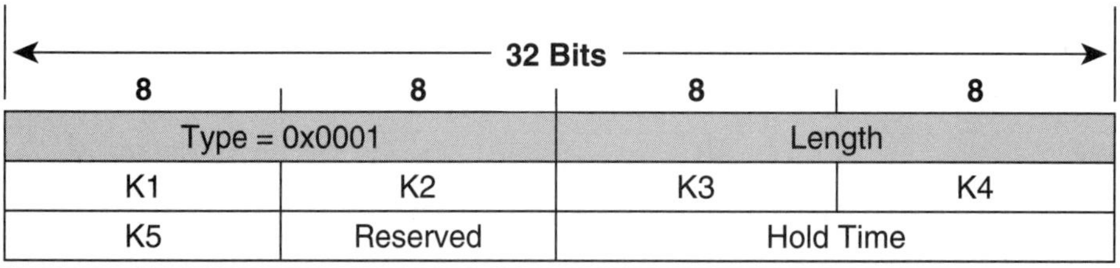

Figure 8.29
The EIGRP Parameters TLV.

IP-Specific TLV Fields

Each Internal and External Routes TLV contains one route entry. Every Update, Query, and Reply packet contains at least one Routes TLV.

The Internal and External Routes TLVs include metric information for the route. As noted earlier, the metrics used by EIGRP are the same metrics used by IGRP, although scaled by 256, and are discussed in more detail—along with the calculation of the composite metric—in Chapter 6.

IP Internal Routes TLV

An internal route is a path to a destination within the EIGRP autonomous system. The format of the Internal Routes TLV is shown in Figure 8.30.

Next Hop is the next-hop IP address. This address may or may not be the address of the originating router. *Delay* is the sum of the configured delays expressed in units of 10 microseconds. Notice that unlike the 24-bit delay field of the IGRP packet, this field is 32 bits. This larger field accommodates the 256 multiplier used by EIGRP. A delay of 0xFFFFFFFF indicates an unreachable route.

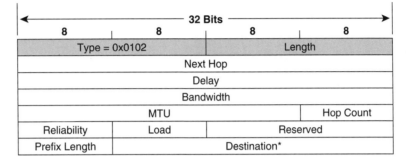

*This field is variable. If it is less than or more than three octets, the TLV will be padded with zeros to the next four-octet boundary. For example, if the destination address is 10.1, the Destination field will be two octets and will be followed with a pad of 0x00. If the address is 192.168.16.64, the Destination field will be four octets and will be followed with a pad of 0x000000.

Figure 8.30
The IP Internal Routes TLV.

Bandwidth is 256 * $BW_{IGRP(min)}$, or 2,560,000,000 divided by the lowest configured bandwidth of any interface along the route. Like Delay, this field is also eight bits larger than the IGRP field.

MTU is the smallest Maximum Transmission Unit of any link along the route to the destination. Although an included parameter, it has never been used in the calculation of metrics.

Hop Count is a number between 0x01 and 0xFF indicating the number of hops to the destination. A router will advertise a directly connected network with a hop count of 0; subsequent routers will record and advertise the route relative to the next-hop router.

Reliability is a number between 0x01 and 0xFF that reflects the total outgoing error rates of the interfaces along the route, calculated on a 5-minute exponentially weighted average. 0xFF indicates a 100% reliable link.

Load is also a number between 0x01 and 0xFF, reflecting the total outgoing load of the interfaces along the route, calculated on a 5-minute exponentially weighted average. 0x01 indicates a minimally loaded link.

Reserved is an unused field and is always 0x0000.

Prefix Length specifies the number of network bits of the address mask. *Destination* is the destination address of the route. Although the field is shown as a three-octet field in Figures 8.30 and 8.31, the field varies with the specific address. For example, if the route is to 10.1.0.0/16, the prefix length will be 16 and the destination will be a two-octet field containing 10.1. If the route is to 192.168.17.64/27, the prefix length will be 27 and the destination will be a four-octet field containing 192.168.16.64. If this field is not exactly three octets, the TLV will be padded with zeros to make it end on a four-octet boundary.

IP External Routes TLV

An external route is a path that leads to a destination outside of the EIGRP autonomous system and that has been redistributed into the EIGRP domain. Figure 8.31 shows the format of the External Routes TLV.

Next Hop is the next-hop IP address. On a multiaccess network, the router advertising the route may not be the best next-hop router to the destination. For example, an EIGRP-speaking router on an Ethernet link may also be speaking BGP and may be advertising a BGP-learned route into the EIGRP autonomous system. Because other routers on the link do not speak BGP, they may have no way of knowing that the interface to the BGP speaker is the best next-hop address. The Next Hop field allows the "bilingual" router to tell its EIGRP neighbors, "Use address A.B.C.D as the next hop instead of using my interface address." *Originating Router* is the IP address or router ID of the router that redistributed the external route into the EIGRP autonomous system.

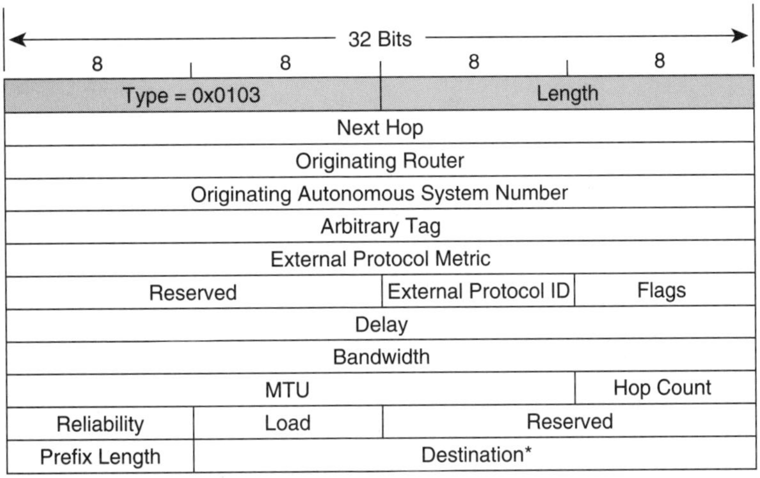

32 Bits			
8	8	8	8
Type = 0x0103		Length	
Next Hop			
Originating Router			
Originating Autonomous System Number			
Arbitrary Tag			
External Protocol Metric			
Reserved		External Protocol ID	Flags
Delay			
Bandwidth			
MTU			Hop Count
Reliability	Load	Reserved	
Prefix Length	Destination*		

*This field is variable. If it is less than or more than three octets, the TLV will be padded with zeros to the next four-octet boundary. For example, if the destination address is 10.1, the Destination field will be two octets and will be followed with a pad of 0x00. If the address is 192.168.16.64, the Destination field will be four octets and will be followed with a pad of 0x000000.

Figure 8.31
The IP External Routes TLV.

Originating Autonomous System Number is the autonomous system number of the router originating the route.

Arbitrary Tag may be used to carry a tag set by route maps. See Chapter 14, "Route Maps," for information on the use of route maps.

External Protocol metric is, as the name implies, the metric of the external protocol. This field is used, when redistributing with IGRP, to track the IGRP metric.

Reserved is an unused field and is always 0x0000.

External Protocol ID specifies the protocol from which the external route was learned. Table 8.4 lists the possible values of this field.

Table 8.4   *Values of the External protocol ID field.*

Code	External Protocol
0x01	IGRP
0x02	EIGRP
0x03	Static Route
0x04	RIP
0x05	Hello
0x06	OSPF
0x07	IS-IS
0x08	EGP
0x09	BGP
0x0A	IDRP
0x0B	Connected Link

Flags currently constitute just two flags. If the right-most bit of the eight-bit field is set (0x01), the route is an external route. If the second bit is set (0x02), the route is a candidate default route. Default routes are discussed in Chapter 12, "Default Routes and On-Demand Routing."

The remaining fields describe the metrics and the destination address. The descriptions of these fields are the same as those given in the discussion of the Internal Routes TLV.

Address Aggregation

Chapter 2, "TCP/IP Review," introduced the practice of subnetting, in which the address mask is extended into the host space in order to address multiple data links under one major network address. Chapter 7 introduced the practice of variable-length subnet masking, in which the address mask is extended even more to create subnets within subnets.

From an opposite perspective, a subnet address may be thought of as a summarization of a group of sub-subnets. And a major network address may be thought of as a summarization of a group of subnet addresses. In each case, the summarization is achieved by reducing the length of the address mask.

Address aggregation takes summarization a step further by breaking the class limits of major network addresses. An aggregate address represents a numerically contiguous group of network addresses, known as a supernet.[13] Figure 8.32 shows an example of an aggregate address.

> An aggregate address summarizes a group of network or subnet addresses.

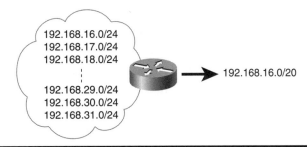

Figure 8.32

This group of network addresses can be represented with a single aggregate address, or subnet.

---

[13] *An aggregate is, more correctly, any summarized group of addresses. For clarity, in this book the term* aggregate *refers to a summarization of a group of major network addresses.*

Figure 8.33 shows how the aggregate address of Figure 8.32 is derived. For a group of network addresses, find the bits that are common to all of the addresses and mask these bits. The masked portion is the aggregate address.

```
11111111111111111111111100000000 =  24-bit mask
11000000101010000001000000000000 =  192.168.16.0/24
11000000101010000001000100000000 =  192.168.17.0/24
11000000101010000001001000000000 =  192.168.18.0/24
11000000101010000001001100000000 =  192.168.19.0/24
11000000101010000001010000000000 =  192.168.20.0/24
11000000101010000001010100000000 =  192.168.21.0/24
11000000101010000001011000000000 =  192.168.22.0/24
11000000101010000001011100000000 =  192.168.23.0/24
11000000101010000001100000000000 =  192.168.24.0/24
11000000101010000001100100000000 =  192.168.25.0/24
11000000101010000001101000000000 =  192.168.26.0/24
11000000101010000001101100000000 =  192.168.27.0/24
11000000101010000001110000000000 =  192.168.28.0/24
11000000101010000001110100000000 =  192.168.29.0/24
11000000101010000001111000000000 =  192.168.30.0/24
11000000101010000001111100000000 =  192.168.31.0/24
11000000101010000001000000000000 =  192.168.16.0/20
```

Figure 8.33

The aggregate address is derived by masking all the common bits of a group of numerically contiguous network addresses.

A design rule for aggregate addressing

When designing a supernet, it is important that the member addresses should form a complete, contiguous set of the formerly masked bits. In Figure 8.33, for example, the 20-bit mask of the aggregate address is four bits less than the mask of the member addresses. Of the four "difference" bits, notice that they include every possible bit combination from 0000 to 1111. Failure to follow this design rule will make the addressing scheme confusing, can reduce the efficiency of aggregate routes, and may lead to routing loops and black holes.

The obvious advantage of summary addressing is the conservation of network resources. Bandwidth is conserved by advertising fewer routes, and CPU cycles are conserved by processing fewer routes. Most important, memory is conserved by reducing the size of the route tables.

Classless routing, VLSM, and aggregate addressing together provide the means to maximize resource conservation by building address hierarchies. Unlike IGRP, EIGRP supports all of these addressing strategies. In Figure 8.34, the engineering division of Treetop Aviation has been assigned 16 class C addresses. These addresses have been assigned to the various departments according to need.

Addressing capabilities of EIGRP compared to IGRP

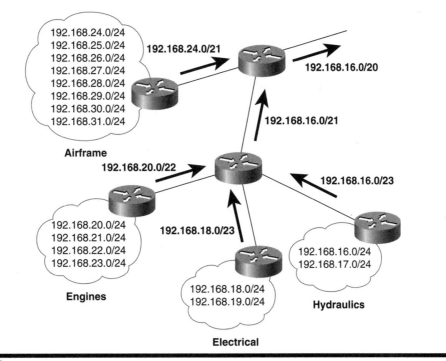

192.168.24.0/24
192.168.25.0/24
192.168.26.0/24   192.168.24.0/21
192.168.27.0/24
192.168.28.0/24   192.168.16.0/20
192.168.29.0/24
192.168.30.0/24
192.168.31.0/24
                                192.168.16.0/21

Airframe
        192.168.20.0/22
                                    192.168.16.0/23

192.168.20.0/24
192.168.21.0/24   192.168.18.0/23
192.168.22.0/24
192.168.23.0/24   192.168.16.0/24
                                    192.168.17.0/24

Engines
                192.168.18.0/24
                192.168.19.0/24   **Hydraulics**

                Electrical

Figure 8.34

At Treetop Aviation, several departments within a larger division are aggregating addresses. In turn, the entire division can be advertised with a single aggregate address (192.168.16.0/20).

The aggregate addresses of the engines, electrical, and hydraulics departments are themselves aggregated into a single address, 192.168.16.0/21. That address and the aggregate address of the airframe department are aggregated into the single address 192.168.16.0/20, which represents the entire engineering division.

Other divisions may be similarly represented. For example, if Treetop Aviation has a total of eight divisions and if those divisions are all addressed similarly to the engineering division, the backbone router at the top of the hierarchy may have as few as eight routes (Figure 8.35).

The hierarchical design is continued within each department of each division by subnetting the individual network addresses. VLSM may be used to further divide the subnets. The routing protocols will automatically summarize the subnets at network boundaries, as discussed in previous chapters.

Address aggregation also allows both address conservation and address hierarchies in the Internet. With the exponential growth of the Internet, two increasing concerns have been the depletion of available IP addresses (particularly class B addresses) and the huge databases needed to store the Internet routing information.

A solution to this problem is an initiative known as *Classless Interdomain Routing* (CIDR).[14] Under CIDR, aggregates of class C addresses are allocated by the InterNIC to the various worldwide address assignment authorities such as Network Solutions in the United States and Rèseaux IP Europèens (RIPE) in Europe. The aggregates are organized geographically, as shown in Table 8.5.

---

[14] *V. Fuller, T. Li, J. I. Yu, and K. Varadhan. "Classless Inter-Domain Routing (CIDR):*
   An Address Assignment and Aggregation Strategy." RFC 1519, September 1993.

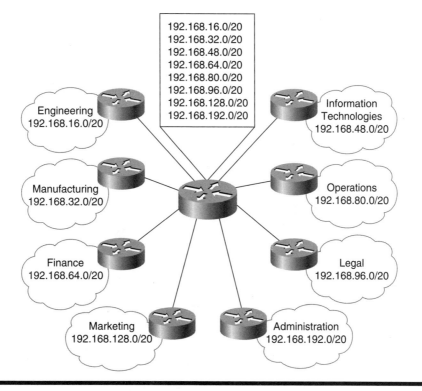

Figure 8.35

Although there are 128 major network addresses and possibly over 32,000 hosts in this internetwork, the backbone router has only eight aggregate addresses in its route table.

Table 8.5   *CIDR address allocations by geographic region.*

Region	Address Range
Multiregional	192.0.0.0–193.255.255.255
Europe	194.0.0.0–195.255.255.255
Others	196.0.0.0–197.255.255.255
North America	198.0.0.0–199.255.255.255
Central/South America	200.0.0.0–201.255.255.255
Pacific Rim	202.0.0.0–203.255.255.255
Others	204.0.0.0–205.255.255.255
Others	206.0.0.0–207.255.255.255

The address assignment authorities in turn divide their portions among the regional Internet service providers (ISPs). When an organization applies for an IP address and requires addressing for less than 32 subnets and 4096 hosts, it will be given a contiguous group of class C addresses called a *CIDR block*.

In this way, the Internet routers of individual organizations might advertise a single summary address to their ISP. The ISP, in turn, aggregates all of its addresses, and all ISPs in a region of the world may be summarized by the addresses of Table 8.5.

This chapter's case studies include some examples of address aggregation; further examples are included in Chapter 9, "Open Shortest Path First."

CONFIGURING EIGRP

The basic configuration of EIGRP is so similar to the basic configuration of IGRP that instructors occasionally will instruct beginners to "configure IGRP, but add an *E*." As mentioned in the previous section, the **metric weights** command is used the same way with EIGRP and IGRP. The **traffic-share** and **variance** commands are also used identically. For a review of these commands, please refer to Chapter 6.

The case studies in this section demonstrate a basic EIGRP configuration and then examine summarization techniques and interoperability with IGRP.

Case Study: A Basic EIGRP Configuration

Like IGRP, EIGRP requires only two steps to begin the routing process:

1. Enable EIGRP with the command **router eigrp** *process-id*.
2. Specify each major network on which to run EIGRP with the **network** command.

The process ID may be any number between 1 and 65535 (0 is not allowed), and it may be arbitrarily chosen by the network administrator, as long as it is the same for all EIGRP processes in all routers that must share information. Alternatively, the number may be an InterNIC-assigned autonomous system number. Figure 8.36 shows a simple internetwork; the configurations for the three routers are as follows:

Earhart:

```
router eigrp 15
   network 172.20.0.0
```

Cochran:

```
router eigrp 15
   network 172.20.0.0
   network 192.168.17.0
```

Lindbergh:

```
router eigrp 15
   network 172.20.0.0
   network 192.168.16.0
```

Earhart's route table is shown in Figure 8.37. The table shows that the default EIGRP administrative distance is 90 and that network 172.20.0.0 is variably subnetted.

The internetwork of Figure 8.36 uses default metrics, unlike the earlier examples in this chapter, so a review of the EIGRP metric calculation in a more realistic scenario may be useful.

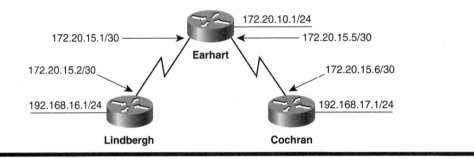

Figure 8.36

Unlike IGRP, EIGRP will support the VLSM requirements of this internetwork.

```
Earhart#show ip route
Codes: C - connected, S - static, I - IGRP, R - RIP, M - mobile, B - BGP
       D - EIGRP, EX - EIGRP external, O - OSPF, IA - OSPF inter area
       N1 - OSPF NSSA external type 1, N2 - OSPF NSSA external type 2
       E1 - OSPF external type 1, E2 - OSPF external type 2, E - EGP
       i - IS-IS, L1 - IS-IS level-1, L2 - IS-IS level-2, * - candidate default
       U - per-user static route, o - ODR

Gateway of last resort is not set

D      192.168.16.0/24 [90/2195456] via 172.20.15.2, 00:02:06, Serial0
D      192.168.17.0/24 [90/2195456] via 172.20.15.6, 00:02:06, Serial1
       172.20.0.0/16 is variably subnetted, 3 subnets, 2 masks
C         172.20.10.0/24 is directly connected, Ethernet0
C         172.20.15.4/30 is directly connected, Serial1
C         172.20.15.0/30 is directly connected, Serial0
Earhart#
```

Figure 8.37

Earhart's route table.

Tracing the route from Earhart to network 192.168.16.0, the path traverses a serial interface and an Ethernet interface, each with default metric values. The metric calculation is the same as for IGRP, as discussed in Chapter 6, except that EIGRP will multiply the final result by 256. The minimum bandwidth of the route will be that of the serial interface,[15] and the delay will be the sum of the two interface delays. Referring back to Table 6.1:

$$BW_{EIGRP(min)} = 256 * 6476 = 1657856$$

$$DLY_{EIGRP(sum)} = 256 * (2000 + 100) = 537600$$

Therefore,

$$Metric = 1657856 + 537600 = 2195456$$

Case Study: Redistribution with IGRP

Redistribution between routing protocols is covered in Chapter 11, but it is worth noting here that if an IGRP process and an EIGRP process have the same process IDs, they will redistribute automatically. In Figure 8.38, router Curtiss has the following configuration:

```
router igrp 15
  network 172.25.0.0
  network 172.20.0.0
```

Earhart is configured as follows:

```
router eigrp 15
  passive-interface Ethernet0
  network 172.20.0.0
!
router igrp 15
  passive-interface Serial0
  passive-interface Serial1
  network 172.20.0.0
```

The IGRP process speaks to Curtiss, and the EIGRP process speaks to Lindbergh and Cochran. Note that because Earhart's interfaces are all in network 172.20.0.0, the **passive-interface** command is used to restrict unnecessary routing protocol traffic. For EIGRP, this command is only needed to block unnecessary

---

[15] *Remember that the default bandwidth of a serial interface is 1544K.*

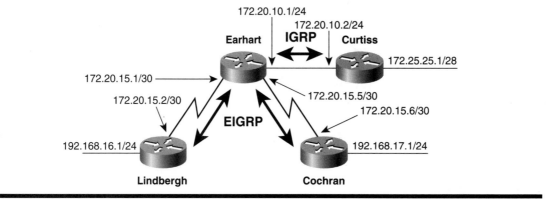

Figure 8.38

If Earhart is configured with both EIGRP and with IGRP, using the same process ID for both, route information will be redistributed.

Hellos. If no neighbors are found on an interface, no other EIGRP traffic will be sent.

Figure 8.39 shows Curtiss's route table. Notice that not only are routes to 192.168.16.0 and 192.168.17.0 present, but the metrics have been adjusted by the redistribution process to remove the EIGRP multiplier. Conversely, the metrics of routes redistributed into EIGRP from IGRP will be multiplied by 256.

Figure 8.39 also shows that information is missing. Earhart's classful IGRP process will not accept the variably subnetted routes to 172.20.15.0/30 and 172.20.15.4/30. Using the command **ip summary-address eigrp,** Earhart can be configured to send a summary advertisement to Curtiss:

```
interface Ethernet0
  ip address 172.20.10.1 255.255.255.0
  ip summary-address eigrp 15 172.20.15.0 255.255.255.0
!
router eigrp 15
  passive-interface Ethernet0
  network 172.20.0.0
!
```

```
Curtiss#show ip route
Codes: C - connected, S - static, I - IGRP, R - RIP, M - mobile, B - BGP
       D - EIGRP, EX - EIGRP external, O - OSPF, IA - OSPF inter area
       N1 - OSPF NSSA external type 1, N2 - OSPF NSSA external type 2
       E1 - OSPF external type 1, E2 - OSPF external type 2, E - EGP
       i - IS-IS, L1 - IS-IS level-1, L2 - IS-IS level-2, * - candidate default
       U - per-user static route, o - ODR

Gateway of last resort is not set

I    192.168.16.0/24 [100/8676] via 172.20.10.1, 00:00:06, Ethernet0
I    192.168.17.0/24 [100/8676] via 172.20.10.1, 00:00:06, Ethernet0
     172.25.0.0/28 is subnetted, 1 subnets
C       172.25.25.0 is directly connected, Ethernet1
     172.20.0.0/24 is subnetted, 1 subnets
C       172.20.10.0 is directly connected, Ethernet0
Curtiss#
```

Figure 8.39

The route table in Curtiss after the IGRP process is added to Earhart.

```
router igrp 15
  passive-interface Serial0
  passive-interface Serial1
  network 172.20.0.0
```

Curtiss's IGRP process will read the EIGRP summary, resulting in the route table shown in Figure 8.40.

Figure 8.41 shows Cochran's route table with the redistributed IGRP route. As this table shows, EIGRP explicitly tags externally learned routes. This information can be an aid when reading a route table because routes learned by redistribution are easily recognized.

Also of interest in Figure 8.41 is the last entry, a summary route pointing to the Null interface. This route helps to prevent potential black holes when default and summary routes are used. The technique is discussed in Chapters 11 and 12.

```
Curtiss#show ip route
Codes: C - connected, S - static, I - IGRP, R - RIP, M - mobile, B - BGP
       D - EIGRP, EX - EIGRP external, O - OSPF, IA - OSPF inter area
       N1 - OSPF NSSA external type 1, N2 - OSPF NSSA external type 2
       E1 - OSPF external type 1, E2 - OSPF external type 2, E - EGP
       i - IS-IS, L1 - IS-IS level-1, L2 - IS-IS level-2, * - candidate default
       U - per-user static route, o - ODR

Gateway of last resort is not set

I    192.168.16.0/24 [100/10676] via 172.20.10.1, 00:00:18, Ethernet0
I    192.168.17.0/24 [100/8676] via 172.20.10.1, 00:00:18, Ethernet0
     172.25.0.0/28 is subnetted, 1 subnets
C       172.25.25.0 is directly connected, Loopback0
     172.20.0.0/24 is subnetted, 2 subnets
C       172.20.10.0 is directly connected, Ethernet0
I       172.20.15.0 [100/8576] via 172.20.10.1, 00:00:18, Ethernet0
Curtiss#
```

Figure 8.40

With Earhart configured to send a summary route, Curtiss can now reach the two serial links.

```
Cochran#show ip route
Codes: C - connected, S - static, I - IGRP, R - RIP, M - mobile, B - BGP
       D - EIGRP, EX - EIGRP external, O - OSPF, IA - OSPF inter area
       E1 - OSPF external type 1, E2 - OSPF external type 2, E - EGP
       i - IS-IS, L1 - IS-IS level-1, L2 - IS-IS level-2, * - candidate default
       U - per-user static route

Gateway of last resort is not set

D    192.168.16.0/24 [90/3219456] via 172.20.15.5, 00:41:41, Serial0
C    192.168.17.0/24 is directly connected, Ethernet0
     192.168.18.0/24 is variably subnetted, 2 subnets, 2 masks
D EX 172.25.0.0/16 [170/2221056] via 172.20.15.5, 00:41:48, Serial0
     172.20.0.0/16 is variably subnetted, 3 subnets, 2 masks
D       172.20.10.0/24 [90/2195456] via 172.20.15.5, 00:41:48, Serial0
C       172.20.15.4/30 is directly connected, Serial0
D       172.20.15.0/30 [90/2681856] via 172.20.15.5, 00:41:48, Serial0
D       172.20.0.0/16 is a summary, 00:00:09, Null0
```

Figure 8.41

EIGRP tags externally learned routes, as Cochran's route table shows.

Case Study: Disabling Automatic Summarization

By default, EIGRP summarizes at network boundaries as do the protocols covered in previous chapters. Unlike those protocols, however, EIGRP's automatic summarization can be disabled. Figure 8.42 shows a situation in which disabling summarization is useful.

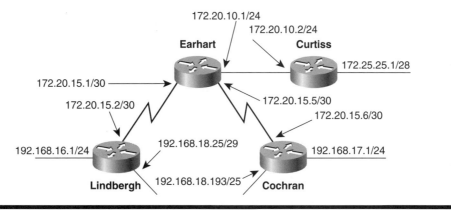

Figure 8.42

Disabling automatic summarization at Cochran and Lindbergh prevents ambiguous routing to network 192.168.18.0.

New Ethernet links have been added to routers Cochran and Lindbergh, and their addresses create a discontiguous subnet. The default behavior of both routers is to see themselves as border routers between major networks 172.20.0.0 and 192.168.18.0. As a result, Earhart will receive summary advertisements to 192.168.18.0 on both of its serial interfaces. The result is an ambiguous routing situation in which Earhart records two equal-cost paths to 192.168.18.0; a packet destined for one of the subnets may or may not be routed to the correct link.

Automatic summarization is turned off with the command **no auto-summary**. For example, Lindbergh's configuration will be:

```
router eigrp 15
  network 172.20.0.0
  network 192.168.16.0
  network 192.168.18.0
  no auto-summary
```

By turning off summarization at Lindbergh and Cochran, the individual subnets 192.168.18.24/29 and 192.168.18.128/25 will be advertised into network 172.20.0.0, eliminating the ambiguities at Earhart.

Case Study: Address Aggregation

A new router is added to the internetwork in Figure 8.43. The five network addresses that Earhart must advertise to Yeager can be summarized with two aggregate addresses. Earhart's configuration will be:

```
interface Ethernet1
  ip address 10.15.15.254 255.255.255.252
  ip summary-address eigrp 15 172.0.0.0 255.0.0.0
  ip summary-address eigrp 15 192.168.16.0 255.255.240.0
```

The ip **summary-address eigrp** command will automatically suppress the advertisement of the more specific networks to Yeager. Figure 8.44 shows the route table of Yeager before and after the aggregate addresses are configured. Even in this small internetwork, the number of EIGRP-learned entries has been reduced by half; in a large internetwork, the impact on route tables and the memory required to store them can be significant.

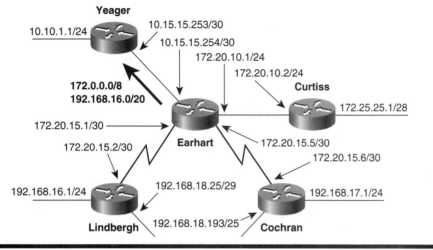

Figure 8.43

Earhart is advertising two aggregate addresses to Yeager.

Authentication

Authentication of EIGRP packets is supported in IOS versions 11.3 and later. MD5 cryptographic checksums are the only authentication supported, which on first consideration may seem less flexible than RIPv2 and OSPF, which support both MD5 and clear-text passwords. However, clear-text password authentication should be used only when a neighboring device does not support the more secure MD5. Because EIGRP will be spoken only between two Cisco devices, this situation will never arise.

Authentication method of EIGRP compared to OSPF and RIPv2

The steps for configuring EIGRP authentication are:

1. Define a key chain with a name.
2. Define the key or keys on the key chain.
3. Enable authentication on an interface and specify the key chain to be used.
4. Optionally configure key management.

```
Yeager#show ip route
Codes: C - connected, S - static, I - IGRP, R - RIP, M - mobile, B - BGP
       D - EIGRP, EX - EIGRP external, O - OSPF, IA - OSPF inter area
       E1 - OSPF external type 1, E2 - OSPF external type 2, E - EGP
       i - IS-IS, L1 - IS-IS level-1, L2 - IS-IS level-2, * - candidate default
       U - per-user static route

Gateway of last resort is not set

     10.0.0.0/8 is variably subnetted, 2 subnets, 2 masks
C       10.10.1.0/24 is directly connected, Ethernet1
C       10.15.15.252/30 is directly connected, Ethernet0
D     192.168.16.0/24 [90/2733056] via 10.15.15.254, 00:00:13, Ethernet0
D     192.168.17.0/24 [90/2221056] via 10.15.15.254, 00:00:13, Ethernet0
      192.168.18.0/24 is variably subnetted, 2 subnets, 2 masks
D        192.168.18.24/29 [90/2221056] via 10.15.15.254, 00:00:13, Ethernet0
D        192.168.18.128/25 [90/2323456] via 10.15.15.254, 00:00:13, Ethernet0
D EX 172.25.0.0/16 [170/332800] via 10.15.15.254, 00:00:13, Ethernet0
D 172.20.0.0/16 [90/307200] via 10.15.15.254, 00:00:14, Ethernet0
```

```
Yeager#show ip route
Codes: C - connected, S - static, I - IGRP, R - RIP, M - mobile, B - BGP
       D - EIGRP, EX - EIGRP external, O - OSPF, IA - OSPF inter area
       E1 - OSPF external type 1, E2 - OSPF external type 2, E - EGP
       i - IS-IS, L1 - IS-IS level-1, L2 - IS-IS level-2, * - candidate default
       U - per-user static route

Gateway of last resort is not set

     10.0.0.0/8 is variably subnetted, 2 subnets, 2 masks
C       10.10.1.0/24 is directly connected, Ethernet1
C       10.15.15.252/30 is directly connected, Ethernet0
   D  192.168.16.0/20 [90/435200] via 10.15.15.254, 00:00:26, Ethernet0
   D  172.0.0.0/8 [90/307200] via 10.15.15.254, 00:00:26, Ethernet0
```

Figure 8.44

Yeager's route table before and after aggregate addresses are configured at Earhart.

Key chain configuration and management are described in Chapter 7. EIGRP authentication is enabled and linked to a key chain on an interface with the commands **ip authentication key-chain eigrp** and **ip authentication mode eigrp md5**.[16]

Referring to Figure 8.43, the following configuration enables EIGRP authentication on Cochran's interface to Earhart:

Cochran

```
key chain Edwards
  key 1
    key-string PanchoBarnes
!
interface Serial0
  ip address 172.20.15.6 255.255.255.252
  ip authentication key-chain eigrp 15 Edwards
  ip authentication mode eigrp 15 md5
```

A similar configuration would be necessary on Earhart. The commands **accept-lifetime** and **send-lifetime** are used for key chain management as described in Chapter 7.

TROUBLESHOOTING EIGRP

Troubleshooting the exchange of IGRP or RIP route information is a reasonably simple procedure. Routing updates are either propagated or they are not, and they either contain accurate information or they do not. The added complexity of EIGRP means an added complexity to the troubleshooting procedure. Neighbor tables and adjacencies must be verified, the query/response procedure of DUAL must be followed, and the influences of VLSM on automatic summarization must be considered.

This section's case study describes a sequence of events that typically can be used when pursuing an EIGRP problem. Following the case study is a discussion of an occasional cause of instabilities in larger EIGRP internets.

---

[16] *Although MD5 is the only authentication mode available, the* **ip authentication mode eigrp md5** *command anticipates the possibility of another mode being available in the future.*

Case Study: A Missing Neighbor

Figure 8.45 shows a small EIGRP internetwork. Users are complaining that subnet 192.168.16.224/28 is unreachable. An examination of the route tables reveals that something is wrong at router Grissom (Figure 8.46).[17]

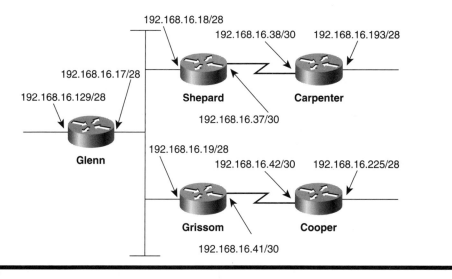

Figure 8.45

Subnet 192.168.16.224/28 is not reachable through Grissom in this example of an EIGRP internetwork.

The following observations are made from the two route tables of Figure 8.46:

- Shepard does not have subnets 192.168.16.40/30 and 192.168.16.224/28 in its route table, although Grissom does.

---

[17] *When troubleshooting an internetwork, it is a good practice to verify that the addresses of all router interfaces belong to the correct subnet.*

```
Grissom#show ip route
Codes: C - connected, S - static, I - IGRP, R - RIP, M - mobile, B - BGP
       D - EIGRP, EX - EIGRP external, O - OSPF, IA - OSPF inter area
       N1 - OSPF NSSA external type 1, N2 - OSPF NSSA external type 2
       E1 - OSPF external type 1, E2 - OSPF external type 2, E - EGP
       i - IS-IS, L1 - IS-IS level-1, L2 - IS-IS level-2, * - candidate default
       U - per-user static route, o - ODR

Gateway of last resort is not set

     192.168.16.0/24 is variably subnetted, 3 subnets, 2 masks
C       192.168.16.40/30 is directly connected, Serial0
C       192.168.16.16/28 is directly connected, Ethernet0
D       192.168.16.224/28 [90/2195456] via 192.168.16.42, 01:07:26, Serial0
```

```
Shepard#show ip route
Codes: C - connected, S - static, I - IGRP, R - RIP, M - mobile, B - BGP
       D - EIGRP, EX - EIGRP external, O - OSPF, IA - OSPF inter area
       N1 - OSPF NSSA external type 1, N2 - OSPF NSSA external type 2
       E1 - OSPF external type 1, E2 - OSPF external type 2, E - EGP
       i - IS-IS, L1 - IS-IS level-1, L2 - IS-IS level-2, * - candidate default
       U - per-user static route, o - ODR

Gateway of last resort is not set

     192.168.16.0/24 is variably subnetted, 4 subnets, 2 masks
C       192.168.16.36/30 is directly connected, Serial0
C       192.168.16.16/28 is directly connected, Ethernet0
D       192.168.16.192/28 [90/2297856] via 192.168.16.38, 01:07:20, Serial0
D       192.168.16.128/28 [90/307200] via 192.168.16.17, 01:07:20, Ethernet0
```

Figure 8.46

The route tables of Shepard and Grissom show that Grissom's EIGRP process is not advertising or receiving routes on subnet 192.168.16.16/28.

- Grissom's route table does not contain any of the subnets that should be advertised by Glenn or Shepard.

- Shepard's route table contains the subnets advertised by Glenn (and Glenn's table contains the subnets advertised by Shepard, although its route table is not included in the figure).

The conclusion to be drawn from these observations is that Grissom is not advertising or receiving routes correctly over subnet 192.168.16.16/28.

Among the possible causes, the simplest causes should be examined first. These are:

- An incorrect interface address or mask

- An incorrect EIGRP process ID

- A missing or incorrect network statement

In this case, there are no EIGRP or address configuration errors.

Next, the neighbor tables should be examined. Looking at the neighbor tables at Grissom, Shepard, and Glenn (Figure 8.47), two facts stand out:

- Grissom (192.168.16.19) is in its neighbors' tables, but its neighbors are not in Grissom's neighbor table.

- The entire internetwork has been up for more than five hours; this information is reflected in the *uptime* statistic for all neighbors except Grissom. However, Grissom's uptime shows approximately one minute.

If Grissom is in Shepard's neighbor table, Shepard must be receiving Hellos from it. Grissom, however, is apparently not receiving Hellos from Shepard. Without this two-way exchange of Hello packets, an adjacency will not be established and route information will not be exchanged.

A closer examination of Shepard's and Glenn's neighbor tables reinforces this hypothesis:

- The SRTT for Grissom is 0, indicating that a packet has never made the round-trip.

```
Grissom#show ip eigrp neighbors
IP-EIGRP neighbors for process 75
H   Address            Interface    Hold Uptime   SRTT   RTO  Q   Seq
                                    (sec)         (ms)        Cnt Num
0   192.168.16.42      Se0            11 05:27:11    23    200  0   8
```

```
Shepard#show ip eigrp neighbors
IP-EIGRP neighbors for process 75
H   Address            Interface    Hold Uptime   SRTT   RTO  Q   Seq
                                    (sec)         (ms)        Cnt Num
1   192.168.16.19      Et0            12 00:01:01     0   5000  1   0
2   192.168.16.17      Et0            11 05:27:33     8    200  0   6
0   192.168.16.38      Se0            14 05:27:34    22    200  0  10
```

```
Glenn#show ip eigrp neighbors
IP-EIGRP neighbors for process 75
H   Address            Interface    Hold Uptime   SRTT   RTO  Q   Seq
                                    (sec)         (ms)        Cnt Num
1   192.168.16.19      Et0            14 00:00:59     0   8000  1   0
2   192.168.16.18      Et0            10 05:30:11     9     20  0   7
0   192.168.16.129     Et1            12 05:30:58     6     20  0   7
```

Figure 8.47

Subnet 192.168.16.224/28 is not reachable through Grissom in this example of an EIGRP internetwork.

- The RTO for Grissom has increased to five and eight seconds, respectively.

- There is a packet enqueued for Grissom (Q Cnt).

- The sequence number recorded for Grissom is 0, indicating that no reliable packets have ever been received from it.

These factors indicate that the two routers are trying to send a packet reliably to Grissom, but are not receiving an ACK.

In Figure 8.48, **debug eigrp packets** is used at Shepard to get a better look at what is happening. All EIGRP packet types will be displayed, but a second debug command is used with it: **debug ip eigrp neighbor 75 192.168.16.19**. This command adds a filter to the first command. It tells **debug eigrp packet** to display only IP packets of EIGRP 75 (the process ID of the routers in Figure 8.45) and only those packets that concern neighbor 192.168.16.19 (Grissom).

```
Shepard#debug eigrp packets
EIGRP Packets debugging is on
    (UPDATE, REQUEST, QUERY, REPLY, HELLO, IPXSAP, PROBE, ACK)
Shepard#debug ip eigrp neighbor 75 192.168.16.19
IP Neighbor target enabled on AS 75 for 192.168.16.19
IP-EIGRP Neighbor Target Events debugging is on
EIGRP: Sending UPDATE on Ethernet0 nbr 192.168.16.19, retry 14, RTO 5000
   AS 75, Flags 0x1, Seq 22/0 idbQ 1/0 iidbQ un/rely 0/0 peerQ un/rely 0/1 serno
1-4
EIGRP: Received HELLO on Ethernet0 nbr 192.168.16.19
   AS 75, Flags 0x0, Seq 0/0 idbQ 0/0 iidbQ un/rely 0/0 peerQ un/rely 0/1
EIGRP: Sending UPDATE on Ethernet0 nbr 192.168.16.19, retry 15, RTO 5000
AS 75, Flags 0x1, Seq 22/0 idbQ 1/0 iidbQ un/rely 0/0 peerQ un/rely 0/1 serno
1-4
EIGRP: Received HELLO on Ethernet0 nbr 192.168.16.19
   AS 75, Flags 0x0, Seq 0/0 idbQ 0/0 iidbQ un/rely 0/0 peerQ un/rely 0/1
EIGRP: Sending UPDATE on Ethernet0 nbr 192.168.16.19, retry 16, RTO 5000
   AS 75, Flags 0x1, Seq 22/0 idbQ 1/0 iidbQ un/rely 0/0 peerQ un/rely 0/1 serno
1-4
EIGRP: Received HELLO on Ethernet0 nbr 192.168.16.19
   AS 75, Flags 0x0, Seq 0/0 idbQ 0/0 iidbQ un/rely 0/0 peerQ un/rely 0/1
EIGRP: Retransmission retry limit exceeded
EIGRP: Received HELLO on Ethernet0 nbr 192.168.16.19
   AS 75, Flags 0x0, Seq 0/0 idbQ 0/0
EIGRP: Enqueueing UPDATE on Ethernet0 nbr 192.168.16.19 iidbQ un/rely 0/1 peerQ
un/rely 0/0 serno 1-4
EIGRP: Sending UPDATE on Ethernet0 nbr 192.168.16.19
   AS 75, Flags 0x1, Seq 23/0 idbQ 1/0 iidbQ un/rely 0/0 peerQ un/rely 0/1 serno
1-4
```

Figure 8.48

The command **debug ip eigrp neighbor** is used to control the packets displayed by **debug eigrp packets**.

Figure 8.48 shows that Hello packets are being received from Grissom. It also shows that Shepard is attempting to send updates to Grissom; Grissom is not acknowledging them. After the 16th retry, the message "Retransmission retry limit exceeded" is displayed. This exceeded limit accounts for the low uptime shown for Grissom in the neighbor tables—when the retransmission retry limit is exceeded, Grissom is removed from the neighbor table. But because Hellos are still being received from Grissom, it quickly reappears in the table and the process begins again.

Figure 8.49 shows the output from **debug eigrp neighbors** at Shepard. This command is not IP specific, but instead shows EIGRP neighbor events. Here, two instances of the events described in the previous paragraph are displayed: Grissom is declared dead as the retransmission limit is exceeded but is immediately "revived" when its next Hello is received.

```
Shepard#debug eigrp neighbors
EIGRP Neighbors debugging is on
Shepard#
EIGRP: Retransmission retry limit exceeded
EIGRP: Holdtime expired
EIGRP: Neighbor 192.168.16.19 went down on Ethernet0
EIGRP: New peer 192.168.16.19
EIGRP: Retransmission retry limit exceeded
EIGRP: Holdtime expired
EIGRP: Neighbor 192.168.16.19 went down on Ethernet0
EIGRP: New peer 192.168.16.19
```

Figure 8.49

Debug eigrp neighbors *displays neighbor events.*

Although Figure 8.48 shows that update packets are being sent to Grissom, observation of EIGRP packets at that router show that they are not being received (Figure 8.50). Because Grissom is successfully exchanging Hellos with Cooper, Grissom's EIGRP process must be working. Suspicion therefore falls on Grissom's Ethernet interface. An inspection of the configuration file shows that an access list is configured as an incoming filter on E0:

```
interface Ethernet0
  ip address 192.168.16.19 255.255.255.240
  ip access-group 150 in
!
!
access-list 150 permit tcp any any established
access-list 150 permit tcp any host 192.168.16.238 eq ftp
access-list 150 permit tcp host 192.168.16.201 any eq telnet
access-list 150 permit tcp any host 192.168.16.230 eq pop3
access-list 150 permit udp any any eq snmp access-list 150 permit
icmp any 192.168.16.224 0.0.0.15
```

```
Grissom#debug eigrp packets
EIGRP Packets debugging is on
     (UPDATE, REQUEST, QUERY, REPLY, HELLO, IPXSAP, PROBE, ACK)
Grissom#
EIGRP: Sending HELLO on Serial0
  AS 75, Flags 0x0, Seq 0/0 idbQ 0/0 iidbQ un/rely 0/0
EIGRP: Received HELLO on Serial0 nbr 192.168.16.42
  AS 75, Flags 0x0, Seq 0/0 idbQ 0/0 iidbQ un/rely 0/0 peerQ un/rely 0/0
EIGRP: Sending HELLO on Ethernet0
  AS 75, Flags 0x0, Seq 0/0 idbQ 0/0 iidbQ un/rely 0/0
EIGRP: Sending HELLO on Serial0
  AS 75, Flags 0x0, Seq 0/0 idbQ 0/0 iidbQ un/rely 0/0
EIGRP: Received HELLO on Serial0 nbr 192.168.16.42
  AS 75, Flags 0x0, Seq 0/0 idbQ 0/0 iidbQ un/rely 0/0 peerQ un/rely 0/0
EIGRP: Sending HELLO on Ethernet0
  AS 75, Flags 0x0, Seq 0/0 idbQ 0/0 iidbQ un/rely 0/0
EIGRP: Sending HELLO on Serial0
  AS 75, Flags 0x0, Seq 0/0 idbQ 0/0 iidbQ un/rely 0/0
EIGRP: Sending HELLO on Ethernet0
  AS 75, Flags 0x0, Seq 0/0 idbQ 0/0 iidbQ un/rely 0/0
EIGRP: Received HELLO on Serial0 nbr 192.168.16.42
  AS 75, Flags 0x0, Seq 0/0 idbQ 0/0 iidbQ un/rely 0/0 peerQ un/rely 0/0
EIGRP: Sending HELLO on Serial0
  AS 75, Flags 0x0, Seq 0/0 idbQ 0/0 iidbQ un/rely 0/0
EIGRP: Sending HELLO on Ethernet0
  AS 75, Flags 0x0, Seq 0/0 idbQ 0/0 iidbQ un/rely 0/0
```

Figure 8.50

Grissom is exchanging Hellos with Cooper via interface S0 and is sending Hellos out E0. However, Grissom is not receiving any EIGRP packets on interface EO.

When EIGRP packets are received at Grissom's E0 interface, they are first filtered through access list 150. They will not match any entry on the list and are therefore being dropped. The problem is resolved (Figure 8.51) by adding the following entry to the access list:

```
access-list 150 permit eigrp 192.168.16.16 0.0.0.15 any
```

Stuck-in-Active Neighbors

When a route goes active and queries are sent to neighbors, the route will remain active until a reply is received for every query.

```
Grissom#show ip eigrp neighbors
IP-EIGRP neighbors for process 75
H   Address              Interface   Hold Uptime    SRTT   RTO    Q     Seq
                                     (sec)          (ms)          Cnt   Num
2   192.168.16.17        Et0           10 00:06:20    4    200    0     41
1   192.168.16.18        Et0           14 00:06:24   15    200    0     85
0   192.168.16.42        Se0           10 06:22:56   22    200    0     12
Grissom#show ip route
Codes: C - connected, S - static, I - IGRP, R - RIP, M - mobile, B - BGP
       D - EIGRP, EX - EIGRP external, O - OSPF, IA - OSPF inter area
       N1 - OSPF NSSA external type 1, N2 - OSPF NSSA external type 2
       E1 - OSPF external type 1, E2 - OSPF external type 2, E - EGP
       i - IS-IS, L1 - IS-IS level-1, L2 - IS-IS level-2, * - candidate default
       U - per-user static route, o - ODR

Gateway of last resort is not set

     192.168.16.0/24 is variably subnetted, 6 subnets, 2 masks
C       192.168.16.40/30 is directly connected, Serial0
D       192.168.16.36/30 [90/2195456] via 192.168.16.18, 00:06:27, Ethernet0
C       192.168.16.16/28 is directly connected, Ethernet0
D       192.168.16.224/28 [90/2195456] via 192.168.16.42, 00:06:12, Serial0
D       192.168.16.192/28 [90/2323456] via 192.168.16.18, 00:06:27, Ethernet0
D       192.168.16.128/28 [90/307200] via 192.168.16.17, 00:06:12, Ethernet0
Grissom#
```

Figure 8.51

When an entry is added to the access list to permit EIGRP packets, Grissom's neighbor and route tables show that it now has routes to all subnets.

But what happens if a neighbor is dead or otherwise incapacitated and cannot reply? The route would stay permanently active. The active timer is designed to prevent this situation. The timer is set when a query is sent. If the timer expires before a reply to the query is received, the route is declared *stuck-in-active*, the neighbor is presumed dead, and it is flushed from the neighbor table.[18] The SIA route and any other routes via that neighbor are eliminated from the route table. DUAL will be satisfied by considering the neighbor to have replied with an infinite metric.

---

[18] *As mentioned previously, the default active time is 3 minutes and can be changed with the command* **timers active-time.**

In reality, this sequence of events should never happen. The loss of Hellos should identify a disabled neighbor long before the active timer expires.

But what happens in large EIGRP networks where a query might, like the bunny in the battery advertisement, keep going and going? Remember that queries cause the diffusing calculation to grow larger, whereas replies cause it to grow smaller (refer to Figure 8.10). Queries must eventually reach the edge of the internetwork, and replies must eventually begin coming back, but if the diameter of the diffusing calculation grows large enough, an active timer may expire before all replies are received. The result, flushing a legitimate neighbor from the neighbor table, is obviously destabilizing.

When neighbors mysteriously disappear from neighbor tables and then reappear, or users complain of intermittently unreachable destinations, SIA routes may be the culprit. Checking the error logs of routers is a good way to find out whether SIAs have occurred (Figure 8.52).

When chasing the cause of SIAs, close attention should be paid to the topology table in routers. If routes can be "caught" in the active state, the neighbors from whom queries have not yet been received should be noted. For example, Figure 8.53 shows a topology table in which several routes are active. Notice that most of them have been active for 15 seconds and that one (10.6.1.0) has been active for 41 seconds.

Notice also that in each case, the neighbor 10.1.2.1 has its reply status flag (r) set. That is the neighbor from which replies have not yet been received. There may be no problem with the neighbor itself or with the link to the neighbor, but this information points to the direction within the internetwork topology in which the investigation should proceed.

Common causes of SIAs in larger EIGRP internetworks are heavily congested, low-bandwidth data links and routers with low mem-

```
Gagarin#show logging
Syslog logging: enabled (0 messages dropped, 0 flushes, 0 overruns)
    Console logging: level debugging, 3369 messages logged
    Monitor logging: level debugging, 0 messages logged
    Trap logging: level informational, 71 message lines logged
    Buffer logging: level debugging, 3369 messages logged

Log Buffer (4096 bytes):
   ...
   ...
   ...
DUAL: dual_rcvupdate(): 10.51.1.0/24 via 10.1.2.1 metric 409600/128256
DUAL: Find FS for dest 10.51.1.0/24. FD is 4294967295, RD is 4294967295 found
DUAL: RT installed 10.51.1.0/24 via 10.1.2.1
DUAL: Send update about 10.51.1.0/24. Reason: metric chg
DUAL: Send update about 10.51.1.0/24. Reason: new if
DUAL: dual_rcvupdate(): 10.52.1.0/24 via 10.1.2.1 metric 409600/128256
DUAL: Find FS for dest 10.52.1.0/24. FD is 4294967295, RD is 4294967295 found
%DUAL-3-SIA: Route 10.11.1.0/24 stuck-in-active state in IP-EIGRP 1. Cleaning up
Gagarin#
```

Figure 8.52
The final entry of this error log shows a SIA message.

ory or overutilized CPUs. The problem will be exacerbated if these limited resources must handle very large numbers of queries.

The careless adjustment of the bandwidth parameter on interfaces may be another cause of SIAs. Recall that EIGRP is designed to use no more than 50% of the available bandwidth of a link. This restriction means that EIGRP's pacing is keyed to the configured bandwidth. If the bandwidth is set artificially low in an attempt to manipulate routing choices, the EIGRP process may be starved. If IOS 11.2 or later is being run, the command **ip bandwidth-percent eigrp** may be used to adjust the percentage of bandwidth used.

For example, suppose that an interface is connected to a 56K serial link, but the bandwidth is set to 14K. EIGRP would limit itself to 50% of this amount, or 7K. The following commands adjust the

Changing the percentage of bandwidth used by EIGRP

```
Gagarin#show ip eigrp topology
IP-EIGRP Topology Table for process 1

Codes: P - Passive, A - Active, U - Update, Q - Query, R - Reply
       r - Reply Status

A 10.11.1.0/24, 0 successors, FD is 3072128000, Q
    1 replies, active 00:00:15, query-origin: Local origin
    Remaining replies:
        via 10.1.2.1, r, Ethernet0
A 10.10.1.0/24, 0 successors, FD is 3584128000, Q
    1 replies, active 00:00:15, query-origin: Local origin
    Remaining replies:
        via 10.1.2.1, r, Ethernet0
A 10.9.1.0/24, 0 successors, FD is 4096128000, Q
    1 replies, active 00:00:15, query-origin: Local origin
    Remaining replies:
        via 10.1.2.1, r, Ethernet0
A 10.2.1.0/24, 1 successors, FD is Inaccessible, Q
    1 replies, active ve 00:00:15, query-origin: Local origin
    Remaining res:
        via 10.1.2.1, r, Ethernet0
P 10.1.2.0/24, 1 successors, FD is 281600
        via Connected, Ethernet0
A 10.6.1.0/24, 0 successors, FD is 3385160704, Q
    1 replies, active 00:00:41, query-origin: Local origin
    Remaining replies:
        via 10.1.2.1, r, Ethernet0
A 10.27.1.0/24, 0 successors, FD is 3897160704, Q
--More-
```

Figure 8.53

This topology table shows several active routes, all of which are waiting for a reply from neighbor 10.1.2.1.

EIGRP bandwidth percent to 200%—200% of 14K, which is 50% of the actual bandwidth of the 56K link:

```
interface Serial 3
    ip address 172.18.107.210 255.255.255.240
    bandwidth 14
    ip bandwidth-percent eigrp 1 200
```

Increasing the active timer period with the **timers active-time** command may help avoid SIAs in some situations, but this step should not be taken without careful consideration of the effects it may have on reconvergence.

A good internetwork design is the best solution to instabilities such as SIA routes. By using a combination of intelligent address assignment, route filtering, default routes, and summarization, boundaries may be constructed in a large EIGRP internetwork to restrict the size and scope of diffusing computations. Chapter 13, "Route Filtering," includes an example of such a design.

LOOKING AHEAD

When comparing EIGRP and OSPF, it is often said that an advantage of EIGRP is that it is simpler to configure. This observation is true for many internetworks, but this chapter's discussion of troubleshooting shows that as an internetwork grows, efforts must be made to "compartmentalize" the EIGRP topology. Ironically, the very complexity of OSPF may make it easier to configure in large internetworks, as the next chapter shows.

SUMMARY TABLE: CHAPTER 8 COMMAND REVIEW

Command	Description
accept-lifetime *start-time* {infinite|*end-time*|duration *seconds*}	Specifies the time period during which the authentication key on a key chain is received as valid.
auto-summary	Enables automatic summarization at network boundaries. This command is enabled by default.
bandwidth *kilobits*	Specifies the bandwidth parameter, in kilobits per second, on an interface.
debug eigrp packets	Displays EIGRP packet activity.
debug ip eigrp neighbor *process-id address*	Adds a filter to the **debug eigrp packets** command, telling it to display only IP packets for the indicated process and neighbor.
delay *tens-of-microseconds*	Specifies the delay parameter, in tens of microseconds, on an interface.
ip authentication key-chain eigrp *process-id key-chain*	Configures a key chain on an EIGRP interface and specifies the name of the key chain to be used.

Command	Description
ip authentication mode eigrp *process-id* **md5**	Enables EIGRP authentication on an interface.
ip bandwidth-percent eigrp *process-id percent*	Configures the percentage of bandwidth used by EIGRP; the default is 50%.
ip hello-interval eigrp *process-id seconds*	Configures the EIGRP hello interval.
ip hold-time eigrp *process-id seconds*	Configures the EIGRP hold time.
ip summary-address eigrp *process-id address mask*	Configures a router to send a summary EIGRP advertisement.
key *number*	Specifies a key on a key chain.
key chain *name-of-chain*	Specifies a group of authentication keys.
key-string *text*	Specifies the authentication string, or password, used by a key.
metric weights *tos k1 k2 k3 k4 k5*	Specifies how much weight the bandwidth, load, delay, and reliability parameters should be given in the IGRP and EIGRP metric calculations.
network *network-number*	Specifies the network address of one or more interfaces on which IGRP, EIGRP, or RIP processes should be enabled.
passive-interface *type number*	Disables the transmission of broadcast or multicast routing updates on an interface.
router eigrp *process-id*	Enables an EIGRP process.
send-lifetime *start-time* {**infinite**|*end-time*|**duration** *seconds*}	Specifies the time period during which the authentication key on a key chain may be sent.
show ip eigrp neighbors [*type number*]	Displays the EIGRP neighbor table.
show ip eigrp topology [*process-id*|[[*ip address*]*mask*]]	Displays the EIGRP topology table.
timers active-time {*minutes*|**disabled**}	Changes or disables the default 3-minute active time.
traffic-share {**balanced**|**min**}	Specifies whether an IGRP or EIGRP routing process should use unequal-cost load-balancing or equal-cost load balancing only.
variance *multiplier*	Specifies a route multiplier by which a route metric can vary from the lowest-cost metric and still be included in an unequal-cost load-balancing group.

REVIEW QUESTIONS

1. Is EIGRP a distance vector or a link state routing protocol?

2. What is the maximum configured bandwidth EIGRP will use on a link? Can this percentage be changed?

3. How do EIGRP and IGRP differ in the way they calculate the composite metric?

4. What are the four basic components of EIGRP?

5. In the context of EIGRP, what does the term *reliable delivery* mean? Which two methods ensure reliable delivery of EIGRP packets?

6. Which mechanism ensures that a router is accepting the most recent route entry?

7. What is the multicast IP address used by EIGRP?

8. What are the packet types used by EIGRP?

9. At what interval, by default, are EIGRP Hello packets sent?

10. What is the default hold time?

11. What is the difference between the neighbor table and the topology table?

12. What is a feasible distance?

13. What is the feasibility condition?

14. What is a feasible successor?

15. What is a successor?

16. What is the difference between an active route and a passive route?

17. What causes a passive route to become active?

18. What causes an active route to become passive?

19. What does *stuck-in-active* mean?

20. What is the difference between subnetting and address aggregation?

CONFIGURATION EXERCISES

1. In Figure 8.42 and the accompanying case study, automatic summarization is turned off in routers Cochran and Lindbergh. As a result, the variably masked subnets 192.168.18.24/29 and 192.168.18.128/25 will be recorded in Earhart's route table. Is any further configuration required so that Curtiss's classful IGRP process will correctly route to these subnets?

2. Write EIGRP configurations for routers A, B, and C in Figure 8.54. Use process ID 5.

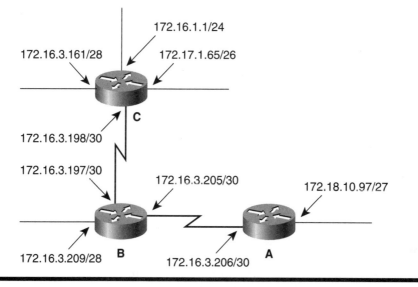

172.16.1.1/24

172.16.3.161/28   172.17.1.65/26

C

172.16.3.198/30

172.16.3.197/30

172.16.3.205/30   172.18.10.97/27

172.16.3.209/28   B   172.16.3.206/30   A

Figure 8.54

The internetwork for Configuration Exercises 2 and 3.

3. The serial interfaces connecting routers A and B in Figure 8.54 are both S0. Configure authentication between these two routers, using the first key 2 days from today's date. Configure a second key to be used beginning 30 days after the first key.

4. Router D is added in Figure 8.55. Add this router to the configurations written in Configuration Exercise 3.

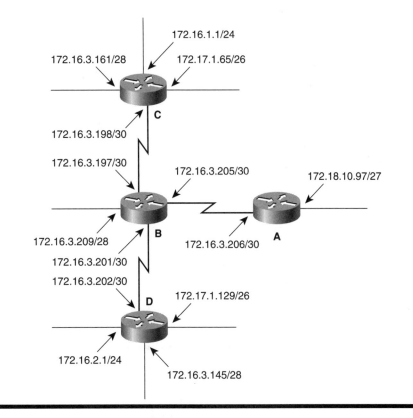

172.16.1.1/24

172.16.3.161/28   172.17.1.65/26

C

172.16.3.198/30

172.16.3.197/30

172.16.3.205/30   172.18.10.97/27

B

172.16.3.209/28   172.16.3.206/30   A

172.16.3.201/30

172.16.3.202/30   D

172.17.1.129/26

172.16.2.1/24

172.16.3.145/28

Figure 8.55
The internetwork for Configuration Exercise 4.

5. Router E has been added in Figure 8.56 and is running IGRP only. Add this router to the configurations written in Configuration Exercises 3 and 4.

6. Router F has been added in Figure 8.57. Configure this router to run EIGRP with the routers configured in Configuration Exercises 3, 4, and 5.

7. Configure route summarization wherever possible in the internetwork of Figure 8.57.

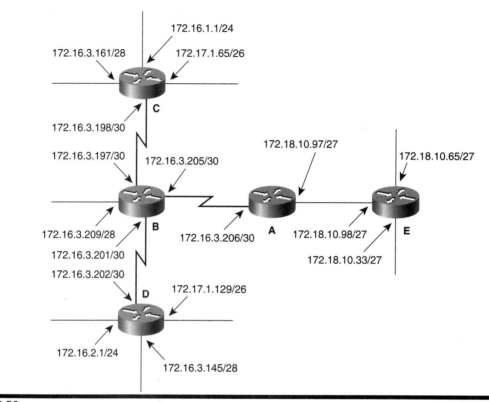

172.16.1.1/24

172.16.3.161/28   172.17.1.65/26

172.16.3.198/30

172.18.10.97/27

172.18.10.65/27

172.16.3.197/30   172.16.3.205/30

172.16.3.209/28

172.16.3.206/30   172.18.10.98/27

172.16.3.201/30

172.18.10.33/27

172.16.3.202/30

172.17.1.129/26

172.16.2.1/24

172.16.3.145/28

Figure 8.56

The internetwork for Configuration Exercise 5.

TROUBLESHOOTING EXERCISES

1. A router is configured to redistribute between EIGRP and IGRP, as follows:

```
router eigrp 15
 network 192.168.5.0
 no auto-summary
 metric weights 0 1 1 0 1 1
!
router igrp 5
 network 172.16.0.0
 metric weights 0 0 0 1 1 1
```

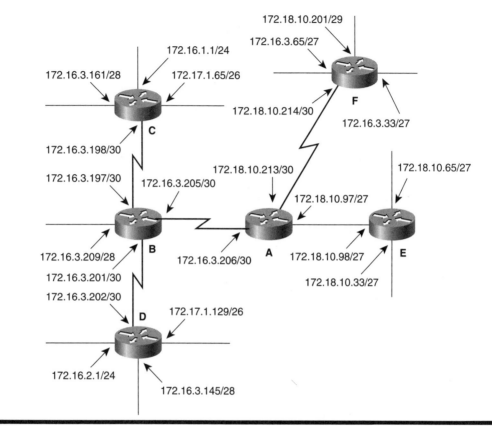

Figure 8.57

The internetwork for Configuration Exercises 6 and 7.

The routers in the EIGRP domain are not learning routes into the IGRP domain, and routers in the IGRP domain are not learning routes into the EIGRP domain. What is wrong?

2. Table 8.6 shows the values displayed in the **show interface** command for every interface in Figure 8.58. Which router will router F use as the successor to subnet A?

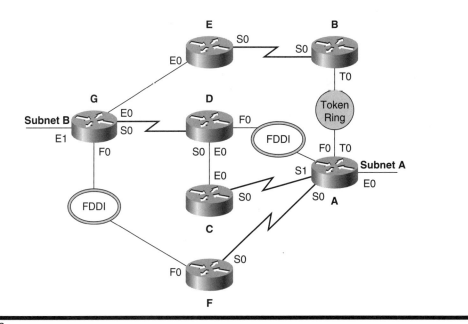

Figure 8.58

The internetwork for Troubleshooting Exercises 2 through 6.

Table 8.6   *The metric values for all interfaces in Figure 8.58, as displayed in the **show interface** command.*

Router	Interface	BW(k)	DLY(μS)
A	E0	10000	1000
	F0	100000	100
	T0	16000	630
	S0	512	20000
	S1	1544	20000
B	T0	16000	630
	S0	1544	20000
C	E0	10000	1000
	S0	1544	20000

Table 8.6 *The metric values for all interfaces in Figure 8.58, as displayed in the* **show interface** *command, continued.*

Router	Interface	BW(k)	DLY(µS)
D	E0	10000	1000
	F0	100000	100
	S0	1544	20000
E	E0	10000	1000
	S0	1544	20000
F	F0	100000	100
	S0	512	20000
G	E0	10000	1000
	E1	10000	1000
	F0	100000	100
	S0	56	20000

3. In Figure 8.58, what is router C's feasible distance to subnet A?

4. In Figure 8.58, what is router G's feasible distance to subnet A?

5. In Figure 8.58, which routers will router G show in its topology table as feasible successors?

6. In Figure 8.58, what is router A's feasible distance to subnet B?

- **Operation of OSPF**
    - Neighbors and Adjacencies
    - Areas
    - The Link State Database
    - The Route Table
    - Authentication
    - OSPF Over Demand Circuits
    - OSPF Packet Formats
    - OSPF LSA Formats
    - The NSSA External LSA
    - The Options Field
- **Configuring OSPF**
    - Case Study: A Basic OSPF Configuration
    - Case Study: Setting Router IDs with Loopback Interfaces
    - Case Study: DNS Lookups
    - Case Study: OSPF and Secondary Addresses
    - Case Study: Stub Areas
    - Case Study: Totally Stubby Areas
    - Case Study: Not-so-Stubby Areas
    - Case Study: Address Summarization
    - Case Study: Authentication
    - Case Study: Virtual Links
    - Case Study: OSPF on NBMA Networks
    - Case Study: OSPF Over Demand Circuits
- **Troubleshooting OSPF**
    - Case Study: An Isolated Area
    - Case Study: Misconfigured Summarization

CHAPTER 9

Open Shortest Path First

Open Shortest Path First (OSPF) was developed by the Internet Engineering Task Force (IETF) as a replacement for the problematic RIP and is now the IETF-recommended Interior Gateway Protocol (IGP). OSPF is a link state protocol that, as the name implies, uses Dijkstra's Shortest Path First (SPF) algorithm and that is *open*—that is, it isn't proprietary to any vendor or organization. OSPF has evolved through several RFCs, all of which were written by John Moy. Version 1 of the protocol was specified in RFC 1131; this version never progressed beyond the experimental stage. Version 2, which is still the current version, was first specified in RFC 1247, and the most recent specification is RFC 2328.[1]

Like all link state protocols, OSPF's major advantages over distance vector protocols are fast reconvergence, support for much larger internetworks, and less susceptibility to bad routing information. Other features of OSPF are:

- The use of areas, which reduces the protocol's impact on CPU and memory, contains the flow of routing protocol traffic, and makes possible the construction of hierarchical internetwork topologies

---

[1] *RFC 2328 was released as this chapter was being written, and obsoletes RFC 2178.*

- Fully classless behavior, eliminating such classful problems as discontiguous subnets

- Support of classless route table lookups, VLSM, and supernetting for efficient address management

- A dimensionless, arbitrary metric

- Equal-cost load balancing for more efficient use of multiple paths[2]

- The use of reserved multicast addresses to reduce the impact on non-OSPF-speaking devices

- Support of authentication for more secure routing

- The use of route tagging for the tracking of external routes

OSPF also has the capability of supporting Type of Service (TOS) routing, although it was never widely implemented. RFC 2328 has deleted the TOS routing option for this reason.

OPERATION OF OSPF[3]

At a very high level, the operation of OSPF is easily explained:

1. OSPF-speaking routers send Hello packets out all OSPF-enabled interfaces. If two routers sharing a common data link agree on certain parameters specified in their respective Hello packets, they will become *neighbors*.

---

[2] *More accurately, the RFC calls for equal-cost multipath, the discovery and use of multiple equal-cost paths, without prescribing how the protocol should route individual packets across these multiple paths. Cisco's OSPF implementation performs equal-cost load balancing as described in previous chapters.*

[3] *Because of the interrelationship of OSPF terms and concepts, this chapter frequently uses terms before they are fully defined. The reader is advised to read this section more than once to ensure a complete understanding of OSPF operation. It will also be useful to review the section "Link State Routing Protocols" in Chapter 4, "Dynamic Routing Protocols."*

2. *Adjacencies*, which may be thought of as virtual point-to-point links, are formed between some neighbors. OSPF defines several network types and several router types. The establishment of an adjacency is determined by the types of routers exchanging Hellos and the type of network over which the Hellos are exchanged.

3. Each router sends *link state advertisements* (LSAs) over all adjacencies. The LSAs describe all of the router's links, or interfaces, and the state of the links. These links may be to stub networks (networks with no other router attached), to other OSPF routers, to networks in other areas, or to external networks (networks learned from another routing process). Because of the varying types of link state information, OSPF defines multiple LSA types.

4. Each router receiving an LSA from a neighbor records the LSA in its *link state database* and sends a copy of the LSA to all of its other neighbors.

5. By flooding LSAs throughout an area, all routers will build identical link state databases.

6. When the databases are complete, each router uses the SPF algorithm to calculate a loop-free graph describing the shortest (lowest cost) path to every known destination, with itself as the root. This graph is the SPF tree.

7. Each router builds its route table from its SPF tree.[4]

When all link state information has been flooded to all routers in an area—that is, the link state databases have been synchronized—and the route tables have been built, OSPF is a quiet protocol. Hello packets are exchanged between neighbors as

---

[4] *This fundamental procedure of calculating routes from the link state database, rather than by exchanging routes with neighbors, has repercussions for route filtering. See Chapter 13, "Route Filtering," for more information.*

keepalives, and LSAs are retransmitted every 30 minutes. If the internetwork topology is stable, no other activity should occur.

Neighbors and Adjacencies

Before any LSAs can be sent, OSPF routers must discover their neighbors and establish adjacencies. The neighbors will be recorded in a *neighbor table*, along with the link (interface) on which each neighbor is located and other information necessary for the maintenance of the neighbor (Figure 9.1).

```
Monet#show ip ospf neighbor

Neighbor ID      Pri   State       Dead Time   Address          Interface
192.168.30.70     1    FULL/DR     00:00:34    192.168.17.73    Ethernet0
192.168.30.254    1    FULL/DR     00:00:34    192.168.32.2     Ethernet1
192.168.30.70     1    FULL/BDR    00:00:34    192.168.32.4     Ethernet1
192.168.30.30     1    FULL/ -     00:00:33    192.168.17.50    Serial0.23
192.168.30.10     1    FULL/ -     00:00:32    192.168.17.9     Serial1
192.168.30.68     1    FULL/ -     00:00:39    192.168.21.134   Serial2.824
192.168.30.18     1    FULL/ -     00:00:30    192.168.21.142   Serial2.826
192.168.30.78     1    FULL/ -     00:00:36    192.168.21.170   Serial2.836
```

Figure 9.1

The neighbor table records all OSPF-speaking neighbors.

Router ID

The tracking of other OSPF routers requires that each router have a *Router ID*, an IP address by which the router is uniquely identified within the OSPF domain. Cisco routers derive their Router IDs by the following means:

1. The router chooses the numerically highest IP address on any of its loopback interfaces.
2. If no loopback interfaces are configured with IP addresses, the router chooses the numerically highest IP address on any of its physical interfaces. The interface from which the Router ID is taken does not have to be running OSPF.

Using addresses associated with loopback interfaces has two advantages:

- The loopback interface is more stable than any physical interface. It is active when the router boots up, and it only fails if the entire router fails.

- The network administrator has more leeway in assigning predictable or recognizable addresses as the Router IDs.

Cisco's OSPF will continue to use a Router ID learned from a physical interface even if the interface subsequently fails or is deleted (see "Case Study: Setting Router IDs with Loopback Interfaces," later in this chapter). Therefore, the stability of a loopback interface is only a minor advantage. The primary benefit is the ability to control the Router ID.

The OSPF router begins a neighbor relationship by advertising its Router ID in Hello packets.

The Hello Protocol

The Hello protocol serves several purposes:

- It is the means by which neighbors are discovered.

- It advertises several parameters on which two routers must agree before they can become neighbors.

- Hello packets act as keepalives between neighbors.

- It ensures bi-directional communication between neighbors.

- It elects Designated Routers (DRs) and Backup Designated Routers (BDRs) on Broadcast and Nonbroadcast Multi-access (NBMA) networks.

OSPF-speaking routers periodically send a Hello packet out each OSPF-enabled interface. This period is known as the *HelloInterval* and is configured on a per interface basis. Cisco uses a default HelloInterval of 10 seconds;[5] the value can be changed with the command **ip ospf hello-interval**. If a router has not heard a Hello from a neighbor within a period of time known as the *Router-DeadInterval*, it will declare the neighbor down. Cisco's default RouterDeadInterval is four times the HelloInterval and can be changed with the command **ip ospf dead-interval**.[6]

Each Hello packet contains the following information:

- The Router ID of the originating router

- The Area ID of the originating router interface

- The address mask of the originating interface

- The authentication type and authentication information for the originating interface

- The HelloInterval of the originating interface

- The RouterDeadInterval of the originating interface

- The Router Priority

- The DR and BDR

- Five flag bits signifying optional capabilities

- The Router IDs of the originating router's neighbors. This list contains only routers from which Hellos were heard on the originating interface within the last RouterDeadInterval.

---

[5] *The default is 30 seconds on NBMA interfaces.*

[6] *RFC 2328 does not set a required value for either the HelloInterval or the Router-DeadInterval, although it does suggest respective values of 10 seconds and 4X HelloInterval.*

This section overviews the meaning and use of most of the information listed. Subsequent sections discuss the DR, BDR, and Router Priority and illustrate the precise format of the Hello packet. When a router receives a Hello from a neighbor, it will verify that the Area ID, Authentication, Network Mask, HelloInterval, RouterDeadInterval, and Options values match the values configured on the receiving interface. If they do not, the packet is dropped and no adjacency is established.

If everything matches, the Hello packet is declared valid. If the ID of the originating router is already listed in the neighbor table for that receiving interface, the RouterDeadInterval timer is reset. If the Router ID is not listed, it is added to the neighbor table.

Whenever a router sends a Hello, it includes in the packet the Router IDs of all neighbors listed for the link on which the packet is to be transmitted. If a router receives a valid Hello in which it finds its own Router ID listed, the router knows that two-way communication has been established.

Once two-way communication has been established, adjacencies may be established. However, as mentioned earlier, not all neighbors will become adjacent. Whether an adjacency is formed or not depends on the type of network to which the two neighbors are attached. Network types also influence the way in which OSPF packets are transmitted; therefore, before discussing adjacencies, it is necessary to discuss network types.

Network Types

OSPF defines five network types:

1. Point-to-point networks
2. Broadcast networks
3. Non-broadcast Multi-access (NBMA) networks

4. Point-to-multipoint networks

5. Virtual links

Point-to-point networks, such as a T1 or subrate link, connect a single pair of routers. Valid neighbors on point-to-point networks will always become adjacent. The destination address of OSPF packets on these networks will always be the reserved class D address 224.0.0.5, known as *AllSPFRouters*.[7]

Broadcast networks, such as Ethernet, Token Ring, and FDDI, might be better defined as broadcast multi-access networks to distinguish them from NBMA networks. Broadcast networks are multi-access in that they are capable of connecting more than two devices, and they are broadcast in that all attached devices can receive a single transmitted packet. OSPF routers on broadcast networks will elect a DR and a BDR, as described in the next section, "Designated Routers and Backup Designated Routers." Hello packets are multicast with the AllSPFRouters destination address 224.0.0.5, as are all OSPF packets originated by the DR and BDR. The destination Media Access Control (MAC) identifier of the frames carrying these packets is 0100.5E00.0005. All other routers will multicast link state update and link state acknowledgment packets (described later) to the reserved class D address 224.0.0.6, known as *AllDRouters*. The destination MAC identifier of the frames carrying these packets is 0100.5E00.0006.

NBMA networks, such as X.25, Frame Relay, and ATM, are capable of connecting more than two routers but have no broadcast capability. A packet sent by one of the attached routers would not be received by all other attached routers. As a result, extra configuration may be necessary for routers on these networks to acquire

---

[7] *The exception to this rule is retransmitted LSAs, which are always unicast on all network types. This exception is covered later, in the section "Reliable Flooding: Acknowledgments."*

their neighbors. OSPF routers on NBMA networks elect a DR and BDR, and all OSPF packets are unicast.

Point-to-multipoint networks are a special configuration of NBMA networks in which the networks are treated as a collection of point-to-point links. Routers on these networks do not elect a DR and BDR, and because the networks are seen as point-to-point links, the OSPF packets are multicast.

Virtual links, described in a later section, are special configurations that are interpreted by the router as unnumbered point-to-point networks. OSPF packets are unicast over virtual links.

In addition to these five network types, it should be noted that all networks fall into one of two more-general types:

1. *Transit* networks have two or more attached routers. They may carry packets that are "just passing through"—packets that were originated on and are destined for a network other than the transit network.

   Transit and stub networks

2. *Stub* networks have only a single attached router.[8] Packets on a stub network always have either a source or a destination address belonging to that network. That is, all packets were either originated by a device on the network or are destined for a device on the network. OSPF advertises host routes (routes with a mask of 255.255.255.255) as stub networks. Loopback interfaces are also considered stub networks and are advertised as host routes.[9]

---

[8] *Do not confuse stub networks with stub areas, discussed later in the chapter.*

[9] *Beginning with IOS 11.3, this default behavior can be changed by adding the command* **ip ospf network point-to-point** *to the loopback interface. This will cause the loopback interface's address to be advertised as a subnet route.*

Designated Routers and Backup Designated Routers

Multiaccess networks present two problems for OSPF, relating to the flooding of LSAs (described in a later section):

1. The formation of an adjacency between every attached router would create many unnecessary LSAs. If n is the number of routers on a multiaccess network, there would be $n(n - 1)/2$ adjacencies (Figure 9.2). Each router would flood $n - 1$ LSAs for its adjacent neighbors, plus one LSA for the network, resulting in n^2 LSAs originating from the network.

2. Flooding on the network itself would be chaotic. A router would flood an LSA to all its adjacent neighbors, which in turn would flood it to all their adjacent neighbors, creating many copies of the same LSA on the same network.

Designated Router (DR)

To prevent these problems a Designated Router is elected on multi-access networks. The DR has the following duties:

- To represent the multi-access network and its attached routers to the rest of the internetwork

- To manage the flooding process on the multi-access network

The concept behind the DR is that the network itself is considered a "pseudonode," or a virtual router. Each router on the network forms an adjacency with the DR (Figure 9.3), which represents the pseudonode. Only the DR will send LSAs to the rest of the internetwork. Keep in mind that a router might be a DR on one of its attached multi-access networks, and it might not be the DR on another of its attached multi-access networks. In other words, the DR is a property of a router's interface, not the entire router.

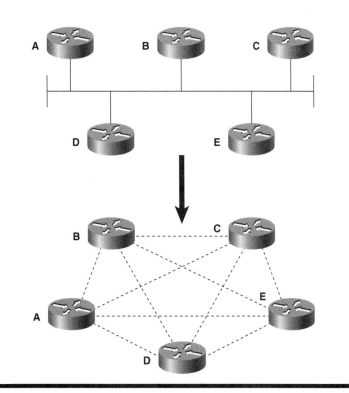

Figure 9.2

Ten adjacencies would be required for each of the five routers on this OSPF network to become fully adjacent with all of its neighbors; 25 LSAs would be originated from the network.

A significant problem with the DR scheme as described so far is that if the DR fails, a new DR must be elected. New adjacencies must be established, and all routers on the network must synchronize their databases with the new DR (part of the adjacency-building process). While all this is happening, the network is unavailable for transit packets.

To prevent this problem, a Backup Designated Router is elected in addition to the DR. All routers form adjacencies not only with the DR but also with the BDR. The DR and BDR also become adjacent with each other. If the DR fails, the BDR becomes the new

Backup Designated Router (BDR)

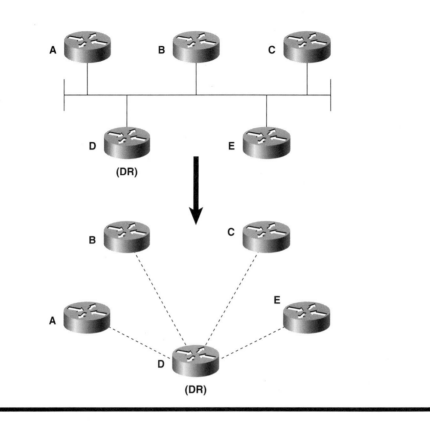

Figure 9.3

The Designated Router represents the multi-access network. Other routers on the network will form adjacencies with the DR, not with each other.

DR. Because the other routers on the network are already adjacent with the BDR, network unavailability is minimized.

The election of the DR and BDR is triggered by the interface state machine, which is described in a later section. For the election process to function properly, the following preconditions must exist:

- Each multi-access interface of each router has a *Router Priority*, which is an 8-bit unsigned integer ranging from 0 to 255. The default priority on Cisco routers is 1 and can be changed on a per multi-access-interface basis with the command **ip ospf priority**. Routers with a priority of 0 are ineligible to become the DR or BDR.

- Hello packets include fields for the originating router to specify its Router Priority and for the IP addresses of the connected interfaces of the routers it considers the DR and BDR.

- When an interface first becomes active on a multi-access network, it sets the DR and BDR to 0.0.0.0. It also sets a *wait timer* with a value equal to the RouterDeadInterval.

- Existing interfaces on a multi-access network record the addresses of the DR and the BDR in the interface data structure, described in a later section.

The election procedure of the DR and BDR is as follows:

1. After 2-Way communication has been established with one or more neighbors, examine the Priority, DR, and BDR fields of each neighbor's Hello. List all routers eligible for election (that is, routers with priority greater than 0 and whose neighbor state is at least 2-Way); all routers declaring themselves to be the DR (their own interface address is in the DR field of the Hello packet); and all routers declaring themselves to be the BDR (their own interface address is in the BDR field of the Hello packet). The calculating router will include itself on this list unless it is ineligible.

2. From the list of eligible routers, create a subset of all routers not claiming to be the DR (routers declaring themselves to be the DR cannot be elected BDR).

3. If one or more neighbors in this subset include its own interface address in the BDR field, the neighbor with the highest priority will be declared the BDR. In a tie, the neighbor with the highest Router ID will be chosen.

4. If no router in the subset claims to be the BDR, the neighbor with the highest priority will become the BDR. In a tie, the neighbor with the highest Router ID will be chosen.

5. If one or more of the eligible routers include their own address in the DR field, the neighbor with the highest priority will be declared the DR. In a tie, the neighbor with the highest Router ID will be chosen.

6. If no router has declared itself the DR, the newly elected BDR will become the DR.

7. If the router performing the calculation is the newly elected DR or BDR, or if it is no longer the DR or BDR, repeat steps 2 through 6.

In simpler language, when an OSPF router becomes active and discovers its neighbors, it checks for an active DR and BDR. If a DR and BDR exist, the router accepts them. If there is no BDR, an election is held in which the router with the highest priority becomes the BDR. If more than one router has the same priority, the one with the numerically highest Router ID wins. If there is no active DR, the BDR is promoted to DR and a new election is held for the BDR.

It should be noted that the priority can influence an election, but will not override an active DR or BDR. That is, if a router with a higher priority becomes active after a DR and BDR have been elected, the new router will not replace either of them. So the first two DR-eligible routers to initialize on a multiaccess network will become the DR and BDR.

Once the DR and BDR have been elected, the other routers (known as DRothers) will establish adjacencies with the DR and BDR only. All routers continue to multicast Hellos to the AllSP-FRouters address 224.0.0.5 so that they can track neighbors, but DRothers multicast update packets to the AllDRouters address 224.0.0.6. Only the DR and BDR will listen to this address; in turn, the DR will flood the updates to the DRothers on 224.0.0.5.

Note that if only one eligible router is attached to a multiaccess network, that router will become the DR and there will be no BDR. Any other routers will form adjacencies only with the DR. If none of the routers attached to a multi-access network are eligible, there will be no DR or BDR and no adjacencies will form. The neighbor states of all routers will remain 2-Way (explained later, in "The Neighbor State Machine").

The duties performed by the DR and BDR are described more fully in subsequent sections.

OSPF Interfaces

The essence of a link state protocol is that it is concerned with links and the state of those links. Before Hellos can be sent, before adjacencies can be formed, and before LSAs can be sent, an OSPF router must understand its own links. A router's interfaces are the means by which OSPF interprets links. As a result, when speaking of OSPF it is not uncommon to hear the terms *interface* and *link* used synonymously. This section examines the data structure OSPF associates with each interface and the various states of an OSPF interface.

The Interface Data Structure

An OSPF router maintains a data structure for each OSPF-enabled interface. In Figure 9.4, the command **show ip ospf interface** has been used to observe the components of an interface data structure.

```
Renoir#show ip ospf interface Serial1.738
Serial1.738 is up, line protocol is up
  Internet Address 192.168.21.21/30, Area 7
  Process ID 1, Router ID 192.168.30.70, Network Type POINT_TO_POINT, Cost: 781
  Transmit Delay is 1 sec, State POINT_TO_POINT,
  Timer intervals configured, Hello 10, Dead 40, Wait 40, Retransmit 5
    Hello due in 00:00:07
  Neighbor Count is 1, Adjacent neighbor count is 1
    Adjacent with neighbor 192.168.30.77
  Message digest authentication enabled
    Youngest key id is 10
```

Figure 9.4

*The OSPF-specific data related to an interface can be observed with the command **show ip ospf interface**. In this example, the interface is attached to a point-to-point network type.*

The components of the interface data structure are as follows:

IP Address and Mask. This component is the configured address and mask of the interface. OSPF packets originated from this interface will have this source address. In Figure 9.4, the address/mask pair is 192.168.21.21/30.

Area ID. The area to which the interface, and the network to which it is attached, belong. OSPF packets originated from this interface will have this Area ID. In Figure 9.4, the area ID is 7.

Process ID. This Cisco-specific feature is not part of the open standard. Cisco routers are capable of running multiple OSPF processes and use the Process ID to distinguish them. The Process ID has no significance outside the router on which it is configured. In Figure 9.4, the Process ID is 1.

Router ID. In Figure 9.4, the Router ID is 192.168.30.70.

Network Type. The type of network to which the interface is connected: broadcast, point-to-point, NBMA, point-to-multipoint, or virtual link. In Figure 9.4, the network type is point-to-point.[10]

---

[10] *Note that this interface is attached to a Frame Relay network. But because this is a point-to-point sub-interface, the OSPF network type is point-to-point instead of NBMA.*

Cost. The outgoing cost for packets transmitted from this interface. Cost is the OSPF metric, expressed as an unsigned 16-bit integer in the range of 1 to 65535. Cisco uses a default cost of 10^8/BW, expressed in whole numbers, where BW is the configured bandwidth of the interface and 10^8 is the *reference bandwidth*. The interface in Figure 9.4 has a configured bandwidth of 128K (not shown in the figure), so the cost is 10^8/128K = 781.

The cost can be changed with the command **ip ospf cost**. This command is especially important when configuring Cisco routers in a multivendor environment. Bay and other vendors, for example, use a default cost of 1 on all interfaces (essentially making OSPF cost reflect hop counts). If all routers do not assign costs in the same manner, OSPF can route improperly.

Changing the
default cost.

The reference bandwidth of 10^8 creates a problem for some modern media with bandwidths higher than 100M (such as OC-3 and Gigabit Ethernet). 10^8/100M = 1, meaning that higher bandwidths calculate to a fraction of 1, which is not allowed. Beginning with IOS 11.2, Cisco has remedied this with the command **ospf auto-cost reference-bandwidth**, which allows the default reference bandwidth to be changed.

InfTransDelay. The seconds by which LSAs exiting the interface will have their age incremented. In Figure 9.4, this is displayed as Transmit Delay and is shown to be the Cisco default, 1 second. InfTransDelay can be changed with the command **ip ospf transmit-delay**.

State. The functional state of the interface, which is described in the following section, "The Interface State Machine."

Router Priority. This 8-bit unsigned integer in the range of 0 to 255 elects the DR and BDR. The priority is not displayed in Figure 9.4 because the network type is point-to-point; no DR or BDR is elected on this network type. Figure 9.5 shows another OSPF interface in the same router. This interface shows an attached network type of broadcast, so a DR and BDR will be elected. The priority shown is 1, the Cisco default. The command **ip ospf priority** is used to change the Router Priority.

```
Renoir#show ip ospf interface Ethernet0
Ethernet0 is up, line protocol is up
   Internet Address 192.168.17.73/29, Area 0
   Process ID 1, Router ID 192.168.30.70, Network Type BROADCAST, Cost: 10
   Transmit Delay is 1 sec, State DR, Priority 1
   Designated Router (ID) 192.168.30.70, Interface address 192.168.17.73
   Backup Designated router (ID) 192.168.30.80, Interface address 192.168.17.74
   Timer intervals configured, Hello 10, Dead 40, Wait 40, Retransmit 5
      Hello due in 00:00:03
   Neighbor Count is 1, Adjacent neighbor count is 1
      Adjacent with neighbor 192.168.30.80 (Backup Designated Router)
   Message digest authentication enabled
      Youngest key id is 10
```

Figure 9.5

This interface is attached to a broadcast network type, and the router is the DR on this network.

Designated Router. The DR for the network to which the interface is attached is recorded both by its Router ID and by the address of the interface attached to the shared network. Note that no DR is displayed in Figure 9.4; it will be displayed only for multi-access network types. In Figure 9.5, the DR is 192.168.30.70. The address of its attached interface is 192.168.17.73. A look at the Router ID, the interface address, and the interface state show that Renoir is the DR.

Backup Designated Router. The BDR for the network to which the interface is attached is also recorded both by its Router ID and by the address of the attached interface. In Figure 9.5, the BDR is 192.168.30.80, and its interface address is 192.168.17.74.

HelloInterval. The period, in seconds, between transmissions of Hello packets on the interface. This period is advertised in Hello packets that are transmitted from the interface. Cisco uses a default of 10 seconds, which can be changed with the command **ip ospf hello-interval**. Figure 9.5 displays HelloInterval as Hello and shows that the default is being used.

RouterDeadInterval. The period, in seconds, that the router will wait to hear a Hello from a neighbor on the network to which the interface is connected before declaring the neighbor down. The RouterDeadInterval is advertised in Hello packets transmitted from the interface. Cisco uses a default of four times the HelloInterval; the default can be changed with the command **ip ospf dead-interval**. Figure 9.5 displays the RouterDeadInterval as Dead and shows that the default is being used.

Wait Timer. The length of time the router will wait for a DR and BDR to be advertised in a neighbor's Hello packet before beginning a DR and BDR selection. The period of the wait timer is the RouterDeadInterval. In Figure 9.4, the wait time is irrelevant because the interface is attached to a point-to-point network; no DR or BDR will be used.

RxmtInterval. The period, in seconds, the router will wait between retransmissions of OSPF packets that have not been acknowledged. Figure 9.5 displays this period as retransmit and shows that the Cisco default of 5 seconds is being used. An interface's RxmtInterval can be changed with the command **ip ospf retransmit-interval**.

Hello Timer. A timer that is set to the HelloInterval. When it expires, a Hello packet is transmitted from the interface. Figure 9.5 shows that the Hello timer will expire in three seconds.

Neighboring Routers. A list of all valid neighbors (neighbors whose Hellos have been seen within the past RouterDeadInterval) on the attached network. Figure 9.6 shows yet another interface on the same router. Here, five neighbors are known on the network, but only two are adjacent (the Router IDs of only the adjacent neighbors are displayed). As a DRother on this network, the router has established an adjacency only with the DR and the BDR, in keeping with the DR protocol.

```
Renoir#show ip ospf interface Ethernet1
Ethernet1 is up, line protocol is up
   Internet Address 192.168.32.4/24, Area 78
   Process ID 1, Router ID 192.168.30.70, Network Type BROADCAST, Cost: 10
   Transmit Delay is 1 sec, State DROTHER, Priority 1
   Designated Router (ID) 192.168.30.254, Interface address 192.168.32.2
   Backup Designated router (ID) 192.168.30.80, Interface address 192.168.32.1
   Timer intervals configured, Hello 10, Dead 40, Wait 40, Retransmit 5
      Hello due in 00:00:01
   Neighbor Count is 5, Adjacent neighbor count is 2
      Adjacent with neighbor 192.168.30.80 (Backup Designated Router)
      Adjacent with neighbor 192.168.30.254 (Designated Router)
   Message digest authentication enabled
      Youngest key id is 10
```

Figure 9.6

On this network, the router sees five neighbors but has only formed adjacencies with the DR and the BDR.

AuType. Describes the type of authentication used on the network. The authentication type may be Null (no authentication), Simple Password, or Cryptographic (Message Digest). Figure 9.6 shows that Message Digest authentication is being used. If Null authentication is used, no authentication type or key information will be displayed when **show ip ospf interface** is invoked.

Authentication Key. A 64-bit password if simple authentication has been enabled for the interface or a message digest key if Cryptographic authentication is used. Figure 9.6 shows that the "youngest key ID" is 10. This alludes to the fact that Cryptographic authentication allows the configuration of multiple keys on an interface to ensure smooth and secure key changes.

Figure 9.7 shows an interface that is connected to an NBMA network. Notice that the HelloInterval is 30 seconds, the default for NBMA, and that the RouterDeadInterval is at the default of four times the HelloInterval.

```
Renoir#show ip ospf interface Serial3
Serial3 is up, line protocol is up
   Internet Address 192.168.16.41/30, Area 0
   Process ID 1, Router ID 192.168.30.105, Network Type NON_BROADCAST, Cost: 64
   Transmit Delay is 1 sec, State BDR, Priority 1
   Designated Router (ID) 192.168.30.210, Interface address 192.168.16.42
   Backup Designated router (ID) 192.168.30.105, Interface address 192.168.16.41
   Timer intervals configured, Hello 30, Dead 120, Wait 120, Retransmit 5
      Hello due in 00:00:08
   Neighbor Count is 1, Adjacent neighbor count is 1
      Adjacent with neighbor 192.168.30.210 (Designated Router)
```

Figure 9.7

This interface is attached to a NBMA Frame Relay network and is the BDR for this network.

It is worthwhile to spend some time comparing Figures 9.4 through 9.7. All four interfaces are on the same router, yet on each network the router performs a different role. In each case, the interface state dictates the role of the OSPF router on a network. The next section describes the various interface states and the interface state machine.

The Interface State Machine

An OSPF-enabled interface will transition through several states before it becomes fully functional. Those states are Down, Point-to-Point, Waiting, DR, Backup, DRother, and Loopback.

Down. This is the initial interface state. The interface is not functional, all interface parameters are set to their initial values, and no protocol traffic is transmitted or received on the interface.

Point-to-Point. This state is applicable only to interfaces connected to point-to-point, point-to-multipoint, and virtual link network types. When an interface transitions to this state, it is fully functional. It will begin sending Hello packets every HelloInterval and will attempt to establish an adjacency with the neighbor at the other end of the link.

Waiting. This state is applicable only to interfaces connected to broadcast and NBMA network types. When an interface transitions to this state, it will begin sending and receiving Hello packets and will set the wait timer. The router will attempt to identify the network's DR and BDR while in this state.

DR. In this state, the router is the DR on the attached network and will establish adjacencies with the other routers on the multi-access network.

Backup. In this state, the router is the BDR on the attached network and will establish adjacencies with the other routers on the multi-access network.

DRother. In this state, the router is neither the DR nor the BDR on the attached network. It will form adjacencies only with the DR and BDR, although it will track all neighbors on the network.

Loopback. In this state, the interface is looped back via software or hardware. Although packets cannot transit an interface in this state, the interface address is still advertised in router LSAs (described later) so that test packets can find their way to the interface.

Figure 9.8 shows the OSPF interface states and the input events that will cause a state transition. The input events are described in Table 9.1.

OSPF Neighbors

The preceding section discussed a router's relationship with the attached network. Although a router's interaction with other routers was discussed in the context of electing DRs and BDRs, the

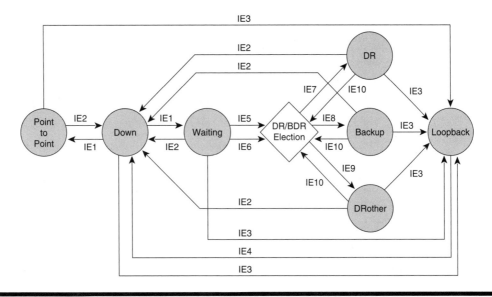

Figure 9.8
The OSPF interface state machine; see Table 9.1 for a description of input events (IEs).

Table 9.1 *Input events for the interface state machine.*

Input Event	Description
IE1	Lower-level protocols indicate that the network interface is operational.
IE2	Lower-level protocols indicate that the network interface is not operational.
IE3	Network management or lower-level protocols indicate that the interface is looped up.
IE4	Network management or lower-level protocols indicate that the interface is looped down.
IE5	A Hello packet is received in which either the originating neighbor lists itself as the BDR or the originating neighbor lists itself as the DR and indicates no BDR.
IE6	The wait timer has expired.
IE7	The router is elected as the DR for this network.
IE8	The router is elected as the BDR for this network.
IE9	The router has not been elected as the DR or BDR for this network.

Table 9.1 *Input events for the interface state machine, continued.*

Input Event	Description
IE10	A change has occurred in the set of valid neighbors on this network. This change may be one of the following: (1) The establishment of two-way communication with a neighbor (2) The loss of two-way communication with a neighbor (3) The receipt of a Hello in which the originating neighbor newly lists itself as the DR or BDR (4) The receipt of a Hello from the DR in which that router is no longer listed as the DR (5) The receipt of a Hello from the BDR in which that router is no longer listed as the BDR (6) The expiration of the RouterDeadInterval without having received a Hello from the DR or the BDR or both

purpose of the DR election process is still to establish a relationship with a network. This section discusses a router's relationship with the neighbors on the network. The ultimate purpose of the neighbor relationship is the formation of adjacencies over which to pass routing information.

An adjacency is established in four general phases:

The phases of establishing an adjacency

1. *Neighbor discovery.*
2. *Bidirectional communication.* This communication is accomplished when two neighbors list each other's Router IDs in their Hello packets.
3. *Database synchronization.* Database Description, Link State Request, and Link State Update packets (described in a later section) are exchanged to ensure that both neighbors have identical information in their link state databases. For the purposes of this process, one neighbor will

become the master and the other will become the slave. As the name implies, the master will control the exchange of Database Description packets.

4. *Full adjacency.*

As previously discussed, neighbor relationships are established and maintained through the exchange of Hello packets. On broadcast and point-to-point network types, Hellos are multicast to AllSPFRouters (224.0.0.5). On NBMA, point-to-multipoint, and virtual link network types, Hellos are unicast to individual neighbors. The implication of unicasting is that the router must first learn of the existence of its neighbors either through manual configuration or an underlying mechanism such as Inverse ARP. The configuration of neighbors on these network types is covered in the appropriate sections.

Hellos are sent every HelloInterval on every network type, with one exception: On NBMA networks, a router will send Hellos to neighbors whose neighbor state is down every PollInterval. On Cisco routers, the default PollInterval is 60 seconds.

The Neighbor Data Structure

An OSPF router builds the Hello packets for each network using the information stored in the interface data structure of the attached interface. By sending the Hello packets containing this information, the router informs neighbors about itself. Likewise, for each neighbor the router will maintain a neighbor data structure consisting of the information learned from other routers' Hello packets. This two-way exchange of information with a neighbor can be thought of as a conversation.

In Figure 9.9, the command **show ip ospf neighbor** is used to observe some of the information in the neighbor data structure for a single neighbor.[11]

---

[11] *Compare this usage with Figure 9.1.*

```
Seurat#show ip ospf neighbor 192.168.30.105
Neighbor 192.168.30.105, interface address 192.168.16.41
   In the area 0 via interface Serial0
   Neighbor priority is 1, State is FULL
   Poll interval 60
   Options 2
   Dead timer due in 00:01:40
```

Figure 9.9

An OSPF router describes each conversation with each neighbor by a neighbor data structure.

Actually, the data structure records more information about each neighbor than is shown in the figure. The components of the neighbor data structure are as follows:

Neighbor ID. The router ID of the neighbor. In Figure 9.9, the neighbor ID is 192.168.30.105.

Neighbor IP Address. The IP address of the neighbor's interface attached to the network. When OSPF packets are unicasted to the neighbor, this address will be the destination address. In Figure 9.9, the neighbor's IP address is 192.168.16.41.

Area ID. In order for two routers to become neighbors, the Area ID carried in a received Hello packet must match the Area ID of the receiving interface. The Area ID of the neighbor in Figure 9.9 is 0 (0.0.0.0).

Interface. The interface attached to the network on which the neighbor is located. In Figure 9.9, the neighbor is reached via S0.

Neighbor Priority. This component is the Router Priority of the neighbor, as advertised in the neighbor's Hello packets. The priority is used in the DR/BDR election process. The neighbor in Figure 9.9 has a priority of 1, the Cisco default.

State. This component is the functional state of the neighbor, as described in the following section, "The Neighbor State Machine." The state of the neighbor in Figure 9.9 is Full.

PollInterval. This value is recorded only for neighbors on NBMA networks. Because neighbors may not be automatically discovered on NBMA networks, if the neighbor state is Down, a Hello will be sent to the neighbor every PollInterval—some period longer than the HelloInterval. The neighbor in Figure 9.9 is on an NBMA network, as indicated by the default Cisco PollInterval of 60 seconds.

Neighbor Options. The optional OSPF capabilities supported by the neighbor. Options are discussed in the section describing the Hello packet format.

Inactivity Timer. A timer whose period is the RouterDeadInterval, as defined in the interface data structure. The timer is reset whenever a Hello is received from the neighbor. If the inactivity timer expires before a Hello is heard from the neighbor, the neighbor is declared Down. In Figure 9.9, the inactivity timer is shown as the Dead Timer and will expire in 100 seconds.

Components of the neighbor data structure that are not displayed by the **show ip ospf neighbor** command are as follows:

Designated Router. This address is included in the DR field of the neighbor's Hello packets.

Backup Designated Router. This address is included in the BDR field of the neighbor's Hello packets.

Master/Slave. The master/slave relationship, negotiated with neighbors in the ExStart state, establishes which neighbor will control the database synchronization.

DD Sequence Number. The Sequence Number of the Database Description (DD) packet currently being sent to the neighbor.

Last Received Database Description Packet. The Initialize, More, and Master bits; the options; and the sequence number of the last received database description packet are recorded. This information is used to determine whether the next DD packet is a duplicate.

Link State Retransmission List. This component is a list of LSAs that have been flooded on the adjacency, but have not yet been acknowledged. The LSAs are retransmitted every RxmtInterval, as defined in the interface data structure, until they are acknowledged or until the adjacency is destroyed.

Database Summary List. This component is the list of LSAs sent to the neighbor in Database Description packets during database synchronization. These LSAs make up the link state database when the router goes into exchange state.

Link State Request List. This list records LSAs from the neighbor's Database Description packets which are more recent than the LSAs in the link state database. Link State Request packets are sent to the neighbor for copies of these LSAs; as the requested LSAs are received in Link State Update packets, the Request List is depleted.

The Neighbor State Machine

An OSPF router will transition a neighbor (as described in the neighbor data structure) through several states before the neighbor is considered fully adjacent.

Down. The initial state of a neighbor conversation indicates that no Hellos have been heard from the neighbor in the last Router-DeadInterval. Hellos are not sent to down neighbors unless those neighbors are on NBMA networks; in this case, Hellos are sent every PollInterval. If a neighbor transitions to the Down state from some higher state, the link state Retransmission List, Database Summary List, and link state request list are cleared.

Attempt. This state applies only to neighbors on NBMA networks, where neighbors are manually configured. A DR-eligible router will transition a neighbor to the Attempt state when the interface to the neighbor first becomes Active or when the router is the DR or BDR. A router will send packets to a neighbor in Attempt state at the HelloInterval instead of the PollInterval.

Init. This state indicates that a Hello packet has been seen from the neighbor in the last RouterDeadInterval, but 2-Way communication has not yet been established. A router will include the Router IDs of all neighbors in this state or higher in the Neighbor field of the Hello packets.

2-Way. This state indicates that the router has seen its own Router ID in the Neighbor field of the neighbor's Hello packets, which means that a bidirectional conversation has been established. On multi-access networks, neighbors must be in this state or higher to be eligible to be elected as the DR or BDR. The reception of a Database Description packet from a neighbor in the init state will also cause a transition to 2-Way.

ExStart. In this state, the router and its neighbor establish a master/slave relationship and determine the initial DD sequence number in preparation for the exchange of Database Description packets. The neighbor with the highest interface address becomes the master.

Exchange. The router sends Database Description packets describing its entire link state database to neighbors that are in the Exchange state. The router may also send Link State Request packets, requesting more recent LSAs, to neighbors in this state.

Loading. The router will send Link State Request packets to neighbors that are in the Loading state, requesting more recent LSAs that have been discovered in the Exchange state but have not yet been received.

Full. Neighbors in this state are fully adjacent, and the adjacencies will appear in Router LSAs and Network LSAs.

Figures 9.10 through 9.12 show the OSPF neighbor states and the input events that will cause a state transition. The input events are described in Table 9.2, and the decision points are defined in Table 9.3. Figure 9.10 shows the normal progression from the least functional state to the fully functional state, and Figure 9.11 and Figure 9.12 show the complete OSPF neighbor state machine.

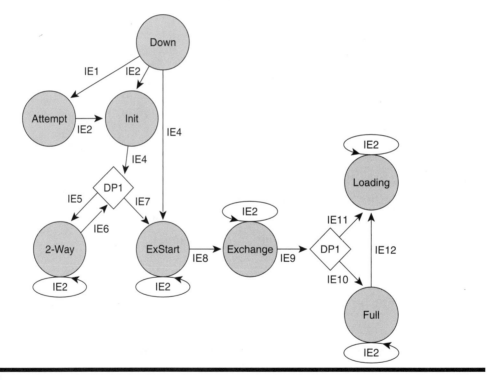

Figure 9.10

The normal series of transitions in the OSPF neighbor state machine which take a neighbor from Down to Full.

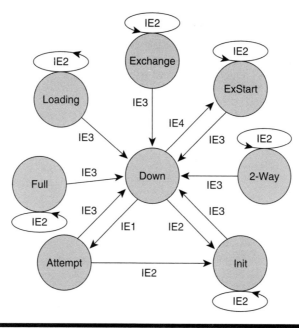

Figure 9.11

The neighbor state machine, from Down to Init.

Building an Adjacency

Neighbors on point-to-point, point-to-multipoint, and virtual link networks always become adjacent unless the parameters of their Hellos don't match. On broadcast and NBMA networks, the DR and BDR become adjacent with all neighbors, but no adjacencies will exist between DRothers.

The adjacency building process uses three OSPF packet types:

1. Database Description packets (type 2)
2. Link State Request packets (type 3)
3. Link State Update packets (type 4)

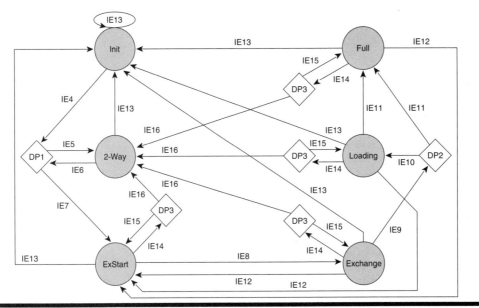

Figure 9.12

The neighbor state machine, from Init to Full.

Table 9.2   *Input events for Figures 9.10, 9.11, and 9.12.*

Input Event	Description
IE1	This event occurs only for NBMA-connected neighbors. The input event will be triggered under either of the following conditions: (1) The interface to the NBMA network first becomes active, and the neighbor is eligible for DR election. (2) The router becomes either DR or BDR, and the neighbor is not eligible for DR election.
IE2	A valid Hello packet has been received from the neighbor.
IE3	The neighbor is no longer reachable, as determined by the lower level protocols, by an explicit instruction from the OSPF process itself, or by the expiration of the inactivity timer.
IE4	The router first sees its own Router ID listed in the Neighbor field of the neighbor's Hello packet or receives a Database Description packet from the neighbor.

Table 9.2 *Input events for Figures 9.10, 9.11, and 9.12, continued.*

Input Event	Description
IE5	The neighbor should not become adjacent.
IE6	This input event occurs under either of the following conditions: (1) The neighbor state first transitions to 2-Way. (2) The interface state changes.
IE7	An adjacency should be formed with this neighbor.
IE8	The master/slave relationship has been established and DD sequence numbers have been exchanged.
IE9	The exchange of Database Description packets has been completed.
IE10	Entries exist in the Link State Request list.
IE11	The Link State Request list is empty.
IE12	The adjacency should be broken and then restarted. This input event may be triggered by any of the following: (1) The reception of a Database Description packet with an unexpected DD sequence number (2) The reception of a Database Description packet with the Options field set differently than the Options field of the last DD packet (3) The reception of a Database Description packet, other than the first packet, in which the Init bit is set (4) The reception of a Link State Request packet for an LSA that is not in the database
IE13	A Hello packet has been received from the neighbor in which the receiving router's Router ID is not listed in the Neighbor field.
IE14	This event occurs when the interface state changes.
IE15	The existing or forming adjacency with this neighbor should continue.
IE16	The existing or forming adjacency with this neighbor should not continue.

Table 9.3   *Decision points for Figures 9.10 and 9.12.*

Decision	Description
DP1	Should an adjacency be established with the neighbor? An adjacency should be formed if one or more of the following conditions is true: (1) The network type is point-to-point. (2) The network type is point-to-multipoint. (3) The network type is virtual link. (4) The router is the DR for the network on which the neighbor is located. (5) The router is the BDR for the network on which the neighbor is located. (6) The neighbor is the DR. (7) The neighbor is the BDR.
DP2	Is the Link State Request list for this neighbor empty?
DP3	Should the existing or forming adjacency with the neighbor continue?

The formats of these packet types are described in detail in a subsequent section, "OSPF Packet Formats."

The Database Description packet is of particular importance to the adjacency building process. As the name implies, the packets carry a summary description of each LSA in the originating router's link state database. These descriptions are not the complete LSAs, but merely their headers—enough information for the receiving router to decide whether it has the latest copy of the LSA in its own database. In addition, three flags in the DD packet are used to manage the adjacency building process:

1. The I-bit, or Initial bit, which when set indicates the first DD packet sent

2. The M-bit, or More bit, which when set indicates that this is not the last DD packet to be sent
3. The MS-bit, or Master/Slave bit, which is set in the DD packets originated by the master

When the master/slave negotiation begins in the ExStart state, both neighbors will claim to be the master by sending an empty DD packet with the MS-bit set to one. The DD sequence number in these two packets will be set to the originating router's idea of what the sequence number should be. The neighbor with the lower Router ID will become the slave and will reply with a DD packet in which the MS-bit is zero and the DD sequence number is set to the master's sequence number. This DD packet will be the first packet populated with LSA summaries. When the master/slave negotiation is completed, the neighbor state will transition to Exchange.

In the Exchange state, the neighbors will synchronize their link state databases by describing all entries in their respective link state databases. The Database Summary List is populated with the headers of all LSAs in the router's database; Database Description packets containing the listed LSA headers are sent to the neighbor.

If either router sees that its neighbor has an LSA that is not in its own database, or that the neighbor has a more recent copy of a known LSA, it places the LSA on the Link State Request list. It then sends a Link State Request packet asking for a complete copy of the LSA in question. Link State Update packets convey the requested LSAs. As the requested LSAs are received, they are removed from the Link State Request list.

All LSAs sent in Update packets must be individually acknowledged. Therefore, the transmitted LSAs are entered into the Link

State Retransmission list. As they are acknowledged, they are removed from the list. The LSA may be acknowledged by one of two means:

- *Explicit Acknowledgment.* A Link State Acknowledgment packet containing the LSA header is received.

- *Implicit Acknowledgment.* An Update packet that contains the same instance of the LSA (neither LSA is more recent than the other) is received.

The master controls the synchronization process and ensures that only one DD packet is outstanding at a time. When the slave receives a DD packet from the master, the slave acknowledges the packet by sending a DD packet with the same sequence number. If the master does not receive an acknowledgment of an outstanding DD packet within the RxmtInterval, as specified in the interface data structure, the master will send a new copy of the packet.

The slave sends DD packets only in response to DD packets it receives from the master. If the received DD packet has a new sequence number, the slave sends a DD packet with the same sequence number. If the received sequence number is the same as a previously acknowledged DD packet, the acknowledging packet is re-sent.

When the database synchronization process is complete, one of two state transitions will occur:

- If there are still entries of the Link State Request list, the router will transition the state of the neighbor to Loading.

- If the Link State Request list is empty, the router will transition the state of the neighbor to Full.

The master knows that the synchronization process is complete when it has sent all the DD packets necessary to fully describe its link state database and has received a DD packet with the M-bit set to zero. The slave knows that the process is complete when it receives a DD packet with the M-bit set to zero and sends an acknowledging DD packet that also has its M-bit set to zero (that is, the slave has fully described its own database). Because the slave must acknowledge each received DD packet, the slave will always be the first to know that the synchronization process is complete.

Figure 9.13 shows the adjacency building process. This example is taken directly from RFC 2328.

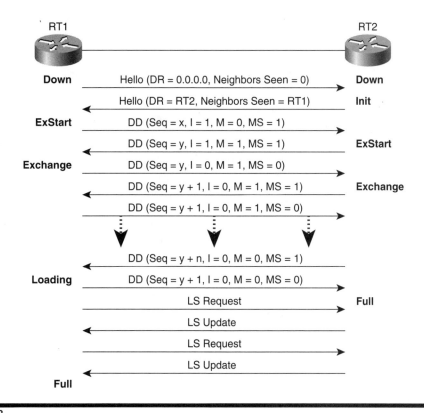

Figure 9.13

The link state database synchronization process and associated neighbor states.

The following steps are illustrated in Figure 9.13:

1. RT1 becomes active on the multi-access network and sends a Hello packet. It has not yet heard from any neighbors, so the Neighbor field of the packet is empty, and the DR and BDR fields are set to 0.0.0.0.

2. Upon reception of the Hello from RT1, RT2 creates a neighbor data structure for RT1 and sets RT1's state to Init. RT2 sends a Hello packet with RT1's Router ID in the Neighbor field; as the DR, RT2 also includes its own interface address in the DR field.

3. Seeing its Router ID in the received Hello packet (IE 4 in Table 9.2), RT1 creates a neighbor data structure for RT2 and sets RT2's state to ExStart for the master/slave negotiation. It then generates an empty (no LSA summaries) Database Description packet; the DD sequence number is set to x, the I-bit is set to indicate that this is RT1's initial DD packet for this exchange, the M-bit is set to indicate that this is not the last DD packet, and the MS-bit is set to indicate that RT1 is asserting itself as the master.

4. RT2 transitions RT1's state to ExStart upon reception of the DD packet. It then sends a responding DD packet with a DD sequence number of y; RT2 has a higher router ID than RT1, so it sets the MS-bit. Like the first DD packet, this one is used for the master/slave negotiation and therefore is empty.

5. Agreeing that RT2 is the master, RT1 transitions RT2's state to Exchange. RT1 will generate a DD packet with RT2's DD sequence number of y and the MS = 0, indicating that RT1 is the slave. This packet will be populated with LSA headers from RT1's Link State Summary list.

6. RT2 transitions its neighbor state to Exchange upon receipt of RT1's DD packet. It will send a DD packet containing LSA headers from its Link State Summary list and will increment the DD sequence number to y+1.

7. RT1 sends an acknowledging packet containing the same sequence number as in the DD packet it just received from RT2. The process continues, with RT2 sending a single DD packet and then waiting for an acknowledging packet from RT1 containing the same sequence number before sending the next packet. When RT2 sends the DD packet with the last of its LSA summaries, it sets M = 0.

8. Receiving this packet and knowing that the acknowledging packet it will send contains the last of its own LSA summaries, RT1 knows the Exchange process is done. However, it has entries in its Link State Request list; therefore, it will transition to Loading.

9. When RT2 receives RT1's last DD packet, RT2 transitions RT1's state to full because it has no entries in its Link State Request list.

10. RT1 sends Link State Request packets, and RT2 sends the requested LSAs in Link State Update packets, until RT1's Link State Request list is empty. RT1 will then transition RT2's state to Full.

Note that if either router has entries in its Link State Request list, it does not need to wait for the Loading state to send Link State Request packets; it may do so while the neighbor is still in the Exchange state. Consequently, the synchronization process is not as tidy as depicted in Figure 9.13, but it is more efficient.

Figure 9.14 shows an analyzer capture of an adjacency being built between two routers. Although Link State Request and Link State Update packets are being sent while both neighbors are still in the Exchange state, attention to the I-, M-, and MS-bits and the sequence numbers reveals that the real-life process follows the generic procedure of Figure 9.13.

Number	Packet Type	Router ID	I-bit	M-bit	MS-bit	Sequence Number
8	Hello	192.168.30.70	–	–	–	–
10	Hello	192.168.30.175	–	–	–	–
11	Database Description	192.168.30.70	1	1	1	0x20E0
12	Database Description	192.168.30.175	1	1	1	0xB17
13	Database Description	192.168.30.70	0	1	0	0xB17
14	Database Description	192.168.30.175	0	1	1	0xB18
15	Link State Request	192.168.30.175	–	–	–	–
16	Database Description	192.168.30.70	0	0	0	0xB18
17	Link State Request	192.168.30.70	–	–	–	–
18	Link State Update	192.168.30.70	–	–	–	–
19	Database Description	192.168.30.175	0	0	1	0xB19
20	Link State Update	192.168.30.175	–	–	–	–
21	Database Description	192.168.30.70	0	0	0	0xB19
22	Link State Update	192.168.30.175	–	–	–	–
23	Link State Update	192.168.30.175	–	–	–	–
24	State Acknowledgement	192.168.30.175	–	–	–	–
25	State Acknowledgement	192.168.30.70	–	–	–	–
26	Link State Update	192.168.30.70	–	–	–	–
28	Link State Update	192.168.30.175	–	–	–	–
30	State Acknowledgement	192.168.30.70	–	–	–	–
33	Link State Update	192.160.30.70	–	–	–	–
34	State Acknowledgement	192.168.30.175	–	–	–	–
40	Hello	192.168.30.70	–	–	–	–
46	Hello	192.168.30.175	–	–	–	–

Figure 9.14

This analyzer capture shows an adjacency being built.

In Figure 9.15, the output of the command **debug ip ospf adj** shows the adjacency of Figure 9.14 being built from the perspective of one of the routers (router ID 192.168.30.175).

```
Degas#debug ip ospf adj
OSPF adjacency events debugging is on
OSPF: Rcv DBD from 192.168.30.70 on Ethernet0 seq 0x20E0 opt 0x2 flag 0x7 len 32
  state INIT
OSPF: 2 Way Communication to 192.168.30.70 on Ethernet0,
state 2WAY
OSPF: Neighbor change Event on interface Ethernet0
OSPF: DR/BDR election on Ethernet0
OSPF: Elect BDR 192.168.30.70
OSPF: Elect DR 192.168.30.175
    DR: 192.168.30.175 (Id) BDR: 192.168.30.70 (Id)
OSPF: Send DBD to 192.168.30.70 on Ethernet0 seq 0xB17 opt 0x2 flag 0x7 len 32
OSPF: First DBD and we are not SLAVE
OSPF: Rcv DBD from 192.168.30.70 on Ethernet0 seq 0xB17 opt 0x2 flag 0x2 len 92
state EXSTART
OSPF: NBR Negotiation Done. We are the MASTER
OSPF: Send DBD to 192.168.30.70 on Ethernet0 seq 0xB18 opt 0x2 flag 0x3 len 72
OSPF: Database request to 192.168.30.70
OSPF: Rcv DBD from 192.168.30.70 on Ethernet0 seq 0xB18 opt 0x2 flag 0x0 len 32
state EXCHANGE
OSPF: Send DBD to 192.168.30.70 on Ethernet0 seq 0xB19 opt 0x2 flag 0x1 len 32
OSPF: Rcv DBD from 192.168.30.70 on Ethernet0 seq 0xB19 opt 0x2 flag 0x0 len 32
state EXCHANGE
OSPF: Exchange Done with 192.168.30.70 on Ethernet0
OSPF: Synchronized with 192.168.30.70 on Ethernet0,
state FULL
```

Figure 9.15

This debug output shows the adjacency events of Figure 9.14 from the perspective of one of the routers.

At the end of the synchronization process in Figure 9.14, a series of Link State Update and Link State Acknowledgment packets can be observed. These are part of the LSA flooding process, discussed in the next section.

Flooding

The entire OSPF topology may be depicted as a group of routers, or nodes, interconnected not by physical links but by logical adjacencies (Figure 9.16). For the nodes to route properly over this logical topology, each node must possess an identical map of the topology. This map is the topological database.

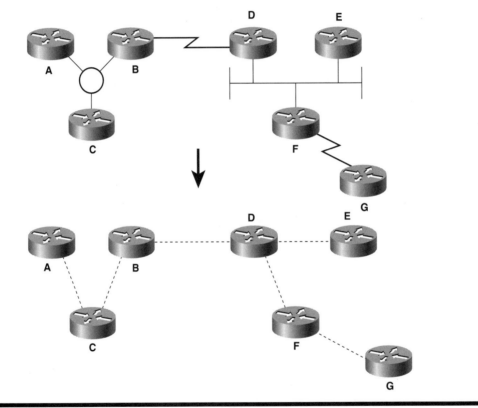

Figure 9.16

A group of routers interconnected by data links will be viewed by OSPF as a group of nodes interconnected by adjacencies.

The OSPF topological database is better known as the link state database. This database consists of all the LSAs the router has received. A change in the topology is represented as a change in one or more of the LSAs. Flooding is the process by which these changed or new LSAs are sent throughout the network, to ensure that the database of every node is updated and remains identical to all other nodes' databases.

Flooding makes use of the following two OSPF packet types:

- Link State Update packets (type 4)

- Link State Acknowledgment packets (type 5)

As Figure 9.17 shows, each Link State Update and Acknowledgment packet may carry multiple LSAs. Although the LSAs themselves are flooded throughout the internetwork, the Update and Acknowledgment packets travel only between two nodes across an adjacency.

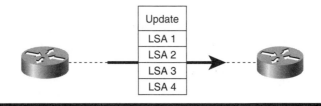

Figure 9.17
LSAs are sent across adjacencies within link state update packets.

On point-to-point networks, updates are sent to the multicast address AllSPFRouters (224.0.0.5). On point-to-multipoint and virtual link networks, updates are unicasted to the interface addresses of the adjacent neighbors.

On broadcast networks, DRothers form adjacencies only with the DR and BDR. Therefore, updates are sent to the address All-DRouters (224.0.0.6). The DR in turn multicasts an Update packets containing the LSA to all adjacent routers on the network using the address AllSPFRouters. All routers then flood the LSA out all other interfaces (Figure 9.18). Although the BDR hears and records LSAs multicast from DRothers, it will not reflood or acknowledge them unless the DR fails to do so. The same DR/BDR functionality exists on NBMA networks, except that LSAs are unicast from DRothers to the DR and BDR, and the DR unicasts a copy of the LSA to all adjacent neighbors.

Because identical link state databases are essential to correct OSPF operation, flooding must be reliable. Transmitting routers must know that their LSAs were received successfully, and receiving routers must know that they are accepting the correct LSAs.

Reliable Flooding: Acknowledgments

Implicit acknowledgment

Each individual transmitted LSA must be acknowledged. This may be accomplished by either an *implicit* acknowledgment or an *explicit* acknowledgment.

A neighbor can implicitly acknowledge the receipt of an LSA by including a duplicate of the LSA in an update back to the originator. Implicit acknowledgments are more efficient than explicit acknowledgments in some situations, for instance, when the neighbor was intending to send an update to the originator anyway.

Explicit acknowledgment

A neighbor explicitly acknowledges the receipt of an LSA by sending a Link State Acknowledgment packet. A single Link State Acknowledgment packet is capable of acknowledging multiple LSAs. The packet carries only LSA headers—enough to completely identify the LSA—not the complete LSA.

When a router first sends an LSA, a copy of the LSA is entered into the Link State Retransmission list of every neighbor to which it

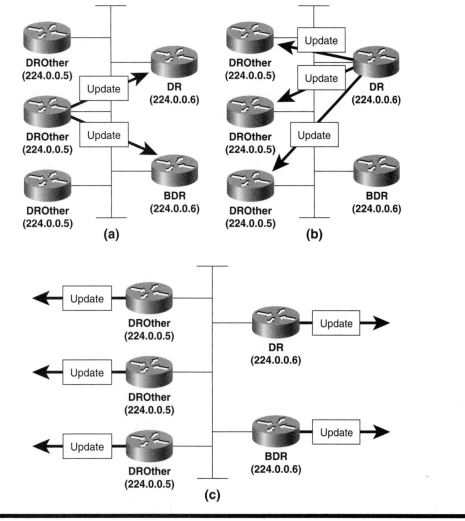

Figure 9.18

On a broadcast network, a DRother sends an LSA only to the DR and BDR (a); the DR refloods the LSA to all adjacent neighbors (b); all routers then flood the LSA on all other interfaces (c).

was sent. The LSA is retransmitted every RxmtInterval until it is acknowledged or until the adjacency is broken. The Link State Update packets containing retransmissions are always unicast, regardless of the network type.

Delayed acknowledgments

Acknowledgments may be either *delayed* or *direct*. By delaying an acknowledgment, more LSAs can be acknowledged in a single Link State Acknowledgment packet; on a broadcast network, LSAs from multiple neighbors can be acknowledged in a single multicast Link State Acknowledgment packet. The period by which an acknowledgment is delayed must be less than the RxmtInterval to prevent unnecessary retransmissions. Under normal circumstances, the unicast/multicast addressing conventions used for Link State Update packets on various network types also apply to Link State Acknowledgments.

Direct acknowledgments

Direct acknowledgments are always sent immediately and are always unicast. Direct acknowledgments are sent whenever the following conditions occur:

1. A duplicate LSA is received from a neighbor, possibly indicating that it has not yet received an acknowledgment.
2. The LSA's age is MaxAge (described in the next section), and there is no instance of the LSA in the receiving router's link state database.

Reliable Flooding: Sequencing, Checksums, and Aging

Each LSA contains three values that are used to ensure that the most recent copy of the LSA exists in every database. These values are sequence number, checksum, and age.

OSPF uses a linear sequence number space (discussed in Chapter 4, "Dynamic Routing Protocols") and 32-bit signed sequence numbers ranging from InitialSequenceNumber (0x80000001) to MaxSequenceNumber (0x7fffffff). When a router originates an LSA, the router sets the LSA's sequence number to InitialSequenceNumber. Each time the router produces a new instance of the LSA, the router increments the sequence number by one.

Sequence number

If the present sequence number is MaxSequenceNumber and a new instance of the LSA must be created, the router must first flush the old LSA from all databases. This is done by setting the age of the existing LSA to MaxAge (defined later in this section) and reflooding it over all adjacencies. As soon as all adjacent neighbors have acknowledged the prematurely aged LSA, the new instance of the LSA with a sequence number of InitialSequence-Number may be flooded.

The checksum is a 16-bit integer calculated using a Fletcher algorithm.[12] The checksum is calculated over the entire LSA with the exception of the Age field (which changes as the LSA passes from node to node and would therefore require recalculation of the checksum at each node). The checksum of each LSA is also verified every five minutes as it resides in the link state database, to ensure that it has not been corrupted in the database.

Checksum

The age is an unsigned 16-bit integer that indicates the age of the LSA in seconds. The range is 0 to 3600 (1 hour, known as Max-Age). When a router originates an LSA, the router sets the age to 0. As the flooded LSA transits a router, the age is incremented by a number of seconds specified by InfTransDelay. Cisco routers

MaxAge

---

[12] Alex McKenzie, "ISO Transport Protocol Specification ISO DP 8073," RFC 905, April 1984, Annex B.

have a default InfTransDelay of 1 second, which can be changed with the command **ip ospf transmit-delay**. The age is also incremented as it resides in the database.

When an LSA reaches MaxAge, the LSA is reflooded and then flushed from the database. When a router needs to flush an LSA from all databases, it prematurely sets the age to MaxAge and refloods it. Only the router that originated the LSA can prematurely age it.

Figure 9.19 shows a portion of a link state database; the age, sequence number, and checksum of each LSA can be observed. More detailed discussion of the database and the various LSA types is in "The Link State Database," later in this chapter.

```
Manet#show ip ospf database

        OSPF Router with ID (192.168.30.43) (Process ID 1)

                Router Link States (Area 3)

Link ID         ADV Router      Age     Seq#        Checksum   Link Count
192.168.30.13   192.168.30.13   910     0x80000F29  0xA94E     2
192.168.30.23   192.168.30.23   1334    0x80000F55  0x8D53     3
192.168.30.30   192.168.30.30   327     0x800011CA  0x523      8
192.168.30.33   192.168.30.33   70      0x80000AF4  0x94DD     3
192.168.30.43   192.168.30.43   1697    0x80000F2F  0x1DA1     2
```

Figure 9.19

The age, sequence number, and checksum for each LSA is recorded in the link state database. The age is incremented in seconds.

When multiple instances of the same LSA are received, a router determines which is the most recent by the following algorithm:

1. Compare the sequence numbers. The LSA with the highest sequence number is more recent.

2. If the sequence numbers are equal, then compare the checksums. The LSA with the highest unsigned checksum is the more recent.

3. If the checksums are equal, then compare the age. If only one of the LSAs has an age of MaxAge (3600 seconds), it is considered the more recent. Else:

4. If the ages of the LSAs differ by more than 15 minutes (known as MaxAgeDiff), the LSA with the lower age is more recent.

5. If none of the preceding conditions are met, the two LSAs are considered identical.

Areas

The reader should by now have a good feel for why OSPF, with its multiple databases and complex algorithms, can put greater demands on the memory and processors of a router than the previously examined protocols can. As an internetwork grows, these demands can become significant or even crippling. And although flooding is more efficient than the periodic, full-table updates of RIP and IGRP, it can still place an unacceptable burden on the data links of a large internetwork. Contrary to popular belief, the SPF algorithm itself is not particularly processor intensive. It is the related processes, such as flooding and database maintenance, that burden the CPU.

Benefits of areas

OSPF uses areas to reduce these adverse effects. In the context of OSPF, an *area* is a logical grouping of OSPF routers and links that effectively divide an OSPF domain into sub-domains (Figure 9.20). Routers within an area will have no detailed knowledge of the topology outside of their area. Because of this condition:

- A router must share an identical link state database only with the other routers in its area, not with the entire internetwork. The reduced size of the database reduces the impact on a router's memory.

- The smaller link state databases mean fewer LSAs to process and therefore less impact on the CPU.

- Because the link state database must be maintained only within an area, most flooding is also limited to the area.

Area ID

Areas are identified by a 32-bit *Area ID*. As Figure 9.20 shows, the Area ID may be expressed either as a decimal number or in dotted decimal, and the two formats may be used together on Cisco routers. The choice usually depends on which format is more convenient for identifying the particular Area ID. For example, area 0 and area 0.0.0.0 are equivalent, as are area 16 and area 0.0.0.16, and area 271 and area 0.0.1.15. In each of these cases, the decimal format would probably be preferred. However, given the choice of area 3232243229 and area 192.168.30.29, the latter would probably be chosen.

Classifying traffic in relation to areas

Three types of traffic may be defined in relation to areas:

- *Intra-area* traffic consists of packets that are passed between routers within a single area.

- *Inter-area* traffic consists of packets that are passed between routers in different areas.

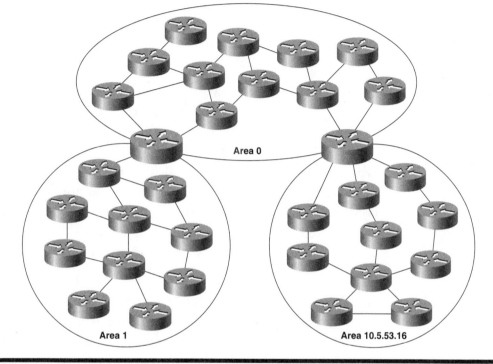

Area 0

Area 1

Area 10.5.53.16

Figure 9.20

An OSPF area is a logical grouping of OSPF routers. Each area is described by its own link state database, and each router must maintain a database only for the area to which it belongs.

- *External* traffic consists of packets that are passed between a router within the OSPF domain and a router within another autonomous system.

Area ID 0 (or 0.0.0.0) is reserved for the backbone. The *backbone* is responsible for summarizing the topographies of each area to every other area. For this reason, all inter-area traffic must pass through the backbone; non-backbone areas cannot exchange packets directly.

Backbone

Another special type of area is the *stub area*. Because stub areas cannot be sufficiently explained without first describing the various types of LSAs, this subject will be addressed in the section "The Link State Database."

Many OSPF designers have a favorite rule of thumb concerning the maximum number of routers that an area can handle. This number might range from 30 to 200. However, the number of routers has little actual bearing on the maximum size of an area. Far more important factors include the number of links in an area, the stability of the topology, the memory and horsepower of the routers, the use of summarization, and the number of summary LSAs entering the area. Because of these factors, 25 routers may be too many for some areas, and other areas may accommodate well over 500 routers.

It is perfectly reasonable to design a small OSPF internetwork with only a single area. Regardless of number of areas, a potential problem arises when an area is so underpopulated that no redundant links exist within it. If such an area becomes partitioned, service disruptions may occur. Partitioned areas are discussed in more detail in a later section.

Router Types

Routers, like traffic, can be categorized in relation to areas. All OSPF routers will be one of four router types, as shown in Figure 9.21.

Internal Routers are routers whose interfaces all belong to the same area. These routers have a single link state database.

Area Border Routers (ABRs) connect one or more areas to the backbone and act as a gateway for inter-area traffic. An ABR always has at least one interface that belongs to the backbone, and must maintain a separate link state database for each of its connected areas. For this reason, ABRs often have more memory and perhaps more powerful processors than internal routers. An ABR will summarize the topological information of its attached areas into the backbone, which will then propagate the summary information to the other areas.

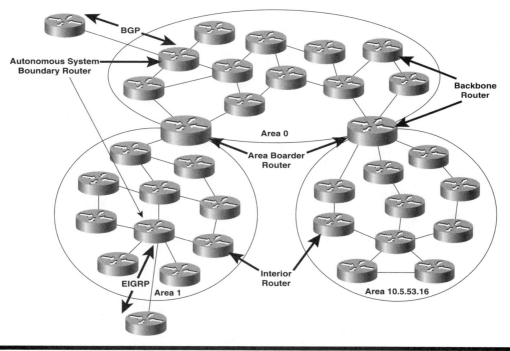

Figure 9.21

All OSPF routers can be classified as an Internal Router, a Backbone Router, an Area Border Router (ABR), or an Autonomous System Boundary Router (ASBR). Note that any of the first three router types may also be an ASBR.

Backbone Routers are routers with at least one interface attached to the backbone. Although this requirement means that ABRs are also Backbone Routers, Figure 9.21 shows that not all Backbone Routers are ABRs. An Internal Router whose interfaces all belong to area 0 is also a Backbone Router.

Autonomous System Boundary Routers (ASBRs) are gateways for external traffic, injecting routes into the OSPF domain that were learned (redistributed) from some other protocol, such as the BGP and EIGRP processes shown in Figure 9.21. An ASBR can be located anywhere within the OSPF autonomous system; it may be an Internal, Backbone, or ABR.

Partitioned Areas

A *partitioned area* is an area in which a link failure causes one part of the area to become isolated from another. If a non-backbone area becomes partitioned and if all routers on either side of the partition can still find an ABR, as in Figure 9.22, no service disruptions will occur. The backbone will merely treat the partitioned area as two separate areas. Intra-area traffic from one side of the partition to the other side will become inter-area traffic, passing through the backbone to circumvent the partition. Note that a partitioned area is not the same as an *isolated* area, in which no path exists to the rest of the internetwork.

A partition of the backbone itself is a more serious matter. As Figure 9.23 shows, a partitioned backbone area will isolate the areas on each side of the partition, creating two separate OSPF domains.

Figure 9.24 shows some better area designs. Both area 0 and area 2 are designed so that neither of them can be partitioned by a single link failure. The vulnerability of area 2, however, is that if the ABR fails, the area will be isolated. Area 3 uses two ABRs; here, neither a single link failure nor a single ABR failure will isolate any part of the area.

Partitioned areas
versus isolated areas

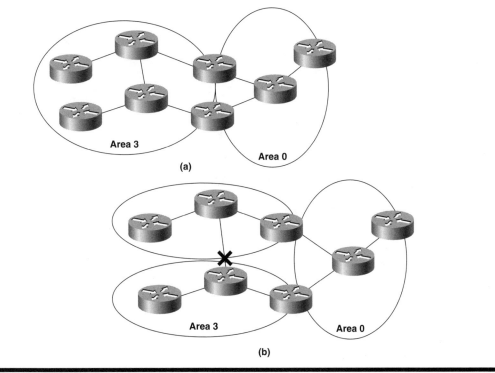

Figure 9.22

(a) Area 3 is connected to the backbone (area 0) by two ABRs. (b) A link failure in area 3 creates a partitioned area, but all routers within area 3 can still reach an ABR. In these circumstances, traffic can still be routed between the two sides of the partitioned area.

Virtual Links

A virtual link is a link to the backbone through a non-backbone area. Virtual links are used for the following purposes:

1. To link an area to the backbone through a non-backbone area (Figure 9.25)
2. To connect the two parts of a partitioned backbone through a non-backbone area (Figure 9.26)

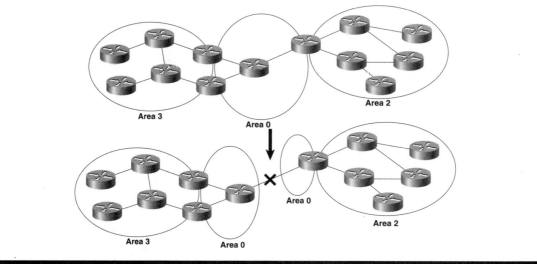

Figure 9.23

If a backbone becomes partitioned, each side of the partition and any connected areas become isolated from the other side.

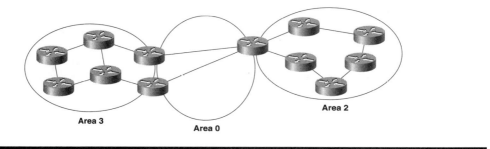

Figure 9.24

In areas 0 and 2, no single link failure can partition the area. In area 3, no single ABR or link failure can isolate the area.

In both examples, the virtual link is not associated with a particular physical link. The virtual link is a tunnel through which packets may be routed on the optimal path from one endpoint to the other.

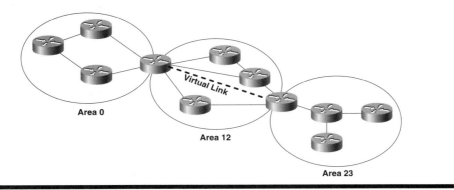

Figure 9.25

A virtual link connects area 23 to the backbone through area 12.

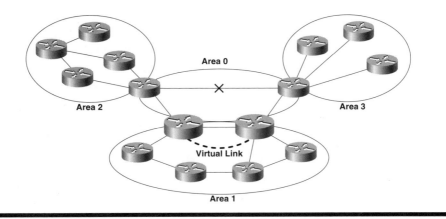

Figure 9.26

A virtual link reconnects a partitioned backbone through a nonbackbone area.

Several rules are associated with the configuration of virtual links:

- Virtual links must be configured between two ABRs.

- The area through which the virtual link is configured, known as the *transit area*, must have full routing information.

- The transit area cannot be a stub area.

As mentioned previously, OSPF classifies a virtual link as a network type. Specifically, the link is considered an unnumbered—that is, unaddressed—link, belonging to the backbone, between two ABRs. These ABRs are considered neighbors by virtue of the virtual link between them, although they are not linked physically. Within each ABR, the virtual link will transition to the fully functional point-to-point interface state when a route to the neighboring ABR is found in the route table. The cost of the link is the cost of the route to the neighbor. When the interface state becomes point-to-point, an adjacency will be established across the virtual link.

Virtual links add a layer of complexity and troubleshooting difficulty to any internetwork. It is best to avoid the need for them by ensuring that areas, particularly backbone areas, are designed with redundant links to prevent partitioning. When two or more internetworks are merged, sufficient planning should take place beforehand so that no area is left without a direct link to the backbone.

If a virtual link is configured, it should be used only as a temporary fix to an unavoidable topology problem. A virtual link is a flag marking a part of the internetwork that needs to be reengineered. Permanent virtual links are virtually always a sign of a poorly designed internetwork.

The Link State Database

All valid LSAs received by a router are stored in its link state database. The collected LSAs will describe a graph of the area topology. Because each router in an area calculates its shortest path tree from this database, it is imperative for accurate routing that all area databases are identical.

A list of the LSAs in a link state database can be observed with the command **show ip ospf database**, as shown in Figure 9.27. This list does not show all of the information stored for each LSA, but shows only the information in the LSA header. Note that this database contains LSAs from multiple areas, indicating that the router is an ABR.

Most of the entries in Figure 9.27 have been deleted for brevity; the actual link state database contains 1,445 entries and four areas, as shown in Figure 9.28.

As mentioned earlier in "Reliable Flooding: Sequencing, Checksums, and Aging," the LSAs are aged as they reside in the link state database. If they reach MaxAge (1 hour), they are flushed from the OSPF domain. The implication here is that there must be a mechanism for preventing legitimate LSAs from reaching MaxAge and being flushed. This mechanism is the *link state refresh*. Every 30 minutes, known as the LSRefreshTime, the router that originated the LSA will flood a new copy of the LSA with an incremented sequence number and an age of zero. Upon receipt, the other OSPF routers will replace the old copy of the LSA and begin aging the new copy.

So the link state refresh process can be thought of as a keepalive for each LSA. An additional benefit is that any LSAs that might have become corrupted in a router's LS database will be replaced with the refreshed copy of the legitimate LSA.

The idea behind associating an individual refresh timer with each LSA is that the LSRefreshTime of the LSAs will not expire all at once, reflooding all LSAs every 30 minutes. Instead, the reflooding will be spread out in a semirandom pattern. The problem with this approach is that with each individual LSA being reflooded as its

```
Homer#show ip ospf database

        OSPF Router with ID (192.168.30.50) (Process ID 1)

                    Router Link States (Area 0)

Link ID              ADV Router        Age     Seq#         Checksum   Link count
192.168.30.10        192.100.30.10     1010    0x80001416   0xA818     3
192.168.30.20        192.168.30.20     677     0x800013C9   0xDE18     3
192.168.30.70        192.168.30.70     857     0x80001448   0xFD79     3
192.168.30.80        192.168.30.80     1010    0x800014D1   0xEB5C     5

                    Net Link States (Area 0)

Link ID              ADV Router        Age      Seq#         Checksum
192.168.17.18        192.168.30.20     677      0x800001AD   0x849A
192.168.17.34        192.168.30.60     695      0x800003E2   0x4619
192.168.17.58        192.168.30.40     579      0x8000113C   0xF0D
192.168.17.73        192.168.30.40     857      0x8000044F   0xB0E7

                    Summary Net Link States (Area 0)

Link ID              ADV Router        Age     Seq#         Checksum
172.16.121.0         192.168.30.60     421     0x8000009F   0xD52
172.16.121.0         192.168.30.70     656     0x8000037F   0x86A
10.63.65.0           192.168.30.10     983     0x80000004   0x1EAA
10.63.65.0           192.168.30.80     962     0x80000004   0x780A

                    Summary ASB Link States (Area 0)

Link ID              ADV Router        Age     Seq#         Checksum
192.168.30.12        192.168.30.20     584     0x80000005   0xFC4C
192.168.30.12        192.168.30.30     56      0x80000004   0x45BA
172.20.57.254        192.168.30.70     664     0x800000CE   0xF2CF
172.20.57.254        192.168.30.80     963     0x80000295   0x23CC

                    Router Link States (Area 4)

Link ID              ADV Router        Age     Seq#         Checksum   Link count
192.168.30.14        192.168.30.14     311     0x80000EA5   0x93A0     7
192.168.30.24        192.168.30.24     685     0x80001333   0x6F56     6
192.168.30.50        192.168.30.50     116     0x80001056   0x42BF     2
192.168.30.54        192.168.30.54     1213    0x80000D1F   0x3385     2

                    Summary Net Link States (Area 4)

Link ID              ADV Router        Age     Seq#         Checksum
172.16.121.0         192.168.30.40     1231    0x80000D88   0x73BF
172.16.121.0         192.168.30.50     34      0x800003F4   0xF90D
10.63.65.0           192.168.30.40     1240    0x80000003   0x5110
10.63.65.0           192.168.30.50     42      0x80000005   0x1144

                    Summary ASB Link States (Area 4)

Link ID              ADV Router        Age     Seq#         Checksum
192.168.30.12        192.168.30.40     1240    0x80000006   0x6980
192.168.30.12        192.168.30.50     42      0x80000008   0xC423
172.20.57.254        192.168.30.40     1241    0x8000029B   0xEED8
172.20.57.254        192.168.30.50     43      0x800002A8   0x9818

                    AS External Link States

Link ID              ADV Router        Age     Seq#         Checksum   Tag
10.83.10.0           192.168.30.60     459     0x80000D49   0x9C0B     0
10.1.27.0            192.168.30.62     785     0x800000EB   0xB5CE     0
10.22.85.0           192.168.30.70     902     0x8000037D   0x1EC0     65502
10.22.85.0           192.168.30.80     1056    0x800001F7   0x6B4B     65502
Homer#
```

Figure 9.27

*The command **show ip ospf database** displays a list of all LSAs in the link state database.*

```
Homer#show ip ospf database database-summary

            OSPF Router with ID (192.168.30.50) (Process ID 1)

Area ID        Router    Network   Sum-Net   Sum-ASBR   Subtotal   Delete   Maxage
0                 8          4        185        27         224        0        0
4                 7          0        216        26         249        0        0
5                 7          0        107        13         127        0        0
56                2          1        236        26         265        0        0
AS External                                                 580        0        0
Total            24          5        744        92        1445
Homer#
```

Figure 9.28

*The command **show ip ospf database database-summary** displays the number of LSAs in a link state database by area and by LSA type.*

LSRefreshTime expires, bandwidth is used inefficiently. Update packets can be transmitted with only a few, or even a single, LSA.

Prior to IOS 11.3, Cisco chose to have a single LSRefreshTime associated with the entire LS database. Every 30 minutes, each router refreshes all of the LSAs it originated, regardless of their actual age. Although this strategy avoids the problem of inefficiency, it reintroduces the problem the individual refresh timers were meant to solve. If the LS database is large, each router can create spikes in the area traffic and CPU usage every half hour.

IOS 11.3AA introduced a mechanism known as *LSA group pacing* to reach a compromise between the problems of individual refresh timers and a single monolithic timer. Each LSA has its own refresh timer, but as the individual refresh timers expire, a delay is introduced before the LSAs are flooded. By delaying the refresh, more LSAs can be grouped together before being flooded, so that Update packets are carrying a larger number of LSAs. By default, the group-pacing interval is 240 seconds (4 minutes), and it can be changed with the command **timers lsa-group-pacing**. If the database is very large, decreasing the group pacing interval is beneficial; if the database is small, increasing the interval can be useful. The range of the group pacing timer is 10 to 1800 seconds.

LSA group pacing

LSA Types

Because of the multiple router types defined by OSPF, multiple types of LSA are also necessary. For example, a DR must advertise the multi-access link and all the routers attached to the link. Other router types would not advertise this type of information. Both Figure 9.27 and Figure 9.28 show that there are multiple types of LSA. Each type describes a different aspect of an OSPF internetwork. Table 9.4 lists the LSA types and the type codes that identify them.

Table 9.4   *LSA types.*

Type Code	Description
1	Router LSA
2	Network LSA
3	Network Summary LSA
4	ASBR Summary LSA
5	AS External LSA
6	Group Membership LSA
7	NSSA External LSA
8	External Attributes LSA
9	Opaque LSA (link-local scope)
10	Opaque LSA (area-local scope)
11	Opaque LSA (AS scope)

Router LSAs are produced by every router (Figure 9.29). This most fundamental LSA lists all of a router's links, or interfaces, along with the state and outgoing cost of each link. These LSAs are flooded only within the area in which they are originated. The command **show ip ospf database router** will list all of the Router LSAs in a database. Figure 9.30 shows a variant of the command, in which a single router LSA is observed by specifying the router's ID. As this and the subsequent illustrations show, the complete LSA is recorded in the link state database. For a description of all the LSA fields, see the "OSPF Packet Formats" section later in this chapter.

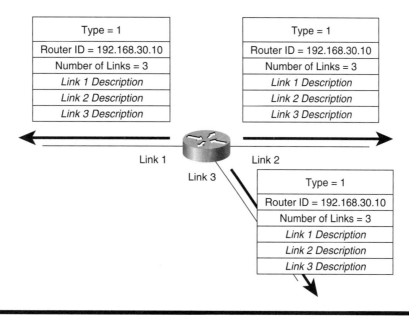

Figure 9.29
The Router LSA describes all of a router's interfaces.

Network LSAs are produced by the DR on every multi-access network (Figure 9.31). As discussed earlier, the DR represents the multi-access network and all attached routers as a "pseudonode," or a single virtual router. In this sense, a Network LSA represents a pseudonode just as a Router LSA represents a single physical router. The Network LSA lists all attached routers, including the DR itself. Like Router LSAs, network LSAs are flooded only within the originating area. In Figure 9.31, the command **show ip ospf database network** is used to observe a Network LSA.

```
Homer#show ip ospf database router 192.168.30.10

        OSPF Router with ID (192.168.30.50) (Process ID 1)

                 Router Link States (Area 0)

Routing Bit Set on this LSA
LS age: 680
Options: (No TOS-capability)
LS Type: Router Links
Link State ID: 192.168.30.10
Advertising Router: 192.168.30.10
LS Seq Number: 80001428
Checksum: 0x842A
Length: 60
Area Border Router
 Number of Links: 3

   Link connected to: another Router (point-to-point)
    (Link ID) Neighboring Router ID: 192.168.30.80
    (Link Data) Router Interface address: 192.168.17.9
     Number of TOS metrics: 0
      TOS 0 Metrics: 64

   Link connected to: a Stub Network
    (Link ID) Network/subnet number: 192.168.17.8
    (Link Data) Network Mask: 255.255.255.248
     Number of TOS metrics: 0
      TOS 0 Metrics: 64

   Link connected to: a Transit Network
    (Link ID) Designated Router address: 192.168.17.18
    (Link Data) Router Interface address: 192.168.17.17
     Number of TOS metrics: 0
      TOS 0 Metrics: 10

Homer#
```

Figure 9.30

The command **show ip ospf database router** displays Router LSAs from the link state database.

Network Summary LSAs are originated by ABRs. They are sent into a single area to advertise destinations outside that area (Figure 9.33). In effect, these LSAs are the means by which an ABR

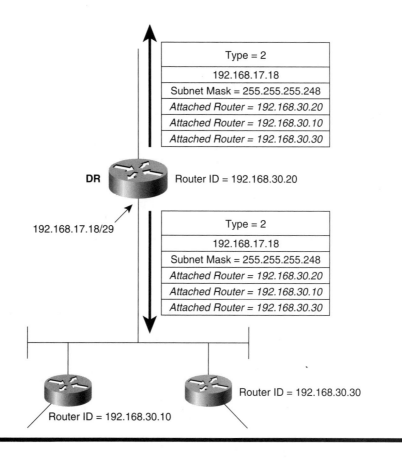

Figure 9.31

A DR originates a network LSA to represent a multi-access network and all attached routers.

tells the Internal Routers of an attached area what destinations the ABR can reach. An ABR also advertises the destinations within its attached areas into the backbone with Network Summary LSAs. Default routes external to the area but internal to the OSPF autonomous system are also advertised by this LSA type. The command **show ip ospf database summary** is used to display the network summary LSAs in the database, as shown in Figure 9.34.

```
Homer#show ip ospf database network 192.168.17.18

        OSPF Router with ID (192.168.30.50) (Process ID 1)

                Net Link States (Area 0)

Routing Bit Set on this LSA
LS age: 244
Options: (No TOS-capability)
LS Type: Network Links
Link State ID: 192.168.17.18 (address of Designated Router)
Advertising Router: 192.168.30.20
LS Seq Number: 800001BF
Checksum: 0x60AC
Length: 32
Network Mask: /29
      Attached Router: 192.168.30.20
      Attached Router: 192.168.30.10
      Attached Router: 192.168.30.30

Homer#
```

Figure 9.32

Network LSAs can be observed with the command **show ip ospf database network**.

When an ABR originates a Network Summary LSA, it includes the cost from itself to the destination the LSA is advertising. The ABR will originate only a single Network Summary LSA for each destination even if it knows of multiple routes to the destination. Therefore, if an ABR knows of multiple routes to a destination within its own attached area, it originates a single Network Summary LSA into the backbone with the lowest cost of the multiple routes. Likewise, if an ABR receives multiple Network Summary LSAs from other ABRs across the backbone, the original ABR will choose the lowest cost advertised in the LSAs and advertise that one cost into its attached non-backbone areas.

When another router receives a Network Summary LSA from an ABR, it does not run the SPF algorithm. Rather, it simply adds the cost of the route to the ABR and the cost included in the LSA. A route to the advertised destination, via the ABR, is entered into the route table along with the calculated cost. This behavior—depending on an intermediate router instead of determining the full route to the destination—is distance vector behavior. So, while OSPF is a link state protocol within an area, it uses a distance vector algorithm to find inter-area routes.[13]

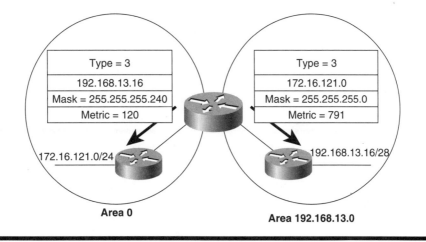

Figure 9.33
An ABR will originate a Network Summary LSA to describe inter-area destinations.

ASBR Summary LSAs are also originated by ABRs. ASBR Summary LSAs are identical to Network Summary LSAs except that the destination they advertise is an ASBR (Figure 9.35), not a network. The command **show ip ospf database asbr-summary** is used to display ASBR Summary LSAs (Figure 9.36). Note in the illustration that the destination is a host address, and the mask is zero; the destination advertised by an ASBR Summary LSA will always be a host address because it is a route to a router.

---

[13] *This distance vector behavior is the reason for requiring a backbone area and requiring that all inter-area traffic pass through the backbone. By forming the areas into what is essentially a hub-and-spoke topology, the route loops to which distance vector protocols are prone are avoided.*

```
Homer#show ip ospf database summary 172.16.121.0

   OSPF Router with ID (192.168.30.50) (Process ID 1)

     Summary Net Link States (Area 0)

Routing Bit Set on this LSA
LS age: 214
Options: (No TOS-capability)
LS Type: Summary Links(Network)
Link State ID: 172.16.121.0 (summary Network Number)
Advertising Router: 192.168.30.60
LS Seq Number: 800000B1
Checksum: 0xE864
Length: 28
Network Mask: /24
   TOS: 0 Metric: 791
```

Figure 9.34

Network Summary LSAs can be observed with the command **show ip ospf database summary**.

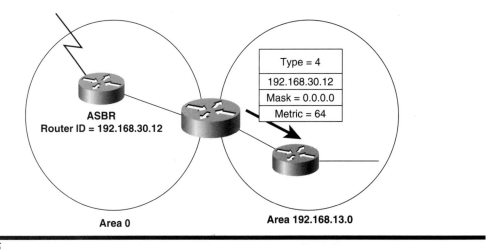

Figure 9.35

ASBR summary LSAs advertise routes to ASBRs.

Autonomous System External LSAs, or *External LSAs*, are originated by ASBRs and advertise either a destination external to the

```
Homer#show ip ospf database asbr-summary

   OSPF Router with ID (192.168.30.50) (Process ID 1)

     Summary ASB Link States (Area 0)

Routing Bit Set on this LSA
LS age: 1640
Options: (No TOS-capability)
LS Type: Summary Links (AS Boundary Router)
Link State ID: 192.168.30.12 (AS Boundary Router address)
Advertising Router: 192.168.30.20
LS Seq Number: 80000009
Checksum: 0xF450
Length: 28
Network Mask: /0
   TOS: 0 Metric: 64

--More-
```

Figure 9.36

*ASBR Summary LSAs can be observed with the command **show ip ospf database asbr-summary**.*

OSPF autonomous system, or a default route[14] external to the OSPF autonomous system (Figure 9.37). Referring back to Figure 9.27, you can see that the AS External LSAs are the only LSA types in the database that are not associated with a particular area; external LSAs are flooded throughout the autonomous system. The command **show ip ospf database external** displays AS External LSAs (Figure 9.38).

Group Membership LSAs are used in an enhancement of OSPF known as *Multicast OSPF* (MOSPF).[15] MOSPF routes packets from a single source to multiple destinations, or group members, which share a class D multicast address. Although Cisco supports other multicast routing protocols, MOSPF is not supported as of

---

[14] *Default routes are routes that are chosen if no more specific route exists in the route table. OSPF and RIP use an IP address of 0.0.0.0 to identify a default route. See Chapter 12 for more information.*

[15] *John Moy, "Multicast Extensions to OSPF," RFC 1584, March 1994.*

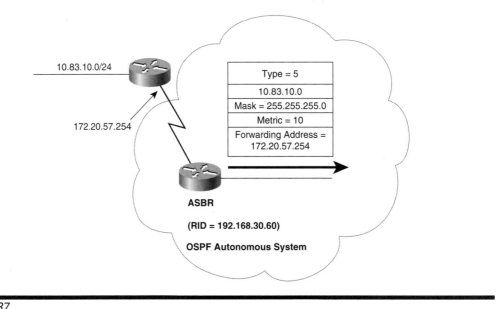

10.83.10.0/24

172.20.57.254

| Type = 5 |
| 10.83.10.0 |
| Mask = 255.255.255.0 |
| Metric = 10 |
| Forwarding Address = 172.20.57.254 |

ASBR

(RID = 192.168.30.60)

OSPF Autonomous System

Figure 9.37
AS External LSAs advertise destinations external to the OSPF autonomous system.

this writing. For this reason, neither MOSPF nor the Group Membership LSA is covered in this book.

NSSA External LSAs are originated by ASBRs within not-so-stubby areas (NSSAs). NSSAs are described in the following section. An NSSA External LSA is almost identical to an AS External LSA, as the section on OSPF packet formats shows. Unlike AS External LSAs, which are flooded throughout an OSPF autonomous system, NSSA external LSAs are flooded only within the not-so-stubby area in which it was originated. The command **show ip ospf database nssa-external** displays NSSA external LSAs (Figure 9.39).

External Attributes LSAs are proposed as an alternative to running Internal BGP (iBGP) in order to transport BGP information across an OSPF domain. As of this writing, type 8 LSAs have not yet been implemented, and no RFC or Internet draft has been published yet on the subject.

```
Homer#show ip ospf database external 10.83.10.0

        OSPF Router with ID (192.168.30.50) (Process ID 1)

                    AS External Link States

Routing Bit Set on this LSA
LS age: 1680
Options: (No TOS-capability)
LS Type: AS External Link
Link State ID: 10.83.10.0 (External Network Number )
Advertising Router: 192.168.30.60
LS Seq Number: 80000D5A
Checksum: 0x7A1C
Length: 36
Network Mask: /24
        Metric Type: 1 (Comparable directly to link state metric)
        TOS: 0
        Metric: 10
        Forward Address: 172.20.57.254
        External Route Tag: 0

Homer#
```

Figure 9.38

*AS External LSAs can be observed with the command **show ip ospf database external**.*

Opaque LSAs are a proposed class of LSAs that consist of a standard LSA header followed by application-specific information.[16] The Information field can be used directly by OSPF or indirectly by other applications to distribute information throughout the OSPF domain. As of this writing, Opaque LSAs have not been deployed.

Stub Areas

An ASBR learning external destinations will advertise those destinations by flooding AS External LSAs throughout the OSPF autonomous system. In many cases, these External LSAs may make up a large percentage of the LSAs in the databases of every

---

[16] *Rob Coltun, "The OSPF Opaque LSA Option," RFC 2370, July 1998.*

```
Morisot#show ip ospf database nssa-external

        OSPF Router with ID (10.3.0.1) (Process ID 1)

                Type-7 AS External Link States (Area 15)

LS age: 532
Options: (No TOS-capability, No Type 7/5 translation, DC)
LS Type: AS External Link
Link State ID: 10.0.0.0 (External Network Number)
Advertising Router: 10.3.0.1
LS Seq Number: 80000001
Checksum: 0x9493
Length: 36
Network Mask: /16
      Metric Type: 2 (Larger than any link state path)
      TOS: 0
      Metric: 100
      Forward Address: 10.3.0.1
      External Route Tag: 0

--More-
```

Figure 9.39

*NSSA external LSAs can be observed with the command **show ip ospf database nssa-external**.*

router. For example, Figure 9.28 shows that 580 of the LSAs in that database—40%—are external LSAs.

In Figure 9.40, not every router needs to know about all the external destinations. The routers in area 2 must send a packet to an ABR to reach the ASBR, no matter what the external destination may be. For this reason, area 2 can be configured as a *stub area*.

A *stub area* is an area into which AS External LSAs are not flooded. And if type 5 LSAs are not known inside an area, type 4 LSAs are unnecessary; these LSAs are also blocked. ABRs at the edge of a stub area will use Network Summary LSAs to advertise a single default route (destination 0.0.0.0) into the area. Any destination that the Internal Routers cannot match to an intra- or inter-area route will match the default route. Because the default

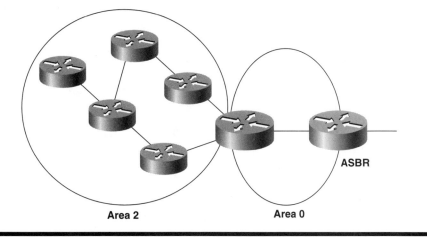

Figure 9.40

Memory can be conserved and performance improved by making area 2 a stub area.

route is carried in type 3 LSAs, it will not be advertised outside of the area.

The performance of routers within a stub area can be improved, and memory conserved, by the reduced size of their databases. Of course, the improvement will be more marked in internetworks with a large number of type 5 LSAs. There are, however, four restrictions on stub areas:

Restrictions on stub areas

1. As in any area, all routers in a stub area must have identical link state databases. To ensure this condition, all stub routers will set a flag (the E-bit) in their Hello packets to zero; they will not accept any Hello from a router in which the E-bit is set to one. As a result, adjacencies will not be established with any router that is not configured as a stub router.

2. Virtual links cannot be configured within, or transit, a stub area.

3. No router within a stub area can be an ASBR. This restriction is intuitively understandable because ASBRs produce type 5 LSAs and type 5 LSAs cannot exist within a stub area.

4. A stub area may have more than one ABR, but because of the default route, the Internal Routers cannot determine which router is the optimal gateway to the ASBR.

Totally Stubby Areas

If memory is saved by blocking the propagation of type 5 and type 4 LSAs into an area, wouldn't more memory be saved by blocking type 3 LSAs? In addressing this question, Cisco carries the concept of stub areas to its logical conclusion with a scheme known as *totally stubby areas*.

Totally stubby areas use a default route to reach not only destinations external to the autonomous system but also all destinations external to the area. The ABR of a totally stubby area will block not only AS External LSAs but also all Summary LSAs—with the exception of a single type 3 LSA to advertise the default route.

Not-So-Stubby Areas

In Figure 9.41, a router with a few stub networks must be attached to the OSPF internetwork via one of the area 2 routers. The router supports only RIP, so the area 2 router will run RIP and redistribute the networks into OSPF. Unfortunately, this configuration makes the area 2 router an ASBR, and therefore area 2 can no longer be a stub area.

The RIP speaker does not need to learn routes from OSPF—a default route pointing to the area 2 router is all it needs. But all OSPF routers must know about the networks attached to the RIP router to route packets to them.

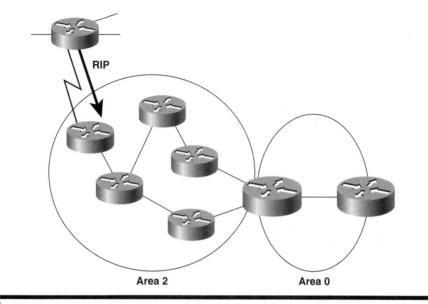

Figure 9.41

Because a few external destinations must be redistributed into OSPF at one of the area 2 routers, all of area 2 is ineligible to be a stub area.

Not-so-stubby areas (NSSAs)[17] allow external routes to be advertised into the OSPF autonomous system while retaining the characteristics of a stub area to the rest of the autonomous system. To do this, the ASBR in an NSSA will originate type 7 LSAs to advertise the external destinations. These NSSA External LSAs are flooded throughout the NSSA but are blocked at the ABR.

The NSSA External LSA has a flag in its header known as the P-bit. The NSSA ASBR has the option of setting or clearing the P-bit. If the NSSA's ABR receives a type 7 LSA with the P-bit set to one, it will translate the type 7 LSA into a type 5 LSA and flood it throughout the other areas (see Figure 9.42). If the P-bit is set to zero, no translation will take place and the destination in the type 7 LSA will not be advertised outside of the NSSA.

[17] *Rob Coltun and Vince Fuller, "The OSPF NSSA Option," RFC 1587, March 1994.*

NSSAs are supported in IOS 11.2 and later.

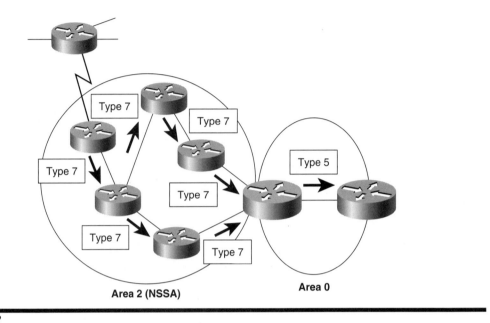

Figure 9.42

An ASBR within an NSSA will originate NSSA External LSAs. If the P-bit of an NSSA External LSA is set, the ABR will translate the LSA into an AS External LSA.

Table 9.5 summarizes which LSAs are allowed in which areas.

Table 9.5   *LSA types allowed per area type.*

Area Type	1&2	3&4	5	7
Backbone (area 0)	Yes	Yes	Yes	No
Non-backbone, non-stub	Yes	Yes	Yes	No
Stub	Yes	Yes	No	No
Totally stubby	Yes	No[*]	No	No
Not-so-stubby	Yes	Yes	No	Yes

---

[*] *Except for a single type 3 LSA per ABR, advertising the default route.*

The Route Table

The Dijkstra algorithm is used to calculate the Shortest Path Tree from the LSAs in the link state database. Chapter 4 has a somewhat detailed discussion of the Dijkstra algorithm; for a full description of the OSPF calculation of the SPF tree, see section 16.1 of RFC 2328. The SPF algorithm is run once to build the branches of the tree, which are the links to each node (router) in the area. The algorithm is then run a second time to add the leaves to the tree—the stub networks attached to each router.

OPSF determines the shortest path based on an arbitrary metric called *cost*, which is assigned to each interface. The cost of a route is the sum of the costs of all the outgoing interfaces to a destination. RFC 2328 does not specify any values for cost. Cisco routers calculate a default OSPF cost as 10^8/BW, where BW is the configured bandwidth of the interface. Fractional costs are rounded down to the nearest whole number. The cost of an interface may be changed with the command **ip ospf cost**. LSAs record cost in a 16-bit field, so the total cost of an interface can range from 1 to 65535. Table 9.6 shows the default costs for some typical interfaces.

Cisco default cost

Table 9.6 *Cisco default interface costs.*

Interface Type	Cost (10^8/BW)
FDDI, Fast Ethernet	1
HSSI (45M)	2
16M Token Ring	6
Ethernet	10
4M Token Ring	25
T1 (1.544M)	64
DS0 (64K)*	1562

Table 9.6   *Cisco default interface costs, continued.*

Interface Type	Cost (10^8/BW)
56K[*]	1785
Tunnel (9K)	11111

[*] *Assumes the default bandwidth of the serial interface has been changed.*

Destination Types

Each route entry will be classified according to a *destination type*. The destination type will be either *network* or *router*.

Network entries are the addresses of networks to which packets can be routed. These are the destinations that are entered into the route table (Figure 9.43).

Router entries are routes to ABRs and ASBRs. If a router needs to send a packet to an inter-area destination, it must know how to find an ABR; if a packet must go to an external destination, the router must know how to find an ASBR. Router entries contain this information, and are kept in a separate, internal route table. This table can be observed with the command **show ip ospf border-routers** (Figure 9.44).

As Figure 9.44 shows, the internal route table looks very similar to any other route table—there are destinations, metrics, next-hop addresses, and exit interfaces. The difference is that all destinations are the Router IDs of ABRs and ASBRs. Each entry is tagged as intra-area (i) or inter-area (I), and the entry indicates whether the destination is an ABR, an ASBR, or both. The area is recorded, as is the iteration of the SPF algorithm that installed the entry.

```
Homer#show ip route
Codes: C - connected, S - static, I - IGRP, R - RIP, M - mobile, B - BGP
       D - EIGRP, EX - EIGRP external, O - OSPF, IA - OSPF inter area
       E1 - OSPF external type 1, E2 - OSPF external type 2, E - EGP
       i - IS-IS, L1 - IS-IS level-1, L2 - IS-IS level-2, * - candidate default
       U - per-user static route

Gateway of last resort is 192.168.32.2 to network 0.0.0.0

O E1 192.168.118.0/24 [110/94] via 192.168.17.74, 02:15:01, Ethernet0
O E1 10.0.0.0/8 [110/84] via 192.168.17.41, 02:15:01, Serial0.19
O E1 192.168.119.0/24 [110/94] via 192.168.17.74, 02:15:01, Ethernet0
O E2 172.19.0.0/16 [110/21] via 192.168.32.2, 02:15:01, Ethernet1
     172.21.0.0/16 is variably subnetted, 2 subnets, 2 masks
O E2    172.21.0.0/16 [110/801] via 192.168.21.6, 02:15:01, Serial1.724
O       172.21.121.0/24 [110/791] via 192.168.21.6, 04:18:30, Serial1.724
     172.16.0.0/16 is variably subnetted, 104 subnets, 7 masks
O       172.16.21.48/30 [110/844] via 192.168.21.10, 04:18:48, Serial1.725
O IA    172.16.30.61/32 [110/856] via 192.168.17.74, 02:15:19, Ethernet0
O IA    172.16.35.0/24 [110/865] via 192.168.17.74, 02:15:19, Ethernet0
C       172.16.32.0/24 is directly connected, Ethernet1
O       172.16.17.48/29 [110/74] via 192.168.17.74, 06:19:46, Ethernet0
O E1    172.16.46.0/24 [110/30] via 192.168.32.2, 02:15:19, Ethernet1
O       172.16.45.0/24 [110/20] via 192.168.32.2, 3d10h, Ethernet1
O IA    172.16.30.54/32 [110/1061] via 192.168.17.74, 02:15:21, Ethernet0
O       172.16.17.56/29 [110/84] via 192.168.17.74, 06:19:48, Ethernet0
O       172.16.54.0/24 [110/11] via 192.168.32.2, 3d10h, Ethernet1
O       172.16.55.0/24 [110/11] via 192.168.32.2, 3d10h, Ethernet1
O       172.16.52.0/24 [110/11] via 192.168.32.2, 3d10h, Ethernet1
O       172.16.53.0/24 [110/11] via 192.168.32.2, 3d10h, Ethernet1
C       172.16.25.28/30 is directly connected, Tunnel29
--More-
```

Figure 9.43

The OSPF entries in the route table are network destination types.

Path Types

Each route to a network destination will also be classified as one of four *path types*. These path types are intra-area, inter-area, type 1 external, and type 2 external.

Intra-area paths are to destinations within one of the router's attached areas.

```
Homer#show ip ospf border-routers

OSPF Process 1 internal Routing Table

Codes:  i - Intra-area route, I - Inter-area route
i 192.168.30.10 [74] via 192.168.17.74, Ethernet0, ABR, Area 0, SPF 391
I 192.168.30.12 [148] via 192.168.17.74, Ethernet0, ASBR, Area 0, SPF 391
I 192.168.30.18 [205] via 192.168.17.74, Ethernet0, ASBR, Area 0, SPF 391
i 192.168.30.20 [84] via 192.168.17.74, Ethernet0, ABR, Area 0, SPF 391
i 192.168.30.27 [781] via 192.168.21.6, Serial1.724, ASBR, Area 7, SPF 631
i 192.168.30.30 [74] via 192.168.17.74, Ethernet0, ABR/ASBR, Area 0, SPF 391
I 192.168.30.38 [269] via 192.168.17.74, Ethernet0, ASBR, Area 0, SPF 391
i 192.168.30.37 [390] via 192.168.21.10, Serial1.725, ASBR, Area 7, SPF 631
i 192.168.30.40 [84] via 192.168.17.74, Ethernet0, ABR/ASBR, Area 0, SPF 391
i 192.168.30.47 [400] via 192.168.21.10, Serial1.725, ASBR, Area 7, SPF 631
i 192.168.30.50 [74] via 192.168.17.41, Serial0.19, ABR/ASBR, Area 0, SPF 391
I 192.168.30.62 [94] via 192.168.17.74, Ethernet0, ASBR, Area 0, SPF 391
i 192.168.30.60 [64] via 192.168.17.41, Serial0.19, ABR/ASBR, Area 0, SPF 391
i 192.168.30.60 [790] via 192.168.21.10, Serial1.725, ABR/ASBR, Area 7, SPF 631
i 192.168.30.80 [10] via 192.168.32.5, Ethernet1, ABR/ASBR, Area 78, SPF 158
i 192.168.30.80 [10] via 192.168.17.74, Ethernet0, ABR/ASBR, Area 0, SPF 391
i 172.20.57.254 [10] via 192.168.32.2, Ethernet1, ASBR, Area 78, SPF 158
Homer#
```

Figure 9.44

Router entries, kept in a separate table from network entries, are routes to ABRs and ASBRs.

Inter-area paths are to destinations in another area but within the OSPF autonomous system. An inter-area path, tagged with an IA in Figure 9.43, will always pass through at least one ABR.

Type 1 external paths (E1 in Figure 9.43) are to destinations outside the OSPF autonomous system. When an external route is redistributed into any autonomous system, it must be assigned a metric that is meaningful to the routing protocol of the autonomous system. Within OSPF, the ASBR is responsible for assigning a cost to the external routes they advertise. Type 1 external paths have a cost that is the sum of this external cost plus the cost of the path to the ASBR. Configuring an ASBR to advertise an external (redistributed) route with an E1 metric is covered in Chapter 11, "Route Redistribution."

Type 2 external paths (E2) are also to destinations outside the OSPF autonomous system, but do not take into account the cost of the path to the ASBR. E2 routes provide the network administrator with the option of telling OSPF to consider only the external cost of an external route, disregarding the internal cost of reaching the ASBR. OSPF external routes are, by default, E2 paths.

In Figure 9.45, router A has two paths to external destination 10.1.2.0. If the destination is advertised as E1, the A-B-D path will have a cost of 35 (5 + 20 + 10) and will be preferred over the A-C-D path whose cost is 50 (30 + 10 + 10). If the destination is advertised as E2, the cost of the two internal links to the ASBRs will be disregarded. In this case, the A-B-D path has a cost of 30 (20 + 10) and the A-C-D path has a cost of 20 (10 + 10). The latter will be the preferred path.

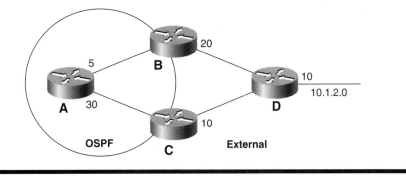

Figure 9.45

If the route to external network 10.1.2.0 is advertised with an E1 metric, router A will choose B as the "closest" ASBR. If the destination is advertised with an E2 metric, C will be chosen as the ASBR.

Route Table Lookups

When an OSPF router examines the destination address of a packet, it takes the following steps to select the best route:[18]

1. Select the route or routes with the most specific match to the destination address. For example, if there are route entries for 172.16.64.0/18, 172.16.64.0/24, and 172.16.64.192/27 and the destination address is 172.16.64.205, the last entry will be chosen. The most specific match should always be the longest match—the route with the longest address mask. The entries may be host, subnet, network, supernet, or default addresses. If no match can be found, an ICMP Destination Unreachable message will be sent to the source address and the packet will be dropped.

2. Prune the set of selected entries by eliminating less-preferred path types. Path types are prioritized in the following order, with 1 being the most-preferred and 4 being the least-preferred:
   1. Intra-area paths
   2. Inter-area paths
   3. E1 external paths
   4. E2 external paths

Cisco's OSPF performs equal-cost load balancing

If multiple equal-cost, equal-path-type routes exist in the final set, OSPF will utilize them. By default, Cisco's OSPF implementation will load balance over a maximum of four equal-cost paths; this number may be changed within the range of one to six with the command **maximum-paths**.

---

[18] *The lookup procedure described here adheres to RFC 2328. The earlier OSPF RFCs specify creating a set of matching routes first, then choosing the preferred path type, and choosing the longest match last.*

Authentication

OSPF has the capability of authenticating all packets exchanged between neighbors. Authentication may be by simple passwords or by MD5 cryptographic checksums. These authentication methods are discussed in Chapter 7, "Routing Information Protocol Version 2," and examples of configuring OSPF authentication are given in the configuration section.

OSPF over Demand Circuits

OSPF sends Hellos every 10 seconds and refreshes its LSAs every 30 minutes. These functions maintain the neighbor relationships, ensure that the link state databases are accurate, and use far less bandwidth than RIP or IGRP. However, even this minimal traffic is undesirable on *demand circuits*—usage-sensitive connections such as X.25 SVCs, ISDN, and dialup lines. The recurring charges for such links may be determined by connect time or traffic volume or both, thus motivating the network manager to minimize their uptime.

An enhancement that makes OSPF practical over demand circuits is the capability of suppressing the Hello and LSA refresh functions so that a link does not have to be constantly up.[19] Although this enhancement is designed specifically for usage-sensitive circuits, it may be useful on any bandwidth-limited link.[20] OSPF over demand circuits is supported in IOS 11.2 and later.

OSPF over demand circuits will bring up a demand link to perform the initial database synchronization and will subsequently

---

[19] John Moy, "Extending OSPF to Support Demand Circuits," RFC 1793, April 1995.

[20] Although OSPF over demand circuits may be configured on any interface, Hellos are not suppressed on multi-access network types; doing so would prevent the DR processes from functioning properly. As a result, the enhancement is really useful only on point-to-point and point-to-multipoint network types.

bring up the link to flood only LSAs in which certain changes have occurred. These changes are:

1. A change in the LSA Options field
2. A new instance of an existing LSA is received in which the age is MaxAge;
3. A change in the Length field of the LSA header
4. A change in the contents of the LSA, excluding the 20-octet header, the checksum, or the sequence number

Because no periodic Hellos are exchanged (Hellos are used only to bring up the link), OSPF must make a *presumption of reachability*. That is, it must presume that the demand circuit will be available when needed. In some instances, however, the link may not be immediately accessible. For example, a dialup link may be in use, both B channels of a BRI link may be in use, or the maximum number of allowed X.25 SVCs may already be up. In these situations, where the link is unavailable not because it is down but because of normal operational characteristics, the link is *oversubscribed*.

OSPF will not report an oversubscribed demand link as down, and packets routed to an oversubscribed link will be dropped rather than being queued. This behavior makes sense because there is no way to predict when the link will again become available; a stream of packets to an unavailable interface could overflow the buffers.

Several changes to the interface and neighbor state machines and to the flooding procedure must be made to support OSPF over demand circuits (see RFC 1793 for more details). Within the LSA format, two changes are made.

First, if LSAs are not periodically refreshed across a demand circuit, no routers on the other side of the link should declare the LSA invalid after MaxAge. The semantics of the LSA's Age field are changed to accomplish this by designating the high bit as the

DoNotAge bit. When an LSA is flooded over a demand circuit, the transmitting router will set DoNotAge = 1. As the LSA is flooded to all routers on the other side of the link, the Age field will be incremented normally by InfTransDelay seconds.[21] However, after being installed in a database, an LSA will not be aged like the other LSAs.

The second change derives from the first change. Because all routers must be capable of correctly interpreting the DoNotAge bit, a new flag known as the *Demand Circuit bit* (DC-bit) is added to all LSAs. By setting this flag in all LSAs it originates, a router signals to the other routers that it is capable of supporting OSPF over demand circuits.

OSPF Packet Formats

The OSPF packet consists of multiple encapsulations, and deconstructing one is like peeling an onion. As shown in Figure 9.46, the outside of the onion is the IP header. Cisco's maximum OSPF packet size is 1500 octets. Encapsulated within the IP header is one of five OSPF packet types. Each packet type begins with an OSPF packet header, whose format is the same for all packet types. The OSPF packet data following the header varies according to the packet type. Each packet type will have a number of type-specific fields, followed by more data. The data contained in a Hello packet will be a list of neighbors. LS Request packets will contain a series of fields describing the requested LSAs. LS Update packets will contain a list of LSAs, as shown in Figure 9.46. These LSAs in turn have their own headers and type-specific data fields. Database Description and LS Acknowledgment packets will contain a list of LSA headers.

---

[21] *Note that this means MaxAge will actually be MaxAge + DoNotAge.*

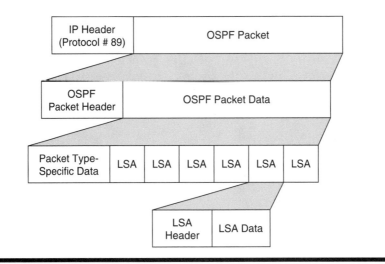

Figure 9.46

An OSPF packet is composed of a series of encapsulations.

Note that OSPF packets are exchanged only between neighbors on a network. They are never routed beyond the network on which they originate.

Figure 9.47 shows an analyzer capture of an IP header for a packet carrying OSPF data, indicated by the protocol number of 89. OSPF packets are sent with a TTL of 1, as can be seen here. Since an OSPF packet should never be routed past an immediate neighbor, setting the TTL to 1 helps to ensure that the packet never travels more than a single hop. Some routers run processes that prioritize packets according to the Precedence bits (Weighted Fair Queuing and Weighted Random Early Detection, for example). OSPF sets the Precedence bits to Internetwork Control (110b), as shown in Figure 9.47, so that these processes will give a high priority to OSPF packets.

This section details the five OSPF packet types, beginning with the header. The following section details the LSA types. An Options

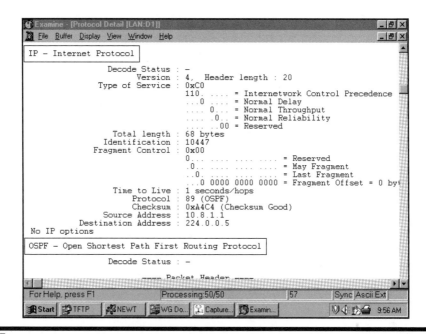

Figure 9.47

OSPF uses a protocol number of 89. It also sets the TTL value in the IP header to 1 and the Precedence bits to Internetwork Control.

field is carried in Hello, Database Description packets, and in all LSAs. The format of this field is the same in all cases and is detailed in its own section.

The Packet Header

All OSPF packets begin with a 24-octet header, as shown in Figure 9.48.

Version is the OSPF version number. As of this writing, the most recent OSPF version number is 2.

Type specifies the packet type following the header. Table 9.7 lists the five packet types by the number appearing in the Type field.

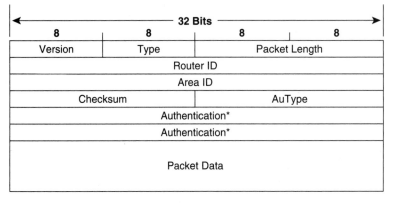

Figure 9.48
The OSPF packet header.

Table 9.7 *OSPF packet types.*

Type Code	Description
1	Hello
2	Database Description
3	Link State Request
4	Link State Update
5	Link State Acknowledgment

Packet length is the length of the OSPF packet, in octets, including the header.

Router ID is the ID of the originating router.

Area ID is the area from which the packet originated. If the packet is sent over a virtual link, the Area ID will be 0.0.0.0, the backbone Area ID, because virtual links are considered part of the backbone.

Checksum is a standard IP checksum of the entire packet, including the header.

AuType is the authentication mode being used. Table 9.8 lists the possible authentication modes.

Table 9.8   *OSPF authentication types.*

AuType	Authentication Type
0	Null (no authentication)
1	Simple (clear text) Password Authentication
2	Cryptographic (MD5) Checksum

Authentication is the information necessary for the packet to be authenticated by whatever mode is specified in the AuType field. If AuType = 0, the field is not examined and therefore may contain anything. If AuType = 1, the field will contain a password of up to 64 bits. If AuType = 2, the Authentication field will contain a Key ID, the Authentication Data Length, and a nondecreasing Cryptographic sequence number. The message digest is appended to the end of the OSPF packet, and is not considered part of the packet itself.

Key ID identifies the authentication algorithm and the secret key used to create the message digest.

Authentication Data Length specifies the length, in octets, of the message digest appended to the end of the packet.

Cryptographic Sequence Number is a nondecreasing number used to prevent replay attacks.

The Hello Packet

The Hello packet (Figure 9.49) establishes and maintains adjacencies. The Hello carries parameters on which neighbors must agree in order to form an adjacency.

8	8	8	8
Version	Type = 1	Packet Length	
Router ID			
Area ID			
Checksum		AuType	
Authentication			
Authentication			
Network Mask			
Hello Interval		Options	Router Priority
Router Dead Interval			
Designated Router			
Backup Designated Router			
Neighbor			
Neighbor			

Figure 9.49
The OSPF Hello packet.

Network Mask is the address mask of the interface from which the packet was sent. If this mask does not match the mask of the interface on which the packet is received, the packet will be dropped. This technique ensures that routers will become neighbors only if they agree on the exact address of their shared network.

Hello Interval, as discussed earlier, is the period, in seconds, between transmissions of Hello packets on the interface. If the sending and receiving routers don't have the same value for this parameter, they will not establish a neighbor relationship.

Options are described in "The Options Field," later in this chapter. This field is included in the Hello packet to ensure that neighbors have compatible capabilities. A router may reject a neighbor because of a capabilities mismatch.

Router Priority is used in the election of the DR and BDR. If set to zero, the originating router is ineligible to become the DR or BDR.

Router Dead Interval is the number of seconds the originating router will wait for a Hello from a neighbor before declaring the neighbor dead. If a Hello is received in which this number does not match the RouterDeadInterval of the receiving interface, the packet will be dropped. This technique ensures that neighbors agree on this parameter.

Designated Router is the IP address of the interface of the DR on the network (not its Router ID). During the DR election process, this may only be the originating router's idea of the DR, not the finally elected DR. If there is no DR (because one has not been elected or because the network type does not require DRs), this field will be set to 0.0.0.0.

Backup DR is the IP address of the interface of the BDR on the network. Again, during the DR election process, this may only be the originating router's idea of the BDR. If there is no BDR, this field is set to 0.0.0.0.

Neighbor is a recurring field that lists all neighbors on the network from which the originating router has received a valid Hello in the past RouterDeadInterval.

The Database Description Packet

The Database Description packet (Figure 9.50) is used when an adjacency is being established (see "Building an Adjacency," earlier in this chapter). The primary purpose of the DD packet is to describe some or all of the LSAs in the originator's database so that the receiver can determine whether it has a matching LSA in its own database. This is done by listing only the headers of the LSAs. Because multiple DD packets may be exchanged during this process, flags are included for managing the exchange via a master/slave polling relationship.

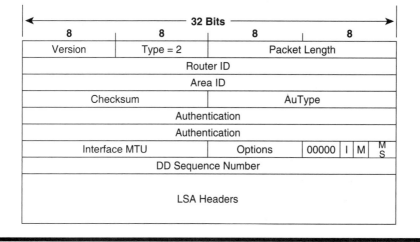

Figure 9.50
The OSPF Database Description packet.

Interface MTU is the size, in octets, of the largest IP packet that can be sent out the originator's interface without fragmentation. This field will be set to 0x0000 when the packet is sent over virtual links.

Options are described in "The Options Field." The field is included in the Database Description packet so that a router may choose not to forward certain LSAs to a neighbor that doesn't support the necessary capabilities.

The first five bits of the next octet are unused and are always set to 00000b.

I-bit, or Initial bit, is set to 1 when the packet is the initial packet in series of DD packets. Subsequent DD packets will have I-bit = 0.

M-bit, or More bit, is set to 1 to indicate that the packet is not the last in a series of DD packets. The last DD packet will have M-bit = 0.

MS-bit, or Master/Slave bit, is set to 1 to indicate that the originator is the master (that is, is in control of the polling process) during a database synchronization. The slave will have MS-bit = 0.

DD Sequence Number ensures that the full sequence of DD packets are received in the database synchronization process. The sequence number will be set by the master to some unique value in the first DD packet, and the sequence will be incremented in subsequent packets.

LSA Headers list some or all of the headers of the LSAs in the originator's link state database. See "The Link State Header," for a full description of the LSA header; the header contains enough information to uniquely identify the LSA and the particular instance of the LSA.

The Link State Request Packet

As Database Description packets are received during the database synchronization process, a router will take note of any listed LSAs that are not in its database or are more recent than its own LSA. These LSAs are recorded in the Link State Request list. The router will then send one or more Link State Request packets (Figure 9.51) asking the neighbor for its copy of the LSA. Note that the packet uniquely identifies the LSA by Type, ID, and advertising router fields of its header, but it does not request a specific instance of the LSA (identified by the header's sequence number, checksum, and age). Therefore, the request is for the most recent instance of the LSA, whether the requester is aware of that instance or not.

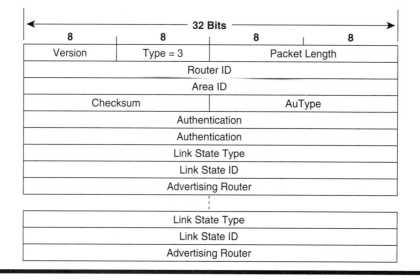

Figure 9.51
The OSPF link state request packet.

Link State Type is the LS type number, which identifies the LSA as a router LSA, network LSA, and so on. Type numbers are listed in Table 9.4.

Link State ID is a type-dependent field of the LSA header. See "The Link State Header" and the LSA-specific sections for a full description of how the various LSAs use this field.

Advertising Router is the Router ID of the router which originated the LSA.

The Link State Update Packet

The Link State Update packet, shown in Figure 9.52, is used in the flooding of LSAs and to send LSAs in response to Link State Requests. Recall that OSPF packets do not leave the network on which they were originated. Consequently, a Link State Update packet, carrying one or many LSAs, only carries the LSAs only one hop further from their originating router. The receiving neighbor is responsible for re-encapsulating the appropriate LSAs in new LS Update packets for further flooding.

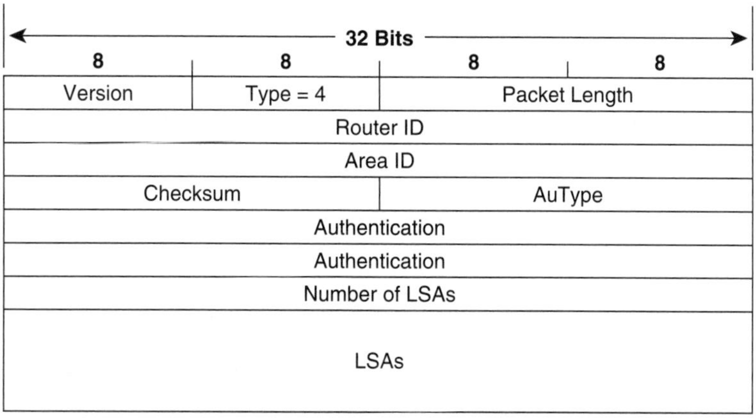

32 Bits			
8	8	8	8
Version	Type = 4	Packet Length	
Router ID			
Area ID			
Checksum		AuType	
Authentication			
Authentication			
Number of LSAs			
LSAs			

Figure 9.52

The OSPF Link State Update packet.

Number of LSAs specifies the number of LSAs included in this packet.

LSAs are the full LSAs as described in OSPF LSA formats. Each update may carry multiple LSAs, up to the maximum packet size allowed on the link.

The Link State Acknowledgment Packet

Link State Acknowledgment packets are used to make the flooding of LSAs reliable. Each LSA received by a router from a neighbor must be explicitly acknowledged in a Link State Acknowledgment packet. The LSA being acknowledged is identified by including its header in the LS ACK packet, and multiple LSAs may be acknowledged in a single packet. As Figure 9.53

shows, the LS ACK packet consists of nothing more than an OSPF packet header and a list of LSA headers.

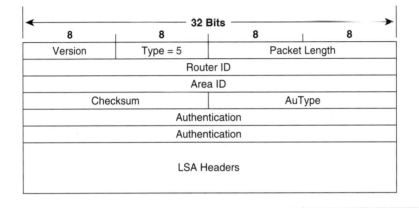

Figure 9.53
The OSPF Link State Acknowledgment packet.

OSPF LSA Formats

This section details the fields of each LSA type. The exception is the Group Membership LSA (type 6); because MOSPF is not covered in this book, details of its associated LSA are also not covered. LSA types 8 through 11 are also not covered because they are currently only proposed types and have not yet been deployed.

The LSA Header

The LSA header (Figure 9.54) begins all LSAs and is also used by itself in Database Description and Link State Acknowledgment packets. Three fields in the header uniquely identify every LSA: the Type, Link State ID, and Advertising Router. Additionally, three other fields uniquely identify the most recent instance of an LSA: the Age, Sequence Number, and Checksum.

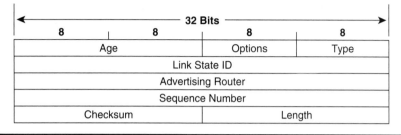

Figure 9.54
The OSPF LSA header.

Age is the time, in seconds, since the LSA was originated. As the LSA is flooded, the age is incremented by InfTransDelay seconds at each router interface it exits. The age is also incremented in seconds as it resides in a link state database.

Options is described in "The Options Field." In the LSA header, the Options field specifies the optional capabilities supported by the portion of the OSPF domain described by the LSA.

Type is the LSA type. The type codes are shown in Table 9.4.

Link State ID identifies the portion of the OSPF domain being described by the LSA. The specific usage of this field varies according to the LSA type; the descriptions of each LSA include a description of how the LSA uses this field.

Advertising Router is the router ID of the router that originated the LSA.

Sequence Number is incremented each time a new instance of the LSA is originated. This update helps other routers identify the most recent instance of the LSA.

Checksum is the Fletcher checksum of the complete contents of the LSA except the Age field. If the Age field were included, the checksum would have to be recalculated every time the age was incremented.

Length is the number of octets of the LSA, including the header.

The Router LSA

A Router LSA (Figure 9.55) is produced by every router. It lists a router's links, or interfaces, along with the state and the outgoing cost of each link. These LSAs are flooded only within the area in which they are originated. The command **show ip ospf database router** (refer to Figure 9.30) lists the Router LSAs in a database. Note that Router LSAs advertise host routes as stub networks; the Link ID field carries the host IP address, and the Link Data field carries the host address mask of 255.255.255.255.

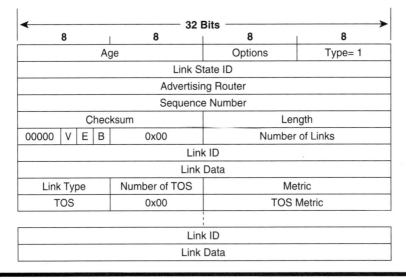

Figure 9.55
The OSPF Router LSA.

Link State ID for router LSAs is the originating router's Router ID.

V, or *Virtual Link Endpoint* bit, is set to one when the originating router is an endpoint of one or more fully adjacent virtual links having the described area as the transit area.

E, or *External* bit, is set to one when the originating router is an ASBR.

B, or *Border* bit, is set to one when the originating router is an ABR.

Number of Links specifies the number of router links the LSA describes. The router LSA must describe all of the originating router's links, or interfaces, to the area in which the LSA is flooded.

Subsequent fields in the Router LSA describe each link and appear one or more times, corresponding to the number in the Number of Links field. This discussion covers the Link Type field first, although that field does not appear until after the Link Data field. Understanding link type first is important because the descriptions of the Link ID and Link Data fields vary according to the value of the Link Type field.

Link Type describes the general type of connection the link provides. Table 9.9 lists the possible values of the field and the associated connection types.

Table 9.9 *Link type values.*

Link Type	Connection
1	Point-to-point connection to another router
2	Connection to a transit network
3	Connection to a stub network
4	Virtual link

Link ID identifies the object to which the link connects. This is dependent on the link type, as shown in Table 9.10. Note that when the connected object is another router, the Link ID is the same as the Link State ID in the header of the neighboring router's LSA. During the routing table calculation, this value is used to find the neighbor's LSA in the link state database.

Table 9.10   *Link ID values.*

Link Type	Value of Link ID Field
1	Neighboring router's Router ID.
2	IP address of the DR's interface.
3	IP network or subnet address.
4	Neighboring router's Router ID.

Link Data also depends on the value of the Link Type field, as shown in Table 9.11.

Table 9.11   *Link data values.*

Link Type	Value of Link Data Field
1	IP address of the originating router's interface to the network.*
2	IP address of the originating router's interface to the network.
3	Network's IP address or subnet mask.
4	The MIB-II ifIndex value for the originating router's interface.

---

* *If the point-to-point link is unnumbered, this field will instead carry the MIB-II ifIndex value of the interface.*

Number of TOS specifies the number of Type of Service metrics listed for this link. Although TOS is no longer supported in RFC 2328, the TOS fields are still included for backward compatibility with earlier OSPF implementations. If no TOS metrics are associated with a link, this field is set to 0x00.

Metric is the cost of the link (interface).

The next two fields are associated with a link corresponding to the number (#) of TOS field. For example, if # of TOS = 3, there will be three 32-bit words containing three instances of these fields. If # of TOS = 0, there will be no instances of these fields.

Note that Cisco supports only TOS = 0.

TOS specifies the Type of Service to which the following metric refers.[22] Table 9.12 lists the TOS values (as specified in RFC 1349), the bit values of the corresponding TOS field in the IP header, and the corresponding value used in the OSPF TOS field.

Table 9.12 *OSPF TOS values.*

RFC TOS Value	IP Header TOS Field	OSPF TOS Encoding
Normal Service	0000	0
Minimize Monetary Cost	0001	2
Maximize Reliability	0010	4
Maximize Throughput	0100	8
Minimize Delay	1000	16

TOS Metric is the metric associated with the specified TOS value.

The Network LSA

Network LSAs (Figure 9.56) are originated by DRs. These LSAs advertise the multi-access network, and all routers (including the

---

[22] *Philip Almquist, "Type of Service in the Internet Protocol Suite," RFC 1349, July 1992.*

DR) attached to the network. Like Router LSAs, Network LSAs are flooded only within the originating area. The command **show ip ospf database network** (Figure 9.32) is used to observe a Network LSA.

32 Bits			
8	8	8	8
Age		Options	Type = 2
Link State ID			
Advertising Router			
Sequence Number			
Checksum		Length	
Network Mask			
Attached Router			
Attached Router			
Attached Router			

Figure 9.56
The OSPF Network LSA.

Link State ID for Network LSAs is the IP address of the DR's interface to the network.

Network Mask specifies the address or subnet mask used on this network.

Attached Router lists the Router IDs of all routers on the network that are fully adjacent with the DR, and the Router ID of the DR itself. The number of instances of this field (and hence the number of routers listed) can be deduced from the LSA header's Length field.

The Network and ASBR Summary LSAs

The Network Summary LSA (type 3) and the ASBR Summary LSA (type 4) have an identical format, shown in Figure 9.57. The only difference in field contents is the Type and the Link State ID. ABRs produce both types of Summary LSA; Network Summary LSAs advertise networks external to an area (including default routes), whereas ASBR Summary LSAs advertise ASBRs external to an area. Both types are flooded only into a single area. The Network Summary LSAs in a router's database can be observed with the command **show ip ospf database summary** (Figure 9.34), and ASBR Summary LSAs can be observed with **show ip ospf database asbr-summary** (Figure 9.36).

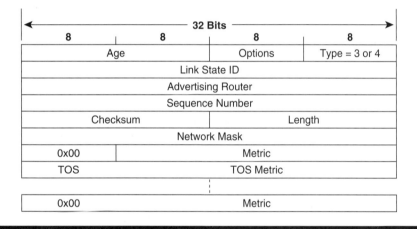

Figure 9.57

The OSPF Summary LSA. The format is the same for both type 3 and type 4 Summary LSAs.

Link State ID, for type 3 LSAs, is the IP address of the network or subnet being advertised. If the LSA is type 4, the Link State ID is the Router ID of the ASBR being advertised.

Network Mask is the address or subnet mask of the network being advertised in type 3 LSAs. In type 4 LSAs, this field has no meaning and is set to 0.0.0.0.

If a type 3 LSA is advertising a default route, both the Link State ID and the Network Mask fields will be 0.0.0.0.

Metric is the cost of the route to this destination.

The TOS and TOS Metric fields are optional and are described in "The Router LSA." Again, Cisco supports only TOS = 0.

The Autonomous System External LSA

Autonomous System External LSAs (Figure 9.58) are originated by ASBRs. These LSAs are used to advertise destinations external to the OSPF autonomous system, including default routes to external destinations, and are flooded into all nonstub areas of the OSPF domain. The command **show ip ospf database external** is used to display AS External LSAs (Figure 9.38).

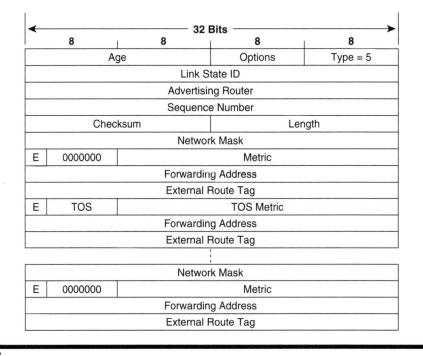

Figure 9.58

The OSPF Autonomous System External LSA.

Link State ID for AS External LSAs is the IP address of the destination.

Network Mask is the address or subnet mask for the destination being advertised.

If the type 5 LSA is advertising a default route, the Link State ID and the network mask will both be 0.0.0.0.

E, or *External Metric* bit, specifies the type of external metric to be used with this route. If the E-bit is set to 1, the metric type is E2. If the E-bit = 0, the metric type is E1. See the section "Path Types," earlier in this chapter, for more information on E1 and E2 external metrics.

Metric is the cost of the route, as set by the ASBR.

Forwarding Address is the address to which packets for the advertised destination should be forwarded. If the forwarding address is 0.0.0.0, packets will be forwarded to the originating ASBR.

External Route Tag is an arbitrary tag that may be applied to the external route. This field is not used by the OSPF protocol itself, but is instead provided for external route management. The setting and use of such tags are discussed in Chapter 14, "Route Maps."

Optionally, TOS fields may be associated with the destination. These fields are the same as discussed previously, except each TOS metric also has its own E-bit, Forwarding Address, and External Route Tag.

The NSSA External LSA

NSSA External LSAs are originated by ASBRs within an NSSA (not-so-stubby area). All fields of the NSSA External LSA (Figure

9.59) are identical to an AS External LSA's fields, with the exception of the Forwarding Address field. Unlike AS External LSAs, which are flooded throughout an OSPF autonomous system, NSSA external LSAs are flooded only within the not-so-stubby area in which it was originated. The command **show ip ospf database nssa-external** is used to display NSSA External LSAs (Figure 9.39).

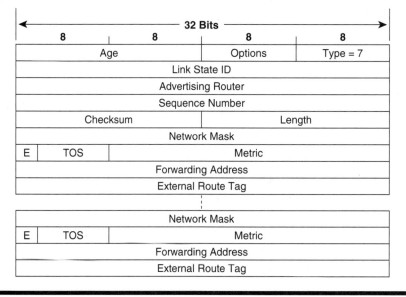

Figure 9.59
The OSPF NSSA LSA.

Forwarding Address, if the network between the NSSA ASBR and the adjacent autonomous system is advertised as an internal route, is the next hop address on the network. If the network is not advertised as an internal route, the forwarding address will be the NSSA ASBR's Router ID.

The Options Field

The Options field (Figure 9.60) is present in every Hello and Database Description packet and in every LSA. The Options field allows routers to communicate their optional capabilities to other routers.

*	*	DC	EA	N/P	MC	E	T

Figure 9.60
The OSPF Options field.

The asterisk, *, indicates an unused bit, normally set to zero.

DC is set when the originating router is capable of supporting OSPF over demand circuits.

EA is set when the originating router is capable of receiving and forwarding External Attributes LSAs. These LSAs are not yet in general usage and are not covered in this book.

N is used only in Hello packets. A router will set N-bit = 1 to indicate support for NSSA External LSAs. If N-bit = 0, the router will not accept or send these LSAs. Neighboring routers with mismatched N-bits will not become adjacent; this restriction ensures that all routers in an area support NSSA capabilities equally. If the N-bit = 1, the E-bit must be 0.

P is used only in NSSA External LSA headers. (For this reason, the N- and P-bit can use the same position.) This bit tells the ABR of a not-so-stubby area to translate type 7 LSAs into type 5 LSAs.

MC is set when the originating router is capable of forwarding IP multicast packets. This bit is used by MOSPF.

E is set when the originating router is capable of accepting AS External LSAs. It will be set to 1 in all AS External LSAs and in all LSAs originated in the backbone and nonstub areas. E-bit = 0 in all LSAs originated within a stub area. Additionally, the bit is used in the Hello packet to indicate an interface's capability of sending and receiving type 5 LSAs. Neighboring routers with mismatched E-bits will not become adjacent; this restriction ensures that all routers in an area support stub capabilities equally.

T is set when the originating router is capable of supporting TOS.

CONFIGURING OSPF

The many options and configuration variables available to OSPF frequently make it the IGP of choice in large IP internetworks. However, the opinion is occasionally expressed that OSPF configuration is "too complex" to be a good choice for small internets. This is nonsense. As the first case study shows, getting a basic OSPF configuration up and running involves only a few extra keystrokes in the **network** command; if the operation of OSPF is reasonably well understood, these extra keystrokes will be intuitive.

Case Study: A Basic OSPF Configuration

The three steps necessary to begin a basic OSPF process are:

1. Determine the area to which each router interface will be attached.
2. Enable OSPF with the command **router ospf** *process-id*.
3. Specify the interfaces on which to run OSPF, and their areas, with the **network area** command.

Unlike the process ID associated with IGRP and EIGRP, the OSPF process ID is not an autonomous system number. The process ID can be any positive integer and has no significance outside the router on which it is configured. Cisco IOS allows multiple OSPF processes to run on the same router;[23] the process ID merely distinguishes one process from another within the device.

The **network** command used with the previously discussed protocols allows only the specification of a major network address. If some interfaces within the network should not run the routing protocol, the **passive-interface** command has to be used with those protocols. The **network area** command is much more flexible, reflecting the fully classless nature of OSPF. Any address range can be specified with an (address, inverse mask) pair. The inverse mask is the same as the inverse mask used with access lists.[24] The area can be specified in either decimal or dotted decimal.

Figure 9.61 shows an OSPF internetwork. Note that each area has an assigned IP address from which its subnets are derived. Limiting an area to a single address or subnet is not necessary, but doing so has significant advantages, as will be seen in a later case study on address summarization. Note also that this example is designed to demonstrate the configuration of multiple areas. In "real life," it would be much wiser to put such a small internetwork within a single area. Further, that single area does not have to be area 0. The rule is that all areas must connect to the backbone; therefore, a backbone area is needed only if there is more than one area.

---

[23] *Although the use of multiple processes on one router is possible, it is highly discouraged because of the demands that the multiple databases will place on router resources.*

[24] *See Appendix B, "Tutorial: Access Lists," for a tutorial on the use of inverse masks.*

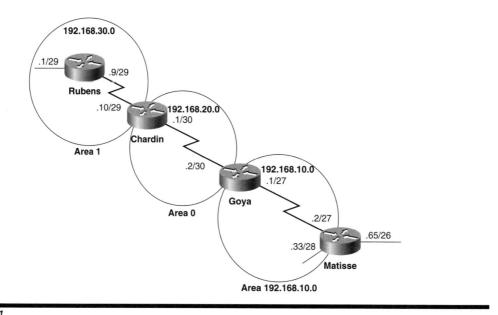

Figure 9.61

Chardin and Goya are ABRs; Rubens and Matisse are Internal Routers.

Each of the four routers in Figure 9.61 is configured differently to demonstrate the flexibility of the **network area** command. The configurations are:

Rubens

```
router ospf 10
  network 0.0.0.0 255.255.255.255 area 1
```

Chardin

```
router ospf 20
  network 192.168.30.0 0.0.0.255 area 1
  network 192.168.20.0 0.0.0.255 area 0
```

Goya

```
router ospf 30
  network 192.168.20.0 0.0.0.3 area 0.0.0.0
  network 192.168.10.0 0.0.0.31 area 192.168.10.0
```

Matisse

```
router ospf 40
  network 192.168.10.2 0.0.0.0 area 192.168.10.0
  network 192.168.10.33 0.0.0.0 area 192.168.10.0
```

The first thing to note is that the process IDs are different for each router. Usually these numbers are the same across an internet for consistency of configuration. Here the process IDs are configured differently merely to demonstrate that they have no meaning outside of the router. These four differently numbered processes are able to communicate.

The next thing to notice is the format of the **network area** command. Following the **network** portion is an IP address and an inverse mask. When the OSPF process first becomes active, it will "run" the IP addresses of all active interfaces against the (address, inverse mask) pair of the first network statement. All interfaces that match will be assigned to the area specified by the **area** portion of the command. The process will then run the addresses of any interfaces that did not match the first network statement against the second network statement. The process of running IP addresses against network statements continues until all interfaces have been matched or until all network statements have been used. It is important to note that this process is consecutive, beginning with the first network statement. As a result, the order of the statements can be important, as is shown in the troubleshooting section.

The process of matching IP addresses to areas is consecutive, beginning with the first **network** statement.

Rubens' network statement will match all interfaces on the router. The address 0.0.0.0 is really just a placeholder; the inverse mask of 255.255.255.255 is the element that does all of the work here. With "don't care" bits placed across the entire four octets, the mask will find a match with any address and place the corresponding interface into area 1. This method provides the least precision in controlling which interfaces will run OSPF.

Chardin is an ABR between area 1 and area 0. This fact is reflected in its network statements. Here the (address, inverse mask) pairs will place any interface that is connected to any subnet of major network 192.168.30.0 in area 1 and any interface that is connected to any subnet of major network 192.168.20.0 in the backbone area.

Goya is also an ABR. Here the (address, inverse mask) pairs will match only the specific subnets configured on the two interfaces. Notice also that the backbone area is specified in dotted decimal. Both this format and the decimal format used at Chardin will cause the associated area fields of the OSPF packets to be 0x00000000, so they are compatible.

Matisse has one interface, 192.168.10.65/26, which is not running OSPF. The network statements for this router are configured to the individual interface addresses, and the inverse mask indicates that all 32 bits must match exactly. This method provides the most precise control over which interfaces will run OSPF.

Finally, note that although Matisse's interface 192.168.10.65/26 is not running OSPF, that address is numerically the highest on the router. As a result, Matisse's Router ID is 192.168.10.65 (Figure 9.62).

Case Study: Setting Router IDs with Loopback Interfaces

Suppose router Matisse from Figure 9.61 has been configured in a staging center and then sent to the field to be installed. During the bootup, the router reports that it cannot allocate a Router ID, and it seems to report the **network area** commands as configuration errors (Figure 9.63). Worse, the OSPF commands are no longer in the running configuration.

The problem here is that during bootup all the interfaces on the router were administratively shut down. If OSPF cannot find an

```
Matisse#show ip ospf 40
Routing Process "ospf 40" with ID 192.168.10.65
Supports only single TOS(TOS0) routes
SPF schedule delay 5 secs, Hold time between two SPFs 10 secs
Number of DCbitless external LSA 0
Number of DoNotAge external LSA 0
Number of areas in this router is 1. 1 normal 0 stub 0 nssa
    Area 192.168.10.0
        Number of interfaces in this area is 2
        Area has no authentication
        SPF algorithm executed 3 times
        Area ranges are
        Link State Update Interval is 00:30:00 and due in 00:27:59
        Link State Age Interval is 00:20:00 and due in 00:17:58
        Number of DCbitless LSA 1
        Number of indication LSA 1
        Number of DoNotAge LSA 0

Matisse#
```

Figure 9.62

*The command **show ip ospf** process-id displays process-specific information. The first line here shows that the Router ID is 192.168.10.65.*

active IP address for its Router ID, it cannot start. And if the OSPF process isn't active, the subsequent **network area** commands will be invalid.

The solution to this problem (assuming you have a valid reason for having all physical interfaces in shutdown) is to use a loopback interface. The loopback interface, which is a virtual, software-only interface, is always up. Therefore, its IP address is always available.

The more common reason for using loopback interfaces on OSPF routers is that the interfaces allow the network administrator to control the Router IDs. When the OSPF process looks for a Router ID, OSPF will prefer the address of a loopback interface over the addresses of all physical interfaces, regardless of the numerical

```
Cisco Internetwork Operating System Software
IOS (tm) 2500 Software (C2500-J-L), Version 11.2(7a), RELEASE SOFTWARE (fc1)
Copyright (c) 1986-1997 by cisco Systems, Inc.
Compiled Tue 01-Jul-97 15:31 by kuong
Image text-base: 0x0303E1EC, data-base: 0x00001000

cisco 2509 (68030) processor (revision C) with 16384K/2048K bytes of memory.
Processor board ID 01210416, with hardware revision 00000000
Bridging software.
SuperLAT software copyright 1990 by Meridian Technology Corp).
X.25 software, Version 2.0, NET2, BFE and GOSIP compliant.
TN3270 Emulation software.
1 Ethernet/IEEE 802.3 interface(s)
2 Serial network interface(s)
32K bytes of non-volatile configuration memory.
8192K bytes of processor board System flash (Read ONLY)

OSPF: Could not allocate router id
 network 192.168.10.2 0.0.0.0 area 192.168.10.0
    ^

% Invalid input detected at '^' marker.

 network 192.168.10.334 0.0.0.0 area 192.168.10.0
    ^

% Invalid input detected at '^' marker.



Press RETURN to get started!
```

Figure 9.63

OSPF will not boot if it cannot find an active IP address for its Router ID.

order. If there are multiple loopback interfaces with IP addresses, OSPF will choose the numerically highest loopback address.

Controlling the Router IDs so that individual OSPF routers are more easily identified facilitates management and troubleshooting. The Router IDs are usually managed by one of two methods:

- Set aside a legitimate network or subnet address to be used strictly for Router IDs

- Use a "bogus" IP address range

The first method has the disadvantage of using up the assigned network address space. The second method will preserve the legitimate addresses, but one must remember that what is bogus in one internet is legitimate in another. Using easily recognized addresses such as 1.1.1.1, 2.2.1.1, and so on is fine as long as you remember that these are not public addresses. Care must be taken that the bogus addresses do not leak out to the public Internet.

The configurations of the last section are modified to use loopback addresses as follows:

Rubens
```
interface Loopback0
  ip address 192.168.50.1 255.255.255.255
!
router ospf 10
  network 192.168.30.0 0.0.0.255 area 1
```

Chardin
```
interface Loopback0
  ip address 192.168.50.2 255.255.255.255
!
router ospf 20
  network 192.168.30.0 0.0.0.255 area 1
  network 192.168.20.0 0.0.0.255 area 0
```

Goya
```
interface Loopback0
  ip address 192.168.50.3 255.255.255.255
!
router ospf 30
  network 192.168.20.0 0.0.0.3 area 0.0.0.0
  network 192.168.10.0 0.0.0.31 area 192.168.10.0
```

Matisse
```
interface Loopback0
  ip address 192.168.50.4 255.255.255.255
!
router ospf 40
  network 192.168.10.2 0.0.0.0 area 192.168.10.0
  network 192.168.10.33 0.0.0.0 area 192.168.10.0
```

For this example, the network address 192.168.50.0 has been set aside for exclusive use as Router IDs. Router IDs are thus easily distinguished from other IP addresses in this internet.

The first thing to note about this configuration is the address masks used with the loopback addresses: Each mask is configured as a host address. This step is not really necessary, because OSPF treats a loopback interface as a stub host; whatever (address, mask) pair is configured, the address of the loopback interface will be advertised as a host route. The host mask is used merely to keep things neat, and to reflect the way in which the address is advertised.

OSPF advertises loopback interface addresses as host routes

However, the second point of interest makes the first somewhat irrelevant. Remember that OSPF does not have to be running on an interface for its IP address to be used as the Router ID. In fact, having OSPF advertise the loopback addresses just creates unnecessary LSAs. In the example shown, notice that the **network area** statements do not refer to the loopback addresses. In fact, the configuration at Rubens had to be changed. Rubens' previous command, **network 0.0.0.0 255.255.255.255 area 1**, would have picked up the loopback address.

Benefits of loopback addresses

In addition to aiding management and troubleshooting, using loopback interfaces will also make an OSPF internet more stable. If a physical interface from which the Router ID was taken experiences a hardware failure,[25] if the interface is administratively shut down, or if the IP address is inadvertently deleted, the OSPF process must acquire a new Router ID. Therefore, the router must prematurely age and flood its old LSAs and then flood LSAs containing the new ID. A loopback interface has no hardware components to fail. The Router ID will still have to be recalculated if the loopback interface or its IP address is inadvertently deleted, but the likelihood of a change in the loopback interface is reduced because routine configuration activity should not concern this interface.

---

[25] *Merely disconnecting the interface will not cause the Router ID to change.*

Case Study: Domain Name Service Lookups

Loopback interfaces simplify the management and troubleshooting of OSPF internets by providing predictable Router IDs. This simplification can be taken even further by recording the Router IDs in a Domain Name Service (DNS) database. The router can then be configured to consult the server address-to-name mappings, or Reverse DNS lookups, and then display the routers by name instead of by Router ID (Figure 9.64).

```
Goya#show ip ospf neighbor

Neighbor ID     Pri  State     Dead Time   Address        Interface
chardin          1   FULL/ -   00:00:38    192.168.20.1   Serial0
matisse          1   FULL/ -   00:00:36    192.168.10.2   Serial1
Goya#show ip ospf database

        OSPF Router with ID (192.168.50.3) (Process ID 30)

                Router Link States (Area 0.0.0.0)

   Link ID           ADV Router     Age      Seq#         Checksum    Link count
   192.168.50.2      chardin        151      0x80000097   0x1B3F      2
   192.168.50.3      goya           1568     0x8000000C   0x2A1C      3

                Summary Net Link States (Area 0.0.0.0)

   Link ID           ADV Router    Age      Seq#         Checksum
   192.168.10.0      goya          1568     0x80000009   0xA35E
   192.168.10.33     goya          1568     0x80000009   0x1DA3
   192.168.30.1      chardin       1058     0x80000009   0x6984
   192.168.30.8      chardin       1059      0x80000009 0xEEFF

                Router Link States (Area 192.168.10.0)

   Link ID           ADV Router    Age      Seq#         Checksum    Link count
   192.168.50.3      goya          1569     0x8000001C   0xF9E8      2
   192.168.50.4      matisse       688      0x8000000B   0xB597      3
   --More-
```

Figure 9.64

*OSPF can be configured to use DNS to map Router IDs to names for use in some **show** commands.*

Goya was configured to perform DNS lookups as follows:

```
ip name-server 172.19.35.2
!
ip ospf name-lookup
```

The first command specifies the address of the DNS server, and the second enables the OSPF process to perform DNS lookups. In some cases, a router is identified by an interface address instead of a Router ID. Adding entries to the DNS database for the router interfaces, such as *rubens-e0*, allows the interfaces to also be identified by name while differentiating them from the Router IDs.

The address of the name server used in this example does not belong to one of the subnets shown in Figure 9.61. The method by which this network is reached is the subject of the next case study.

Case Study: OSPF and Secondary Addresses

Two rules are related to the use of secondary addresses in an OSPF environment:

1. OSPF will advertise a secondary network or subnet only if it is also running on the primary network or subnet.
2. OSPF sees secondary networks as stub networks (networks on which there are no OSPF neighbors) and therefore will not send Hellos on them. Consequently, no adjacencies can be established on secondary networks.

Figure 9.65 shows the DNS server and an additional router attached to the E0 interface of Matisse. The server and the new router have addresses in subnet 172.19.35.0/25, so Matisse's E0 has been given a secondary address of 172.19.35.15/25:

```
interface Ethernet0
  ip address 172.19.35.15 255.255.255.128 secondary
  ip address 192.168.10.33 255.255.255.240
!
```

```
router ospf 40
  network 192.168.10.2 0.0.0.0 area 192.168.10.0
  network 192.168.10.33 0.0.0.0 area 192.168.10.0
  network 172.19.35.15 0.0.0.0 area 192.168.10.0
```

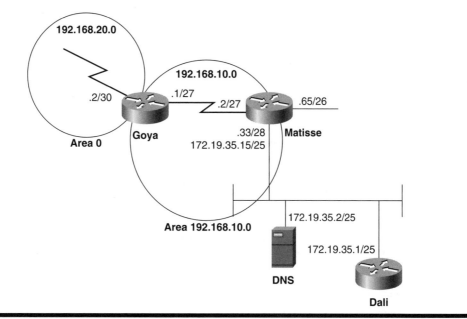

Figure 9.65

Router Dali and the DNS server are not part of the OSPF domain and are attached to Matisse via a secondary network address.

With this configuration, Matisse will advertise subnet 172.19.35.0/25 to its neighbors. However, if the **network area** statement for 192.168.10.33 should be deleted, subnet 172.19.35.0/25 will no longer be advertised.

Because Matisse is attached to subnet 172.19.35.0/25 via a secondary address, it cannot establish an adjacency with any routers on that subnet (Figure 9.66). However, the DNS server uses Dali as its default gateway. Therefore Matisse and Dali must be able to route packets to each other.

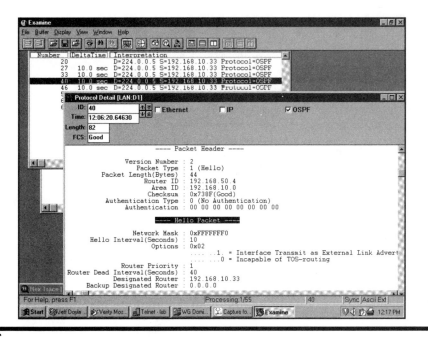

Figure 9.66
This analyzer capture is from the network to which Matisse, Dali, and the DNS server are attached. The smaller window shows that Hellos are only being sourced from Matisse's primary address of 192.168.10.33. The larger window shows a decode of one of the Hellos.

An assessment of the internet as it has been described so far shows that:

- Subnet 172.19.35.0/25 is being advertised into the OSPF domain; a packet with a destination address of 172.19.35.2 will be routed to Matisse's E0 interface and from there directly to the DNS server (Figure 9.67).

- Because the DNS server must send replies to network addresses different than its own, it will send the replies to Dali for routing.

- Dali is not exchanging routing information with Matisse, so it does not know how to reach the networks within the OSPF autonomous system.

```
Matisse#show arp
Protocol   Address          Age (min)   Hardware Addr   Type   Interface
Internet   192.168.10.33          -     0000.0c0a.2c51  ARPA   Ethernet0
Internet   172.19.35.15           -     0000.0c0a.2c51  ARPA   Ethernet0
Internet   172.19.35.1          167     0000.0c0a.2aa9  ARPA   Ethernet0
Internet   172.19.35.2           26     0002.6779.0f4c  ARPA   Ethernet0
Matisse#
```

Figure 9.67

The MAC identifier of the DNS server is recorded in Matisse's ARP cache, indicating that the server can be reached directly. If packets destined for the server had to be routed through Dali, the MAC identifier for both the server and for Dali would be 0000.0c0a.2aa9 in this cache.

So the one step needed to "close the circuit" is to tell Dali how to reach the OSPF networks. This is easily done with a static route:

```
Dali(config)#ip route 192.168.0.0 255.255.0.0 172.19.35.15
```

Note that static routes are classless, so the one supernet entry can be used to match all addresses within the OSPF autonomous system.

In this example, Matisse is not an ASBR. Although it sends packets to destinations outside of the autonomous system, it is not accepting any information about exterior destinations and therefore is not originating any type 5 LSAs.

Figure 9.68 shows a new set of destinations reachable via Dali. Matisse must now become an ASBR and advertise the routes into the OSPF domain. However, it must first learn the routes. This task can be done by configuring static routes or by running a routing protocol that will communicate over the secondary network. In either case, the routes must then be redistributed into OSPF.

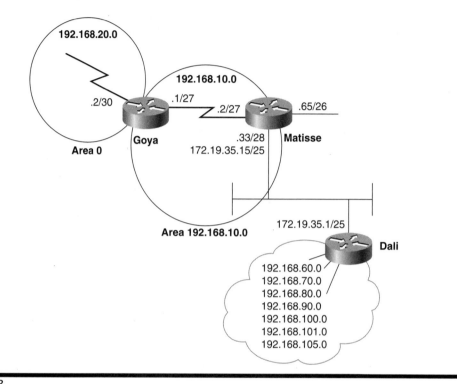

Figure 9.68

*The OSPF autonomous system must learn about the destinations reachable via Dali, but Matisse's
secondary address to Dali prevents the two routers from sharing information via OSPF.*

RIP, which has no difficulties with secondary addresses, is chosen
to communicate with Dali. Matisse's configuration is as follows:

```
interface Ethernet0
  ip address 172.19.35.15 255.255.255.128 secondary
  ip address 192.168.10.33 255.255.255.240
!
router ospf 40
  redistribute rip metric 10
  network 192.168.10.2 0.0.0.0 area 192.168.10.0
  network 192.168.10.33 0.0.0.0 area 192.168.10.0
!
router rip
  network 172.19.0.0
```

This configuration enables RIP on the secondary network of E0, allowing Matisse to learn routes from Dali (Figure 9.69). The routes are redistributed into OSPF, (which is no longer running on the secondary address) and assigned an OSPF cost of 10, with the command **redistribute rip metric 10**. See Chapter 11 for more details on redistribution. Figure 9.70 shows that the routes are advertised into the OSPF domain with default external type 2 (E2) metrics; notice that at Rubens the cost of these routes is still 10. Matisse advertises these external destinations with type 5 LSAs, making it an ASBR (Figure 9.71).

Case Study: Stub Areas

Because no type 5 LSAs are being originated within area 1, it can be configured as a stub area. Note that when an attached area is configured as a stub area, the Hellos originated by the router into that area will have E = 0 in the Options field. Any router receiving these Hellos, which is not similarly configured, will drop the packets, and an adjacency will not be established. If there is an existing adjacency, it will be broken. Consequently, if an operational area is going to be reconfigured as a stub area, downtime should be scheduled; routing will be disrupted until all routers are reconfigured.

A stub area is configured by adding the **area stub** command to the OSPF process:

Rubens
```
router ospf 10
  network 0.0.0.0 255.255.255.255 area 1
  area 1 stub
```

Chardin
```
router ospf 20
  network 192.168.30.0 0.0.0.255 area 1
  network 192.168.20.0 0.0.0.255 area 0
  area 1 stub
```

```
Matisse#show ip route
Codes:  C - connected, S - static, I - IGRP, R - RIP, M - mobile, B - BGP
        D - EIGRP, EX - EIGRP external, O - OSPF, IA - OSPF inter area
        N1 - OSPF NSSA external type 1, N2 - OSPF NSSA external type 2
        E1 - OSPF external type 1, E2 - OSPF external type 2, E - EGP
        i - IS-IS, L1 - IS-IS level-1, L2 - IS-IS level-2, * - candidate default
        U - per-user static route, o - ODR

Gateway of last resort is not set

R    192.168.105.0/24 [120/1] via 172.19.35.1, 00:00:13, Ethernet0
R    192.168.100.0/24 [120/1] via 172.19.35.1, 00:00:14, Ethernet0
R    192.168.101.0/24 [120/1] via 172.19.35.1, 00:00:14, Ethernet0
R    192.168.70.0/24 [120/1] via 172.19.35.1, 00:00:14, Ethernet0
R    192.168.90.0/24 [120/1] via 172.19.35.1, 00:00:14, Ethernet0
R    192.168.80.0/24 [120/1] via 172.19.35.1, 00:00:14, Ethernet0
R    192.168.60.0/24 [120/1] via 172.19.35.1, 00:00:14, Ethernet0
     192.168.50.0/32 is subnetted, 1 subnets
C       192.168.50.4 is directly connected, Loopback0
     192.168.10.0/24 is variably subnetted, 3 subnets, 3 masks
C       192.168.10.64/26 is directly connected, Ethernet1
C       192.168.10.32/28 is directly connected, Ethernet0
C       192.168.10.0/27 is directly connected, Serial1
     192.168.30.0/24 is variably subnetted, 2 subnets, 2 masks
O IA    192.168.30.1/32 [110/193] via 192.168.10.1, 01:16:02, Serial1
O IA    192.168.30.8/29 [110/192] via 192.168.10.1, 01:16:02, Serial1
     192.168.20.0/30 is subnetted, 1 subnets
O IA    192.168.20.0 [110/128] via 192.168.10.1, 01:16:02, Serial1
     172.19.0.0/25 is subnetted, 1 subnets
C       172.19.35.0 is directly connected, Ethernet0
```

Figure 9.69

Dali has passed its routing information to Matisse via RIP.

Comparing the link state database of Rubens before (Figure 9.72) and after (Figure 9.73) the configured stub area shows that all autonomous system external LSAs and ASBR summary LSAs have been eliminated from the database. In this case, the size of the database has been reduced by 50%.

When a stub area is attached to an ABR, the router will automatically advertise a default route (destination 0.0.0.0) into the area via a Network Summary LSA. The database summary in Figure

```
Rubens#show ip route
Codes: C - connected, S - static, I - IGRP, R - RIP, M - mobile, B - BGP
       D - EIGRP, EX - EIGRP external, O - OSPF, IA - OSPF inter area
       E1 - OSPF external type 1, E2 - OSPF external type 2, E - EGP
       i - IS-IS, L1 - IS-IS level-1, L2 - IS-IS level-2, * - candidate default
       U - per-user static route

Gateway of last resort is not set

O E2 192.168.105.0/24 [110/10] via 192.168.30.10, 01:21:35, Serial1
O E2 192.168.100.0/24 [110/10] via 192.168.30.10, 01:21:35, Serial1
O E2 192.168.101.0/24 [110/10] via 192.168.30.10, 01:21:35, Serial1
O E2 192.168.70.0/24 [110/10] via 192.168.30.10, 01:21:35, Serial1
O E2 192.168.90.0/24 [110/10] via 192.168.30.10, 01:21:35, Serial1
O E2 192.168.80.0/24 [110/10] via 192.168.30.10, 01:21:35, Serial1
O E2 192.168.60.0/24 [110/10] via 192.168.30.10, 01:21:35, Serial1
     192.168.50.0/24 is subnetted, 1 subnets
C        192.168.50.1 is directly connected, Loopback1
     192.168.10.0/24 is variably subnetted, 2 subnets, 2 masks
O IA     192.168.10.32/28 [110/202] via 192.168.30.10, 02:01:21, Serial1
O IA     192.168.10.0/27 [110/192] via 192.168.30.10, 02:01:22, Serial1
     192.168.30.0/24 is subnetted, 2 subnets
C        192.168.30.0 is directly connected, Ethernet0
C        192.168.30.8 is directly connected, Serial1
     192.168.20.0/24 is subnetted, 1 subnets
O IA     192.168.20.0 [110/128] via 192.168.30.10, 02:01:22, Serial1
     172.19.0.0/16 is subnetted, 1 subnets
O IA     172.19.35.0 [110/202] via 192.168.30.10, 02:01:22, Serial1
Rubens#
```

Figure 9.70

The RIP-learned routes are redistributed into the OSPF autonomous system as path type E2.

```
Rubens#show ip ospf border-routers

OSPF Process 10 internal Routing Table

Codes: i - Intra-area route, I - Inter-area route
i    192.168.50.2 [64] via 192.168.30.10, Serial1, ABR, Area 1, SPF 60
I    192.168.50.4 [192] via 192.168.30.10, Serial1, ASBR, Area 1, SPF 60
Rubens#
```

Figure 9.71

Matisse (RID = 192.168.50.4) is now an ASBR because it is originating autonomous system external LSAs to advertise the external routes.

```
Rubens#show ip ospf database database-summary

            OSPF Router with ID (192.168.50.1) (Process ID 10)

Area ID        Router    Network  Sum-Net  Sum-ASBR   Subtotal  Delete  Maxage
1              2         0        4        1          7         0       0
AS External                                           7         0       0
Total          2         0        4        1          14
Rubens#
```

Figure 9.72

Reubens's database has a total of 14 LSAs before area 1 is configured as a stub area.

```
Rubens#show ip ospf database database-summary

            OSPF Router with ID (192.168.50.1) (Process ID 10)

Area ID        Router    Network  Sum-Net  Sum-ASBR   Subtotal  Delete  Maxage
1              2         0        5        0          7         0       0
AS External                                           0         0       0
Total          2         0        5        0          7
Rubens#
```

Figure 9.73

The stub area configuration eliminates the seven type 5 LSAs and the single type 4 LSA from Rubens's database. One type 3 LSA, which advertises the default route, has been added.

9.73 indicates this additional type 3 LSA. The last entry in Rubens's route table (Figure 9.74) shows the default route advertised by Chardin.

The ABR will advertise a default route with a cost of 1. The cost of the serial link between Rubens and Chardin is 64; Figure 9.74 shows the total cost of the default route to be 64 + 1 = 65. This default cost can be changed with the **area default-cost** command. For example, Chardin can be configured to advertise the default route with a cost of 20 as follows:

```
router ospf 20
  network 192.168.30.0 0.0.0.255 area 1
  network 192.168.20.0 0.0.0.255 area 0
  area 1 stub
  area 1 default-cost 20
```

```
Rubens#show ip route
Codes: C - connected, S - static, I - IGRP, R - RIP, M - mobile, B - BGP
       D - EIGRP, EX - EIGRP external, O - OSPF, IA - OSPF inter area
       E1 - OSPF external type 1, E2 - OSPF external type 2, E - EGP
       i - IS-IS, L1 - IS-IS level-1, L2 - IS-IS level-2, * - candidate default
       U - per-user static route

Gateway of last resort is 192.168.30.10 to network 0.0.0.0

     192.168.50.0/24 is subnetted, 1 subnets
C       192.168.50.1 is directly connected, Loopback1
     192.168.10.0/24 is variably subnetted, 2 subnets, 2 masks
O IA    192.168.10.32/28 [110/202] via 192.168.30.10, 00:05:43, Serial1
O IA    192.168.10.0/27 [110/192] via 192.168.30.10, 00:05:43, Serial1
     192.168.30.0/24 is subnetted, 2 subnets
C       192.168.30.0 is directly connected, Loopback0
C       192.168.30.8 is directly connected, Serial1
     192.168.20.0/24 is subnetted, 1 subnets
O IA    192.168.20.0 [110/128] via 192.168.30.10, 00:05:43, Serial1
     172.19.0.0/16 is subnetted, 1 subnets
O IA    172.19.35.0 [110/202] via 192.168.30.10, 00:05:43, Serial1
O*IA 0.0.0.0/0 [110/65] via 192.168.30.10, 00:05:44, Serial1
Rubens#
```

Figure 9.74

*Rubens's route table shows that all external routes have been eliminated (compare this to Figure 9.70)
and that a default route has been added.*

The resulting cost increase, 64 + 20 = 84, can be seen in Figure
9.75. Changing the cost of the default route has no real benefit
here but may be useful in stub areas with more than one ABR.
Normally, each Internal Router would merely choose the default
route with the lowest cost. By manipulating the advertised cost,
the network administrator could cause all Internal Routers to use
the same ABR. The second ABR, advertising a higher cost, would
be used only if the first were to fail.

```
Rubens#show ip route
Codes: C - connected, S - static, I - IGRP, R - RIP, M - mobile, B - BGP
       D - EIGRP, EX - EIGRP external, O - OSPF, IA - OSPF inter area
       E1 - OSPF external type 1, E2 - OSPF external type 2, E - EGP
       i - IS-IS, L1 - IS-IS level-1, L2 - IS-IS level-2, * - candidate default
       U - per-user static route

Gateway of last resort is 192.168.30.10 to network 0.0.0.0

     192.168.50.0/24 is subnetted, 1 subnets
C       192.168.50.1 is directly connected, Loopback1
     192.168.10.0/24 is variably subnetted, 2 subnets, 2 masks
O IA    192.168.10.32/28 [110/202] via 192.168.30.10, 00:01:08, Serial1
O IA    192.168.10.0/27 [110/192] via 192.168.30.10, 00:01:08, Serial1
     192.168.30.0/24 is subnetted, 2 subnets
C       192.168.30.0 is directly connected, Ethernet0
C       192.168.30.8 is directly connected, Serial1
     192.168.20.0/24 is subnetted, 1 subnets
O IA    192.168.20.0 [110/128] via 192.168.30.10, 00:01:08, Serial1
     172.19.0.0/16 is subnetted, 1 subnets
O IA    172.19.35.0 [110/202] via 192.168.30.10, 00:01:08, Serial1
O*IA 0.0.0.0/0 [110/84] via 192.168.30.10, 00:01:03, Serial1
Rubens#
```

Figure 9.75
Rubens's route table reflects the results of changing the cost of the default route.

Case Study: Totally Stubby Areas

Totally stubby areas are configured by placing the keyword **no-summary** at the end of the **area stub** command. This step is necessary only at the ABR; the Internal Routers use the standard stub area configuration. To make area 1 of the sample internet a totally stubby area, Chardin's configuration would be:

```
router ospf 20
  network 192.168.30.0 0.0.0.255 area 1
  network 192.168.20.0 0.0.0.255 area 0
  area 1 stub no-summary
```

Figure 9.76 shows that the LSAs in Rubens' database have been reduced to three; Figure 9.77 shows the route table.

```
Rubens#show ip ospf database database-summary

      OSPF Router with ID (192.168.50.1) (Process ID 10)

Area ID  Router   Network  Sum-Net  Sum-ASBR  Subtotal  Delete  Maxage
1        2        0        1        0         3         0       0
AS External                                   0         0       0
Total    2        0        1        0         3
Rubens#
```

Figure 9.76
Changing area 1 to a totally stubby area eliminates all but one of the type 3 LSAs (the default route).

```
Rubens#show ip route
Codes: C - connected, S - static, I - IGRP, R - RIP, M - mobile, B - BGP
       D - EIGRP, EX - EIGRP external, O - OSPF, IA - OSPF inter area
       E1 - OSPF external type 1, E2 - OSPF external type 2, E - EGP
       i - IS-IS, L1 - IS-IS level-1, L2 - IS-IS level-2, * - candidate default
       U - per-user static route

Gateway of last resort is 192.168.30.10 to network 0.0.0.0

     192.168.50.0/24 is subnetted, 1 subnets
C       192.168.50.1 is directly connected, Loopback1
     192.168.30.0/24 is subnetted, 2 subnets
C       192.168.30.0 is directly connected, Ethernet0
C       192.168.30.8 is directly connected, Serial1
O*IA 0.0.0.0/0 [110/65] via 192.168.30.10, 00:03:33, Serial1
Rubens#
```

Figure 9.77
A route table in a totally stubby area will contain only intra-area routes and the default route.

Case Study: Not-So-Stubby Areas

The earlier case study, "OSPF and Secondary Interfaces," left off with Matisse accepting routes from Dali via RIP and redistributing them into the OSPF domain (see Figure 9.68). This step makes Matisse an ASBR and by extension makes area 192.168.10.0 ineligible to become a stub or totally stubby area. However, there is no need for AS External LSAs to enter the area from the backbone area; therefore area 192.168.10.0 can be configured as an NSSA. The configuration at Matisse is:

```
router ospf 40
  redistribute rip metric 10
  network 192.168.10.2 0.0.0.0 area 192.168.10.0
  network 192.168.10.33 0.0.0.0 area 192.168.10.0
  area 192.168.10.0 nssa
!
router rip
  network 172.19.0.0
```

The same **area nssa** statement shown here is configured at Goya. Since Goya is an ABR, it will translate type 7 LSAs received on the NSSA-attached interface into type 5 LSAs. These translated LSAs will be flooded into the backbone and hence to the other areas. Comparing the route tables of Goya and Chardin shows that Goya has tagged the external routes as NSSA[26] (Figure 9.78). Chardin has tagged the routes as E2 (Figure 9.79), indicating that they have been learned from type 5 LSAs.

This translation can also be observed by examining Goya's database. Figure 9.80 shows that the database contains both type 7 and type 5 LSAs to the same external routes. The originating router for the type 7 LSAs is Matisse, whereas the originating router for the type 5 LSAs is Goya.

Several configuration options are available for the ABR. First, the **no-summary** option can be used with the **area nssa** command to block the flooding of type 3 and type 4 LSAs into the NSSA. To turn area 192.168.10.0 into a somewhat schizophrenically named "totally stubby not-so-stubby" area, Goya's configuration would be:

```
router ospf 30
  network 192.168.20.0 0.0.0.3 area 0
  network 192.168.10.0 0.0.0.31 area 192.168.10.0
  area 192.168.10.0 nssa no-summary
```

---

[26] *N2 indicates the same metric calculation as E2—that is, only the external cost is used. A subsequent example will demonstrate E1 and N1 metric types.*

```
Goya#show ip route
Codes: C - connected, S - static, I - IGRP, R - RIP, M - mobile, B - BGP
       D - EIGRP, EX - EIGRP external, O - OSPF, IA - OSPF inter area
       N1 - OSPF NSSA external type 1, N2 - OSPF NSSA external type 2
       E1 - OSPF external type 1, E2 - OSPF external type 2, E - EGP
       i - IS-IS, L1 - IS-IS level-1, L2 - IS-IS level-2, * - candidate default
       U - per-user static route, o - ODR

Gateway of last resort is not set

O N2 192.168.105.0/24 [110/10] via 192.168.10.2, 00:38:32, Serial1
O N2 192.168.100.0/24 [110/10] via 192.168.10.2, 00:38:33, Serial1
O N2 192.168.101.0/24 [110/10] via 192.168.10.2, 00:38:33, Serial1
O N2 192.168.70.0/24 [110/10] via 192.168.10.2, 00:38:33, Serial1
O N2 192.168.90.0/24 [110/10] via 192.168.10.2, 00:38:33, Serial1
O N2 192.168.80.0/24 [110/10] via 192.168.10.2, 00:38:33, Serial1
O N2 192.168.60.0/24 [110/10] via 192.168.10.2, 00:38:33, Serial1
     192.168.50.0/32 is subnetted, 1 subnets
C       192.168.50.3 is directly connected, Loopback0
     192.168.10.0/24 is variably subnetted, 2 subnets, 2 masks
O       192.168.10.32/28 [110/74] via 192.168.10.2, 00:38:33, Serial1
C       192.168.10.0/27 is directly connected, Serial1
     192.168.30.0/24 is variably subnetted, 2 subnets, 2 masks
O IA    192.168.30.1/32 [110/129] via 192.168.20.1, 00:38:33, Serial0
O IA    192.168.30.8/29 [110/128] via 192.168.20.1, 00:38:35, Serial0
     192.168.20.0/30 is subnetted, 1 subnets
C       192.168.20.0 is directly connected, Serial0
```

Figure 9.78

The external routes learned from Matisse are tagged as NSSA routes at Goya.

Matisse's route table (Figure 9.81) shows the elimination of all inter-area routes and the addition of a default route advertised by Goya.

In Figure 9.82, the link to Dali has been moved from Matisse to Goya; the IP address has also moved. Goya is now an ASBR redistributing RIP-learned routes into OSPF.

When an ABR is also an ASBR and is connected to a not-so-stubby area, the default behavior is to advertise the redistributed routes into the NSSA as shown in Figure 9.83.

```
Chardin#show ip route
Codes:   C - connected, S - static, I - IGRP, R - RIP, M - mobile, B - BGP
         D - EIGRP, EX - EIGRP external, O - OSPF, IA - OSPF inter area
         E1 - OSPF external type 1, E2 - OSPF external type 2, E - EGP
         i - IS-IS, L1 - IS-IS level-1, L2 - IS-IS level-2, * - candidate default
         U - per-user static route

Gateway of last resort is not set

O E2 192.168.105.0/24 [110/10] via 192.168.20.2, 00:00:58, Serial0
O E2 192.168.100.0/24 [110/10] via 192.168.20.2, 00:00:58, Serial0
O E2 192.168.101.0/24 [110/10] via 192.168.20.2, 00:00:58, Serial0
O E2 192.168.70.0/24 [110/10] via 192.168.20.2, 00:00:58, Serial0
O E2 192.168.90.0/24 [110/10] via 192.168.20.2, 00:00:58, Serial0
O E2 192.168.80.0/24 [110/10] via 192.168.20.2, 00:00:58, Serial0
O E2 192.168.60.0/24 [110/10] via 192.168.20.2, 00:00:58, Serial0
     192.168.50.0/24 is subnetted, 1 subnets
C        192.168.50.2 is directly connected, Loopback0
     192.168.10.0/24 is variably subnetted, 2 subnets, 2 masks
O IA     192.168.10.32/28 [110/138] via 192.168.20.2, 00:00:59, Serial0
O IA     192.168.10.0/27 [110/128] via 192.168.20.2, 00:01:10, Serial0
     192.168.30.0/24 is variably subnetted, 2 subnets, 2 masks
O        192.168.30.1/32 [110/65] via 192.168.30.9, 00:01:30, Serial1
C        192.168.30.8/29 is directly connected, Serial1
     192.168.20.0/24 is subnetted, 1 subnets
C        192.168.20.0 is directly connected, Serial0
```

Figure 9.79
Chardin has tagged the same routes as E2, indicating they have been learned from autonomous system external LSAs.

The default redistribution may be turned off on an ABR/ASBR by adding the statement **no-redistribution** to the **area nssa** command. In the sample internet, no types 3, 4, 5, or 7 LSAs should be sent into area 192.168.10.0 from the ABR. The desired redistribution is accomplished by the following configuration at Goya:[27]

---

[27] *Note the metric-type 1 statement in the redistribution command. This statement causes the external destinations to be advertised with an E1 metric; within the NSSA, the metric type becomes N1, as shown in Figure 9.82.*

```
Type-7 AS External Link States (Area 192.168.10.0)

Link ID         ADV Router     Age    Seq#           Checksum  Tag
192.168.60.0    192.168.50.4   1476   0x800000E6     0xD907    0
192.168.70.0    192.168.50.4   1485   0x800000E6     0x6B6B    0
192.168.80.0    192.168.50.4   1494   0x800000E6     0xFCCF    0
192.168.90.0    192.168.50.4   1503   0x800000E6     0x8E34    0
192.168.100.0   192.168.50.4   1512   0x800000E6     0x2098    0
192.168.101.0   192.168.50.4   1521   0x800000E6     0x15A2    0
192.168.105.0   192.168.50.4   1530   0x800000E6     0xE8CA    0

             Type-5 AS External Link States

Link ID         ADV Router     Age    Seq#           Checksum  Tag
192.168.60.0    192.168.50.3   2695   0x80000001     0x4091    0
192.168.70.0    192.168.50.3   2704   0x80000001     0xD1F5    0
192.168.80.0    192.168.50.3   2713   0x80000001     0x635A    0
192.168.90.0    192.168.50.3   2722   0x80000001     0xF4BE    0
192.168.100.0   192.168.50.3   2731   0x80000001     0x8623    0
192.168.101.0   192.168.50.3   2740   0x80000001     0x7B2D    0
192.168.105.0   192.168.50.3   2749   0x80000001     0x4F55    0
Goya#
```

Figure 9.80

Goya's link state database indicates that the type 7 LSAs from Matisse (192.168.50.4) have been translated into type 5 LSAs by Goya (192.168.50.3).

```
interface Ethernet0
  ip address 172.19.35.15 255.255.255.128
!
router ospf 30
  redistribute rip metric 10 metric-type 1
  network 192.168.20.0 0.0.0.3 area 0
  network 192.168.10.0 0.0.0.31 area 192.168.10.0
  area 192.168.10.0 nssa no-redistribution no-summary
!
router rip
  network 172.19.0.0
```

```
Matisse#show ip route
Codes: C - connected, S - static, I - IGRP, R - RIP, M - mobile, B - BGP
       D - EIGRP, EX - EIGRP external, O - OSPF, IA - OSPF inter area
       N1 - OSPF NSSA external type 1, N2 - OSPF NSSA external type 2
       E1 - OSPF external type 1, E2 - OSPF external type 2, E - EGP
       i - IS-IS, L1 - IS-IS level-1, L2 - IS-IS level-2, * - candidate default
       U - per-user static route, o - ODR

Gateway of last resort is 192.168.10.1 to network 0.0.0.0

R    192.168.105.0/24 [120/1] via 172.19.35.1, 00:00:13, Ethernet0
R    192.168.100.0/24 [120/1] via 172.19.35.1, 00:00:13, Ethernet0
R    192.168.101.0/24 [120/1] via 172.19.35.1, 00:00:13, Ethernet0
R    192.168.70.0/24 [120/1] via 172.19.35.1, 00:00:13, Ethernet0
R    192.168.90.0/24 [120/1] via 172.19.35.1, 00:00:13, Ethernet0
R    192.168.80.0/24 [120/1] via 172.19.35.1, 00:00:13, Ethernet0
R    192.168.60.0/24 [120/1] via 172.19.35.1, 00:00:13, Ethernet0
     192.168.50.0/32 is subnetted, 1 subnets
C       192.168.50.4 is directly connected, Loopback0
     192.168.10.0/24 is variably subnetted, 3 subnets, 3 masks
C       192.168.10.64/26 is directly connected, Loopback1
C       192.168.10.32/28 is directly connected, Ethernet0
C       192.168.10.0/27 is directly connected, Serial1
     172.19.0.0/25 is subnetted, 1 subnets
C       172.19.35.0 is directly connected, Ethernet0
O*IA 0.0.0.0/0 [110/65] via 192.168.10.1, 00:36:50, Serial1
Matisse#
```

Figure 9.81

All inter-area routes have been replaced with a default route to the ABR.

Here the **area nssa** command blocks type 5 LSAs from entering the area through Goya; **no-redistribution** blocks type 7 LSAs, and **no-summary** blocks types 3 and 4. As before, the **no-summary** command also causes Goya to send a single type 3 LSA into the area to advertise a default route. Figure 9.84 shows Matisse's route table after type 7 redistribution is disabled at Goya. Note that the external networks are still reachable, even though they are not in the table, because of the default route.

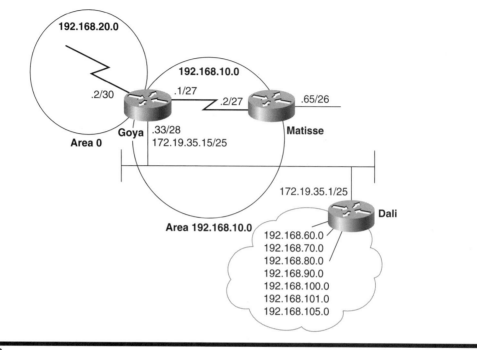

Figure 9.82

The link to Dali has moved to Goya, which now speaks RIP to Dali and redistributes the learned routes into OSPF.

In the final example, Goya is to allow types 3 and 4 LSAs into the NSSA, but not types 5 and 7. The problem is that when the **no-summary** statement is removed, the ABR will no longer originate a type 3 LSA advertising a default route. Without a default route, the exterior destinations will not be reachable from within the NSSA. The statement **default-information-originate**, added to the **area nssa** command, will cause the ABR to advertise a default

```
Matisse#show ip route
Codes: C - connected, S - static, I - IGRP, R - RIP, M - mobile, B - BGP
       D - EIGRP, EX - EIGRP external, O - OSPF, IA - OSPF inter area
       N1 - OSPF NSSA external type 1, N2 - OSPF NSSA external type 2
       E1 - OSPF external type 1, E2 - OSPF external type 2, E - EGP
       i - IS-IS, L1 - IS-IS level-1, L2 - IS-IS level-2, * - candidate default
       U - per-user static route, o - ODR

Gateway of last resort is 192.168.10.1 to network 0.0.0.0

O N1 192.168.105.0/24 [110/74] via 192.168.10.1, 00:03:03, Serial1
O N1 192.168.100.0/24 [110/74] via 192.168.10.1, 00:03:03, Serial1
O N1 192.168.101.0/24 [110/74] via 192.168.10.1, 00:03:03, Serial1
O N1 192.168.70.0/24 [110/74] via 192.168.10.1, 00:03:03, Serial1
O N1 192.168.90.0/24 [110/74] via 192.168.10.1, 00:03:03, Serial1
O N1 192.168.80.0/24 [110/74] via 192.168.10.1, 00:03:03, Serial1
O N1 192.168.60.0/24 [110/74] via 192.168.10.1, 00:03:03, Serial1
     192.168.50.0/32 is subnetted, 1 subnets
C       192.168.50.4 is directly connected, Loopback0
     192.168.10.0/24 is variably subnetted, 3 subnets, 3 masks
C       192.168.10.64/26 is directly connected, Loopback1
C       192.168.10.32/28 is directly connected, Ethernet0
C       192.168.10.0/27 is directly connected, Serial1
O*IA 0.0.0.0/0 [110/65] via 192.168.10.1, 00:03:04, Serial1
Matisse#
```

Figure 9.83

An ABR that is also an ASBR will advertise the external routes into an NSSA with type 7 LSAs. In this example, Goya is advertising the external routes with an N1 metric type.

route into the NSSA—this time, with a type 7 LSA. Using this statement, Goya's OSPF configuration is:

```
router ospf 30
  redistribute rip metric 10 metric-type 1
  network 192.168.20.0 0.0.0.3 area 0
  network 192.168.10.0 0.0.0.31 area 192.168.10.0
  area 192.168.10.0 nssa no-redistribution default-information-originate
```

Figure 9.85 shows Matisse's route table after the reconfiguration. The table contains inter-area routes and a default route with an N2 tag indicating that the route was learned from a type 7 LSA.

```
Matisse#show ip route
Codes: C - connected, S - static, I - IGRP, R - RIP, M - mobile, B - BGP
       D - EIGRP, EX - EIGRP external, O - OSPF, IA - OSPF inter area
       N1 - OSPF NSSA external type 1, N2 - OSPF NSSA external type 2
       E1 - OSPF external type 1, E2 - OSPF external type 2, E - EGP
       i - IS-IS, L1 - IS-IS level-1, L2 - IS-IS level-2, * - candidate default
       U - per-user static route, o - ODR

Gateway of last resort is 192.168.10.1 to network 0.0.0.0

     192.168.50.0/32 is subnetted, 1 subnets
C       192.168.50.4 is directly connected, Loopback0
     192.168.10.0/24 is variably subnetted, 3 subnets, 3 masks
C       192.168.10.64/26 is directly connected, Loopback1
C       192.168.10.32/28 is directly connected, Ethernet0
C       192.168.10.0/27 is directly connected, Serial1
O*IA 0.0.0.0/0 [110/65] via 192.168.10.1, 00:00:10, Serial1
Matisse#
```

Figure 9.84

After **no-redistribution** is added to Goya's **area nssa** command, the route table of Figure 9.83 no longer contains routes learned from type 7 LSAs.

Case Study: Address Summarization

Although stub areas conserve resources within non-backbone areas by preventing certain LSAs from entering, these areas do nothing to conserve resources on the backbone. All addresses within an area are still advertised out to the backbone. This situation is where address summarization can help. Like stub areas, address summarization conserves resources by reducing the number of LSAs flooded. It also conserves resources by hiding instabilities. For example, a "flapping" subnet will cause LSAs to be flooded throughout the internetwork at each state transition. However, if that subnet address is subsumed by a summary address, the individual subnet and its instabilities are no longer advertised.

```
Matisse#show ip route
Codes: C - connected, S - static, I - IGRP, R - RIP, M - mobile, B - BGP
       D - EIGRP, EX - EIGRP external, O - OSPF, IA - OSPF inter area
       N1 - OSPF NSSA external type 1, N2 - OSPF NSSA external type 2
       E1 - OSPF external type 1, E2 - OSPF external type 2, E - EGP
       i - IS-IS, L1 - IS-IS level-1, L2 - IS-IS level-2, * - candidate default
       U - per-user static route, o - ODR

Gateway of last resort is 192.168.10.1 to network 0.0.0.0

     192.168.50.0/32 is subnetted, 1 subnets
C       192.168.50.4 is directly connected, Loopback0
     192.168.10.0/24 is variably subnetted, 3 subnets, 3 masks
C       192.168.10.64/26 is directly connected, Loopback1
C       192.168.10.32/28 is directly connected, Ethernet0
C       192.168.10.0/27 is directly connected, Serial1
     192.168.30.0/24 is variably subnetted, 2 subnets, 2 masks
O IA    192.168.30.1/32 [110/193] via 192.168.10.1, 00:00:13, Serial1
O IA    192.168.30.8/29 [110/192] via 192.168.10.1, 00:00:13, Serial1
     192.168.20.0/30 is subnetted, 1 subnets
O IA    192.168.20.0 [110/128] via 192.168.10.1, 00:00:14, Serial1
O*N2 0.0.0.0/0 [110/1] via 192.168.10.1, 00:00:14, Serial1
Matisse#
```

Figure 9.85

*Adding the **default-information-originate** statement to the **area nssa** command causes the ABR to advertise a default route into an NSSA.*

Inter-area and external router summarization

Cisco's OSPF can perform two types of address summarization: inter-area summarization and external route summarization. *Inter-area summarization* is, as the name implies, the summarization of addresses between areas; this type of summarization is always configured on ABRs. *External route summarization* allows a set of external addresses to be redistributed into an OSPF domain as a summary address and is configured on ASBRs. Inter-area summarization is covered in this section, and external route summarization is covered in Chapter 11.

In Figure 9.86, area 15 contains eight subnets: 10.0.0.0/16 through 10.7.0.0/16. Figure 9.87 shows that these addresses can be represented with the single summary address 10.0.0.0/13.

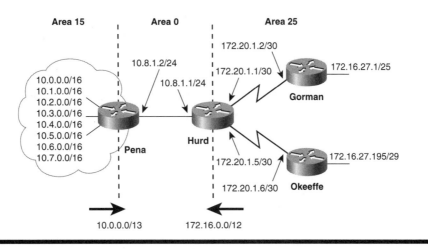

Figure 9.86

The addresses in areas 15 and 25 can summarized into the backbone area.

```
11111111111111110000000000000000   =  16-bit mask
00001010000000000000000000000000   =  10.0.0.0/16
00001010000000010000000000000000   =  10.1.0.0/16
00001010000000100000000000000000   =  10.2.0.0/16
00001010000000110000000000000000   =  10.3.0.0/16
00001010000001000000000000000000   =  10.4.0.0/16
00001010000001010000000000000000   =  10.5.0.0/16
00001010000001100000000000000000   =  10.6.0.0/16
00001010000001110000000000000000   =  10.7.0.0/16
00001010000000000000000000000000   =  10.0.0.0/13
```

Figure 9.87

The summary address 10.0.0.0/13 represents the range of addresses from 10.0.0.0/16 to 10.7.0.0/16.

An ABR can be configured to advertise a summary address either into the backbone area or into a non-backbone area. Best practice dictates that a non-backbone area's addresses should be summarized into the backbone by its own ABR, as opposed to having all other ABRs summarize the area into their areas. Then, from the backbone area, the summary will be advertised across the backbone and into the other areas. This both simplifies the router configurations and reduces the size of the LS database in the backbone.

The **area range** command specifies the area to which the summary address belongs, the summary address, and the address mask. Recall from Chapter 8, "Enhanced Interior Gateway Routing Protocol (EIGRP)," that when a summary route is configured for EIGRP, a route to the null interface is automatically entered into the route table to prevent black holes and route loops.[28] Unlike EIGRP, OSPF does not enter this route automatically. Therefore, whenever you are configuring summary routes within an OSPF domain, be sure to add a static route for the summary address, pointing to the null interface.

Pena's OSPF configuration is:

```
router ospf 1
  network 10.0.0.0 0.7.255.255 area 15
  network 10.8.0.0 0.7.255.255 area 0
  area 15 range 10.0.0.0 255.248.0.0
!
ip route 10.0.0.0 255.248.0.0 Null0
```

Figure 9.87 shows that the range of addresses represented by 10.0.0.0/13 is contiguous—that is, the three bits that are summarized constitute every combination from 000 to 111. The addresses in area 25 are different. These do not form a contiguous range. They may, however, still be summarized with the following configuration at Hurd:

```
router ospf 1
  network 10.8.0.0 0.0.255.255 area 0
  network 172.20.0.0 0.0.255.255 area 25
  area 25 range 172.16.0.0 255.240.0.0
!
ip route 172.16.0.0 255.240.0.0 Null0
```

This summary will work, even if some of the addresses in the range appear elsewhere in the internetwork. In Figure 9.88, network 172.17.0.0/16 is in area 15, although it belongs to the set of addresses being summarized from area 25. Pena advertises this

---

[28] *The reasons for this route are discussed in more detail, with examples, in Chapters 11, "Route Redistribution," and 12, "Default Routes and On-Demand Routing."*

address into the backbone area, where Hurd learns it and advertises it into area 25. The accompanying mask is more specific (that is, longer) than the mask of the summary address 172.16.0.0/12; because OSPF is classless, it will route destination addresses belonging to 172.17.0.0 to the correct destination.

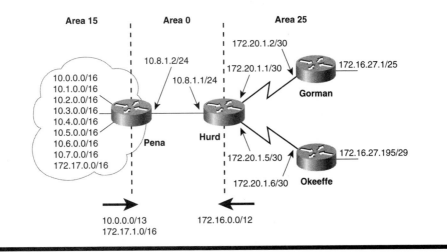

Figure 9.88

Network 172.17.0.0 is in area 15, although it is within the range of addresses summarized by 172.16.0.0/12.

Although the address configuration of Figure 9.88 will work, it is an undesirable design practice. The point of summarization is to conserve resources; network 172.17.0.0/16 must be advertised across the backbone independently of 172.16.0.0/12. Such a design also creates the potential for route loops if default addresses are used. This problem is discussed in Chapter 12, "Default Routes and On-Demand Routing."

Notice also in Figure 9.88 that subnets 172.16.27.0/25 (at Gorman) and 172.16.27.192/29 (at Okeeffe) are discontiguous. Again because OSPF is a classless routing protocol, Gorman and Okeeffe do not act as network border routers. The subnets and their masks are advertised into network 172.20.0.0, and no routing ambiguities will occur.

Case Study: Authentication

OSPF packets can be authenticated to prevent inadvertent or intentional introduction of bad routing information. Table 9.8 lists the types of authentication available. Null authentication (type 0), which means no authentication information is included in the packet header, is the default. Authentication using simple clear-text passwords (type 1) or MD5 cryptographic checksums (type 2) can be configured. When authentication is configured, it must be configured for an entire area.

If increased network security is the objective, type 1 authentication should be used only when devices within an area cannot support the more secure type 2 authentication. Clear-text authentication leaves the internetwork vulnerable to a "sniffer attack," in which packets are captured by a protocol analyzer and the passwords are read (see Chapter 7 and especially Figure 7.8). However, type 1 authentication can be useful when performing OSPF reconfigurations. For example, separate passwords can be used on "old" OSPF routers and "new" OSPF routers sharing a common broadcast network to prevent them from talking to each other.

To configure type 1 authentication for an area, the command **ip ospf authentication-key** is used to assign a password of up to eight octets to each interface attached to the area. The passwords do not have to be the same throughout the area, but must be the same between neighbors. Type 1 authentication is then enabled by entering the **area authentication** command to the OSPF configuration.

Referring to Figure 9.88, type 1 authentication is enabled for areas 0 and 25. Hurd's configuration is:

```
interface Ethernet0
  ip address 10.8.1.1 255.255.255.0
  ip ospf authentication santafe
!
interface Serial0
  ip address 172.20.1.1 255.255.255.252
  ip ospf authentication taos
!
interface Serial1
  ip address 172.20.1.5 255.255.255.252
  ip ospf authentication abiquiu
!
router ospf 1
  network 10.8.0.0 0.0.255.255 area 0
  network 172.20.0.0 0.0.255.255 area 25
  area 25 range 172.16.0.0 255.240.0.0
  area 0 authentication
  area 25 authentication
```

The password "santafe" is used between Hurd and Pena; "taos" is used between Hurd and Gorman, and "abiquiu" is used between Hurd and Okeeffe.

The MD5 algorithm, used by type 2 authentication, computes a hash value from the OSPF packet contents and a password (or key). This hash value is transmitted in the packet, along with a key ID and a non-decreasing sequence number. The receiver, knowing the same password, will calculate its own hash value. If nothing in the message has changed, the receiver's hash value should match the sender's value transmitted with the message. The key ID allows routers to reference multiple passwords, making password changes easier and more secure. An example of password migration is included in this case study. The sequence number prevents "replay attacks," in which OSPF packets are captured, modified, and retransmitted to a router.

To configure type 2 authentication for an area, the command **ip ospf message-digest-key md5** assigns a password of up to 16 bytes and key ID between 1 and 255 to each interface attached to the area. Like type 1, the passwords do not have to be the same throughout the area, but both the key ID and the password must be the same between neighbors. Type 2 authentication is then enabled by entering the **area authentication message-digest** command to the OSPF configuration.

Hurd is configured to use type 2 authentication as follows:

```
interface Ethernet0
  ip address 10.8.1.1 255.255.255.0
  ip ospf message-digest-key 5 md5 santafe
!
interface Serial0
  ip address 172.20.1.1 255.255.255.252
  ip ospf message-digest-key 10 md5 taos
!
interface Serial1
  ip address 172.20.1.5 255.255.255.252
  ip ospf message-digest-key 15 md5 abiquiu
!
router ospf 1
  network 10.8.0.0 0.0.255.255 area 0
  network 172.20.0.0 0.0.255.255 area 25
  area 25 range 172.16.0.0 255.240.0.0
  area 0 authentication message-digest
  area 25 authentication message-digest
```

Changing passwords without disabling authentication

The key allows the password to be changed without having to disable authentication. For example, to change the password between Hurd and Okeeffe, the new password would be configured with a different key. Hurd's configuration would be:

```
interface Serial1
  ip address 172.20.1.5 255.255.255.252
  ip ospf message-digest-key 15 md5 abiquiu
  ip ospf message-digest-key 20 md5 steiglitz
```

Hurd will now send duplicate copies of each OSPF packet out S1; one will be authenticated with key 15, the other with key 20.

When Hurd begins receiving OSPF packets from Okeeffe authenticated with key 20, it will stop sending packets with key 15. Once the new key is in use, the old key can be removed from both routers with the command **no ip ospf message-digest-key 15 md5 abiquiu.**

The passwords in an operational internetwork should never be as predictable as the ones used in these examples. Adding the command **service password-encryption** to the configuration file of all routers using authentication is also wise. This change will cause the router to encrypt the passwords in any display of the configuration file, thereby guarding against the password being learned by simply observing a text copy of the router's configuration. With encryption, a display of Hurd's configuration would include:

```
service password-encryption
!
interface Ethernet0
  ip address 10.8.1.1 255.255.255.0
  ip ospf message-digest-key 5 md5 7 001712008105A0D03
!
interface Serial0
  ip address 172.20.1.1 255.255.255.252
  ip ospf message-digest-key 10 md5 7 03105A0415
!
interface Serial1
  ip address 172.20.1.5 255.255.255.252
  ip ospf message-digest-key 20 md5 7 070E23455F1C1010
```

Case Study: Virtual Links

Figure 9.89 shows an internetwork with a poorly designed backbone area. If the link between routers Hokusai and Hiroshige fails, the backbone will be partitioned. As a result, routers Sesshiu and Okyo will be unable to communicate with each other. If these two routers are ABRs to separate areas, inter-area traffic between those areas will also be blocked.

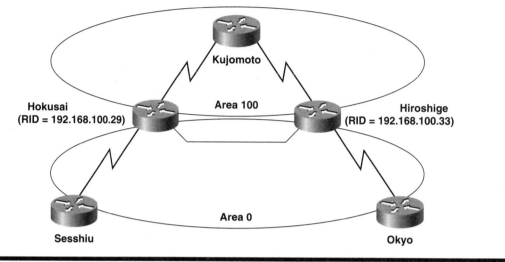

Figure 9.89
A failure of the link between Hokusai and Hiroshige will partition the backbone area.

The best solution to this vulnerability is to add another link to the backbone area—between Sesshiu and Okyo, for instance. An interim solution, until the backbone can be improved, is to create a virtual link between Hokusai and Hiroshige through area 100.

Virtual links are always created between ABRs, at least one of which must be connected to area 0.[29] At each ABR, the **area virtual-link** command, added to the OSPF configuration, specifies the area through which the virtual link will transit and the Router ID of the ABR at the far end of the link. A virtual link is configured between Hokusai and Hiroshige as follows:

Hokusai

```
router ospf 10
  network 192.168.100.1 0.0.0.0 area 0
  network 192.168.100.29 0.0.0.0 area 0
  network 192.168.100.21 0.0.0.0 area 100
  area 100 virtual-link 192.168.100.33
```

---

[29] *When a virtual link is used to connect an area to the backbone through a non-backbone area, one of the ABRs will be between the two non-backbone areas.*

Hiroshige

```
router ospf 10
  network 192.168.100.2 0.0.0.0 area 0
  network 192.168.100.33 0.0.0.0 area 0
  network 192.168.100.25 0.0.0.0 area 100
  area 100 virtual-link 192.168.100.29
```

Packets will normally travel between Sesshiu and Okyo on the backbone link between Hokusai and Hiroshige. If that link fails, the virtual link will be used. Although each router sees the link as an unnumbered point-to-point network (Figure 9.90), in reality the packets are being routed via Kujomoto.

```
Hokusai#show ip ospf virtual-link
Virtual Link OSPF_VL1 to router 192.168.100.33 is up
  Run as demand circuit
  DoNotAge LSA not allowed (Number of DCbitless LSA is 2).
  Transit area 100, via interface Serial0, Cost of using 128
  Transmit Delay is 1 sec, State POINT_TO_POINT,
  Timer intervals configured, Hello 10, Dead 40, Wait 40, Retransmit 5
    Hello due in 00:00:00
    Adjacency State FULL (Hello suppressed)
Hokusai#
```

Figure 9.90

The state of a virtual link can be observed with the command **show ip ospf virtual-link**.

Case Study: OSPF on NBMA Networks

Non-broadcast multi-access networks such as X.25, frame relay, and ATM present a problem for OSPF. *Multi-access* means that the NBMA "cloud" is a single network to which multiple devices are attached, the same as Ethernet or Token Ring networks (Figure 9.91). But unlike Ethernet and Token Ring, which are broadcast networks, *non-broadcast* means a packet sent into the network might not be seen by all other routers attached to the network. Because an NBMA network is multi-access, OSPF will want to elect a DR and BDR. But since an NBMA network is non-broadcast, there is no guarantee that all attached routers will receive the Hellos of all other routers. Therefore, all routers may not automatically learn about all its neighbors, and DR election would not function correctly.

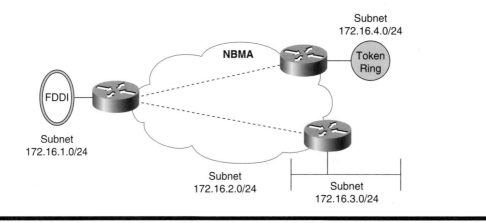

Figure 9.91

Routing protocols view NBMA networks as a single subnet to which multiple devices are connected. But when an NBMA network is partially meshed, as it is here, not all attached routers have direct connectivity with all other attached routers.

This section examines several solutions to the NBMA problem. The selection of a particular solution depends on the characteristics of the internetwork upon which the solution is to be implemented.

The oldest solution, pertinent to pre-10.0 versions of the Cisco IOS, is to manually identify each router's neighbors and establish the DR, using the **neighbor** command. Figure 9.92 shows a frame relay network with four attached routers.

Because of the partially-meshed hub-and-spoke configuration of the PVCs in Figure 9.92, Rembrandt must become the DR. As the hub, it is the only router directly connected to all the other routers. The configurations of the four routers are:

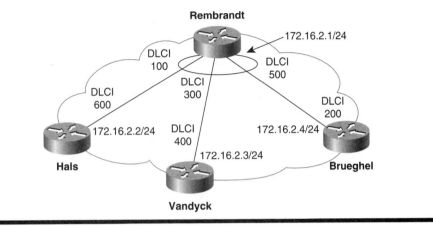

Figure 9.92

Several options exist for configuring OSPF on this NBMA network.

Rembrandt

```
interface Serial0
  encapsulation frame-relay
  ip address 172.16.2.1 255.255.255.0
  frame-relay map ip 172.16.2.2 100
  frame-realy map ip 172.16.2.3 300
  frame-relay map ip 172.16.2.4 500
!
router ospf 1
  network 172.16.0.0 0.0.255.255 area 0
  neighbor 172.16.2.2
  neighbor 172.16.2.3
  neighbor 172.16.2.4
```

Hals

```
interface Serial0
  encapsulation frame-relay
  ip address 172.16.2.2 255.255.255.0
  frame-relay map ip 172.16.2.1 600
  frame-relay map ip 172.16.2.3 600
  frame-relay map ip 172.16.2.4 600
!
router ospf 1
  network 172.16.0.0 0.0.255.255 area 0
  neighbor 172.16.2.1 priority 10
```

Vandyck

```
interface Serial0
  encapsulation frame-relay
  ip address 172.16.2.3 255.255.255.0
  frame-relay map ip 172.16.2.1 400
  frame-relay map ip 172.16.2.2 400
  frame-relay map ip 172.16.2.4 400
!
router ospf 1
  network 172.16.0.0 0.0.255.255 area 0
  neighbor 172.16.2.1 priority 10
```

Brueghel

```
interface Serial0
  encapsulation frame-relay
  ip address 172.16.2.4 255.255.255.0
  frame-relay map ip 172.16.2.1 200
  frame-relay map ip 172.16.2.2 200
  frame-relay map ip 172.16.2.3 200
!
router ospf 1
  network 172.16.0.0 0.0.255.255 area 0
  neighbor 172.16.2.1 priority 10
```

The **neighbor** command configures Rembrandt with the IP addresses of the interfaces of its three neighbors. The default priority is zero; by not changing the default at Rembrandt, none of its neighbors is eligible to become the DR or BDR.

The other three routers are configured with only Rembrandt as a neighbor; the priority is set to 10, which means Rembrandt will become the DR. By making Rembrandt the DR, the PVCs exactly emulate the adjacencies that would have formed if the four routers had been connected to a broadcast multi-access network. OSPF packets will now be unicast to the configured neighbor addresses.

To repeat, the **neighbor** command is necessary only with old (pre-10.0) versions of IOS. A newer solution is to use the **ip ospf network** command to change the default OSPF network type.

One option with this command is to change the network type to broadcast, with **ip ospf network broadcast** entered at every frame relay interface. This change will cause the NBMA cloud to be viewed as a broadcast network; the configuration of the four routers is:

Rembrandt

```
interface Serial0
  encapsulation frame-relay
  ip address 172.16.2.1 255.255.255.0
  ip ospf network broadcast
  ip ospf priority 10
  frame-relay map ip 172.16.2.2 100 broadcast
  frame-realy map ip 172.16.2.3 300 broadcast
  frame-relay map ip 172.16.2.4 500 broadcast
!
router ospf 1
  network 172.16.0.0 0.0.255.255 area 0
```

Hals

```
interface Serial0
  encapsulation frame-relay
  ip address 172.16.2.2 255.255.255.0
  ip ospf network broadcast
  ip ospf priority 0
  frame-relay map ip 172.16.2.1 600 broadcast
  frame-relay map ip 172.16.2.3 600 broadcast
  frame-relay map ip 172.16.2.4 600 broadcast
!
router ospf 1
  network 172.16.0.0 0.0.255.255 area 0
```

Vandyck

```
interface Serial0
  encapsulation frame-relay
  ip address 172.16.2.3 255.255.255.0
  ip ospf network broadcast
  ip ospf priority 0
  frame-relay map ip 172.16.2.1 400 broadcast
  frame-relay map ip 172.16.2.2 400 broadcast
  frame-relay map ip 172.16.2.4 400 broadcast
!
router ospf 1
  network 172.16.0.0 0.0.255.255 area 0
```

Brueghel
```
interface Serial0
  encapsulation frame-relay
  ip address 172.16.2.4 255.255.255.0
  ip ospf network broadcast
  ip ospf priority 0
  frame-relay map ip 172.16.2.1 200 broadcast
  frame-relay map ip 172.16.2.2 200 broadcast
  frame-relay map ip 172.16.2.3 200 broadcast
!
router ospf 1
  network 172.16.0.0 0.0.255.255 area 0
```

Note in this example that the priority of Rembrandt's interface is set to 10, and the priority of the other interfaces is set to 0. This will, again, ensure that Rembrandt is the DR. Note also that the static frame relay mapping commands are set to forward broadcast and multicast addresses.

An alternative to influencing the DR election is to implement a fully meshed topology in which every router has a PVC to every other router. From the standpoint of the router, this solution is actually the most efficient of all the NBMA implementation alternatives. The obvious drawback of this approach is monetary cost. If there are n routers, $n(n - 1)/2$ PVCs will be necessary to create a fully meshed topology. For example, the 4 routers of Figure 9.92 would need 6 PVCs for a full mesh; 16 routers would require 120 PVCs.

Another option is to avoid the DR/BDR election process altogether, by changing the network type to point-to-multipoint. Point-to-multipoint networks treat the PVCs as a collection of point-to-point links; therefore, no DR/BDR election takes place. In multivendor environments, point-to-multipoint may be the only alternative to broadcast networks.

In the following configurations, the OSPF network type associated with each interface is changed to point-to-multipoint:

Rembrandt

```
interface Serial0
  encapsulation frame-relay
  ip address 172.16.2.1 255.255.255.0
  ip ospf network point-to-multipoint
!
router ospf 1
  network 172.16.0.0 0.0.255.255 area 0
```

Hals

```
interface Serial0
  encapsulation frame-relay
  ip address 172.16.2.2 255.255.255.0
  ip ospf network point-to-multipoint
!
router ospf 1
  network 172.16.0.0 0.0.255.255 area 0
```

Vandyck

```
interface Serial0
  encapsulation frame-relay
  ip address 172.16.2.3 255.255.255.0
  ip ospf network point-to-multipoint
!
router ospf 1
  network 172.16.0.0 0.0.255.255 area 0
```

Brueghel

```
interface Serial0
  encapsulation frame-relay
  ip address 172.16.2.4 255.255.255.0
  ip ospf network point-to-multipoint
!
router ospf 1
  network 172.16.0.0 0.0.255.255 area 0
```

These configurations take advantage of the frame relay inverse ARP function to dynamically map network-level addresses to the DLCIs, instead of using the static map commands shown in the previous examples. Static maps can still be used if desired.

The OSPF point-to-multipoint network type treats the underlying network as a collection of point-to-point links rather than a multi-access network, and OSPF packets are multicast to the neighbors. This situation can be problematic for networks whose connections are dynamic, such as frame relay SVCs or ATM SVCs.

Beginning with IOS 11.3AA, this problem can be solved by declaring a network to be both point-to-multipoint and non-broadcast:

Rembrandt

```
interface Serial0
  ip address 172.16.2.1 255.255.255.0
  encapsulation frame-relay
  ip ospf network point-to-multipoint non-broadcast
  map-group Leiden
  frame-relay lmi-type q933a
  frame-relay svc
!
router ospf 1
  network 172.16.0.0 0.0.255.255 area 0
  neighbor 172.16.2.2 cost 30
  neighbor 172.16.2.3 cost 20
  neighbor 172.16.2.4 cost 50
```

Hals

```
interface Serial0
  ip address 172.16.2.2 255.255.255.0
  encapsulation frame-relay
  ip ospf network point-to-multipoint non-broadcast
  map-group Haarlem
  frame-relay lmi-type q933a
  frame-relay svc
!
router ospf 1
  network 172.16.0.0 0.0.255.255 area 0
  neighbor 172.16.2.1 priority 10
```

Vandyck

```
interface Serial0
  ip address 172.16.2.3 255.255.255.0
  encapsulation frame-relay
  ip ospf network point-to-multipoint non-broadcast
  map-group Antwerp
  frame-relay lmi-type q933a
  frame-relay svc
!
router ospf 1
  network 172.16.0.0 0.0.255.255 area 0
  neighbor 172.16.2.1 priority 10
```

Brueghel
```
interface Serial0
  ip address 172.16.2.4 255.255.255.0
  encapsulation frame-relay
  ip ospf network point-to-multipoint non-broadcast
  map-group Brussels
  frame-relay lmi-type q933a
  frame-relay svc
!
router ospf 1
  network 172.16.0.0 0.0.255.255 area 0
  neighbor 172.16.2.1 priority 10
```

Because the network is non-broadcast, neighbors are not discovered automatically and must be manually configured. Another feature introduced in IOS 11.3AA can be seen in Rembrandt's configuration: Cost can be assigned on a per VC basis with the **neighbor** command.

The last solution is to establish each PVC as an individual point-to-point network with its own subnet (Figure 9.93). This solution is accomplished with subinterfaces:

Rembrandt
```
interface Serial0
  no ip address
  encapsulation frame-relay
interface Serial0.100 point-to-point
  description ----------------------- to Hals
  ip address 172.16.2.1 255.255.255.252
  frame-relay interface-dlci 100
interface Serial0.300 point-to-point
  description ----------------------- to Vandyck
  ip address 172.16.2.5 255.255.255.252
  frame-relay interface-dlci 300
interface Serial0.500 point-to-point
  description ----------------------- to Brueghels
  ip address 172.16.2.9 255.255.255.252
  frame-relay interface-dlci 500
!
router ospf 1
  network 172.16.0.0 0.0.255.255 area 0
```

Hals

```
interface Serial0
  no ip address
  encapsulation frame-relay
interface Serial0.600
  description ------------------------ to Rembrandt
  ip address 172.16.2.2 255.255.255.252
  frame-relay interface-dlci 600
  !
router ospf 1
  network 172.16.0.0 0.0.255.255 area 0
```

Vandyck

```
interface Serial0
  no ip address
  encapsulation frame-relay
interface Serial0.400
  description ------------------------ to Rembrandt
  ip address 172.16.2.6 255.255.255.252
  frame-relay interface-dlci 400
  !
router ospf 1
  network 172.16.0.0 0.0.255.255 area 0
```

Brueghel

```
interface Serial0
  no ip address
  encapsulation frame-relay
interface Serial0.200
  description ------------------------ to Rembrandt
  ip address 172.16.2.10 255.255.255.252
  frame-relay interface-dlci 200
  !
router ospf 1
  network 172.16.0.0 0.0.255.255 area 0
```

Benefits of establishing each PVC as a point-to-point network for OSPF over NBMA

This configuration is the most easily managed of all the configurations of OSPF over NBMA networks. Some of the advantages are evident in the configuration code, such as the ability to use an interface number that corresponds to the DLCI and the inclusion of a description line. The major advantage, however, is the simple one-to-one relationship between routers.

An occasional objection to the use of subinterfaces is that each PVC must have its own subnet address. In most cases, this require-

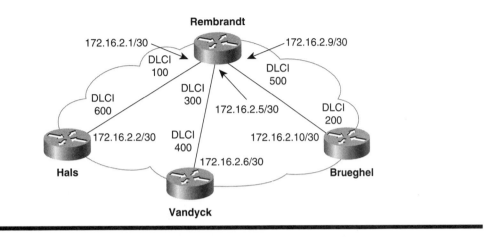

Figure 9.93

Point-to-point sub-interfaces allow each PVC to be configured as an individual subnet and eliminate the problem of DR/BDR election on NBMA networks.

ment should not be a problem, because OSPF supports VLSM. As the example shows, creating sub-subnets from the subnet address that was assigned to the cloud is an easy matter. And because the PVCs are now point-to-point links, IP unnumbered may be used as an alternative to subnet addresses. A more serious concern with subinterfaces is that they require more memory. The burden can be significant on small routers with limited memory.

Case Study: OSPF over Demand Circuits

OSPF over demand circuits is easily configured by adding the command **ip ospf demand-circuit** to the interface connected to the demand circuit. Only one end of a point-to-point circuit, or the multipoint side of a point-to-multipoint circuit, needs to be declared a demand circuit. In most cases, OSPF over demand circuits should not be implemented across a broadcast medium. On such a network, the Hello packets cannot be suppressed, and the link will stay up.

If the virtual circuits in Figure 9.92 are frame relay SVCs, Rembrandt's configuration might be as follows:

```
interface Serial0
  ip address 172.16.2.1 255.255.255.0
  encapsulation frame-relay
  ip ospf network point-to-multipoint non-broadcast
  ip ospf demand-circuit
   map-group Leiden
  frame-relay lmi-type q933a
  frame-relay svc
!
router ospf 1
  network 172.16.0.0 0.0.255.255 area 0
  neighbor 172.16.2.2 cost 30
  neighbor 172.16.2.3 cost 20
  neighbor 172.16.2.4 cost 50
```

Keep the following points in mind when implementing OSPF over demand circuits:

- LSAs with the DoNotAge bit set will be allowed into an area only if all LSAs in the area's link state database have the DC-bit set. This setting ensures that all routers in the area are capable of understanding the DoNotAge bit.

- All routers of an area in which OSPF over demand circuits is implemented must be capable of supporting it.

- If OSPF over demand circuits is implemented in a non-stub area, the routers in all non-stub areas must support it. The reason is that the DC-bit in type 5 LSAs will be set, and these LSAs are flooded into all non-stub areas.

- An effort should be made to implement demand circuits only within stub, totally stubby, or NSSA areas. Such an implementation negates the need for all routers within the OSPF domain to support OSPF over demand circuits. It also minimizes the number of changed LSAs received as the result of topology changes in other areas and hence prevents excess uptime of the demand circuit.

- If OSPF over demand circuits is configured and a virtual link is configured to cross the demand circuit, the virtual link will also be treated as a demand circuit. Otherwise, the virtual link traffic would keep the circuit up.

- OSPF refreshes its LSAs every 30 minutes to guard against an LSA becoming corrupted while it resides in the link state database. Because DoNotAge LSAs are not refreshed across a demand circuit, this robustness feature is lost.

- The refresh process occurs on each side of a demand circuit out all other interfaces, but LSAs are not refreshed across the link. As a result, the sequence numbers of otherwise identical LSAs on each side of the link may be different. Network management stations may use certain MIB variables[30] to verify database synchronization; if the sequence numbers do not match across the databases, an error may be falsely reported.

TROUBLESHOOTING OSPF

Troubleshooting OSPF can sometimes be daunting, especially in a large internetwork. However, a routing problem with OSPF is no different than a routing problem with any other routing protocol; the cause will be one of the following:

- Missing route information

- Inaccurate route information

---

[30] *Specifically, ospfExternLSACksumSum and ospfAreaLSACksumSum. These are sums of the individual LSA checksum fields. Because the checksum calculation includes the sequence number, and because the sequence numbers may be different, the checksums will also be different.*

An examination of the route table is still the primary source of troubleshooting information. Using the **show ip ospf database** command to examine the various LSAs will also yield important information. For example, if a link is unstable, the LSA advertising it will change frequently. This condition is reflected in a sequence number that is conspicuously higher than that of the other LSAs. Another sign of instability is an LSA whose age never gets very high.

Keep in mind that the LS database of every router within an area is the same. So unless you suspect that the database itself is being corrupted on some routers, you can examine the LS database for the entire area by examining a single router's LS database. Another good practice is to keep a copy (hard or soft) of the link state database for each area.

Troubleshooting router configuration

When examining an individual router's configuration, consider the following:

- Do all interfaces have the correct addresses and masks?

- Do the **network area** statements have the correct inverse masks to match the correct interfaces?

- Do the **network area** statements put all interfaces into the correct areas?

- Are the **network area** statements in the correct order?

Troubleshooting adjacencies

When examining adjacencies (or the lack thereof), consider these questions:

- Are Hellos being sent from both neighbors?

- Are the timers set the same between neighbors?

- Are the optional capabilities set the same between neighbors?

- Are the interfaces configured on the same subnet (that is, do the address/mask pairs belong to the same subnet)?

- Are the neighboring interfaces of the same network type?

- Is a router attempting to form an adjacency with a neighbor's secondary address?

- If authentication is being used, is the authentication type the same between neighbors? Are the passwords and (in the case of MD5) the keys the same? Is authentication enabled on all routers within the area?

- Are any access lists blocking OSPF?

- If the adjacency is across a virtual link, is the link configured within a stub area?

If a neighbor or adjacency is suspected of being unstable, adjacencies can be monitored with the command **debug ip ospf adj**. However, this command can often present more information than you want, as Figure 9.94 shows. Not only are the state changes of a neighbor recorded in great detail, but regular Hello processing is recorded. If monitoring is to be performed over an extended period, this wealth of information can overflow a router's internal logging buffers. Beginning with IOS 11.2, adjacencies can be monitored by adding the command **ospf log-adjacency-changes** under a router's OSPF configuration. This command will keep a simpler log of adjacency changes, as shown in Figure 9.95.

```
Hurd#debug ip ospf adj
OSPF adjacency events debugging is on
Hurd#
OSPF: Rcv hello from 172.20.1.2 area 25 from Serial0 172.20.1.2
OSPF: End of hello processing
OSPF: Rcv hello from 10.3.0.1 area 0 from Ethernet0 10.8.1.2
OSPF: Cannot see ourself in hello from 10.3.0.1 on Ethernet0, state INIT
%OSPF-5-ADJCHG: Process 1, Nbr 10.3.0.1 on Ethernet0 from FULL to INIT, 1-Way
OSPF: Neighbor change Event on interface Ethernet0
OSPF: DR/BDR election on Ethernet0
OSPF: Elect BDR 0.0.0.0
OSPF: Elect DR 172.20.1.5
         DR: 172.20.1.5 (Id) BDR: none
OSPF: End of hello processing
OSPF: Build router LSA for area 0, router ID 172.20.1.5
OSPF: Build network LSA for Ethernet0, router ID 172.20.1.5
OSPF: No full nbrs to build Net Lsa
OSPF: Flush network LSA on Ethernet0 for area 0
OSPF: Schedule SPF to remove network route
OSPF: Rcv hello from 172.20.1.2 area 25 from Serial0 172.20.1.2
OSPF: End of hello processing
OSPF: Rcv hello from 10.3.0.1 area 0 from Ethernet0 10.8.1.2
OSPF: End of hello processing
OSPF: Rcv DBD from 10.3.0.1 on Ethernet0 seq 0x2653 opt 0x2 flag 0x7 len 32
state INIT
%OSPF-5-ADJCHG: Process 1, Nbr 10.3.0.1 on Ethernet0 from INIT to 2WAY, 2-Way
Received
OSPF: 2 Way Communication to 10.3.0.1 on Ethernet0, state 2WAY
OSPF: Neighbor change Event on interface Ethernet0
OSPF: DR/BDR election on Ethernet0
OSPF: Elect BDR 10.3.0.1
OSPF: Elect DR 172.20.1.5
         DR: 172.20.1.5 (Id)     BDR: 10.3.0.1 (Id)
%OSPF-5-ADJCHG: Process 1, Nbr 10.3.0.1 on Ethernet0 from 2WAY to EXSTART,
AdjOK?
OSPF: Send DBD to 10.3.0.1 on Ethernet0 seq 0x25D7 opt 0x2 flag 0x7 len 32
OSPF: First DBD and we are not SLAVE
OSPF: Rcv DBD from 10.3.0.1 on Ethernet0 seq 0x25D7 opt 0x2 flag 0x2 len 312
state EXSTART
OSPF: NBR Negotiation Done. We are the MASTER
%OSPF-5-ADJCHG: Process 1, Nbr 10.3.0.1 on Ethernet0 from EXSTART to EXCHANGE,
Negotiation Done
OSPF: Send DBD to 10.3.0.1 on Ethernet0 seq 0x25D8 opt 0x2 flag 0x3 len 292
OSPF: Database request to 10.3.0.1
OSPF:sent LS REQ packet to 10.8.1.2, length 36
OSPF: Rcv DBD from 10.3.0.1 on Etherneto seq 0x25DB opt 0x2 flag 0x0 len 32
state EXCHANGE
OSPF: Send DBD to 10.3.0.1 on Ethernet0 seq 0x25D9 opt 0x2 flag 0x1 len 32
OSPF: Rcv DBD from 10.3.0.1 on Ethernet0 seq 0x25D9 opt 0x2 flag 0x0 len 32
state EXCHANGE
OSPF: Exchange Done with 10.3.0.1 on Ethernet0
%OSPF-5-ADJCHG: Process 1, Nbr 10.3.0.1 on Ethernet0 from EXCHANGE to LOADING,
Exchange Done
OSPF: Synchronized with 10.3.0.1 on Ethernet0, state FULL
%OSPF-5-ADJCHG: Process 1, Nbr 10.3.0.1 on Ethernet0 from LOADING to FULL,
Loading Done
OSPF: Build router LSA for area 0, router ID 172.20.1.5
OSPF: Build network LSA for Ethernet0, router ID 172.20.1.5
OSPF: Rcv hello from 172.20.1.2 area 25 from Serial0 172.20.1.2
OSPF: End of hello processing
OSPF: Rcv hello from 10.3.0.1 area 0 from Ethernet0 10.8.1.2
OSPF: Neighbor change Event on interface Ethernet0
OSPF: DR/BDR election on Ethernet0
OSPF: Elect BDR 10.3.0.1
OSPF: Elect DR 172.20.1.5
         DR: 172.20.1.5 (Id) BDR: 10.3.0.1 (Id)
OSPF: End of hello processing
OSPF: Build router LSA for area 0, router ID 172.20.1.
```

Figure 9.94

*This debug output from **debug ip ospf adj** shows the result of temporarily disconnecting and then reconnecting a neighbor's ethernet interface.*

```
Hurd#show logging
Syslog logging: enabled (0 messages dropped, 0 flushes, 0 overruns)
    Console logging: level debugging, 19 messages logged
    Monitor logging: level debugging, 0 messages logged
    Trap logging: level informational, 23 message lines logged
    Buffer logging: level debugging, 19 messages logged

Log Buffer (4096 bytes):

%OSPF-5-ADJCHG: Process 1, Nbr 10.3.0.1 on Ethernet0 from FULL to INIT, 1-Way
%OSPF-5-ADJCHG: Process 1, Nbr 10.3.0.1 on Ethernet0 from INIT to 2WAY, 2-Way Received
%OSPF-5-ADJCHG: Process 1, Nbr 10.3.0.1 on Ethernet0 from 2WAY to EXSTART, AdjOK?
%OSPF-5-ADJCHG: Process 1, Nbr 10.3.0.1 on Ethernet0 from EXSTART to EXCHANGE, Negotiation Done
%OSPF-5-ADJCHG: Process 1, Nbr 10.3.0.1 on Ethernet0 from EXCHANGE to LOADING, Exchange Done
%OSPF-5-ADJCHG: Process 1, Nbr 10.3.0.1 on Ethernet0 from LOADING to FULL, Loading Done
Hurd#
```

Figure 9.95

*These logging messages, resulting from the command **ospf log-adjacency-changes**, show the same neighbor failure as depicted in Figure 9.94, but with much less detail.*

Troubleshooting the link state database

If you suspect that a link state database is corrupted or that two databases are not synchronized, you can use the **show ip ospf database database-summary** command to observe the number of LSAs in each router's database. For a given area, the number of each LSA type should be the same in all routers. Next the command **show ip ospf database** will show the checksums for every LSA in a router's database. Within a given area, each LSA's checksum should be the same in every router's database. Verifying this status can be excruciatingly tedious for all but the smallest databases. Luckily, there are MIBs,[31] which can report the sum of a database's checksums to an SNMP management platform. If all databases in an area are synchronized, this sum should be the same for each database.

---

[31] *Namely, ospfExternLsaCksumSum and ospfAreaLsaCksumSum.*

Troubleshooting
area-wide problems

When examining an area-wide problem, keep in mind the following issues:

- Is the ABR configured correctly?

- Are all routers configured for the same area type? For example, if the area is a stub area, all routers must have the **area stub** command.

- If address summarization is configured, is it correct?

Troubleshooting
performance

If performance is a problem, check the memory and CPU utilization on the routers. If memory utilization is above 70%, the link state database may be too large; if CPU utilization is consistently above 60%, instabilities may exist in the topology. If memory and/or CPU surpasses the 50% mark, the network administrator should begin an analysis of the cause of the performance stress and, based on the results of the analysis, should begin planning corrective upgrades.

Stub areas and address summarization can help to both reduce the size of the link state database and to contain instabilities. The processing of LSAs, not the SPF algorithm, puts the most burden on an OSPF router. Taken individually, type 1 and type 2 LSAs would be more processor intensive than summary LSAs. However, type 1 and 2 LSAs tend to be grouped, whereas summary LSAs are sent in individual packets. As a result, in reality summary LSAs are more processor intensive.

The following case studies demonstrate the most frequently used techniques and tools for troubleshooting OSPF.

Case Study: An Isolated Area

Intra-area packets can be routed within area 1 of Figure 9.96, but all attempts at inter-area communications fail. Suspicion should immediately fall on area 1's ABR. This suspicion is reinforced by the fact that the Internal Routers have no router entry for an ABR (Figure 9.97).

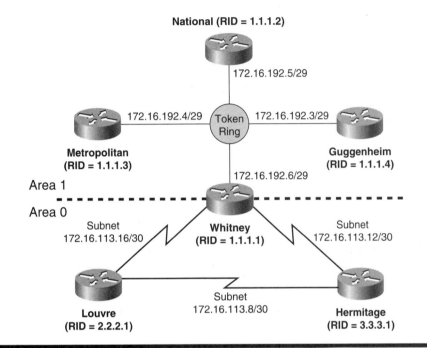

Figure 9.96

The end systems and routers within area 1 can communicate, but no traffic is being passed to or from area 0.

```
National#show ip ospf border-routers

OSPF Process 8 internal Routing Table

Codes: i - Intra-area route, I - Inter-area route

National#
```

Figure 9.97

*The command **show ip ospf border-routers** checks the internal route table of the internal routers. No router entry for an ABR is shown.*

The next step is to verify that the physical link to the ABR is operational and that OSPF is working properly. The same Internal Router's neighbor table (Figure 9.98) shows that the neighbor state of the ABR is full, indicating that an adjacency exists. In fact, the ABR is the DR for the Token Ring network. The existence of an adjacency confirms that the link is good and that OSPF Hellos are being exchanged with the proper parameters.

```
National#show ip ospf neighbor

Neighbor ID    Pri   State      Dead Time    Address        Interface
1.1.1.1          1   FULL/DR    00:00:33     172.16.192.6   TokenRing0
1.1.1.3          1   FULL/BDR   00:00:34     172.16.192.4   TokenRing0
1.1.1.4          1   FULL/ -    00:00:30     172.16.192.3   TokenRing0
National#
```

Figure 9.98

The neighbor table of router National indicates that the ABR (1.1.1.1) is fully adjacent.

Other evidence relevant to the problem can be found in National's database and its route table. The database (Figure 9.99) contains only Router (type 1) and Network (type 2) LSAs. No Network Summary (type 3) LSAs, which advertise destinations outside of the area, are recorded. At the same time, there are LSAs originated by Whitney (1.1.1.1). This information again indicates that Whitney is adjacent but is not passing information from area 0 into area 1.

The only destinations outside of area 1 in National's route table (Figure 9.100) are the serial links attached to Whitney. Yet another clue is revealed here: The route entries are tagged as intra-area routes (O); if they were in area 0, as Figure 9.96 shows they should be, they would be tagged as inter-area routes (O IA). The problem is apparently on the area 0 side of the ABR.

An examination of Whitney's serial interfaces (Figure 9.101) reveals the problem, if not the cause of the problem. Both interfaces, which should be in area 0, are instead in area 1. Both inter-

```
National#show ip ospf database

        OSPF Router with ID (1.1.1.2) (Process ID 8)

             Router Link States (Area 1)

Link ID        ADV Router  Age   Seq#        Checksum   Link count
172.16.192.6   1.1.1.1     132   0x80000034  0xAC4D     3
172.16.219.120 1.1.1.2 1   458   0x8000002B  0x6B46     2

             Net Link States (Area 1)

Link ID        ADV Router  Age   Seq#        Checksum
172.16.192.6   1.1.1.1     132   0x8000002E  0x2078
National#
```

Figure 9.99

National's link state database also shows that Whitney is adjacent, but is not advertising inter-area destinations.

```
National#show ip route
Codes: C - connected, S - static, I - IGRP, R - RIP, M - mobile, B - BGP
       D - EIGRP, EX - EIGRP external, O - OSPF, IA - OSPF inter area
       E1 - OSPF external type 1, E2 - OSPF external type 2, E - EGP
       i - IS-IS, L1 - IS-IS level-1, L2 - IS-IS level-2, * - candidate default
       U - per-user static route

Gateway of last resort is not set

     172.16.0.0/16 is variably subnetted, 4 subnets, 3 masks
C       172.16.219.112/28 is directly connected, Serial0
C       172.16.192.0/29 is directly connected, TokenRing0
O       172.16.113.12/30 [110/70] via 172.16.192.6, 03:01:43, TokenRing0
O       172.16.113.16/30 [110/70] via 172.16.192.6, 03:01:43, TokenRing0
National#
```

Figure 9.100

Whitney is advertising the subnets of its serial interfaces, but they are being advertised as intra-area destinations.

faces are connected to topological neighbors (Louvre and Hermitage), but no OSPF neighbors are recorded. Error messages are being displayed regularly, indicating that Whitney is receiving

Hellos from Louvre and Hermitage; those Hellos have their Area fields set to zero, causing a mismatch.

```
Whitney#show ip ospf interface serial0
Serial0 is up, line protocol is up
   Internet Address 172.16.113.18/30, Area 1
   Process ID 8, Router ID 1.1.1.1, Network Type POINT_TO_POINT, Cost: 64
   Transmit Delay is 1 sec, State POINT_TO_POINT,
   Timer intervals configured, Hello 10, Dead 40, Wait 40, Retransmit 5
     Hello due in 00:00:05
   Neighbor Count is 0, Adjacent neighbor count is 0
Whitney#show ip ospf interface serial 1
Serial1 is up, line protocol is up
   Internet Address 172.16.113.14/30, Area 1
   Process ID 8, Router ID 1.1.1.1, Network Type POINT_TO_POINT, Cost: 64
   Transmit Delay is 1 sec, State POINT_TO_POINT,
   Timer intervals configured, Hello 10, Dead 40, Wait 40, Retransmit 5
     Hello due in 00:00:09
   Neighbor Count is 0, Adjacent neighbor count is 0
Whitney#
%OSPF-4-ERRRCV: Received invalid packet: mismatch area ID, from backbone area
must be virtual-link but not found from 172.16.113.13, Serial1
%OSPF-4-ERRRCV: Received invalid packet: mismatch area ID, from backbone area
must be virtual-link but not found from 172.16.113.17, Serial0
```

Figure 9.101

Whitney's serial interfaces are configured in area 1 instead of area 0; this configuration is causing error messages when area 0 Hellos are received.

Whitney's OSPF configuration is:

```
router ospf 8
   network 172.16.0.0 0.0.255.255 area 1
   network 172.16.113.0 0.0.0.255 area 0
```

At first glance, this configuration may appear to be fine. However, recall from the first configuration case study that the **network area** commands are executed consecutively. The second **network area** command affects only interfaces that do not match the first command. With this configuration, all interfaces match the first **network area** command and are placed into area 1. The second command is never applied.

A correct configuration is:

```
router ospf 8
  network 172.16.192.0 0.0.0.255 area 1
  network 172.16.113.0 0.0.0.255 area 0
```

There are, of course, several valid configurations. The important point is that the first **network area** command must be specific enough to match only the address of the area 1 interface, and not the addresses of the area 0 interfaces.

Case Study: Misconfigured Summarization

Figure 9.102 shows a backbone area and three attached areas. To reduce the size of the link state database and to increase the stability of the internetwork, summarization will be used between areas.

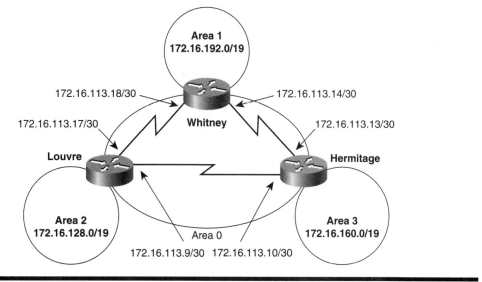

Figure 9.102

The summary addresses shown for each area will be advertised into area 0. Area 0 will also be summarized into the other areas.

The individual subnets of the three nonbackbone areas are summarized with the addresses shown in the figure. For example, a few of the subnets of area 1 may be:

172.16.192.0/29

172.16.192.160/29

172.16.192.248/30

172.16.217.0/24

172.16.199.160/29

172.16.210.248/30

Figure 9.103 shows that these subnet addresses can all be summarized with 172.16.192.0/19.

```
10101100000010000110000000000000000   = 172.16.192.0/29
10101100000010000110000001111000     = 172.16.192.248/30
10101100000010000110110010000000     = 172.16.217.0/24
10101100000010000110001111010000000  = 172.16.199.160/29
10101100000010000110100101111100000  = 172.16.210.248/30
10101100000010000110000000000000000  = 172.16.192.0/19
```

Figure 9.103
A few of the subnet addresses that are summarized with 172.16.192.0/19. The bold type indicates the network bits of each address.

Whitney's configuration is:
```
router ospf 8
  network 172.16.192.0 0.0.0.255 area 1
  network 172.16.113.0 0.0.0.255 area 0
  area 1 range 172.16.192.0 255.255.224.0
  area 0 range 172.16.113.0 255.255.224.0
```

The other three ABRs are configured similarly. Each ABR will advertise the summary address of its attached non-backbone area into area 0 and will also summarize area 0 into the non-backbone area.

Figure 9.104 shows that there is a problem. When the route table of one of area 1's Internal Routers is examined, area 0 is not being summarized properly (area 1's internal subnets are not shown, for clarity). Although the summary addresses for areas 2 and 3 are present, the individual subnets of area 0 are in the table instead of its summary address.

```
National#show ip route
Codes: C - connected, S - static, I - IGRP, R - RIP, M - mobile, B - BGP
       D - EIGRP, EX - EIGRP external, O - OSPF, IA - OSPF inter area
       E1 - OSPF external type 1, E2 - OSPF external type 2, E - EGP
       i - IS-IS, L1 - IS-IS level-1, L2 - IS-IS level-2, * - candidate default
       U - per-user static route

Gateway of last resort is not set

     172.16.0.0/16 is variably subnetted, 7 subnets, 4 masks
O IA    172.16.160.0/19 [110/80] via 172.16.192.6, 1d22h, TokenRing0
O IA    172.16.128.0/19 [110/80] via 172.16.192.6, 1d22h, TokenRing0
C       172.16.192.0/29 is directly connected, TokenRing0
O IA    172.16.113.12/30 [110/70] via 172.16.192.6, 00:39:46, TokenRing0
O IA    172.16.113.8/30 [110/134] via 172.16.192.6, 00:39:46, TokenRing0
O IA    172.16.113.16/30 [110/70] via 172.16.192.6, 00:39:46, TokenRing0
National#
```

Figure 9.104

The individual subnets of area 0, instead of the expected summary address, are recorded in the route table of one of area 1's internal routers.

You can see that the **area range** command for area 0 is the problem when you examine the three subnets of area 0 in binary (Figure 9.105).

```
10101100000010000011100010001000   = 172.16.113.8/30
10101100000010000011100010001100   = 172.16.113.12/30
10101100000010000011100010010000   = 172.16.113.16/30
11111111111111111110000000000000   = 255.255.224.0
10101100000010000011000000000000   = 172.16.96.0
```

Figure 9.105

The subnets of area 0, the configured summary mask, and the correct summary address.

The problem is that the summary address specified in the **area range** command (172.16.113.0) is more specific than the accompanying mask (255.255.224.0). The correct address to use with the 19-bit mask is 172.16.96.0:

```
router ospf 8
  network 172.16.192.0 0.0.0.255 area 1
  network 172.16.113.0 0.0.0.255 area 0
  area 1 range 172.16.192.0 255.255.224.0
  area 0 range 172.16.96.0 255.255.224.0
```

Figure 9.106 shows the resulting route table. There are other options for area 0's summary address. For example, 172.16.113.0/24 and 172.16.113.0/27 are both legitimate. The most appropriate summary address depends on the priorities of the internetwork design. In the case of the internetwork of Figure 9.99, 172.16.96.0/19 might be selected for consistency—all summary addresses have a 19-bit mask. On the other hand, 172.16.113.0/27 might be selected for better scalability; five more subnets can be added to the backbone under this summary address, leaving a wider range of addresses to be used elsewhere in the internetwork.

```
National#show ip route
Codes:  C - connected, S - static, I - IGRP, R - RIP, M - mobile, B - BGP
        D - EIGRP, EX - EIGRP external, O - OSPF, IA - OSPF inter area
        E1 - OSPF external type 1, E2 - OSPF external type 2, E - EGP
        i - IS-IS, L1 - IS-IS level-1, L2 - IS-IS level-2, * - candidate default
        U - per-user static route

Gateway of last resort is not set

     172.16.0.0/16 is variably subnetted, 5 subnets, 3 masks
O IA    172.16.160.0/19 [110/80] via 172.16.192.6, 00:38:11, TokenRing0
O IA    172.16.128.0/19 [110/80] via 172.16.192.6, 1d23h, TokenRing0
C       172.16.192.0/29 is directly connected, TokenRing0
O IA    172.16.96.0/19 [110/70] via 172.16.192.6, 00:00:23, TokenRing0
National#
```

Figure 9.106

Area 0 is now being summarized correctly.

Looking Ahead

When link state routing protocols are mentioned, most people first think of OSPF. However, it is not the only link state protocol for IP. The ISO's Intermediate-System to Intermediate-System (IS-IS), although designed to route other protocols, can route IP. Chapter 10, "Integrated IS-IS," examines this lesser known link state routing protocol.

Summary Table: Chapter 9 Command Review

Command	Description
area *area-id* authentication[message-digest]	Enables type 1 or type 2 authentication for an area.
area *area-id* default-cost *cost*	Specifies a cost for the default route sent into a stub area by an ABR.
area *area-id* nssa [no-redistribution][default-information-originate][no-summary]	Configures an area as not-so-stubby (NSSA).
area *area-id* range *address mask*	Summarizes addresses into or out of an area.
area area-id *stub* [no-summary]	Configures an area as a stub or totally stubby area.
area *area-id* virtual-link *router-id*	Defines a virtual link between ABRs.
debug ip ospf adj	Shows the events involved in the building or breaking of an OSPF adjacency.
ip ospf authentication-key *password*	Assigns a password to an OSPF interface for use with type 1 authentication.
ip ospf cost *cost*	Specifies the outgoing cost of an OSPF interface.
ip ospf dead-interval *seconds*	Specifies the OSPF RouterDeadInterval for an interface.
ip ospf demand-circuit	Configures an interface as an OSPF demand circuit.

Command	Description
ip ospf hello-interval *seconds*	Specifies the OSPF HelloInterval for an interface.
ip ospf message-digest-key *key-id* md5 *key*	Specifies an interface's key ID and key (password) for use with type 2 authentication.
ip ospf name-lookup	Enables the reverse DNS lookup of names to match Router IDs in certain **show** commands.
ip ospf network [broadcast] [nonbroadcast][point-to-multipoint]	Configures the OSPF network type.
ip ospf priority *number*	Sets the router priority of an interface for use in the DR/BDR election process.
ip ospf retransmit-interval *seconds*	Sets an interface's OSPF RxmtInterval.
ip ospf transmit-delay *seconds*	Sets an interface's OSPF InfTransDelay.
maximum-paths	Sets the number of paths over which OSPF performs load balancing.
neighbor *ip-address*[priority *number*][poll-interval *seconds*] [cost *cost*]	Manually informs a router of its neighbors on a non-broadcast network.
network *address inverse-mask* area *area-id*	Specifies the interfaces on which OSPF is to run and specifies the area to which the interface is connected.
ospf auto-cost reference-bandwidth *reference-bandwidth*	Changes the default OSPF reference bandwidth used for the calculation of link costs.
ospf log-adjacency-changes	Logs neighbor state changes.
router ospf *process-id*	Enables an OSPF routing process.
show ip ospf [*process-id*]	Displays general information about an OSPF routing process.
show ip ospf border-routers	Displays a router's internal OSPF route table.
show ip ospf [*process-id area-id*] database	Displays all entries in the OSPF link state database.
show ip ospf [*process-id area-id*] database router [*link state-id*]	Displays type 1 LSAs in the OSPF link state database.

Command	Description
show ip ospf [*process-id area-id*] **database network** [*link state-id*]	Displays type 2 LSAs in the OSPF link state database.
show ip ospf [*process-id area-id*] **database summary** [*link state-id*]	Displays type 3 LSAs in the OSPF link state database.
show ip ospf [*process-id area-id*] **database asbr-summary**[*link state-id*]	Displays type 4 LSAs in the OSPF link state database.
show ip ospf [*process-id area-id*] **database nssa-external**[*link state-id*]	Displays type 7 LSAs in the OSPF link state database.
show ip ospf [*process-id*] **database external** [*link state-id*]	Displays type 5 LSAs in the OSPF link state database.
show ip ospf [*process-id area-id*] **database database-summary**	Displays the number of LSAs in the OSPF link state database by type and by area ID.
show ip ospf **interface** [*type number*]	Displays OSPF-specific information about an interface.
show ip ospf **neighbor** [*type number*][*neighbor-id*] [**detail**]	Displays information from the OSPF neighbor table.
show ip ospf **virtual-links**	Displays information about OSPF virtual links.
timer lsa-group-pacing *pacing-time*	Sets the minimum pacing time between two groups of LSAs whose refresh timers have expired.

RECOMMENDED READING

John Moy, "OSPF Version 2," RFC 2328, April 1998.

John Moy, *OSPF: Anatomy of an Internet Routing Protocol.* Reading, Massachusetts: Addison-Wesley; 1998.

Written by one of the original designers of OSPF and the author of the RFCs, this book is good reading not only for its excellent coverage of the protocol but also for its historic perspective. Chapter 3 is especially interesting, with its insider's perspective on the design, testing, and standardization of a routing protocol.

REVIEW QUESTIONS

1. What is an OSPF neighbor?
2. What is an OSPF adjacency?
3. What are the five OSPF packet types? What is the purpose of each type?
4. What is an LSA? How does an LSA differ from an OSPF Update packet?
5. What are LSA types 1 to 5 and LSA type 7? What is the purpose of each type?
6. What is a link state database? What is link state database synchronization?
7. What is the default HelloInterval?
8. What is the default RouterDeadInterval?
9. What is a Router ID? How is a Router ID determined?
10. What is an area?
11. What is the significance of area 0?
12. What is MaxAge?
13. What are the four OSPF router types?
14. What are the four OSPF path types?
15. What are the five OSPF network types?
16. What is a Designated Router?
17. How does a Cisco router calculate the outgoing cost of an interface?
18. What is a partitioned area?
19. What is a virtual link?

20. What is the difference between a stub area, a totally stubby area, and a not-so-stubby area?

21. What is the difference between OSPF network entries and OSPF router entries?

22. Why is type 2 authentication preferable over type 1 authentication?

23. Which three fields in the LSA header distinguish different LSAs? Which three fields in the LSA header distinguish different instances of the same LSA?

CONFIGURATION EXERCISES

1. Table 9.13 shows the interfaces and addresses of 14 routers. Also shown is the OSPF area to which each interface is connected. The following facts apply:

   ○ All interfaces of each router are shown in the table.

   ○ If no area is shown (-), OSPF should not be running on the associated interface.

   ○ The second octet of the subnet address is the same as the area ID.

   ○ The first 16 bits of the address of every OSPF interface are specific to the area. For example, addresses with the prefix 10.30.x.x will be found only within area 30.

   Write OSPF configurations for the routers in Table 9.13. (Tip: Draw a picture of the routers and subnets first.)

Table 9.13   *The router information for Configuration Exercises 1 through 6.*

Router	Interface	Address/Mask	Area ID
A	L0	10.100.100.1/32	-
	E0	10.0.1.1/24	0
	E1	10.0.2.1/24	0
	E2	10.0.3.1/24	0
	E3	10.0.4.1/24	0
B	L0	10.100.100.2/32	-
	E0	10.0.1.2/24	0
	E1	10.5.1.1/24	5
	S0	10.5.255.13/30	5
	S1	10.5.255.129/30	5
C	L0	10.100.100.3/32	-
	E0	10.0.2.2/24	0
	E1	10.10.1.1/24	10
	S0	10.30.255.249/30	30
D	L0	10.100.100.4/32	-
	E0	10.0.3.2/24	0
	E1	10.20.1.1/24	20
E	L0	10.100.100.5/32	-
	E0	10.0.4.2/24	0
	S0	10.15.255.1/30	15
F	L0	10.100.100.6/32	-
	E0	10.5.5.1/24	5
	S0	10.5.255.130/30	5
	S1	10.5.255.65/30	5
G	L0	10.100.100.7/32	-

Table 9.13 *The router information for Configuration Exercises 1 through 6, continued.*

Router	Interface	Address/Mask	Area ID
	E0	10.10.1.58/24	10
	S0	10.10.255.5/30	-
H	L0	10.100.100.8/32	-
	E0	10.20.1.2/24	20
	E1	10.20.100.100/27	20
	S0	10.20.255.225/30	-
I	L0	10.100.100.9/32	-
	E0	10.35.1.1/24	35
	S0	10.5.255.66/30	5
J	L0	10.100.100.10/32	-
	E0	10.15.227.50/24	15
	S0	10.15.225.2	15
K	L0	10.100.100.11/32	-
	E0	10.30.1.1/24	30
	S0*	10.30.254.193/26	30
L	L0	10.100.100.12/32	-
	E0	10.30.2.1/24	30
	S0*	10.30.254.194/26	30
M	L0	10.100.100.13/32	-
	E0	10.30.3.1/24	30
	S0*	10.30.254.195/26	30
	S1	10.30.255.250/30	30
N	L0	10.100.100.14/32	-
	E0	10.30.4.1/24	30
	S0*	10.30.254.196/26	30

---

* *Indicates frame relay encapsulation.*

2. Configure summarization on all ABRs in Table 9.13.
3. Modify the configurations to make area 15 a stub area.
4. Modify the configurations to make area 30 a totally stubby area.
5. Interface S0 of router H is connected to a router running another routing protocol, and the routes learned from that protocol are being redistributed into OSPF. Modify the configurations as necessary to allow these redistributed routes to be advertised throughout the OSPF domain, but do not allow any type 5 LSAs to enter area 20.
6. The serial link between routers C and M is a very low bandwidth link. Modify the configurations so that OSPF treats this link as a demand circuit.

TROUBLESHOOTING EXERCISES

1. OSPF is not working between two routers. When debugging is turned on, the messages shown in Figure 9.107 are received every 10 seconds. What is the problem?

```
RTR_EX1#debug ip ospf adj
OSPF adjacency events debugging is on
RTR_EX1#
OSPF: Rcv pkt from 172.16.27.1, TokenRing0, area 0.0.0.25 : src not on the same network
OSPF: Rcv pkt from 172.16.27.1, TokenRing0, area 0.0.0.25 : src not on the same network
OSPF: Rcv pkt from 172.16.27.1, TokenRing0, area 0.0.0.25 : src not on the same network
OSPF: Rcv pkt from 172.16.27.1, TokenRing0, area 0.0.0.25 : src not on the same network
OSPF: Rcv pkt from 172.16.27.1, TokenRing0, area 0.0.0.25 : src not on the same network
```

Figure 9.107

The debug messages for Troubleshooting Exercise 1.

2. Explain what problem is indicated by the debug messages in Figure 9.108.

```
RTR_EX2#debug ip ospf adj
OSPF adjacency events debugging is on
RTR_EX2#
OSPF: Hello from 172.16.27.195 with mismatched Stub/Transit area option bit
OSPF: Hello from 172.20.1.1 with mismatched Stub/Transit area option bit
OSPF: Hello from 172.16.27.195 with mismatched Stub/Transit area option bit
OSPF: Hello from 172.20.1.1 with mismatched Stub/Transit area option bit
OSPF: Hello from 172.16.27.195 with mismatched Stub/Transit area option bit
OSPF: Hello from 172.20.1.1 with mismatched Stub/Transit area option bit
OSPF: Hello from 172.16.27.195 with mismatched Stub/Transit area option bit
OSPF: Hello from 172.20.1.1 with mismatched Stub/Transit area option bit
```

Figure 9.108

The debug messages for Troubleshooting Exercise 2.

3. Explain what problem is indicated by the error messages in Figure 9.109.

```
RTR_EX3#
OSPF: Send with youngest Key 10
OSPF: Rcv pkt from 10.8.1.1, Ethernet0 : Mismatch Authentication type. Input
packet specified type 0, we use type 2
OSPF: Send with youngest Key 10
OSPF: Rcv pkt from 10.8.1.1, Ethernet0 : Mismatch Authentication type. Input
packet specified type 0, we use type 2
RTR_EX3#
```

Figure 9.109

The error messages for Troubleshooting Exercise 3.

4. Explain what problem is indicated by the error messages in Figure 9.110.

```
RTR EX4#
OSPF: Send with youngest Key 10
OSPF: Rcv pkt from 10.8.1.1, Ethernet0 : Mismatch Authentication Key - Message D
igest Key 10
OSPF: Send with youngest Key 10
OSPF: Rcv pkt from 10.8.1.1, Ethernet0 : Mismatch Authentication Key - Message D
igest Key 10
RTR_EX4#
```

Figure 9.110

The error messages for Troubleshooting Exercise 4.

5. Explain what problem is indicated by the error messages in Figure 9.111.

```
RTR_EX5#
%OSPF-4-ERRRCV: Received invalid packet: mismatch area ID, from backbone area must be virtual-link
but not found from 10.8.1.1, Ethernet0
%OSPF-4-ERRRCV: Received invalid packet: mismatch area ID, from backbone area must be virtual-link
but not found from 10.8.1.1, Ethernet0
RTR_EX5#
```

Figure 9.111

The error messages for Troubleshooting Exercise 5.

6. The configurations for the routers in Figure 9.112 follow.

A
```
router ospf 15
  network 192.168.50.224 0.0.0.31 area 192.168.50.0
  network 192.168.50.240 0.0.0.15 area 0.0.0.0
  area 192.168.50.0 authentication message-digest
```

B
```
router ospf 51
  network 192.168.50.0 0.0.0.255 area 0
```

Routers A and B are not forming an adjacency. What is wrong?

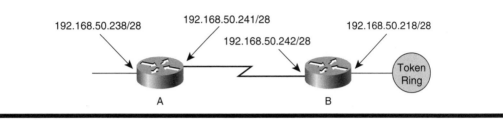

Figure 9.112

The internetwork for Troubleshooting Problem 6.

7. Figure 9.113 shows a link state database from an area in which an unstable link exists. Based on the information shown, which link is the likely culprit?

```
RTR_EX7#show ip ospf database

        OSPF Router with ID (10.8.20.1) (Process ID 1)

            Router Link States (Area 0)

Link ID        ADV Router      Age   Seq#        Checksum  Link count
10.3.0.1       10.3.0.1        18    0x8000001B  0x6AF8    5
10.8.5.1       10.8.5.1        15    0x80000267  0xFDA0    6
10.8.20.1      10.8.20.1       478   0x800000    1E 0xD451 4

            Net Link States (Area 0)

Link ID        ADV Router      Age   Seq#        Checksum
10.8.1.2       10.3.0.1        18    0x80000013  0xA747
RTR_EX2#
```

Figure 9.113

The link state database for Troubleshooting Exercise 7.

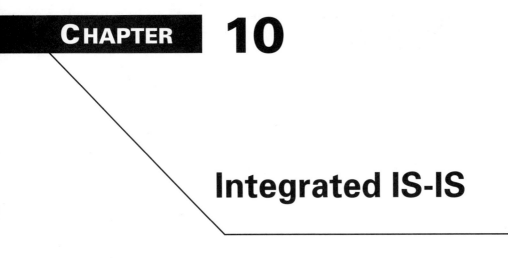

CHAPTER 10

Integrated IS-IS

When the terms *link state protocol* and *IP* are mentioned together, almost everyone thinks of OSPF. Some may say, "Oh, yeah, there's also IS-IS, but Idunnomuch-aboutit." Only a few will think of Integrated IS-IS as a serious alternative to OSPF. However, those few do exist, and there are internetworks—including a few ISPs—that route IP with IS-IS.

IS-IS, which stands for Intermediate System to Intermediate System, is the routing protocol for the ISO's Connectionless Network Protocol (CLNP) and is described in ISO 10589.[1] The protocol was developed by Digital Equipment Corporation for its DECnet Phase V.

The ISO was working on IS-IS at more or less the same time that the Internet Architecture Board (IAB) was working on OSPF, and there was a proposal that IS-IS be adopted as the routing protocol for TCP/IP in place of OSPF. This proposal was driven by the opinion, popularly held in the late 1980s and early 1990s, that TCP/IP was an interim protocol suite that would eventually be replaced by the OSI suite. Adding impetus to this movement toward OSI were specifications such as the United States'

---

[1] *International Organization for Standardization, "Intermediate System to Intermediate System Intra-Domain Routeing Information Exchange Protocol for Use in Conjunction with the Protocol for Providing the Connectionless-mode Network Service (ISO 8473)," ISO/IEC 10589, 1992.*

Government Open Systems Interconnection Profile (GOSIP) and the European Procurement Handbook for Open Systems (EPHOS).

To support the predicted transition from TCP/IP to OSI, an extension to IS-IS, known as Integrated IS-IS, was proposed.[2] The purpose of Integrated IS-IS, also known as Dual IS-IS, was to provide a single routing protocol with the capabilities of routing both CLNS[3] and IP. The protocol was designed to operate in a pure CLNS environment, a pure IP environment, or a dual CLNS/IP environment.

Saying that battle lines were drawn may be overly dramatic, but at the least strong pro-ISO and pro-OSPF factions developed. It can be enlightening to read and contrast the coverage of OSPF and IS-IS in the well-known books by Christian Huitema,[4] a past chairman of the IAB, and Radia Perlman,[5] the chief designer of IS-IS. In the end, the Internet Engineering Task Force (IETF) adopted OSPF as the recommended IGP. Technical differences certainly influenced the decision, but so did political considerations. ISO standardization is a slow, four-step process that depends upon the voted approval of many committees. The IETF, on the other hand, is much more freewheeling. A statement made in 1992 has been its informal motto: "We reject kings, presidents, and voting; we believe in rough consensus and running code."[6] Letting OSPF evolve through the RFC process made more sense than adopting the more formalized IS-IS.

---

[2] Ross Callon, "Use of OSI IS-IS for Routing in TCP/IP and Dual Environments," RFC 1195, December 1990.

[3] Connectionless-Mode Network Service—the network layer protocol of CLNP.

[4] Christian Huitema, Routing in the Internet, Prentice Hall PTR, Englewood Cliffs, NJ, 1995.

[5] Radia Perlman, Interconnections: Bridges and Routers, Addison-Wesley, Reading, MA, 1992.

[6] Dave Clark, quoted in Huitema, p.23.

Despite the political friction, the OSPF Working Group learned from and capitalized on many of the basic mechanisms designed for IS-IS. On the surface, OSPF and IS-IS have many features in common:

- They both maintain a link state database from which a Dijkstra-based SPF algorithm computes a shortest-path tree.

- They both use Hello packets to form and maintain adjacencies.

- They both use areas to form a two-level hierarchical topology.

- They both have the capability of providing address summarization between areas.

- They both are classless protocols.

- They both elect a designated router to represent broadcast networks.

- They both have authentication capabilities.

Below these similarities, there are distinct differences. This chapter begins by examining those differences. Integrated IS-IS (henceforth referred to simply as IS-IS) is covered only as an IP routing protocol; CLNS is discussed only when it is relevant to using IS-IS to route IP.

OPERATION OF INTEGRATED IS-IS

The ISO often uses different terms than the IETF to describe the same entities, a fact that can sometimes cause confusion. ISO terms are introduced and defined in this section, but in most cases the more familiar IETF terminology used throughout the rest of this book is used in this chapter.[7] Some ISO terms are so fundamental that they should be discussed before getting into any specifics of the IS-IS protocol.

ES-IS

A router is an *Intermediate System* (IS), and a host is an *End System* (ES). Accordingly, a protocol that provides communication between a host and a router is known as ES-IS, and a protocol that routers use to speak to each other (a routing protocol) is IS-IS (Figure 10.1). Whereas IP uses router discovery mechanisms, such as Proxy ARP or IRDP, or simply has a default gateway configured on hosts, CLNP uses ES-IS to form adjacencies between End Systems and Intermediate Systems. ES-IS has no relevance to IS-IS for IP and is not covered in this book.

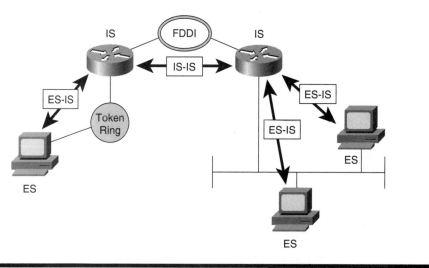

Figure 10.1

Hosts are end systems in ISO terminology, and routers are Intermediate Systems.

---

[7] *The temptation to use the ISO/European spelling of certain common terms such as "routeing" and "neighbour" was successfully resisted.*

An interface attached to a subnetwork is a *Subnetwork Point of Attachment* (SNPA). An SNPA is somewhat conceptual because it actually defines the point at which subnetwork services are provided, rather than an actual physical interface. The conceptual nature of SNPAs fits with the conceptual nature of subnetworks themselves, which can consist of multiple data links connected by data link switches.

SNPA

A data unit passed from an OSI layer of one node to the peer OSI layer of another node is called a *Protocol Data Unit* (PDU). So a frame is a Data Link PDU (DLPDU), and a packet is a Network PDU (NPDU). The data unit that performs the equivalent function of the OSPF LSA is the Link State PDU (LSP).[8] Unlike LSAs, which are encapsulated behind an OSPF header and then an IP packet, an LSP is itself a packet.

PDU

IS-IS Areas

Although both IS-IS and OSPF use areas to create a two-level hierarchical topology, a fundamental difference exists in the way in which the two protocols define their areas. OSPF area borders are marked by routers, as shown in Figure 10.2. Some interfaces are in one area, and other interfaces are in another area. When an OSPF router has interfaces in more than one area, it is an Area Border Router (ABR).

Figure 10.3 shows the same topology as shown in Figure 10.2 but with IS-IS areas. Notice that all the routers are completely within an area, and the area borders are on links, not on routers. The routers that connect the areas are *level 2* routers, and routers that have no direct connectivity to another area are *level 1* routers.

Level 1 and level 2 routers

---

[8]   *Some documentation, such as RFC 1195, define the LSP as Link State Packet.*

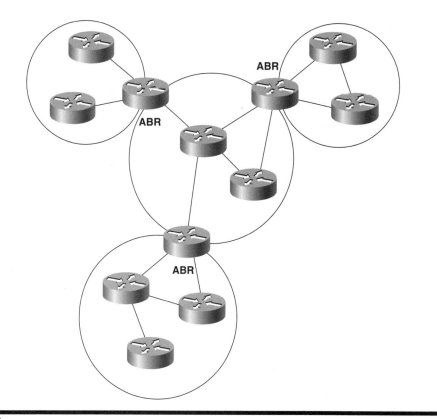

Figure 10.2
OSPF area borders fall within routers, and the routers that connect the areas are ABRs.

An intermediate system can be a level 1 (L1) router, a level 2 (L2) router, or both (L1/L2). L1 routers are analogous to OSPF non-backbone Internal Routers, L2 routers are analogous to OSPF backbone routers, and L1/L2 routers are analogous to OSPF ABRs. In Figure 10.3, the L1/L2 routers are connected to L1 routers and to L2 routers. These L1/L2 routers must maintain both a level 1 link state database and a level 2 link state database, in much the same way that an OSPF ABR must maintain a separate database for each area to which it is attached.

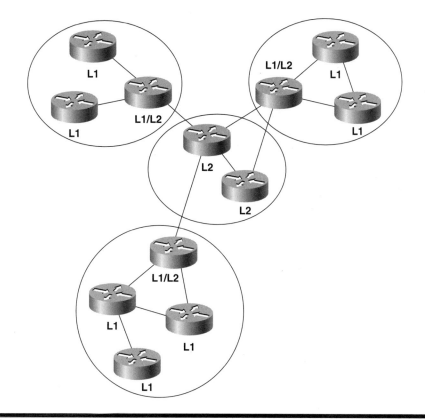

Figure 10.3
IS-IS areas fall on links, and the routers that connect the areas are level 2 routers.

The set of L2 routers (including L1/L2 routers) and their interconnecting links is the IS-IS backbone; as with OSPF, inter-area traffic must traverse this backbone. Every level 1 router within an area (including the area's L1/L2 routers) maintains an identical link state database. Unlike OSPF ABRs, L1/L2 routers do not advertise L2 routes to L1 routers. Therefore, an L1 router has no knowledge of destinations outside of its own area. In this sense, an L1 router is similar to a router in an OSPF totally stubby area. To route a packet to another area, an L1 router must forward the packet to an L1/L2 router. When an L1/L2 router sends its level 1 LSP into an area, it signals other L1 routers that it can reach another area by setting a bit known as the *Attached* (ATT) bit[9] in the LSP.

Recall from Chapter 9, "Open Shortest Path First," that OSPF runs its SPF algorithm to compute routes within an area, but that inter-area routes are computed using a distance vector algorithm. This situation is not true of IS-IS. L1/L2 routers, maintaining separate level 1 and level 2 link state databases, will calculate separate SPF trees for the level 1 and level 2 topology.

ISO 10589 describes a procedure by which IS-IS routers can create virtual links to repair partitioned areas, just as OSPF can. This feature is not supported by Cisco or by most other router vendors and is not further described here.

Area ID

Because an IS-IS router resides completely within a single area, the Area ID (or area address) is associated with the entire router rather than an interface. A unique feature of IS-IS is that a router can have up to three area addresses, which can be useful during area transitions. A configuration case study later in this chapter, "An Area Migration," demonstrates the use of multiple area addresses. Each IS-IS router must also have a way to uniquely identify itself within the routing domain. This identification is the function of the *System ID*, which is analogous to the OSPF Router

System ID

ID. Both the Area ID and the System ID are defined on an IS-IS router by a single address, the Network Entity Title (NET).

Network Entity Titles

Even when IS-IS is used to route only TCP/IP, IS-IS is still an ISO CLNP protocol. Consequently, the packets by which IS-IS communicates with its peers are CLNS PDUs, which in turn means

---

[9]   *There are actually four ATT bits, relevant to different metrics. These bits are further explained in the section "IS-IS PDU Formats."*

that even in an IP-only environment, an IS-IS router must have an ISO address. The ISO address is a network address, a NET, described in ISO 8348.[10] The length of a NET can range from 8 to 20 octets; the NET describes both the Area ID and the System ID of a device, as shown in Figure 10.4.

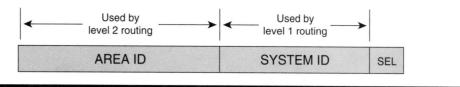

Figure 10.4
The NET specifies the Area ID and the System ID of an IS or ES.

The ISO designed the NET to be many things to many systems, and depending upon your viewpoint, the address format is either extremely flexible and scalable or it is a cumbersome muddle of variable fields. Figure 10.5 shows just three of the many forms an ISO NET can take. Although the fields preceding the System ID are different in each example, the System ID itself is the same. ISO 10589 specifies that the field can be from one to eight octets in length, but that the System ID of all nodes within the routing domain must use the same length. Most commonly, the length is six octets[11] and is usually the Media Access Control (MAC) identifier of an interface on the device. The System ID must be unique for each node within the routing domain.

Also of interest in the examples of Figure 10.5 is the NSAP Selector (SEL). In each case, this one-octet field is set to 0x00. A Network Service Access Point (NSAP) describes an attachment to a

---

[10] *International Organization for Standardization, "Network Service Definition Addendum 2: Network Layer Addressing," ISO/IEC 8348/Add.2, 1988.*
[11] *Cisco's IS-IS implementation requires a System ID of 6 octets.*

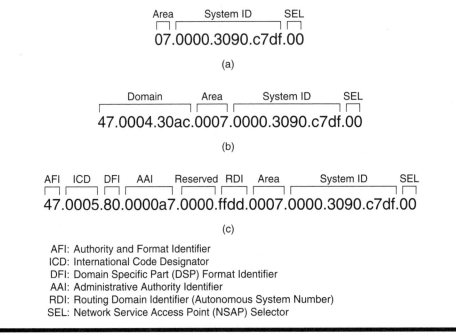

Figure 10.5

Three NET formats: A simple eight-octet Area ID/System ID format (a); an OSI NSAP format (b); and a GOSIP NSAP format[12] (c).

[12]   GOSIP Advanced Requirements Group, "Government Open Systems Interconnection Profile (GOSIP) Version 2.0 [Final Text]," Federal Information Processing Standard, U.S. Department of Commerce, National Institute of Standards and Technology, October 1990.

particular service at the network layer of a node. So when the SEL is set to something other than 0x00 in an ISO address the address is an NSAP address. This situation is similar to the combination of IP destination address and IP protocol number in an IP packet, which addresses a particular service at the network layer of a particular device's TCP/IP stack. When the SEL is set to 0x00 in an ISO address, the address is a NET, the address of a node's network layer itself.

As the variety of formats in Figure 10.5 implies, a detailed discussion of the configuration of NETs is beyond the scope of this book.

A good reference for further study is RFC 1237.[13] In most cases, Integrated IS-IS will be run in a dual CLNP/IP environment, and the NET will be assigned based on the CLNP requirements. In an IP-only environment, the NET might be assigned based on a standard such as GOSIP. If you are free to choose any NET for an IP-only environment, choose the simplest format that will serve the needs of your internetwork.

Regardless of the format, the following three rules apply:

- The NET must begin with a single octet (for example, 47.xxxx...).

- The NET must end with a single octet, which should be set to 0x00 (...xxxx.00). IS-IS will function if the SEL is non-zero but a dual CLNP/IP router may experience problems.

- On Cisco routers, the System ID of the NET must be six octets.

IS-IS Functional Organization

One of the primary reasons for having a layered network architecture like the OSI model is so that the functions of each layer are independent from the layer below. The network layer, for example, must adapt to many types of data links, or subnetworks. To further this adaptability, the network layer consists of two sublayers (Figure 10.6). The *Subnetwork-Independent sublayer* provides consistent, uniform network services to the transport layer. The *Subnetwork-Dependent sublayer* accesses the services of the data link layer on behalf of the Subnetwork-Independent sublayer. As

---

the two names imply, the Subnetwork-Dependent sublayer depends upon a specific type of data link, so that the subnetwork-independent sublayer can be independent of the data link.

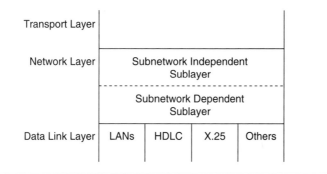

Figure 10.6

The OSI network layer consists of two sublayers.

The organization of the network layer, specified in ISO 8648,[14] is actually more complex than that shown in Figure 10.6. The two basic sublayers are introduced here because ISO 10589 presents much of its description of the operation of IS-IS within the framework of the functions of these sublayers.

Subnetwork Dependent Functions

The subnetwork dependent functions are, of course, the functions of the subnetwork dependent sublayer. Their job is to hide the characteristics of different kinds of data links (subnetworks) from the functions of the subnetwork independent sublayer. The following subnetwork dependent functions are important to routing:

- The transmission and reception of PDUs over the specific attached subnetwork

---

[14] *International Organization for Standardization, "Internal Organisation of the Network Layer," ISO 8648, 1990.*

- The exchange of IS-IS Hello PDUs to discover neighbors and establish adjacencies on the subnetwork

- The maintenance of the adjacencies

- Link demultiplexing, or the transfer of OSI PDUs to the OSI process and the transfer of IP packets to the IP process

In contrast to the four network types defined by OSPF, IS-IS defines only two: broadcast subnetworks and point-to-point or general topology subnetworks. *Broadcast subnetworks* are defined the same as they are under OSPF—multi-access data links that support multicasting. Point-to-point (nonbroadcast) subnetworks can be permanent, such as a T1 link, or dynamically established, such as X.25 SVCs.

IS-IS network types

Neighbors and Adjacencies

IS-IS routers discover neighbors and form adjacencies by exchanging IS-IS Hello PDUs. Hellos are transmitted every 10 seconds, and on Cisco routers this interval can be changed on a per interface basis with the command **isis hello-interval**. Although IS-IS Hellos are slightly different for broadcast and point-to-point subnetworks, the Hellos include the same essential information, described in the section "IS-IS PDU Formats." An IS-IS router uses its Hello PDUs to identify itself and its capabilities and to describe the parameters of the interface on which the Hellos are sent. If two neighbors are in agreement about their respective capabilities and interface parameters, they become adjacent.

IS-IS forms separate adjacencies for level 1 and level 2 neighbors. L1 routers form L1 adjacencies with L1 and L1/L2 neighbors, and L2 routers form L2 adjacencies with L2 and L1/L2 neighbors. Neighboring L1/L2 routers form both an L1 adjacency and an L2 adjacency. An L1 router and an L2 router will not establish an adjacency.

Once an adjacency is established, the Hellos act as keepalives. Each router sends a *hold time* in its Hellos, informing its neighbors how long they should wait to hear the next Hello before declaring the router dead. The default hold time on Cisco routers is three times the Hello interval and can be changed on a per interface basis with the command **isis hello-multiplier**.

The IS-IS neighbor table can be observed with the command **show clns is-neighbors** (Figure 10.7). The first four columns of the display show the System ID of each neighbor, the interface on which the neighbor is located, the state of the adjacency, and the adjacency type. The state will be either Init, indicating that the neighbor is known, but is not adjacent, or Up, indicating that the neighbor is adjacent. The priority is the router priority used for electing a Designated Router on a broadcast network, as described in the next section.

```
Brussels#show clns is-neighbors

System Id       Interface  State  Type Priority  Circuit Id       Format
0000.0C04.DCC0  Se0        Up     L1   0          06               Phase V
0000.0C04.DCC0  Et1        Up     L1   64         0000.0C76.5B7C.03 Phase V
0000.0C0A.2C51  Et0        Up     L2   64         0000.0C76.5B7C.02 Phase V
0000.0C0A.2AA9  Et0        Up     L1L2 64/64      0000.0C76.5B7C.02 Phase V
Brussels#
```

Figure 10.7

The command ***show clns is-neighbors*** *displays the IS-IS neighbor table.*

| Circuit ID, LAN ID, and Pseudonode ID | The sixth column shows the *Circuit ID*, a one-octet number that the router uses to uniquely identify the IS-IS interface. If the interface is attached to a broadcast multiaccess network, the Circuit ID is concatenated with the System ID of the network's Designated Router, and the complete number is known as the *LAN ID*. In this |

usage, the Circuit ID is more correctly called the *Pseudonode ID*. For example, in Figure 10.7 the LAN ID of the link attached to interface E0 is 0000.0c76.5b7c.02. The System ID of the Designated Router is 0000.0c76.5b7c, and the Pseudonode ID is 02.

The last column indicates the format of the adjacency. For Integrated IS-IS the format will always be Phase V, indicating OSI/DECnet Phase V. The only other adjacency format is DECnet Phase IV.

Designated Routers

IS-IS elects a Designated Router (or more officially, a Designated IS) on broadcast multi-access networks for the same reason OSPF does. Rather than having each router connected to the LAN advertise an adjacency with every other router on the network, the network itself is considered a router—a pseudonode. Each router, including the Designated Router, advertises a single link to the pseudonode. The DR also advertises, as the representative of the pseudonode, a link to all of the attached routers.

Unlike OSPF, however, an IS-IS router attached to a broadcast multi-access network establishes adjacencies with all of its neighbors on the network, not just the DR. Each router multicasts its LSPs to all of its neighbors, and the DR uses a system of PDUs called Sequence Number PDUs (SNPs) to ensure that the flooding of LSPs is reliable. The reliable flooding process, and SNPs, are described in a later section, "The Update Process."

The IS-IS Designated Router election process is quite simple. Every IS-IS router interface is assigned both an L1 priority and an L2 priority in the range of 0 to 127. Cisco router interfaces have a default priority of 64 for both levels, and this value can be changed with the command **isis priority**.

The router advertises its priority in the Hellos sent from each interface—the L1 priority is advertised in L1 Hellos, and the L2 priority is advertised in L2 Hellos. If the priority is 0, the router is ineligible to become the DR. Interfaces to nonbroadcast networks, on which a DR is not elected, also have a priority of 0 (notice the priority of the serial interface in Figure 10.7). The router with the highest priority becomes the DR. In a tie, the router with the numerically highest System ID becomes the DR.

As the L1 and L2 priorities suggest, separate DRs are elected on a network for level 1 and level 2. This outcome is necessary because of the separate L1 and L2 adjacencies that can exist on a single LAN, as shown in Figure 10.8. Because an interface can have separate priorities for each level, the L1 DR and the L2 DR on a LAN might or might not be the same router.

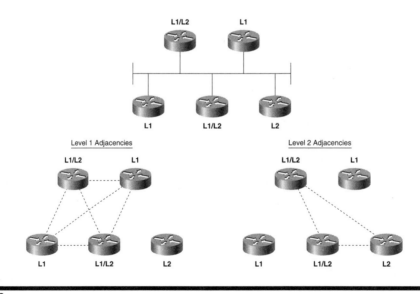

Figure 10.8

Separate adjacencies are established for level 1 and for level 2, so separate DRs must be elected for level 1 and level 2.

The DR assigns the LAN ID to the network. As discussed in the preceding section, the LAN ID is a concatenation of the DR's System ID and its Pseudonode ID for the attached network. All other routers on the network will use the LAN ID assigned by the DR.

Figure 10.9 shows the neighbor table of a router whose E0 interface is attached to the same network as the E0 interface of the router of Figure 10.7. By comparing these two tables, you can see that three routers are attached to the Ethernet: 0000.0c0a.2aa9, 0000.0c0a.2c51, and 0000.0c76.5b7c. All have a priority of 64, so the one with the numerically highest System ID is the DR. That router, 0000.0c76.5b7c, identifies the network with Circuit ID 02. Therefore, the LAN ID shown in both Figure 10.7 and Figure 10.9 is 0000.0c76.5b7c.02.

```
London#show clns is-neighbors

System Id        Interface   State  Type Priority  Circuit Id         Format
0000.0C76.5B7C Et0          Up     L2   64         0000.0C76.5B7C.02  Phase V
0000.0C0A.2AA9 Et0          Up     L2   64         0000.0C76.5B7C.02  Phase V
0000.3090.6756 Se0          Up     L1   0          02                 Phase V
London#
```

Figure 10.9

The E0 interface of this router is attached to the same network as the E0 interface of the router in Figure 10.7.

Appending the Circuit ID to the System ID is necessary because the same router can be the DR on more than one network. Notice in Figure 10.7 that the same router is the DR on the network attached to E0 and the network attached to E1. It is the Circuit ID, 02 on E0 and 03 on E1, which makes the LAN ID unique for each network.

The IS-IS DR process is more primitive (or less complex, depending upon one's viewpoint) than the OSPF DR process in two ways. First, IS-IS does not elect a Backup Designated Router. If the IS-IS

IS-IS Designated Router process compared to OSPF

DR fails, a new DR is elected. Second, the IS-IS DR is not as stable as the OSPF DR. If an OSPF router becomes active on a network with an existing DR, the new router will not become the DR even if its priority or Router ID is higher. As a result, the OSPF DR usually is the router that has been active on the network for the longest time. In contrast to the OSPF rules, a new IS-IS router with a higher priority than the existing DR, or an equal priority and a higher System ID, will become the new DR. Each time the DR is changed, a new set of LSPs must be flooded.

Subnetwork Independent Functions

The functions of the subnetwork-independent sublayer define how CLNS delivers packets throughout the CLNP internetwork and how these services are offered to the transport layer. The routing function itself is divided into four processes: the Update process, the Decision process, the Forwarding process, and the Receive process. As the names of the last two processes suggest, the Forwarding process is responsible for transmitting PDUs, and the Receive process is responsible for the reception of PDUs. These two processes, as described in ISO 10589, are more relevant to CLNS NPDUs than to IP packets, and so are not described further.

The Update Process

The Update process is responsible for constructing the L1 and L2 link state databases. To do so, L1 LSPs are flooded throughout an area, and L2 LSPs are flooded over all L2 adjacencies. The specific fields of the LSPs are described in the section "IS-IS PDU Formats."

Each LSP contains a Remaining Lifetime, a Sequence Number, and a Checksum. The Remaining Lifetime is an age. The difference between an IS-IS LSP's Remaining Lifetime and an OSPF LSA's Age parameter is that the LSA Age increments from zero to MaxAge, whereas the LSP Remaining Lifetime begins at MaxAge and decrements to zero. The IS-IS MaxAge is 1200 seconds (20 minutes). Like OSPF, IS-IS ages each LSP as it resides in the link state database, and the originator must periodically refresh its LSAs to prevent the Remaining Lifetime from reaching zero. The IS-IS refresh interval is 15 minutes minus a random jitter of up to 25%. If the Remaining Lifetime reaches zero, the expired LSP will be kept in the link state database for 60 seconds, known as the *ZeroAgeLifetime*.

If any router receives a LSP with an incorrect Checksum, the router will purge the LSP by setting the LSP's Remaining Lifetime to zero and reflooding it. The purge causes the LSP's originator to send a new instance of the LSP. This procedure is yet another way that IS-IS differs from OSPF, where only the originator can purge an OSPF LSA.

On error-prone subnetworks, allowing receiving routers to initiate purges can significantly increase the LSP traffic. To override this behavior, the command **ignore-lsp-errors** can be added to the IS-IS routing configuration. When a router with this option enabled receives a corrupted LSP, it ignores it rather than purging it. The originator of the corrupted LSP will still know that the LSP was not received through the use of SNPs, described later in this section.

The Sequence Number is an unsigned, 32-bit linear number. When a router first originates an LSP, it uses a Sequence Number of one, and each subsequent instance of the LSP has its Sequence Number incremented by one. If the Sequence Number increments to the maximum (0xFFFFFFFF), the IS-IS process must shut down for at least 21 minutes (MaxAge + ZeroAgeLifetime) to allow the old LSPs to age out of all databases.

Sequence Number

On point-to-point subnetworks, routers send L1 and L2 LSPs directly to the neighboring router. On broadcast subnetworks, the LSPs are multicast to all neighbors. Frames carrying L1 LSPs have

MAC identifiers for
broadcasting L1 and
L2 LSPs

a destination MAC identifier of 0180.c200.0014, known as AllL1ISs. Frames carrying L2 LSPs have a destination MAC identifier of 0180.c200.0015, known as AllL2ISs.

IS-IS uses SNPs both to acknowledge the receipt of LSPs and to maintain link state database synchronization. There are two types of SNPs: *Partial SNPs* (PSNPs) and *Complete SNPs* (CSNPs). On a point-to-point subnetwork, a router uses a PSNP to explicitly acknowledge each LSP it receives.[15] The PSNP describes the LSP it is acknowledging by including the following information:

- The LSP ID

- The LSP's Sequence Number

- The LSP's Checksum

- The LSP's Remaining Lifetime

When a router sends an LSP on a point-to-point subnetwork, it sets a timer for a period known as *minimumLSPTransmission-Interval*. If the timer expires before the router receives a PSNP acknowledging receipt of the LSP, a new LSP will be sent. On Cisco routers, the default minimumLSPTransmissionInterval is five seconds and can be changed on a per interface basis with the command **isis retransmit-interval**.

On broadcast subnetworks, LSPs are not acknowledged by each receiving router. Instead, the DR periodically multicasts a CSNP that describes every LSP in the link state database. The default CSNP period is 10 seconds and can be changed with the command **isis csnp-interval**. L1 CSNPs are multicast to AllL1ISs (0180.c200.0014), and L2 CSNPs are multicast to AllL2ISs (0180.c200.0015).

---

[15] *The exception is if a router receives an instance of an LSP that is older than an instance of the same LSP in its database. In that case, the router will reply with the newer LSP.*

When a router receives a CSNP, it compares the LSPs summarized in the PDU with the LSPs in its database. If the router has an LSP that is missing from the CSNP or a newer instance of an LSP, the router multicasts the LSP onto the network. If another router sends the updated LSP first, however, the router will not send another copy of the same LSP. If the router's database does not contain a copy of every LSP listed in the CSNP or if the database contains an older instance of an LSP, the router multicasts a PSNP listing the LSPs it needs. Although the PSNP is multicast, only the DR responds with the appropriate LSPs.

An interesting feature of IS-IS is its ability to signal other routers if it runs out of memory and cannot record the complete link state database. The memory overload might be due to an area that has been allowed to grow too large, a router with insufficient memory, or a transitory condition such as the failure of a DR. If a router cannot store the complete link state database, it will set a bit in its LSP called the *Overload* (OL) bit.

The OL bit signals that the router might not be able to make correct routing decisions because of its incomplete database. The other routers still route packets to the overloaded router's directly connected networks, but do not use the router for transit traffic until it has issued an LSP with the OL bit cleared. Because a set OL bit prevents the router from being used as a hop along a route, the bit is frequently called the *hippity* bit (as in hippity-hop, believe it or not).

Memory should be allocated equally to the L1 and the L2 database, but a router can be in an overload condition at one level and normal in the other. If you want to intentionally set an IS-IS router to act only as an end node, the OL bit can be set manually with the command **set-overload-bit**.

The command **show isis database** displays a summary of the IS-IS link state database, as shown in Figure 10.10. The router Brussels in this figure is an L1/L2 router, so it has both L1 and L2 databases. The LSP ID shown in the first column consists of the System ID of the originating router, concatenated with two more octets. The first octet following the System ID is the Pseudonode ID. If this octet is nonzero, the LSP was originated by a DR. The System ID and the nonzero Pseudonode ID together make the LAN ID of a broadcast subnetwork.

The last octet is the LSP Number. Occasionally, an LSP can be so large that it exceeds the MTU that can be supported by the router buffers or the data link. In this case, the LSP is *fragmented*—that is, the information is conveyed in multiple LSPs. The LSP IDs of these multiple LSPs consist of identical System IDs and Pseudonode IDs, and distinct LSP Numbers.

```
Brussels#show isis database
IS-IS Level-1 Link State Database
LSPID                   LSP Seq Num    LSP Checksum   LSP Holdtime   ATT/P/OL
0000.0C04.DCC0.00-00    0x00000036     0x78AE         1152           0/0/0
0000.0C0A.2AA9.00-00    0x0000011B     0x057B         416            0/0/0
0000.0C76.5B7C.00-00*   0x00000150     0xD5D4         961            1/0/0
0000.0C76.5B7C.02-00*   0x00000119     0xD9C3         407            0/0/0
0000.0C76.5B7C.03-00*   0x000000FA     0x896E         847            0/0/0

IS-IS Level-2 Link State Database
LSPID                   LSP Seq Num    LSP Checksum   LSP Holdtime   ATT/P/OL
0000.0C0A.2AA9.00-00    0x0000013E     0x319A         666            0/0/0
0000.0C0A.2C51.00-00    0x00000133     0x762D         654            0/0/0
0000.0C76.5B7C.00-00*   0x0000014C     0x4E91         886            0/0/0
0000.0C76.5B7C.02-00*   0x0000011F     0x3CC3         1174           0/0/0
0000.3090.C7DF.00-00    0x0000011A     0xDDF0         858            0/0/0
Brussels#
```

Figure 10.10

The IS-IS database can be observed with the command **show isis database**.

An asterisk following the LSP ID indicates that the LSP is originated by the router on which the database is being observed. For example, the database shown in Figure 10.10 is taken from a router named Brussels. The L1 LSP with an ID of 0000.0c76.5bB7c.00-00 is originated by Brussels, as are four other LSPs.

The second and third columns of the database display shows the Sequence Number and Checksum of each LSP. The fourth column, LSP Holdtime, is the Remaining Lifetime of the LSP in seconds. If you enter the **show isis database** command repeatedly, you can observe the numbers decrementing. When the LSP is refreshed, the Remaining Lifetime is reset to 1200 seconds and the Sequence Number is incremented by one.

The last column indicates the state of the Attached (ATT) bit, the Partition (P) bit, and the Overload (OL) bit of each LSP. L2 and L1/L2 routers will set the OL bit to one to indicate that they have a route to another area. The P bit indicates that the originating router has partition repair capability. Cisco (and most other vendors) does not support this function, so the bit is always set to zero. The OL bit is set to one if the originating router is experiencing a memory overload and has an incomplete link state database.

A complete LSP can be observed by using the command **show isis database detail** along with the level and the LSP ID, as shown in Figure 10.11. The meanings of the individual fields of the LSP are given in "IS-IS PDU Formats."

The Decision Process

Once the Update process has built the link state database, the Decision process uses the information in the database to calculate a shortest path tree. The process then uses the shortest path tree to construct a forwarding database (route table). Separate SPF calculations are run for the L1 routes and the L2 routes.

```
London#show isis database detail level-2 0000.0C0A.2C51.00-00

IS-IS Level-2 LSP 0000.0C0A.2C51.00-00
LSPID                    LSP Seq Num  LSP Checksum  LSP Holdtime  ATT/P/OL
0000.0C0A.2C51.00-00* 0x0000013B     0x6635        815           0/0/0
  Area Address: 47.0001
  NLPID:        0x81 0xCC
  IP Address:   10.1.3.2
  Metric: 10 IS 0000.0C76.5B7C.02
  Metric: 10 IP 10.1.3.0 255.255.255.0
  Metric: 20 IP 10.1.2.0 255.255.255.0
  Metric: 10 IP 10.1.255.4 255.255.255.252
  Metric: 20 IP 10.1.255.0 255.255.255.0
  Metric: 30 IP 10.1.255.8 255.255.255.252
London#
```

Figure 10.11

*The command **show isis database detail** is used to observe complete LSPs in the database.*

ISO 10589 specifies the following metrics (one required and three optional) to be used by IS-IS to calculate the shortest path:

IS-IS metrics

- *Default.* This metric must be supported and understood by every IS-IS router.

- *Delay.* This optional metric reflects the transit delay of a subnetwork.

- *Expense.* This optional metric reflects the monetary cost of using the subnetwork.

- *Error.* This optional metric reflects the residual error probability of the subnetwork, similar to the IGRP/EIGRP reliability metric.

Each metric is expressed as an integer between 0 and 63, and a separate route is calculated for each metric. Therefore, if a system supports all four metrics, the SPF calculation must be run four times for both L1 routes and L2 routes. Because of the potential for many iterations of the SPF calculation for every destination, resulting in many different route tables, and because the optional metrics provide rudimentary Type of Service routing at best, Cisco supports only the default metric.

Cisco assigns a default metric of 10 to every interface, regardless of the interface type. The command **isis metric** changes the value of the default metric, and the default can be changed separately for level 1 and level 2. If the metrics are left at 10 for every interface, every subnetwork is considered equal and the IS-IS metric becomes a simple measure of hop count, where each hop has a cost of 10.

The total cost of a route is a simple sum of the individual metrics at each outgoing interface, and the maximum metric value that can be assigned to any route is 1023. This small maximum is frequently pointed out as a limitation of IS-IS because it leaves little room for metric granularity in large internetworks. The flip side of this criticism, however, is that limiting the metric to 1023 makes the SPF algorithm more efficient.

IS-IS not only classifies routes as L1 or L2 but also classifies routes as *internal* or *external*. Internal routes are paths to destinations within the IS-IS routing domain, and external routes are paths to destinations external to the routing domain. Whereas L2 routes may be either internal or external, L1 routes are always internal.

Internal and external routes

Given multiple possible routes to a particular destination, an L1 path is preferred over an L2 path. Within each level, a path that supports the optional metrics is preferred over a path that supports only the default metric. (Again, Cisco supports only the default metric, so the second order of preference is not relevant to Cisco routers.) Within each level of metric support, the path with the lowest metric is preferred. If multiple equal-cost, equal-level paths are found by the Decision process, they are all entered into the route table. Cisco's IS-IS implementation will perform equal-cost load balancing on up to six paths.

The previous section, "The Update Process," discussed the last octet of the LSP ID, known as the LSP Number, used to track fragmented LSPs. The Decision process pays attention to the LSP Number for several reasons. First, if an LSP with an LSP Number of zero and a nonzero Remaining Lifetime is not present in the database, the Decision process will not process any LSPs from the same system that have nonzero LSP Numbers. For example, if the LSP IDs 0000.0c76.5b7c.00-01 and 0000.0c76.5b7c.00-02 exist in the database, but the database contains no LSP with an LSP ID of 0000.0c76.5b7c.00-00, the first two LSPs are not processed. This approach ensures that incomplete LSPs do not cause inaccurate routing decisions.

Also, the Decision process will accept the following information only from LSPs whose LSP Number is zero:

- The setting of the Database Overload bit

- The setting of the IS Type field

- The setting of the Area Addresses option field

The Decision process ignores these settings in LSPs whose LSP Number is nonzero. In other words, the first LSP in a series of fragments speaks for all the fragments for these three settings.

Figure 10.12 shows a route table from a Cisco IS-IS router. Notice that the L1 and L2 routes are indicated and that three destinations have multiple paths. A mask is associated with each route, indicating support for VLSM. Finally, the route table indicates that the administrative distance of IS-IS routes is 115.

Another duty of the Decision process in L1 routers is to calculate the path to the nearest L2 router, for inter-area routing. As previously discussed, when an L2 or L1/L2 router is attached to another area, the router will advertise the fact by setting the ATT

```
Brussels#show ip route
Codes: C - connected, S - static, I - IGRP, R - RIP, M - mobile, B - BGP
       D - EIGRP, EX - EIGRP external, O - OSPF, IA - OSPF inter area
       E1 - OSPF external type 1, E2 - OSPF external type 2, E - EGP
       i - IS-IS, L1 - IS-IS level-1, L2 - IS-IS level-2, * - candidate default

Gateway of last resort is not set

     10.0.0.0 is variably subnetted, 8 subnets, 3 masks
C       10.1.3.0 255.255.255.0 is directly connected, Ethernet0
i L2    10.1.2.0 255.255.255.0 [115/30] via 10.1.3.2, Ethernet0
                               [115/30] via 10.1.3.3, Ethernet0
i L1    10.1.5.0 255.255.255.0 [115/20] via 0.0.0.0, Serial0
                               [115/20] via 10.1.4.2, Ethernet1
C       10.1.4.0 255.255.255.0 is directly connected, Ethernet1
i L2    10.1.255.4 255.255.255.252 [115/20] via 10.1.3.2, Ethernet0
i L2    10.1.255.0 255.255.255.0 [115/30] via 10.1.3.2, Ethernet0
i L1    10.1.255.8 255.255.255.252 [115/20] via 10.1.3.3, Ethernet0
i L1    10.1.6.240 255.255.255.240 [115/20] via 0.0.0.0, Serial0
                               [115/20] via 10.1.4.2, Ethernet1
Brussels#
```

Figure 10.12

This route table shows both level 1 and level 2 IS-IS routes.

bit in its LSP to one. The Decision process in L1 routers will choose the metrically closest L1/L2 router as the default inter-area router. When IS-IS is used to route IP, a default IP route to the L1/L2 is entered into the route table. For example, Figure 10.13 shows a link state database for an L1 router and its associated route table. LSP 0000.0c0a.2c51.00-00 has an ATT = 1. Based upon this information, the Decision process has chosen the router with System ID 0000.0c0a.2c51 as the default inter-area router. The route table shows a default route (0.0.0.0) via 10.1.255.6, with a metric of 10. Although it is not readily apparent from the information shown in Figure 10.13, 10.1.255.6 and System ID 0000.0c0a.2c51 refer to the same router.

The information in Figure 10.13 illustrates a basic problem of working with Integrated IS-IS, particularly when troubleshooting.

```
Paris#show isis database
IS-IS Level-1 Link State Database
LSPID                LSP Seq Num  LSP Checksum  LSP Holdtime  ATT/P/OL
0000.0C0A.2C51.00-00  0x0000016D   0xA093        730           1/0/0
0000.3090.6756.00-00* 0x00000167   0xC103        813           0/0/0
0000.3090.6756.04-00* 0x0000014E   0x227F        801           0/0/0
0000.3090.C7DF.00-00  0x00000158   0x78A6        442           0/0/0
Paris#show ip route
Codes: C - connected, S - static, I - IGRP, R - RIP, M - mobile, B - BGP
       D - EIGRP, EX - EIGRP external, O - OSPF, IA - OSPF inter area
       E1 - OSPF external type 1, E2 - OSPF external type 2, E - EGP
       i - IS-IS, L1 - IS-IS level-1, L2 - IS-IS level-2, * - candidate default

Gateway of last resort is 10.1.255.6 to network 0.0.0.0

     10.0.0.0 is variably subnetted, 5 subnets, 2 masks
i L1    10.1.3.0 255.255.255.0 [115/20] via 10.1.255.6, Serial0
C       10.1.2.0 255.255.255.0 is directly connected, TokenRing0
i L1    10.1.255.4 255.255.255.252 [115/20] via 10.1.255.6, Serial0
C       10.1.255.0 255.255.255.0 is directly connected, Serial0
i L1    10.1.255.8 255.255.255.252 [115/20] via 10.1.2.2, TokenRing0
i*L1 0.0.0.0 0.0.0.0 [115/10] via 10.1.255.6, Serial0
Paris#
```

Figure 10.13

Integrated IS-IS adds a default IP route to the nearest L1/L2 router whose ATT bit is set to one.

Although TCP/IP is the protocol being routed, the protocol determining the routes, including all the route control packets and addresses, is a CLNS protocol. Sometimes correlating the CLNS information with the IP information can be difficult. One command that can be useful is **which-route.**

The command is used primarily to determine the route table in which a particular CLNS destination is located. However, **which route** can also yield useful information about the IP addresses associated with a particular CLNS address. In Figure 10.14 the System ID/Circuit ID 0000.0c0a.2c51.00, shown in the database of Figure 10.13 as having ATT = 1, is used as the argument to **which-route.** The result shows, among other things, that the next-hop address for the queried System ID is 10.1.255.6.

```
Paris#which-route 0000.0C0A.2C51.00
Route look-up for destination 00.000c.0a2c.5100
  Using route to closest IS-IS level-2 router

Adjacency entry used:
System Id       SNPA              Interface   State  Holdtime  Type Protocol
0000.0C0A.2C51 *HDLC*            Se0         Up     26        L1   IS-IS
  Area Address(es): 47.0001
  IP Address(es):  10.1.255.6
  Uptime: 22:08:52
Paris#
```

Figure 10.14

*The command **which-route** can reveal some information tying CLNS addresses to IP addresses.*

IS-IS PDU Formats

IS-IS uses nine PDU types in its processes, and each PDU is identified by a five-bit type number. The PDUs fall into three categories, as shown in Table 10.1.

Table 10.1 *IS-IS PDU types.*

IS-IS PDU	Type Number
Hello PDUs	
Level 1 LAN IS-IS Hello PDU	15
Level 2 LAN IS-IS Hello PDU	16
Point-to-point IS-IS Hello PDU	17
Link State PDUs	
Level 1 LSP	18
Level 2 LSP	20
Sequence Numbers PDUs	
Level 1 CSNP	24
Level 2 CNSP	25
Level 1 PSNP	26
Level 2 PSNP	27

The first eight octets of all of the IS-IS PDUs are header fields that are common to all PDU types, as shown in Figure 10.15. These first fields are described here, and the PDU-specific fields are described in subsequent sections.

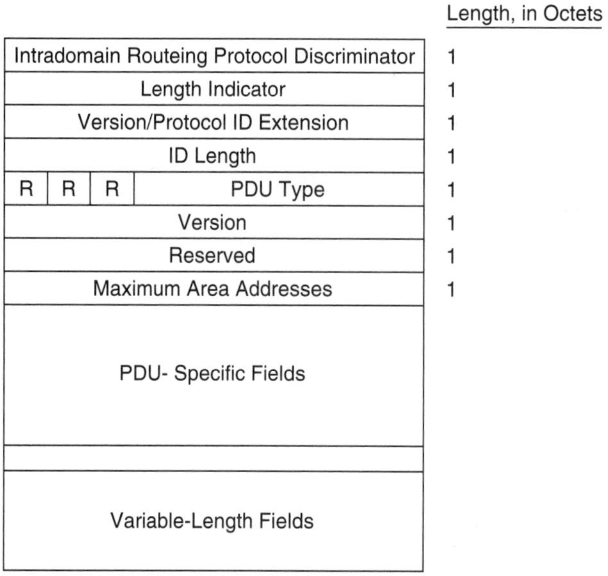

Length, in Octets

Intradomain Routeing Protocol Discriminator	1
Length Indicator	1
Version/Protocol ID Extension	1
ID Length	1
R R R PDU Type	1
Version	1
Reserved	1
Maximum Area Addresses	1
PDU- Specific Fields	
Variable-Length Fields	

Figure 10.15

The first eight octets of the IS-IS PDUs.

Intradomain Routeing Protocol Discriminator is a constant assigned by ISO 9577[16] to identify NPDUs. All IS-IS PDUs have a value of 0x83 in this field.

Length Indicator specifies the length of the fixed header in octets.

Version/Protocol ID Extension is always set to one.

---

[16] *International Organization for Standardization, "Protocol Identification in the Network Layer," ISO/IEC TR 9577, 1990.*

ID Length describes the length of the System ID field of NSAP addresses and NETs used in this routing domain. This field is set to one of the following values:

- An integer between 1 and 8 inclusive, indicating a System ID field of the same length in octets

- 0, indicating a System ID field of six octets

- 255, indicating a null System ID field (zero octets)

The System ID of Cisco routers must be six octets, so the ID Length field of a Cisco-originated PDU will always be zero.

PDU Type is a five-bit field containing one of the PDU type numbers shown in Table 10.1. The preceding three bits (R) are reserved and are always set to zero.

Version is always set to one, just like the Version/Protocol ID Extension in the third octet.

Reserved is always set to all zeroes.

Maximum Area Addresses describes the number of area addresses permitted for this IS area. The number is set to one of the following values:

- An integer between 1 and 254 inclusive, indicating the number of areas allowed

- 0, indicating that the IS only supports a maximum of three addresses

Cisco IOS supports a maximum of three areas, so the Maximum Area Addresses field in IS-IS PDUs originated by Cisco routers will always be zero.

In Figure 10.16, an analyzer capture of an IS-IS PDU shows the first eight octets of the PDU.

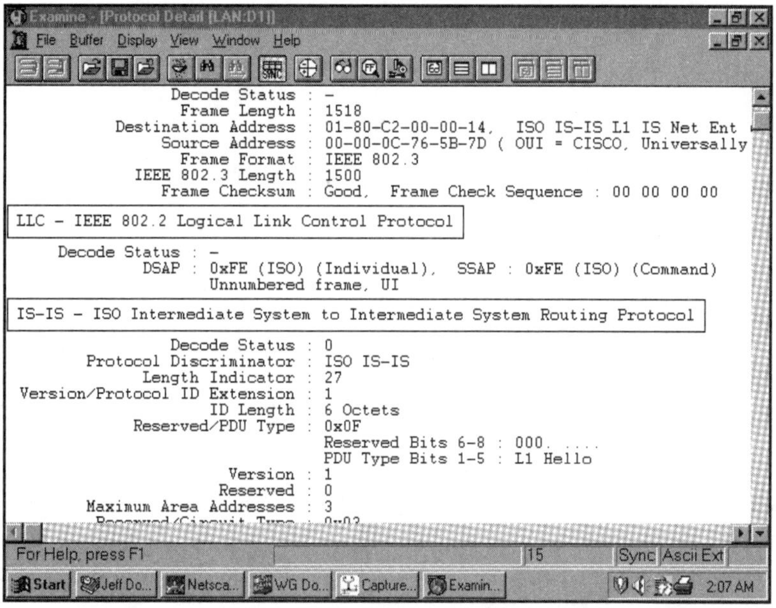

Figure 10.16

This analyzer capture shows the first eight fields of an IS-IS PDU, along with its data link header.

The PDU-specific fields following the common header fields are also part of the header; they vary according to PDU type and are discussed in the sections dealing with specific PDU types.

CLV Fields

The variable-length fields following the PDU-specific fields are *Code/Length/Value* (CLV)[17] triplets, as shown in Figure 10.17.

---

[17] *The acronym CLV is not used in ISO 10589, but is used here for convenience. You are already familiar with the concept of CLVs from the coverage of EIGRP TLVs in Chapter 8, "Enhanced Interior Gateway Routing Protocol (EIGRP)." In fact, RFC 1195 refers to Integrated IS-IS CLVs as TLVs.*

The Code is a number specifying the information content of the value field, the Length specifies the length of the Value field, and the Value field is the information itself. As the one-octet size of the Length field implies, the maximum size of the Value field is 255 octets.

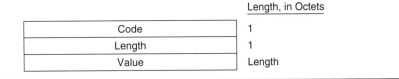

	Length, in Octets
Code	1
Length	1
Value	Length

Figure 10.17
IS-IS Code/Length/Value triplets perform the same function for IS-IS as Type/Length/Value triplets perform for EIGRP.

Table 10.2 lists the IS-IS CLV codes. The table also indicates whether the CLV is specified in ISO 10589 or in RFC 1195. The ISO-specified CLVs are designed for use with CLNP, although most of them are also used with IP. The RFC-specified CLVs are designed only for IP. If a router does not recognize a particular CLV code, it will ignore the CLV. This arrangement allows CLVs for CLNP, IP, or both to be carried in the same PDU.

Table 10.2 *CLV codes used with IS-IS.*

Code	CLV Type	ISO 10589	RFC 1195
1	Area Addresses	X	
2	IS Neighbors (LSPs)	X	
3	ES Neighbors[*]	X	
4	Partition Designated level 2 IS[†]	X	
5	Prefix Neighbors[*]	X	
6	IS Neighbors (Hellos)	X	
8	Padding	X	
9	LSP Entries	X	

Table 10.2   CLV codes used with IS-IS, continued.

Code	CLV Type	ISO 10589	RFC 1195
10	Authentication Information	X	
128	IP Internal Reachability Information		X
129	Protocols Supported		X
130	IP External Reachability Information		X
131	Inter-Domain Routing Protocol Information		X
132	IP Interface Address		X
133	Authentication Information‡		X

* The ES-Neighbors and Prefix Neighbors CLVs are not relevant to IP routing and are not covered in this book.
† This CLV is used for partition repair, which Cisco does not support.
‡ RFC 1195 specifies this code for IP authentication, but Cisco uses the ISO code of 10.

Although many of the CLVs are used by more than one IS-IS PDU type, only one (Authentication) is used by all PDUs. As the formats of the IS-IS PDUs are described in the following sections, the CLVs used by each PDU are listed. The format of each CLV is described only once, the first time it is listed. Table 10.3 summarizes which CLVs are used with which PDUs.

Table 10.3   The CLVs used by each IS-IS PDU.

CLV Type	PDU Type								
	15	16	17	18	20	24	25	26	27
Area addresses	X	X	X	X	X				
IS Neighbors (LSPs)				X	X				
ES Neighbors				X					
Partition Designated Level 2 IS					X				
Prefix Neighbors					X				
IS Neighbors (Hellos)	X	X							
Padding	X	X	X						
LSP Entries						X	X	X	X

Table 10.3 *The CLVs used by each IS-IS PDU, continued.*

CLV Type	PDU Type								
	15	16	17	18	20	24	25	26	27
Authentication Information	X	X	X	X	X	X	X	X	X
IP Internal Reachability Information				X	X				
Protocols Supported	X	X	X	X	X				
IP External Reachability Information					X				
Inter-Domain Routing Protocol Information					X				
IP Interface Address	X	X	X	X	X				

The IS-IS Hello PDU Format

The purpose of the IS-IS Hello PDU is to allow IS-IS routers to discover IS-IS neighbors on a link. Once the neighbors have been discovered and have become adjacent, the job of the Hello PDU is to act as a keepalive to maintain the adjacency and to inform the neighbors of any changes in the adjacency parameters.

The upper limit on the size of an IS-IS PDU is defined by either the buffer size of the originating router or the MTU of the data link on which the PDU is transmitted. ISO 10589 specifies that IS-IS Hellos must be padded to within one octet less than this maximum, partly to allow a router to implicitly communicate its MTU to its neighbors. More important, sending Hellos at or near the link MTU is intended to help detect link failure modes in which small PDUs pass but larger PDUs are dropped. The benefit of this design decision, weighed against the expense of sending such large Hellos over low-speed serial links, is debatable.

There are two kinds of IS-IS Hellos: LAN Hellos and point-to-point Hellos. The LAN Hellos can be further divided into

L1 and L2 LAN Hellos. The format of the two types of LAN Hellos is identical, as shown in Figure 10.18. Figure 10.19 shows an analyzer capture of a level 2 LAN Hello.

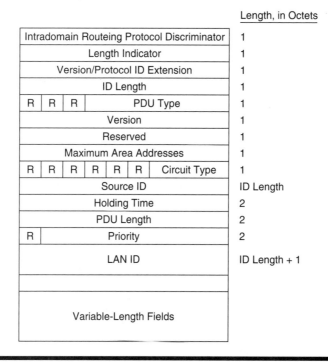

Length, in Octets

Intradomain Routeing Protocol Discriminator	1
Length Indicator	1
Version/Protocol ID Extension	1
ID Length	1
R R R PDU Type	1
Version	1
Reserved	1
Maximum Area Addresses	1
R R R R R R Circuit Type	1
Source ID	ID Length
Holding Time	2
PDU Length	2
R Priority	2
LAN ID	ID Length + 1
Variable-Length Fields	

Figure 10.18

The IS-IS LAN Hello PDU format.

Circuit Type is a two-bit field (the preceding six bits are reserved and are always zero) specifying whether the router is an L1 (01), L2 (10), or L1/L2 (11). If both bits are zero (00), the entire PDU is ignored.

Source ID is the System ID of the router that originated the Hello.

Holding Time is the period a neighbor should wait to hear the next Hello before declaring the originating router dead.

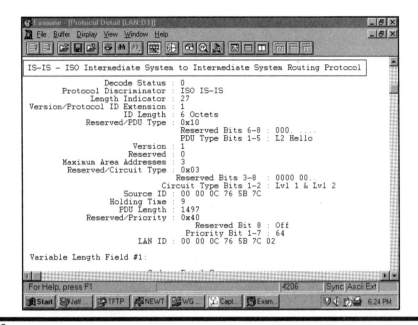

Figure 10.19

This analyzer capture of a LAN Hello shows the fields unique to a Hello PDU.

PDU Length is the length of the entire PDU in octets.

Priority is a seven-bit field used for the election of a DR. The field carries a value between 0 and 127 with the higher number having the higher priority. L1 DRs are elected by the priority in L1 LAN Hellos, and L2 DRs are elected by the priority in L2 LAN Hellos.

LAN ID is the System ID of the DR plus one more octet (the Pseudonode ID) to differentiate this LAN ID from another LAN ID that might have the same DR.

The following CLVs can be used by an IS-IS LAN Hello:[18]

- Area Addresses (type 1)

- Intermediate System Neighbors (type 6)

- Padding (type 8)

- Authentication Information (type 10)

- Protocols Supported (type 129)

- IP Interface Address (type 132)

Figure 10.20 shows the format of the IS-IS point-to-point Hello PDU. It is almost identical to the LAN Hello except that there is no Priority field and there is a Local Circuit ID field instead of a LAN ID field. Unlike LAN Hellos, L1 and L2 information is carried in the same point-to-point Hello PDU.

Local Circuit ID is a one-octet ID assigned to this circuit by the router originating the Hello and is unique among the router's interfaces. The Local Circuit ID in the Hellos at the other end of the point-to-point link may or may not contain the same value.

The IS-IS point-to-point Hello does not use the IS Neighbors CLV. With that exception, the same CLVs are used as the LAN Hello.

Area Addresses CLV

The Area Addresses CLV (Figure 10.21) is used to advertise the area addresses configured on the originating router. As the multiple Address Length/Area Address fields imply, a router can be configured with multiple area addresses. There will never be more than three Address Length/Area Address fields in PDUs originated

---

[18] *As a reminder, RFC 1195 also specifies an Authentication Information CLV with a type number of 133. Cisco uses the ISO-specified type number of 10 to identify its Authentication Information CLVs.*

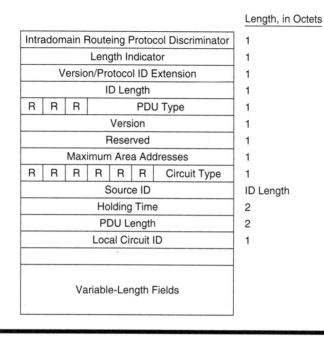

Length, in Octets

Intradomain Routeing Protocol Discriminator	1
Length Indicator	1
Version/Protocol ID Extension	1
ID Length	1
R R R PDU Type	1
Version	1
Reserved	1
Maximum Area Addresses	1
R R R R R R Circuit Type	1
Source ID	ID Length
Holding Time	2
PDU Length	2
Local Circuit ID	1
Variable-Length Fields	

Figure 10.20
The IS-IS point-to-point Hello PDU.

by Cisco routers because that is the maximum number of area addresses supported.

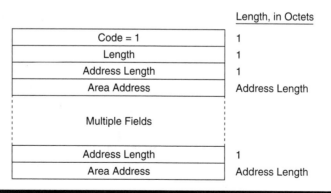

Length, in Octets

Code = 1	1
Length	1
Address Length	1
Area Address	Address Length
Multiple Fields	
Address Length	1
Area Address	Address Length

Figure 10.21
The Area Addresses CLV.

Figure 10.22 shows part of an IS-IS Hello PDU; Variable Length Field #3 is an Area Addresses CLV with a total length of six octets. There are two area addresses: 47.0002 (three octets), and 0 (one octet).

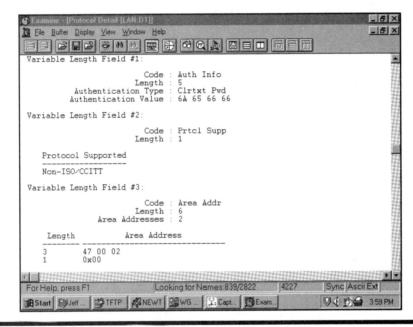

Figure 10.22

An Area Addresses CLV is shown as Variable Length Field #3. The analyzer also indicates the total addresses listed in the CLV (2) for convenience, but this information is not one of the CLV fields.

Intermediate System Neighbors CLV (Hello)

The IS Neighbors CLV (Figure 10.23) lists the System IDs of all neighbors from whom a Hello has been heard within the last Hold Time. Note that this CLV gives the IS-IS LAN Hello a function similar to the OSPF function of listing all recently-heard-from neighbors in order to verify two-way communication.

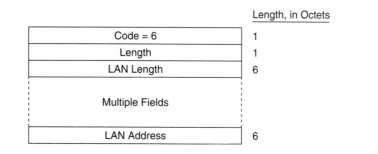

Figure 10.23
The IS Neighbors CLV for Hello PDUs.

This CLV is used only in LAN Hellos; it is not carried in point-to-point Hellos, where no DR election is performed. It is also different from the IS Neighbors CLV used by LSPs, and the two are distinguished by their type numbers. L1 LAN Hellos list L1 neighbors only, and L2 LAN Hellos list L2 neighbors. Although fields carrying System IDs are frequently of variable length, the fields of this CLV are always six octets. The length can be fixed because the System IDs always belong to routers on LANs, and are therefore always MAC identifiers. Variable Length Field #5 in Figure 10.24 shows an IS Neighbors CLV in which a single neighbor, 0000.0c0a.2aa9, is listed.

Padding CLV

The Padding CLV is used to pad a Hello PDU out to at least its minimum-allowed size. Since the maximum size of a Value field is 255 octets, multiple Padding CLVs are often used. The bits in the Value field can be arbitrary because they are ignored; Cisco sets all these bits to zero (Figure 10.25).

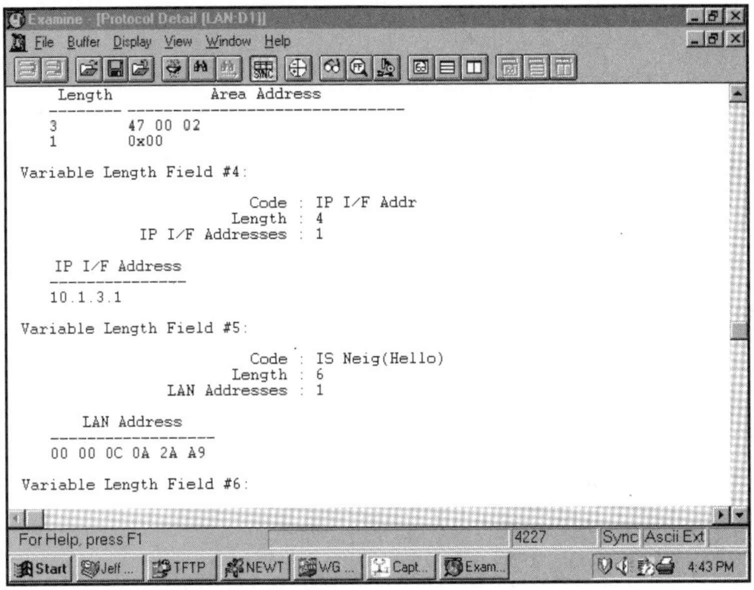

Figure 10.24

An IS Neighbors CLV is shown as Variable Length Field #5.

Authentication Information CLV

The Authentication Information CLV (Figure 10.26) is used when authentication is configured. The Authentication Type field contains a number between 0 and 255 that specifies the type of authentication used and hence the type of information contained in the Authentication Value field. The only authentication type currently defined by ISO 10589 or supported by Cisco is a clear-text password, which is Authentication Type 1.

Variable Length Field #1 in Figure 10.22 is an Authentication Information CLV. The password is "jeff," which is displayed as the hex representation of its ASCII characters.

```
 Examine - [Protocol Detail [LAN:D1]]                                    _ 8 X
 File  Buffer  Display  View  Window  Help                               _ 8 X

                              Code   :  Padding
                              Length :  255
                              Padding :  00 00 00 00 00 00 00 00 00...
 Variable Length Field #8:

                              Code   :  Padding
                              Length :  255
                              Padding :  00 00 00 00 00 00 00 00 00...

 Variable Length Field #9:

                              Code   :  Padding
                              Length :  255
                              Padding :  00 00 00 00 00 00 00 00 00...

 Variable Length Field #10:

                              Code   :  Padding
                              Length :  152
                              Padding :  00 00 00 00 00 00 00 00 00...


 For Help, press F1                                  4206    Sync Ascii Ext
 Start   Jeff...   TFTP   NEWT   WG...   Capt...   Exam...          9:34 PM
```

Figure 10.25

The last Variable Length Fields of the Hello PDU shown in Figure 10.19 are Padding CLVs, which bring the size of the PDU to the 1497-octet length shown in Figure 10.19. With the addition of the 3-octet LLC header and the 18-octet Ethernet header, the entire frame size is the 1518-octet Ethernet MTU.

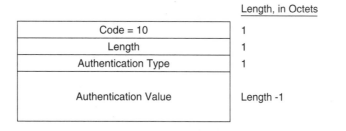

	Length, in Octets
Code = 10	1
Length	1
Authentication Type	1
Authentication Value	Length -1

Figure 10.26

The Authentication Information CLV.

Protocols Supported CLV

The Protocols Supported CLV (Figure 10.27) is specified in RFC 1195, and its purpose is to indicate whether the originator of the PDU supports CLNP only, IP only, or both. For each protocol supported, the corresponding one-octet Network Layer Protocol Identifier (NLPID), specified in ISO/TR 9577, is listed in the CLV. IP is 0x81. Variable Length Field #2 in Figure 10.22 is a Protocols Supported CLV.

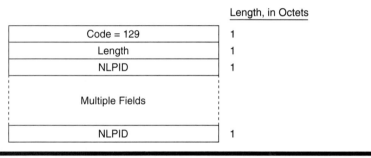

Figure 10.27
The Protocols Supported CLV.

IP Interface Address CLV

The IP Interface Address CLV (Figure 10.28) contains the IP address or addresses of the interface out which the PDU was sent. Because the Length field is one octet, an interface of an IS-IS router can theoretically have up to 255 IP addresses. Variable Length Field #4 in Figure 10.24 is an IP Interface Address CLV, indicating that the captured Hello PDU was transmitted from an interface with an address of 10.1.3.1.

The IS-IS Link State PDU Format

The IS-IS LSP performs essentially the same function as the OSPF LSA. An L1 router floods a L1 LSP throughout an area to identify

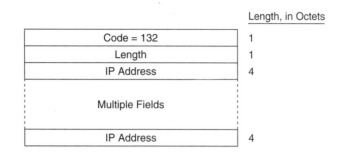

Figure 10.28
The IP Interface Address CLV.

its adjacencies and the state of those adjacencies. An L2 router floods L2 LSPs throughout the level 2 domain, identifying adjacencies to other L2 routers and address prefixes that the advertising L2 router can reach.

Figure 10.29 shows the format of the IS-IS LSP. The format is the same for both L1 LSPs and L2 LSPs.

PDU Length is the length of the entire PDU in octets.

Remaining Lifetime is the number of seconds before the LSP is considered to be expired.

LSP ID is the System ID, the Pseudonode ID, and the LSP Number of the LSP. The LSP ID is described in more detail in "The Update Process."

Sequence Number is a 32-bit unsigned integer.

Checksum is the checksum of the contents of the LSP.

P is the Partition Repair bit. Although the bit exists in both L1 and L2 LSPs, it is relevant only in L2 LSPs. When this bit is set, it indicates that the originating router supports the automatic repair of area partitions. Cisco IOS does not support this function, so the P bit of LSPs originated by Cisco routers will always be zero.

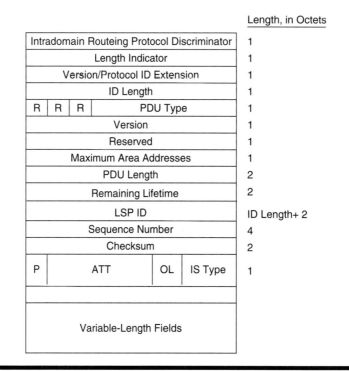

Figure 10.29
The IS-IS LSP format.

ATT is a four-bit field indicating that the originating router is attached to one or more other areas. Although the bits exist in both L1 and L2 LSPs, they are relevant only in L1 LSPs that have been originated by L1/L2 routers. The four bits indicate which metrics are supported by the attachment. Reading from left to right, the bits indicate:

- Bit 7: The Error metric
- Bit 6: The Expense metric
- Bit 5: The Delay metric
- Bit 4: The Default metric

Cisco IOS supports only the default metric, so bits 5 through 7 will always be zero.

OL is the Link State Database Overload bit. Under normal circumstances, this bit will be zero. If the originating router is experiencing a memory overload condition, it will set the OL bit to one. Routers receiving an LSP with the OL bit set will not use the originating router as a transit router, although they will still route to destinations on the originator's directly connected links.

IS Type is a two-bit field indicating whether the originating router is an L1 or an L2:

- 00 = Unused value

- 01 = L1

- 10 = Unused value

- 11 = L2

An L1/L2 router sets the bits according to whether the LSP is an L1 or an L2 LSP.

The following CLVs can be used by an L1 LSP:

- Area Addresses (type 1)

- IS Neighbors (type 2)

- ES Neighbors (type 3);

- Authentication Information (type 10)

- IP Internal Reachability Information (type 128)

- Protocols Supported (type 129)

- IP Interface Address (type 132)

The following CLVs can be used by an L2 LSP:

- Area Addresses (type 1)

- IS Neighbors (type 2)

- Partition Designated Level 2 IS (type 4)

- Prefix Neighbors (type 5)

- Authentication Information (type 10)

- IP Internal Reachability Information (type 128)

- IP External Reachability Information (type 130)

- Inter-Domain Routing Protocol Information (type 131)

- Protocols Supported (type 129)

- IP Interface Address (type 132)

Figure 10.30 shows an L1 LSP that was originated by an L1/L2 router.

Intermediate System Neighbors CLV (LSP)

The Intermediate System Neighbors CLV used by LSPs (Figure 10.31) lists the originating router's IS-IS neighbors (including pseudonodes) and the metrics of the router's link to each of its neighbors.

Virtual Flag, although eight bits long, has a value of either 0x01 or 0x00. A 0x01 in this field indicates that the link is a level 2 virtual link to repair an area partition. The field is relevant only to L2 routers that support area partition repair; Cisco does not, so the field will always be 0x00 in Cisco-originated LSPs.

R is a reserved bit and is always zero.

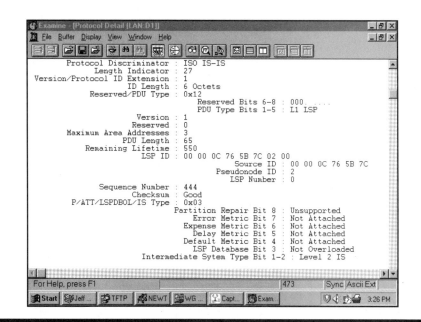

Figure 10.30
An analyzer capture of an LSP.

I/E, associated with each of the metrics, indicates whether the associated metric is internal or external. The bit has no meaning in IS Neighbors CLVs because all neighbors are by definition internal to the IS-IS domain. Therefore, this bit is always zero in IS Neighbors CLVs.

Default Metric is the six-bit default metric for the originating router's link to the listed neighbor and contains a value between 0 and 63.

S, associated with each of the optional metrics, indicates whether the metric is supported (zero) or unsupported (one). Cisco does not support any of the three optional metrics, so the bit is always set to one and the associated six-bit metric fields are all zeroes.

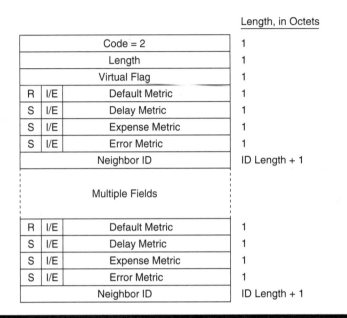

Figure 10.31

The Intermediate System Neighbors CLV for LSPs.

Neighbor ID is the System ID of the neighbor, plus one more octet. If the neighbor is a router, the last octet is 0x00. If the neighbor is a pseudonode, the System ID is that of the DR and the last octet is the Pseudonode ID.

Figure 10.32 shows part of an IS Neighbors CLV.

IP Internal Reachability Information CLV

The IP Internal Reachability Information CLV (Figure 10.33) lists IP addresses and associated masks within the routing domain that are directly connected to the advertising router. The CLV is used by both L1 and L2 LSPs, but never appears in an LSP describing a pseudonode. The metric fields are identical to the IS Neighbors CLV, except that no I/E bit is associated with the optional metrics.

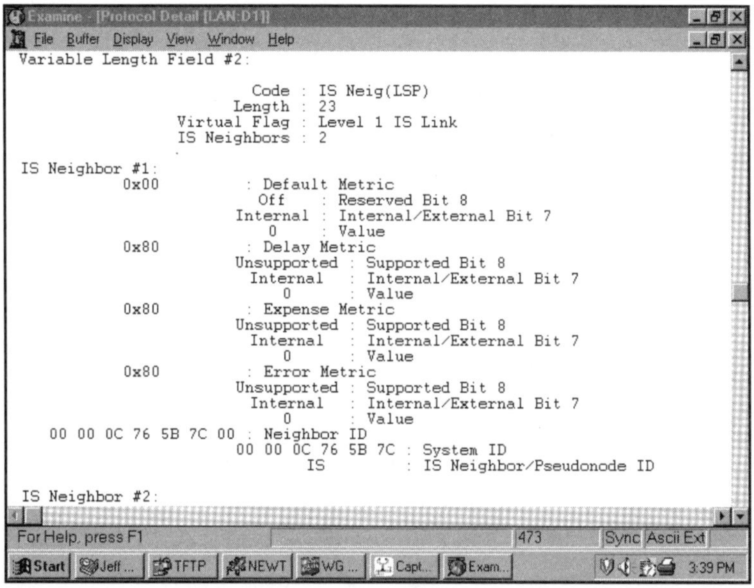

Figure 10.32
Part of an IS Neighbors CLV in an LSP.

Instead, the bit is reserved and is always zero. Like the IS Neighbors CLV, the I/E bit in this CLV is always zero because the addresses advertised in the CLV are always internal. Figure 10.34 shows an analyzer capture of an IP Internal Reachability Information CLV.

IP External Reachability Information CLV

The IP External Reachability Information CLV lists IP addresses and associated masks external to the routing domain, which can be reached via one of the originating router's interfaces. Its format is identical to the Internal Reachability Information CLV shown in Figure 10.33 except for the code, which is 130. However, unlike the Internal Reachability Information CLV, this CLV can be used only

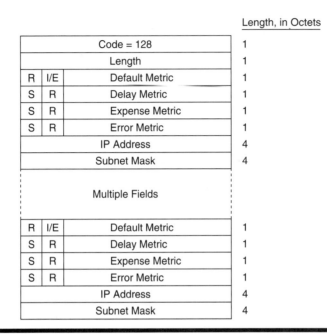

Length, in Octets

		Field	Length
		Code = 128	1
		Length	1
R	I/E	Default Metric	1
S	R	Delay Metric	1
S	R	Expense Metric	1
S	R	Error Metric	1
		IP Address	4
		Subnet Mask	4
		Multiple Fields	
R	I/E	Default Metric	1
S	R	Delay Metric	1
S	R	Expense Metric	1
S	R	Error Metric	1
		IP Address	4
		Subnet Mask	4

Figure 10.33

The IP Internal Reachability Information CLV.

by L2 LSPs. The I/E bit determines the metric type for all four metrics—I/E = 0 for internal metrics, and I/E = 1 for external metrics.

Inter-Domain Routing Protocol Information CLV

The Inter-Domain Routing Protocol Information CLV (Figure 10.35) allows L2 LSPs to transparently carry information from external routing protocols through the IS-IS domain. The CLV serves the same purpose as the Route Tag fields of RIPv2, EIGRP, and OSPF packets. Route tagging is covered in Chapter 14, "Route Maps."

Inter-Domain Information Type specifies the type of information contained in the variable-length External Information field. If the type field is 0x01, the External Information is of a format used by

```
Examine - [Protocol Detail [LAN:D1]]                                    _ 8 X
File  Buffer  Display  View  Window  Help                               _ 8 X
Variable Length Field #4:

                      Code : Intn Rch Info
                    Length : 24
Internal Reachability Information : 2

Internal Reachability Info #1:
       0x0A      : Default Metric
                Off      : Reserved Bit 8
                Internal : Internal/External Bit 7
                10       : Value
       0x80      : Delay Metric
                Unsupported : Supported Bit 8
                      Off   : Reserved Bit 7
                      0     : Value
       0x80      : Expense Metric
                Unsupported : Supported Bit 8
                      Off   : Reserved Bit 7
                      0     : Value
       0x80      : Error Metric
                Unsupported : Supported Bit 8
                      Off   : Reserved Bit 7
                      0     : Value
       10.1.3.0   : IP Address
       255.255.255.0 : Subnet Mask

Internal Reachability Info #2:
       0x0A      : Default Metric
                Off      : Reserved Bit 8

For Help, press F1                              471      Sync Ascii Ext
Start  Jeff Do...  TFTP  NEWT  W/G Do...  Capture...  Examin...   4:41 PM
```

Figure 10.34

An analyzer capture of an IP Internal Reachability Information CLV.

	Length, in Octets
Code = 131	1
Length	1
Inter-Domain Information Type	1
External Information	Variable

Figure 10.35

The Inter-Domain Routing Protocol Information CLV.

the local interdomain routing protocol. Chapter 14 includes examples of using route maps to set such local information. If the type field is 0x02, the External Information is a 16-bit autonomous system number, which is used to tag all subsequent External IP Reachability entries until either the end of the LSP or the next occurrence of the Inter-Domain Routing Protocol Information CLV.

The IS-IS Sequence Numbers PDU Format

SNPs are used to maintain the IS-IS link state database by describing some or all of the LSPs in the database. A DR periodically multicasts a CSNP (Figure 10.36) to describe all the LSPs in the pseudonode's database. Because there is an L1 database and an L2 database, CSNPs are also either L1 or L2. Some link state databases can be so large that the LSPs cannot all be described in a single CSNP. For this reason, the last two fields of the CSNP header are the *Start LSP ID* field and the *End LSP ID* field, which together describe the range of LSPs described in the CSNP. Figure 10.37 shows how these two fields are used. In this CSNP, the full database is described; therefore, the LSP ID range starts with 0000.0000.0000.00.00 and ends with ffff.ffff.ffff.ff.ff. If two CSNPs were required to describe the database, the range of the first CSNP might be something like 0000.0000.0000.00 to 0000.0c0a.1234.00.00 and the range of the second CSNP might be 0000.0c0a.1235.00.00 to ffff.ffff.ffff.ff.ff.

A PSNP (Figure 10.38) is similar to a CSNP, except that the former describes only some LSPs rather than the entire database. Therefore, no Start and End fields are necessary as they are with CSNPs. A router sends a PSNP on a point-to-point subnetwork to acknowledge received LSPs. On a broadcast subnetwork, PSNPs request missing or more recent LSPs. Like CSNPs, there are both L1 and L2 PSNPs.

Only two CLVs are used by SNPs, whether they are CSNP or PSNP and whether they are L1 or L2:

- LSP Entries (type 9)

- Authentication Information (type 10)

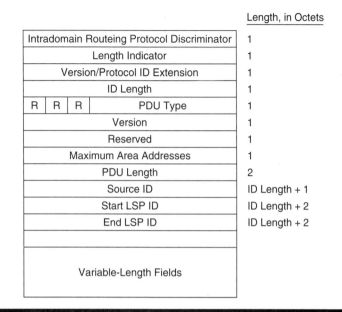

Figure 10.36
The IS-IS CSNP format.

LSP Entries CLV

The LSP Entries CLV (Figure 10.39) summarizes an LSP by listing its Remaining Lifetime, LSP ID, Sequence Number, and Checksum. These fields not only identify the LSP but also completely identify a particular instance of an LSP. Figure 10.40 shows part of an LSP Entries CLV.

CONFIGURING INTEGRATED IS-IS

Integrated IS-IS is unique among the IP routing protocols covered in this book for a couple of reasons. First, it is the only protocol

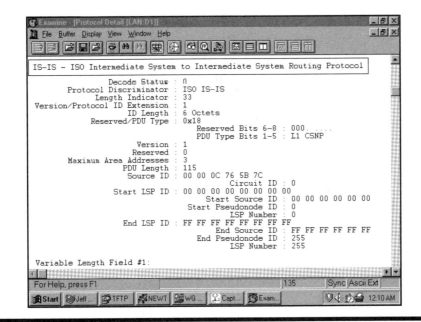

Figure 10.37

This analyzer capture shows the header of an L1 CSNP.

that must be enabled both as a process and on individual interfaces. Second, it is the only IP routing protocol that was not originally designed for IP. Because Integrated IS-IS uses CLNS PDUs rather than IP packets, the configuration is not always as obvious as that of the other protocols.

An interesting side effect of the fact that Integrated IS-IS is a CLNS protocol is that the IP addresses of neighboring routers have no influence on the formation of adjacencies. As a result, IS-IS does not have the adjacency restrictions concerning secondary IP addresses that OSPF has. However, another result is that two interfaces with IP addresses from completely different subnets can become adjacent. IP will not work in such a situation, but the fact

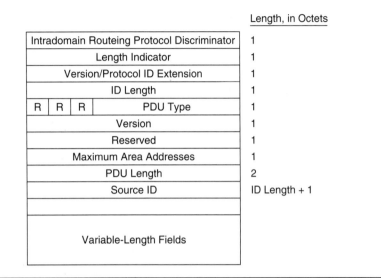

	Length, in Octets
Intradomain Routeing Protocol Discriminator	1
Length Indicator	1
Version/Protocol ID Extension	1
ID Length	1
R R R PDU Type	1
Version	1
Reserved	1
Maximum Area Addresses	1
PDU Length	2
Source ID	ID Length + 1
Variable-Length Fields	

Figure 10.38
The IS-IS PSNP format.

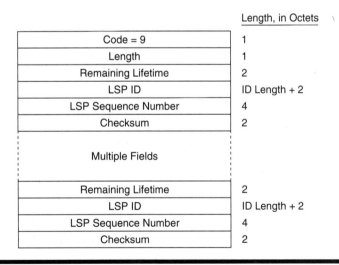

	Length, in Octets
Code = 9	1
Length	1
Remaining Lifetime	2
LSP ID	ID Length + 2
LSP Sequence Number	4
Checksum	2
Multiple Fields	
Remaining Lifetime	2
LSP ID	ID Length + 2
LSP Sequence Number	4
Checksum	2

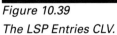

Figure 10.39
The LSP Entries CLV.

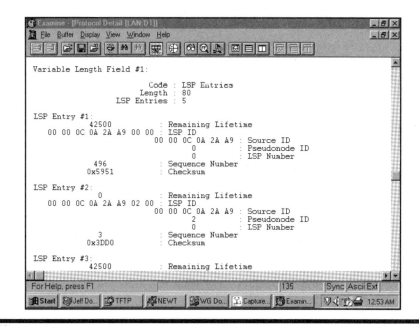

Figure 10.40

Part of the LSP Entries CLV of the CSNP in Figure 10.37.

that the adjacency makes the link only "half broken" can cause some troubleshooting confusion.

Case Study: A Basic Integrated IS-IS Configuration

A basic Integrated IS-IS process is configured on a Cisco router in four steps:

1. Determine the area in which the router is to be located and the interfaces on which IS-IS is to be enabled.
2. Enable IS-IS with the command **router isis**.[19]

---

[19] *The* **router isis** *command can also be given a name, such as* router isis **Warsaw**. *If IS-IS and ISO-IGRP are configured on the same router, one or both of the processes must be named. If ISO-IGRFP is not configured, naming is unnecessary.*

3. Configure the NET with the **net** command.

4. Enable Integrated IS-IS on the proper interfaces with the command **ip router isis**. This command must be added not only to transit interfaces (interfaces connected to IS-IS neighbors) but also to interfaces connected to stub networks whose IP addresses should be advertised by IS-IS.

Figure 10.41 shows a small six-router internetwork divided into two areas. In the NETs, areas 1 and 2 will be encoded as 00.0001 and 00.0002, respectively, and the System IDs will be the MAC identifiers of the E0 or TO0 interfaces of each router. Table 10.4 shows the NETs encoded with this information.

The configurations of Paris, London, Brussels, and Amsterdam are:

Paris

```
clns routing
!
interface Serial0
  ip address 10.1.255.5 255.255.255.252
  ip router isis
!
interface TokenRing0
  ip address 10.1.2.1 255.255.255.0
  ip router isis
  ring-speed 16
!
interface TokenRing1
  ip address 10.1.7.1 255.255.255.0
  ip router isis
  ring-speed 16
!
router isis
  net 00.0001.0000.3090.6756.00
```

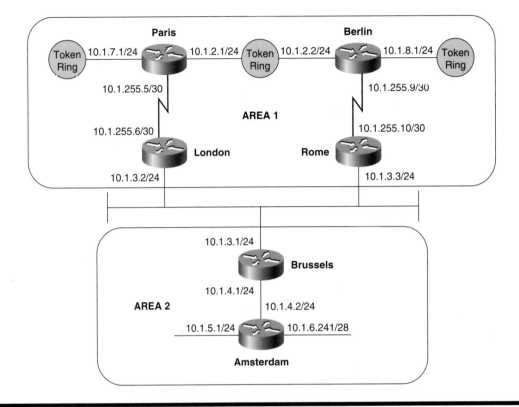

Figure 10.41

Area 1 is encoded as 00.0001 in the NET, and area 2 is encoded as 00.0002. The System ID of each NET is the E0 or T00 MAC identifier.

Table 10.4   *The NETs used for the IS-IS configurations of the routers in Figure 10.41 .*

Router	Area	MAC	Net
Paris	00.0001	0000.3090.6756	00.0001.0000.3090.6756.00
Berlin	00.0001	0000.3090.c7df	00.0001.0000.3090.c7df.00
London	00.0001	0000.0c0a.2c51	00.0001.0000.0c0a.2c51.00
Rome	00.0001	0000.0c0a.2aa9	00.0001.0000.0c0a.2aa9.00
Brussels	00.0002	0000.0c76.5b7c	00.0002.0000.0c76.5b7c.00
Amsterdam	00.0002	0000.0c04.dcc0	00.0002.0000.0c04.dcc0.00

London

```
clns routing
!
interface Ethernet0
  ip address 10.1.3.2 255.255.255.0
  ip router isis
!
interface Serial0
  ip address 10.1.255.6 255.255.255.252
  ip router isis
!
router isis
  net 00.0001.0000.0c0a.2c51.00
```

Brussels

```
clns routing
!
interface Ethernet0
  ip address 10.1.3.1 255.255.255.0
  ip router isis
!
interface Ethernet1
  ip address 10.1.4.1 255.255.255.0
  ip router isis
!
router isis
  net 00.0002.0000.0c76.5b7c.00
```

Amsterdam

```
clns routing
!
interface Ethernet0
  ip address 10.1.4.2 255.255.255.0
  ip router isis
!
interface Ethernet1
  ip address 10.1.5.1 255.255.255.0
  ip router isis
!
interface Ethernet2
  ip address 10.1.6.241 255.255.255.240
  ip router isis
!
router isis
  net 00.0002.0000.0c04.dcc0.00
```

The configurations of Berlin and Rome are similar. A detail that you should notice is that CLNS routing is enabled in these configurations. The CLNS routing is necessary to handle the CLNS PDUs used by IS-IS. However, the **clns routing** command was not entered as a configuration step. Rather, the router entered it automatically when IS-IS was enabled.

Figure 10.42 shows Paris' route table. Notice that the table contains both L1 and L2 routes. By default, Cisco routers are L1/L2 routers. This fact is also apparent by observing the routers' IS neighbor tables, as in Figure 10.43.

```
Paris#show ip route
Codes: C - connected, S - static, I - IGRP, R - RIP, M - mobile, B - BGP
       D - EIGRP, EX - EIGRP external, O - OSPF, IA - OSPF inter area
       E1 - OSPF external type 1, E2 - OSPF external type 2, E - EGP
       i - IS-IS, L1 - IS-IS level-1, L2 - IS-IS level-2, * - candidate default

Gateway of last resort is not set

     10.0.0.0 is variably subnetted, 9 subnets, 3 masks
i L1    10.1.8.0 255.255.255.0 [115/20] via 10.1.2.2, TokenRing0
i L1    10.1.3.0 255.255.255.0 [115/20] via 10.1.255.6, Serial0
C       10.1.2.0 255.255.255.0 is directly connected, TokenRing0
C       10.1.7.0 255.255.255.0 is directly connected, TokenRing1
i L2    10.1.5.0 255.255.255.0 [115/40] via 10.1.255.6, Serial0
i L2    10.1.4.0 255.255.255.0 [115/30] via 10.1.255.6, Serial0
C       10.1.255.4 255.255.255.252 is directly connected, Serial0
i L1    10.1.255.8 255.255.255.252 [115/20] via 10.1.2.2, TokenRing0
i L2    10.1.6.240 255.255.255.240 [115/40] via 10.1.255.6, Serial0
Paris#
```

Figure 10.42

Paris' route table shows both L1 and L2 routes, indicating that this router is an L1/L2 router.

Because every router in the internetwork of Figure 10.41 is an L1/L2, every router has formed both an L1 adjacency and an L2 adjacency. Consequently, every router has both an L1 and an L2 LS database. For example, Figure 10.44 shows the LS databases of Amsterdam. The L1 database contains an LSP originated by

```
Berlin#show clns is-neighbors

System Id        Interface   State   Type Priority   Circuit Id          Format
0000.0C0A.2AA9 Se0           Up      L1L2 0  /0       03                  Phase V
0000.3090.6756 To0           Up      L1L2 64/64       0000.3090.6756.04   Phase V
Berlin#
```

Figure 10.43

Berlin's IS neighbor table shows that both Paris and Rome are L1/L2 routers.

Amsterdam (0000.0c04.dcc0.00-00)[20] and an LSP originated by Brussels (0000.0c76.5b7c.00-00). It also contains a pseudonode LSP (0000.0c76.5b7c.03-00) originated by Brussels, representing the Ethernet link between Brussels and Amsterdam. Remember that the LSP ID is recognizable as that of a pseudonode LSP because the next-to-last octet, the Pseudonode ID, is non-zero.

The three LSPs indicate that Amsterdam's only L1 adjacency is with Brussels. This single adjacency is expected because Brussels is the only other router in area 2. Comparing Amsterdam's L2 database with the System IDs in Table 10.4 reveals that Amsterdam has an L2 adjacency with every router in the IS-IS domain, which is also expected because every router is an L1/L2.

Case Study: Changing the Router Types

In a small internetwork like the one in Figure 10.41, leaving all routers at their default type is acceptable. As the internetwork grows, these defaults become less and less acceptable. Not only is the processing and maintenance of two LS databases a burden on the router's CPU and memory, the L1 and L2 IS-IS PDUs being originated by every router become a burden on the buffers and bandwidth.

---

[20] *As discussed earlier, the asterisk after the LSP ID indicates that the LSP was originated by this router.*

```
Amsterdam#show isis database
IS-IS Level-1 Link State Database
LSPID                  LSP Seq Num  LSP Checksum  LSP Holdtime  ATT/P/OL
0000.0C04.DCC0.00-00*  0x00000025   0x3E6C        1078          0/0/0
0000.0C76.5B7C.00-00   0x00000023   0xD30E        1074          1/0/0
0000.0C76.5B7C.03-00   0x00000020   0x3F93        1074          0/0/0

IS-IS Level-2 Link State Database
LSPID                  LSP Seq Num  LSP Checksum  LSP Holdtime  ATT/P/OL
0000.0C04.DCC0.00-00*  0x0000005B   0x9A66        1080          0/0/0
0000.0C0A.2AA9.00-00   0x00000034   0xE971        371           0/0/0
0000.0C0A.2C51.00-00   0x00000031   0x732C        1135          0/0/0
0000.0C76.5B7C.00-00   0x0000002F   0xBEC6        1078          0/0/0
0000.0C76.5B7C.02-00   0x0000001F   0x3FC1        366           0/0/0
0000.0C76.5B7C.03-00   0x00000021   0xCC8D        1073          0/0/0
0000.3090.6756.00-00   0x0000002C   0xEF9F        365           0/0/0
0000.3090.6756.04-00   0x0000001D   0x1941        1143          0/0/0
0000.3090.C7DF.00-00   0x0000002D   0x4C01        359           0/0/0
Amsterdam#
```

Figure 10.44

Amsterdam has both a level 1 LS database and a level 2 LS database, indicating that the router is an L1/L2 router.

Paris, Berlin, and Amsterdam in Figure 10.41 can be configured as L1 routers, because they have no direct connection to another area. To change the default router type, use the command **is-type**. For example, to make Berlin an L1 router its configuration is:

```
router isis
  net 00.0001.0000.3090.c7df.00
  is-type level-1
```

Paris and Amsterdam are configured similarly. Comparing Paris' route table in Figure 10.45 with its route table in Figure 10.42 shows that the L2 routes have been deleted. Similarly, comparing Figure 10.46 with Figure 10.44 shows that Amsterdam now has only an L1 LS database.

With the L1 configurations shown so far, IP routing is not completely functional. Recall from the earlier discussion of the ATT bit in the LSPs that an L1/L2 router uses the ATT bit to tell L1

```
Paris#show ip route
Codes: C - connected, S - static, I - IGRP, R - RIP, M - mobile, B - BGP
       D - EIGRP, EX - EIGRP external, O - OSPF, IA - OSPF inter area
       E1 - OSPF external type 1, E2 - OSPF external type 2, E - EGP
       i - IS-IS, L1 - IS-IS level-1, L2 - IS-IS level-2, * - candidate default

Gateway of last resort is not set

     10.0.0.0 is variably subnetted, 6 subnets, 2 masks
i L1    10.1.8.0 255.255.255.0 [115/20] via 10.1.2.2, TokenRing0
i L1    10.1.3.0 255.255.255.0 [115/20] via 10.1.255.6, Serial0
C       10.1.2.0 255.255.255.0 is directly connected, TokenRing0
C       10.1.7.0 255.255.255.0 is directly connected, TokenRing1
C       10.1.255.4 255.255.255.252 is directly connected, Serial0
i L1    10.1.255.8 255.255.255.252 [115/20] via 10.1.2.2, TokenRing0
Paris#
```

Figure 10.45

After Paris is configured as an L1 router, its route table contains routes only to destinations within its own area.

```
Amsterdam#show isis database
IS-IS Level-1 Link State Database
LSPID                  LSP Seq Num   LSP Checksum   LSP Holdtime   ATT/P/OL
0000.0C04.DCC0.00-00*  0x0000002C    0x2E77         726            0/0/0
0000.0C76.5B7C.00-00   0x0000002A    0xC515         733            1/0/0
0000.0C76.5B7C.03-00   0x00000026    0x3399         733            0/0/0
Amsterdam#
```

Figure 10.46

After Amsterdam is configured as an L1 router, it has only a level 1 link state database.

routers that it has an inter-area connection. Figure 10.47 shows that both London's LSP (0000.0c0a.2c51.00-00) and Rome's LSP (0000.0c0aA.2aa9.00-00) have ATT = 1. So Paris should know to send inter-area traffic to either London or Rome. In other words, Paris should have a default route to London or Rome, with London being preferred because it is metrically closer. Unfortunately, Figure 10.45 shows that there is no default route (0.0.0.0) in Paris' route table.

```
Paris#show isis database
IS-IS Level-1 Link State Database
LSPID                 LSP Seq Num   LSP Checksum   LSP Holdtime   ATT/P/OL
0000.0C0A.2AA9.00-00  0x0000000F    0x63B0         837            1/0/0
0000.0C0A.2C51.00-00  0x00000013    0x8922         784            1/0/0
0000.0C0A.2C51.01-00  0x0000000A    0x69D2         646            0/0/0
0000.3090.6756.00-00* 0x00000016    0x4A66         650            0/0/0
0000.3090.6756.04-00* 0x0000000E    0xA53D         864            0/0/0
0000.3090.C7DF.00-00  0x00000014    0x047E         1119           0/0/0
Paris#
```

Figure 10.47

The L1 LSPs of London and Rome have ATT = 1, indicating a connection to another area.

The problem is that the ATT bit is a CLNS function, and the IP process cannot directly interpret the bit. There are two solutions to the problem. The first solution is to enable IS-IS for CLNS on the interfaces in addition to IS-IS for IP. For example, the serial interface configurations for London and Paris are:

London

```
interface Serial0
  ip address 10.1.255.6 255.255.255.252
  ip router isis
  clns router isis
```

Paris

```
interface Serial0
  ip address 10.1.255.5 255.255.255.252
  ip router isis
  clns router isis
```

Figure 10.48 shows that Paris now has a default IP route pointing to London and that a ping to an inter-area destination is successful.

This first solution works in a dual CLNP/IP environment, but if IS-IS is being used as an IP-only routing protocol, enabling CLNS routing just for default IP routes may be undesirable. A second solution to the default route problem is to configure a static

```
Paris#show ip route
Codes: C - connected, S - static, I - IGRP, R - RIP, M - mobile, B - BGP
       D - EIGRP, EX - EIGRP external, O - OSPF, IA - OSPF inter area
       E1 - OSPF external type 1, E2 - OSPF external type 2, E - EGP
       i - IS-IS, L1 - IS-IS level-1, L2 - IS-IS level-2, * - candidate default

Gateway of last resort is 10.1.255.6 to network 0.0.0.0

     10.0.0.0 is variably subnetted, 6 subnets, 2 masks
i L1    10.1.8.0 255.255.255.0 [115/20] via 10.1.2.2, TokenRing0
i L1    10.1.3.0 255.255.255.0 [115/20] via 10.1.255.6, Serial0
C       10.1.2.0 255.255.255.0 is directly connected, TokenRing0
C       10.1.7.0 255.255.255.0 is directly connected, TokenRing1
C       10.1.255.4 255.255.255.252 is directly connected, Serial0
i L1    10.1.255.8 255.255.255.252 [115/20] via 10.1.2.2, TokenRing0
i*L1 0.0.0.0 0.0.0.0 [115/10] via 10.1.255.6, Serial0
Paris#ping 10.1.6.241
Type escape sequence to abort.
Sending 5, 100-byte ICMP Echos to 10.1.6.241, timeout is 2 seconds:
!!!!!
Success rate is 100 percent (5/5), round-trip min/avg/max = 32/36/40 ms
Paris#
```

Figure 10.48

After London and Paris have been configured as dual CLNP/IP routers, Paris understands the ATT bit and adds a default route to its route table.

default route on the L1/L2 router and configure IS-IS to advertise the default with the command **default-information originate**. Using this method in area 2 of Figure 10.41, the Brussels' configuration is:

```
router isis
  net 00.0002.0000.0c76.5b7c.00
  default-information originate
!
ip route 0.0.0.0 0.0.0.0 Null0
```

Figure 10.49 shows Amsterdam's route table with the default route that has been advertised by Brussels and a successful ping to an inter-area destination. Default routes and the **default-information** originate command are discussed in more detail in Chapter 12, "Default Routes and On-Demand Routing."

```
Amsterdam#show ip route
Codes: C - connected, S - static, I - IGRP, R - RIP, M - mobile, B - BGP
       D - EIGRP, EX - EIGRP external, O - OSPF, IA - OSPF inter area
       E1 - OSPF external type 1, E2 - OSPF external type 2, E - EGP
       i - IS-IS, L1 - IS-IS level-1, L2 - IS-IS level-2, * - candidate default

Gateway of last resort is 10.1.4.1 to network 0.0.0.0

     10.0.0.0 is variably subnetted, 4 subnets, 2 masks
i L1    10.1.3.0 255.255.255.0 [115/20] via 10.1.4.1, Ethernet0
C       10.1.5.0 255.255.255.0 is directly connected, Ethernet1
C       10.1.4.0 255.255.255.0 is directly connected, Ethernet0
C       10.1.6.240 255.255.255.240 is directly connected, Ethernet2
i*L1 0.0.0.0 0.0.0.0 [115/10] via 10.1.4.1, Ethernet0
Amsterdam#ping 10.1.8.1
Type escape sequence to abort.
Sending 5, 100-byte ICMP Echos to 10.1.8.1, timeout is 2 seconds:
!!!!!
Success rate is 100 percent (5/5), round-trip min/avg/max = 32/36/40 ms
Amsterdam#
```

Figure 10.49
Amsterdam's route table contains the default route statically configured at Brussels.

Case Study: An Area Migration

To change area addresses in an OSPF domain, downtime must be scheduled. However, IS-IS is designed to allow areas to be changed nondisruptively. As discussed in "Operation of Integrated IS-IS," Cisco routers can be configured with up to three area addresses. For two routers to form an L1 adjacency, they must have at least one area address in common. With multiple area addresses allowed, a new adjacency can take over while an old adjacency is being broken. This approach is useful when areas are being consolidated or split, when an area is being renumbered, or when area addresses assigned by multiple addressing authorities are being used in the same IS-IS domain.

For example, the routers in Figure 10.50(a) all have an area address of 01. (A NET of one of these routers would look like 01.0000.0c12.3456.00.) In Figure 10.50(b), the routers have been assigned an additional area address of 03. Although multiple adjacencies are not actually formed, the routers do recognize that they have multiple area addresses in common. In Figure 10.50(c), area 01 has been removed from one of the routers. All three routers remain adjacent, because they all have at least one area address in common. Finally, in Figure 10.50(d), all of the 01 area addresses have been removed and the routers are all in area 03. At no time during the area migration was an adjacency lost.

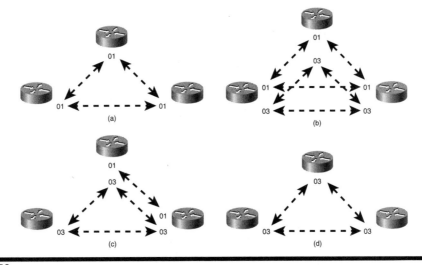

Figure 10.50
The support of multiple area addresses per router eases area changes.

Suppose that the "powers that be" over the internetwork in Figure 10.41 decree that the area addressing scheme being used is inappropriate and should become GOSIP compliant. After registering with the U.S. GSA, the following components are to be used to construct the NETs:

AFI:	47
IDI:	0005
DFI:	80
AAI:	00ab7c
Reserved:	0000
RDI:	fffe9
Areas:	0001 (area 1), 0002 (area 2)

The new NETs are shown in Table 10.5.

Table 10.5   *The new GOSIP-format NETs to be assigned to the routers in Figure 10.41 .*

Router	NET
Paris	47.0005.80.00ab7c.0000.ffe9.0001.0000.3090.6756.00
Berlin	47.0005.80.00ab7c.0000.ffe9.0001.0000.3090.c7df.00
London	47.0005.80.00ab7c.0000.ffe9.0001.0000.0c0a.2c51.00
Rome	47.0005.80.00ab7c.0000.ffe9.0001.0000.0c0a.2aa9.00
Brussels	47.0005.80.00ab7c.0000.ffe9.0002.0000.0c76.5b7c.00
Amsterdam	47.0005.80.00ab7c.0000.ffe9.0002.0000.0c04.dcc0.00

The first step in changing the area addresses is to add the new NETs to the routers without changing the old NETs. Rome's IS-IS configuration is:

```
router isis
  net 00.0001.0000.0c0a.2aa9.00
  net 47.0005.8000.ab7c.0000.ffe9.0001.0000.0c0a.2aa9.00
```

The other five routers are configured similarly. The results can be observed by using the **detail** keyword with either the **show isis database** command (Figure 10.51) or the **show clns is-neighbors** command (Figure 10.52). In both databases, multiple areas are associated with each router in the internetwork.

```
Rome#show isis database detail
IS-IS Level-1 Link State Database
LSPID                LSP Seq Num  LSP Checksum  LSP Holdtime  ATT/P/OL
0000.0C0A.2AA9.00-00* 0x00000059   0x705E        592           1/0/0
  Area Address: 00.0001
  Area Address: 47.0005.8000.ab7c.0000.ffe9.0001
  NLPID:       0x81 0xCC
  IP Address:  10.1.3.3
  Metric: 10 IP 10.1.3.0 255.255.255.0
  Metric: 10 IP 10.1.255.8 255.255.255.252
  Metric: 10 IS 0000.0C0A.2C51.01
  Metric: 10 IS 0000.3090.C7DF.00
  Metric: 0  ES 0000.0C0A.2AA9
0000.0C0A.2C51.00-00  0x00000059   0xD495        652           1/0/0
  Area Address: 00.0001
  Area Address: 47.0005.8000.ab7c.0000.ffe9.0001
  NLPID:       0x81 0xCC
  IP Address:  10.1.3.2
  Metric: 10 IP 10.1.3.0 255.255.255.0
  Metric: 10 IP 10.1.255.4 255.255.255.252
  Metric: 10 IS 0000.0C0A.2C51.01
  Metric: 10 IS 0000.3090.6756.00
  Metric: 0  ES 0000.0C0A.2C51
0000.0C0A.2C51.01-00  0x00000052   0xD81B        507           0/0/0
  Metric: 0  IS 0000.0C0A.2C51.00
  Metric: 0  IS 0000.0C0A.2AA9.00
0000.3090.6756.00-00  0x0000005C   0xDB0D        678           0/0/0
  Area Address: 00.0001
  Area Address: 47.0005.8000.ab7c.0000.ffe9.0001
  NLPID:       0x81 0xCC
  IP Address:  10.1.7.1
  Metric: 10 IP 10.1.7.0 255.255.255.0
  Metric: 10 IP 10.1.255.4 255.255.255.252
  Metric: 10 IP 10.1.2.0 255.255.255.0
  Metric: 10 IS 0000.3090.6756.04
  Metric: 10 IS 0000.0C0A.2C51.00
  Metric: 0  ES 0000.3090.6756
0000.3090.6756.04-00  0x00000054   0x1983        835           0/0/0
  Metric: 0  IS 0000.3090.6756.00
  Metric: 0  IS 0000.3090.C7DF.00
0000.3090.C7DF.00-00  0x0000005B   0x18A5        545           0/0/0
  Area Address: 00.0001
  Area Address: 47.0005.8000.ab7c.0000.ffe9.0001
  --More--
```

Figure 10.51

The LSPs in Rome's link state database show that all routers in the internetwork of Figure 10.41 are advertising two area addresses.

```
Rome#show clns is-neighbors detail

System Id       Interface   State  Type Priority  Circuit Id         Format
0000.0C76.5B7C Et0          Up     L2   64         0000.0C76.5B7C.02  Phase V
  Area Address(es): 00.0002 47.0005.8000.ab7c.0000.ffe9.0002
  IP Address(es):  10.1.3.1
  Uptime: 0:27:22
0000.0C0A.2C51 Et0          Up     L1L2 64/64      0000.0C0A.2C51.01  Phase V
  Area Address(es): 00.0001 47.0005.8000.ab7c.0000.ffe9.0001
  IP Address(es):  10.1.3.2
  Uptime: 0:27:21
0000.3090.C7DF Se0          Up     L1   0          02                 Phase V
  Area Address(es): 00.0001 47.0005.8000.ab7c.0000.ffe9.0001
  IP Address(es):  10.1.255.9
  Uptime: 0:27:24
Rome#
```

Figure 10.52

Rome's IS-IS neighbor table also shows multiple addresses associated with each neighbor.

The last step of the migration is to delete the old NET statements from all routers. For example, under Rome's IS-IS configuration the command **no net 00.0001.0000.0c0a.2aa9.00** is entered. Figure 10.53 shows some of the LSPs in Rome's database after the old NET statements have been removed from the routers.

Case Study: Route Summarization

Route summarization between areas in a link state protocol is introduced in Chapter 9. A more complete discussion of summarization, in the context of default routes, is presented in Chapter 12. Briefly, summary routes are useful because:

- They reduce the size of LSPs, which reduces the size of the link state database; consequently, memory and CPU are conserved.

- They hide instabilities within areas. If an address within a summary range changes or a link changes state, the change is not advertised outside of the summarized area.

```
Rome#show isis data detail
IS-IS Level-1 Link State Database
LSPID                   LSP Seq Num  LSP Checksum  LSP Holdtime  ATT/P/OL
0000.0C0A.2AA9.00-00* 0x00000069    0x02C4         809           1/0/0
  Area Address: 47.0005.8000.ab7c.0000.ffe9.0001
  NLPID:        0x81 0xCC
  IP Address:   10.1.3.3
  Metric: 10 IP 10.1.3.0 255.255.255.0
  Metric: 10 IP 10.1.255.8 255.255.255.252
  Metric: 10 IS 0000.0C0A.2C51.01
  Metric: 10 IS 0000.3090.C7DF.00
  Metric: 0  ES 0000.0C0A.2AA9
0000.0C0A.2C51.00-00  0x0000006C    0x75E9         719           1/0/0
  Area Address: 47.0005.8000.ab7c.0000.ffe9.0001
  NLPID:        0x81 0xCC
  IP Address:   10.1.3.2
  Metric: 10 IP 10.1.3.0 255.255.255.0
  Metric: 10 IP 10.1.255.4 255.255.255.252
  Metric: 10 IS 0000.0C0A.2C51.01
  Metric: 10 IS 0000.3090.6756.00
  Metric: 0  ES 0000.0C0A.2C51
0000.0C0A.2C51.01-00  0x0000005F    0xBE28         628           0/0/0
  Metric: 0  IS 0000.0C0A.2C51.00
  Metric: 0  IS 0000.0C0A.2AA9.00
0000.3090.6756.00-00  0x00000067    0x9936         896           0/0/0
  Area Address: 47.0005.8000.ab7c.0000.ffe9.0001
  NLPID:        0x81 0xCC
  IP Address:   10.1.7.1
  Metric: 10 IP 10.1.7.0 255.255.255.0
  Metric: 10 IP 10.1.255.4 255.255.255.252
  Metric: 10 IP 10.1.2.0 255.255.255.0
  Metric: 10 IS 0000.3090.6756.04
  Metric: 10 IS 0000.3090.6756.05
  Metric: 10 IS 0000.0C0A.2C51.00
  Metric: 0  ES 0000.3090.6756
0000.3090.6756.04-00  0x0000005B    0x0B8A         730           0/0/0
  Metric: 0  IS 0000.3090.6756.00
  Metric: 0  IS 0000.3090.C7DF.00
0000.3090.6756.05-00  0x00000004    0xDF01         857           0/0/0
  Metric: 0  IS 0000.3090.6756.00
0000.3090.C7DF.00-00  0x00000069    0xECC6         646           0/0/0
  Area Address: 47.0005.8000.ab7c.0000.ffe9.0001
  NLPID:        0x81 0xCC
  IP Address:   10.1.8.1
  Metric: 10 IP 10.1.8.0 255.255.255.0
  Metric: 10 IP 10.1.255.8 255.255.255.252
  Metric: 10 IP 10.1.2.0 255.255.255.0
  Metric: 10 IS 0000.3090.C7DF.05
  --More--
```

Figure 10.53

The LSPs in Rome's database show only a single area address.

The primary disadvantages of summary routes are:

- Their effectiveness is dependent on being able to summarize a contiguous range of IP addresses, so addresses must be planned carefully.

- They can reduce route precision by hiding the details of the area. If there are multiple paths into a summarized area, the best path cannot be determined.

Summarization is enabled under the IS-IS configuration with the **summary-address** command. Any more-specific destination addresses that fall within the summarization range are suppressed, and the metric of the summary route is the smallest metric of all the more-specific addresses.

Figure 10.54 shows an IS-IS internetwork with three areas. The addresses within area 1 can be summarized with 172.16.0.0/21, and the addresses within area 3 can be summarized with 172.16.16.0/21. The configurations of Zurich, Madrid, and Bonn are[21]:

Zurich

```
router isis
  net 01.0000.0c76.5b7c.00
  summary-address 172.16.0.0 255.255.248.0
```

Madrid

```
router isis
  net 02.0000.3090.6756.00
  is-type level-2-only
```

Bonn

```
router isis
  net 03.0000.0c0a.2aa9.00
  summary-address 172.16.16.0 255.255.248.0
```

---

[21] *Notice that Madrid, which has no L1 neighbors, is configured as an L2 router.*

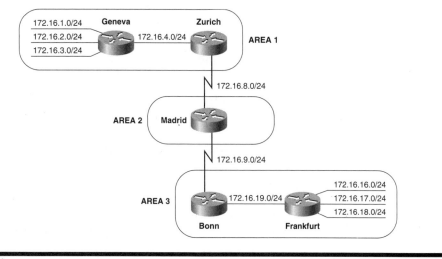

Figure 10.54

Zurich and Bonn are summarizing areas 1 and 3 into area 2.

Notice that Madrid, which has no L1 neighbors, is configured as an L2 router. Zurich and Bonn are summarizing their areas into the level 2 backbone. The results of the summarization can be seen in Madrid's route table (Figure 10.55).

```
Madrid#show ip route
Codes: C - connected, S - static, I - IGRP, R - RIP, M - mobile, B - BGP
       D - EIGRP, EX - EIGRP external, O - OSPF, IA - OSPF inter area
       E1 - OSPF external type 1, E2 - OSPF external type 2, E - EGP
       i - IS-IS, L1 - IS-IS level-1, L2 - IS-IS level-2, * - candidate default

Gateway of last resort is not set

     172.16.0.0 is variably subnetted, 4 subnets, 2 masks
i L2    172.16.16.0 255.255.248.0 [115/20] via 172.16.9.2, Serial0
C       172.16.8.0 255.255.255.0 is directly connected, Serial1
C       172.16.9.0 255.255.255.0 is directly connected, Serial0
i L2    172.16.0.0 255.255.248.0 [115/20] via 172.16.8.2, Serial1
Madrid#
```

Figure 10.55

Madrid's route table shows the summary addresses advertised by Bonn and Zurich.

Case Study: Authentication

IS-IS authentication is limited to cleartext passwords only. This mode of authentication provides weak security against a determined attack on the internetwork but is effective for preventing service disruptions from misconfigured or unauthorized routers.

Cisco IOS supports IS-IS authentication on three levels: between neighbors, area wide, and domain wide. The three authentication levels can be used by themselves or together. The rules for IS-IS authentication are:

- When authenticating between neighbors, the same password must be configured on the connecting interfaces.

- When authenticating between neighbors, authentication must be configured separately for L1 and L2 adjacencies.

- When performing area-wide authentication, every router in the area must perform authentication and must have the same password.

- When performing domain-wide authentication, every L2 and L1/L2 router in the IS-IS domain must perform authentication and must have the same password.

To authenticate between neighbors, the **isis password** command is used to configure a password on the connected interfaces. The command specifies a password and specifies whether the password is for L1 or L2 adjacencies. Passwords for either or both levels can be specified on an interface, and the passwords for each level can be the same or different passwords. When configured, the passwords are carried in authentication information CLVs in the L1 or L2 Hellos between IS-IS neighbors.

For example, to authenticate between Geneva, Zurich, and Madrid in Figure 10.54, the configurations are:

Geneva

```
interface Ethernet0
  ip address 172.16.4.1 255.255.255.0
  ip router isis
  isis password Alps level-1
```

Zurich

```
interface Ethernet0
  ip address 172.16.4.2 255.255.255.0
  ip router isis
  isis password Alps level-1
!
interface Serial0
  ip address 172.16.8.2 255.255.255.0
  ip router isis
  isis password Pyrenees level-2
```

Madrid

```
interface Serial1
  ip address 172.16.8.1 255.255.255.0
  ip router isis
  isis password Pyrenees level-2
```

Since the adjacency between Geneva and Zurich is L1, only a level 1 password (Alps) is specified. Between Zurich and Madrid, only an L2 adjacency exists, so a level 2 password (Pyranees) is used. Note that if no **level-1** or **level-2** keyword is specified, the **isis password** command defaults to level 1.

To authenticate within an area, the **area-password** command is used to specify a password under the IS-IS configuration. Whereas the password specified by the **isis password** command is carried in Hellos, the password specified by the **area-password** command is carried in all L1 LSPs, CSNPs, and PSNPs. So the neighbor-level password regulates the establishment of adjacencies, and the area-level password regulates the exchange of level 1 link state information. If area authentication is not configured correctly, routers will still become adjacent but L1 LSPs will not be exchanged.

To configure area passwords in area 3 of Figure 10.54, the configurations of Bonn and Frankfurt are:

Bonn

```
router isis
  net 03.0000.0c0a.2aa9.00
  area-password Rhine
  summary-address 172.16.16.0 255.255.248.0
```

Frankfurt

```
router isis
  net 03.0000.0c04.dcc0.00
  is-type level-1
  area-password Rhine
```

To authenticate domain wide, the **domain-password** command is used. The password specified by this command is carried in L2 LSPs, CSNPs, and PSNPs. As a result, domain authentication regulates the exchange of level 2 route information. Like area authentication, domain authentication does not authenticate L2 adjacencies, but does authenticate the exchange of L2 LSPs.

To configure domain authentication in the internetwork of Figure 10.54, only Zurich, Madrid, and Bonn must be configured because Geneva and Frankfurt are L1 routers. The configurations are:

Zurich

```
router isis
  net 01.0000.0c76.5b7c.00
  domain-password BlackForest
  area-password Switzerland
  summary-address 172.16.0.0 255.255.248.0
```

Madrid

```
router isis
  net 02.0000.3090.6756.00
  is-type level-2-only
  domain-password BlackForest
```

Bonn
```
router isis
  net 03.0000.0c0a.2aa9.00
  domain-password Blackforest
  area-password Rhine
  summary-address 172.16.16.0 255.255.248.0
```

TROUBLESHOOTING INTEGRATED IS-IS

The basic methods for troubleshooting IS-IS are very similar to the methods for troubleshooting OSPF, as discussed in Chapter 9. A major aspect of troubleshooting Integrated IS-IS that is different from the other IP routing protocols is that IS-IS uses CLNS PDUs rather than IP packets. If you are troubleshooting the protocol itself, remember that you are troubleshooting CLNS, not IP.

As with all routing protocols, the first troubleshooting step is to check the route table for accurate information. If an expected route entry is missing or incorrect, the remainder of the trouble-shooting task is to determine the source of the problem.

After the routing table, the link state database is the most important source of troubleshooting information. As recommended in Chapter 9, it is good practice to keep a copy of the L1 link state database for every area, and a copy of the L2 link state database. These stored copies of the databases should be updated regularly, as part of your routine baselining procedures. When things go wrong, these stored databases provide a steady-state reference.

When examining an individual router's configuration, consider the following:

- Does the **net** statement under the IS-IS configuration specify the correct NET? Are the Area ID and System ID correct for this router? Does the NET comply with whatever CLNS addressing convention is being used in this internetwork?

- Is IS-IS enabled on the correct interfaces with the **ip router isis** command?

- Are the IP addresses and subnet masks correct? It is doubly important to check these in an Integrated IS-IS environment because a misconfigured IP address will not prevent an IS-IS adjacency from being established.

Troubleshooting IS-IS Adjacencies

The command **show clns is-neighbors** displays the IS-IS neighbor table. The entire table is displayed by default, or you can specify a particular interface. From this table, you can observe whether all expected neighbors are present and whether they are the correct type. For more information, such as the area addresses and IP addresses associated with each neighbor and the uptime of each neighbor, use the **show clns is-neighbors detail** command.

When examining adjacencies, consider the following:

- Are the router levels configured correctly? L1 routers can establish adjacencies only with L1 and L1/L2 routers, and L2 routers can establish adjacencies only with L2 and L1/L2 routers.

- Are Hellos being sent from both neighbors? Are the Hellos the correct level, and do they contain the correct parameters? The command **debug isis adj-packets** (Figure 10.56) is useful for observing Hellos.

- Are the values set by **isis hello-interval** and **isis hello-multiplier** the same between neighbors?

- If authentication is being used, are the passwords the same between neighbors? Remember that area (level 1) and domain (level 2) authentication do not regulate adjacencies, only the exchange of LSPs.

- Are any access lists blocking IS-IS or CLNS?

```
Bonn#debug isis adj-packets
IS-IS Adjacency related packets debugging is on
Bonn#
ISIS-Adj: Sending serial IIH on Serial0
ISIS-Adj: Rec L1 IIH from 0000.0c04.dcc0 (Ethernet0), cir type 1, cir id 0000.0C
0A.2AA9.02
ISIS-Adj: Sending L1 IIH on Ethernet0
ISIS-Adj: Rec serial IIH from *HDLC* on Serial0, cir type 2, cir id 02
ISIS-Adj: rcvd state 0, old state 0, new state 0
ISIS-Adj: Action = 2, new_type = 0
ISIS-Adj: Sending L1 IIH on Ethernet0
ISIS-Adj: Sending L2 IIH on Ethernet0
ISIS-Adj: Sending serial IIH on Serial0
ISIS-Adj: Sending L1 IIH on Ethernet0
ISIS-Adj: Rec serial IIH from *HDLC* on Serial0, cir type 2, cir id 02
ISIS-Adj: rcvd state 0, old state 0, new state 0
ISIS-Adj: Action = 2, new_type = 0
ISIS-Adj: Sending L1 IIH on Ethernet0
ISIS-Adj: Rec L1 IIH from 0000.0c04.dcc0 (Etheir type 1, cir id 0000.0C0A.2AA9.0
2
ISIS-Adj: Sending L1 IIH on Ethernet0
ISIS-Adj: Sending L2 IIH on Ethernet0
ISIS-Adj: Sending serial IIH on Serial0
```

Figure 10.56

*The details of IS-IS Hellos (IIHs) can be observed with the **debug isis adj-packets** command. This display is from router Bonn in Figure 10.54.*

Troubleshooting the IS-IS Link State Database

The IS-IS link state database is examined with the command **show isis database**. If the router is an L1/L2, both of the databases are displayed by default. To observe only one of the databases, use the **level-1** or **level-2** keywords. To examine the LSPs in more detail, use the **detail** keyword. A single LSP can be observed by specifying its LSPID, as in Figure 10.57.

```
Zurich#show isis database detail 0000.3090.6756.00-00

IS-IS Level-2 LSP 0000.3090.6756.00-00
LSPID                    LSP Seq Num  LSP Checksum  LSP Holdtime  ATT/P/OL
0000.3090.6756.00-00  0x00000080    0x9EA1        480           0/0/0
  Auth:        Length: 12
  Area Address: 02
  NLPID:       0xCC
  IP Address:  172.16.8.1
  Metric: 10 IS 0000.0C76.5B7C.00
  Metric: 10 IS 0000.0C0A.2AA9.00
  Metric: 10 IP 172.16.8.0 255.255.255.0
  Metric: 10 IP 172.16.9.0 255.255.255.0
Zurich#
```

Figure 10.57

This LSP is from the L2 database of router Zurich in Figure 10.54.

A sequence number that is noticeably higher than the sequence numbers of other LSPs might indicate instability either within the area or on the level 2 backbone. Another hint of instability is an LSP Holdtime that never gets very small. If instability is suspected, use the command **show isis spf-log** to list all SPF calculations recently performed by the router.

In Figure 10.58, the SPF log for router Geneva in Figure 10.54 is shown. Nothing but the periodic SPF calculations triggered by the 15-minute database refreshes are shown until approximately three minutes before the log was displayed. At that time, frequent SPF calculations began occurring, indicating frequent changes of some sort in the internetwork.[22]

To further investigate instabilities revealed by the SPF log, three useful debug commands are available. Figures 10.59, 10.60, and 10.61 show output from these three debug functions. In each case,

---

[22] *The first four triggering events were caused by "bouncing" Zurich's serial interface several times, and the next three events were caused by deleting and then misconfiguring the link password. The last event was caused when the correct password was configured.*

```
Geneva#sh isis spf-log

   Level 1 SPF log
   When   Duration  Nodes  Count    Last trigger LSP    Triggers
02:43:09     12       3      1                           PERIODIC
02:28:08     12       3      1                           PERIODIC
02:13:06     12       3      1                           PERIODIC
01:58:05     12       3      1                           PERIODIC
01:43:03     12       3      1                           PERIODIC
01:28:02     12       3      1                           PERIODIC
01:13:00     12       3      1                           PERIODIC
00:57:59     12       3      1                           PERIODIC
00:42:58     12       3      1                           PERIODIC
00:27:56     12       3      1                           PERIODIC
00:12:55     12       3      1                           PERIODIC
00:03:08      8       3      1     0000.0C76.5B7C.00-00  LSPHEADER
00:02:35      8       3      1     0000.0C76.5B7C.00-00  LSPHEADER
00:02:23      8       3      1     0000.0C76.5B7C.00-00  LSPHEADER
00:01:50      8       3      1     0000.0C76.5B7C.00-00  LSPHEADER
00:01:14      4       1      1     0000.0C0A.2C51.00-00  TLVCONTENT
00:00:46      4       2      2     0000.0C0A.2C51.04-00  NEWLSP TLVCONTENT
00:00:20      4       1      3     0000.0C0A.2C51.00-00  NEWADJ TLVCONTENT
00:00:08      8       3      1     0000.0C76.5B7C.02-00  TLVCONTENT
Geneva#
```

Figure 10.58

This SPF log reveals instability in area 1 of Figure 10.54..

the debug messages show the results of disconnecting and reconnecting the serial interface of Zurich in Figure 10.54 from the perspective of Geneva. The first, **debug isis spf-triggers** (Figure 10.59), displays messages pertaining to events that trigger an SPF calculation. The second command is **debug isis spf-events** (Figure 10.60). This command displays a detailed account of the SPF calculations caused by a triggering event. The third command, **debug isis spf-statistics** (Figure 10.61), displays information about the SPF calculation itself. Of particular interest is the time taken to complete the calculation, which can reveal performance problems on the router.

```
Geneva#debug isis spf-triggers
IS-IS SPF triggering events debugging is on
Geneva#
ISIS-SPF-TRIG: L1, LSP fields changed 0000.0C76.5B7C.00-00
ISIS-SPF-TRIG: L1, LSP fields changed 0000.0C76.5B7C.00-00
Geneva#
```

Figure 10.59

debug isis spf-triggers displays messages about events that trigger an SPF calculation..

```
Geneva#debug isis spf-events
IS-IS SPF events debugging is on
Geneva#
ISIS-SPF: L1 LSP 3 (0000.0C76.5B7C.00-00) flagged for recalculation
from 34F561A
ISIS-SPF: Calculating routes for L1 LSP 3 (0000.0C76.5B7C.00-00)
ISIS-SPF: Add 172.16.4.0/255.255.255.0 to IP route table, metric 20
ISIS-SPF: Next hop 0000.0C76.5B7C/172.16.4.2 (Ethernet0) (rejected)
ISIS-SPF: Add 0000.0C76.5B7C to L1 route table, metric 10
ISIS-SPF:    Next hop 0000.0C76.5B7C (Ethernet0)
ISIS-SPF: Aging L1 LSP 3 (0000.0C76.5B7C.00-00), version 132
ISIS-SPF: Aging IP 172.16.8.0/255.255.255.0, next hop 172.16.4.2
ISIS-SPF: Deleted NDB
ISIS-SPF: Compute L1 SPT
ISIS-SPF: Move 0000.0C0A.2C51.00-00 to PATHS, metric 0
ISIS-SPF: thru 2147483647/2147483647/2147483647, delay 0/0/0, mtu 2147483647/214
7483647/2147483647, hops 0/0/0, ticks 0/0/0
ISIS-SPF: Add 0000.0C76.5B7C.02-00 to TENT, metric 10
ISIS-SPF:    Next hop local
ISIS-SPF: Add 0000.0C0A.2C51 to L1 route table, metric 0
ISIS-SPF: Move 0000.0C76.5B7C.02-00 to PATHS, metric 10
ISIS-SPF: thru 2147483647/2147483647/2147483647, delay 0/0/0, mtu 2147483647/214
7483647/2147483647, hops 0/0/0, ticks 0/0/0
ISIS-SPF: considering adj to 0000.0C76.5B7C (Ethernet0) metric 10
ISIS-SPF:    (accepted)
ISIS-SPF: Add 0000.0C76.5B7C.00-00 to TENT, metric 10
ISIS-SPF:    Next hop 0000.0C76.5B7C (Ethernet0)
ISIS-SPF: Move 0000.0C76.5B7C.00-00 to PATHS, metric 10
ISIS-SPF: Add 172.16.4.0/255.255.255.0 to IP route table, metric 20
ISIS-SPF: N0C76.5B7C/172.16.4.2 (Ethernet0) (rejected)
ISIS-SPF: Add 0000.0C76.5B7C to L1 route table, metric 10
ISIS-SPF:    Next hop 0000.0C76.5B7C (Ethernet0)
ISIS-SPF: Aging L1 LSP 1 (0000.0C0A.2C51.00-00), version 126
ISIS-SPF: Aging L1 LSP 2 (0000.0C76.5B7C.02-00), version 127
ISIS-SPF: Aging L1 LSP 3 (0000.0C76.5B7C.00-00), version 133
```

Figure 10.60

debug isis spf-events displays the details of an SPF calculation.

```
Geneva#debug isis spf-statistics
IS-IS SPF Timing and Statistics Data debugging is on
Geneva#
ISIS-Stats: Compute L1 SPT
ISIS-Stats: Complete L1 SPT, Compute time 0.008, 3 nodes, 2 links on SPT, 0 suspends
ISIS-Stats: Compute L1 SPT
ISIS-Stats: Complete L1 SPT, Compute time 0.008, 3 nodes, 2 links on SPT, 0 suspends
```

Figure 10.61

debug isis spf-statistics *displays statistical information about the SPF calculation..*

Within each area, every router must have an identical link state database. Additionally, every L1/L2 and L2 router in the IS-IS domain must have an identical L2 database. If you suspect that a router's link state database is not correctly synchronized, examine the LSP IDs and the checksums. The same LSP IDs should exist in every database, and the checksum of each LSP should be identical in every database.

Two debug commands can help you observe the synchronization process. The first is **debug isis update-packets** (Figure 10.62), which displays information about SNPs and LSPs the router sends and receives. The second command, **debug isis snp-packets** (Figure 10.63), displays information specific to the CSNPs and PSNPs the router sends and receives.

```
Geneva#debug isis update-packets
IS-IS Update related packet debugging is on
Geneva#
ISIS-Update: Rec L1 LSP 0000.0C76.5B7C.00-00, seq A7, ht 1199,
ISIS-Update: from SNPA 0000.0c76.5b7c (Ethernet0)
ISIS-Update: LSP newer than database copy
ISIS-Update: Important fields changed
ISIS-Update: Populating FastPSNP cache (index 245 lspix 3 chksm EF1A)
ISIS-Update: Full SPF required
ISIS-SNP: Rec L1 CSNP from 0000.0C76.5B7C (Ethernet0)
ISIS-SNP: Rec L1 CSNP from 0000.0C76.5B7C (Ethernet0)
Geneva#
```

Figure 10.62

debug isis update-packets *displays information about SNPs and LSPs.*

```
Geneva#debug isis snp-packets
IS-IS CSNP/PSNP packets debugging is on
Geneva#
ISIS-SNP: Rec L1 CSNP from 0000.0C76.5B7C (Ethernet0)
ISIS-SNP: CSNP range 0000.0000.0000.00-00 to FFFF.FFFF.FFFF.FF-FF
ISIS-SNP: Same entry 0000.0C0A.2C51.00-00, seq 82
ISIS-SNP: Same entry 0000.0C76.5B7C.00-00, seq A7
ISIS-SNP: Same entry 0000.0C76.5B7C.02-00, seq 65
ISIS-SNP: Rec L1 CSNP from 0000.0C76.5B7C (Ethernet0)
ISIS-SNP: CSNP range 0000.0000.0000.00-00 to FFFF.FFFF.FFFF.FF-FF
ISIS-SNP: Same entry 0000.0C0A.2C51.00-00, seq 82
ISIS-SNP: Entry 0000.0C76.5B7C.00-00, seq AD is newer than ours (seq A8), sending PSNP
ISIS-SNP: Same entry 0000.0C76.5B7C.02-00, seq 65
ISIS-SNP: Rec L1 CSNP from 0000.0C76.5B7C (Ethernet0)
ISIS-SNP: CSNP range 0000.0000.0000.00-00 to FFFF.FFFF.FFFF.FF-FF
ISIS-SNP: Same entry 0000.0C0A.2C51.00-00, seq 82
ISIS-SNP: Same entry 0000.0C76.5B7C.00-00, seq AE
ISIS-SNP: Same entry 0000.0C76.5B7C.02-00, seq 65
ISIS-SNP: Rec L1 CSNP from 0000.0C76.5B7C (Ethernet0)
ISIS-SNP: CSNP range 0000.0000.0000.00-00 to FFFF.FFFF.FFFF.FF-FF
ISIS-SNP: Same entry 0000.0C0A.2C51.00-00, seq 82
ISIS-SNP: Same entry 0000.0C76.5B7C.00-00, seq AE
ISIS-SNP: Same entry 0000.0C76.5B7C.02-00, seq 65
```

Figure 10.63

debug isis snp-packets *displays detailed information about CSNPs and PSNPs.*

Case Study: Integrated IS-IS on NBMA Networks

Figure 10.64 shows four routers running IS-IS connected by a partially meshed Frame Relay network. The IP addresses, DLCIs, and NETs are shown. The IS-IS configurations of all routers have been verified as correct, and no authentication is configured.

The problem with this internetwork is that no routes are being discovered (Figure 10.65). The IP addresses of neighbors' Frame Relay interfaces can be pinged, but the addresses of the routers' other interfaces cannot be pinged (Figure 10.66). The pings show that the Frame Relay PVCs are operational and that IP is working, but that the routers are not routing.

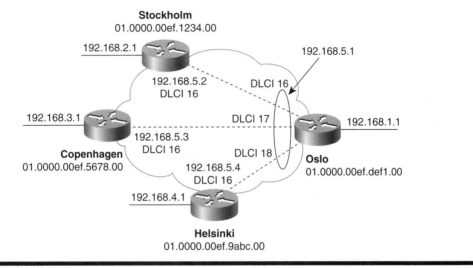

Figure 10.64

IS-IS is not establishing adjacencies across the Frame Relay network.

```
Oslo#show ip route
Codes: C - connected, S - static, I - IGRP, R - RIP, M - mobile, B - BGP
       D - EIGRP, EX - EIGRP external, O - OSPF, IA - OSPF inter area
       E1 - OSPF external type 1, E2 - OSPF external type 2, E - EGP
       i - IS-IS, L1 - IS-IS level-1, L2 - IS-IS level-2, * - candidate default

Gateway of last resort is not set

C    192.168.1.0 is directly connected, TokenRing0
C    192.168.5.0 is directly connected, Serial0
Oslo#
```

Figure 10.65

The route table of Oslo in Figure 10.64 does not contain any IS-IS routes.

The next step is to check the IS-IS neighbor table. Oslo's neighbor table shows that Hellos have been received (Figure 10.67) and that the router knows the System IDs of its neighbors. It also shows that the IP addresses and the area addresses of the neighbors are correct. However, the state of all of the neighbors is *Init*, indicating that a full adjacency has not been established. A look at the

```
Oslo#ping 192.168.5.2
Type escape sequence to abort.
Sending 5, 100-byte ICMP Echos to 192.168.5.2, timeout is 2 seconds:
!!!!!
Success rate is 100 percent (5/5), round-trip min/avg/max = 64/65/68 ms
Oslo#ping 192.168.2.1
Type escape sequence to abort.
Sending 5, 100-byte ICMP Echos to 192.168.2.1, timeout is 2 seconds:
.....
Success rate is 0 percent (0/5)
Oslo#ping 192.168.5.3
Type escape sequence to 5, 100-byte ICMP Echos to 192.168.5.3, timeout is 2 seconds:
!!!!!
Success rate is 100 percent (5/5), round-trip min/avg/max = 64/66/68 ms
Oslo#ping 192.168.3.1
Type escape sequence to abort.
Sending 5, 100-byte ICMP Echos to 192.168.3.1, timeout is 2 seconds:
.....
Success rate is 0 percent (0/5)
Oslo#ping 192.168.5.4
Type escape sequence to abort.
Sending 5, 100-byte ICMP Echos to 192.168.5.4, timeout is 2 seconds:
!!!!!
Success rate is 100 percent (5/5), round-trip min/avg/max = 64/65/68 ms
Oslo#ping 192.168.4.1
Type escape sequence to abort.
Sending 5, 100-byte ICMP Echos to 192.168.4.1, timeout is 2 seconds:
.....
Success rate is 0 percent (0/5)
Oslo#
```

Figure 10.66

Pings are successful to other interfaces connected to the Frame Relay network, but addresses reachable through the routers cannot be pinged.

link state database verifies the absence of adjacencies; the only LSPs in Oslo's database are the router's own LSPs (Figure 10.68).

The fact that Hellos are being received, but adjacencies are not being established, points to a problem with the Hellos themselves. If the parameters in the Hellos are not correct, the PDU is dropped. So **debug isis adj-packets** is enabled to observe the Hellos. Of particular interest in the debug output (Figure 10.69) are the "encapsulation failed" messages. These messages show that the router apparently cannot interpret the received Hellos and is dropping them.

```
Oslo#show clns is-neighbors detail

System Id       Interface    State Type Priority  Circuit Id          Format
0000.00EF.5678 Se0           Init  L1L2 0 /0      0000.0000.0000.00   Phase V
  Area Address(es): 01
  IP Address(es):  192.168.5.3
  Uptime: 1:11:20
0000.00EF.1234 Se0           Init  L1L2 0 /0      0500.0000.0000.00   Phase V
  Area Address(es): 01
  IP Address(es):  192.168.5.2
  Uptime: 1:11:15
0000.00EF.9ABC Se0           Init  L1L2 0 /0      0700.0000.0000.00   Phase V
  Area Address(es): 01
  IP Address(es):  192.168.5.4
  Uptime: 1:11:20
Oslo#
```

Figure 10.67

Oslo's IS-IS neighbor table shows that Hellos are being received but that the adjacency is not complete.

```
Oslo#show isis database
IS-IS Level-1 Link State Database
LSPID                  LSP SeqChecksum  LSP Holdtime  ATT/P/OL
0000.00EF.DEF1.00-00* 0x0000001F  0x8460       947          0/0/0
0000.00EF.DEF1.02-00* 0x00000010  0x695E       896          0/0/0
0000.00EF.DEF1.04-00* 0x00000002  0x2F2E       887          0/0/0
0000.00EF.DEF1.05-00* 0x00000008  0x1C3A       847          0/0/0

IS-IS Level-2 Link State Database
LSPID                  LSP Seq Num  LSP Checksum  LSP Holdtime  ATT/P/OL
0000.00EF.DEF1.00-00* 0x00000013  0x81BE       829          0/0/0
Oslo#
```

Figure 10.68

Oslo's link state database does not contain any LSPs from any of its neighbors.

```
Oslo#debug isis adj-packets
IS-IS Adjacency related packets debugging is on
Oslo#
ISIS-Adj: Sending L1 IIH on TokenRing0
ISIS-Adj: Encapsulation failed for level 2 IIH on Serial0
ISIS-Adj: Rec serial IIH from DLCI 17 on Serial0, cir type 3, cir id 00
ISIS-Adj: rcvd state 2, old state 1, new state 1
ISIS-Adj: Action = 1, new_type = 3
ISIS-Adj: Sending L2 IIH on TokenRing0
ISIS-Adj: Encapsulation failed for level 1 IIH on Serial0
ISIS-Adj: Sending L1 IIH on TokenRing0
ISIS-Adj: Rec serial IIH from DLCI 18 on Serial0, cir type 3, cir id 07
ISIS-Adj: rcvd state 2, old state 1, new state 1
ISIS-Adj: Action = 1, new_type = 3
ISIS-Adj: Encapsulation failed for level 2 IIH on Serial0
ISIS-Adj: Sending L2 IIH on TokenRing0
ISIS-Adj: Encapsulation failed for level 1 IIH on Serial0
ISIS-Adj: Rec serial IIH from DLCI 16 on Serial0, cir type 3, cir id 05
ISIS-Adj: rcvd state 2, old state 1, new state 1
ISIS-Adj: Action = 1, new_type = 3
ISIS-Adj: Sending L1 IIH on TokenRing0
ISIS-Adj: Encapsulation failed for level 2 IIH on Serial0no debu
ISIS-Adj: Sending L2 IIH on TokenRing0
ISIS-Adj: Encapsulation failed for level 1 IIH on Serial0g a
ISIS-Adj: Sending L1 IIH on TokenRing0
ISIS-Adj: Rec serial IIH from DLCI 17 on Serial0, cir type 3, cir id 00
ISIS-Adj: rcvd state 2, old state 1, new state 1
ISIS-Adj: Action = 1, new_type = 3
ISIS-Adj: Encapsulation failed for level 2 IIH on Serial0ll
```

Figure 10.69

*The results of enabling **debug isis adj-packets** show that Hellos are being dropped because of encapsulation failures.*

Any time an encapsulation failed message is received, suspicion should fall on the data link and its connected interfaces. Examining the interfaces with the **show interface serial** command reveals no significant error rates, so it is unlikely that the Hellos are being corrupted on the Frame Relay PVCs. The next step is to examine the interface configurations. The interface configurations for the four routers in Figure 10.64 are:

Oslo

```
interface Serial0
  ip address 192.168.5.1 255.255.255.0
  ip router isis
  encapsulation frame-relay
  frame-relay interface-dlci 16
  frame-relay interface-dlci 17
  frame-relay interface-dlci 18
```

Stockholm

```
interface Serial0
  no ip address
  encapsulation frame-relay
!
interface Serial0.16 point-to-point
  ip address 192.168.5.2 255.255.255.0
  ip router isis
  frame-relay interface-dlci 16
```

Copenhagen

```
interface Serial0
  no ip address
  encapsulation frame-relay
!
interface Serial0.16 point-to-point
  ip address 192.168.5.3 255.255.255.0
  ip router isis
  frame-relay interface-dlci 16
```

Helsinki

```
interface Serial0
  no ip address
  encapsulation frame-relay
!
interface Serial0.16 point-to-point
  ip address 192.168.5.4 255.255.255.0
  ip router isis
  frame-relay interface-dlci 16
```

A comparison of these configurations reveals the problem, although it may not be readily apparent. Stockholm, Copenhagen, and Helsinki are all configured with point-to-point subinterfaces. Oslo is not using subinterfaces. By default, a Cisco serial interface with Frame Relay encapsulation is a multi-point interface. Therefore, Stockholm, Copenhagen, and Helsinki are sending point-to-point IS-IS Hellos, and Oslo is sending L1 and L2 IS-IS LAN Hellos.

IS-IS does not have a configuration option similar to OSPF's **ip ospf network** command; therefore, Oslo must be reconfigured with point-to-point subinterfaces, and the IP addresses must be changed so that each PVC is a different subnet (Figure 10.70).

```
Oslo#show ip route
Codes: C - connected, S - static, I - IGRP, R - RIP, M - mobile, B - BGP
       D - EIGRP, EX - EIGRP external, O - OSPF, IA - OSPF inter area
       E1 - OSPF external type 1, E2 - OSPF external type 2, E - EGP
       i - IS-IS, L1 - IS-IS level-1, L2 - IS-IS level-2, * - candidate default

Gateway of last resort is not set

C    192.168.1.0 is directly connected, TokenRing0
i L1 192.168.2.0 [115/20] via 192.168.5.5, Serial0.16
i L1 192.168.3.0 [115/20] via 192.168.5.9, Serial0.17
i L1 192.168.4.0 [115/20] via 192.168.5.13, Serial0.18
     192.168.5.0 is variably subnetted, 4 subnets, 2 masks
C       192.168.5.12 255.255.255.252 is directly connected, Serial0.18
C       192.168.5.8 255.255.255.252 is directly connected, Serial0.17
C       192.168.5.4 255.255.255.252 is directly connected, Serial0.16
C       192.168.5.0 255.255.255.0 is directly connected, Serial0
Oslo#
```

Figure 10.70
After Oslo has been configured with point-to-point subinterfaces and the PVCs have been readdressed as individual subnets, IS-IS routing is functioning.

LOOKING AHEAD

Now that all of the IP IGPs have been examined, the next step is to study the tools available to help you control your internetwork. Part III covers redistribution, default routes, On-Demand Routing, route filters, and route maps.

SUMMARY TABLE: CHAPTER 10 COMMAND REVIEW

Command	Description
area-password *password*	Configures IS-IS area (level 1) authentication.
clns routing	Enables the routing of CLNS PDUs.
debug isis adj-packets	Displays IS-IS Hello PDU activity.
debug isis spf-events	Displays details of events triggering an IS-IS SPF calculation.
debug isis snp-packets	Displays information about SNPs sent and received by the router.
debug isis spf-statistics	Displays statistical information about IS-IS SPF calculations.
debug isis spf-triggers	Displays events that trigger IS-IS SPF calculations.
debug isis update-packets	Displays information about LSPs, CSNPs, and PSNPs sent and received by the router.
default-information originate [route-map *map-name*]	Generates a default IP route into an IS-IS domain.
domain-password *password*	Configures IS-IS domain (level 2) authentication.
ignore-lsp-errors	Configures an IS-IS router to ignore errored LSPs rather than triggering a purge of the LSPs.
ip router isis [*tag*]	Enables IS-IS routing on an interface.
isis csnp-interval *seconds* {**level-1**|**level-2**}	Specifies the interval in which an IS-IS Designated Router sends CSNPs.
isis hello-interval *seconds* {**level-1**|**level-2**}	Specifies the interval between transmissions of IS-IS Hello PDUs.
isis hello-multiplier *multiplier* {**level-1**|**level-2**}	Specifies the number of IS-SI Hello PDUs a neighbor must miss before declaring its adjacency to the originating router down.
isis metric *default-metric* {**level-1**|**level-2**}	Specifies an interface's IS-IS default metric.
isis password *password* {**level-1**|**level-2**}	Configures authentication between two IS-IS neighbors.
isis priority *value* {**level-1**|**level-2**}	Specifies the priority of an interface to be used for DR election.

Command	Description
isis retransmit-interval *seconds*	Specifies the time a router will wait for an acknowledgment after sending an LSP on a point-to-point link before retransmitting the LSP.
is-type {level-1|level-1-2|level-2-only}	Configures the router as an L1, L1/L2, or L2 IS-IS router.
net *network-entity-title*	Configures an IS-IS router's NET.
router isis [*tag*]	Enables an IS-IS routing process.
set-overload-bit	Manually sets the Overload bit in a router's LSP to one.
show clns is-neighbor [*type number*][detail]	Displays the IS-IS neighbor table.
show isis database [level-1][level-2][l1][l2][detail] [*lspid*]	Displays an IS-IS link state database.
show isis spf-log	Displays how often and why the router has run a full SPF calculation.
summary-address *address-mask* {level-1|level-1-2|level-2}	Configures IP address summarization.
which-route {*nsap-address|clns-name*}	Displays the routing table in which the specified CLNS destination is found and displays details of the associated IP addresses and area addresses.

REVIEW QUESTIONS

1. What is an intermediate system?
2. What is a network protocol data unit?
3. What is the difference between an L1, an L2, and an L1/L2 router?
4. Explain the basic difference between an IS-IS area and an OSPF area.

   5. What is a network entity title (NET)?

   6. To what value must the NSAP Selector be set in a NET?

   7. What is the purpose of a System ID?

   8. How does a router determine what area it is in?

   9. Does IS-IS elect a Backup Designated Router on a broadcast subnetwork?

   10. What is the purpose of the Pseudonode ID?

   11. What is the maximum age (MaxAge) of an IS-IS LSP?

   12. What is the basic difference between the way OSPF ages its LSAs and the way IS-IS ages its LSPs?

   13. How often does an IS-IS router refresh its LSPs?

   14. What is a Complete Sequence Number Packet (CSNP)? How is it used?

   15. What is a Partial Sequence Number Packet (PSNP)? How is it used?

   16. What is the purpose of the Overload (OL) bit?

   17. What is the purpose of the Attached (ATT) bit?

   18. What metrics are specified by the ISO for IS-IS? How many of these metrics does the Cisco IOS support?

   19. What is the maximum value of the IS-IS default metric?

   20. What is the maximum metric value of an IS-IS route?

   21. What is the difference between a level 1 IS-IS metric and a level 2 IS-IS metric?

   22. What is the difference between an internal IS-IS metric and an external IS-IS metric?

CONFIGURATION EXERCISES

1. Table 10.6 shows the interfaces, interface addresses, and subnet masks of 11 routers. The table also designates that routers belong in the same area. Write Integrated IS-IS configurations for the routers, using the following guidelines:

   ○ Make up your own System IDs for the routers

   ○ Use the shortest NETs possible

   ○ Configure routers as L1, L2, or L1/L2 as appropriate

   Tip: Draw a picture of the routers and subnets first.

Table 10.6   *Router information for Configuration Exercises 1 through 5.*

Router	Area	Interface	Address/Mask
A	0	E0	192.168.1.17/28
		E1	192.168.1.50/28
B	0	E0	192.168.1.33/28
		E1	192.168.1.51/28
C	0	E0	192.168.1.49/28
		S0	192.168.1.133/30
D	2	S0	192.168.1.134/30
		S1	192.168.1.137/30
E	2	S0	192.168.1.142/30
		S1	192.168.1.145/30
		S2	192.168.1.138/30
F	2	S0	192.168.1.141/30
		S1	192.168.1.158/30
G	1	E0	192.168.1.111/27

Table 10.6 *Router information for Configuration Exercises 1 through 5, continued.*

Router	Area	Interface	Address/Mask
		S0	192.168.1.157/30
H	1	E0	192.168.1.73/27
		E1	192.168.1.97/27
I	3	E0	192.168.1.225/29
		E1	192.168.1.221/29
		S0	192.168.1.249/30
		S1	192.168.1.146/30
J	3	E0	192.168.1.201/29
		E1	192.168.1.217/29
K	3	EO	192.168.1.209/29
		S0	192.168.1.250/30

2. Configure authentication between all routers in area 2 of Table 10.6. Use the password "Eiffel" between routers D and E; use the password "Tower" between routers D and F.

3. Configure level 1 authentication in area 1 of Table 10.6. Use the password "Scotland."

4. Configure level 2 authentication on the routers in Table 10.6. Use the password "Vienna."

5. Configure the L1/L2 routers in areas 0, 1, and 3 in Table 10.6 to summarize their area addresses.

TROUBLESHOOTING EXERCISES

1. Figures 10.71 and 10.72 show the IS-IS neighbor tables of two routers, router A and router B, connected to a Token Ring network. IS-IS is exchanging routes between the two routers and entering them into the route tables, but no IP traffic is passing between the routers. What is wrong?

```
Router_A#show clns is-neighbors detail

System Id       Interface   State  Type Priority  Circuit Id        Format
0000.00EF.DCBA To0          Up     L1L2 64/64      0000.00EF.DCBA.04 Phase V
  Area Address(es): 01
  IP Address(es):  192.168.11.2
  Uptime: 0:09:25
0000.00EF.5678 Se0.17       Up     L1L2 0 /0       00                Phase V
  Area Address(es): 01
  IP Address(es):  192.168.5.9
  Uptime: 1:28:22
0000.00EF.9ABC Se0.18       Up     L1L2 0 /0       07                Phase V
  Area Address(es): 01
  IP Address(es):  192.168.5.13
  Uptime: 1:29:45
0000.00EF.1234 Se0.16       Up     L1L2 0 /0       06                Phase V
  Area Address(es): 01
  IP Address(es):  192.168.5.5
  Uptime: 1:29:45
Router_A#
```

Figure 10.71

The IS-IS neighbor table of router A, Troubleshooting Exercise 1.

```
Router_B#show clns is-neighbors detail

System Id       Interface   State  Type Priority  Circuit Id        Format
0000.00EF.DEF1 To0          Up     L1L2 64/64      0000.00EF.DCBA.04 Phase V
  Area Address(es): 01
  IP Address(es):  192.168.1.1
  Uptime: 0:11:06
Router_B#
```

Figure 10.72

The IS-IS neighbor table of router B, Troubleshooting Exercise 1.

2. Figure 10.73 shows debug messages from a router that is not establishing an adjacency with a neighbor on its interface TO0. What is wrong?

```
Router_B#debug isis adj-packets
IS-IS Adjacency related packets debugging is on
Router_B#
ISIS-Adj: Sending L1 IIH on TokenRing0
ISIS-Adj: Sending L1 IIH on TokenRing1
ISIS-Adj: Sending L1 IIH on TokenRing0
ISIS-Adj: Sending L1 IIH on TokenRing1
ISIS-Adj: Sending L1 IIH on TokenRing0
ISIS-Adj: Sending L1 IIH on TokenRing1
ISIS-Adj: Rec L2 IIH from 0000.3090.c7df (TokenRing0), cir type 2, cir id 0000.0
0EF.DCBA.04
ISIS-Adj: is-type mismatch
ISIS-Adj: Sending L1 IIH on TokenRing0
ISIS-Adj: Sending L1 IIH on TokenRing1
ISIS-Adj: Sending L1 IIH on TokenRing0
ISIS-Adj: Sending L1 IIH on TokenRing1
ISIS-Adj: Sending L1 IIH on TokenRing1
ISIS-Adj: Sending L1 IIH on TokenRing0
ISIS-Adj: Rec L2 IIH from 0000.3090.c7df (TokenRing0), cir type 2, cir id 0000.0
0EF.DCBA.04
ISIS-Adj: is-type mismatch
ISIS-Adj: Sending L1 IIH on TokenRing1
ISIS-Adj: Sending L1 IIH on TokenRing0
ISIS-Adj: Sending L1 IIH on TokenRing1
ISIS-Adj: Sending L1 IIH on TokenRing0
 IIH on TokenRing0L1 IIH on TokenRing1
```

Figure 10.73

The debug output for Troubleshooting Exercise 2.

PART III

Route Control
and Interoperability

- **Principles of Redistribution**

    Metrics

    Administrative Distances

    Redistributing from Classless to Classful Protocols

- **Configuring Redistribution**

    Case Study: Redistributing IGRP and RIP

    Case Study: Redistributing EIGRP and OSPF

    Case Study: Redistribution and Route Summarization

    Case Study: Redistributing IS-IS and RIP

    Case Study: Redistributing Static Routes

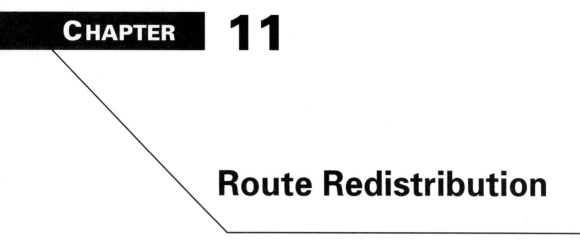

Route Redistribution

A router performs redistribution when it uses a routing protocol to advertise routes that were learned by some other means. Those "other means" may be another routing protocol, static routes, or a direct connection to the destination network. For example, a router may be running both an OSPF process and a RIP process. If the OSPF process is configured to advertise routes learned by the RIP process, it is said to be "redistributing RIP."

Running a single routing protocol throughout the entire IP internetwork is usually more desirable than running multiple protocols, both from a configuration management perspective and from a fault management perspective. However, the realities of modern internetworking frequently force the acceptance of multiprotocol IP routing domains. As departments, divisions, and entire companies merge, their formerly autonomous internetworks must be consolidated.

In most cases, the internets that are to be consolidated were implemented differently and have evolved differently, to meet different needs or merely as the result of different design philosophies. This diversity can make the migration to a single routing protocol a complex undertaking. In some cases, corporate politics can force the use of multiple routing protocols. And in a few cases, multiple routing protocols may be the result of network administrators who do not work and play well together.

Multi-vendor environments are another factor that can necessitate redistribution. For example, an internet running Cisco's IGRP or EIGRP may be merged with an internet using another manufacturer's routers, which support only RIP or Open Shortest Path First. Without redistribution, either the Cisco routers would have to be reconfigured to an open protocol or the non-Cisco routers would have to be replaced with Cisco routers.

Redistribution is necessary when multiple routing protocols are "thrown together," but redistribution may also be part of a well-thought-out internetwork design. Figure 11.1 shows an example. Here two OSPF process domains are connected, but the OSPF processes do not directly communicate. Instead, static routes are configured on each router to selected networks in the other OSPF domain.

For instance, router Spalding has static routes to networks 192.168.11.0 and 192.168.12.0. Spalding then redistributes these static routes into OSPF, and OSPF advertises the routes to the other routers in OSPF 10. The result is that the other networks in OSPF 20 are hidden from OSPF 10. Redistribution has allowed the dynamic characteristics of OSPF to be mixed with the precise control of static routes.

Static routes redistributed into a dynamic routing protocol are also very useful, if not essential, in dial-up environments. The periodic management traffic of a dynamic protocol can cause the dial-up line to be "always up." By blocking routing updates or hellos across the link and configuring static routes on each side, the administrator can ensure that the link will only come up when user traffic must traverse it. And by redistributing the static routes into the dynamic routing protocol, all routers on both sides of the dial-up link have full knowledge of all networks on the opposite side of the link.

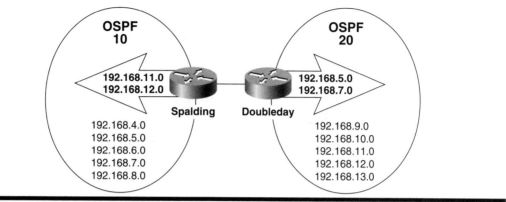

Figure 11.1

In this internetwork, static routes are configured on each router and redistributed into OSPF. As a result, the advertisement of networks between the two OSPF domains is carefully controlled.

Note that with few exceptions,[1] the existence of more than one routing protocol on the same router does not mean that redistribution will automatically occur. Redistribution must be explicitly configured. The configuration of multiple routing protocols on a single router without redistribution is called *ships in the night* (SIN) routing. The router will pass routes to its peers in each process domain, but the process domains will have no knowledge of each other—like ships passing in the night. Although SIN routing usually refers to multiple routing protocols routing multiple routed protocols on the same router (such as OSPF routing IP and NLSP routing IPX), it can also refer to two IP protocols routing for separate IP domains on a single router.

---

[1]   *Within IP, IGRP and EIGRP processes with the same autonomous system number will redistribute automatically. An example is given in the Chapter 8, "Enhanced Interior Gateway Routing Protocol (EIGRP)," section, "Case Study: Redistribution with IGRP."*

PRINCIPLES OF REDISTRIBUTION

The capabilities of the IP routing protocols vary widely. The protocol characteristics that have the most bearing on redistribution are the differences in metrics and administrative distances, and each protocol's classful or classless capabilities. Failure to give careful consideration to these differences when redistributing can lead to, at best, a failure to exchange some or all routes or, at worst, routing loops and black holes.

Metrics

The routers of Figure 11.1 are redistributing static routes into OSPF, which then advertises the routes to other OSPF-speaking routers. Static routes have no metric associated with them, but every OSPF route must have a cost. Another example of conflicting metrics is the redistribution of RIP routes into IGRP. RIP's metric is hop count, whereas IGRP uses bandwidth and delay. In both cases, the protocol into which routes are redistributed must be able to associate its own metrics with those routes.

So the router performing the redistribution must assign a metric to the redistributed routes. Figure 11.2 shows an example. Here EIGRP is being redistributed into OSPF, and OSPF is being redistributed into EIGRP. OSPF does not understand the composite metric of EIGRP, and EIGRP does not understand cost. As a result, part of the redistribution process is that the router must assign a cost to each EIGRP route before passing it to OSPF. Likewise, the router must assign a bandwidth, delay, reliability, load, and MTU to each OSPF route before passing it to EIGRP. If incorrect metrics are assigned, redistribution will fail.

Case studies later in this chapter show how to configure routers to assign metrics for purposes of redistribution.

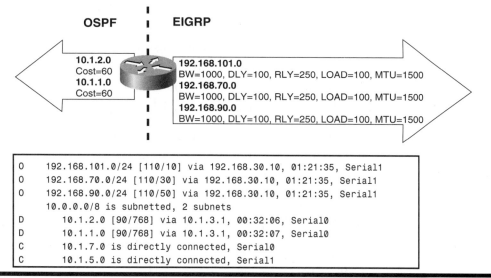

Figure 11.2

When routes are redistributed, a metric that is understandable to the receiving protocol must be assigned to the routes.

Administrative Distances

The diversity of metrics presents another problem: If a router is running more than one routing protocol and learns a route to the same destination from each of the protocols, which route should be selected? Each protocol uses its own metric scheme to define the best route. Comparing routes with different metrics, such as cost and hop count, is like comparing apples and oranges.

The answer to the problem is administrative distances. Just as metrics are assigned to routes so that the most preferred route may be determined, administrative distances are assigned to route sources so that the most preferred source may be determined. Think of an administrative distance as a measure of believability. The lower the administrative distance, the more believable the protocol.

For example, suppose a router running RIP and EIGRP learns of a route to network 192.168.5.0 from a RIP-speaking neighbor and another route to the same destination from an EIGRP-speaking neighbor. Because of EIGRP's composite metric, that protocol is more likely to have determined the optimum route. Therefore, EIGRP should be believed over RIP. [2]

Table 11.1 shows the default Cisco administrative distances. EIGRP has an administrative distance of 90, whereas RIP has an administrative distance of 120. Therefore, EIGRP is deemed more trustworthy than RIP.

Table 11.1 *Cisco default administrative distances.*

Route Source	Administrative Distance
Connected interface[2]	0
Static route	1
EIGRP summary route	5
External BGP	20
EIGRP	90
IGRP	100
OSPF	110
IS-IS	115
RIP	120
EGP	140
External EIGRP	170
Internal BGP	200
Unknown	255

---

[2] *Recall from Chapter 3 that when a static route refers to an interface instead of a next-hop address, the destination is considered to be a directly connected network.*

Although administrative distances help resolve the confusion of diverse metrics, they can cause problems for redistribution. For example, in Figure 11.3 both Gehrig and Ruth are redistributing RIP-learned routes into IGRP. Gehrig learns about network 192.168.1.0 via RIP and advertises the network into the IGRP domain. As a result, Ruth learns about network 192.168.1.0 not only from Combs via RIP but also from Meusel via IGRP.

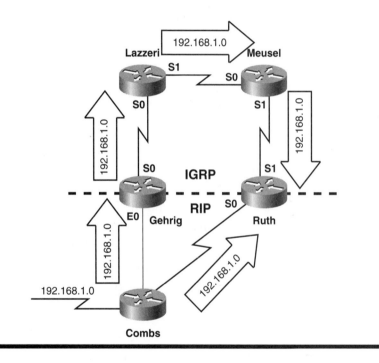

Figure 11.3

Network 192.168.1.0 is being advertised to Ruth via both RIP and IGRP.

Figure 11.4 shows Ruth's routing table. Notice that the route to 192.168.1.0 is an IGRP route. Ruth has chosen the IGRP route because, compared to RIP, IGRP has a lower administrative distance. Ruth will send all packets to 192.168.1.0 over the "scenic route" through Meusel, instead of sending them directly to Combs.

```
Ruth#show ip route
Codes: C - connected, S - static, I - IGRP, R - RIP, M - mobile, B - BGP
       D - EIGRP, EX - EIGRP external, O - OSPF, IA - OSPF inter area
       E1 - OSPF external type 1, E2 - OSPF external type 2, E - EGP
       i - IS-IS, L1 - IS-IS level-1, L2 - IS-IS level-2, * - candidate default
       U - per-user static route

Gateway of last resort is not set

I     192.168.1.0/24 [100/16100] via 192.168.5.1, 00:00:00, Serial1
I     192.168.2.0/24 [100/12576] via 192.168.5.1, 00:00:00, Serial1
I     192.168.3.0/24 [100/12476] via 192.168.5.1, 00:00:01, Serial1
I     192.168.4.0/24 [100/10476] via 192.168.5.1, 00:00:01, Serial1
C     192.168.5.0/24 is directly connected, Serial1
C     192.168.6.0/24 is directly connected, Serial0
Ruth#
```

Figure 11.4

Although the optimal route to network 192.168.1.0 from Ruth is through Combs, out S0, Ruth is instead routing to that network through Meusel, out S1.

Split horizon prevents a routing loop in the internet of Figure 11.3. Both Gehrig and Ruth initially advertise network 192.168.1.0 into the IGRP domain, and the four IGRP routers eventually converge on a single path to that network. However, the convergence is unpredictable. This condition can be seen by rebooting routers Lazzeri and Meusel. After the reboot, Ruth's routing table shows that it is using Combs as the next-hop router to reach 192.168.1.0 (Figure 11.5).

Convergence after the reboot is not only unpredictable but also slow. Figure 11.6 shows Gehrig's routing table approximately three minutes after the reboot. It is using Lazzeri as a next-hop router to network 192.168.1.0, but pings to a working address on that network fail. Lazzeri's routing table (Figure 11.7) shows the problem: Lazzeri is using Gehrig as a next-hop router. A routing loop exists.

```
Ruth#show ip route
Codes: C - connected, S - static, I - IGRP, R - RIP, M - mobile, B - BGP
       D - EIGRP, EX - EIGRP external, O - OSPF, IA - OSPF inter area
       E1 - OSPF external type 1, E2 - OSPF external type 2, E - EGP
       i - IS-IS, L1 - IS-IS level-1, L2 - IS-IS level-2, * - candidate default
       U - per-user static route

Gateway of last resort is not set

R     192.168.1.0/24 [120/1] via 192.168.6.2, 00:00:23, Serial0
I     192.168.2.0/24 [100/12576] via 192.168.5.1, 00:00:22, Serial1
I     192.168.3.0/24 [100/12476] via 192.168.5.1, 00:00:22, Serial1
I     192.168.4.0/24 [100/10476] via 192.168.5.1, 00:00:22, Serial1
C     192.168.5.0/24 is directly connected, Serial1
C     192.168.6.0/24 is directly connected, Serial0
Ruth#
```

Figure 11.5

The convergence of the internet in Figure 11.3 is unpredictable. After a reboot of the routers, Ruth is now routing to 192.168.1.0 through Combs.

```
Gehrig#show ip route
Codes: C - connected, S - static, I - IGRP, R - RIP, M - mobile, B - BGP
       D - EIGRP, EX - EIGRP external, O - OSPF, IA - OSPF inter area
       N1 - OSPF NSSA external type 1, N2 - OSPF NSSA external type 2
       E1 - OSPF external type 1, E2 - OSPF external type 2, E - EGP
       i - IS-IS, L1 - IS-IS level-1, L2 - IS-IS level-2, * - candidate default
       U - per-user static route, o - ODR

Gateway of last resort is not set

I     192.168.1.0/24 [100/16100] via 192.168.3.2, 00:02:38, Serial0
C     192.168.2.0/24 is directly connected, Ethernet0
C     192.168.3.0/24 is directly connected, Serial0
I     192.168.4.0/24 [100/10476] via 192.168.3.2, 00:00:29, Serial0
I     192.168.5.0/24 [100/12476] via 192.168.3.2, 00:00:29, Serial0
I     192.168.6.0/24 [100/14476] via 192.168.3.2, 00:00:39, Serial0
Gehrig#ping 192.168.1.1

Type escape sequence to abort.
Sending 5, 100-byte ICMP Echos to 192.168.1.1, timeout is 2 seconds:
.....
Success rate is 0 percent (0/5)
Gehrig#
```

Figure 11.6

Soon after the reboot, Gehrig is routing packets to 192.168.1.0 via Lazzeri.

```
Lazzeri#show ip route
Codes: C - connected, S - static, I - IGRP, R - RIP, M - mobile, B - BGP
       D - EIGRP, EX - EIGRP external, O - OSPF, IA - OSPF inter area
       E1 - OSPF external type 1, E2 - OSPF external type 2, E - EGP
       i - IS-IS, L1 - IS-IS level-1, L2 - IS-IS level-2, * - candidate default
       U - per-user static route

Gateway of last resort is not set

I    192.168.1.0/24 [100/12100] via 192.168.3.1, 00:04:21, Serial0
I    192.168.2.0/24 [100/8576] via 192.168.3.1, 00:00:33, Serial0
C    192.168.3.0/24 is directly connected, Serial0
C    192.168.4.0/24 is directly connected, Serial1
I    192.168.5.0/24 [100/10476] via 192.168.4.2, 00:00:53, Serial1
I    192.168.6.0/24 [100/12100] via 192.168.3.1, 00:02:32, Serial0
Lazzeri#
```

Figure 11.7

Lazzeri is routing packets to 192.168.1.0 via Gerig, creating a routing loop. Notice the age of the route.

Here's the sequence of events leading to the loop:

1. While Lazzeri and Meusel are rebooting, both Gehrig and Ruth have routing table entries showing network 192.168.1.0 as reachable via Combs.

2. As Lazzeri and Meusel become active, both Gehrig and Ruth send IGRP updates that include network 192.168.1.0. Simply by the "luck of the draw," Ruth sends its update slightly earlier than Gehrig does.

3. Meusel, receiving Ruth's update, makes Ruth the next-hop router and sends an update to Lazzeri.

4. Lazzeri, receiving Meusel's update, makes Meusel the next-hop router.

5. Lazzeri and Gehrig send updates to each other at about the same time. Lazzeri makes Gehrig the next-hop router to 192.168.1.0 because its route is metrically closer than Meusel's route. Gehrig makes Lazzeri the next-hop router

to 192.168.1.0 because its IGRP advertisement has a lower administrative distance than Combs's RIP advertisement. The loop is now in effect.

Split horizon and the invalid timers will eventually sort things out. Lazzeri is advertising 192.168.1.0 to Meusel, but Meusel continues to use the metrically closer route via Ruth. And since Ruth is the next-hop router, split horizon is in effect for 192.168.1.0 at Meusel's S1 interface. Meusel is also advertising 192.168.1.0 to Lazzeri, but Lazzeri sees Gehrig as metrically closer.

Lazzeri and Gehrig see each other as the next-hop router to 192.168.1.0, so they will not advertise the route to each other. The route will age in both of their routing tables until the invalid timer expires (Figure 11.8).

```
Lazzeri#show ip route
Codes: C - connected, S - static, I - IGRP, R - RIP, M - mobile, B - BGP
       D - EIGRP, EX - EIGRP external, O - OSPF, IA - OSPF inter area
       E1 - OSPF external type 1, E2 - OSPF external type 2, E - EGP
       i - IS-IS, L1 - IS-IS level-1, L2 - IS-IS level-2, * - candidate default
       U - per-user static route

Gateway of last resort is not set

I    192.168.1.0/24 is possibly down, routing via 192.168.3.1, Serial0
I    192.168.2.0/24 [100/8576] via 192.168.3.1, 00:00:57, Serial0
C    192.168.3.0/24 is directly connected, Serial0
C    192.168.4.0/24 is directly connected, Serial1
I    192.168.5.0/24 [100/10476] via 192.168.4.2, 00:01:25, Serial1
I    192.168.6.0/24 is possibly down, routing via 192.168.3.1, Serial0
Lazzeri#
```

Figure 11.8

When the invalid timer for the route to 192.168.1.0 expires, the route is declared unreachable and the holddown timer is started.

When Lazzeri's invalid timer expires, the route to 192.168.1.0 will be put into holddown. Although Meusel is advertising a route to that network, Lazzeri cannot accept it until the holddown timer expires. Figure 11.9 shows that Lazzeri has finally accepted the route from Meusel, and Figure 11.10 shows that Gehrig is successfully reaching 192.168.1.0 through Lazzeri. It took more than nine minutes for these two routers to converge, and the route they are using is still not the optimal route.

```
Lazzeri#show ip route
Codes: C - connected, S - static, I - IGRP, R - RIP, M - mobile, B - BGP
       D - EIGRP, EX - EIGRP external, O - OSPF, IA - OSPF inter area
       E1 - OSPF external type 1, E2 - OSPF external type 2, E - EGP
       i - IS-IS, L1 - IS-IS level-1, L2 - IS-IS level-2, * - candidate default
       U - per-user static route

Gateway of last resort is not set

I     192.168.1.0/24 [100/14100] via 192.168.4.2, 00:00:27, Serial1
I     192.168.2.0/24 [100/8576] via 192.168.3.1, 00:00:02, Serial0
C     192.168.3.0/24 is directly connected, Serial0
C     192.168.4.0/24 is directly connected, Serial1
I     192.168.5.0/24 [100/10476] via 192.168.4.2, 00:00:28, Serial1
I     192.168.6.0/24 [100/12476] via 192.168.4.2, 00:00:28, Serial1
Lazzeri#
```

Figure 11.9

After the holddown timer for 192.168.1.0 expires, Lazzeri accepts the route advertised by Meusel.

Administrative distances can contribute to routing loops.

Administrative distances can cause even worse problems than the sub-optimal routes, unpredictable behavior, and slow convergence of the previous example. For example, Figure 11.11 shows essentially the same internetwork as in Figure 11.3 except the links between the IGRP routers are frame relay PVCs. By default, IP split horizon is turned off on Frame Relay interfaces. As a result, permanent routing loops will form between Lazzeri and Gehrig and between Meusel and Ruth. Network 192.168.1.0 is unreachable from the IGRP domain.

Several tools and strategies exist to prevent routing loops when redistributing. The administrative distances can be manipulated, and route filters or route maps can be used. Chapter 13 covers route filters, and Chapter 14 covers route maps. These chapters also demonstrate techniques for changing administrative distances.

```
Gehrig#show ip route
Codes: C - connected, S - static, I - IGRP, R - RIP, M - mobile, B - BGP
       D - EIGRP, EX - EIGRP external, O - OSPF, IA - OSPF inter area
       N1 - OSPF NSSA external type 1, N2 - OSPF NSSA external type 2
       E1 - OSPF external type 1, E2 - OSPF external type 2, E - EGP
       i - IS-IS, L1 - IS-IS level-1, L2 - IS-IS level-2, * - candidate default
       U - per-user static route, o - ODR

Gateway of last resort is not set

I    192.168.1.0/24 [100/16100] via 192.168.3.2, 00:00:32, Serial0
C    192.168.2.0/24 is directly connected, Ethernet0
C    192.168.3.0/24 is directly connected, Serial0
I    192.168.4.0/24 [100/10476] via 192.168.3.2, 00:00:33, Serial0
I    192.168.5.0/24 [100/12476] via 192.168.3.2, 00:00:33, Serial0
I    192.168.6.0/24 [100/14476] via 192.168.3.2, 00:00:33, Serial0
Gehrig#ping 192.168.1.1

Type escape sequence to abort.
Sending 5, 100-byte ICMP Echos to 192.168.1.1, timeout is 2 seconds:
!!!!!
Success rate is 100 percent (5/5), round-trip min/avg/max = 52/72/108 ms
Gehrig#
```

Figure 11.10
Gehrig can now reach network 192.168.1.0 via Lazzeri.

Redistributing from Classless to Classful Protocols

Careful consideration must be given to the effects of redistributing routes from a classless routing process domain into a classful domain. To understand why, it is necessary to first understand how a classful routing protocol reacts to variable subnetting. Recall from Chapter 5, "Routing Information Protocol (RIP)," that classful routing protocols do not advertise a mask with each route. For every route a classful router receives, one of two situations will apply:

- The router will have one or more interfaces attached to the major network.

- The router will have no interfaces attached to the major network.

In the first case, the router must use its own configured mask for that major network to correctly determine the subnet of a packet's destination address. In the second case, only the major network address itself can be included in the advertisement because the router has no way of knowing which subnet mask to use.

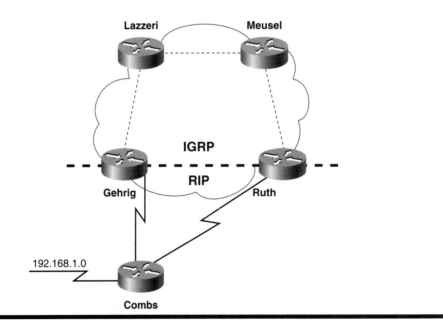

Figure 11.11

Because IP split horizon is turned off by default on Frame Relay interfaces, permanent routing loops will form in this internetwork.

Figure 11.12 shows a router with four interfaces connected to subnets of 192.168.100.0. The network is variably subnetted—two interfaces have 27-bit masks, and two interfaces have 30-bit masks. If the router is running a classful protocol such as IGRP, it cannot use the 27-bit mask to derive 30-bit subnets, and it cannot use the 30-bit mask to derive 27-bit subnets. So, how does the protocol cope with the conflicting masks?

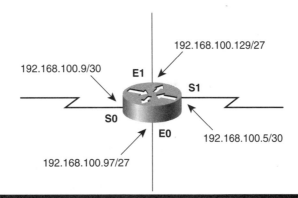

192.168.100.129/27

192.168.100.9/30

E1

S1

S0

E0

192.168.100.5/30

192.168.100.97/27

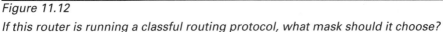

Figure 11.12

If this router is running a classful routing protocol, what mask should it choose?

In Figure 11.13, debugging is used to observe the IGRP advertisements sent by the router in Figure 11.12. Notice that subnet 192.168.100.128/27 is advertised out interface E0, which has a 27-bit mask, but neither 192.168.100.4/30 nor 192.168.100.8/30 is advertised out that interface. Similarly, 192.168.100.8/30 is advertised out interface S1, which has a 30-bit mask, but neither 192.168.100.96/27 nor 192.168.100.128/27 is advertised out that interface. The same situation applies to all four interfaces. Only subnets of 192.168.100.0 whose masks match the interface mask are advertised. As a result, IGRP-speaking neighbors on interfaces E0 and E1 will have no knowledge of the 30-bit subnets, and IGRP-speaking neighbors on interfaces S0 and S1 will have no knowledge of the 27-bit subnets.

```
O'Neil#debug ip igrp transactions
IGRP protocol debugging is on
O'Neil#
IGRP: sending update to 255.255.255.255 via Ethernet0 (192.168.100.97)
     subnet 192.168.100.128, metric=1100
IGRP: sending update to 255.255.255.255 via Ethernet1 (192.168.100.129)
     subnet 192.168.100.96, metric=1100
IGRP: sending update to 255.255.255.255 via Serial0 (192.168.100.9)
     subnet 192.168.100.4, metric=8476
IGRP: sending update to 255.255.255.255 via Serial1 (192.168.100.5)
     subnet 192.168.100.8, metric=8476
O'Neil#
```

Figure 11.13

A classful routing protocol will not advertise routes between interfaces whose masks do not match.

This behavior of only advertising routes between interfaces with matching masks also applies when redistributing from a classless routing protocol into a classful routing protocol. In Figure 11.14, the subnets of the OSPF domain are variably subnetted, and Paige is redistributing OSPF-learned routes into IGRP.

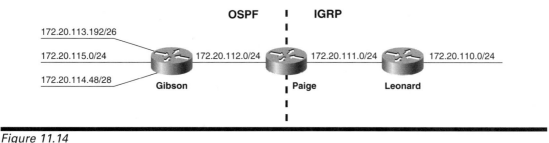

Figure 11.14

Paige is redistributing its OSPF-learned routes into IGRP.

As Figure 11.15 shows, Paige knows about all of the subnets in both the OSPF and the IGRP domain. And because OSPF is classless, the router knows which masks are associated with each subnet connected to Gibson. Paige's IGRP process is using a 24-bit mask; therefore, 172.20.113.192/26 and 172.20.114.48/28 are not compatible and are not advertised (Figure 11.16). Notice that

IGRP does advertise 172.20.112.0/24 and 172.20.115.0/24. The result is that the only subnets within the OSPF domain that Leonard knows of are the ones with a 24-bit mask (Figure 11.17).

```
Paige#show ip route
Codes: C - connected, S - static, I - IGRP, R - RIP, M - mobile, B - BGP
       D - EIGRP, EX - EIGRP external, O - OSPF, IA - OSPF inter area
       N1 - OSPF NSSA external type 1, N2 - OSPF NSSA external type 2
       E1 - OSPF external type 1, E2 - OSPF external type 2, E - EGP
       i - IS-IS, L1 - IS-IS level-1, L2 - IS-IS level-2, * - candidate default
       U - per-user static route, o - ODR

Gateway of last resort is not set

     172.20.0.0/16 is variably subnetted, 6 subnets, 3 masks
O       172.20.113.192/26 [110/74] via 172.20.112.1, 00:01:35, Ethernet1
C       172.20.112.0/24 is directly connected, Ethernet1
O       172.20.115.0/24 [110/80] via 172.20.112.1, 00:01:35, Ethernet1
I       172.20.110.0/24 [100/1600] via 172.20.111.1, 00:00:33, Ethernet0
C       172.20.111.0/24 is directly connected, Ethernet0
O       172.20.114.48/28 [110/74] via 172.20.112.1, 00:01:35, Ethernet1
Paige#
```

Figure 11.15

Paige knows about all six subnets of Figure 11.14, either from OSPF, IGRP, or a direct connection.

```
Paige#debug ip igrp transactions
IGRP protocol debugging is on
Paige#
IGRP: received update from 172.20.111.1 on Ethernet0
      subnet 172.20.110.0, metric 1600 (neighbor 501)
IGRP: sending update to 255.255.255.255 via Ethernet0 (172.20.111.2)
      subnet 172.20.112.0, metric=1100
      subnet 172.20.115.0, metric=1100
Paige#
```

Figure 11.16

Only the OSPF-learned routes with a 24-bit mask are successfully redistributed into the IGRP domain, which is also using a 24-bit mask.

```
Leonard#show ip route
Codes: C - connected, S - static, I - IGRP, R - RIP, M - mobile, B - BGP
       D - EIGRP, EX - EIGRP external, O - OSPF, IA - OSPF inter area
       N1 - OSPF NSSA external type 1, N2 - OSPF NSSA external type 2
       E1 - OSPF external type 1, E2 - OSPF external type 2, E - EGP
       i - IS-IS, L1 - IS-IS level-1, L2 - IS-IS level-2, * - candidate default
       U - per-user static route, o - ODR

Gateway of last resort is not set

     172.20.0.0/24 is subnetted, 4 subnets
I       172.20.112.0 [100/1200] via 172.20.111.2, 00:00:48, Ethernet1
I       172.20.115.0 [100/1200] via 172.20.111.2, 00:00:48, Ethernet1
C       172.20.110.0 is directly connected, Ethernet0
C       172.20.111.0 is directly connected, Ethernet1
Leonard#
```

Figure 11.17

The only subnets within the OSPF domain known at Leonard are the ones with a 24-bit mask.
172.20.113.192/26 and 172.20.114.48/28 are unreachable from here.

The configuration section includes case studies that demonstrate methods for reliably redistributing from a classless routing protocol to a classful routing protocol.

CONFIGURING REDISTRIBUTION

Redistribution is configured in two steps:

1. In the routing protocol configuration that is to receive the redistributed routes, use the **redistribute** command to specify the source of the routes.
2. Specify the metric to be assigned to the redistributed routes.

For example, the IGRP configuration of Paige in Figure 11.14 is:

```
router igrp 1
  redistribute ospf 1 metric 10000 100 255 1 1500
  passive-interface Ethernet1
  network 172.20.0.0
```

This configuration redistributes routes discovered by OSPF process 1 into IGRP process 1. The **metric** portion of the command assigns IGRP metrics to the routes. In order, the numbers specify:

- Bandwidth, in kilobits per second

- Delay, in tens of microseconds

- Reliability, as a fraction of 255

- Load, as a fraction of 255

- MTU, in octets

The OSPF configuration of Paige is:

```
router ospf 1
 redistribute igrp 1 metric 30 metric-type 1 subnets
 network 172.20.112.2 0.0.0.0 area 0
```

This configuration redistributes routes discovered by IGRP process 1 into OSPF process 1. The **metric** portion of the command assigns an OSPF cost of 30 to each redistributed route. The redistribution makes Paige an ASBR in the OSPF domain, and the redistributed routes are advertised as external routes. The **metric-type** portion of the command specifies that the external type of the routes is E1. The **subnets** keyword, used only when redistributing routes into OSPF, specifies that subnet details will be redistributed. Without it, only major network addresses are redistributed. More will be said about the **subnets** keyword in the case studies.

An alternative method of specifying the metrics to be assigned to redistributed routes is to use the **default-metric** command. For example, the previous OSPF configuration can also be written as follows:

```
router ospf 1
 redistribute igrp 1 metric-type 1 subnets
 default-metric 30
 network 172.20.112.2 0.0.0.0 area 0
```

The results of this configuration are exactly the same as the previous configuration. The **default-metric** command is useful when routes are being redistributed from more than one source. For example, suppose router Paige in Figure 11.14 was running not only IGRP and OSPF but also RIP and EIGRP. The OSPF configuration might be:

```
router ospf 1
  redistribute igrp 1 metric-type 1 subnets
  redistribute rip metric-type 1 subnets
  redistribute eigrp 2 metric-type 1 subnets
  default-metric 30
  network 172.20.112.2 0.0.0.0 area 0
```

Here an OSPF cost of 30 will be assigned to all IGRP-, RIP- and EIGRP-learned routes.

The two methods of assigning metrics can also be used with each other. For example, suppose Paige were to be configured to redistribute OSPF, RIP, and EIGRP into IGRP, but that RIP routes were to be advertised with a different set of metrics than the OSPF and EIGRP routes. The configuration might be:

```
router igrp 1
  redistribute ospf 1
  redistribute rip metric 50000 500 255 1 1500
  redistribute eigrp 2
  default-metric 10000 100 255 1 1500
  passive-interface Ethernet1
  network 172.20.0.0
```

The metrics assigned using the **metric** keyword with the **redistribute** command take precedence over metrics assigned with the **default-metric** command. RIP-learned routes will be advertised into IGRP with the metrics specified on the **redistribute rip** line, and the OSPF- and EIGRP-learned routes will be advertised with the metrics specified by the **default-metric** command.

Default metric quantities for redistribution

If neither the **metric** keyword nor the **default-metric** command specifies a metric, the metric will default to 20 for routes redistributed into OSPF and to 0 for routes redistributed into other protocols. The 0 metric will be understood by IS-IS, but not by RIP, whose hop count must be between 1 and 16. The 0 metric is also incompatible with the IGRP and EIGRP multi-metric format. These three protocols must have the appropriate metrics assigned to any redistributed routes, or redistribution will not work. The following case studies examine techniques for configuring redistribution into the various IP IGPs. In addition, they are arranged so that the more generic issues of redistributing classful to classful, classless to classless, and classless to classful can be examined.

Case Study: Redistributing IGRP and RIP

In the internetwork of Figure 11.18, Ford is running IGRP, and Berra is running RIP. Mantle's routing configuration is:

```
router rip
 redistribute igrp 1 metric 5
 passive-interface Ethernet1
 network 10.0.0.0
!
router igrp 1
 redistribute rip
 default-metric 1000 100 255 1 1500
 passive-interface Ethernet0
 network 10.0.0.0
```

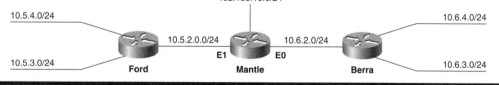

Figure 11.18

Ford is running IGRP, and Berra is running RIP. Mantle is performing redistribution.

Both methods of assigning metrics are used here for demonstration purposes. In most cases, a redistribution scheme as simple as this will use one method or the other.

Notice that Mantle is also connected to a stub network (192.168.10.0/24). In this case, the stub network should be advertised into the IGRP domain, but not into the RIP domain. One way to accomplish this configuration is to simply add the appropriate network statement under IGRP. However, doing so will create unnecessary IGRP broadcasts on the stub network. Another way to achieve the desired configuration is to use redistribution:

```
router rip
 redistribute igrp 1 metric 5
 passive-interface Ethernet1
 network 10.0.0.0
!
router igrp 1
 redistribute connected
 redistribute rip
 default-metric 1000 100 255 1 1500
 passive-interface Ethernet0
 network 10.0.0.0
```

The **redistribute connected** command will redistribute all directly connected networks. If network 192.168.10.0/24 is to be advertised into the IGRP domain and the RIP domain, the configuration is:

```
router rip
 redistribute connected metric 5
 redistribute igrp 1 metric 5
 passive-interface Ethernet1
 network 10.0.0.0
!
router igrp 1
 redistribute connected
 redistribute rip
 default-metric 1000 100 255 1 1500
 passive-interface Ethernet0
 network 10.0.0.0
```

Case Study: Redistributing EIGRP and OSPF

The internetwork of Figure 11.19 has an OSPF domain and two EIGRP domains. Router Hodges is running OSPF process 1. Podres is running EIGRP process 1, and EIGRP process 2 is running on Snider and Campanella. Robinson has the following configuration:

```
router eigrp 1
 redistribute ospf 1 metric 1000 100 1 255 1500
 redistribute eigrp 2
 passive-interface Ethernet0
 network 192.168.3.0
!
router eigrp 2
 redistribute ospf 1 metric 1000 100 1 255 1500
 redistribute eigrp 1
 network 192.168.4.0
 network 172.16.0.0
!
router ospf 1
 redistribute eigrp 1 metric 50
 redistribute eigrp 2 metric 100
 network 192.168.3.33 0.0.0.0 area 0
```

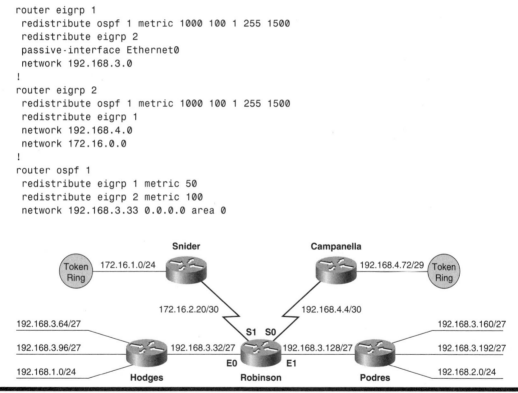

Figure 11.19

Hodges is running OSPF, and Podres is running EIGRP 1. Snider and Campanella are running EIGRP 2.

Notice that although redistribution must be configured between the EIGRP processes, no metrics are configured. The processes use the same metrics, so the metrics can be tracked accurately across the redistribution boundary. Figure 11.20 shows Podres' routing table. The redistributed routes are tagged as EIGRP external routes.

```
Podres#show ip route
Codes: C - connected, S - static, I - IGRP, R - RIP, M - mobile, B - BGP
       D - EIGRP, EX - EIGRP external, O - OSPF, IA - OSPF inter area
       E1 - OSPF external type 1, E2 - OSPF external type 2, E - EGP
       i - IS-IS, L1 - IS-IS level-1, L2 - IS-IS level-2, * - candidate default
       U - per-user static route

Gateway of last resort is not set

D EX 192.168.1.0/24 [170/2611200] via 192.168.3.129, 00:39:14, Ethernet0
C    192.168.2.0/24 is directly connected, Ethernet3
     192.168.3.0/24 is variably subnetted, 7 subnets, 3 masks
D EX    192.168.3.96/27 [170/2611200] via 192.168.3.129, 00:41:18, Ethernet0
D EX    192.168.3.64/27 [170/2611200] via 192.168.3.129, 00:41:18, Ethernet0
D       192.168.3.32/27 [90/307200] via 192.168.3.129, 00:44:06, Ethernet0
D       192.168.3.0/24 is a summary, 00:52:21, Null0
C       192.168.3.192/27 is directly connected, Ethernet2
C       192.168.3.160/27 is directly connected, Ethernet1
C       192.168.3.128/27 is directly connected, Ethernet0
     192.168.4.0/24 is variably subnetted, 3 subnets, 3 masks
D EX    192.168.4.72/29 [170/2211584] via 192.168.3.129, 00:07:25, Ethernet0
D EX    192.168.4.4/30 [170/281600] via 192.168.3.129, 00:07:25, Ethernet0
D EX    192.168.4.0/24 [170/2195456] via 192.168.3.129, 00:07:25, Ethernet0
     172.16.0.0/16 is variably subnetted, 3 subnets, 3 masks
D EX    172.16.2.20/30 [170/281600] via 192.168.3.129, 00:07:27, Ethernet0
D EX    172.16.0.0/16 [170/2195456] via 192.168.3.129, 00:07:27, Ethernet0
D EX    172.16.1.0/24 [170/2211584] via 192.168.3.129, 00:07:27, Ethernet0
Podres#
```

Figure 11.20

The routing table of Podres in Figure 11.19.

Figure 11.21 shows Hodges' routing table, which has some problems. Recall from Chapter 9, "Open Shortest Path First," that routes redistributed into OSPF are either type 1 (E1) or type 2 (E2) external routes. The only route that seems to have been redistributed, indicated by the E2 tag, is the major network address 192.168.2.0/24. The reason for this is the absence of the **subnets** keyword in Robinson's redistribution statements. Without this keyword, only major network addresses that are not directly connected to the redistributing router will be redistributed.

```
Hodges#show ip route
Codes: C - connected, S - static, I - IGRP, R - RIP, M - mobile, B - BGP
       D - EIGRP, EX - EIGRP external, O - OSPF, IA - OSPF inter area
       N1 - OSPF NSSA external type 1, N2 - OSPF NSSA external type 2
       E1 - OSPF external type 1, E2 - OSPF external type 2, E - EGP
       i - IS-IS, L1 - IS-IS level-1, L2 - IS-IS level-2, * - candidate default
       U - per-user static route, o - ODR

Gateway of last resort is not set

C    192.168.1.0/24 is directly connected, Ethernet2
O E2 192.168.2.0/24 [110/50] via 192.168.3.33, 00:11:59, Ethernet0
     192.168.3.0/27 is subnetted, 3 subnets
C       192.168.3.96 is directly connected, Ethernet1
C       192.168.3.64 is directly connected, Ethernet3
C       192.168.3.32 is directly connected, Ethernet0
Hodges#
```

Figure 11.21

The routing table of Hodges contains only a single redistributed route, indicated by the E2 tag.

Robinson's configuration is changed to include the **subnets** keyword:

```
router eigrp 1
  redistribute ospf 1 metric 1000 100 1 255 1500
  redistribute eigrp 2
  passive-interface Ethernet0
  network 192.168.3.0
!
router eigrp 2
  redistribute ospf 1 metric 1000 100 1 255 1500
  redistribute eigrp 1
  network 192.168.4.0
  network 172.16.0.0
!
router ospf 1
  redistribute eigrp 1 metric 50 subnets
  redistribute eigrp 2 metric 100 subnets
  network 192.168.3.33 0.0.0.0 area 0
```

As a result of this change, all subnets in Figure 11.19 are in Hodges' routing table (Figure 11.22).

```
Hodges#show ip route
Codes: C - connected, S - static, I - IGRP, R - RIP, M - mobile, B - BGP
       D - EIGRP, EX - EIGRP external, O - OSPF, IA - OSPF inter area
       N1 - OSPF NSSA external type 1, N2 - OSPF NSSA external type 2
       E1 - OSPF external type 1, E2 - OSPF external type 2, E - EGP
       i - IS-IS, L1 - IS-IS level-1, L2 - IS-IS level 2, * - candidate default
       U - per-user static route, o - ODR

Gateway of last resort is not set

C    192.168.1.0/24 is directly connected, Ethernet2
O E2 192.168.2.0/24 [110/50] via 192.168.3.33, 00:17:31, Ethernet0
     192.168.3.0/27 is subnetted, 6 subnets
C       192.168.3.96 is directly connected, Ethernet1
C       192.168.3.64 is directly connected, Ethernet3
C       192.168.3.32 is directly connected, Ethernet0
O E2    192.168.3.192 [110/50] via 192.168.3.33, 00:02:51, Ethernet0
O E2    192.168.3.160 [110/50] via 192.168.3.33, 00:02:51, Ethernet0
O E2    192.168.3.128 [110/50] via 192.168.3.33, 00:00:36, Ethernet0
     192.168.4.0/24 is variably subnetted, 3 subnets, 3 masks
O E2    192.168.4.72/29 [110/100] via 192.168.3.33, 00:00:19, Ethernet0
O E2    192.168.4.4/30 [110/100] via 192.168.3.33, 00:00:19, Ethernet0
O E2    192.168.4.0/24 [110/100] via 192.168.3.33, 00:00:19, Ethernet0
     172.16.0.0/16 is variably subnetted, 3 subnets, 3 masks
O E2    172.16.2.20/30 [110/100] via 192.168.3.33, 00:00:20, Ethernet0
O E2    172.16.0.0/16 [110/100] via 192.168.3.33, 00:00:20, Ethernet0
O E2    172.16.1.0/24 [110/100] via 192.168.3.33, 00:00:20, Ethernet0
Hodges#
```

Figure 11.22

*After the **subnets** keyword is added to Robinson's redistribution configuration, Hodges has knowledge of all subnets.*

By default, external routes are redistributed into OSPF as type 2 routes. As discussed in Chapter 9, E2 routes include only the external cost of the route. This fact can be important when a single destination is reachable by more than one external route, as shown in Figure 11.23. In this internetwork, one router is redistributing the route to 10.2.3.0/24 with a cost of 50, and the other router is redistributing a different route to the same destination with a cost of 100. If the routes are advertised as E2, the costs of the links within the OSPF domain will not be added. As a result, the router internal to the OSPF domain will choose route 1 to reach 10.2.3.0/24.

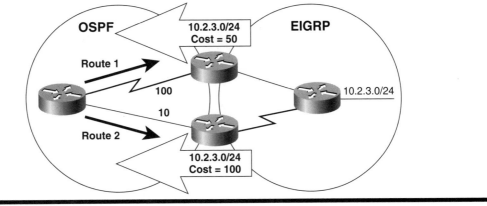

Figure 11.23
If the routes to 10.2.3.0/24 are advertised as E2, route 1 will have a cost of 50 and route 2 will have a cost of 100. If the routes are advertised as E1, route 1 will have a cost of 150 and route 2 will have a cost of 110.

If the routes to 10.2.3.0/24 in Figure 11.23 are redistributed as E1, the costs of the links within the OSPF domain will be added to the redistributed costs. As a result, the router internal to the OSPF domain would choose route 2, with a cost of 110 (100 + 10) over route 1, with a cost of 150 (50 + 100).

Robinson, in Figure 11.19, is redistributing EIGRP 1 with a cost of 50 and redistributing EIGRP 2 with a cost of 100. Figure 11.22 shows that, at Hodges, the routes to the EIGRP 1 subnets still have a cost of 50, and the routes to the EIGRP 2 subnets still have a cost of 100. The cost of the Ethernet link between Hodges and Robinson has not been added to the routes.

To redistribute routes into OSPF as E1, the keyword **metric-type 1** is added to the redistribution command. In the following config-

Redistributing external routes into OSPF as E1 instead of E2.

uration, Robinson continues to redistribute EIGRP 1 as E2, but EIGRP 2 is redistributed as E1:

```
router eigrp 1
  redistribute ospf 1 metric 1000 100 1 255 1500
  redistribute eigrp 2
  passive-interface Ethernet0
  network 192.168.3.0
!
router eigrp 2
  redistribute ospf 1 metric 1000 100 1 255 1500
  redistribute eigrp 1
  network 192.168.4.0
  network 172.16.0.0
!
router ospf 1
  redistribute eigrp 1 metric 50 subnets
  redistribute eigrp 2 metric 100 metric-type 1 subnets
  network 192.168.3.33 0.0.0.0 area 0
```

Figure 11.24 shows Hodges' routing table after Robinson is reconfigured. All the routes to destinations within the EIGRP 1 domain still have a cost of 50, but the routes to destinations within the EIGRP 2 domain now have a cost of 110 (the redistributed cost plus the default cost of 10 for the Ethernet link between Robinson and Hodges).

Case Study: Redistribution and Route Summarization

Cisco's EIGRP, OSPF, and IS-IS implementations have the capability to summarize redistributed routes. This case study examines summarization for EIGRP and OSPF; the following case study examines IS-IS summarization.

The first thing to note is that summarization is useful only if the IP subnet addresses have been planned for summarization. For example, the subnets of 192.168.3.0 within the OSPF domain in Figure 11.19 all fall under the summary address 192.168.3.0/25. The subnets of the same major address within the EIGRP 1 domain all fall under the summary address 192.168.3.128/25. If subnet 192.168.3.0/27 were to be connected to Podres, that single

```
Hodges#sh ip rou
Codes: C - connected, S - static, I - IGRP, R - RIP, M - mobile, B - BGP
       D - EIGRP, EX - EIGRP external, O - OSPF, IA - OSPF inter area
       N1 - OSPF NSSA external type 1, N2 - OSPF NSSA external type 2
       E1 - OSPF external type 1, E2 - OSPF external type 2, E - EGP
       i - IS-IS, L1 - IS-IS level-1, L2 - IS-IS level-2, * - candidate default
       U - per-user static route, o - ODR

Gateway of last resort is not set

C    192.168.1.0/24 is directly connected, Ethernet2
O E2 192.168.2.0/24 [110/50] via 192.168.3.33, 00:21:20, Ethernet0
     192.168.3.0/27 is subnetted, 6 subnets
C       192.168.3.96 is directly connected, Ethernet1
C       192.168.3.64 is directly connected, Ethernet3
C       192.168.3.32 is directly connected, Ethernet0
O E2    192.168.3.192 [110/50] via 192.168.3.33, 00:06:40, Ethernet0
O E2    192.168.3.160 [110/50] via 192.168.3.33, 00:06:40, Ethernet0
O E2    192.168.3.128 [110/50] via 192.168.3.33, 00:04:24, Ethernet0
     192.168.4.0/24 is variably subnetted, 3 subnets, 3 masks
O E1    192.168.4.72/29 [110/110] via 192.168.3.33, 00:00:54, Ethernet0
O E1    192.168.4.4/30 [110/110] via 192.168.3.33, 00:00:54, Ethernet0
O E1    192.168.4.0/24 [110/110] via 192.168.3.33, 00:00:54, Ethernet0
     172.16.0.0/16 is variably subnetted, 3 subnets, 3 masks
O E1    172.16.2.20/30 [110/110] via 192.168.3.33, 00:00:55, Ethernet0
O E1    172.16.0.0/16 [110/110] via 192.168.3.33, 00:00:55, Ethernet0
O E1    172.16.1.0/24 [110/110] via 192.168.3.33, 00:00:55, Ethernet0
Hodges#
```

Figure 11.24

Robinson's configuration has been changed so that the subnets of 192.168.4.0 and 172.16.0.0 are being advertised as type 1 external routes.

destination would have to be advertised separately from the summary address. Although advertising such a single destination will have little adverse impact, advertising a large number of subnets outside of the range of the summary address will reduce the benefits of summarization.

The command **summary-address** specifies a summary address and mask to an OSPF process. Any more-specific subnet addresses that fall within the range of the specified summary address will be suppressed. Note that this command is used only to summarize external routes at ASBRs; summarization of internal OSPF routes at

ABRs is accomplished with the **area range** command, as discussed in Chapter 9.

At Robinson in Figure 11.19, the EIGRP 1 subnets are summarized into the OSPF domain with 192.168.3.128/25, and the EIGRP 2 subnets are summarized with 172.16.0.0/16:

```
router eigrp 1
  redistribute ospf 1 metric 1000 100 1 255 1500
  redistribute eigrp 2
  passive-interface Ethernet0
  network 192.168.3.0
!
router eigrp 2
  redistribute eigrp 1
  network 192.168.4.0
  network 172.16.0.0
!
router ospf 1
  summary-address 192.168.3.128 255.255.255.128
  summary-address 172.16.0.0 255.255.0.0
  redistribute eigrp 1 metric 50 subnets
  redistribute eigrp 2 metric 100 metric-type 1 subnets
  network 192.168.3.33 0.0.0.0 area 0
```

Compare Figure 11.25 with Figure 11.24. In Figure 11.25, Hodges' routing table contains the specified summary addresses. The subnet addresses within the summary range have been suppressed at the redistribution point. Notice, also, that no summarization was configured for 92.168.4.0/24, so the subnets of that major address are still in the routing table.

Summarization for EIGRP is interface-specific. That is, instead of specifying the summary address and mask under the routing process, they are specified under individual interfaces. This system provides the flexibility to advertise different summary routes out different interfaces of the same process. The command **ip summary-address eigrp** *process-id* specifies the summary address and mask and the EIGRP process into which the summary is to be advertised.

```
Hodges#show ip route
Codes: C - connected, S - static, I - IGRP, R - RIP, M - mobile, B - BGP
       D - EIGRP, EX - EIGRP external, O - OSPF, IA - OSPF inter area
       N1 - OSPF NSSA external type 1, N2 - OSPF NSSA external type 2
       E1 - OSPF external type 1, E2 - OSPF external type 2, E - EGP
       i - IS-IS, L1 - IS-IS level-1, L2 - IS-IS level-2, * - candidate default
       U - per-user static route, o - ODR

Gateway of last resort is not set

C    192.168.1.0/24 is directly connected, Ethernet2
O E2 192.168.2.0/24 [110/50] via 192.168.3.33, 00:25:01, Ethernet0
     192.168.3.0/24 is variably subnetted, 4 subnets, 2 masks
C        192.168.3.96/27 is directly connected, Ethernet1
C        192.168.3.64/27 is directly connected, Ethernet3
C        192.168.3.32/27 is directly connected, Ethernet0
O E2     192.168.3.128/25 [110/50] via 192.168.3.33, 00:01:45, Ethernet0
     192.168.4.0/24 is variably subnetted, 3 subnets, 3 masks
O E1     192.168.4.72/29 [110/110] via 192.168.3.33, 00:04:35, Ethernet0
O E1     192.168.4.4/30 [110/110] via 192.168.3.33, 00:04:35, Ethernet0
O E1     192.168.4.0/24 [110/110] via 192.168.3.33, 00:04:36, Ethernet0
O E1 172.16.0.0/16 [110/110] via 192.168.3.33, 00:04:36, Ethernet0
Hodges#
```

Figure 11.25

Robinson is summarizing 192.168.3.128/25 and 172.16.0.0/26, so no more-specific subnets within those ranges appear in the routing table of Hodges.

In the following configuration, Robinson will advertise summary addresses 192.168.3.0/25, 172.16.0.0/16, and 192.168.4.0/24 into EIGRP 1:

```
interface Ethernet0
  ip address 192.168.3.33 255.255.255.224
!
interface Ethernet1
  ip address 192.168.3.129 255.255.255.224
  ip summary-address eigrp 1 192.168.3.0 255.255.255.128
  ip summary-address eigrp 1 172.16.0.0 255.255.0.0
  ip summary-address eigrp 1 192.168.4.0 255.255.255.0
!
interface Serial0
  ip address 192.168.4.5 255.255.255.252
  ip summary-address eigrp 2 192.168.3.0 255.255.255.0
!
interface Serial1
  ip address 172.16.2.21 255.255.255.252
  ip summary-address eigrp 2 192.168.0.0 255.255.0.0
!
```

```
router eigrp 1
 redistribute ospf 1 metric 1000 100 1 255 1500
 redistribute eigrp 2
 passive-interface Ethernet0
 network 192.168.3.0
!
router eigrp 2
 redistribute eigrp 1
 network 192.168.4.0
 network 172.16.0.0
!
router ospf 1
 summary-address 192.168.3.128 255.255.255.128
 summary-address 172.16.0.0 255.255.0.0
 redistribute eigrp 1 metric 50 subnets
 redistribute eigrp 2 metric 100 metric-type 1 subnets
 network 192.168.3.33 0.0.0.0 area 0
```

Figure 11.26 shows the routing table of Podres. As with OSPF summarization, EIGRP summarization suppresses the advertisement of subnets within the summary range. Unlike OSPF, Podres' routing table shows that summary routes advertised into EIGRP are not tagged as external routes.

Robinson is advertising EIGRP summary routes of 192.168.3.0/24 to Campanella and 192.168.0.0/16 to Snider. Figure 11.27 shows Campanella's routing table, and Figure 11.28 shows Snider's routing table.

A point of interest in Snider's routing table is the entry for 192.168.4.0/24. You might expect this route to be suppressed by the summary address of 192.168.0.0/16. However, 192.168.4.0/24 is internal to the EIGRP 2 process domain; the summarization applies only to routes being redistributed into the process domain.

Looking again at Figure 11.26, notice the entry for the summary route 192.168.3.128/25. This entry may surprise you because that summary address is advertised into OSPF, not EIGRP. Notice also that the route is marked as an external route, indicating that it was redistributed into the EIGRP domain. What has happened is that

```
Podres#show ip route
Codes: C - connected, S - static, I - IGRP, R - RIP, M - mobile, B - BGP
       D - EIGRP, EX - EIGRP external, O - OSPF, IA - OSPF inter area
       E1 - OSPF external type 1, E2 - OSPF external type 2, E - EGP
       i - IS-IS, L1 - IS-IS level-1, L2 - IS-IS level-2, * - candidate default
       U - per-user static route

Gateway of last resort is not set

D EX 192.168.1.0/24 [170/2611200] via 192.168.3.129, 00:00:52, Ethernet0
C    192.168.2.0/24 is directly connected, Ethernet3
     192.168.3.0/24 is variably subnetted, 6 subnets, 3 masks
D        192.168.3.0/24 is a summary, 00:00:52, Null0
D        192.168.3.0/25 [90/307200] via 192.168.3.129, 00:00:52, Ethernet0
C        192.168.3.192/27 is directly connected, Ethernet2
C        192.168.3.160/27 is directly connected, Ethernet1
D EX     192.168.3.128/25 [170/2611200] via 192.168.3.129, 00:00:52, Ethernet0
C        192.168.3.128/27 is directly connected, Ethernet0
D    192.168.4.0/24 [90/281600] via 192.168.3.129, 00:00:52, Ethernet0
D    172.16.0.0/16 [90/281600] via 192.168.3.129, 00:00:52, Ethernet0
D EX 192.168.0.0/16 [170/281600] via 192.168.3.129, 00:00:53, Ethernet0
Podres#
```

Figure 11.26

The routing table of Podres, showing summary routes 192.168.3.0/25, 192.168.4.0/24, and 172.16.0.0/16.

```
Campanella#show ip route
Codes: C - connected, S - static, I - IGRP, R - RIP, M - mobile, B - BGP
       D - EIGRP, EX - EIGRP external, O - OSPF, IA - OSPF inter area
       E1 - OSPF external type 1, E2 - OSPF external type 2, E - EGP
       i - IS-IS, L1 - IS-IS level-1, L2 - IS-IS level-2, * - candidate default
       U - per-user static route

Gateway of last resort is not set

D EX 192.168.2.0/24 [170/2323456] via 192.168.4.5, 00:03:15, Serial0
D    192.168.3.0/24 [90/2169856] via 192.168.4.5, 00:04:26, Serial0
     192.168.4.0/24 is variably subnetted, 2 subnets, 2 masks
C        192.168.4.72/29 is directly connected, TokenRing0
C        192.168.4.4/30 is directly connected, Serial0
D    172.16.0.0/16 [90/2681856] via 192.168.4.5, 00:03:13, Serial0
Campanella#
```

Figure 11.27

Campanella's routing table after summarization is configured at Robinson.

```
Snider#show ip route
Codes: C - connected, S - static, I - IGRP, R - RIP, M - mobile, B - BGP
       D - EIGRP, EX - EIGRP external, O - OSPF, IA - OSPF inter area
       E1 - OSPF external type 1, E2 - OSPF external type 2, E - EGP
       i - IS-IS, L1 - IS-IS level-1, L2 - IS-IS level-2, * - candidate default
       U - per-user static route

Gateway of last resort is not set

D    192.168.4.0/24 [90/2681856] via 172.16.2.21, 00:05:26, Serial0
     172.16.0.0/16 is variably subnetted, 3 subnets, 3 masks
C       172.16.2.20/30 is directly connected, Serial0
D       172.16.0.0/16 is a summary, 00:05:24, Null0
C       172.16.1.0/24 is directly connected, TokenRing0
D    192.168.0.0/16 [90/2169856] via 172.16.2.21, 00:07:37, Serial0
Snider#
```

Figure 11.28

Snider's routing table after summarization is configured at Robinson.

the summary route was advertised into OSPF and was then redistributed back into EIGRP from the OSPF domain. Hence the unexpected entry at Podres.

Now suppose subnet 192.168.3.192/27 were to become inaccessible. Podres would forward packets destined for that subnet to the less-specific route 192.168.3.128/25. The packet would be sent into the OSPF domain, where you might expect the summary route 192.168.3.128/25 to cause the packet to be sent right back to Podres.

Using null interfaces to protect against routing loops caused by summarization.

In fact, this situation will not occur. Robinson's routing table (Figure 11.29) has numerous entries for summary routes that show interface Null0 as a connected interface. The null interface is a software-only interface to nowhere—packets routed to it are dropped. With some exceptions,[3] whenever a router generates a summary address, the router will also create a route for that

---

[3]   *OSPF inter-area summarization, for example, does not automatically create a summary route to the null interface. It must be configured statically, as demonstrated in Chapter 9, "Open Shortest Path First."*

address that goes to the null interface. If Robinson receives a packet destined for 192.168.3.192/27 and that subnet is no longer reachable, the router will forward the packet to the null interface. The routing loop is broken in one hop.

```
Robinson#show ip route
Codes: C - connected, S - static, I - IGRP, R - RIP, M - mobile, B - BGP
       D - EIGRP, EX - EIGRP external, O - OSPF, IA - OSPF inter area
       N1 - OSPF NSSA external type 1, N2 - OSPF NSSA external type 2
       E1 - OSPF external type 1, E2 - OSPF external type 2, E - EGP
       i - IS-IS, L1 - IS-IS level-1, L2 - IS-IS level-2, * - candidate default
       U - per-user static route, o - ODR

Gateway of last resort is not set

O    192.168.1.0/24 [110/74] via 192.168.3.34, 02:28:09, Ethernet0
D    192.168.2.0/24 [90/409600] via 192.168.3.130, 02:04:15, Ethernet1
     192.168.3.0/24 is variably subnetted, 9 subnets, 4 masks
O       192.168.3.96/27 [110/11] via 192.168.3.34, 02:28:09, Ethernet0
O       192.168.3.64/27 [110/74] via 192.168.3.34, 02:28:09, Ethernet0
C       192.168.3.32/27 is directly connected, Ethernet0
D       192.168.3.0/24 is a summary, 00:58:14, Null0
D       192.168.3.0/25 is a summary, 00:58:14, Null0
D       192.168.3.192/27 [90/435200] via 192.168.3.130, 02:04:15, Ethernet1
D       192.168.3.160/27 [90/460800] via 192.168.3.130, 02:04:15, Ethernet1
O       192.168.3.128/25 is a summary, 01:21:18, Null0
C       192.168.3.128/27 is directly connected, Ethernet1
     192.168.4.0/24 is variably subnetted, 3 subnets, 3 masks
D       192.168.4.72/29 [90/2185984] via 192.168.4.6, 00:58:15, Serial0
C       192.168.4.4/30 is directly connected, Serial0
D       192.168.4.0/24 is a summary, 01:21:08, Null0
     172.16.0.0/16 is variably subnetted, 3 subnets, 3 masks
C       172.16.2.20/30 is directly connected, Serial1
D       172.16.0.0/16 is a summary, 00:58:16, Null0
D       172.16.1.0/24 [90/2185984] via 172.16.2.22, 01:21:10, Serial1
D    192.168.0.0/16 is a summary, 01:21:08, Null0
Robinson#
```

Figure 11.29

Robinson's routing table. Because the router is originating many summary routes, there are many entries for summaries whose connected interface is Null0. This is a safeguard against routing loops.

Summary routes to null interfaces are very helpful for preventing loops, and their use is described in greater detail in Chapter 12, "Default Routes and On-Demand Routing." However, the redistribution of incorrect routing information should not be allowed to happen at all. Suppose that instead of being one hop away from Robinson, Podres is 10 hops away. The misdirected packet would have to travel a long way before being dropped. This example demonstrates the need to carefully regulate route advertisements when using *mutual redistribution*—that is, when two routing protocols are redistributing their routes into each other. In such cases the use of route filters, described in Chapter 13, or route maps, as described in Chapter 14, is essential.

The previous scenario also demonstrates the trade-off of using summarization. Although the size of the routing table is reduced, saving memory and processor cycles, route precision is also reduced. As the internetwork grows more complex, that loss of detail increases the possibility of routing errors.

Case Study: Redistributing IS-IS and RIP

In the internetwork of Figure 11.30, Aaron is running IS-IS, Williams is running RIPv1, and Mays is redistributing. Mays' IS-IS configuration is:

```
router isis
 redistribute rip metric 0 metric-type internal level-2
 net 01.0001.0000.0c76.5432.00
!
router rip
 redistribute isis level-1-2 metric 1
 passive-interface Ethernet0
 network 10.0.0.0
```

Routes may be redistributed into IS-IS as either internal or external routes (internal is the default) and as either level 1 or level 2 routes (level 2 is the default). In the example shown, the RIP routes are redistributed as internal, level 2 routes with the default metric of 0. Figure 11.31 shows the redistributed routes in Aaron's routing table.

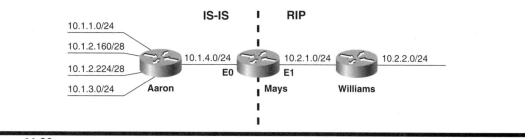

Figure 11.30

Router Mays is redistributing RIP into IS-IS and IS-IS into RIP.

```
Aaron#show ip route
Codes: C - connected, S - static, I - IGRP, R - RIP, M - mobile, B - BGP
       D - EIGRP, EX - EIGRP external, O - OSPF, IA - OSPF inter area
       N1 - OSPF NSSA external type 1, N2 - OSPF NSSA external type 2
       E1 - OSPF external type 1, E2 - OSPF external type 2, E - EGP
       i - IS-IS, L1 - IS-IS level-1, L2 - IS-IS level-2, * - candidate default
       U - per-user static route, o - ODR

Gateway of last resort is not set

     10.0.0.0/8 is variably subnetted, 7 subnets, 2 masks
C       10.1.3.0/24 is directly connected, Ethernet4
i L2    10.2.1.0/24 [115/10] via 10.1.4.2, Ethernet0
i L2    10.2.2.0/24 [115/10] via 10.1.4.2, Ethernet0
C       10.1.1.0/24 is directly connected, Ethernet1
C       10.1.4.0/24 is directly connected, Ethernet0
C       10.1.2.160/28 is directly connected, Ethernet2
C       10.1.2.224/28 is directly connected, Ethernet3
Aaron#
```

Figure 11.31

Aaron's routing table shows the redistributed RIP routes.

Since the RIP routes are external to the IS-IS routing domain, it is best to reflect this by having them redistributed into the domain as external routes:

```
router isis
  redistribute rip metric 0 metric-type external level-2
  net 01.0001.0000.0c76.5432.00
!
router rip
  redistribute isis level-1-2 metric 1
  passive-interface Ethernet0
  network 10.0.0.0
```

Figure 11.32 shows Aaron's routing table after the change. The only change from Figure 11.31 is that the metrics of the redistributed routes have increased to greater than 64, indicating (in this small internetwork) external routes.

```
Aaron#show ip route
Codes: C - connected, S - static, I - IGRP, R - RIP, M - mobile, B - BGP
       D - EIGRP, EX - EIGRP external, O - OSPF, IA - OSPF inter area
       N1 - OSPF NSSA external type 1, N2 - OSPF NSSA external type 2
       E1 - OSPF external type 1, E2 - OSPF external type 2, E - EGP
       i - IS-IS, L1 - IS-IS level-1, L2 - IS-IS level-2, * - candidate default
       U - per-user static route, o - ODR

Gateway of last resort is not set

     10.0.0.0/8 is variably subnetted, 6 subnets, 2 masks
C       10.1.3.0/24 is directly connected, Ethernet4
i L2    10.2.1.0/24 [115/138] via 10.1.4.2, Ethernet0
i L2    10.2.2.0/24 [115/138] via 10.1.4.2, Ethernet0
C       10.1.1.0/24 is directly connected, Ethernet1
C       10.1.4.0/24 is directly connected, Ethernet0
C       10.1.2.160/28 is directly connected, Ethernet2
C       10.1.2.224/28 is directly connected, Ethernet3
Aaron#
```

Figure 11.32
The metrics of the routes to 10.2.1.0/24 and 10.2.2.0/24 change to 138 after the routes are advertised as external.

Another look at Figure 11.30 shows that both subnets of the RIP domain can be summarized with a single address of 10.2.0.0/16. Route summarization into IS-IS is configured with the same **summary-address** command that is used with OSPF. However, the level into which the summary is being sent must also be specified. In the following configuration, RIP routes are redistributed as level 1 and summarized:

```
router isis
 summary-address 10.2.0.0 255.255.0.0 level-1
 redistribute rip metric 0 metric-type external level-1
 net 01.0001.0000.0c76.5432.00
!
```

```
router rip
 redistribute isis level-1-2 metric 1
 passive-interface Ethernet0
 network 10.0.0.0
```

Figure 11.33 shows the summary route in Aaron's routing table. Like OSPF and EIGRP, the summarization causes more-specific routes in the summary range to be suppressed.

```
Aaron#show ip route
Codes: C - connected, S - static, I - IGRP, R - RIP, M - mobile, B - BGP
       D - EIGRP, EX - EIGRP external, O - OSPF, IA - OSPF inter area
       N1 - OSPF NSSA external type 1, N2 - OSPF NSSA external type 2
       E1 - OSPF external type 1, E2 - OSPF external type 2, E - EGP
       i - IS-IS, L1 - IS-IS level-1, L2 - IS-IS level-2, * - candidate default
       U - per-user static route, o - ODR

Gateway of last resort is not set

     10.0.0.0/8 is variably subnetted, 6 subnets, 3 masks
i L1    10.2.0.0/16 [115/138] via 10.1.4.2, Ethernet0
C       10.1.3.0/24 is directly connected, Ethernet4
C       10.1.1.0/24 is directly connected, Ethernet1
C       10.1.4.0/24 is directly connected, Ethernet0
C       10.1.2.160/28 is directly connected, Ethernet2
C       10.1.2.224/28 is directly connected, Ethernet3
Aaron#
```

Figure 11.33

Aaron's routing table with a summary route to the subnets within the RIP domain.

When IS-IS is redistributed into another protocol, the route level to be redistributed must be specified. In the examples shown so far, both level 1 and level 2 routes have been specified to be redistributed into RIP.

Case Study: Redistributing Static Routes

Figure 11.34 shows the routing table of Williams in Figure 11.30. Notice that subnets 10.1.2.160/28 and 10.1.2.224/28 are missing; their subnet masks are inconsistent with the 24-bit mask configured on Mays' E1 interface, so the routes have not been included in the RIP updates sent out that interface. This scenario again illustrates the problem of redistributing variably subnetted routes from a classless protocol into a classful protocol, as discussed earlier in this chapter.

```
Williams#show ip route
Codes: C - connected, S - static, I - IGRP, R - RIP, M - mobile, B - BGP
       D - EIGRP, EX - EIGRP external, O - OSPF, IA - OSPF inter area
       E1 - OSPF external type 1, E2 - OSPF external type 2, E - EGP
       i - IS-IS, L1 - IS-IS level-1, L2 - IS-IS level-2, * - candidate default
       U - per-user static route

Gateway of last resort is not set

     10.0.0.0/8 is subnetted, 5 subnets
R       10.1.3.0 [120/1] via 10.2.1.2, 00:00:01, Ethernet0
C       10.2.1.0 is directly connected, Ethernet0
R       10.1.1.0 [120/1] via 10.2.1.2, 00:00:02, Ethernet0
C       10.2.2.0 is directly connected, Ethernet1
R       10.1.4.0 [120/1] via 10.2.1.2, 00:00:02, Ethernet0
Williams#
```

Figure 11.34

The routes with subnets other than /24 are not redistributed into the RIP domain.

A solution to this problem is to summarize the two 28-bit subnets with a single 24-bit address of 10.1.2.0/24. RIP does not have a summarization command, so the way to accomplish summarization is to configure a static route to the summary address and then redistribute that route into RIP:

```
router isis
  summary-address 10.2.0.0 255.255.0.0 level-1
  redistribute rip metric 0 metric-type external level-1
  net 01.0001.0000.0c76.5432.00
!
router rip
  redistribute static metric 1
  redistribute isis level-1-2 metric 1
  passive-interface Ethernet0
  network 10.0.0.0
!
ip route 10.1.2.0 255.255.255.0 10.1.4.1
```

Figure 11.35 shows Williams' routing table with the summary route included.

```
Williams#show ip route
Codes: C - connected, S - static, I - IGRP, R - RIP, M - mobile, B - BGP
       D - EIGRP, EX - EIGRP external, O - OSPF, IA - OSPF inter area
       E1 - OSPF external type 1, E2 - OSPF external type 2, E - EGP
       i - IS-IS, L1 - IS-IS level-1, L2 - IS-IS level-2, * - candidate default
       U - per-user static route

Gateway of last resort is not set

     10.0.0.0/8 is subnetted, 6 subnets
R       10.1.3.0 [120/1] via 10.2.1.2, 00:00:03, Ethernet0
R       10.1.2.0 [120/1] via 10.2.1.2, 00:00:03, Ethernet0
C       10.2.1.0 is directly connected, Ethernet0
R       10.1.1.0 [120/1] via 10.2.1.2, 00:00:03, Ethernet0
C       10.2.2.0 is directly connected, Ethernet1
R       10.1.4.0 [120/1] via 10.2.1.2, 00:00:03, Ethernet0
Williams#
```

Figure 11.35

Subnets 10.1.2.160/28 and 10.1.2.224/28 have been summarized with the address 10.1.2.0/24.

As discussed in Chapter 3, "Static Routing," a variant of the static route is an entry that points to an outgoing interface instead of a next-hop address. These static routes can also be redistributed, but the configuration is somewhat different. For example, the configuration of Mays can be:

```
router isis
  summary-address 10.2.0.0 255.255.0.0 level-1
  redistribute rip metric 0 metric-type external level-1
  net 01.0001.0000.0c76.5432.00
!
router rip
  redistribute isis level-1-2 metric 1
  passive-interface Ethernet0
  network 10.0.0.0
!
ip route 10.1.2.0 255.255.255.0 Ethernet0
```

Here the static route now points to Mays' E0 interface instead of to the next-hop address 10.1.4.1. Also, the **redistribute static** command is no longer used under the RIP configuration, yet Williams' routing table still looks the same as in Figure 11.35.

The reason this static route still gets redistributed is that when a static route points to an outgoing interface, the destination is considered by the router to be directly connected (Figure 11.36). And because a network statement for 10.0.0.0 appears under the RIP configuration, RIP will advertise this "directly connected" subnet of 10.0.0.0.

```
Mays#show ip route
Codes: C - connected, S - static, I - IGRP, R - RIP, M - mobile, B - BGP
       D - EIGRP, EX - EIGRP external, O - OSPF, IA - OSPF inter area
       N1 - OSPF NSSA external type 1, N2 - OSPF NSSA external type 2
       E1 - OSPF external type 1, E2 - OSPF external type 2, E - EGP
       i - IS-IS, L1 - IS-IS level-1, L2 - IS-IS level-2, * - candidate default
       U - per-user static route, o - ODR

Gateway of last resort is not set

     10.0.0.0/8 is variably subnetted, 8 subnets, 2 masks
i L1    10.1.3.0/24 [115/20] via 10.1.4.1, Ethernet0
S       10.1.2.0/24 is directly connected, Ethernet0
C       10.2.1.0/24 is directly connected, Ethernet1
i L1    10.1.1.0/24 [115/20] via 10.1.4.1, Ethernet0
R       10.2.2.0/24 [120/1] via 10.2.1.1, 00:00:21, Ethernet1
C       10.1.4.0/24 is directly connected, Ethernet0
i L1    10.1.2.160/28 [115/20] via 10.1.4.1, Ethernet0
i L1    10.1.2.224/28 [115/20] via 10.1.4.1, Ethernet0
Mays#
```

Figure 11.36
Mays considers the summary address 10.1.2.0/24 to be directly connected to Ethernet 0.

Suppose Williams receives a packet with a destination address of 10.1.2.5. The summary address of 10.1.2.0/24 will be matched, and the packet will be forwarded to Mays. At Mays, the destination address does not match a more-specific subnet, and therefore will match the static route. Mays will send ARP requests out E0 in an attempt to find host 10.1.2.5 (or a router that will send a Proxy ARP reply). Finding none, the router does not know what to do with the packet. An ICMP Destination Unreachable message will not be sent to the originator.

Recall that when the summarization commands are used, they create an entry in the routing table to Null 0. The same can and should be done with static summary routes:

> Null interfaces should be configured in conjunction with static summary routes.

```
router isis
 summary-address 10.2.0.0 255.255.0.0 level-1
 redistribute rip metric 0 metric-type external level-1
 net 01.0001.0000.0c76.5432.00
!
router rip
 redistribute isis level-1-2 metric 1
 passive-interface Ethernet0
 network 10.0.0.0
!
ip route 10.1.2.0 255.255.255.0 Null0
```

Now any destination address that doesn't find a more-specific match at Mays will be routed to the null interface and dropped, and an ICMP Destination Unreachable message will be sent to the originator.

LOOKING AHEAD

This chapter touches on several problems that can arise when redistributing routes. Avoiding or correcting trouble in all but the simplest redistribution schemes usually involves the use of route filters, which are discussed in Chapter 13, or route maps, discussed in Chapter 14. Those chapters include examples of more complex redistribution schemes and how to troubleshoot them. First, though, Chapter 12 examines default routes—which may be thought of as the most generic form of summary routes.

SUMMARY TABLE:
CHAPTER 11 COMMAND REVIEW

Command	Description
default-metric *bandwidth delay reliability load mtu*	Specifies a default metric to be associated with routes redistributed into IGRP and EIGRP.
default-metric *number*	Specifies a default metric to be associated with routes redistributed into RIP and OSPF.
ip summary-address eigrp *autonomous-system-number address mask*	Configures an EIGRP summary route on an interface.
redistribute connected	Redistributes all directly connected networks.
redistribute *protocol* [*process-id*]{level-1|level-1-2| level-2}[**metric** *metric-value*][**metric-type** *type-value*][**match**{**internal**| **external 1**|**external 2**}][**tag** *tag-value*] [**route-map** *map-tag*][**weight** *weight*][**subnets**]	Configures redistribution into a routing protocol and specifies the source of the redistributed routes.
summary-address *address mask* {**level-1**|**level-1-2**|**level-2**} *prefix mask* [**not-advertise**] [**tag** *tag*]	Configures route summarization for IS-IS and OSPF.

REVIEW QUESTIONS

1. From what sources can a route be redistributed?
2. What is the purpose of an administrative distance?
3. How can administrative distances cause problems when redistributing?

4. How can redistribution from a classless to a classful routing protocol cause problems?

5. Which IP IGPs can use the default redistribution metric, and which IGPs must have a metric configured in order for redistribution to work?

6. What is the difference between using the **metric** keyword with the **redistribute** command and using the **default-metric** command?

7. What is the purpose of the **subnets** keyword when redistributing OSPF?

8. How is the null interface useful when summarizing routes?

CONFIGURATION EXERCISES

1. Router A in Figure 11.37 is running IGRP and router C is running RIPv1. Write a configuration for router B that will provide full connectivity for all subnets.

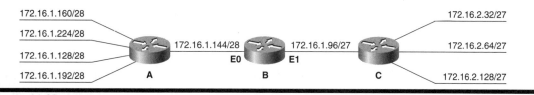

172.16.1.160/28
172.16.1.224/28
172.16.1.128/28
172.16.1.192/28

172.16.1.144/28
E0

172.16.1.96/27
E1

172.16.2.32/27
172.16.2.64/27
172.16.2.128/27

A   B   C

Figure 11.37

The internetwork for Configuration Exercises 1, 2, and 3.

2. Router A in Figure 11.37 is running OSPF and router C is running RIPv1. Write a configuration for router B that will provide full connectivity for all subnets.

3. Router A in Figure 11.37 is running EIGRP, and router C is running IS-IS. At router B, all the IS-IS routes are level 1. Configure mutual redistribution at router B by using summarization wherever possible. The EIGRP routes should be advertised into the IS-IS domain as external routes.

TROUBLESHOOTING EXERCISES

1. In the case study "Redistributing IGRP and RIP," the following configuration is given for router Mantle of Figure 11.18:

```
router rip
  redistribute igrp 1 metric 5
  passive-interface Ethernet1
  network 10.0.0.0
!
router igrp 1
  redistribute connected
  redistribute rip
  default-metric 1000 100 255 1 1500
  passive-interface Ethernet0
  network 10.0.0.0
```

Will the RIP domain know about the stub network 192.168.10.0/24 by virtue of the fact that it is redistributed into IGRP, which is then redistributed into RIP?

2. In Troubleshooting Exercise 1, if the **redistribute rip** command is eliminated under the IGRP configuration, will the **redistribute connected** command be sufficient to advertise the RIP domain?

3. In Figure 11.20, why isn't subnet 192.168.3.32/27 tagged as an EIGRP external route?

4. In Figure 11.20, there is a summary route to 192.168.3.0. What caused this entry?

5. In Figure 11.27, why isn't 192.168.1.0/24 in Campanella's routing table?

- **Fundamentals of Default Routes**

- **Fundamentals of On-Demand Routing**

- **Configuring Default Routes and ODR**

    Case Study: Static Default Routes

    Case Study: The Default-Network Command

    Case Study: The Default-Information-Originate Command

    Case Study: Configuring On-Demand Routing

CHAPTER 12

Default Routes and On-Demand Routing

Summarization has been examined in several chapters so far. *Summarization* conserves internetwork resources by reducing the size of routing tables and route advertisements. The smaller, simpler routing tables can also make management and troubleshooting easier.

A *summary address* is an address that represents several, sometimes many, more-specific addresses. For example, the following four subnets:

> 192.168.200.128/27
>
> 192.168.200.160/27
>
> 192.168.200.192/27
>
> 192.168.200.224/27

can be summarized with the single address 192.168.200.128/25.

When examined in binary, the addresses reveal that the summary address is less specific because it consists of fewer network and subnet bits than the addresses being summarized. So put crudely, it might be said that as more zeros are added to the host space and as fewer network bits are used, more addresses are summarized. Taking this concept to its limit, what if so many zeros are added to the host space that no network bits remain? In other words, what if the summary address consists of 32 zeros (0.0.0.0)? This address summarizes every possible IP address.

0.0.0.0 is the IP default address, and a route to 0.0.0.0 is a default route.[1] Every other IP address is more specific than the default address, so when a default route exists in a routing table, that route will be matched only if a more specific match cannot be made.

FUNDAMENTALS OF DEFAULT ROUTES

When a router is connected to the Internet, a default route is immensely useful. Without a default, the router will have to have a route entry for every destination address reachable over the Internet. As of this writing, such a routing table consists of more than 55,000 entries. With a default route, the router need only know about the destinations internal to its own administrative system. The default route will forward packets destined for any other address to the Internet service provider. In dealing with large routing tables, topology changes are an even bigger concern than the demands on memory. In a large internetwork, topology changes will occur more frequently, resulting in increased system activity to advertise and process those changes. Using a default route effectively "hides" the changes of more-specific routes, making the internetwork into which the default is advertised more stable.

Default routes are also useful on a smaller scale, within single autonomous systems. The same benefits of decreased memory and processor utilization can be gained in smaller internetworks, although the benefits decrease as the number of routes decreases.

---

[1] *This address is used by all the open IP routing protocols. Cisco's IGRP and EIGRP use an actual network address, advertised as an external route.*

Default routes are also very useful in hub-and-spoke topologies, such as the one in Figure 12.1. Here the hub router has a static route to every remote subnet. Entering new static routes in the hub router when a new subnet is brought online is a fairly trivial administrative task, but adding the routes to every spoke router might be much more time-consuming. By using default routes at the spoke routers, only the hub needs entries for every subnet. When a spoke router receives a packet for an unknown destination, it will forward the packet to the hub, which can in turn forward the packet to the correct destination.

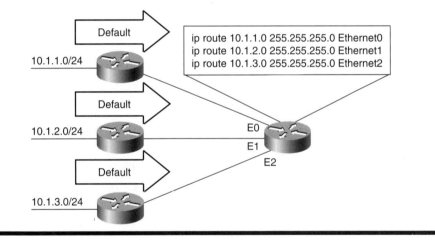

Figure 12.1

Default routes greatly simplify the administration of static routing in a hub-and-spoke internetwork.

The spoke routers in Figure 12.1 are more correctly called "stub" routers. A *stub router* has only a single connection to another router. The routing decisions become very simple in such a device: The destination is either one of the router's directly connected networks (*stub networks*), or it is reachable via its single neighbor. And if the single neighbor is the only next-hop routing choice, the stub router has little need for a detailed routing table. A default route may be sufficient.

As with other summary routes, the trade-off with default routes is a loss of routing detail. The stub routers in Figure 12.1, for instance, have no way of knowing whether a destination is unreachable. All packets to unknown destinations are forwarded to the hub router and only then is reachability determined. Packets to nonexistent addresses should be infrequent in an internetwork. If for some reason they are not, a better design choice might be to allow the stub routers to have a full routing table so that unknown destinations can be determined as soon as possible.

Another problem with loss of routing detail is shown in Figure 12.2. These routers form a nationwide corporate backbone, and large local internetworks are connected to each of the backbone routers. The Los Angeles backbone router is receiving default routes from both San Francisco and San Diego. If Los Angeles must forward a packet to Seattle and has only the two default routes, it has no way of knowing that the best route is via San Francisco. Los Angeles may forward the packet to San Diego, in which case the packet will use a small portion of some very expensive bandwidth before it belatedly reaches its destination. Using default routes on this backbone is a bad design decision[2] but illustrates how hiding route details with a default route can lead to suboptimal routing.

FUNDAMENTALS OF ON-DEMAND ROUTING

Although the configuration of static routes is simple in a hub router such as the one in Figure 12.1, many network administrators still see static routes as administratively undesirable. The difficulty is not so much adding routes as new stub networks are brought online, as it is remembering to remove routes when stub

---

[2]   *Having each backbone router advertise only a default route into its local internetwork, on the other hand, can be a very good design choice.*

networks or stub routers are taken offline. Beginning with IOS 11.2, Cisco offers a proprietary alternative for hub routers called *On-Demand Routing* (ODR).

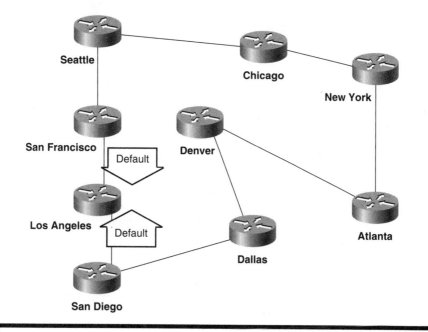

Figure 12.2

If the Los Angeles router knows only the default routes advertised by San Francisco and San Diego and has no more specific details about the topology behind those two routers, it cannot route efficiently.

With ODR a hub router can automatically discover stub networks while the stub routers still use a default route to the hub. ODR conveys address prefixes—that is, only the network portion of the address—rather than the entire address—so VLSM is supported. And because only minimal route information is traversing the link between the stub and hub routers, bandwidth is conserved.

ODR is not a true routing protocol. It discovers information about stub networks, but does not provide any routing information to the stub routers. The link information is conveyed by a data link protocol and, therefore, does not go further than from the stub router to the hub router. However, as a case study will show, ODR-discovered routes can be redistributed into dynamic routing protocols.

Figure 12.3 shows a routing table containing ODR entries. The table shows that the administrative distance is 160; the metric of the routes is 1. Because ODR routes are always from a hub router to a stub router, the metric (hop count) will never be more than 1. The routes also show that VLSM is supported.

```
Router#show ip route
Codes: C - connected, S - static, I - IGRP, R - RIP, M - mobile, B - BGP
       D - EIGRP, EX - EIGRP external, O - OSPF, IA - OSPF inter area
       N1 - OSPF NSSA external type 1, N2 - OSPF NSSA external type 2
       E1 - OSPF external type 1, E2 - OSPF external type 2, E - EGP
       i - IS-IS, L1 - IS-IS level-1, L2 - IS-IS level-2, * - candidate default
       U - per-user static route, o - ODR

Gateway of last resort is not set

     192.168.1.0/24 is variably subnetted, 3 subnets, 2 masks
o       192.168.1.40/30 [160/1] via 192.168.1.37, 00:00:27, Serial0
C       192.168.1.36/30 is directly connected, Serial0
C       192.168.1.192/27 is directly connected, Ethernet1
o    192.168.3.0/24 [160/1] via 192.168.1.37, 00:00:27, Serial0
     192.168.4.0/24 is variably subnetted, 2 subnets, 2 masks
o       192.168.4.48/29 [160/1] via 192.168.1.37, 00:00:27, Serial0
o       192.168.4.128/27 [160/1] via 192.168.1.37, 00:00:27, Serial0
Router#
```

Figure 12.3

This routing table shows several ODR entries.

ODR and Cisco Discovery Protocol

The transport mechanism for ODR routes is *Cisco Discovery Protocol* (CDP), a proprietary data link protocol that gathers information about neighboring network devices.[3] Figure 12.4 shows the type of information collected by CDP.

---

[3]   *CDP runs not only on routers but also on Cisco switches and access servers.*

CDP runs on any media that supports the subnetwork access protocol (SNAP), which means that ODR also depends on SNAP support. Although CDP is enabled by default on all interfaces of all Cisco devices running IOS 10.3 and later, ODR support begins with IOS 11.2. The configuration case study will show that ODR is configured on the hub router only; however, the stub routers must run IOS 11.2 or later for the hub router to discover their attached networks.

```
reg75k2#show cdp neighbor detail
-----------------------
Device ID: WPI72k
Entry address(es):
  IP address: 192.168.5.2
  Novell address: BA5.0008.f417.1f88
Platform: cisco 7206, Capabilities: Router Source-Route-Bridge
Interface: TokenRing5/1/0, Port ID (outgoing port): TokenRing2/1
Holdtime : 133 sec
Version :
Cisco Internetwork Operating System Software
IOS (tm) 7200 Software (C7200-DR-M), Version 11.1(14)CA1, EARLY DEPLOYMENT RELEASE SOFTWARE (fc1)
Synced to mainline version: 11.1(14)
Copyright (c) 1986-1997 by cisco Systems, Inc.
Compiled Tue 30-Sep-97 16:49 by susingh
-----------------------
Device ID: REG75K1
Entry address(es):
  IP address: 172.23.109.2
  Novell address: AA08.0006.e2b4.8c46
  DECnet address: 16.2
Platform: cisco RSP4, Capabilities: Router Source-Route-Bridge
Interface: TokenRing5/1/3, Port ID (outgoing port): TokenRing3/2
Holdtime : 134 sec
Version :
Cisco Internetwork Operating System Software
IOS (tm) GS Software (RSP-JV-M), Version 11.1(16)CA, EARLY DEPLOYMENT RELEASE SO
FTWARE (fc1)
Synced to mainline version: 11.1(16)
Copyright (c) 1986-1997 by cisco Systems, Inc.
Compiled Sat 20-Dec-97 04:21 by tej
-----------------------
```

Figure 12.4

CDP collects information about neighboring Cisco network devices.

CONFIGURING DEFAULT ROUTES AND ODR

Default routes can be configured either on each router that needs a default route or on one router that in turn advertises the routes to its peers. The case studies of this section examine both methods.

Recall from the discussion in Chapter 5, "Routing Information Protocol (RIP)," of classful route lookups that a router will first match a major network number and then match the subnet. If a subnet cannot be matched, the packet will be dropped. Classful route lookup is the default behavior on Cisco routers; lookups can be changed to classless (even for classful routing protocols) with the global command **ip classless**.

Routers using a default route should perform classless lookups.

Any router using a default route must perform classless route lookups. Figure 12.5 shows why. In this internetwork, Memphis is speaking a dynamic routing protocol to Tanis and Giza, but is not receiving routes from Thebes. Memphis has a default route pointing to Thebes for routing packets to BigNet. If Memphis receives a packet with a destination address of 192.168.1.50 and is performing classful route lookups, it will first match major network 192.168.1.0, of which it has several subnets in its routing table. Memphis will then attempt to find a route for subnet 192.168.1.48/28, but because Memphis is not receiving routes from Thebes, this subnet is not in its routing table. The packet will be dropped.

If Memphis is configured with **ip classless**, it will try to find the most specific match for 192.168.1.48/28 without matching the major network first. Finding no match for this subnet in the routing table, it will match the default route and forward the packet to Thebes.

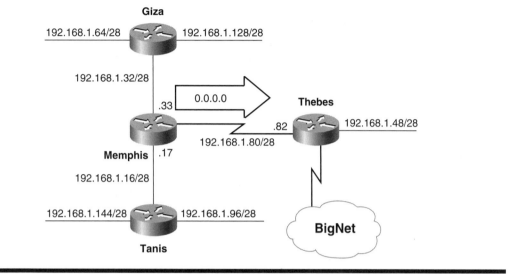

Figure 12.5

Memphis forwards packets to Thebes with a default route. If Memphis uses classful route lookups, subnet 192.168.1.48/28 will be unreachable.

Case Study: Static Default Routes

The configuration of Memphis in Figure 12.5 is:

```
router rip
 network 192.168.1.0
 !
ip classless
ip route 0.0.0.0 0.0.0.0 192.168.1.82
```

The static route configures the default route address of 0.0.0.0, and uses a mask that is also 0.0.0.0. A common mistake made by people configuring default routes for the first time is to use an all-ones mask instead of an all-zeros mask, such as:

```
ip route 0.0.0.0 255.255.255.255 192.168.1.82
```

An all-ones mask would configure a host route to 0.0.0.0, and the only packets that would match this address would be those with a destination address of 0.0.0.0. The all-zeros mask, on the other hand, is a mask made up entirely of "don't care" bits and will match any bit in any position. The beginning of this chapter described the default address as a summary route taken to its extreme, so that every bit is summarized with a zero. The mask of the default route is a summary mask taken to its extreme.

Gateway of last resort

Memphis' default route has a next-hop address at Thebes. This next-hop address is the *gateway of last resort*, or the default router. Figure 12.6 shows the routing table at Memphis. The route to 0.0.0.0 is tagged as a candidate default, and the gateway of last resort is indicated at the top of the table.

```
Memphis#show ip route
Codes: C - connected, S - static, I - IGRP, R - RIP, M - mobile, B - BGP
       D - EIGRP, EX - EIGRP external, O - OSPF, IA - OSPF inter area
       N1 - OSPF NSSA external type 1, N2 - OSPF NSSA external type 2
       E1 - OSPF external type 1, E2 - OSPF external type 2, E - EGP
       i - IS-IS, L1 - IS-IS level-1, L2 - IS-IS level-2, * - candidate default
       U - per-user static route, o - ODR

Gateway of last resort is 192.168.1.82 to network 0.0.0.0

     192.168.1.0/28 is subnetted, 7 subnets
R       192.168.1.96 [120/1] via 192.168.1.18, 00:00:15, Ethernet0
R       192.168.1.64 [120/1] via 192.168.1.34, 00:00:27, Ethernet1
C       192.168.1.80 is directly connected, Serial0
C       192.168.1.32 is directly connected, Ethernet1
C       192.168.1.16 is directly connected, Ethernet0
R       192.168.1.128 [120/1] via 192.168.1.34, 00:00:27, Ethernet1
R       192.168.1.144 [120/1] via 192.168.1.18, 00:00:15, Ethernet0
S*   0.0.0.0/0 [1/0] via 192.168.1.82
Memphis#
```

Figure 12.6

Memphis' routing table, showing the default route and the gateway of last resort.

Memphis will advertise the default route to Tanis and Giza (Figure 12.7). This action may seem surprising at first because no redistribution has been configured at Memphis. However, the static route is not actually the route being redistributed. After a default route is identified in the routing table, RIP, IGRP, and EIGRP will automatically advertise it. OSPF and IS-IS require some additional configuration, as shown in a subsequent case study.

```
Tanis#show ip route
Codes: C - connected, S - static, I - IGRP, R - RIP, M - mobile, B - BGP
       D - EIGRP, EX - EIGRP external, O - OSPF, IA - OSPF inter area
       N1 - OSPF NSSA external type 1, N2 - OSPF NSSA external type 2
       E1 - OSPF external type 1, E2 - OSPF external type 2, E - EGP
       i - IS-IS, L1 - IS-IS level-1, L2 - IS-IS level-2, * - candidate default
       U - per-user static route, o - ODR

Gateway of last resort is 192.168.1.17 to network 0.0.0.0

     192.168.1.0/28 is subnetted, 9 subnets
C       192.168.1.96 is directly connected, Ethernet1
R       192.168.1.64 [120/2] via 192.168.1.17, 00:00:01, Ethernet0
R       192.168.1.80 [120/1] via 192.168.1.17, 00:00:01, Ethernet0
R       192.168.1.32 [120/1] via 192.168.1.17, 00:00:01, Ethernet0
R       192.168.1.48 [120/2] via 192.168.1.17, 00:00:01, Ethernet0
C       192.168.1.16 is directly connected, Ethernet0
R       192.168.1.224 [120/1] via 192.168.1.17, 00:00:01, Ethernet0
R       192.168.1.128 [120/2] via 192.168.1.17, 00:00:01, Ethernet0
C       192.168.1.144 is directly connected, Ethernet2
R*  0.0.0.0/0 [120/1] via 192.168.1.17, 00:00:02, Ethernet0
Tanis#
```

Figure 12.7

The routing table of Tanis shows that the default route has been learned from Memphis via RIP.

Default routes are also useful for connecting classless routing domains. In Figure 12.8, Chimu is connecting a RIP domain with an EIGRP domain. Although the masks of major network 192.168.25.0 are consistent in the RIP domain, they are variably subnetted in the EIGRP domain. Further, the VLSM scheme does not lend itself to summarization into RIP.

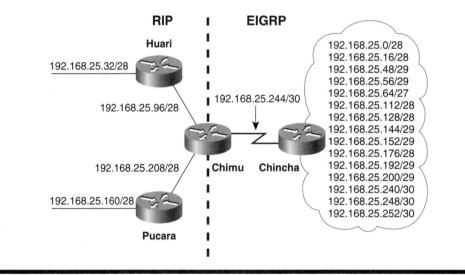

Figure 12.8

A default route enables RIP to route into the variably subnetted EIGRP domain.

Chimu's configuration is:

```
router eigrp 1
 redistribute rip metric 1000 100 255 1 1500
 passive-interface Ethernet0
 passive-interface Ethernet1
 network 192.168.25.0

!
router rip
 passive-interface Serial0
 network 192.168.25.0
!
ip classless
ip route 0.0.0.0 0.0.0.0 Null0
```

Chimu has a full set of routes from the EIGRP domain, but is not redistributing them into RIP. Instead, Chimu is advertising a default route. The RIP routers will forward packets with unknown destinations to Chimu, which can then consult its routing table for a more-specific route into the EIGRP domain.

Chimu's static route is pointing to the null interface rather than a next-hop address. If a packet is forwarded to Chimu with a destination on a nonexistent subnet, such as 192.168.25.224/28, the packet will be dropped instead of being forwarded into the EIGRP domain.

Case Study: The Default-Network Command

An alternative method of configuring default routes is to use the command **ip default-network**. This command specifies a major network address to be used as a default network. The network may be directly connected to the router, specified by a static route, or discovered by a dynamic routing protocol.

The configuration of Athens in Figure 12.9 is:

```
router rip
  network 172.16.0.0
!
ip classless
default-network 10.0.0.0
```

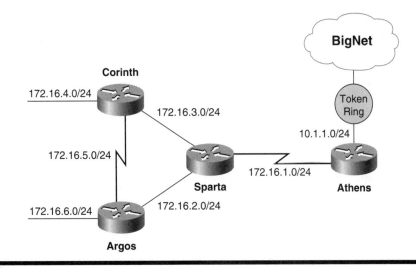

Figure 12.9

*The **default-network** command is used at Athens to generate a default network advertisement.*

Figure 12.10 shows that network 10.0.0.0 has been tagged as a candidate default route in Athens' routing table, but notice that no gateway of last resort is specified. The reason is that Athens is the gateway to the default network. The **ip default-network** command will cause Athens to advertise a default network, even though no network statement for 10.0.0.0 exists under the RIP configuration (Figure 12.11).

```
Athens#show ip route
Codes: C - connected, S - static, I - IGRP, R - RIP, M - mobile, B - BGP
       D - EIGRP, EX - EIGRP external, O - OSPF, IA - OSPF inter area
       E1 - OSPF external type 1, E2 - OSPF external type 2, E - EGP
       i - IS-IS, L1 - IS-IS level-1, L2 - IS-IS level-2, * - candidate default
       U - per-user static route

Gateway of last resort is not set

*      10.0.0.0/8 is subnetted, 1 subnets
C         10.1.1.0 is directly connected, TokenRing0
R      192.168.1.0/24 [120/2] via 172.16.1.2, 00:00:12, Serial0
       172.16.0.0/16 is subnetted, 6 subnets
R         172.16.4.0 [120/2] via 172.16.1.2, 00:00:12, Serial0
R         172.16.5.0 [120/2] via 172.16.1.2, 00:00:12, Serial0
R         172.16.6.0 [120/2] via 172.16.1.2, 00:00:12, Serial0
C         172.16.1.0 is directly connected, Serial0
R         172.16.2.0 [120/1] via 172.16.1.2, 00:00:12, Serial0
R         172.16.3.0 [120/1] via 172.16.1.2, 00:00:12, Serial0
Athens#
```

Figure 12.10

Network 10.0.0.0 is tagged as a candidate default in Athens' routing table.

IGRP and EIGRP do not use 0.0.0.0 to identify a default route.

Default routing is somewhat different for IGRP and EIGRP. These protocols do not understand the address 0.0.0.0. Rather, they advertise an actual address as an external route (see Chapters 6, "Interior Gateway Routing Protocol (IGRP)," and 8, "Enhanced Interior Gateway Routing Protocol"). Destinations advertised as external routes in IGRP and EIGRP are understood to be default

```
Sparta#show ip route
Codes: C - connected, S - static, I - IGRP, R - RIP, M - mobile, B - BGP
       D - EIGRP, EX - EIGRP external, O - OSPF, IA - OSPF inter area
       N1 - OSPF NSSA external type 1, N2 - OSPF NSSA external type 2
       E1 - OSPF external type 1, E2 - OSPF external type 2, E - EGP
       i - IS-IS, L1 - IS-IS level-1, L2 - IS-IS level-2, * - candidate default
       U - per-user static route, o - ODR

Gateway of last resort is 172.16.1.1 to network 0.0.0.0

R     192.168.1.0/24  [120/1] via 172.16.2.2, 00:00:10, Ethernet0
                      [120/1] via 172.16.3.2, 00:00:14, Ethernet1
      172.16.0.0/24 is subnetted, 6 subnets
R        172.16.4.0 [120/1] via 172.16.3.2, 00:00:14, Ethernet1
R        172.16.5.0 [120/1] via 172.16.3.2, 00:00:14, Ethernet1
R        172.16.6.0 [120/1] via 172.16.2.2, 00:00:10, Ethernet0
C        172.16.1.0 is directly connected, Serial0
C        172.16.2.0 is directly connected, Ethernet0
C        172.16.3.0 is directly connected, Ethernet1
R*    0.0.0.0/0 [120/1] via 172.16.1.1, 00:00:17, Serial0
Sparta#
```

Figure 12.11

Sparta's routing table shows that Athens is advertising a default route of 0.0.0.0 and that Athens is Sparta's gateway of last resort.

routes. If the routers in Figure 12.9 are configured to run IGRP, Athens' configuration will be:

```
router igrp 1
 network 10.0.0.0
 network 172.16.0.0
 !
ip classless
ip default-network 10.0.0.0
```

The **ip default-network** command remains the same, but notice that a network statement for 10.0.0.0 is added to the IGRP configuration. Because IGRP uses the actual network address, that address must be configured to be advertised, as shown in Figure 12.12. Because Corinth has learned about the default route from Sparta, that router is Corinth's gateway of last resort. If the link to Sparta fails, Corinth will use Argos as its gateway of last resort.

```
Corinth#show ip route
Codes: C - connected, S - static, I - IGRP, R - RIP, M - mobile, B - BGP
       D - EIGRP, EX - EIGRP external, O - OSPF, IA - OSPF inter area
       E1 - OSPF external type 1, E2 - OSPF external type 2, E - EGP
       i - IS-IS, L1 - IS-IS level-1, L2 - IS-IS level-2, * - candidate default
       U - per-user static route

Gateway of last resort is 172.16.3.1 to network 10.0.0.0

I*  10.0.0.0/8 [100/8639] via 172.16.3.1, 00:00:17, Ethernet0
    172.16.0.0/16 is subnetted, 6 subnets
C       172.16.4.0 is directly connected, Ethernet1
C       172.16.5.0 is directly connected, Serial0
I       172.16.6.0 [100/1700] via 172.16.3.1, 00:00:18, Ethernet0
I       172.16.6.0 [100/1700] via 172.16.3.1, 00:00:18, Ethernet0
I       172.16.2.0 [100/1200] via 172.16.3.1, 00:00:18, Ethernet0
C       172.16.3.0 is directly connected, Ethernet0
```

Figure 12.12

IGRP and EIGRP use an actual network address, rather than 0.0.0.0, as the default network. Corinth's routing table shows that network 10.0.0.0 is tagged as the default network.

Case Study: The Default-Information Originate Command

An OSPF ASBR and an IS-IS interdomain router will not automatically advertise a default route into their routing domains, even when one exists. For example, suppose Athens in Figure 12.9 is configured for OSPF and given a static default route into BigNet:

```
router ospf 1
 network 172.16.0.0 0.0.255.255 area 0
!
ip classless
ip route 0.0.0.0 0.0.0.0 10.1.1.2
```

Figure 12.13 shows the routing tables of Athens and Sparta. Although the static route has caused the gateway of last resort to be set at Athens, Sparta has no knowledge of the default route. The default route must be advertised into the OSPF domain in type 5 LSAs, which means that Athens must be an ASBR. Yet so far, nothing in Athens' configuration tells it to perform this function.

```
Athens#show ip route
Codes: C - connected, S - static, I - IGRP, R - RIP, M - mobile, B - BGP
       D - EIGRP, EX - EIGRP external, O - OSPF, IA - OSPF inter area
       E1 - OSPF external type 1, E2 - OSPF external type 2, E - EGP
       i - IS-IS, L1 - IS-IS level-1, L2 - IS-IS level-2, * - candidate default

Gateway of last resort is 10.1.1.2 to network 0.0.0.0

     10.0.0.0 255.255.255.0 is subnetted, 1 subnets
C       10.1.1.0 is directly connected, TokenRing0
     172.16.0.0 is variably subnetted, 6 subnets, 2 masks
O       172.16.5.0 255.255.255.0 [110/138] via 172.16.1.2, 00:04:17, Serial0
O       172.16.4.1 255.255.255.0 [110/75] via 172.16.1.2, 00:04:17, Serial0
O       172.16.6.1 255.255.255.0 [110/75] via 172.16.1.2, 00:04:17, Serial0
C       172.16.1.0 255.255.255.0 is directly connected, Serial0
O       172.16.2.0 255.255.255.0 [110/74] via 172.16.1.2, 00:04:17, Serial0
O       172.16.3.0 255.255.255.0 [110/74] via 172.16.1.2, 00:04:17, Serial0
S*   0.0.0.0 0.0.0.0 [1/0] via 10.1.1.2
```

```
Sparta#show ip route
Codes: C - connected, S - static, I - IGRP, R - RIP, M - mobile, B - BGP
       D - EIGRP, EX - EIGRP external, O - OSPF, IA - OSPF inter area
       N1 - OSPF NSSA external type 1, N2 - OSPF NSSA external type 2
       E1 - OSPF external type 1, E2 - OSPF external type 2, E - EGP
       i - IS-IS, L1 - IS-IS level-1, L2 - IS-IS level-2, * - candidate default
       U - per-user static route, o - ODR

Gateway of last resort is not set

     172.16.0.0/16 is variably subnetted, 6 subnets, 2 masks
O       172.16.5.0/24 [110/74] via 172.16.2.2, 00:06:00, Ethernet1
                      [110/74] via 172.16.3.2, 00:06:00, Ethernet0
O       172.16.4.1/24 [110/11] via 172.16.3.2, 00:06:00, Ethernet0
O       172.16.6.1/24 [110/11] via 172.16.2.2, 00:06:00, Ethernet1
C       172.16.1.0/24 is directly connected, Serial0
C       172.16.2.0/24 is directly connected, Ethernet1
C       172.16.3.0/24 is directly connected, Ethernet0
```

Figure 12.13

The OSPF process at Athens does not automatically advertise the default route into the OSPF domain.

The **default-information originate** command is a specialized form of the **redistribute** command, causing a default route to be redistributed into OSPF or IS-IS. And like **redistribute**, the **default-information originate** command informs an OSPF router that it is an ASBR, or an IS-IS router that it is an interdomain router. Also like **redistribute**, the metric of the redistributed default can be specified, as can the OSPF external metric type and the IS-IS level. To redistribute the default route into the OSPF domain with a metric of 10 and an external metric type of E1, Athens's configuration will be:

```
router ospf 1
 network 172.16.0.0 0.0.255.255 area 0
 default-information originate metric 10 metric-type 1
!
ip classless
ip route 0.0.0.0 0.0.0.0 10.1.1.2
```

Figure 12.14 shows that the default route is now being redistributed into OSPF. The route can also be observed in Sparta's OSPF database (Figure 12.15).

```
Sparta#show ip route
Codes: C - connected, S - static, I - IGRP, R - RIP, M - mobile, B - BGP
       D - EIGRP, EX - EIGRP external, O - OSPF, IA - OSPF inter area
       N1 - OSPF NSSA external type 1, N2 - OSPF NSSA external type 2
       E1 - OSPF external type 1, E2 - OSPF external type 2, E - EGP
       i - IS-IS, L1 - IS-IS level-1, L2 - IS-IS level-2, * - candidate default
       U - per-user static route, o - ODR

Gateway of last resort is 172.16.1.1 to network 0.0.0.0

     172.16.0.0/16 is variably subnetted, 6 subnets, 2 masks
O       172.16.5.0/24 [110/74] via 172.16.2.2, 00:14:46, Ethernet0
O       172.16.4.1/32 [110/75] via 172.16.2.2, 00:14:46, Ethernet0
O       172.16.6.1/32 [110/11] via 172.16.2.2, 00:14:46, Ethernet0
C       172.16.1.0/24 is directly connected, Serial0
C       172.16.2.0/24 is directly connected, Ethernet0
C       172.16.3.0/24 is directly connected, Ethernet1
O* E1 0.0.0.0/0 [110/74] via 172.16.1.1, 00:02:55, Serial0
Sparta#
```

Figure 12.14

*After **default-information originate** is configured at Athens, the default route is redistributed into the OSPF domain.*

The **default-information originate** command also will redistribute into OSPF or IS-IS a default route that has been discovered by another routing process. In the following configuration, the static

```
Sparta#show ip ospf database external

        OSPF Router with ID (172.16.3.1) (Process ID 1)

                Type-5 AS External Link States

Routing Bit Set on this LSA
LS age: 422
Options: (No TOS-capability, No DC)
LS Type: AS External Link
Link State ID: 0.0.0.0 (External Network Number )
Advertising Router: 172.16.1.1
LS Seq Number: 80000002
Checksum: 0x5238
Length: 36
Network Mask: /0
        Metric Type: 1 (Comparable directly to link state metric)
        TOS: 0
        Metric: 10
        Forward Address: 0.0.0.0
        External Route Tag: 1
Sparta#
```

Figure 12.15

Like other external routes advertised by an ASBR, the default route is advertised in a type 5 LSA.

route to 0.0.0.0 has been eliminated, and Athens is speaking BGP to a router in BigNet:

```
router ospf 1
 network 172.16.0.0 0.0.255.255 area 0
 default-information originate metric 10 metric-type 1
!
router bgp 65501
 network 172.16.0.0
 neighbor 10.1.1.2 remote-as 65502
!
ip classless
```

Athens is now learning a route to 0.0.0.0 from its BGP neighbor and will advertise the route into the OSPF domain via type 5 LSAs (Figure 12.16).

```
Athens#show ip route
Codes: C - connected, S - static, I - IGRP, R - RIP, M - mobile, B - BGP
       D - EIGRP, EX - EIGRP external, O - OSPF, IA - OSPF inter area
       E1 - OSPF external type 1, E2 - OSPF external type 2, E - EGP
       i - IS-IS, L1 - IS-IS level-1, L2 - IS-IS level-2, * - candidate default
       U - per-user static route

Gateway of last resort is 10.1.1.2 to network 0.0.0.0

     10.0.0.0/8 is subnetted, 1 subnets
C       10.1.1.0 is directly connected, TokenRing0
     172.16.0.0/16 is variably subnetted, 6 subnets, 2 masks
O IA    172.16.4.1/32 [110/139] via 172.16.1.2, 00:16:45, Serial0
O IA    172.16.5.0/24 [110/138] via 172.16.1.2, 00:16:45, Serial0
O IA    172.16.6.1/32 [110/75] via 172.16.1.2, 00:16:45, Serial0
C       172.16.1.0/24 is directly connected, Serial0
O IA    172.16.2.0/24 [110/74] via 172.16.1.2, 00:16:45, Serial0
O IA    172.16.3.0/24 [110/74] via 172.16.1.2, 00:16:45, Serial0
B*   0.0.0.0/0 [20/0] via 10.1.1.2, 00:12:02
Athens#
```

Figure 12.16

A BGP-speaking neighbor in BigNet is advertising a default route to Athens.

A benefit of default routes, or any summary route, is that it can add stability to an internetwork. But what if the default route itself is unstable? For example, suppose that the default route advertised to Athens in Figure 12.15 is *flapping*, that is, alternating frequently between reachable and unreachable. With each change, Athens must send a new type 5 LSA into the OSPF domain. This LSA will be advertised into all non-stub areas. Although this flooding and reflooding may have minimal impact on system resources, it still might be undesirable to the network administrator. A solution is to use the **always** keyword:[4]

```
router ospf 1
 network 172.16.0.0 0.0.255.255 area 0
 default-information originate always metric 10 metric-type 1
!
router bgp 65501
 network 172.16.0.0
 neighbor 10.1.1.2 remote-as 65502
!
ip classless
```

---

[4] *This keyword is available only under OSPF. It is not supported under IS-IS.*

With this configuration, Athens will always advertise a default route into the OSPF domain, regardless of whether it actually has a route to 0.0.0.0. If a router within the OSPF domain defaults a packet to Athens and Athens has no default route, it will send an ICMP Destination Unreachable message to the source address and drop the packet.

The **always** keyword can be used safely when there is only a single default route out of the OSPF domain. If more than one ASBR is advertising a default route, the defaults should be dynamic—that is, the loss of a default route should be advertised. If an ASBR claims to have a default when it doesn't, packets can be forwarded to it instead of to a legitimate ASBR.

Case Study: Configuring On-Demand Routing

ODR is enabled with a single command, **router odr**. No networks or other parameters must be specified. CDP is enabled by default; it needs to be enabled only if it has been turned off for some reason. The command to enable the CDP process on a router is **cdp run**; to enable CDP on a specific interface, the command is **cdp enable**.

Figure 12.17 shows a typical hub-and-spoke topology. To configure ODR, the hub router will have the **router odr** command. As long as all routers are running IOS 11.2 or later and the connecting medium supports SNAP (such as the Frame Relay or PVCs shown), ODR is operational and the hub will learn the stub networks. The only configuration necessary at the stub routers is a static default route to the hub.

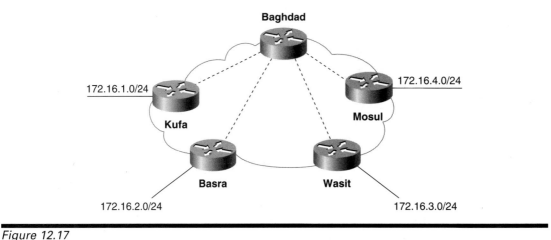

Baghdad

172.16.1.0/24

Kufa

172.16.4.0/24

Mosul

Basra   **Wasit**

172.16.2.0/24   172.16.3.0/24

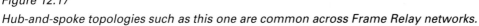

Figure 12.17

Hub-and-spoke topologies such as this one are common across Frame Relay networks.

ODR can also be redistributed. If Baghdad in Figure 12.17 needs to advertise the ODR-discovered routes into OSPF, Baghdad's configuration might be:

```
router odr
!
router ospf 1
 redistribute odr metric 100
 network 172.16.0.0 0.0.255.255 area 5
```

LOOKING AHEAD

Configuration and troubleshooting of default routes are trivial tasks in the simple, loop-free internetworks shown in this chapter. When topologies are more complex, and especially when they include looping paths, the potential for problems with both default routing and with redistribution increases. Chapters 13, "Route Filtering," and 14, "Route Maps," discuss the tools that are vital to controlling routing behavior in complex topologies.

SUMMARY TABLE: CHAPTER 12 COMMAND REVIEW

Command	Description
cdp enable	Enables CDP on an interface.
cdp run	Enables CDP globally on a router.
default-information originate [always][metric metric-value] [metric-type type-value]{level-1|level-1-2 |level-2}[route-map map-name]	Generates a default route into OSPF and IS-IS routing domains.
ip classless	Enables classless route lookups so that the router can forward packets to unknown subnets of directly connected networks.
ip default-network network-number	Specifies a network as a candidate route when determining the gateway of last resort.
ip route prefix mask {address|interface}[distance] [tag tag][permanent]	Specifies a static route entry.
router odr	Enables On-Demand Routing.

REVIEW QUESTIONS

1. What is the destination address of default routes used by the open protocols?
2. How are default routes identified and advertised by IGRP and EIGRP?
3. Can a static route to 0.0.0.0 be used as the default route on a router running IGRP?
4. What is a stub router? What is a stub network?
5. What is an advantage of using default routes instead of a full routing table?

6. What is an advantage of using a full routing table instead of a default route?

7. What data link protocol does On-Demand Routing use to discover routes?

8. What IOS restrictions are placed on ODR?

9. What media restrictions are placed on ODR?

- **Uses of Route Filters**

- **Configuring Route Filters**

  Case Study: Filtering Specific Routes

  Case Study: Route Filtering and Redistribution

  Case Study: A Protocol Migration

  Case Study: Multiple Redistribution Points

  Case Study: Using Distances to Set Router Preferences

13

Route Filtering

Chapter 11, "Route Redistribution," presents several situations in which redistribution causes unwanted or inaccurate routes to exist in a particular router. For instance, in Figure 11.3 and the associated discussion, one or more routers choose a sub-optimal route through an internetwork. The problem in that example is that the routers prefer the lower administrative distance of IGRP to the administrative distance of RIP. More generally, any time routes to the same destination are being redistributed into a routing domain by more than a single router, the potential for inaccurate routing exists. In some cases, routing loops and black holes may occur.

Figure 11.26 shows another example of an unwanted or unexpected route. In this case, the summary route 192.168.3.128/25 is advertised into OSPF but is redistributed into the EIGRP domain—where the summarized subnets exist. This phenomenon, in which a route is advertised in the wrong direction across a redistributing router, is called *route feedback*.

Route filtering enables the network administrator to keep tight control over route advertisements. Any time a router is performing *mutual redistribution*—the mutual sharing of routes between two or more routing protocols—route filters should be used to ensure that routes are advertised in only one direction.

Route feedback

Figure 13.1 shows another use for route filters. Here, a routing domain is broken into sub-domains, each containing multiple routers. The router connecting the two domains is filtering routes so that the routers in sub-domain B know only a subset of the routes in sub-domain A. This filtering may be done for security, so that the B routers only know of authorized subnets. Or it may be done simply to manage the size of the routing tables and updates of the B routers by eliminating unnecessary routes.

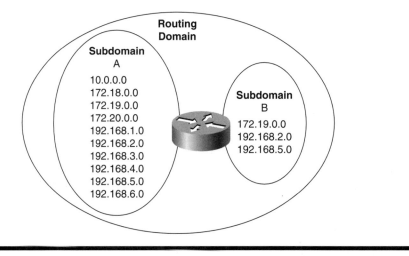

Figure 13.1

Route filters may be used to create routing sub-domains, into which only some of the routing domain's addresses are advertised.

Yet another common use of route filters is to create a "route firewall." Frequently, corporate divisions or government agencies must be interconnected while they remain under separate administrative control. If you do not have control of all parts of the internetwork, you are vulnerable to misconfigured or even malicious routing. Route filters at the interconnecting routers will ensure that routers accept only legitimate routes. This approach is again a form of security, but in this case, incoming routes, instead of outgoing routes, are regulated.

Route filters work by regulating the routes that are entered into, or advertised out of, the route table. They have somewhat different effects on link state routing protocols than they do on distance vector routing protocols. A router running a distance vector protocol advertises routes based on what is in its route table. As a result, a route filter will influence which routes the router advertises to its neighbors.

Route filters and distance vector routing

On the other hand, routers running link state protocols determine their routes based on information in their link state database, rather than the advertised route entries of its neighbors. Route filters have no effect on link state advertisements or the link state database.[1] As a result, a route filter can influence the route table of the router on which the filter is configured, but has no effect on the route entries of neighboring routers. Because of this behavior, route filters are mostly used at redistribution points into link state domains, such as an OSPF ASBR, where they can regulate which routes enter or leave the domain. Within the link state domain, route filters have limited utility.

Route filters and link state routing.

CONFIGURING ROUTE FILTERS

Route filtering is accomplished by one of the following methods:

- Filtering specific routes, using the **distribute-list** command

- Manipulating the administrative distances of routes, using the **distance** command

---

[1] *Remember that a basic requirement of link state protocols is that all routers in an area must have identical link state databases. If a route filter blocked some LSAs, this requirement would be violated.*

Case Study: Filtering Specific Routes

Figure 13.2 shows a portion of an internetwork running RIPv2. Barkis is providing connectivity to the rest of the internet via Traddles. In addition to the 700 specific routes within BigNet, Traddles is advertising a default route to Barkis. Because of the default route, Barkis, Micawber, Peggotty, and Heep do not need to know the other 700 routes in BigNet. So the objective is to configure a filter at Barkis that will accept only the default route from Traddles and reject all other routes. Barkis' configuration is:

```
router rip
 version 2
 network 192.168.75.0
 distribute-list 1 in Serial1
!
ip classless
 access-list 1 permit 0.0.0.0
```

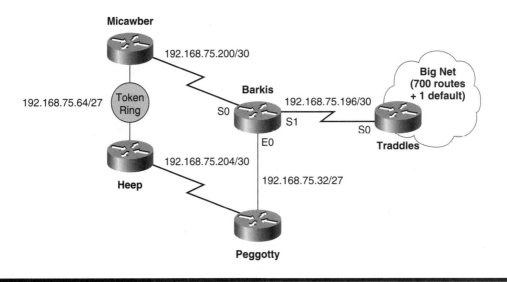

Figure 13.2

A route filter at Barkis will accept only the default route from Traddles and will reject all other BigNet routes.

This route filter examines incoming routes at S1, which is the interface connected to Traddles. It specifies that the only routes accepted by Barkis's RIP process are those permitted by access list 1, and access list 1 specifies that only 0.0.0.0 is permitted.[2] All other routes are implicitly denied by the access list. Figure 13.3 shows the resulting routing table at Barkis.

```
Barkis#show ip route
Codes: C - connected, S - static, I - IGRP, R - RIP, M - mobile, B - BGP
       D - EIGRP, EX - EIGRP external, O - OSPF, IA - OSPF inter area
       N1 - OSPF NSSA external type 1, N2 - OSPF NSSA external type 2
       E1 - OSPF external type 1, E2 - OSPF external type 2, E - EGP
       i - IS-IS, L1 - IS-IS level-1, L2 - IS-IS level-2, * - candidate default
       U - per-user static route, o - ODR

Gateway of last resort is 192.168.75.198 to network 0.0.0.0

     192.168.75.0/24 is variably subnetted, 5 subnets, 2 masks
C       192.168.75.32/27 is directly connected, Ethernet0
R       192.168.75.64/27 [120/1] via 192.168.75.201, 00:00:23, Serial0
C       192.168.75.196/30 is directly connected, Serial1
C       192.168.75.200/30 is directly connected, Serial0
R       192.168.75.204/30 [120/1] via 192.168.75.34, 00:00:13, Ethernet0
R*  0.0.0.0/0 [120/10] via 192.168.75.198, 00:00:03, Serial1
Barkis#
```

Figure 13.3

0.0.0.0 is the only route accepted from Traddles.

Of course, advertising 700 routes across a serial link only to discard them at the far end is a waste of bandwidth. So a better configuration would be to place the filter at Traddles, allowing only the default route to be advertised to Barkis:

```
router rip
 version 2
 network 192.168.63.0
 network 192.168.75.0
 network 192.168.88.0
 distribute-list 1 out Serial0
```

---

[2]   *Note that no inverse mask is shown. An access list's default inverse mask is 0.0.0.0, which is correct for this configuration.*

```
!
ip classless
access-list 1 permit 0.0.0.0
```

Here the filter configuration looks almost the same except that it is filtering outgoing routes instead of incoming routes. Figure 13.4 shows that only the default route is being advertised across the serial link from Traddles.

```
Barkis#debug ip rip
RIP protocol debugging is on
Barkis#
RIP: received v2 update from 192.168.75.198 on Serial1
     0.0.0.0/0 -> 0.0.0.0 in 10 hops
RIP: sending v2 update to 224.0.0.9 via Ethernet0 (192.168.75.33)
     192.168.75.64/27 -> 0.0.0.0, metric 2, tag 0
     192.168.75.196/30 -> 0.0.0.0, metric 1, tag 0
     192.168.75.200/30 -> 0.0.0.0, metric 1, tag 0
     0.0.0.0/0 -> 0.0.0.0, metric 11, tag 0
RIP: sending v2 update to 224.0.0.9 via Serial0 (192.168.75.202)
     192.168.75.32/27 -> 0.0.0.0, metric 1, tag 0
     192.168.75.196/30 -> 0.0.0.0, metric 1, tag 0
     192.168.75.204/30 -> 0.0.0.0, metric 2, tag 0
     0.0.0.0/0 -> 0.0.0.0, metric 11, tag 0
RIP: sending v2 update to 224.0.0.9 via Serial1 (192.168.75.197)
     192.168.75.32/27 -> 0.0.0.0, metric 1, tag 0
     192.168.75.64/27 -> 0.0.0.0, metric 2, tag 0
     192.168.75.200/30 -> 0.0.0.0, metric 1, tag 0
     192.168.75.204/30 -> 0.0.0.0, metric 2, tag 0
RIP: received v2 update from 192.168.75.34 on Ethernet0
     192.168.75.64/27 -> 0.0.0.0 in 2 hops
     192.168.75.204/30 -> 0.0.0.0 in 1 hops
RIP: received v2 update from 192.168.75.201 on Serial0
     192.168.75.64/27 -> 0.0.0.0 in 1 hops
     192.168.75.204/30 -> 0.0.0.0 in 2 hops
```

Figure 13.4

The filter at Traddles allows only the default route to be advertised to Barkis.

In both configurations, Barkis will advertise the default route to Micawber and to Peggotty. Neither configuration affects the routes that Barkis advertises to Traddles.

When the **distribute-list** command is configured under link state protocols such as OSPF, the "out" keyword cannot be used in association with an interface.[3] Because link state protocols do not advertise routes from their routing table as do distance vector protocols, there are no updates to filter. A command such as **distribute-list 1 out Serial1** under a link state protocol is meaningless.

In Figure 13.5, another group of routers has been connected. This internetwork section, ThemNet, is under separate administrative control, as is the router Creakle. Because the BigNet administrator has no access to or control over the routers in ThemNet, route filters should be used to minimize the potential of bad routing information being sent into BigNet from Creakle. For example, notice that ThemNet is using a default route (perhaps to access an internal Internet connection). If this default route should be advertised into BigNet, it could cause packets to be mis-routed into ThemNet. A black hole would exist.

To allow only the routes necessary for communication with ThemNet, Heep's configuration is:

```
router rip
 version 2
 network 192.168.75.0
 distribute-list 2 out Serial1
 distribute-list 1 in Serial1
!
ip classless
access-list 1 permit 192.168.73.0
access-list 1 permit 192.168.65.0
access-list 1 permit 192.168.62.0
access-list 1 permit 10.5.187.208
access-list 2 deny 0.0.0.0
access-list 2 permit any
```

---

[3]   *The "out" keyword can be used in association with a routing protocol, as discussed in the next case study.*

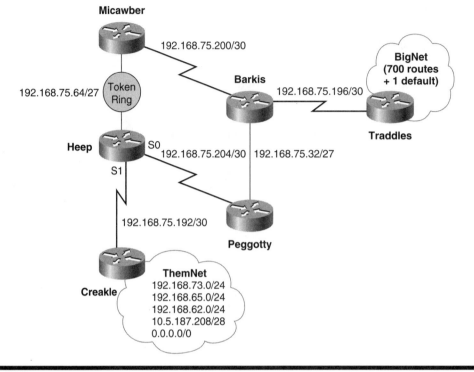

Figure 13.5
The internetwork ThemNet is not under the control of the BigNet administrator.

Distribute list 1 allows only the routes specified in access list 1 to be accepted from Creakle. It blocks the default route and any other routes that may be incorrectly inserted into the routing tables of ThemNet.

Distribute list 2 is in place to ensure that BigNet is a good neighbor. It blocks the BigNet default route, which would cause problems in ThemNet, and allows all other BigNet routes.

Case Study: Route Filtering and Redistribution

Any time a router performs mutual redistribution, the potential for route feedback exists. For example, a route from the RIP side in Figure 13.6 can be redistributed into OSPF and, from there, be redistributed back into RIP. Therefore, using route filters to control the direction of route advertisements is a wise approach.

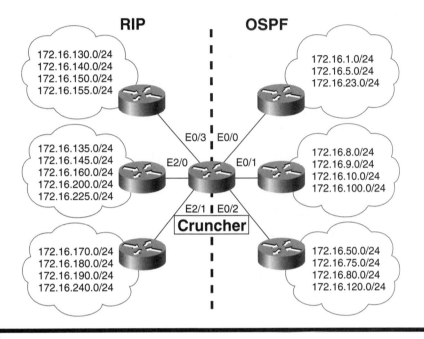

Figure 13.6

Cruncher is redistributing RIP routes into OSPF, and OSPF routes into RIP. Route filters should be used to prevent route feedback.

Cruncher in Figure 13.6 is speaking both RIP and OSPF on several interfaces. Cruncher's configuration is:

```
router ospf 25
  redistribute rip metric 100
  network 172.16.1.254 0.0.0.0 area 25
  network 172.16.8.254 0.0.0.0 area 25
  network 172.16.50.254 0.0.0.0 area 25
  distribute-list 3 in Ethernet0/0
  distribute-list 3 in Ethernet0/1
  distribute-list 3 in Ethernet0/2
!
router rip
  redistribute ospf 25 metric 5
  passive-interface Ethernet0/0
  passive-interface Ethernet0/1
```

```
passive-interface Ethernet0/2
network 172.16.0.0
distribute-list 1 in Ethernet0/3
distribute-list 1 in Ethernet2/0
distribute-list 1 in Ethernet2/1
!
ip classless
access-list 1 permit 172.16.128.0 0.0.127.255
access-list 3 permit 172.16.0.0 0.0.127.255
```

In this configuration, the logic of the access lists is to permit certain routes and deny all others. The logic can also be reversed; to deny certain routes and allow all others:

```
access-list 1 deny 172.16.0.0 0.0.127.255
access-list 1 permit any
access-list 3 deny 172.16.128.0 0.0.127.255
access-list 3 permit any
```

The effect of this second access list configuration is the same as the first. In both cases, routes to destinations in the OSPF domain will not be advertised into OSPF from RIP, and routes to destinations in the RIP domain will not be advertised into RIP from OSPF. However, this second access list configuration is not as easy to administer, because of the *permit any* at the end. To add new entries to the list, the entire list must first be deleted so that the new entry can be placed before the *permit any*.

The small access lists shown are possible because the subnet addresses in Figure 13.6 were carefully assigned for easy summarization. The trade-off is a loss of specificity. More precise control over the routes means larger, more precise access lists at the price of increased administrative attention.

An alternative method of configuring route filters at redistribution points is to filter by route process instead of by interface. For

example, the following configuration allows only certain routes in
Figure 13.6 to be redistributed:

```
router ospf 25
  redistribute rip metric 100
  network 172.16.1.254 0.0.0.0 area 25
  network 172.16.8.254 0.0.0.0 area 25
  network 172.16.50.254 0.0.0.0 area 25
  distribute-list 10 out rip
!
router rip
  redistribute ospf 25 metric 5
  passive-interface Ethernet0/3
  passive-interface Ethernet2/0
  passive-interface Ethernet2/1
  network 172.16.0.0
  distribute-list 20 out ospf 25
!
ip classless
access-list 10 permit 172.16.130.0
access-list 10 permit 172.16.145.0
access-list 10 permit 172.16.240.0
access-list 20 permit 172.16.23.0
access-list 20 permit 172.16.9.0
access-list 20 permit 172.16.75.0
```

The route filter under the OSPF configuration allows OSPF to
advertise RIP-discovered routes only if access list 10 permits them.
Likewise, the filter under the RIP configuration allows RIP to
advertise routes discovered by OSPF 25 only if access list 20 permits them. In both cases, the filters have no effect on routes discovered by other protocols. For example, if OSPF were
redistributing both RIP and EIGRP routes, the distribute list
shown would not apply to EIGRP-discovered routes.

When filtering by route process, only the "out" keyword is
allowed. After all, it makes no sense to specify something like **distribute-list 10 in rip** under OSPF. The route has already been
entered into the route table by RIP, and OSPF either advertises it
("out") or it does not.

Note that although filtering by routing protocol is useful for specifying which routes will be redistributed, it is not a good method for preventing route feedback. For example, consider the following configuration for Cruncher in Figure 13.6:

```
router ospf 25
 redistribute rip metric 100
 network 172.16.1.254 0.0.0.0 area 25
 network 172.16.8.254 0.0.0.0 area 25
 network 172.16.50.254 0.0.0.0 area 25
 distribute-list 1 out rip
!
router rip
 redistribute ospf 25 metric 5
 passive-interface Ethernet0/3
 passive-interface Ethernet2/0
 passive-interface Ethernet2/1
 network 172.16.0.0
 distribute-list 3 out ospf 25
!
ip classless
access-list 1 permit 172.16.128.0 0.0.127.255
access-list 3 permit 172.16.0.0 0.0.127.255
```

Suppose a route from the RIP domain, such as 172.16.190.0/24, redistributed into the OSPF domain, were to be advertised back to Cruncher. Although the distribute list under the RIP configuration will prevent the route from being advertised back into the RIP domain, the list does nothing to prevent the route from being entered into Cruncher's routing table as originating within the OSPF domain. In fact, the filter assumes that the route has already been entered into the table by OSPF. To prevent route feedback, routes must be filtered as they are incoming on an interface, before they are entered into the route table.

Case Study: A Protocol Migration

The **distance** command, when used without any optional parameters, specifies the administrative distance to be assigned to routes learned from a particular routing protocol. On first consideration, this action may not seem to be a route filtering function, but it is.

When multiple routing protocols are running, routes are accepted or rejected based on their administrative distances.

The internetwork in Figure 13.7 is running RIP, and there is a plan to convert to EIGRP. Several methods exist for conducting such a protocol migration. One option is to turn off the old protocol and turn on the new protocol at each router. Although this option is valid for a small internetwork like the one in Figure 13.7, the downtime can be impractical in larger internetworks.

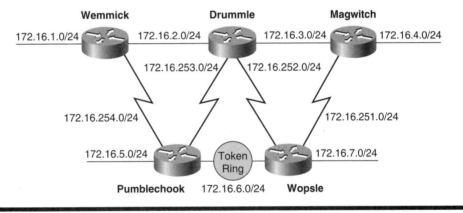

Figure 13.7

These routers are running RIP and are to be converted to EIGRP.

Another option is to add the new protocol without removing the old protocol. If the default administrative distance of the new protocol is lower than that of the old, each router will prefer the routes advertised by the new protocol as they are added. The internetwork will converge to the new protocol as the routers are converted, and after the entire internetwork has converged on the new protocol, the old one can be removed from all routers.

Referring to Table 11.1, the default administrative distance of RIP is 120, and the default administrative distance of EIGRP is 90. If EIGRP is added to each router in addition to RIP, the router will begin preferring the EIGRP routes as its neighbors begin speaking EIGRP. When all RIP routes have disappeared from all routing tables, the internetwork has reconverged on EIGRP. The RIP processes can then be removed from the routers.

The problem with this approach is that the potential for routing loops and black holes exists during the reconfiguration. The five routers in Figure 13.7 can be reconfigured and reconverged in a matter of minutes, so looping may not be as much of a concern here as it would be in a larger internetwork.

A modification of this dual-protocol method is to use the **distance** command to ensure that the routes of the new protocol are rejected until all routers are ready for conversion. The first step in this procedure is to lower the administrative distance of RIP in all routers:

```
router rip
  network 172.16.0.0
  distance 70
```

Note that the administrative distance is relevant only to the routing process of a single router. While RIP is still the only protocol running, the change of administrative distance will have no effect on routing.

Next each router is revisited, and the EIGRP process is added:

```
router eigrp 1
  network 172.16.0.0
!
router rip
  network 172.16.0.0
  distance 70
```

Because EIGRP has a default administrative distance of 90, the RIP routes are preferred (Figure 13.8). No routers are preferring EIGRP, so no network downtime has to be scheduled while the configurations are changed. This approach gives the network administrator time to re-examine the new configurations in each router for accuracy before the conversion.

```
Drummle#show ip route
        D - EIGRP, EX - EIGRP external, O - OSPF, IA - OSPF inter area
        N1 - OSPF NSSA external type 1, N2 - OSPF NSSA external type 2
        E1 - OSPF external type 1, E2 - OSPF external type 2, E - EGP
        i - IS-IS, L1 - IS-IS level-1, L2 - IS-IS level-2, * - candidate default
        U - per-user static route, o - ODR

Gateway of last resort is not set

        172.16.0.0/24 is subnetted, 11 subnets
C          172.16.252.0 is directly connected, Serial0
C          172.16.253.0 is directly connected, Serial1
R          172.16.254.0 [70/1] via 172.16.2.253, 00:00:16, Ethernet0
                        [70/1] via 172.16.253.253, 00:00:05, Serial1
R          172.16.251.0 [70/1] via 172.16.252.253, 00:00:08, Serial0
                        [70/1] via 172.16.3.253, 00:00:01, Ethernet1
R          172.16.4.0 [70/1] via 172.16.3.253, 00:00:01, Ethernet1
R          172.16.5.0 [70/1] via 172.16.253.253, 00:00:05, Serial1
R          172.16.6.0 [70/1] via 172.16.252.253, 00:00:08, Serial0
                        [70/1] via 172.16.253.253, 00:00:05, Serial1
R          172.16.7.0 [70/1] via 172.16.252.253, 00:00:08, Serial0
R          172.16.1.0 [70/1] via 172.16.2.253, 00:00:17, Ethernet0
C          172.16.2.0 is directly connected, Ethernet0
C          172.16.3.0 is directly connected, Ethernet1
Drummle#
```

Figure 13.8

The RIP routes, which have been assigned an administrative distance of 70, are preferred over the EIGRP routes.

Finally, the conversion is performed by revisiting each router and changing the RIP distance back to the default of 120. Network downtime should be scheduled for this step. The RIP routes with the administrative distance of 70 will begin to age out because the new RIP updates will be assigned an administrative distance of 120 (Figure 13.9). At 210 seconds, the RIP routes will be declared

invalid (Figure 13.10), and finally the EIGRP routes will be preferred (Figure 13.11).

```
Drummle#show ip route
Codes: C - connected, S - static, I - IGRP, R - RIP, M - mobile, B - BGP
       D - EIGRP, EX - EIGRP external, O - OSPF, IA - OSPF inter area
       N1 - OSPF NSSA external type 1, N2 - OSPF NSSA external type 2
       E1 - OSPF external type 1, E2 - OSPF external type 2, E - EGP
       i - IS-IS, L1 - IS-IS level-1, L2 - IS-IS level-2, * - candidate default
       U - per-user static route, o - ODR

Gateway of last resort is not set

     172.16.0.0/24 is subnetted, 11 subnets
C       172.16.252.0 is directly connected, Serial0
C       172.16.253.0 is directly connected, Serial1
R       172.16.254.0 [70/1] via 172.16.2.253, 00:02:31, Ethernet0
                     [70/1] via 172.16.253.253, 00:02:18, Serial1
R       172.16.251.0 [70/1] via 172.16.252.253, 00:02:27, Serial0
                     [70/1] via 172.16.3.253, 00:02:32, Ethernet1
R       172.16.4.0 [70/1] via 172.16.3.253, 00:02:32, Ethernet1
R       172.16.5.0 [70/1] via 172.16.253.253, 00:02:19, Serial1
R       172.16.6.0 [70/1] via 172.16.252.253, 00:02:27, Serial0
                   [70/1] via 172.16.253.253, 00:02:19, Serial1
R       172.16.7.0 [70/1] via 172.16.252.253, 00:02:27, Serial0
R       172.16.1.0 [70/1] via 172.16.2.253, 00:02:32, Ethernet0
C       172.16.2.0 is directly connected, Ethernet0
C       172.16.3.0 is directly connected, Ethernet1
```

Figure 13.9
After the RIP administrative distance is changed back to 120, the routes with a distance of 70 begin to age out. Here all the RIP routes are more than two minutes old.

Although routing loops and black holes are still a possibility with
this method, the conversion should be faster and less prone to
human error because the single change of administrative distance
is all that is required.

Another advantage of this method is that a back-out, in case of
problems, is easy. The RIP processes are still in place on all the
routers, so changing the administrative distances back to 70 is all
that is needed to return to RIP. Once the new EIGRP configuration
has been tested and proven stable, the RIP processes can be deleted
from all routers without further service disruptions.

```
Drummle#show ip route
Codes: C - connected, S - static, I - IGRP, R - RIP, M - mobile, B - BGP
       D - EIGRP, EX - EIGRP external, O - OSPF, IA - OSPF inter area
       N1 - OSPF NSSA external type 1, N2 - OSPF NSSA external type 2
       E1 - OSPF external type 1, E2 - OSPF external type 2, E - EGP
       i - IS-IS, L1 - IS-IS level-1, L2 - IS-IS level-2, * - candidate default
       U - per-user static route, o - ODR

Gateway of last resort is not set

     172.16.0.0/24 is subnetted, 11 subnets
C       172.16.252.0 is directly connected, Serial0
C       172.16.253.0 is directly connected, Serial1
R       172.16.254.0/24 is possibly down,
          routing via 172.16.253.253, Serial1
R       172.16.251.0/24 is possibly down,
          routing via 172.16.252.253, Serial0
R       172.16.4.0/24 is possibly down,
          routing via 172.16.3.253, Ethernet1
R       172.16.5.0/24 is possibly down,
          routing via 172.16.253.253, Serial1
R       172.16.6.0/24 is possibly down,
          routing via 172.16.253.253, Serial1
R       172.16.7.0/24 is possibly down,
          routing via 172.16.252.253, Serial0
R       172.16.1.0/24 is possibly down,
          routing via 172.16.2.253, Ethernet0
C       172.16.2.0 is directly connected, Ethernet0
C       172.16.3.0 is directly connected, Ethernet1
Drummle#
```

Figure 13.10
At 3.5 minutes, the RIP routes are declared down.

One thing to consider before using the dual-protocol method is the impact running two protocols concurrently on each router will have on memory and processing. If the utilization of memory or processing or both is averaging above 50% to 60%, careful lab testing and modeling should be performed prior to committing to the conversion to ensure that the routers can handle the additional load. If they can't, a more complex procedure of removing the old protocol before configuring the new protocol may be the only option.

```
Drummle#show ip route
Codes: C - connected, S - static, I - IGRP, R - RIP, M - mobile, B - BGP
       D - EIGRP, EX - EIGRP external, O - OSPF, IA - OSPF inter area
       N1 - OSPF NSSA external type 1, N2 - OSPF NSSA external type 2
       E1 - OSPF external type 1, E2 - OSPF external type 2, E - EGP
       i - IS-IS, L1 - IS-IS level-1, L2 - IS-IS level-2, * - candidate default
       U - per-user static route, o - ODR

Gateway of last resort is not set

     172.16.0.0/24 is subnetted, 11 subnets
C       172.16.252.0 is directly connected, Serial0
C       172.16.253.0 is directly connected, Serial1
D       172.16.254.0 [90/2195456] via 172.16.2.253, 00:01:11, Ethernet0
D       172.16.251.0 [90/2195456] via 172.16.3.253, 00:01:06, Ethernet1
D       172.16.4.0 [90/307200] via 172.16.3.253, 00:01:06, Ethernet1
D       172.16.5.0 [90/2195456] via 172.16.253.253, 00:01:11, Serial1
D       172.16.6.0 [90/2185984] via 172.16.252.253, 00:01:11, Serial0
                   [90/2185984] via 172.16.253.253, 00:01:11, Serial1
D       172.16.7.0 [90/2195456] via 172.16.252.253, 00:01:07, Serial0
D       172.16.1.0 [90/307200] via 172.16.2.253, 00:01:11, Ethernet0
C       172.16.2.0 is directly connected, Ethernet0
C       172.16.3.0 is directly connected, Ethernet1
Drummle#
```

Figure 13.11

The EIGRP routes, with their default distance of 90, replace the RIP routes.

A variant on this procedure is to increase the administrative distance of the new protocol, rather than decrease the distance of the old protocol, and then lower the distance of the new protocol at conversion time. However, be sure to enter the **distance** command before any network commands so that the new protocol won't first activate at its default distance.

Looking again at Table 11.1, notice that EIGRP has two default administrative distances: 90 for internal routes, and 170 for external routes. Therefore, the **distance** command is also different for EIGRP. For example, to raise the EIGRP distance instead of lowering the RIP distance, the configuration is:

```
router eigrp 1
  network 172.16.0.0
  distance eigrp 130 170
!
router rip
  network 172.16.0.0
```

The keyword "eigrp" is added to indicate that EIGRP distances are specified. The administrative distance of internal EIGRP routes is changed to 130, and the distance of external routes is left at 170.

One final note on using the dual-protocol procedure to migrate to a new routing protocol: Be sure you understand the behavior of both protocols. For example, some protocols, such as EIGRP, do not age out their route entries. Therefore, if EIGRP is being replaced, an additional step of the conversion process is to clear the route tables with the **clear ip route** * command after the distances have been changed.

Case Study: Multiple Redistribution Points

Figure 13.12 shows an internetwork very similar to the one depicted in Figure 11.3. Recall from the associated discussion in Chapter 11 that the problem with multiple redistribution points is that administrative distances can cause routers to choose undesirable paths. In some cases, route loops and black holes can result. For example, Bumble's routing table (Figure 13.13) shows that it is routing to network 192.168.6.0 through Blathers, rather than using the preferable route through Monks.

One solution to this problem is to use the **distribute-list** command to control the source of the routes at the redistribution points. The configurations of Bumble and Grimwig are:

Bumble
```
router ospf 1
 redistribute rip metric 100
 network 192.168.3.1 0.0.0.0 area 0
 distribute-list 1 in
!
router rip
 redistribute ospf 1 metric 2
 network 192.168.2.0
 distribute-list 2 in
!
```

```
ip classless
access-list 1 permit 192.168.4.0
access-list 1 permit 192.168.5.0
access-list 2 permit 192.168.1.0
access-list 2 permit 192.168.6.0
```

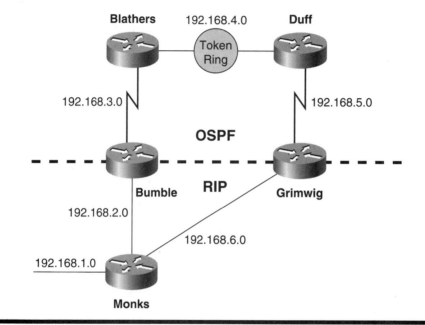

Figure 13.12
When mutual redistribution is performed at more than one point, as in this internetwork,
administrative distances can cause sub-optimal routing, route loops, and black holes.

Grimwig
```
router ospf 1
  redistribute rip metric 100
  network 192.168.5.1 0.0.0.0 area 0
  distribute-list 1 in
!
router rip
  redistribute ospf 1 metric 2
  network 192.168.6.0
  distribute-list 2 in
!
```

```
no ip classless
access-list 1 permit 192.168.3.0
access-list 1 permit 192.168.4.0
access-list 2 permit 192.168.1.0
access-list 2 permit 192.168.2.0
```

In both configurations, access list 1 allows only networks within the OSPF domain to be accepted by OSPF, and access list 2 allows only networks within the RIP domain to be accepted by RIP. Figure 13.14 shows Bumble's route table after the route filter has been configured.

The problem with this configuration is that it eliminates the redundancy inherent in multiple redistribution points. In Figure 13.15, Bumble's Ethernet link has been disconnected. Because routes to the RIP networks are being filtered in OSPF, all of those routes are now unreachable.

```
Bumble#show ip route
Codes: C - connected, S - static, I - IGRP, R - RIP, M - mobile, B - BGP
       D - EIGRP, EX - EIGRP external, O - OSPF, IA - OSPF inter area
       N1 - OSPF NSSA external type 1, N2 - OSPF NSSA external type 2
       E1 - OSPF external type 1, E2 - OSPF external type 2, E - EGP
       i - IS-IS, L1 - IS-IS level-1, L2 - IS-IS level-2, * - candidate default
       U - per-user static route, o - ODR

Gateway of last resort is not set

R    192.168.1.0/24 [120/1] via 192.168.2.1, 00:00:00, Ethernet0
C    192.168.2.0/24 is directly connected, Ethernet0
C    192.168.3.0/24 is directly connected, Serial0
O    192.168.4.0/24 [110/70] via 192.168.3.2, 00:05:09, Serial0
O    192.168.5.0/24 [110/134] via 192.168.3.2, 00:05:09, Serial0
O E2 192.168.6.0/24 [110/100] via 192.168.3.2, 00:05:09, Serial0
Bumble#
```

Figure 13.13

The route Bumble is using to reach to network 192.168.6.0, via Blathers (192.168.3.2) involves crossing two serial links and a Token Ring.

```
Bumble#show ip route
Codes: C - connected, S - static, I - IGRP, R - RIP, M - mobile, B - BGP
       D - EIGRP, EX - EIGRP external, O - OSPF, IA - OSPF inter area
       N1 - OSPF NSSA external type 1, N2 - OSPF NSSA external type 2
       E1 - OSPF external type 1, E2 - OSPF external type 2, E - EGP
       i - IS-IS, L1 - IS-IS level-1, L2 - IS-IS level-2, * - candidate default
       U - per-user static route, o - ODR

Gateway of last resort is not set

R    192.168.1.0/24 [120/1] via 192.168.2.1, 00:00:12, Ethernet0
C    192.168.2.0/24 is directly connected, Ethernet0
C    192.168.3.0/24 is directly connected, Serial0
O    192.168.4.0/24 [110/70] via 192.168.3.2, 00:00:22, Serial0
O    192.168.5.0/24 [110/134] via 192.168.3.2, 00:00:22, Serial0
R    192.168.6.0/24 [120/1] via 192.168.2.1, 00:00:13, Ethernet0
Bumble#
```

Figure 13.14

After the route filters are configured, Bumble is using the preferred route to reach network 192.168.6.0.

```
Bumble#
%LINEPROTO-5-UPDOWN: Line protocol on Interface Ethernet0, changed state to down
Bumble#show ip route
Codes: C - connected, S - static, I - IGRP, R - RIP, M - mobile, B - BGP
       D - EIGRP, EX - EIGRP external, O - OSPF, IA - OSPF inter area
       N1 - OSPF NSSA external type 1, N2 - OSPF NSSA external type 2
       E1 - OSPF external type 1, E2 - OSPF external type 2, E - EGP
       i - IS-IS, L1 - IS-IS level-1, L2 - IS-IS level-2, * - candidate default
       U - per-user static route, o - ODR

Gateway of last resort is not set

C    192.168.3.0/24 is directly connected, Serial0
O    192.168.4.0/24 [110/70] via 192.168.3.2, 00:06:45, Serial0
O    192.168.5.0/24 [110/134] via 192.168.3.2, 00:06:45, Serial0
Bumble#
```

Figure 13.15

When Bumble's Ethernet link fails, the RIP networks become unreachable. The route filters prevent OSPF from entering the alternative routes into the route table.

A better approach is to use two forms of the **distance** command to set preferred routes. The configurations of Bumble and Grimwig are:

Bumble

```
router ospf 1
 redistribute rip metric 100
 network 192.168.3.1 0.0.0.0 area 0
 distance 130
 distance 110 0.0.0.0 255.255.255.255 1
!
router rip
 redistribute ospf 1 metric 2
 network 192.168.2.0
 distance 130
 distance 120 192.168.2.1 0.0.0.0 2
!
ip classless
access-list 1 permit 192.168.4.0
access-list 1 permit 192.168.5.0
access-list 2 permit 192.168.1.0
access-list 2 permit 192.168.6.0
```

Grimwig

```
router ospf 1
 redistribute rip metric 100
 network 192.168.5.1 0.0.0.0 area 0
 distance 130
 distance 110 0.0.0.0 255.255.255.255 1
!
router rip
 redistribute ospf 1 metric 2
 network 192.168.6.0
 distance 130
 distance 120 192.168.6.1 0.0.0.0 2
!
ip classless
access-list 1 permit 192.168.3.0
access-list 1 permit 192.168.4.0
access-list 2 permit 192.168.1.0
access-list 2 permit 192.168.2.0
```

The first **distance** command in both configurations sets the default distance of both OSPF and RIP routes to 130. The second **distance** command sets a different distance according to the advertising router specified and the referenced access list. For instance, Grim-wig's RIP process assigns a distance of 120 to routes advertised by Monks (192.168.6.1) that are permitted by access list 2. All other routes are given a distance of 130. Notice that an inverse mask is used with the address of the advertising router.

OSPF is more problematic. The address of the advertising router is not necessarily the interface address of the next-hop router. Rather, it is the Router ID of the router originating the LSA from which the route is calculated. Therefore the address and inverse mask for the **distance** command under OSPF is 0.0.0.0 255.255.255.255, specifying any router.[4] OSPF routes from all routers that are permitted by access list 1 are assigned a distance of 110; all other routes are given a distance of 130.

The result appears in Figure 13.16. The first route table shows that Grimwig is routing to all networks in the OSPF domain via Duff and to all networks in the RIP domain via Monks. The normal dis-tances of 110 for OSPF and 120 for RIP are assigned to the routes. Next Grimwig's Ethernet connection fails. The second route table shows that all networks are now reachable via Duff. The routes to the networks in the RIP domain have a distance of 130. When the Ethernet connection is restored, the RIP advertisements from Monk, with a distance of 120, will replace the OSPF advertise-ments with a distance of 130.

If one of the serial links in Figure 13.12 fails, the opposite will happen. The networks within the OSPF domain will become reachable through the RIP domain, again with a distance of 130 (Figure 13.17). However, unlike the speedy reconvergence of OSPF, the RIP side will take several minutes to reconverge. This slow reconvergence is due to RIP's split horizon at Monks. That

---

[4] *The same "any" address can be used with RIP. A specific address was used for demon-stration purposes.*

```
Grimwig#show ip route
Codes: C - connected, S - static, I - IGRP, R - RIP, M - mobile, B - BGP
       D - EIGRP, EX - EIGRP external, O - OSPF, IA - OSPF inter area
       E1 - OSPF external type 1, E2 - OSPF external type 2, E - EGP
       i - IS-IS, L1 - IS-IS level-1, L2 - IS-IS level-2, * - candidate default
       U - per-user static route

Gateway of last resort is not set

R    192.168.1.0/24 [120/1] via 192.168.6.1, 00:00:19, Ethernet0
R    192.168.2.0/24 [120/1] via 192.168.6.1, 00:00:19, Ethernet0
O    192.168.3.0/24 [110/134] via 192.168.5.2, 00:15:06, Serial0
O    192.168.4.0/24 [110/70] via 192.168.5.2, 00:15:06, Serial0
C    192.168.5.0/24 is directly connected, Serial0
C    192.168.6.0/24 is directly connected, Ethernet0
Grimwig#
%LINEPROTO-5-UPDOWN: Line protocol on Interface Ethernet0, changed state to down
Grimwig#show ip route
Codes: C - connected, S - static, I - IGRP, R - RIP, M - mobile, B - BGP
       D - EIGRP, EX - EIGRP external, O - OSPF, IA - OSPF inter area
       E1 - OSPF external type 1, E2 - OSPF external type 2, E - EGP
       i - IS-IS, L1 - IS-IS level-1, L2 - IS-IS level-2, * - candidate default
       U - per-user static route

Gateway of last resort is not set

O E2 192.168.1.0/24 [130/100] via 192.168.5.2, 00:00:08, Serial0
O E2 192.168.2.0/24 [130/100] via 192.168.5.2, 00:00:08, Serial0
O    192.168.3.0/24 [110/134] via 192.168.5.2, 00:16:23, Serial0
O    192.168.4.0/24 [110/70] via 192.168.5.2, 00:16:23, Serial0
C    192.168.5.0/24 is directly connected, Serial0
O E2 192.168.6.0/24 [130/100] via 192.168.5.2, 00:00:08, Serial0
Grimwig#
```

Figure 13.16
Grimwig's route table, before and after its Ethernet link to Monks is disconnected.

router will not advertise the OSPF routes to Bumble or Grimwig until the same routes have ceased to be advertised from one of those routers and the existing routes have timed out.

The solution to this problem is to disable split horizon on Monk's two Ethernet interfaces with the command **no ip split-horizon**. Although disabling split horizon is trading some loop protection for shorter reconvergence times, it is a good trade. The distance-based route filters at Bumble and Grimwig will prevent all

```
Grimwig#show ip route
Codes: C - connected, S - static, I - IGRP, R - RIP, M - mobile, B - BGP
       D - EIGRP, EX - EIGRP external, O - OSPF, IA - OSPF inter area
       E1 - OSPF external type 1, E2 - OSPF external type 2, E - EGP
       i - IS-IS, L1 - IS-IS level-1, L2 - IS-IS level-2, * - candidate default
       U - per-user static route

Gateway of last resort is not set

R    192.168.1.0/24 [120/1] via 192.168.6.1, 00:00:04, Ethernet0
R    192.168.2.0/24 [120/1] via 192.168.6.1, 00:00:04, Ethernet0
O    192.168.3.0/24 [110/134] via 192.168.5.2, 00:00:12, Serial0
O    192.168.4.0/24 [110/70] via 192.168.5.2, 00:00:12, Serial0
C    192.168.5.0/24 is directly connected, Serial0
C    192.168.6.0/24 is directly connected, Ethernet0
Grimwig#
%LINEPROTO-5-UPDOWN: Line protocol on Interface Serial0, changed state to down
%LINK-3-UPDOWN: Interface Serial0, changed state to down
Grimwig#show ip route
Codes: C - connected, S - static, I - IGRP, R - RIP, M - mobile, B - BGP
       D - EIGRP, EX - EIGRP external, O - OSPF, IA - OSPF inter area
       E1 - OSPF external type 1, E2 - OSPF external type 2, E - EGP
       i - IS-IS, L1 - IS-IS level-1, L2 - IS-IS level-2, * - candidate default
       U - per-user static route

Gateway of last resort is not set

R    192.168.1.0/24 [120/1] via 192.168.6.1, 00:00:07, Ethernet0
R    192.168.2.0/24 [120/1] via 192.168.6.1, 00:00:07, Ethernet0
R    192.168.3.0/24 [130/3] via 192.168.6.1, 00:00:07, Ethernet0
R    192.168.4.0/24 [130/3] via 192.168.6.1, 00:00:07, Ethernet0
R    192.168.5.0/24 is possibly down, routing via 192.168.6.1, Ethernet0
C    192.168.6.0/24 is directly connected, Ethernet0
Grimwig#
```

Figure 13.17

Grimwig's route table, before and after its serial link to Duff is disconnected.

multi-hop loops, and the split horizon function on the same two routers' Ethernet interfaces will break single-hop loops.

Case Study: Using Distances to Set Router Preferences

Suppose policy states that Monks in Figure 13.12 will use Grimwig as its primary gateway to the OSPF domain and route through

Bumble only if Grimwig becomes unavailable. Presently, Monks is performing equal-cost load balancing between Grimwig and Bumble to reach the OSPF networks (Figure 13.18).

```
Monks#show ip route
Codes: C - connected, S - static, I - IGRP, R - RIP, M - mobile, B - BGP
       D - EIGRP, EX - EIGRP external, O - OSPF, IA - OSPF inter area
       N1 - OSPF NSSA external type 1, N2 - OSPF NSSA external type 2
       E1 - OSPF external type 1, E2 - OSPF external type 2, E - EGP
       i - IS-IS, L1 - IS-IS level-1, L2 - IS-IS level-2, * - candidate default
       U - per-user static route, o - ODR

Gateway of last resort is not set

C    192.168.1.0/24 is directly connected, Ethernet2
C    192.168.2.0/24 is directly connected, Ethernet0
R    192.168.3.0/24 [120/2] via 192.168.2.2, 00:00:26, Ethernet0
                    [120/2] via 192.168.6.2, 00:00:23, Ethernet1
R    192.168.4.0/24 [120/2] via 192.168.2.2, 00:00:26, Ethernet0
                    [120/2] via 192.168.6.2, 00:00:23, Ethernet1
R    192.168.5.0/24 [120/2] via 192.168.2.2, 00:00:26, Ethernet0
                    [120/2] via 192.168.6.2, 00:00:23, Ethernet1
C    192.168.6.0/24 is directly connected, Ethernet1
Monks#
```

Figure 13.18

Monks sees all of the networks in the OSPF domain as equidistant through Bumble and Grimwig.

Monks can be configured to prefer Grimwig by lowering the distance of all routes from that router:

```
router rip
  network 192.168.1.0
  network 192.168.2.0
  network 192.168.6.0
  distance 100 192.168.6.2 0.0.0.0
```

Here, the **distance** command makes no reference to an access list. All routes advertised by Grimwig (192.168.6.2) will be assigned an administrative distance of 100. All other routes (meaning routes from Bumble) will be assigned the default RIP administrative distance of 120. Therefore, Grimwig's routes will be preferred.

Figure 13.19 shows the results. The first route table shows that Monks is now routing to Grimwig only. After a failure of the connection to Grimwig, the bottom route table shows that Monks has switched to Bumble (192.168.2.2).

```
Monks#show ip route
Codes: C - connected, S - static, I - IGRP, R - RIP, M - mobile, B - BGP
       D - EIGRP, EX - EIGRP external, O - OSPF, IA - OSPF inter area
       N1 - OSPF NSSA external type 1, N2 - OSPF NSSA external type 2
       E1 - OSPF external type 1, E2 - OSPF external type 2, E - EGP
       i - IS-IS, L1 - IS-IS level-1, L2 - IS-IS level-2, * - candidate default
       U - per-user static route, o - ODR

Gateway of last resort is not set

C    192.168.1.0/24 is directly connected, Ethernet2
C    192.168.2.0/24 is directly connected, Ethernet0
R    192.168.3.0/24 [100/2] via 192.168.6.2, 00:00:12, Ethernet1
R    192.168.4.0/24 [100/2] via 192.168.6.2, 00:00:12, Ethernet1
R    192.168.5.0/24 [100/2] via 192.168.6.2, 00:00:12, Ethernet1
C    192.168.6.0/24 is directly connected, Ethernet1
Monks#
%LINEPROTO-5-UPDOWN: Line protocol on Interface Ethernet1, changed state to down
Monks#show ip route
Codes: C - connected, S - static, I - IGRP, R - RIP, M - mobile, B - BGP
       D - EIGRP, EX - EIGRP external, O - OSPF, IA - OSPF inter area
       N1 - OSPF NSSA external type 1, N2 - OSPF NSSA external type 2
       E1 - OSPF external type 1, E2 - OSPF external type 2, E - EGP
       i - IS-IS, L1 - IS-IS level-1, L2 - IS-IS level-2, * - candidate default
       U - per-user static route, o - ODR

Gateway of last resort is not set

C    192.168.1.0/24 is directly connected, Ethernet2
C    192.168.2.0/24 is directly connected, Ethernet0
R    192.168.3.0/24 [120/2] via 192.168.2.2, 00:00:00, Ethernet0
R    192.168.4.0/24 [120/2] via 192.168.2.2, 00:00:00, Ethernet0
R    192.168.5.0/24 [120/2] via 192.168.2.2, 00:00:00, Ethernet0
R    192.168.6.0/24 [120/2] via 192.168.2.2, 00:00:00, Ethernet0
Monks#
```

Figure 13.19

Monks' route table, before and after its Ethernet link to Grimwig is disconnected.

LOOKING AHEAD

Route filters are very useful tools for controlling the behavior of your internetwork. In large internetworks, route filters are nearly indispensable. Yet for all their utility, they still can only allow or disallow routes. Chapter 14, "Route Maps," introduces route maps, powerful tools that not only identify routes but also actively modify them.

SUMMARY TABLE: CHAPTER 13 COMMAND REVIEW

Command	Description
access-list access-list-number {**deny**|**permit**} *source* [*source-wildcard*]	Defines a line of a standard IP access list.
distance weight [*address mask* [*access-list-number*|*name*]]	Defines an administrative distance other than the default.
distance eigrp **internal-distance** **external-distance**	Defines the administrative distances other than the default of internal and external EIGRP routes.
distribute-list {*access-list-number*|*name*} **in** [*interface-name*]	Filters the routes in incoming updates.
distribute-list {*access-list-number*|*name*} **out** [*interface-name*|*routing-process*|*autonomous-system-number*]	Filters the routes in outgoing updates.
redistribute *protocol* [*process-id*]{**level-1**|**level-1-2**|**level-2**}[**metric** *metric-value*][**metric-type** *type-value*][**match**{**internal**| **external 1**|**external 2**}][**tag** *tag-value*] [**route-map** *map-tag*][**weight** *weight*][**subnets**]	Configures redistribution into a routing protocol and specifies the source of the redistributed routes.

CONFIGURATION EXERCISES

1. The routing configuration for router A in Figure 13.20 is:

```
router rip
  redistribute igrp 1 metric 3
  passive-interface Ethernet0
  passive-interface Ethernet1
  network 172.16.0.0
!
router igrp 1
  redistribute rip metric 10000 1000 255 1 1500
  passive-interface Ethernet2
  passive-interface Ethernet3
  network 172.16.0.0
```

Configure a route filter at A that will prevent subnet 172.16.12.0/24 from being known by any router other than E.

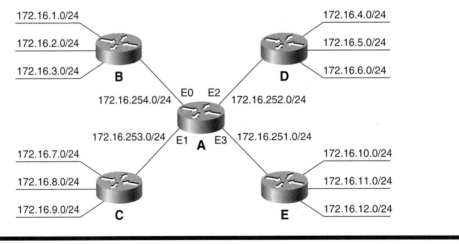

Figure 13.20

The internetwork for Configuration Exercises 1 through 4.

2. Configure a route filter at A in Figure 13.20 that will prevent D from learning about subnet 172.16.10.0/24.

3. Configure a route filter at A in Figure 13.20 that will allow only subnets 172.16.2.0/24, 172.16.8.0/24, and 172.16.9.0/24 to be advertised into the RIP domain.

4. Configure a route filter at A in Figure 13.20 that will prevent B from learning about any of the subnets in the RIP domain.

5. Table 13.1 shows the interface addresses for all routers in Figure 13.21. Routers A and B are running EIGRP, and routers E and F are running IS-IS. C and D are redistributing. Configure **distance** commands for C and D that will prevent loops and route feedback but will still allow redundant paths.

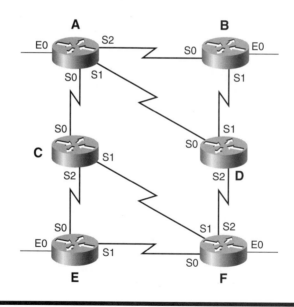

Figure 13.21

The internetwork for Configuration Exercises 5 through 7.

Table 13.1 *The interface addresses of the routers in Figure 13.21.*

Router	Interface	Address	Mask
A	E0	192.168.1.1	255.255.255.0
	S0	192.168.10.254	255.255.255.252
	S1	192.168.10.249	255.255.255.252
	S2	192.168.10.245	255.255.255.252
B	E0	192.168.2.1	255.255.255.0
	S0	192.168.10.246	255.255.255.252
	S1	192.168.10.241	255.255.255.252
C	S0	192.168.10.253	255.255.255.252
	S1	192.168.10.234	255.255.255.252
	S2	192.168.10.225	255.255.255.252
D	S0	192.168.10.250	255.255.255.252
	S1	192.168.10.242	255.255.255.252
	S2	192.168.10.237	255.255.255.252
E	E0	192.168.4.1	255.255.255.0
	S0	192.168.10.226	255.255.255.252
	S1	192.168.10.229	255.255.255.252
F	E0	192.168.3.1	255.255.255.0
	S0	192.168.10.230	255.255.255.252
	S1	192.168.10.233	255.255.255.252
	S2	192.168.10.238	255.255.255.252

6. Using the **distance** command, configure router D in Figure 13.21 to accept EIGRP routes only from router A. If the link to A fails, D should not accept routes from router B, although D should still advertise routes to B.

7. Remove the configuration added to D in Configuration Exercise 6. Configure router C in Figure 13.21 to route to all destinations, including the networks and subnets of the IS-IS domain, via router A. C should route through E and F only if the link to A fails.

TROUBLESHOOTING EXERCISES

1. A router has the following configuration:

```
router igrp 1
  network 10.0.0.0
  distribute-list 1 in Ethernet5/1
!
access-list 1 deny 0.0.0.0 255.255.255.255
access-list 1 permit any
```

The intention is to deny the incoming default route at interface E5/1 and to permit all other routes incoming on that interface. However, no routes are being accepted on E5/1. What is wrong?

2. Grimwig in Figure 13.12 has the following configuration:

```
router ospf 1
  redistribute rip metric 100
  network 192.168.5.1 0.0.0.0 area 0
  distance 255
  distance 110 0.0.0.0 255.255.255.255 1
!
router rip
  redistribute ospf 1 metric 2
  network 192.168.6.0
  distance 255
  distance 120 192.168.6.1 0.0.0.0 2
!
ip classless
access-list 1 permit 192.168.3.0
access-list 1 permit 192.168.4.0
access-list 2 permit 192.168.1.0
access-list 2 permit 192.168.2.0
```

What effect will this configuration have on the routes at Grimwig?

3. The routers in Figure 13.22 are running OSPF. Router B has the following configuration:

```
router ospf 50
  network 0.0.0.0 255.255.255.255 area 1
  distribute-list 1 in
!
access-list 1 deny 172.17.0.0
access-list 1 permit any
```

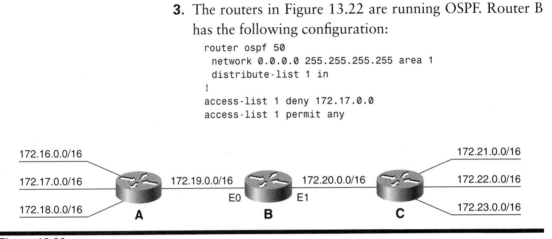

172.16.0.0/16
172.17.0.0/16   172.19.0.0/16   172.20.0.0/16   172.21.0.0/16
                      EO   E1   172.22.0.0/16
172.18.0.0/16   A   B   C   172.23.0.0/16

Figure 13.22
The internetwork for Troubleshooting Exercises 3 and 4.

The intention is to prevent routers B and C from having a route entry for network 172.17.0.0. This plan seems to be working at router B, but router C still has an entry for 172.17.0.0. Why?

4. The routers in Figure 13.22 are running RIP. Router B has the following configuration:

```
router rip
  network 172.19.0.0
  network 172.20.0.0
  distribute-list 1 out Ethernet0
  distribute-list 2 out Ethernet1
!
access-list 1 permit 172.18.0.0
access-list 2 permit 172.22.0.0
```

The intention is to advertise only network 172.22.0.0 to router A and to advertise only network 172.18.0.0 to router C. However, A and C have no RIP entries in their routing table. What is wrong?

- **Basic Uses of Route Maps**

- **Configuring Route Maps**

    Case Study: Policy Routing

    Case Study: Policy Routing and Quality of Service Routing

    Case Study: Route Maps and Redistribution

    Case Study: Route Tagging

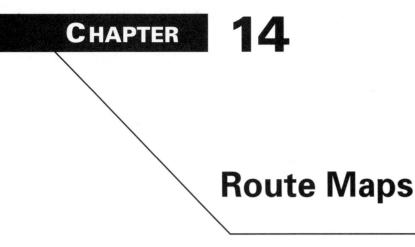

CHAPTER 14

Route Maps

Route maps are similar to access lists; they both have criteria for matching the details of certain packets and an action of permitting or denying those packets. Unlike access lists, though, route maps can add to each "match" criterion a "set" criterion that actually changes the packet in a specified manner, or changes route information in a specified manner.

BASIC USES OF ROUTE MAPS

Route maps can be used for both redistribution and for policy routing. They are also used frequently in large-scale Border Gateway Protocol (BGP) implementations. Although redistribution has been covered extensively in previous chapters, this chapter introduces the topic of policy routing.

Policy routes are nothing more than sophisticated static routes. Whereas static routes forward a packet to a specified next hop based on the destination address of the packet, policy routes forward a packet to a specified next hop based on the source of the packet. Policy routes can also be linked to extended IP access lists so that routing may be based on such things as protocol types and port numbers. Like a static route, a policy route influences the routing only of the router on which it is configured.

Policy routing

Figure 14.1 shows an example of a typical policy routing application. AbnerNet is connected to two Internet service providers via router Dogpatch. AbnerNet's corporate policy dictates that some users' Internet traffic should be sent via ISP 1 and other users' Internet traffic should be sent via ISP 2. If either ISP should become unavailable, the traffic normally using that provider will be sent to the other provider. A policy route at Dogpatch can distribute Internet traffic in accordance with local policy. The distribution of traffic might be based on subnet, specific user, or even user applications.

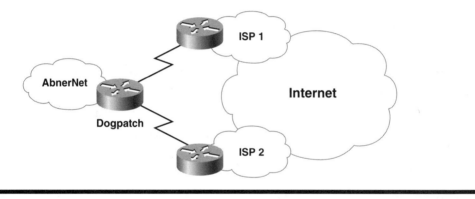

Figure 14.1

Policy routing allows traffic from AbnerNet to be routed to one of its two Internet service providers based on parameters such as source address, source/destination address combinations, packet size, application-level ports, or even packet length.

Figure 14.2 shows another use for policy routing. One of the systems on the right watches for invasion forces from the planet Mongo while the other stores back copies of *Dilbert* comic strips. Policy routes can be configured to route the critical traffic from the Mongo System to Flash_G over the FDDI link and to route the lower-priority Dilbert traffic over the 56K links. Or vice versa.

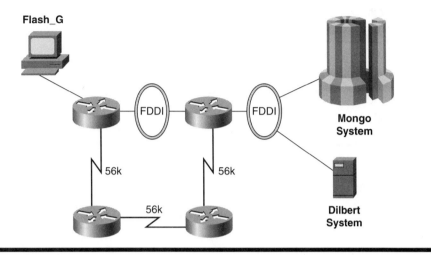

Figure 14.2

Policy routing allows high-priority traffic from the Mongo System to be routed over the FDDI link while low-priority traffic from the Dilbert System is routed over the 56K links.

Tables 14.1 and 14.2 show the **match** and **set** commands that can be used with redistribution, and Tables 14.3 and 14.4 show the **match** and **set** commands that can be used with policy routing.

Table 14.1   *Match commands that can be used with redistribution.*

Command	Description
match interface *type number* [*...type number*]	Matches routes that have their next hop out one of the interfaces specified.
match ip address {*access-list-number\name*} [*...access-list-number\name*]	Matches routes that have a destination address specified by one of the access lists.
match ip next-hop {*access-list-number\name*} [*...access-list-number\name*]	Matches routes that have a next-hop router address specified by one of the access lists.
match ip route-source {*access-list-number\name*} [*...access-list-number\name*]	Matches routes that have been advertised by routers at the addresses specified in the access lists.
match metric *metric-value*	Matches routes with the specified metric.

Table 14.1   *Match* commands that can be used with redistribution, continued.

Command	Description
match route-type {internal|external[type-1| type-2]|level-1|level-2}	Matches OSPF, EIGRP, or IS-IS routes of the specified type.
match tag *tag-value* [...*tag-value*]	Matches routes with the specified tags.

Table 14.2   *Set* commands that can be used with redistribution.

Command	Description
set level {level-1|level-2|level-1-2| stub-area|backbone}	Sets the IS-IS level or the OSPF area into which a matched route is to be redistributed.
set metric {*metric-value|bandwidth delay reliability loading mtu*}	Sets the metric value for a matched route.
set metric-type {internal|external|type-1| type-2}	Sets the metric type for a matched route being redistributed into IS-IS or OSPF.
set next-hop *next-hop*	Sets the next-hop router address for a matched route.
set tag *tag-value*	Sets a tag value for a matched route.

Table 14.3   *Match* commands that can be used with policy routing.

Command	Description
match ip address {*access-list-number|name*} [...*access-list-number|name*]	Matches a packet with the characteristics specified in the standard or extended access lists.
match length *min max*	Matches the level 3 length of a packet.

Table 14.4 *Set* commands that can be used with policy routing.

Command	Description
set default interface *type number* [...*type number*]	Sets the outgoing interface for matched packets when there is no explicit route to the destination.
set interface *type number* [...*type number*]	Sets the outgoing interface for matched packets when there is an explicit route to the destination.
set ip default next-hop *ip-address* [...*ip-address*]	Sets the next-hop router address for matched packets when there is no explicit route to the destination.
set ip next-hop *ip-address* [...*ip-address*]	Sets the next-hop router address for matched packets when there is an explicit route to the destination.
set ip precedence *precedence*	Sets the precedence bits in the Type of Service field of matched IP packets.
set ip tos *type-of-service*	Sets the TOS bits in the Type of Service field of matched packets.

CONFIGURING ROUTE MAPS

Like access lists (see Appendix B, "Tutorial: Access Lists"), route maps by themselves affect nothing; they must be "called" by some command. The command will be either a policy routing command or a redistribution command. Policy routing will send packets to the route map, whereas redistribution will send routes to the route map. The case studies in this section demonstrate the use of route maps for both redistribution and policy routing.

Route maps are identified by a name. For example, the following route map is named Hagar:

```
route-map Hagar permit 10
  match ip address 110
  set metric 100
```

Each route map statement has a "permit" or "deny" action and a sequence number. This route map shows a permit action and a sequence number of 10. These settings are the defaults—that is, if no action or sequence number is specified when the route map is configured, the route map will default to a permit and a sequence number of 10.

The sequence number allows the identification and editing of multiple statements. Consider the following configuration steps:

```
Linus(config)#route-map Hagar 20
Linus(config-route-map)#match ip address 111
Linus(config-route-map)#set metric 50
Linus(config-route-map)#route-map Hagar 15
Linus(config-route-map)#match ip address 112
Linus(config-route-map)#set metric 80
```

Here a second and third set of route map statements, each with their own **match** and **set** statements, have been added to route map Hagar. Notice that a sequence number of 20 was configured first and then a sequence number of 15. In the final configuration, the IOS has placed statement 15 before 20 even though it was entered later:[1]

```
route-map Hagar permit 10
  match ip address 110
  set metric 100
!
route-map Hagar permit 15
  match ip address 112
  set metric 80
!
route-map Hagar permit 20
  match ip address 111
  set metric 50
```

The sequence numbers also allow for the elimination of individual statements. For example, the statement:

```
Linus(config)#no route-map Hagar 15
```

deletes statement 15 and leaves the other statements intact:

```
route-map Hagar permit 10
  match ip address 110
  set metric 100
```

---

[1]   *Notice also that no action was specified in the configuration steps, so the default "permit" appears in the final configuration.*

```
!
route-map Hagar permit 20
  match ip address 111
  set metric 50
```

Caution must be used when editing route maps. In this example, if **no route-map Hagar** had been typed, without specifying a sequence number, the entire route map would have been deleted. Likewise, if no sequence numbers had been specified when the additional **match** and **set** statements were added, they would have simply changed statement 10.

A packet or route is passed sequentially through route map statements. If a match is made, any **set** statements are executed and the permit or deny action is executed. As with access lists, processing stops when a match is made and the specified action is executed; the route or packet is not passed to subsequent statements. Consider the following route map:

```
route-map Sluggo permit 10
  match ip route-source 1
  set next-hop 192.168.1.5
!
route-map Sluggo permit 20
  match ip route-source 2
  set next-hop 192.168.1.10
!
route-map Sluggo permit 30
  match ip route-source 3
  set next-hop 192.168.1.15
```

If a route does not match statement 10, it will be passed to statement 20. If a match is made at statement 20, the **set** command will be executed and the route will be permitted. The matched route will not be passed on to statement 30.

The behavior of a "deny" action depends on whether the route map is being used for policy routing or for redistribution. If a route map is being used for redistribution and a route matches a statement with a deny action, the route will not be redistributed. If the route map is being used for policy routing and a packet matches a statement with a deny action, the packet is not policy routed, but is passed back to the normal routing process for forwarding.

Again as with access lists, there must be a default action for the route map to take in the event that a route or packet passes through every statement without a match. An implicit deny exists at the end of every route map. Routes that pass through a redistribution route map without a match are not redistributed, and packets that pass through a policy route map without a match are sent to the normal routing process.

Implicit deny

If no **match** statement is configured under a route map statement, the default action is to match everything.

Each map statement may have multiple **match** and **set** statements, as follows:

```
route-map Garfield permit 10
   match ip route-source 15
   match interface Serial0
   set metric-type type-1
   set next-hop 10.1.2.3
```

In a case such as this, every **match** statement must be matched for the **set** statements to be executed.

Case Study: Policy Routing

Policy routing is defined with the command **ip policy route-map**. The command is configured on an interface and affects incoming packets only.

Suppose a policy were to be implemented on Linus in Figure 14.3 such that traffic from subnet 172.16.6.0/24 is forwarded to Lucy and traffic from subnet 172.16.7.0/24 is forwarded to Pigpen. Linus's configuration is:

```
interface Serial0
   ip address 172.16.5.1 255.255.255.0
   ip policy route-map Sally
```

```
!
access-list 1 permit 172.16.6.0 0.0.0.255
access-list 2 permit 172.16.7.0 0.0.0.255
!
route-map Sally permit 10
  match ip address 1
  set ip next-hop 172.16.4.2
!
route-map Sally permit 15
  match ip address 2
  set ip next-hop 172.16.4.3
```

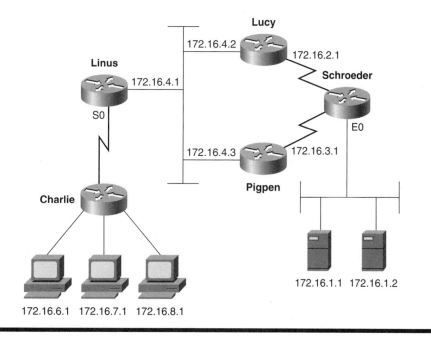

Figure 14.3

Policy routes can be configured at Linus to route some packets through Lucy and other packets through Pigpen.

The policy routing command on S0 sends incoming packets to route map Sally. Statement 10 of route map Sally uses access list 1 to identify source addresses from subnet 172.16.6.0/24. If a match is made, the packet is forwarded to Lucy, whose next-hop interface address is 172.16.4.2. If no match is made, the packet is sent to statement 15. That statement uses access list 2 to match source addresses from subnet 172.16.7.0/24. If a match is made at that statement, the packet is forwarded to Pigpen (172.16.4.3). Any packets that do not match statement 15, such as packets sourced from subnet 172.16.8.0/24, are routed normally. Figure 14.4 shows the results of the policy route.[2]

```
Linus#debug ip packet 5
IP packet debugging is on for access list 5
Linus#
IP: s=172.16.7.1 (Serial0), d=172.16.1.1 (Ethernet0), g=172.16.4.3, len 60, forward
IP: s=172.16.7.1 (Serial0), d=172.16.1.1 (Ethernet0), g=172.16.4.3, len 60, forward
IP: s=172.16.7.1 (Serial0), d=172.16.1.1 (Ethernet0), g=172.16.4.3, len 60, forward
IP: s=172.16.7.1 (Serial0), d=172.16.1.1 (Ethernet0), g=172.16.4.3, len 60, forward
IP: s=172.16.6.1 (Serial0), d=172.16.1.1 (Ethernet0), g=172.16.4.2, len 60, forward
IP: s=172.16.6.1 (Serial0), d=172.16.1.1 (Ethernet0), g=172.16.4.2, len 60, forward
IP: s=172.16.6.1 (Serial0), d=172.16.1.1 (Ethernet0), g=172.16.4.2, len 60, forward
IP: s=172.16.6.1 (Serial0), d=172.16.1.1 (Ethernet0), g=172.16.4.2, len 60, forward
IP: s=172.16.8.1 (Serial0), d=172.16.1.1 (Ethernet0), g=172.16.4.2, len 60, forward
IP: s=172.16.8.1 (Serial0), d=172.16.1.1 (Ethernet0), g=172.16.4.3, len 60, forward
IP: s=172.16.8.1 (Serial0), d=172.16.1.1 (Ethernet0), g=172.16.4.2, len 60, forward
IP: s=172.16.8.1 (Serial0), d=172.16.1.1 (Ethernet0), g=172.16.4.3, len 60, forward
```

Figure 14.4

The policy route configured on Linus's S0 interface routes packets from subnet 172.16.6.0/24 to Lucy (172.16.4.2) and routes packets from subnet 172.16.7.0/24 to Pigpen (172.16.4.3). Packets from subnet 172.16.8.0/24, which do not match the policy route, are routed normally (load balancing between Lucy and Pigpen).

Standard IP access lists are used when policy routing by source address only. To route by both source and destination, an extended IP access list is used. The following configuration causes packets from any subnet to host 172.16.1.1 to be forwarded to Lucy, whereas packets from host 172.16.7.1 to host 172.16.1.2 are forwarded to Pigpen. All other packets are routed normally:

---

[2]   Note that the **debug ip packet** command references an access list 5. This access list permits only the subnets connected to router Charlie so that uninteresting traffic is not displayed by the debug function.

```
interface Serial0
  ip address 172.16.5.1 255.255.255.0
  ip policy route-map Sally
!
access-list 101 permit ip any host 172.16.1.1
access-list 102 permit ip host 172.16.7.1 host 172.16.1.2
!
route-map Sally permit 10
  match ip address 101
  set ip next-hop 172.16.4.2
!
route-map Sally permit 15
  match ip address 102
  set ip next-hop 172.16.4.3
```

Route map Sally is again used, except the **match** statements now reference access lists 101 and 102. Figure 14.5 shows the results.

```
Linus#debug ip packet 5
IP packet debugging is on for access list 5
Linus#
IP: s=172.16.7.1 (Serial0), d=172.16.1.1 (Ethernet0), g=172.16.4.2, len 60, forward
IP: s=172.16.7.1 (Serial0), d=172.16.1.1 (Ethernet0), g=172.16.4.2, len 60, forward
IP: s=172.16.7.1 (Serial0), d=172.16.1.1 (Ethernet0), g=172.16.4.2, len 60, forward
IP: s=172.16.7.1 (Serial0), d=172.16.1.1 (Ethernet0), g=172.16.4.2, len 60, forward
IP: s=172.16.7.1 (Serial0), d=172.16.1.2 (Ethernet0), g=172.16.4.3, len 60, forward
IP: s=172.16.7.1 (Serial0), d=172.16.1.2 (Ethernet0), g=172.16.4.3, len 60, forward
IP: s=172.16.7.1 (Serial0), d=172.16.1.2 (Ethernet0), g=172.16.4.3, len 60, forward
IP: s=172.16.7.1 (Serial0), d=172.16.1.2 (Ethernet0), g=172.16.4.3, len 60, forward
IP: s=172.16.7.254 (Serial0), d=172.16.1.2 (Ethernet0), g=172.16.4.3, len 60, forward
IP: s=172.16.7.254 (Serial0), d=172.16.1.2 (Ethernet0), g=172.16.4.2, len 60, forward
IP: s=172.16.7.254 (Serial0), d=172.16.1.2 (Ethernet0), g=172.16.4.3, len 60, forward
IP: s=172.16.7.254 (Serial0), d=172.16.1.2 (Ethernet0), g=172.16.4.2, len 60, forward
```

Figure 14.5

Packets from host 172.16.7.1 to host 172.16.1.1 match statement 10 of route map Sally and are forwarded to Lucy. Packets from the same host to host 172.16.1.2 are forwarded to Pigpen. Packets from another address on subnet 172.16.7.0/24 to host 172.16.1.2 are not matched by Sally and are routed normally.

Next, suppose your policy states that FTP traffic from the servers on subnet 172.16.1.0/24 should be forwarded to Lucy and that Telnet traffic from the same servers should be forwarded to

Pigpen. This plan allows the bulk FTP traffic and the bursty, inter-active Telnet traffic to be segregated on the two serial links from Schroeder. Schroeder will have the following configuration:

```
interface Ethernet0
  ip address 172.16.1.4 255.255.255.0
  ip policy route-map Rerun
!
access-list 105 permit tcp 172.16.1.0 0.0.0.255 eq ftp any
access-list 105 permit tcp 172.16.1.0 0.0.0.255 eq ftp-data any
access-list 106 permit tcp 172.16.1.0 0.0.0.255 eq telnet any
!
route-map Rerun permit 10
  match ip address 105
  set ip next-hop 172.16.2.1
!
route-map Rerun permit 20
  match ip address 106
  set ip next-hop 172.16.3.1
```

Access lists 105 and 106 are examining not only the source and destination addresses but also the source port. In Figure 14.6, the **detail** option is used with **debug ip packet** to allow observation of the packet types being forwarded by Schroeder. An access list 10 limits the displayed packets to those from 172.16.1.1 to 172.16.6.1.

The purpose of segregating bulk and interactive traffic, as demonstrated in the last example, is so that the small packets characteristic of interactive traffic do not become delayed by the large packets characteristic of bulk traffic. The problem with the approach in this example is that if many types of traffic must be segregated, the access lists identifying the traffic by destination port may become prohibitively large.

If the objective is to segregate small packets from large packets, the length of the packet can be matched:

```
interface Ethernet0
  ip address 172.16.1.4 255.255.255.0
  ip policy route-map Woodstock
!
route-map Woodstock permit 20
```

```
    match length 1000 1600
    set ip next-hop 172.16.2.1
  !
  route-map Woodstock permit 30
    match length 0 400
    set ip next-hop 172.16.3.1
```

Here the **match length** statement specifies a minimum and a maximum packet size. Statement 20 of the route map causes all packets between 1000 and 1600 octets in length to be routed across the serial link to Lucy. Statement 30 causes all packets up to 400 octets in length to be routed across the serial link to Pigpen. Packets between 400 and 1000 octets are routed normally.

```
Schroeder#debug ip packet detail 10
IP packet debugging is on (detailed) for access list 10
Schroeder#
IP: s=172.16.1.2 (Ethernet0), d=172.16.6.1 (Serial0), g=172.16.2.1, len 1064, forward
    TCP src=20, dst=1047, seq=3702770065, ack=591246297, win=14335 ACK PSH
IP: s=172.16.1.2 (Ethernet0), d=172.16.6.1 (Serial0), g=172.16.2.1, len 64, forward
    TCP src=21, dst=1046, seq=3662108731, ack=591205663, win=14335 ACK PSH
IP: s=172.16.1.2 (Ethernet0), d=172.16.6.1 (Serial0), g=172.16.2.1, len 1476, forward
    TCP src=20, dst=1047, seq=3702771089, ack=591246297, win=14335 ACK PSH
IP: s=172.16.1.2 (Ethernet0), d=172.16.6.1 (Serial1), g=172.16.3.1, len 40, forward
    TCP src=23, dst=1048, seq=3734385279, ack=591277873, win=14332 ACK
IP: s=172.16.1.2 (Ethernet0), d=172.16.6.1 (Serial1), g=172.16.3.1, len 52, forward
    TCP src=23, dst=1048, seq=3734385279, ack=591277873, win=14335 ACK PSH
IP: s=172.16.1.2 (Ethernet0), d=172.16.6.1 (Serial1), g=172.16.3.1, len 40, forward
    TCP src=23, dst=1048, seq=3734385291, ack=591277876, win=14332 ACK
IP: s=172.16.1.2 (Ethernet0), d=172.16.6.1 (Serial0), g=172.16.2.1, len 60, forward
    ICMP type=0, code=0
IP: s=172.16.1.2 (Ethernet0), d=172.16.6.1 (Serial1), g=172.16.3.1, len 60, forward
    ICMP type=0, code=0
IP: s=172.16.1.2 (Ethernet0), d=172.16.6.1 (Serial0), g=172.16.2.1, len 60, forward
    ICMP type=0, code=0
IP: s=172.16.1.2 (Ethernet0), d=172.16.6.1 (Serial1), g=172.16.3.1, len 60, forward
    ICMP type=0, code=0
```

Figure 14.6

FTP packets (TCP ports 20 and 21) are being forwarded to Lucy, whereas Telnet packets (TCP port 23) with the same source and destination addresses are forwarded to Pigpen. Echo Reply packets (ICMP type 0), which do not find a match in the policy route, are routed normally.

Figure 14.7 shows the results of the new route map. Again there are FTP, Telnet, and Echo Reply packets from 172.16.1.2 to 172.16.6.1, but now the packets are routed according to their size instead of their addresses and ports.

```
Schroeder#debug ip packet detail 10
IP packet debugging is on (detailed) for access list 10
Schroeder#
IP: s=172.16.1.2 (Ethernet0), d=172.16.6.1 (Serial0), g=172.16.2.1, len 1476, forward
    TCP src=20, dst=1063, seq=1528444161, ack=601956937, win=14335 ACK PSH
IP: s=172.16.1.2 (Ethernet0), d=172.16.6.1 (Serial0), g=172.16.2.1, len 1476, forward
    TCP src=20, dst=1063, seq=1528442725, ack=601956937, win=14335 ACK PSH
IP: s=172.16.1.2 (Ethernet0), d=172.16.6.1 (Serial0), g=172.16.2.1, len 1476, forward
    TCP src=20, dst=1063, seq=1528444161, ack=601956937, win=14335 ACK PSH
IP: s=172.16.1.2 (Ethernet0), d=172.16.6.1 (Serial1), g=172.16.3.1, len 840, forward
    TCP src=20, dst=1063, seq=1528445597, ack=601956937, win=14335 ACK PSH
IP: s=172.16.1.2 (Ethernet0), d=172.16.6.1 (Serial1), g=172.16.3.1, len 40, forward
    TCP src=21, dst=1062, seq=1469372904, ack=601897901, win=14329 ACK
IP: s=172.16.1.2 (Ethernet0), d=172.16.6.1 (Serial1), g=172.16.3.1, len 54, forward
    TCP src=21, dst=1062, seq=1469372904, ack=601897901, win=14335 ACK PSH
IP: s=172.16.1.2 (Ethernet0), d=172.16.6.1 (Serial1), g=172.16.3.1, len 40, forward
    TCP src=21, dst=1062, seq=1469372918, ack=601897901, win=14335 ACK FIN
IP: s=172.16.1.2 (Ethernet0), d=172.16.6.1 (Serial1), g=172.16.3.1, len 44, forward
    TCP src=23, dst=1064, seq=1712116521, ack=602140570, win=14335 ACK SYN
IP: s=172.16.1.2 (Ethernet0), d=172.16.6.1 (Serial1), g=172.16.3.1, len 43, forward
    TCP src=23, dst=1064, seq=1712116522, ack=602140570, win=14335 ACK PSH
IP: s=172.16.1.2 (Ethernet0), d=172.16.6.1 (Serial1), g=172.16.3.1, len 40, forward
    TCP src=23, dst=1064, seq=1712116525, ack=602140573, win=14332 ACK
IP: s=172.16.1.2 (Ethernet0), d=172.16.6.1 (Serial1), g=172.16.3.1, len 52, forward
    TCP src=23, dst=1064, seq=1712116525, ack=602140573, win=14335 ACK PSH
IP: s=172.16.1.2 (Ethernet0), d=172.16.6.1 (Serial1), g=172.16.3.1, len 60, forward
    ICMP type=0, code=0
IP: s=172.16.1.2 (Ethernet0), d=172.16.6.1 (Serial1), g=172.16.3.1, len 60, forward
    ICMP type=0, code=0
IP: s=172.16.1.2 (Ethernet0), d=172.16.6.1 (Serial1), g=172.16.3.1, len 60, forward
    ICMP type=0, code=0
IP: s=172.16.1.2 (Ethernet0), d=172.16.6.1 (Serial1), g=172.16.3.1, len 60, forward
    ICMP type=0, code=0
```

Figure 14.7

Packets of 1000 octets or larger are routed to Lucy, whereas packets of 400 octets or less are routed to Pigpen. Any packets between 400 and 1000 octets are routed normally.

The policy routes demonstrated so far affect packets entering the router from a particular interface. But what about packets generated by the router itself? These can also be policy routed, with the command **ip local policy route-map**. Unlike the **ip policy route-map** command, which is configured on an interface, this command is configured globally on the router.

To apply the previously demonstrated policy to packets generated by Schroeder, the configuration is:

```
interface Ethernet0
  ip address 172.16.1.4 255.255.255.0
  ip policy route-map Woodstock
!
ip local policy route-map Woodstock
!
access-list 120 permit ip any 172.16.1.0 0.0.0.255
access-list 120 permit ospf any any
!
route-map Woodstock permit 10
  match ip address 120
!
route-map Woodstock permit 20
  match length 1000 1600
  set ip next-hop 172.16.2.1
!
route-map Woodstock permit 30
  match length 0 400
  set ip next-hop 172.16.3.1
```

Of particular interest is statement 10. This statement does not have a **set** statement, but merely permits packets that match access list 120. Access list 120, in turn, permits all OSPF packets and all packets destined for subnet 172.16.1.0/24. Without the first line of the access list, some packets originated by Schroeder and destined for subnet 172.16.1.0/24 would be forwarded to the wrong interface by statement 20 or 30. Figure 14.8 shows why the second line of the access list is necessary. The length of Schroeder's OSPF Hellos is 44 octets. If statement 10 were not included, the OSPF Hellos would all match statement 30 and be forwarded to Pigpen, breaking the adjacency between Lucy and Schroeder. By matching statement 10, the OSPF packets are permitted with no changes and are forwarded normally.

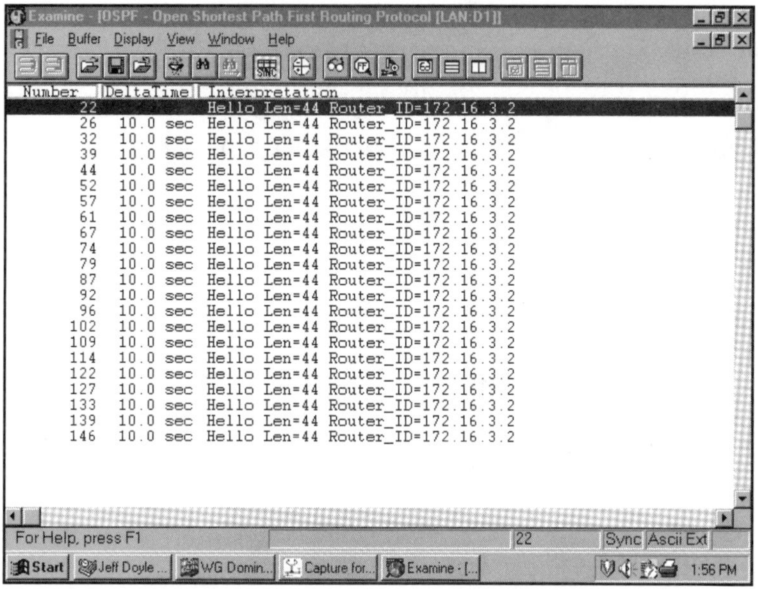

Figure 14.8
The length of the OSPF Hello packets is seen in this analyzer capture.

Case Study: Policy Routing and Quality of Service Routing

Although Quality of Service (QoS) routing is outside the scope of this volume, it must be noted here that policy routing can be an integral part of QoS. Policy routing in conjunction with QoS is done by setting the Precedence or the Type of Service (TOS) bits of the TOS field in the IP headers of packets as they enter a router's interface. Figure 14.9 shows the bits of the TOS field. Although the TOS bits are seldom used in modern internetworks, the Precedence bits have found new life in QoS applications. The TOS bits are used to influence the path a router selects for a packet, whereas the Precedence bits are used to prioritize packets within a router.

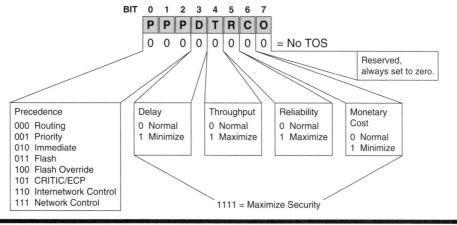

Figure 14.9

The Precedence and TOS bits of the Type of Service field of the IP header.

The Precedence bits are set by using the **set ip Precedence** statement within a route map. The Precedence may be set by specifying the decimal equivalent of the three Precedence bits or by using keywords. Table 14.5 shows the decimal numbers and the keywords that can be used.

Table 14.5   *Precedence values and keywords used with the **set ip precedence** command.*

Bits	Number	Keyword
000	0	routine
001	1	priority
010	2	immediate
011	3	flash
100	4	flash-override
101	5	critical
110	6	internet
111	7	network

Table 14.6   *TOS values and keywords used with the **set ip tos** command.*

Bits	Number (0-15)	Keyword
0000	0	normal
0001	1	min-monetary-cost
0010	2	max-reliability
0100	4	max-throughput
1000	8	min-delay

The TOS bits are set by using the **set ip tos** statement. Like the Precedence statement, the argument of the statement may be a number or a keyword, as shown in Table 14.6. Unlike Precedence, you may use a combination of TOS values. For example, specifying a TOS value of 12 (1100b) means *minimum delay* and *maximum throughput*. Only a single keyword can be used, so to set a combination of TOS values, a number must be specified.

Figure 14.10 shows an example of how policy routes can be used for QoS routing. Here, router Pogo is at the "edge" of the internet OkefenokeeNet. By configuring policy routes on Pogo's serial links, the Precedence and/or TOS bits of incoming packets can be changed so that IP traffic is divided into several traffic classes. For instance:

```
interface Serial0
  ip address 10.1.18.67 255.255.255.252
  ip policy route-map Albert
!
interface Serial1
  ip address 10.34.16.83 255.255.255.252
  ip policy route-map Albert
!
access-list 1 permit 172.16.0.0 0.0.255.255
access-list 110 permit tcp any eq www any
!
route-map Albert permit 10
  match ip address 1 110
  set ip precedence critical
```

```
!
route-map Albert permit 20
  set ip tos 10
  set ip precedence priority
```

Statement 10 says that if packets match both access lists 1 and 110, the Precedence will be set to *critical*. Notice that statement 20 has no **match** statement. This statement will match any packets that haven't been matched by statement 10. There are also two **set** statements under statement 20. These statements will set the TOS bits to *minimum delay* and *maximum reliability* and will set the Precedence bits to *priority*. Figure 14.11 shows a capture of a packet from somewhere inside OkefenokeeNet, which has been modified by the route map at Pogo.

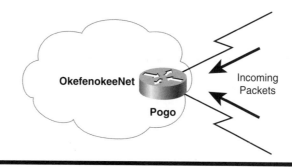

Figure 14.10

Policy routes can be used to set the Precedence or TOS bits of packets entering an internetwork. The routers within the internetwork can then make QoS decisions based on the setting of these bits.

After the Precedence or TOS bits have been set in packets entering the internetwork, the routers within the internet can make QoS decisions based in part or wholly on the class of service these bits define. For example, priority, custom, or weighted fair queuing may be configured to prioritize traffic according to the Precedence or TOS bits. In some implementations, Precedence can be used with congestion avoidance mechanisms such as Weighted Random Early Detection (WRED). Or a crude Class-of-Service routing can be implemented by configuring access lists that permit or

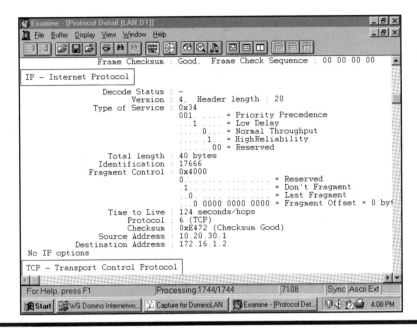

Figure 14.11

Pogo's policy route has set the Precedence bits of this packet to priority (001b) and the TOS bits to minimum delay and maximum reliability (1010b).

deny packets across certain links based on the setting of their Precedence or TOS bits.

Case Study: Route Maps and Redistribution

A route map can be used with redistribution by adding a call to the route map in the **redistribute** command. Figure 14.12 shows an internetwork in which IS-IS and OSPF routes are being mutually redistributed at router Zippy. Of the network and subnet addresses listed in the illustration, only the ones whose third octet is odd-numbered are to be redistributed. Zippy's configuration is:

```
router ospf 1
  redistribute isis level-1 metric 20 subnets route-map Griffy
  network 172.16.10.2 0.0.0.0 area 5
!
router isis
  redistribute ospf 1 metric 25 route-map Toad metric-type internal level-2
  net 47.0001.1234.5678.9056.00
!
access-list 1 permit 192.168.2.0
access-list 1 permit 192.168.4.0
access-list 1 permit 192.168.6.0
access-list 2 permit 172.16.1.0
access-list 2 permit 172.16.3.0
access-list 2 permit 172.16.5.0
access-list 2 permit 172.16.7.0
access-list 2 permit 172.16.9.0
!
route-map Griffy deny 10
  match ip address 1
!
route-map Griffy permit 20
!
route-map Toad permit 10
  match ip address 2
```

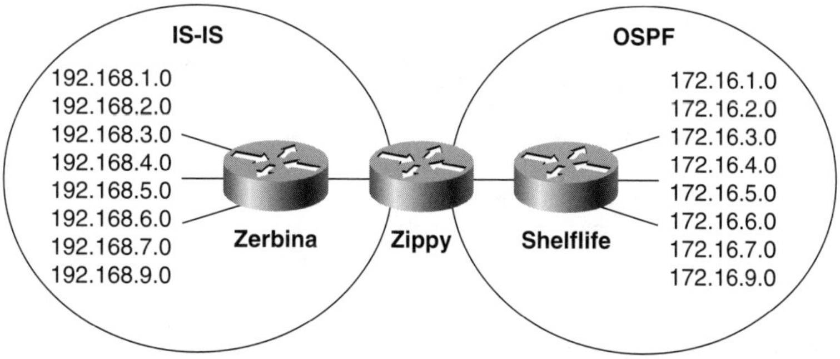

Figure 14.12

The OSPF and IS-IS routes are being mutually redistributed. Route maps can be used with the **redistribute** *command as simple route filters, or they can be used to modify characteristics of the redistributed routes.*

Route maps Griffy and Toad perform the same functions, but with different logic. Griffy uses negative logic, identifying the routes that should not be redistributed, and Toad uses positive logic, identifying the routes that should be redistributed.

Statement 10 of Griffy denies any routes that are permitted by access list 1 (the addresses with an even third octet). Because the addresses with odd-numbered third octets do not find a match at statement 10, they are passed to statement 20. Statement 20 has no **match** statement, so the default is to match everything. Statement 20 has a permit action, so the odd routes are permitted. The result is shown in Figure 14.13.

```
Shelflife#show ip route
Codes: C - connected, S - static, I - IGRP, R - RIP, M - mobile, B - BGP
       D - EIGRP, EX - EIGRP external, O - OSPF, IA - OSPF inter area
       E1 - OSPF external type 1, E2 - OSPF external type 2, E - EGP
       i - IS-IS, L1 - IS-IS level-1, L2 - IS-IS level-2, * - candidate default

Gateway of last resort is not set

O E2 192.168.9.0 [110/20] via 172.16.10.2, 00:24:46, Ethernet0
O E2 192.168.1.0 [110/20] via 172.16.10.2, 00:24:46, Ethernet0
O E2 192.168.3.0 [110/20] via 172.16.10.2, 00:24:46, Ethernet0
O E2 192.168.5.0 [110/20] via 172.16.10.2, 00:24:47, Ethernet0
O E2 192.168.7.0 [110/20] via 172.16.10.2, 00:24:47, Ethernet0
     172.16.0.0 255.255.255.0 is subnetted, 9 subnets
C       172.16.9.0 is directly connected, Serial0
C       172.16.10.0 is directly connected, Ethernet0
O       172.16.4.0 [110/159] via 172.16.9.2, 14:05:33, Serial0
O       172.16.5.0 [110/159] via 172.16.9.2, 14:05:33, Serial0
O       172.16.6.0 [110/159] via 172.16.9.2, 14:05:33, Serial0
O       172.16.7.0 [110/159] via 172.16.9.2, 14:05:33, Serial0
O       172.16.1.0 [110/159] via 172.16.9.2, 14:05:33, Serial0
O       172.16.2.0 [110/159] via 172.16.9.2, 14:05:33, Serial0
O       172.16.3.0 [110/159] via 172.16.9.2, 14:05:33, Serial0
Shelflife#
```

Figure 14.13

The only destinations within the IS-IS domain that are contained in Shelflife's route table are those with an odd-numbered third octet.

Route map Toad has a single statement that permits routes that have been permitted by access list 2 (addresses with an odd third octet). The addresses with an even third octet do not find a match at access list 2. The default route map statement when redistributing is to deny all routes, so the addresses that are not matched by access list 2 are not redistributed. Figure 14.14 shows the results of route map Toad.

```
Zerbina#show ip route
Codes: C - connected, S - static, I - IGRP, R - RIP, M - mobile, B - BGP
       D - EIGRP, EX - EIGRP external, O - OSPF, IA - OSPF inter area
       N1 - OSPF NSSA external type 1, N2 - OSPF NSSA external type 2
       E1 - OSPF external type 1, E2 - OSPF external type 2, E - EGP
       i - IS-IS, L1 - IS-IS level-1, L2 - IS-IS level-2, * - candidate default
       U - per-user static route, o - ODR

Gateway of last resort is not set

C    192.168.9.0/24 is directly connected, Serial0
C    192.168.10.0/24 is directly connected, Ethernet0
i L1 192.168.1.0/24 [115/15] via 192.168.9.2, Serial0
i L1 192.168.2.0/24 [115/15] via 192.168.9.2, Serial0
i L1 192.168.3.0/24 [115/15] via 192.168.9.2, Serial0
i L1 192.168.4.0/24 [115/15] via 192.168.9.2, Serial0
i L1 192.168.5.0/24 [115/15] via 192.168.9.2, Serial0
i L1 192.168.6.0/24 [115/15] via 192.168.9.2, Serial0
i L1 192.168.7.0/24 [115/15] via 192.168.9.2, Serial0
     172.16.0.0/24 is subnetted, 5 subnets
i L2    172.16.9.0 [115/35] via 192.168.10.2, Ethernet0
i L2    172.16.5.0 [115/35] via 192.168.10.2, Ethernet0
i L2    172.16.7.0 [115/35] via 192.168.10.2, Ethernet0
i L2    172.16.1.0 [115/35] via 192.168.10.2, Ethernet0
i L2    172.16.3.0 [115/35] via 192.168.10.2, Ethernet0
Zerbina#
```

Figure 14.14

The only destinations within the OSPF domain that are contained in Zerbina's route table are those with an odd-numbered third octet.

Other configurations will achieve the same ends. For instance, route map Toad will have the same effect with the following access list:

```
access-list 2 deny 172.16.2.0
access-list 2 deny 172.16.4.0
access-list 2 deny 172.16.6.0
access-list 2 permit any
```

Although route maps work fine as simple route filters, their strength lies in their ability to change the routes in various ways. Consider the following configuration of Zippy in Figure 14.12:

```
router ospf 1
  redistribute isis level-1 metric 20 subnets route-map Griffy
  network 172.16.10.2 0.0.0.0 area 5
!
router isis
  redistribute ospf 1 metric 25 route-map Toad metric-type internal level-2
  net 47.0001.1234.5678.9056.00
!
ip classless
access-list 1 permit 192.168.2.0
access-list 1 permit 192.168.4.0
access-list 1 permit 192.168.6.0
access-list 2 permit 172.16.9.0
access-list 2 permit 172.16.5.0
access-list 2 permit 172.16.7.0
access-list 2 permit 172.16.1.0
access-list 2 permit 172.16.3.0
!
route-map Griffy permit 10
  match ip address 1
  set metric-type type-1
!
route-map Griffy permit 20
!
route-map Toad permit 10
  match ip address 2
  set metric 15
  set level level-1
!
route-map Toad permit 20
```

Statement 10 of route map Griffy permits routes to the addresses in access list 1 and redistributes them into OSPF as type 1 external routes. Statement 20 permits all other routes, which will be redistributed with the default external type 2. Figure 14.15 shows the results.

Statement 10 of route map Toad permits routes to addresses in access list 2 and redistributes them into IS-IS as level 1 routes. Their metric is set to 15. Statement 20 permits all other routes,

```
Shelflife#show ip route
Codes: C - connected, S - static, I - IGRP, R - RIP, M - mobile, B - BGP
       D - EIGRP, EX - EIGRP external, O - OSPF, IA - OSPF inter area
       E1 - OSPF external type 1, E2 - OSPF external type 2, E - EGP
       i - IS-IS, L1 - IS-IS level-1, L2 - IS-IS level-2, * - candidate default

Gateway of last resort is not set

O E2 192.168.9.0 [110/20] via 172.16.10.2, 00:13:43, Ethernet0
O E2 192.168.1.0 [110/20] via 172.16.10.2, 00:13:43, Ethernet0
O E1 192.168.2.0 [110/30] via 172.16.10.2, 00:13:43, Ethernet0
O E2 192.168.3.0 [110/20] via 172.16.10.2, 00:13:44, Ethernet0
O E1 192.168.4.0 [110/30] via 172.16.10.2, 00:13:44, Ethernet0
O E2 192.168.5.0 [110/20] via 172.16.10.2, 00:13:44, Ethernet0
O E1 192.168.6.0 [110/30] via 172.16.10.2, 00:13:44, Ethernet0
O E2 192.168.7.0 [110/20] via 172.16.10.2, 00:13:44, Ethernet0
     172.16.0.0 255.255.255.0 is subnetted, 9 subnets
C       172.16.9.0 is directly connected, Serial0
C       172.16.10.0 is directly connected, Ethernet0
O       172.16.4.0 [110/159] via 172.16.9.2, 15:49:29, Serial0
O       172.16.5.0 [110/159] via 172.16.9.2, 15:49:30, Serial0
O       172.16.6.0 [110/159] via 172.16.9.2, 15:49:30, Serial0
O       172.16.7.0 [110/159] via 172.16.9.2, 15:49:30, Serial0
O       172.16.1.0 [110/159] via 172.16.9.2, 15:49:30, Serial0
O       172.16.2.0 [110/159] via 172.16.9.2, 15:49:30, Serial0
O       172.16.3.0 [110/159] via 172.16.9.2, 15:49:30, Serial0
Shelflife#
```

Figure 14.15

The routes to destinations in the IS-IS domain are E1 if the third octet of the address is even and E2 if the third octet is odd.

which will be redistributed as level 2 and with a metric of 25, as specified by the **redistribute** command under the IS-IS configuration (Figure 14.16).

Case Study: Route Tagging

Figure 14.17 shows a situation in which routes from several routing domains, each running a separate routing protocol, are being redistributed into a single transit domain running OSPF. On the other side of the OSPF cloud, the routes must be redistributed back into their respective domains. Route filters can be used at the egress points from the OSPF cloud into each domain to permit only the routes that belong to that domain. However, if each domain has many routes or if the routes within the domain change frequently, the route filters can become difficult to manage.

```
Zerbina#show ip route
Codes: C - connected, S - static, I - IGRP, R - RIP, M - mobile, B - BGP
       D - EIGRP, EX - EIGRP external, O - OSPF, IA - OSPF inter area
       N1 - OSPF NSSA external type 1, N2 - OSPF NSSA external type 2
       E1 - OSPF external type 1, E2 - OSPF external type 2, E - EGP
       i - IS-IS, L1 - IS-IS level-1, L2 - IS-IS level-2, * - candidate default
       U - per-user static route, o - ODR

Gateway of last resort is not set

C      192.168.9.0/24 is directly connected, Serial0
C      192.168.10.0/24 is directly connected, Ethernet0
i L1 192.168.1.0/24 [115/15] via 192.168.9.2, Serial0
i L1 192.168.2.0/24 [115/15] via 192.168.9.2, Serial0
i L1 192.168.3.0/24 [115/15] via 192.168.9.2, Serial0
i L1 192.168.4.0/24 [115/15] via 192.168.9.2, Serial0
i L1 192.168.5.0/24 [115/15] via 192.168.9.2, Serial0
i L1 192.168.6.0/24 [115/15] via 192.168.9.2, Serial0
i L1 192.168.7.0/24 [115/15] via 192.168.9.2, Serial0
       172.16.0.0/24 is subnetted, 8 subnets
i L1     172.16.9.0 [115/25] via 192.168.10.2, Ethernet0
i L2     172.16.4.0 [115/35] via 192.168.10.2, Ethernet0
i L1     172.16.5.0 [115/25] via 192.168.10.2, Ethernet0
i L2     172.16.6.0 [115/35] via 192.168.10.2, Ethernet0
i L1     172.16.7.0 [115/25] via 192.168.10.2, Ethernet0
i L1     172.16.1.0 [115/25] via 192.168.10.2, Ethernet0
i L2     172.16.2.0 [115/35] via 192.168.10.2, Ethernet0
i L1     172.16.3.0 [115/25] via 192.168.10.2, Ethernet0
Zerbina#
```

Figure 14.16
The routes to destinations in the OSPF domain are L2 if the third octet of the address is even and L1 if the third octet is odd. The "odds" are redistributed with a metric of 15, and the "evens" are redistributed with a metric of 25 (10 is added for the hop from Zippy to Zerbina).

Another way of handling this problem is to tag the routes at their ingress points to the OSPF transit domain with a tag that is unique to each domain. At the egress points, the routes can be redistributed by their tags instead of by specific addresses. The routing protocol of the transit network does not use the tag, but merely

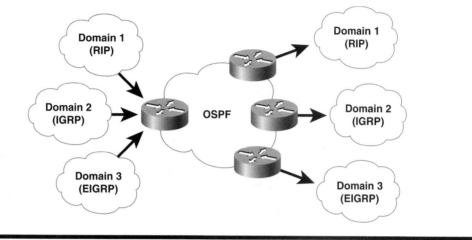

Figure 14.17

Routes from each of the three domains on the left are redistributed into a transit internetwork running OSPF. On the right, the routes for each domain must be redistributed back into their original domains.

conveys it to and from its external networks. RIPv2, EIGRP, Integrated IS-IS and OSPF all support route tags. BGP also supports route tags. Tags are not supported by RIPv1 or IGRP.

A reexamination of the packet formats in Chapters 7, "Routing Information Protocol," 8, "Enhanced Interior Gateway Routing Protocol (EIGRP)," and 9, "Open Shortest Path First," show that RIPv2 messages support 16-bit tags, whereas EIGRP external route TLVs and OSPF type 5 LSAs support 32-bit tags. These tags are expressed as decimal numbers, so tags carried by RIPv2 will be between 0 and 65,535, and tags carried by EIGRP and OSPF will be between 0 and 4,294,967,295.

In Figure 14.18, router Dagwood is accepting routes from three different routing domains and redistributing them into a domain running OSPF. The objective here is to tag the routes from each domain so that their source domain may be identified within the OSPF cloud. Routes from domain 1 will have a tag of 1, domain 2 will have a tag of 2, and so on.

Dagwood's configuration is:

```
router ospf 1
  redistribute igrp 1 metric 10 subnets tag 1
  redistribute rip metric 10 subnets route-map Dithers
network 10.100.200.1 0.0.0.0 area 0
!
router rip
  network 10.0.0.0
!
router igrp 1
  network 10.0.0.0
!
access-list 1 permit 10.1.2.3
access-list 2 permit 10.1.2.4
!
route-map Dithers permit 10
  match ip route-source 1
  set tag 2
!
route-map Dithers permit 20
  match ip route-source 2
  set tag 3
```

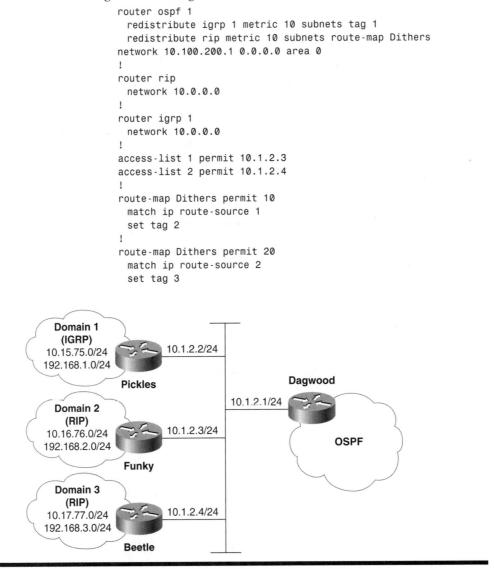

Figure 14.18

Dagwood is configured to tag the routes from each of the three routing domains as they are redistributed into OSPF.

First, notice the **redistribute igrp** command under OSPF. Dagwood is accepting routes from only one IGRP domain, so the tag can be set to 1 directly on the **redistribute** command. However, routes are being learned from two RIP domains. Here a route map is needed. Route map Dithers sets the tag of the RIP routes to either 2 or 3, depending on whether the route was learned from Funky (10.1.2.3) or Beetle (10.1.2.4). Figure 14.19 shows an LSA advertising one of the RIP-learned routes, with the route tag set to 2. The route tags can also be observed in the OSPF link state database (Figure 14.20).

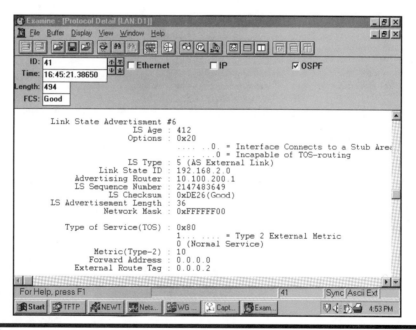

Figure 14.19
This type 5 LSA is advertising network 192.168.2.0, which is in domain 2, within the OSPF domain. The route tag is shown on the last line.

In Figure 14.21, Blondie must redistribute only domain 2 routes to Alley and only domain 1 routes to Oop. Because the routes

```
Blondie#show ip ospf database

     OSPF Router with ID (10.100.200.2) (Process ID 1)


             Router Link States (Area 0)

Link ID        ADV Router      Age   Seq#         Checksum Link count
10.100.200.2   10.100.200.2    39    0x80000002 0x6FF5   1
10.100.200.1   10.100.200.1    40    0x80000033 0x33E1   1

             Net Link States (Area 0)

Link ID        ADV Router      Age   Seq#         Checksum
10.100.200.1   10.100.200.1    40    0x80000001 0xB0A7

             AS External Link States

Link ID        ADV Router      Age   Seq#         Checksum Tag
192.168.2.0    10.100.200.1    641   0x80000028 0x904D   2
10.17.77.0     10.100.200.1    642   0x80000028 0xC817   3
192.168.3.0    10.100.200.1    642   0x80000028 0x9744   3
10.15.75.0     10.100.200.1    642   0x80000028 0xD213   1
10.1.2.0       10.100.200.1    642   0x80000028 0xA19B   1
10.16.76.0     10.100.200.1    642   0x80000028 0xCD15   2
192.168.1.0    10.100.200.1    644   0x80000028 0x8956   1
10.100.200.0   10.100.200.1    644   0x80000028 0x6EA4   1
Blondie#
```

Figure 14.20

The OSPF link state database indicates the tags that were set for each of the external routes by Dagwood's redistribution processes.

were tagged as they entered the OSPF transit domain, this is easily done:

```
router ospf 1
  network 10.100.200.2 0.0.0.0 area 0
!
router rip
  redistribute ospf 1 match external 2 route-map Daisy
  passive-interface Ethernet0
  passive-interface Serial1
  network 10.0.0.0
```

```
    default-metric 5
!
router igrp 1
  redistribute ospf 1 match external 2 route-map Herb
  passive-interface Ethernet0
  passive-interface Serial0
  network 10.0.0.0
  default-metric 10000 1000 255 1 1500
!
route-map Daisy permit 10
  match tag 2
!
route-map Herb permit 10
  match tag 1
```

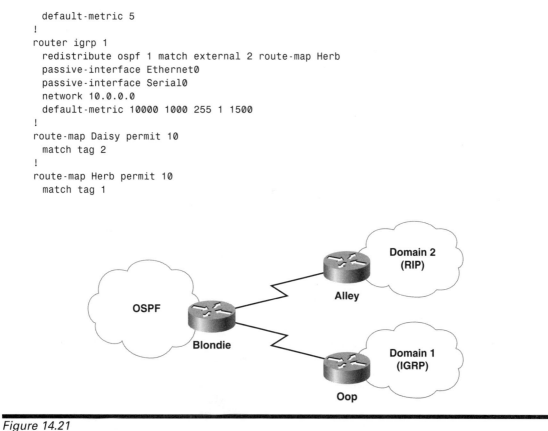

Figure 14.21

Blondie is using route maps to redistribute routes according to their route tag.

Figure 14.22 shows the resulting routes at Alley and Oop. One drawback to the use of route tags to filter routes is that there is no way to filter routes by interface. For example, if Blondie had to send routes to both domain 2 and domain 3, which both run RIP, route maps cannot be configured to send some routes to one RIP process and other routes to another RIP process. The routes would have to be filtered by address with **distribute-list** commands.

```
Alley#show ip route
Codes: C - connected, S - static, I - IGRP, R - RIP, M - mobile, B - BGP
       D - EIGRP, EX - EIGRP external, O - OSPF, IA - OSPF inter area
       E1 - OSPF external type 1, E2 - OSPF external type 2, E - EGP
       i - IS-IS, L1 - IS-IS level-1, L2 - IS-IS level-2, * - candidate default

Gateway of last resort is not set

     10.0.0.0 255.255.255.0 is subnetted, 4 subnets
C        10.1.3.0 is directly connected, Serial0
R        10.1.4.0 [120/1] via 10.1.3.1, 00:00:19, Serial0
R        10.16.76.0 [120/5] via 10.1.3.1, 00:00:19, Serial0
R        10.100.200.0 [120/1] via 10.1.3.1, 00:00:19, Serial0
R     192.168.2.0 [120/5] via 10.1.3.1, 00:00:19, Serial0
Alley#
```

```
Oop#show ip route
Codes: C - connected, S - static, I - IGRP, R - RIP, M - mobile, B - BGP
       D - EIGRP, EX - EIGRP external, O - OSPF, IA - OSPF inter area
       E1 - OSPF external type 1, E2 - OSPF external type 2, E - EGP
       i - IS-IS, L1 - IS-IS level-1, L2 - IS-IS level-2, * - candidate default

Gateway of last resort is not set

     10.0.0.0 255.255.255.0 is subnetted, 5 subnets
I        10.1.3.0 [100/10476] via 10.1.4.1, 00:00:22, Serial0
I        10.1.2.0 [100/8676] via 10.1.4.1, 00:00:22, Serial0
C        10.1.4.0 is directly connected, Serial0
I        10.15.75.0 [100/9176] via 10.1.4.1, 00:00:22, Serial0
I        10.100.200.0 [100/8576] via 10.1.4.1, 00:00:22, Serial0
I     192.168.1.0 [100/9176] via 10.1.4.1, 00:00:22, Serial0
Oop#
```

Figure 14.22
The route tables of Alley and Oop in Figure 14.21 show the results of the redistribution configuration at Blondie.

LOOKING AHEAD

This chapter concludes this book's in-depth look at routing TCP/IP with respect to interior gateway protocols. If you are preparing to become a CCIE, you certainly will want to know this book's topics thoroughly before taking the exam. Use the end-of-chapter problems to test your level of understanding and preparedness. And if you haven't studied routing TCP/IP with respect to Exterior Gateway Protocols, doing so is a next logical step in your preparation.

SUMMARY TABLE: CHAPTER 14 COMMAND REVIEW

Command	Description
access-list *access-list-number* {deny|permit} *source* [*source-wildcard*]	Defines a line of a standard IP access list.
access-list *access-list-number* {deny|permit} *protocol source source-wildcard destination destination-wildcard* [precedence precedence] [tos *tos*] [log]	Defines a line of an extended IP access list.
ip local policy route-map *map-tag*	Defines a policy route for packets originated by the router itself.
ip policy route-map map-tag	Defines a policy route for packets transiting the router.
match interface *type number* [...*type number*]	Matches routes that have their next hop out one of the interfaces specified.
match ip address {*access-list-number|name*} [...*access-list-number|name*]	Matches routes that have a destination address specified by one of the access lists.
match ip next-hop {*access-list-number|name*} [...*access-list-number|name*]	Matches routes that have a next-hop router address specified by one of the access lists.
match ip route-source {*access-list-number|name*} [...*access-list-number|name*]	Matches routes that have been advertised by routers at the addresses specified in the access lists.
match length *min max*	Matches the level 3 length of a packet.
match metric *metric-value*	Matches routes with the specified metric.
match route-type {internal|external[type-1| type-2]|level-1|level-2}	Matches OSPF, EIGRP, or IS-IS routes of the specified type.

Command	Description
match tag *tag-value* [...*tag-value*]	Matches routes with the specified tags.
redistribute *protocol* [*process-id*]{level-1|level-1-2| level-2}[**metric** *metric-value*][**metric-type** *type-value*][**match**{**internal**| **external 1**|**external 2**}][**tag** *tag-value*] [**route-map** *map-tag*][**weight** *weight*][**subnets**]	Configures redistribution into a routing protocol and specifies the source of the redistributed routes.
set level {**level-1**|**level-2**|**level-1-2**| **stub-area**|**backbone**}	Sets the IS-IS level or the OSPF area into which a matched route is to be redistributed.
set default interface *type number* [...*type number*]	Sets the outgoing interface for matched packets when there is no explicit route to the destination.
set interface *type number* [...*type number*]	Sets the outgoing interface for matched packets when there is an explicit route to the destination.
set ip default next-hop *ip-address* [...*ip-address*]	Sets the next-hop router address for matched packets when there is no explicit route to the destination.
set ip next-hop *ip-address* [...*ip-address*]	Sets the next-hop router address for matched packets when there is an explicit route to the destination.
set ip precedence *precedence*	Sets the precedence bits in the Type of Service field of matched IP packets.
set ip tos *type-of-service*	Sets the TOS bits in the Type of Service field of matched packets.
set metric {*metric-value*|*bandwidth delay reliability loading mtu*}	Sets the metric value for a matched route.
set metric-type {**internal**|**external**|**type-1**| **type-2**}	Sets the metric type for a matched route being redistributed into IS-IS or OSPF.
set next-hop *next-hop*	Sets the next-hop router address for a matched route.
set tag *tag-value*	Sets a tag value for a matched route.

REVIEW QUESTIONS

1. How are route maps similar to access lists? How are they different?
2. What are policy routes?
3. What are route tags?
4. In what way do route tags affect routing protocols?

CONFIGURATION EXERCISES

1. Configure policy routes for router A in Figure 14.23 that forward packets from subnets 172.16.1.0/28 through 172.16.1.112/28 to router D and forward packets from subnets 172.16.1.128/28 through 172.16.1.240/28 to router E.

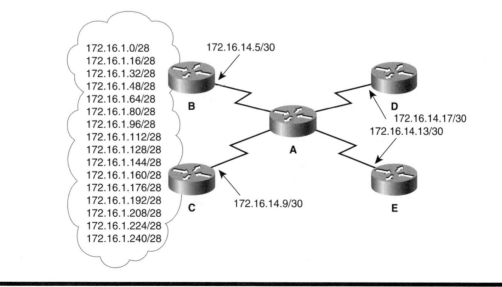

Figure 14.23

The internetwork for Configuration Exercises 1 through 3.

2. Configure policy routes for router A in Figure 14.23 so that packets from subnets 172.16.1.64/28 through 172.16.1.112 are forwarded to router D if they are received from router C. If packets from the same subnets are received from router B, forward them to router E. All other packets should be forwarded normally.

3. Configure policy routes for router A in Figure 14.23 that will forward any packets destined for subnets 172.16.1.0/28 through 172.16.1.240/28, sourced from an SMTP port, to router C. Route any other UDP packets destined for the same subnets to router B. No other packets should be forwarded to routers C or B by either the policy routes or the normal routing protocol.

4. The OSPF and EIGRP configurations for the router in Figure 14.24 is:

```
router eigrp 1
  network 192.168.100.0
!
router ospf 1
  network 192.168.1.0 0.0.0.255 area 16
```

Configure the router to redistribute internal EIGRP routes into OSPF as E1 routes with a metric of 10 and to redistribute external EIGRP routes into OSPF as E2 routes with a metric of 50. Of the networks and subnets shown in the EIGRP domain, all should be redistributed except 10.201.100.0/24.

5. Configure the router in Figure 14.24 to redistribute internal OSPF routes into EIGRP with a lower delay than external OSPF routes. Allow only the three class C networks shown in the OSPF domain to be redistributed.

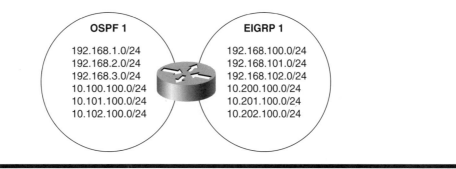

Figure 14.24
The router for Configuration Exercises 4 and 5.

TROUBLESHOOTING EXERCISES

1. Given the following configuration:

```
interface TokenRing1
  ip address 192.168.15.254 255.255.255.0
  ip policy route-map Ex1
!
access-list 1 permit 192.168.0.0 0.0.255.255
access-list 101 permit host 192.168.10.5 any eq telnet
!
route-map Ex1 permit 5
  match ip address 1
  set ip next-hop 192.168.16.254
!
route-map Ex1 permit 10
  match ip address 101
  set ip next-hop 192.168.17.254
```

The intention is to policy route all packets whose source address prefix is 192.168.x.x to 192.168.16.254. The exception is that packets originating from the Telnet port of host 192.168.10.5 should be forwarded to 192.168.17.254. There are two errors in this configuration that are preventing the policy route from working correctly. What are they?

PART IV

Appendixes

Tutorial: Working with Binary and Hex

The best way to gain an understanding of binary and hexadecimal numbering is to begin by examining the decimal numbering system. The decimal system is a base 10 numbering system (the root *deci* means "ten"). *Base 10* means that there are 10 digits with which to represent numbers: *0* through *9*. Most likely, we work in base 10 because our ancient ancestors began counting their cattle and children and enemies on their fingers (in fact, the word *digit* means "finger").

The use of place values allows the representation of large numbers with a few digits, such as the 10 decimal digits. The place values of all numbering systems begin at the right, with the base raised to the power of 0. Reading to the left, each place value is the base raised to a power that is one more than the power of the previous place value:

$$B^4 \ B^3 \ B^2 \ B^1 \ B^0$$

In base 10, the first five place values are:

$$10^4 \ 10^3 \ 10^2 \ 10^1 \ 10^0$$

The first two place values are easy to calculate for any base. Any number raised to the power of 0 is 1; so $10^0 = 1$. Any number raised to the power of 1 is simply that number; so $10^1 = 10$. Working from the left-most place value, simply multiply the number to the right by the base:

$10^0 = 1$

$10^1 = 1 \times 10 = 10$

$10^2 = 10 \times 10 = 100$

$10^3 = 100 \times 10 = 1000$

$10^4 = 1000 \times 10 = 10,000$

So, the first five place values of the base 10 numbering system are:

10,000 1,000 100 10 1

Reading a number such as 57,258 in terms of place values means there are five quantities of 10,000, seven quantities of 1000, two quantities of 100, five quantities of 10, and eight quantities of 1. That is,

$5 \times 10,000 = 50,000$

$7 \times 1,000 = 7,000$

$2 \times 100 = 200$

$5 \times 10 = 50$

$8 \times 1 = 8$

Adding these individual results together, the result is 50,000 + 7,000 + 200 + 50 + 8 = 57,258.

All of us are so acquainted with working in base 10 that we seldom think of breaking a number down into its place values. However, this technique is essential to being able to decipher numbers in other bases.

WORKING WITH BINARY NUMBERS

Computers are, at the most fundamental level, just a collection of electrical switches. Numbers and characters are represented by the positions of these switches. Because a switch has only two positions, on or off, it uses a binary, or base 2, numbering system (the root *bi* means "two"). A base 2 system has just two digits: 0 and 1.

Computers usually group these digits into eight place values, known as a *byte* or an *octet*. The eight place values are:

$$2^7 \; 2^6 \; 2^5 \; 2^4 \; 2^3 \; 2^2 \; 2^1 \; 2^0$$

The place values are calculated:

$2^0 = 1$

$2^1 = 1 \times 2 = 2$

$2^2 = 2 \times 2 = 4$

$2^3 = 4 \times 2 = 8$

$2^4 = 8 \times 2 = 16$

$2^5 = 16 \times 2 = 32$

$2^6 = 32 \times 2 = 64$

$2^7 = 64 \times 2 = 128$

So the place values of a binary octet are:

128 64 32 16 8 4 2 1

Thus the binary octet 10010111 can be read as follows:

1 x 128 = 128

0 x 64 = 0

0 x 32 = 0

$1 \times 16 = 16$

$0 \times 8 = 0$

$1 \times 4 = 4$

$1 \times 2 = 2$

$1 \times 1 = 1$

or $128 + 16 + 4 + 2 + 1 = 151$

Working in binary is easy because for every place value there is either one quantity of that value or none of that value. For another example, $11101001 = 128 + 64 + 32 + 8 + 1 = 233$.

Where converting binary to decimal is a matter of adding the place values, converting from decimal to binary is a matter of subtracting place values. To convert the decimal number 178 to binary, for instance, begin by subtracting the highest base 2 place value possible from the number:

1. 178 is greater than 128, so we know there is a 1 at that place value: $178 - 128 = 50$.
2. 50 is less than 64, so there is a 0 at that place value.
3. 50 is greater than 32, so there is a 1 at that place value: $50 - 32 = 18$.
4. 18 is greater than 16, so there is a 1 at that place value: $18 - 16 = 2$.
5. 2 is less than 8, so there is a 0 at that place value.
6. 2 is less than 4, so there is a 0 at that place value.
7. 2 is equal to 2, so there is a 1 at that place value: $2 - 2 = 0$.
8. 0 is less than 1, so there is a 0 at that place value.

Putting the results of all these steps together, 178 is 10110010 in binary.

Another example may be helpful. Given 110:

1. 110 is less than 128, so there is a 0 at that place value.
2. 110 is greater than 64, so there is a 1 at that place value: 110 − 64 = 46.
3. 46 is greater than 32, so there is a 1 at that place value: 46 − 32 = 14.
4. 14 is less than 16, so there is a 0 at that place value.
5. 14 is greater than 8, so there is a 1 at that place value: 14 − 8 = 6.
6. 6 is greater than 4, so there is a 1 at that place value: 6 − 4 = 2.
7. There is a 1 at the 2 place value: 2 − 2 = 0.
8. 0 is less than 1, so there is a 0 at that place value.

Therefore, 110 is 01101110 in binary.

WORKING WITH HEXADECIMAL NUMBERS

Writing out binary octets isn't much fun. For people who must work with such numbers frequently, a briefer notation is welcome. One possible notation is to have a single character for every possible octet. However, there are $2^8 = 256$ different combinations of eight bits, so a single-character representation of all octets would require 256 digits, or a base 256 numbering system.

Life is much easier if an octet is viewed as two groups of four bits. For instance, 11010011 can be viewed as 1101 and 0011. There are $2^4 = 16$ possible combinations of four bits, so with a base 16, or hexadecimal, numbering system, an octet can be represented with two digits. (The root *hex* means "six," and *deci* means "ten.") Table A.1 shows the hexadecimal digits and their decimal and binary equivalents.

Table A.1   *Hex, decimal, and binary equivalents.*

Hex	Decimal	Binary
0	0	0000
1	1	0001
2	2	0010
3	3	0011
4	4	0100
5	5	0101
6	6	0110
7	7	0111
8	8	1000
9	9	1001
A	10	1010
B	11	1011
C	12	1100
D	13	1101
E	14	1110
F	15	1111

Because the first 10 characters of the decimal and the hexadecimal numbering system are the same, it is customary to precede a hex number with a *0x,* or follow it with an *h,* to distinguish it from a decimal number. For example, the hex number 25 would be written as 0x25 or as 25h. This book uses the 0x convention.

After working with binary for only a short while, it is easy to determine a decimal equivalent of a four-bit binary number in your head. It is also easy to convert a decimal digit to a hex digit in your head. Therefore, converting a binary octet to hex is easily done in three steps:

1. Divide the octet into two, four-bit binary numbers.
2. Convert each four-bit number to decimal.
3. Write each decimal number in its hex equivalent.

For example, to convert 11010011 to hex:

1. 11010011 becomes 1101 and 0011.
2. 1101 = 8 + 4 + 1 = 13, and 0011 = 2 + 1 = 3.
3. 13 = 0xD, and 3 = 0x3.

Therefore, 11010011 in hex is 0xD3.

Converting from hex to binary is a simple matter of working the three steps backwards. For example, to convert 0x7B to binary:

1. 0x7 = 7, and 0xB = 11.
2. 7 = 0111, and 11 = 1011.
3. Putting the four-bit numbers together, 0x7B = 01111011.

Tutorial: Access Lists

Access lists are probably misnamed these days. As the name implies, the original intention of an access list was to permit or deny access of packets into, out of, or through a router. Access lists have become powerful tools for controlling the behavior of packets and frames. Their use falls into three categories (Figure B.1):

- *Security filters* protect the integrity of the router and the networks to which it is passing traffic. Typically, a security filter permits the passage of a few, well-understood packets and denies the passage of everything else.

- *Traffic filters* prevent unnecessary packets from passing onto limited-bandwidth links. These filters look and behave much like security filters, but the logic is generally inverse: Traffic filters deny the passage of a few unwanted packets and permit everything else.

- Many tools available on Cisco routers, such as dialer lists, route filters, route maps, and queuing lists, must be able to identify certain packets to function properly. Access lists may be linked to these and other tools to provide this *packet identification* function.

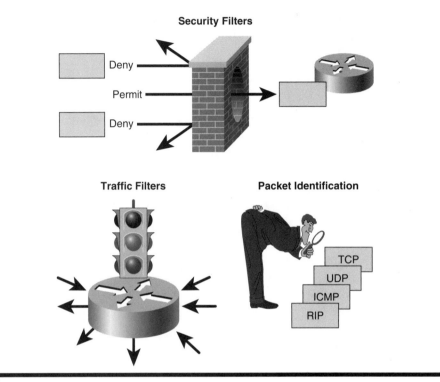

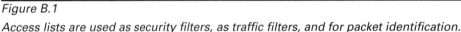

Figure B.1

Access lists are used as security filters, as traffic filters, and for packet identification.

ACCESS LIST BASICS

An access list is a sequential series of filters. Each filter comprises some sort of matching criteria and an action. The action is always either *permit* or *deny*. The matching criteria may be as simple as a source address; alternatively, they may be a more complex combination of source and destination addresses, protocol type, ports or sockets, and specifications of the state of certain flags, such as the TCP ACK bit.

A packet is "dropped into" the top of the stack of filters (Figure B.2). At each filter, the matching criteria is applied. If a match occurs, the specified *permit* or *deny* action is executed. If a match does not occur, the packet "drops down" to the next filter in the stack, and the matching process is applied again.

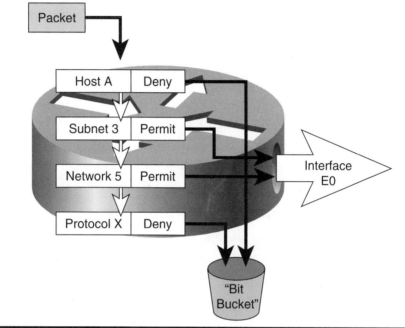

Figure B.2

An access list is a sequential list of filters, each of which defines a matching criteria and an action.

In Figure B.2, a *permit* means that the packet will be allowed to exit on interface E0; a *deny* means that the packet will be dropped. For instance, a packet with a source address of HOST A will be dropped at the first filter. Suppose the packet's source address is HOST D of SUBNET 2 of NETWORK 5. The first filter specifies a match criteria of HOST A, so the packet will not match and will drop to the second layer. The second filter specifies SUBNET 3—again, no match. The packet drops to the third filter, which specifies NETWORK 5. This matches; the action at layer three is permit, so the packet is allowed to exit interface E0.

Implicit Deny Any

What happens if a packet drops through all the filters and a match never occurs? The router has to know what to do with a packet in this situation; that is, there must be a *default action*. The default action could be either to permit all packets that don't match or to deny them. Cisco chose to deny them: Any packet that is referred to an access list and does not find a match is automatically dropped.

This approach is the correct engineering choice, particularly if the access list is being used for security. It is better to drop some packets that shouldn't have been dropped than to permit packets you've inadvertently neglected to filter.

This last filter is called an *implicit deny any* (Figure B.3). As the name implies, the line does not show up in any access list you build. It's simply a default action, and it exists at the end of any and all access lists.

This default can be overridden by making the last line of the list an explicit *permit any*. The implication here is that packets dropping through all the other filters will match the *permit any* before they get to the default *deny any*; therefore, all packets not matching anything else will be permitted—nothing will ever reach the *implicit deny*.

Sequentiality

Access lists are executed sequentially, from the top down. This concept is important: Perhaps the most common cause of malfunctioning access lists is putting the individual filtering lines in the wrong sequence.

In Figure B.4, subnet 10.23.147.0/24 should be denied and the rest of network 10.0.0.0 should be permitted. The list on the left

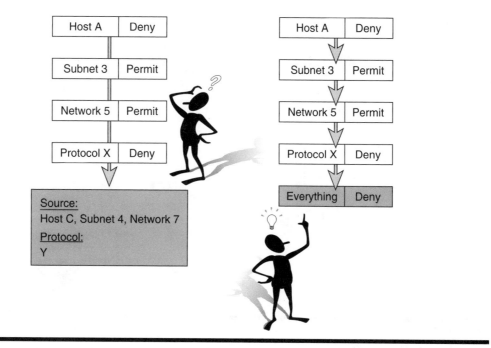

Figure B.3

All access lists end with an implicit deny any, which discards all packets that do not match a line in the list.

is out of sequence; network 10.0.0.0, including its subnet 10.23.147.0, will match the first line and be permitted. Packets with the subnet to be denied will never reach the second line.

The list on the right is correct. Subnet 10.23.147.0 matches the first line and is denied, whereas all other subnets of 10.0.0.0 drop to the next line and are permitted.

Access List Types

The actual configuration lines for the access list shown graphically on the right of Figure B.4 are:

```
access-list 9 deny 10.23.147.0 0.0.0.255
access-list 9 permit 10.0.0.0 0.255.255.255
```

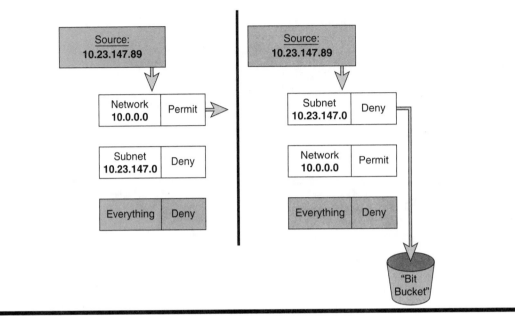

Figure B.4

If the individual filter layers of an access list are not configured in the correct sequence, the access list will not function correctly.

Every filter layer of an access list is represented by one configuration line. The various components of an access list line are discussed shortly, but for now notice the number 9 in both lines. This number is the access list number, and it serves two purposes:

- It links all the lines of this list together and makes the list distinct from any others that might exist in the router's configuration file (it is common to have several access lists on a single router).

- The router has to have a way to distinguish the access list type. Cisco IOS has access lists for IP, IPX, AppleTalk, DEC, NetBIOS, bridging, and many other protocols. Further, many of these protocols have multiple access list types. The access list number tells the router what type of list it is.

Access list types may be identified by either a number or a name. Table B.1 shows the numbered access list types and the range of access list numbers available for each. For example, as shown in the table, **access-list 1010** is identifying IPX SAPs because the number is between 1000 and 1099.

Table B.1 *Cisco access list numbers.*

Access List Type	Range
Standard IP	1–99
Extended IP	100–199
Ethernet type code	200–299
Ethernet address	700–799
Transparent bridging (protocol type)	200–299
Transparent bridging (vendor code)	700–799
Extended transparent bridging	1100–1199
DECnet and extended DECnet	300–399
XNS	400–499
Extended XNS	500–599
AppleTalk	600–699
Source-route bridging (protocol type)	200–299
Source-route bridging (vendor code)	700–799
Standard IPX	800–899
Extended IPX	900–999
IPX SAP	1000–1099
NLSP route summary	1200–1299
Standard VINES	1–99
Extended VINES	100–199
Simple VINES	200–299

Within a range, access list numbers do not have to follow any particular sequence. That is, the first AppleTalk list on a router does not have to be 600, the second 601, and so on. They can be any number between 600 and 699, as long as each list is uniquely numbered on a single router.

Also, notice that some number ranges are the same for different protocols—Ethernet Type Code, Source Route Bridging, and Simple VINES, for instance. In these cases, the router will differentiate between access list types by the format of the access list lines themselves.

The following access list types are identified by names instead of numbers:

- Apollo domain

- Standard IP

- Extended IP

- ISO CLNS

- Source-route bridging NetBIOS

- Standard IPX

- Extended IPX

- IPX Sap

- IPX NetBIOS

- NLSP route summary

An example of an access list named Boo, identifying IPX NetBIOS, is:

```
netbios access-list host Boo deny Atticus
netbios access-list host Boo deny Scout
netbios access-list host Boo deny Jem
netbios access-list host Boo permit *
```

Note that although standard and extended IP access lists normally are numbered, they may also be named access lists. This convention is supported in IOS 11.2 and later. In some environments, a router may be configured with a large number of IP lists. By using names instead of numbers, individual lists may be more easily identified; additionally, the named lists remove the limitation of 99 standard and 100 extended IP access lists.

Named IP access lists currently can be used only with packet and route filters. Refer to the Cisco configuration guides for more information.

Editing Access Lists

Anyone who has edited an access list longer than a few lines from the console will tell you that this process can be an exercise in frustration. There is no way, from the console, to add a line to the middle of the list. All new lines are added to the bottom. And if you happen to type a mistake and try to eliminate a particular line by typing, for instance,

```
no access-list 101 permit tcp 10.2.5.4 0.0.0.255 192.168.3.0 0.0.0.255 eq 25
```

this line, as well as all of access list 101, will be deleted!

A far more convenient technique is to cut and paste the list to the notepad of your PC, or upload the configuration to a TFTP server, and do the editing from there. When finished, the new access list may be loaded back into the router. A word of caution, however: All new lines are added to the bottom of an access list. Always add **no access-list #**, where # is the number of the list you're editing, to the beginning of the edited list. For example:

```
no access-list 5
access-list 5 permit 172.16.5.4 0.0.0.0
access-list 5 permit 172.16.12.0 0.0.0.255
access-list deny 172.16.0.0 0.0.255.255
access-list permit any
```

The line **no access-list 5** will delete the old list 5 from the configuration file before adding the new one. If you omit this step, the new list will simply be added onto the end of the old one.

STANDARD IP ACCESS LISTS

The format of a standard access list line is:

access-list *access-list-number* {**deny**|**permit**} *source* [*source-wildcard*]

This command specifies the access list number, which according to Table B.1 is between 1 and 99; the action (permit or deny); a source IP address; and the wildcard (or inverse) mask. An example of a standard IP access list is:

```
access-list 1 permit 172.22.30.6 0.0.0.0
access-list 1 permit 172.22.30.95 0.0.0.0
access-list 1 deny 172.22.30.0 0.0.0.255
access-list 1 permit 172.22.0.0 0.0.31.255
access-list 1 deny 172.22.0.0 0.0.255.255
access-list 1 permit 0.0.0.0 255.255.255.255
```

The first two lines of the example permit passage of packets whose source addresses belong to two specific hosts, 172.22.30.6 and 172.22.30.95. This seems pretty obvious from looking at the lines, although the inverse mask of 0.0.0.0 may not make sense yet. The third line denies all other hosts on subnet 172.22.30.0. Again, it's fairly intuitive. The purpose of the fourth line is not so obvious. It permits all hosts with addresses in the range of 172.22.0.1 to 172.22.31.255. The inverse mask is what allows the specification of this range of addresses with a single line. The fifth line denies all other subnets of the Class B network 172.22.0.0, and the last line permits all other addresses.

To fully understand this access list, you need to understand inverse masks.

Recall how IP address masks function: To derive a network or subnet address from a host address, a one is set in the mask corresponding to each bit of the network address, and a zero is set for each bit of the host address. A Boolean AND is performed on each bit, and the result is the network or subnet number. Figure B.5(a) includes a truth table for the AND function; in English, the function states:

Compare two bits. The result is one if and only if both bits are one.

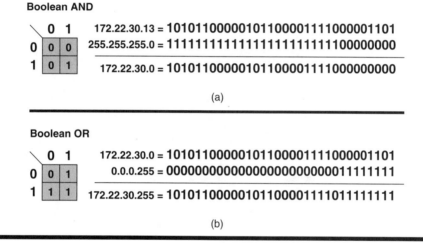

(a)

(b)

Figure B.5

Truth tables and examples of a Boolean AND (a) and a Boolean OR (b).

A Boolean OR is the inverse of this function, as its truth table in Figure B.5(b) shows:

Compare two bits. The result is zero if and only if both bits are zero.

An *inverse mask* (Cisco prefers the term *wildcard mask*) sets a zero for each bit of the address that should be exactly matched and a one for each bit where anything will match—the one bits are frequently referred to as "don't care" bits. The inverse mask is then ORed with the address.

Notice the result of the OR example in Figure B.5(b), 172.22.30.255. In IP terms this result means "all host addresses on subnet 172.22.30.0." Any specific address from 172.22.30.0 will match this address/inverse mask combination.

Figure B.6 shows two shortcuts that may be used when writing standard IP access lists. Figure B.6(a) shows an inverse mask of all zeroes to indicate that all 32 bits of the address in question must match 172.22.30.6 exactly. The default mask for a standard IP access list is 0.0.0.0. So the alternative statement shown, with no mask specified, is the same as the first statement. Note that this default does not apply to extended IP access lists, which are covered in the following section.

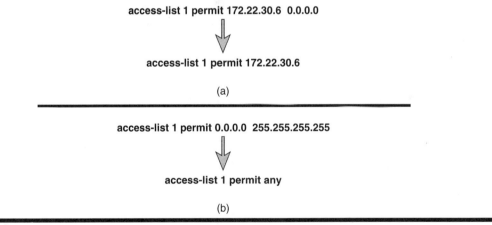

Figure B.6

Two shortcuts may be used when writing standard IP access lists.

Figure B.6(b) shows the permit anything address/inverse mask combination. The address of 0.0.0.0 is actually just a placeholder; the mask, 255.255.255.255, actually does all the work. By placing a one in all 32 bit positions, this mask will match anything. The alternative statement shown uses the keyword **any**, which has the same meaning as the first statement.

EXTENDED IP ACCESS LISTS

Extended IP access lists provide far more flexibility in the specification of what is to be filtered. The basic format of the extended IP access list line is

access-list access-list-number {**deny**|**permit**} *protocol source source-wildcard destination destination-wildcard* [**precedence** *precedence*][**tos**tos][**log**]

Some of the features here are familiar, and some are new.

- *access-list-number*, for extended IP access lists, is between 100 and 199.

- *protocol* is a new variable that looks for a match in the *protocol* field of the IP packet header. The keyword choices are **eigrp**, **gre**, **icmp**, **igmp**, **igrp**, **ip**, **ipinip**, **nos**, **ospf**, **tcp**, or **udp**. An integer in the range 0 to 255 representing an IP protocol number may also be used. **ip** is a generic keyword, which will match any and all IP protocols, in the same way inverse mask 255.255.255.255 will match all addresses.

- Notice that both the *source* and *destination* packet addresses are examined for matches; each has its own inverse mask.

- *precedence* and *tos* are optional variables that look for a match in the *Precedence* and *Type of Service* fields of the IP packet header. Precedence may be an integer from 0 to 7, and TOS may be an integer from 0 to 15, or either field may be described by one of several keywords. Refer to the Cisco documentation for a list of available keywords.

- *log* is an optional specification that turns on informational logging.

An example of an extended IP access list is:
```
access-list 101 permit ip 172.22.30.6 0.0.0.0 10.0.0.0 0.255.255.255
access-list 101 permit ip 172.22.30.95 0.0.0.0 10.11.12.0 0.0.0.255
access-list 101 deny ip 172.22.30.0 0.0.0.255 192.168.18.27 0.0.0.0
access-list 101 permit ip 172.22.0.0 0.0.31.255 192.168.18.0 0.0.0.255
access-list 101 deny ip 172.22.0.0 0.0.255.255 192.168.18.64 0.0.0.63
access-list 101 permit ip 0.0.0.0 255.255.255.255 0.0.0.0 255.255.255.255
```

Line 1: IP packets with a source address of 172.22.30.6 and with a destination address that belongs to network 10.0.0.0 are permitted.

Line 2: IP packets with a source address of 172.22.30.95 and with a destination address that belongs to subnet 10.11.12.0/24 are permitted.

Line 3: IP packets with a source address that belongs to subnet 172.22.30.0/24 and with a destination address of 192.168.18.27 are dropped.

Line 4: IP packets with source addresses between 172.22.0.0 and 172.22.31.255 and with a destination address that belongs to network 192.168.18.0 are permitted.

Line 5: IP packets with a source address that belongs to network 172.22.0.0 and with a destination address whose first 26 bits are 192.168.18.64 are dropped.

Line 6: IP packets from any source to any destination are permitted.

Figure B.7 shows two shortcuts that may be used when writing extended IP access lists. Recall that standard IP access lists have a default mask of 0.0.0.0. This default does not apply to extended access lists; there would be no way for the router to interpret it correctly. An alternative exists for extended lists, however. In Figure B.7(a), packets are permitted if their source is host 172.22.30.6 and their destination is host 10.20.30.40. Any time the mask in an extended IP access list is 0.0.0.0, it may be replaced by adding the keyword **host** before the address.

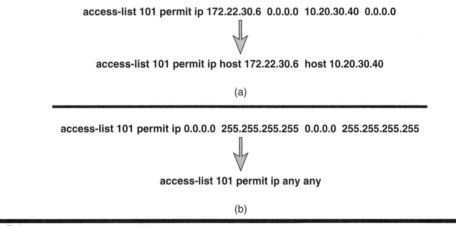

access-list 101 permit ip 172.22.30.6 0.0.0.0 10.20.30.40 0.0.0.0

access-list 101 permit ip host 172.22.30.6 host 10.20.30.40

(a)

access-list 101 permit ip 0.0.0.0 255.255.255.255 0.0.0.0 255.255.255.255

access-list 101 permit ip any any

(b)

Figure B.7

Two shortcuts may be used when writing extended IP access lists.

The example in Figure B.7(b) permits any IP packets from any source to any destination. Just as with standard access lists, the **any** keyword may be used in place of the 0.0.0.0 255.255.255.255 address/inverse mask combination for the source, the destination, or both.

Extended access lists may be more powerful than standard access lists because the former examine more than the packet's source address, but everything has a price. The price you pay with extended lists is increased processing (Figure B.8). Because each line of the access list is examining multiple fields within the packet, multiple CPU interrupts can occur. If the access list is very large or the router is very busy, this requirement may affect performance adversely.

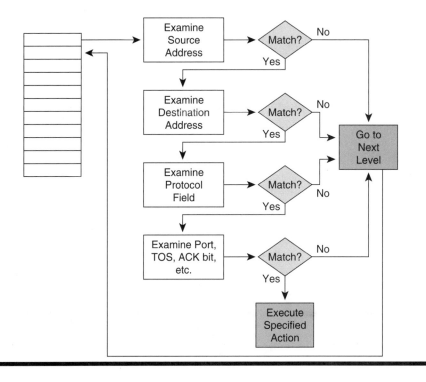

Figure B.8

The decision flow of an extended IP access list.

Keeping access lists as small as possible reduces the processing burden on the router. Also notice that when a match occurs, the specified action is invoked and processing stops. Therefore, if you can write your lists so that most matches occur in the first few lines, performance will be improved. This approach isn't always feasible, but it is something to keep in mind when designing access lists.

As an exercise, try making the access list given as an example at the beginning of this section more elegant. That is, rewrite the list with as few lines as possible without losing any of its functionality. (Hint: A list with the same functionality can be written with only three lines.)

TCP Access Lists

The format for an extended access list line that examines a TCP segment is:

access-list access-list-number {**deny**|**permit**} **tcp** source source-wildcard [*operator port* [*port*]] *destination destination-wildcard* [*operator port* [*port*]] [**established**][**precedence** *precedence*][**tos**tos][**log**]

Notice that the *protocol* variable is **tcp**. Probably the most significant feature here is that the access list can examine the source and destination port numbers in the TCP segment header. As a result, you have the option of filtering packets not only to and from a particular address but also to and from a particular socket (an IP address/application port combination).

- *Operator* specifies a logical operand. The options are **eq** (equal to), **neq** (not equal to), **gt** (greater than), **lt** (less than), and **range** for specifying an inclusive range of ports. If the **range** operator is used, two port numbers are specified.

- *Port* specifies the application layer port to be matched. A few common port numbers are for Telnet (23), FTP (20 and 21), SMTP (25), and SNMP (169). A complete listing of TCP port numbers can be found in RFC 1700.

  What happens if you have implemented an access list to prevent TCP sessions from being established into your network, but you want to ensure that the access list passes the responses if your network establishes a TCP session? The **established** keyword allows this event by checking the

ACK and RST flags in the TCP segment header. If one of these flags is set, a match occurs. If neither bit is set, the source is trying to establish a TCP connection to the destination and a match will not occur. The packet will be denied on a subsequent line of the access list.

An example of a TCP access list line is:

```
access-list 110 permit tcp any 172.22.0.0 0.0.255.255 established
access-list 110 permit tcp any host 172.22.15.83 eq 25
access-list 110 permit tcp 10.0.0.0 0.255.255.255 172.22.114.0 0.0.0.255 eq 23
```

Line 1: Permit TCP packets from any source to network 172.22.0.0 if the connection was established from that network.

Line 2: Permit TCP packets from any source if the destination is port 25 (SMTP) of host 172.22.15.83.

Line 3: Allow any TCP packet with a source address from network 10.0.0.0 to telnet (port 23) to any address on subnet 172.22.114.0/24.

All other packets will be dropped by the implicit *deny any*.

UDP Access Lists

The format for an extended access list line that examines a UDP segment is:

access-list access-list-number {**deny|permit**} **udp** source source-wildcard [*operator port* [*port*]] *destination destination-wildcard* [*operator port* [*port*]] [**precedence** *precedence*][**tos**tos][**log**]

This format is very similar to the TCP format, except that the *protocol* variable now is **udp**. The other difference is that there is no **established** keyword. The reason is that UDP is a connectionless transport service, and no connections are established between hosts.

In the following example, three lines have been added to the previous TCP example:

```
access-list 110 permit tcp any 172.22.0.0 0.0.255.255 established
access-list 110 permit tcp any host 172.22.15.83 eq 25
access-list 110 permit tcp 10.0.0.0 0.255.255.255 172.22.114.0 0.0.0.255 eq 23
access-list 110 permit udp 10.64.32.0 0.0.0.255 host 172.22.15.87 eq 69
access-list 110 permit udp any host 172.22.15.85 eq 53
access-list 110 permit udp any any eq 161
```

Line 4: Permit UDP packets from subnet 10.64.32.0/24 to the TFTP port (69) on host 172.22.15.87.

Line 5: Permit UDP packets from any source to the Domain Name Server (port 53) on host 172.22.15.85.

Line 6: Permit all SNMP packets (port 161) from any source to any destination.

The implicit *deny any* still drops all packets not finding a match in the list.

ICMP Access Lists

The format for an extended access list line that examines an ICMP packet is:

access-list access-list-number {**deny|permit**} **icmp** source source-wildcard destination destination-wildcard [*icmp-type*[*icmp-code*]][**precedence** *precedence*][**tos**tos][**log**]

icmp is now in the *protocol* field. Notice that there are no source or destination ports here; ICMP is a network layer protocol. This line can be used to filter all ICMP messages, or you can use the following options to filter specific ICMP messages:

- *icmp-type* is a number between 0 and 255. All ICMP type numbers can be found in RFC 1700 and in this book in Table 2.5.

- The granularity of filtering may be increased by specifying *icmp-code*. An ICMP code specifies a subset of ICMP packet types; the codes are a number between 0 and 255 and are also found in RFC 1700 or in Table 2.5.

An example of an ICMP access list is:

```
access-list 111 deny icmp 172.22.0.0 0.0.255.255 any 0
access-list 111 deny icmp 172.22.0.0 0.0.255.255 any 3 9
access-list 111 deny icmp 172.22.0.0 0.0.255.255 any 3 10
access-list 111 permit ip any any
```

Line 1: Deny ICMP ping responses (Echo Reply, ICMP type 0) from network 172.22.0.0 to any destination.

Line 2: Deny ICMP destination unreachable packets (type 3) with a code number of 9 (Network Administratively Prohibited) from network 172.22.0.0 to any destination.

Line 3: Deny ICMP destination unreachable packets (type 3) with a code number of 10 (Host Administratively Prohibited) from network 172.22.0.0 to any destination.

Line 4: Permit all other IP packets.

CALLING THE ACCESS LIST

An access list does nothing unless packets are sent to it by a calling command, which defines how the access list is to be used. One such command is:

ip access-group *access-list-number* {in|out}

This command is configured on an interface to create security or traffic filters and may be applied to incoming or outgoing traffic. If neither the **in** nor the **out** keyword is specified, the filter defaults to outgoing. The access list number, of course, is the access list to which this command will send packets. Figure B.9 shows two configurations of this command.

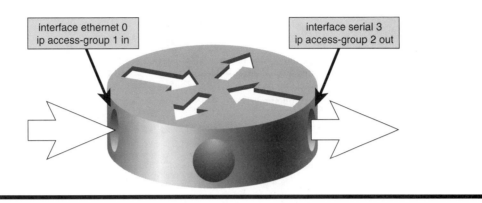

interface ethernet 0
ip access-group 1 in

interface serial 3
ip access-group 2 out

Figure B.9

*The **ip access-group** command uses the specified access list to create a filter on an interface for either incoming or outgoing packets.*

Access list 1 in Figure B.9 filters incoming IP packets on interface E0. It has no effect on outgoing IP traffic and no effect on packets originated by other protocols, such as IPX. Access list 2 filters IP packets going out interface S3. It has no effect on incoming IP packets and no effect on packets originated by other protocols.

Multiple interfaces may make calls to the same access list, but any one interface can have only one incoming and one outgoing access list for each protocol.

In Figure B.10, the TCP, UDP, and ICMP access lists given earlier as examples are used as filters. Access list 110, from the previous two examples, has been applied to the Token Ring 0 interface to check incoming traffic. Access list 111 is applied to the same interface to check outgoing traffic. Analyze the two access lists carefully, including their interrelationship, and consider the following:

- A ping response from 172.23.12.5 to 10.64.32.7 wants to exit interface TO0. Will it be allowed to pass?

- Someone on 172.22.67.4 wants to ping a device at 10.64.32.20, exiting TO0. Will the ping be successful?

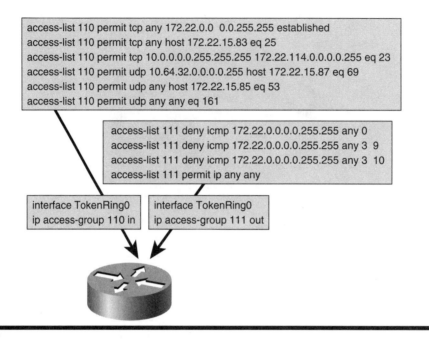

access-list 110 permit tcp any 172.22.0.0 0.0.255.255 established
access-list 110 permit tcp any host 172.22.15.83 eq 25
access-list 110 permit tcp 10.0.0.0.0.255.255.255 172.22.114.0.0.0.0.255 eq 23
access-list 110 permit udp 10.64.32.0.0.0.0.255 host 172.22.15.87 eq 69
access-list 110 permit udp any host 172.22.15.85 eq 53
access-list 110 permit udp any any eq 161

access-list 111 deny icmp 172.22.0.0.0.0.255.255 any 0
access-list 111 deny icmp 172.22.0.0.0.0.255.255 any 3 9
access-list 111 deny icmp 172.22.0.0.0.0.255.255 any 3 10
access-list 111 permit ip any any

interface TokenRing0
ip access-group 110 in

interface TokenRing0
ip access-group 111 out

Figure B.10

Access list 110 is used here to filter incoming packets on the Token Ring interface. Access list 111 is used here to filter outgoing packets on the same interface.

Another command that makes calls to an access list is the **access-class** command. This command is used to regulate telnet sessions to and from the router's virtual terminal lines, not for packet filtering. The format of the command is:

access-class *access-list-number* {in|out}

Figure B.11 shows an example of the **access-class** command. Access list 3 regulates the addresses from which the router's VTY lines will accept telnet sessions. Access list 4 regulates the addresses to which the router's virtual terminal lines may connect.

The **access-class** command has no effect on telnet traffic transiting the router. It only influences telnet sessions to and from the router itself.

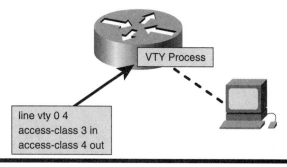

Figure B.11

The **access-class** command uses an access list to regulate telnet traffic to and from the router's virtual terminal lines.

KEYWORD ALTERNATIVES

Most networking professionals know some of the more commonly used TCP port numbers, and maybe a few UDP port numbers. Fewer could say what the ICMP type is for a ping or a destination unreachable, much less what the ICMP codes are for destination unreachable types. Beginning with IOS 10.3, access lists can be configured with keywords in place of many port, type, or code numbers. Using keywords, the access lists 110 and 111 from Figure B.10 are:

```
access-list 110 permit tcp any 172.22.0.0 0.0.255.255 established
access-list 110 permit tcp any host 172.22.15.83 eq smtp
access-list 110 permit tcp 10.0.0.0 0.255.255.255 172.22.114.0 0.0.0.255 eq telnet
access-list 110 permit udp 10.64.32.0 0.0.0.255 host 172.22.15.87 eq tftp
access-list 110 permit udp any host 172.22.15.85 eq domain
access-list 110 permit udp any any eq snmp
!
access-list 111 deny icmp 172.22.0.0 0.0.255.255 any echo-reply
access-list 111 deny icmp 172.22.0.0 0.0.255.255 any net-unreachable administratively-prohibited
access-list 111 deny icmp 172.22.0.0 0.0.255.255 any host-unreachable administratively-prohibited
access-list 111 permit ip any any
```

A word of caution: If you are upgrading a router from a pre-10.3 image, the new IOS, upon bootup, will rewrite the access lists in the configuration file to the new syntax, including keywords. If you subsequently need to reload the original pre-10.3 image, the revised access lists will not be understood. Always upload a copy of the original configuration file to a TFTP server before upgrading.

NAMED ACCESS LISTS

The limit of 99 standard access lists or 100 extended IP access lists per router would seem to be more than enough. However, there are cases, such as with dynamic access lists,[1] in which these maximums may not be sufficient. Named access lists, available beginning with IOS 11.2, extend these limits. The other advantage is that descriptive names can make large numbers of lists more manageable.

To use names, the first line of the access list is of the format:

ip access-list {**standard|extended**} *name*

Because there are no numbers to differentiate list types, this line specifies the list as IP and either standard or extended.

Below the beginning line go the permit and deny statements. The syntax for the standard list is:

{**deny|permit**} *source* [*source-wildcard*]

The syntax for the basic extended list is:

{**deny|permit**} *protocol source source-wildcard destination destination-wildcard* [**precedence** precedence][**tos** *tos*][**log**]

In both cases, the **access-list** access-list-number portion of the command has disappeared, but everything else remains the same. Standard and extended access lists on the same router cannot

---

[1] *Dynamic access lists are not covered in this tutorial. Refer to Cisco's documentation for more information.*

share the same name. The command for establishing a named access list on an interface refers to the name instead of a number but in all other ways remains the same. Figure B.12 shows the access lists of Figure B.10 converted to the named format.

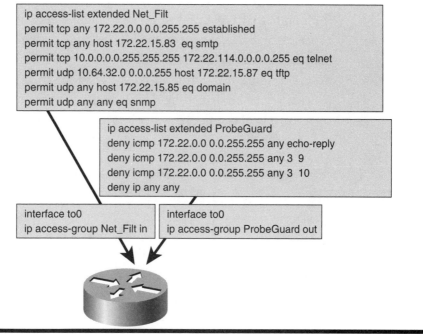

```
ip access-list extended Net_Filt
permit tcp any 172.22.0.0 0.0.255.255 established
permit tcp any host 172.22.15.83  eq smtp
permit tcp 10.0.0.0.0.255.255.255 172.22.114.0.0.0.0.255 eq telnet
permit udp 10.64.32.0 0.0.0.255 host 172.22.15.87 eq tftp
permit udp any host 172.22.15.85 eq domain
permit udp any any eq snmp
```

```
ip access-list extended ProbeGuard
deny icmp 172.22.0.0 0.0.255.255 any echo-reply
deny icmp 172.22.0.0 0.0.255.255 any 3  9
deny icmp 172.22.0.0 0.0.255.255 any 3  10
deny ip any any
```

```
interface to0
ip access-group Net_Filt in
```

```
interface to0
ip access-group ProbeGuard out
```

Figure B.12

The access lists shown in Figure B.10 are now configured as named access lists.

FILTER PLACEMENT CONSIDERATIONS

For the best performance, you must consider not only the efficient design of the access list itself but also the placement of the filter on the router and in the internetwork.

As a rule of thumb, security filters usually are incoming filters. Filtering unwanted or untrusted packets before they reach the routing process, prevents *spoofing attacks*—wherein a packet fools the routing process into thinking it has come from somewhere it hasn't. Traffic filters, on the other hand, usually are outgoing filters. This approach makes sense when you consider that the point of a traffic filter is to prevent unnecessary packets from occupying a particular data link.

Aside from these two rules of thumb, another factor to consider is the number of CPU cycles the combined access list and routing processes will use. An incoming filter is invoked before the routing process, whereas an outgoing filter is invoked after the routing process (Figure B.13). If most packets passing through the routing process are to be denied by the access list, an incoming filter may save some processing cycles.

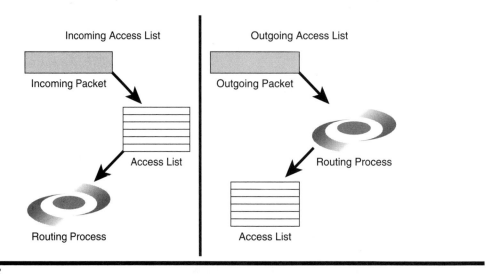

Figure B.13
Incoming packet filters are invoked before the routing process, whereas outgoing packet filters are invoked after the routing process

Standard IP access lists can filter only on source addresses. Consequently, a filter using a standard list must necessarily be placed as close to the destination as possible so that the source still has access to other, nonfiltered destinations (Figure B.14(a)). As a result, bandwidth and CPU cycles may be wasted delivering packets that will ultimately be dropped.

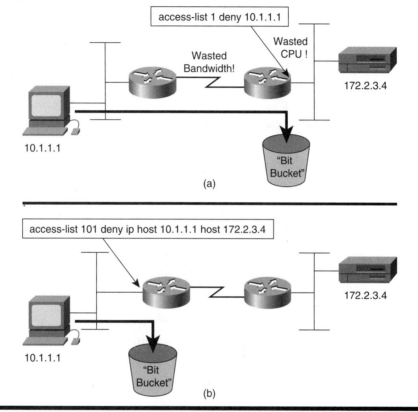

Figure B.14

Filters that use standard access lists generally must be placed close to the destination (a), whereas extended access lists can be placed close to the source (b).

Extended IP access lists, because of their capability to identify very specific packet characteristics, should be placed as close to the source as possible to prevent wasting bandwidth and CPU transporting "doomed" packets (Figure B.14(b)). On the other hand, the complexity of extended lists means more of a processing burden. These tradeoffs must be considered when deciding where on the network to place a filter.

You must also understand how your access list will affect switching on the router. For instance, an interface using an extended IP access list cannot be autonomously switched; dynamic access lists cannot be silicon switched and may affect silicon switching performance. Named access lists are not supported at all before IOS 11.2.

The effect of an access list on switching may be critical on backbone or core routers. Be sure to fully research and understand the effects an access list may have by reading the Cisco Configuration Guide for the IOS being used on your router. In some cases, a *packet filtering router*—a smaller router dedicated to nothing but packet filtering—can be used to offload the filtering burden from a mission-critical router.

ACCESS LIST MONITORING AND ACCOUNTING

It is useful to be able to examine an access list, or even all access lists, without having to display the entire router configuration file. The command **show ip access-list** displays an abbreviated syntax of all IP access lists on the router. If a specific access list is to be observed, the list may be specified by name or number (Figure B.15). If you leave off the **ip** keyword (**show access-list**), all access lists will be displayed.

```
Woody#show ip access-list 110
Extended IP access list 110
    permit tcp any 172.22.0.0 0.0.255.255 established
    permit tcp any host 172.22.15.83 eq smtp
    permit tcp 10.0.0.0 0.255.255.255 172.22.114.0 0.0.0.255 eq telnet
    permit udp 10.64.32.0 0.0.0.255 host 172.22.15.87 eq tftp
    permit udp any host 172.22.15.85 eq domain
    permit udp any any eq snmp
Woody#
```

Figure B.15

The **show ip access-list** command displays an abbreviated syntax of the access lists.

It is also useful, as part of a security plan or a capacity planning strategy, to track packets that have been denied by an access list.

The command **ip accounting access-violations** may be configured on individual interfaces to create a database of all packets that have been denied by any access lists on that interface. To examine the database, use the command **show ip accounting access-violations**. The source and destination addresses, the number of packets and number of bytes matching these addresses, and the access list number that denied the packet will be shown (Figure B.16). The command **clear ip accounting** clears the accounting database.

```
Woody#show ip accounting access-violations
     Source          Destination           Packets           Bytes   ACL
    10.1.4.1       255.255.255.255             13               936   110
    10.1.4.1       172.22.1.1                  12              1088   110

Accounting data age is 10
Woody#
```

Figure B.16

The access list accounting database can be observed with the command **show ip accounting access-violations**.

Accounting will disable autonomous and silicon switching on an interface. Do not use accounting on an interface where these switching modes are required.

As a final "trick," you should be aware that hits accounting does not track packets discarded by the implicit *deny any* at the end of the list. To track these packets, simply configure a deny any at the end of the list:

```
access-list 110 permit tcp any 172.22.0.0 0.0.255.255 established
access-list 110 permit tcp any host 172.22.15.83 eq smtp
access-list 110 permit tcp 10.0.0.0 0.255.255.255 172.22.114.0 0.0.0.255 eq telnet
access-list 110 permit udp 10.64.32.0 0.0.0.255 host 172.22.15.87 eq tftp
access-list 110 permit udp any host 172.22.15.85 eq domain
access-list 110 permit udp any any eq snmp
access-list 110 deny ip any any 1
```

Dynamic access lists are not covered in this book. Refer to Cisco's documentation for more information.

CCIE Preparation Tips

Becoming a Cisco Certified Internetworking Expert (CCIE) is a far cry from the "read a book, take an exam" process of some other industry certifications. You will be required to prove your expertise in a hands-on, notoriously difficult lab exam. While you must be intimately familiar with the Cisco configuration commands, the most difficult challenges of the lab are not Cisco specific; instead, they test the depths of your understanding of switches, routers, and routing protocols. It is for this knowledge that CCIEs are recognized and sought out as proven internetworking experts.

The structured creation of an internetwork involves four phases, and those same four phases are also useful for creating a structured preparation program for the CCIE lab.

Plan: Take a cold, hard look at your present experience level and your shortcomings. Evaluate the daily time you have available for study. Evaluate the resources at your disposal, including lab equipment; funds and time available for training; books; and acquaintances who can serve as coaches, tutors, and subject matter experts. Evaluate your personal strengths and weaknesses: Are you a good test taker? Do you work well under pressure? How do you react to setbacks and disappointments? Do you have good study habits? Do you learn best from reading or from verbal instruction? Using the raw data from your evaluations, write a list of your assets and liabilities.

Develop a plan to fully capitalize on your assets and eliminate as many liabilities as possible.

Design: Design a personalized preparation program that meets your needs while fitting your schedule and resources. Talk to as many CCIEs as possible; ask them about their own preparation programs. Find out what worked and what didn't work for them. Your program should take you from your present experience level right up to the CCIE lab, with definite deadlines and milestones. Build the project from a series of miniprojects, each with a well-defined goal. Be realistic when you design your schedule, taking into consideration the predictability (or lack of) of both your job and your personal life. The level of support you can expect from your employer and your family is an important factor in deciding whether your preparation schedule should be intensive or more relaxed. Exceeding the tolerance of those close to you will hurt your schedule far more than help it.

Implement: Many projects fail because the implementation begins before the design is complete. Your preparation program should be a written document clearly defining all steps of the project from kickoff to completion. Once you begin your preparation program, stick to it. Don't give up, don't be discouraged, and don't be lazy. Check off your goals and milestones as you meet them.

Optimize: Your preparation program should be a living document. As you progress, some subjects will be more difficult than expected, and some subjects will be easier than expected. Always move forward but be flexible enough to add any extra tasks necessary for you to master each topic.

Only you can design a preparation program that best suits you. The advice in the following sections is not meant to be followed unswervingly, but is meant to give you some ideas for creating your study program. These tips come from my personal experience as both a CCIE and as a Cisco Systems Instructor, and from the experiences of associates who have successfully passed the CCIE lab.

LAYING THE FOUNDATIONS

If you are a beginner, or your internetworking experience is limited, your first step is to get a solid grip on the basics of both internetworking and Cisco routers. This effort will involve both classroom training and self-study.

Through its training partners, Cisco offers many hands-on training classes. You should attend as many of these classes as your time and resources allow, but of particular importance are:

- Introduction to Cisco Router Configuration (ICRC)

- Advanced Cisco Router Configuration (ACRC)

- Cisco LAN Switch Configuration (CLSC)

- Cisco Internetwork Troubleshooting

Take full advantage of every class you attend. Ask questions of the instructor and discuss the class topics with your fellow students. Most important, take advantage of the access you have to the lab equipment. Don't just work the labs; be sure you fully understand the whys and hows of the lab exercises. When you finish a lab, don't just stop. Play with the equipment. See what configuration and troubleshooting options are available and try them. If you have time, try building the lab configuration several times to gain proficiency.

The classroom work will help you identify gaps in your internetworking knowledge. Read as much as you can, to fill in the gaps in your knowledge of basic internetworking protocols and technology. Many good tutorials are available on the Internet from both commercial vendors and private individuals. Whenever you begin studying a particular subject, be sure to perform a Web search for the topic.

HANDS-ON EXPERIENCE

Almost all CCIEs will tell you that hands-on experience is an invaluable part of preparing for the lab exam. Never pass up an opportunity to configure or troubleshoot a router. If you do not work with routers and switches on your present job, get friendly with the network engineers and technicians in your organization. Explain your goals to them and offer to assist them whenever possible.

If you have access to lab facilities, take full advantage of them. There is no replacement for the experience you can gain from working in a lab, where you can configure whatever you want to configure and introduce whatever problems you want to introduce, without risk of disrupting a production network.

In some large cities, the local Cisco Systems office may have a customer lab available that you can use by appointment. Ask your local Cisco representative.

Another option is to build your own lab. Although this option is expensive, the salary you can command as a CCIE may make the investment worthwhile. Many sources sell used Cisco equipment at fairly reasonable prices. Subscribe to the Cisco newsgroup on the Internet, at `comp.dcom.sys.cisco`; people frequently post used routers for sale, and you can find some good deals. Although even two routers are useful, you should try to obtain at least four, one of which should have four or more serial interfaces so that you can configure it as a Frame Relay or X.25 switch. Remember that you don't need top-of-the-line equipment; obsolete routers are especially good buys because no one wants them in a production network. You can obtain an AGS+, for instance, for $800 to $1500; it's an excellent lab router if you can stand the noise.

The configurations in this book were all built with five 2500s of various models and one AGS+ equipped with Ethernet, Token Ring, Serial, and FDDI interfaces.

INTENSIFYING THE STUDY

Beyond the basics, and in parallel with your acquisition of practical hands-on experience, you must begin building a deep understanding of the internetworking protocols. At a minimum, you should read the RFCs recommended in this book. Ideally, read as many relevant RFCs as you can. They are available from many sites on the Internet; just do a Web search on "RFC." One of the best sites is www.ietf.com.

Of course, not all internetworking protocols are described in RFCs. Look for advanced books, white papers, and tutorials on the non-IP protocols such as SNA, AppleTalk, IPX, and Banyan VINES. You should also study Ethernet, Token Ring, FDDI, and WAN protocols such as T-1, ISDN, X.25, Frame Relay, and ATM. You'll find a wealth of publicly available information at www.cisco.com.

A very useful study tool, incorporating both theory and practical knowledge, is the Cisco newsgroup at comp.dcom.sys.cisco. Copy particularly challenging questions and problems posted to the newsgroup and find your own answer. Then watch for the answers posted from CCIEs and Cisco engineers and see whether you are right. If not, determine why.

Post questions to the Cisco newsgroup, too. Most regular participants are friendly and willing to share their expertise. Another good source of information, if you are a registered user on Cisco's CCO, is the Open Forum at www.cisco.com/openf/openproj.shtml.

Finally, if you have associates with the same goals, form a study group. Within International Network Services, CCIE study groups have been very effective and have produced many CCIEs.

THE FINAL SIX MONTHS

With a now-solid background combining practical and theoretical knowledge, your final six months of preparation should involve reading the Cisco IOS Configuration Guides from cover to cover. As you read each chapter, review the associated chapter in the Cisco IOS Command Reference to ensure that you are familiar with the full configuration capabilities of the IOS for that protocol. Then use your lab to configure the protocol covered in the chapter in as many ways as you can. Play "what if" games, trying to make the protocol work in unusual situations. You will find that the best learning experiences result not when a configuration works as expected, but when it doesn't.

Keep a notebook of your configurations and your thoughts on how they worked or didn't work. Be sure to explore and record all troubleshooting tools, such as **debug** and **show** commands, relevant to the protocol.

Your goal at each end of chapter is to be able to configure at least the essential elements of the protocol from memory. When you are taking the CCIE lab, it is important to be able to configure the "easy stuff" with little thought so that you can be thinking ahead to the difficult configuration problems. You should also be familiar with how the protocol behaves, what configuration options exist, and how to troubleshoot the protocol. When you meet these goals for one chapter, move to the next.

Early in this final six months, you should take the written portion of the CCIE exam. Don't be fooled by this exam—it is intended primarily to weed out anyone who is completely unprepared so that he or she is only out the price of the written test instead of the much higher price of the lab exam. If you have followed a good study program, you will not find the written exam to be particularly difficult.

Several Cisco training partners offer CCIE preparation courses, which give you experience doing lab work under conditions similar to the CCIE lab exam. Do not mistake these classes as a substitute for diligent study and practice. If you choose to attend one of these classes, you should first be fully prepared to take the CCIE exam. The greatest benefit you will gain from the commercial preparation labs is a feel for being "under the gun," working difficult problems within tight time constraints.

EXAM DAY

The CCIE lab exam tests not only your practical and theoretical knowledge but also your ability to use that knowledge under pressure. You are in for an intense two days, so do not add unnecessarily to that pressure.

- Be aware that most people fail the CCIE exam on their first try. Have a contingency plan for taking the exam a second time. This strategy can help you stay calm during your first try and may make your contingency plan unnecessary.

- Arrange your travel plans so that you arrive in plenty of time the day before the exam. Arrange to leave the day after the exam, not the same evening. You don't want to think about your travel schedule during the exam.

- Locate the test facilities the evening before the exam. You don't want to show up for the exam flustered because you got lost.

- Do no more than a light review on the evening before the exam. If you try to "cram," you will make yourself nervous and sleepless.

- Eat a good dinner, with no alcohol, and get a good night's sleep.

- On the day of the exam, eat a good breakfast. It is an established fact that eating right will help you perform better.

- Dress comfortably. There are no points for appearance.

Before the exam, you will be required to sign a nondisclosure form stating that you will not divulge the details of the lab. The exam is 16 hours long, over two days. (Lunch breaks are scheduled each day.) Although other CCIE candidates will be working on their own labs in the room, you will be working alone. In all likelihood, the other candidates' assignments will be different from yours. The first day and a half (twelve hours) will be spent building an internetwork to given specifications. Be sure to document your work because you may be asked to explain or defend some of your design decisions and configuration choices.

After you have passed the configuration portion of the lab, you will go to lunch. During this time, problems will be introduced into the internetwork you have built. You will have four hours to correct and document the problems. Be sure to also document your troubleshooting procedure. As with the configuration section, you may be asked to explain your methods.

If you do not understand a particular requirement during any part of the exam, do not hesitate to ask your lab proctor. He or she is there not only to test you but also to help you. Most important, relax and stay focused.

When you have won your CCIE, you have accomplished something to be proud of. If this book or the advice in this appendix has helped you reach your goal, please e-mail me so that I can share your pride.

Answers to Review Questions

CHAPTER 1

1. The primary purpose of a local-area network is to allow resource sharing. The resources may be devices, applications, or information. Examples of shared resources are files, databases, e-mail, modems, and printers.

2. A protocol is an agreed-upon set of rules. In data communications, the rules usually govern a procedure or a format.

3. A Media Access Control protocol defines how a given LAN medium is shared, how LAN devices connected to the medium are identified, and how frames transmitted onto the medium are formatted.

4. A frame is a digital "envelope" that provides the information necessary for the delivery of data across a data link. Typical components of a frame are identifiers (addresses) of the source and destination devices on the data link, an indicator of the type of data enclosed in the frame, and error-checking information.

5. A feature common to all frame types is a format for identifying devices on the data link.

6. A Media Access Control address or identifier is a means by which individual devices connected to a data link are uniquely identified for the purpose of delivering data.

7. An address specifies a location. A MAC address is not a true address because it is permanently associated with the interface of a specific device and moves whenever the device moves. A MAC identifies the device, not the location of the device.

8. The three sources of signal degradation on a data link are attenuation, interference, and distortion. Attenuation is a function of the resistance of the medium. Interference is a function of noise entering the medium. Distortion is a function of the reactive characteristics of the medium, which react differently to different frequency components of the signal.

9. A repeater is a device that extends the useful range of a physical medium by reading a degraded signal and producing a "clean" copy of the signal.

10. A bridge is a device that increases the capacity of a LAN. A bridge divides the data link into segments, forwarding only traffic that is generated on one segment and is destined for another segment. By controlling and limiting the traffic on a data link, more devices may be attached to the LAN.

11. A transparent bridge "listens promiscuously" on each of its ports. That is, it examines all frames on all media to which it is attached. It records the source MAC identifiers of the frames, and the ports on which it learns the identifiers, in a bridging table. It can then refer to the table when deciding whether to filter or forward a frame. The bridge is transparent because it performs this learn-

ing function independently of the devices that originate the frames. The end devices themselves have no knowledge of the bridge.

12. Three fundamental differences between local-area and wide-area networks are:

   ○ LANs are limited to a small geographic area, such as a single building or small campus. WANs cover a large geographic area, from citywide to worldwide.

   ○ LANs usually consist entirely of privately owned components. Some components of a WAN, such as a packet switching network or point-to-point serial links, are usually leased from a service provider.

   ○ A LAN provides high bandwidth at a relatively cheap price. The bandwidth across a WAN is significantly more expensive.

13. A broadcast MAC identifier, when used as the destination address of a frame, signifies that the data is for all devices attached to the data link. In binary, the broadcast MAC identifier is all ones. In hex, it is FFFF.FFFF.FFFF.

14. The primary similarity between a bridge and a router is that both devices increase the number of hosts that may be interconnected into a common communications network. The difference is that a bridge works by interconnecting separate segments of a single network, whereas a router interconnects separate networks.

15. A packet is the means by which data is transported from one network to another. The similarity between a frame and a packet is that they both encapsulate data and provide an addressing scheme for delivering the data. The difference between a frame and a packet is that the

frame delivers data between two devices sharing a common data link, whereas a packet delivers data across a logical pathway, or route, spanning multiple data links.

16. Neither the source nor the destination address of a packet changes as it progresses from the source of the packet to the destination.

17. Network addresses are the addresses used in packets. Each network address has a network part, which identifies a particular data link, and a host or node part, which identifies a specific device on the data link identified by the network part.

18. A packet identifies a device from the perspective of the entire internetwork. A frame identifies a device from the perspective of a single data link. Because the connection between two devices across an internetwork is a logical path, a network address is a logical address. Because the connection between two devices across a data link is a physical path, a data link identifier is a physical address.

CHAPTER 2

1. The five layers of the TCP/IP protocol suite are the following:

    ○ Physical layer

    ○ Data link layer

    ○ Internet (or IP) layer

    ○ Host-to-host layer

    ○ Application layer

    The *physical layer* contains the protocols of the physical medium.

The *data link layer* contains the protocols that control the physical layer: How the medium is accessed and shared, how devices on the medium are identified, and how data is framed before being transmitted on the medium.

The *internet layer* contains the protocols that define the logical grouping of data links into an internetwork and the communication across that internetwork.

The *host-to-host layer* contains the protocols that define and control the logical, end-to-end paths across the internetwork.

The *application layer* corresponds to the OSI session, presentation, and application layers.

2. The most common IP version now in use is version 4.

3. Routers perform fragmentation when a packet is longer than the maximum packet length (Maximum Transmission Unit, or MTU) supported by a data link onto which the packet must be transmitted. The data within the packet will be broken into fragments, and each fragment will be encapsulated in its own packet. The receiver uses the Identifier and Fragment Offset fields and the MF bit of the Flags field to reassemble the fragments.

4. The Time to Live (TTL) field prevents "lost" packets from being passed endlessly through the IP internetwork. The field contains an 8-bit integer that is set by the originator of the packet. Each router through which the packet passes will decrement the integer by one. If a router decrements the TTL to zero, it will discard the packet and send an ICMP "time exceeded" error message to the packet's source address.

5. The first octet rule determines the class of an IP address as follows:

   ○ Class A: The first bit of the first octet is always 0.

   ○ Class B: The first two bits of the first octet are always 10.

   ○ Class C: The first three bits of the first octet are always 110.

   ○ Class D: The first four bits of the first octet are always 1110.

   ○ Class E: The first four bits of the first octet are always 1111.

6. The A, B, C IP addresses are recognized in dotted decimal and binary as follows:

Class	Binary Range of First Octet	Decimal Range of First Octet
A	00000001 - 01111110	1 - 126
B	10000000 - 10111111	128 - 191
C	11000000 - 11011111	192 - 223

7. An IP address mask identifies the network part of an IP address. Each one in the 32-bit mask marks the corresponding bit in the IP address as a network bit. A zero in the mask marks the corresponding bit in the IP address as a host bit. A Boolean AND is performed in all 32 bits of the address and the mask; in the result, all network bits of the mask will be repeated, and all host bits will be changed to zero.

8. A subnet is a subgrouping of a class A, B, or C IP address. Without subnetting, the network part of a major class A, B, or C IP address can only identify a single data link. Sub-

netting uses some of the host bits of a major IP address as network bits, allowing the single major address to be "subdivided" into multiple network addresses.

9. A classful routing protocol has no way to differentiate between the all-zeroes subnet and the major IP address, and between the all-ones subnet and the all-hosts, all-subnets broadcast address of the major IP address.

10. ARP, or Address Resolution Protocol, is a function that maps the IP addresses of interfaces on a data link to their corresponding MAC identifiers.

11. Proxy ARP is a function of an IP router. If the router hears an ARP request, and

   ○ The destination network or subnet is in the router's routing table, and

   ○ The table indicates that the destination is reachable via a different router interface than the one on which the ARP request was received,

   ○ The router will respond to the ARP request with its own MAC address.

12. A redirect is an IP router function. If a device has sent a packet to the router and the router must forward the packet to a next-hop router on the same data link, the router will send a redirect to the originating device. The redirect will inform the device that it can reach the next-hop router directly.

13. TCP, or Transmission Control Protocol, provides a connection-oriented service over the connectionless internet layer. UDP, or User Datagram Service, provides a connectionless service.

14. Correct sequencing is accomplished with sequence numbers. Reliability is accomplished by using checksums, acknowledgments, timers, and retransmissions. Flow control is accomplished by windowing.

15. A MAC identifier is a fixed-length binary integer. If IP used MAC identifiers as the host part of the IP address, subnetting would not be possible because there would be no flexibility in using some of the host bits as network bits.

Chapter 3

1. At a minimum, each entry of the routing table must include a destination address and the address of a next-hop router or an indication that the destination address is directly connected.

2. *Variably subnetted* means that the router knows of more than one subnet mask for subnets of the same major IP address.

3. Discontiguous subnets are two or more subnets of a major IP network address that are separated by a different major IP address.

4. **show ip route** is used to examine the routing table of a Cisco router.

5. The first bracketed number is the administrative distance of the routing protocol by which the route was learned. The second number is the metric of the route.

6. When a static route is configured to reference an exit interface instead of a next-hop address, the destination address will be entered into the routing table as directly connected.

7. A summary route is a single route entry that points to multiple subnets or major IP addresses. In the context of static routes, summary routes can reduce the number of static routes that must be configured.

8. An administrative distance is a rating of preference for a routing protocol or a static route. Every routing protocol and every static route has an administrative distance associated with it. When a router learns of a destination via more than one routing protocol or static route, it will use the route with the lowest administrative distance.

9. A floating static route is an alternative route to a destination. The administrative distance is set high enough that the floating static route is used only if a more-preferred route becomes unavailable.

10. Equal-cost load sharing distributes traffic equally among multiple paths with equal metrics. Unequal-cost load sharing distributes packets among multiple paths with different metrics. The traffic will be distributed inversely proportional to the cost of the routes.

11. If an interface is fast switched, per destination load sharing is performed. If an interface is process switched, per packet load sharing is performed.

12. A recursive routing table lookup occurs when a router cannot acquire all the information it needs to forward a packet with a single routing table lookup. For example, the router may perform one lookup to find the route to a destination and then perform another lookup to find a route to the next-hop router of the first route.

CHAPTER 4

1. A routing protocol is a "language" that routers speak to each other to share information about network destinations.

2. At a minimum, a routing protocol should define procedures for:

    ◦ Passing reachability information about networks to other routers

    ◦ Receiving reachability information from other routers

    ◦ Determining optimal routes based on the reachability information it has and for recording this information in a route table

    ◦ Reacting to, compensating for, and advertising topology changes in an internetwork

3. A route metric, also called a route cost or a route distance, is used to determine the best path to a destination. *Best* is defined by the type of metric used.

4. Convergence time is the time a group of routers take to complete the exchange of routing information.

5. Load balancing is the process of sending packets over multiple paths to the same destination. Four types of load balancing are:

    ◦ Equal cost, per packet

    ◦ Equal cost, per destination

    ◦ Unequal cost, per packet

    ◦ Unequal cost, per destination

6. A distance vector protocol is a routing protocol in which each router calculates routes based on the routes of its neighbors and then passes its routes to other neighbors.

7. Several problems associated with distance vector protocols are:

   ○ A susceptibility to incorrect routing information because of its dependence on neighbors for correct information

   ○ Slow convergence

   ○ Route loops

   ○ Counting to infinity

8. Neighbors are routers connected to the same data link.

9. Route invalidation timers delete routes from a route table if they exceed a certain age.

10. Simple split horizon does not send route information back to the source of the route information. Split horizon with poisoned reverse sends the information back to the source but sets the metric to unreachable.

11. Counting to infinity occurs when routes update a route over a loop; each router increases the metric of the route until the metric reaches infinity. The effects of counting to infinity are controlled by defining *infinity* as a fairly low metric so that infinity is reached fairly quickly and the route is declared unreachable.

12. Holddown timers help prevent routing loops. If a route is declared unreachable or if the metric increases beyond a certain threshold, a router will not accept any other information about that route until the holddown timer expires. This approach prevents the router from accepting possibly bad routing information while the internetwork is reconverging.

13. A distance vector router sends its entire route table, but it only sends the table to directly connected neighbors. A link state router sends only information about its directly connected links, but it floods the information

throughout the internetworking area. Distance vector protocols usually use a variant of the Bellman-Ford algorithm to calculate routes, and link state protocols usually use a variant of the Dijkstra algorithm to calculate routes.

14. A topological database holds the link state information originated by all routers in the link state routing domain.

15. Each router floods a link state information advertisement describing its links, the states of its links, and any neighboring routers connected to those links, throughout the internetworking area. All routers store all received copies of the link state advertisement in a link state database. Each router calculates a shortest path tree from the information in the topological database and enters routes in its routing tables based on the shortest path tree.

16. Sequence numbers help a router differentiate between multiple copies of the same link state advertisement and also prevent flooded link state advertisements from circulating endlessly throughout the internetwork.

17. Aging prevents old, possibly obsolete, link state information from residing in a topological database or from being accepted by a router.

18. A router builds a shortest path tree by first adding itself as the root. Using the information in the topological database, the router creates a list of all of its directly connected neighbors. The lowest-cost link to a neighbor becomes a branch of the tree, and that router's neighbors are added to the list. The list is checked for duplicate paths, and if they exist, the higher-cost paths are removed from the list. The lowest-cost router on the list is added to the tree, that router's neighbors are added to

the list, and the list is again checked for duplicate paths. This process continues until no routers remain on the list.

19. Within a routing domain, areas are subdomains. They make link state routing more efficient by limiting the size of the link state database of each router in the area.

20. Depending on the usage, an autonomous system can be defined as an internetwork under a common administrative domain or a single routing domain.

21. An Interior Gateway Protocol is a routing protocol that routes within an autonomous system. An Exterior Gateway Protocol is a routing protocol that routes between autonomous systems.

CHAPTER 5

1. RIP uses UDP port 520.

2. RIP uses a hop count metric. An unreachable network is indicated by setting the hop count to 16, which RIP interprets as an infinite distance.

3. RIP sends periodic updates every 30 seconds minus a small random variable to prevent the updates of neighboring routers from becoming synchronized.

4. A route entry is marked as unreachable if six updates are missed.

5. The garbage collection timer, or flush timer, is set when a route is declared unreachable. When the timer expires, the route is flushed from the route table. This process allows an unreachable route to remain in the routing table long enough for neighbors to be notified of its status.

6. The random timer, whose range is 1 to 5 seconds, prevents a "storm" of triggered updates during a topology change.

7. A Request message asks a router for an update. A Response message is an update.

8. A Request message may either ask for a full update or in some special cases it may ask for specific routes.

9. A Response is sent when the update timer expires, or upon reception of a Request message.

10. RIP updates do not include the subnet mask of the destination address, so a RIP router depends on the subnet masks of its own interfaces to determine how an attached major network address is subnetted. If a router does not have an attachment to a particular major network address, it has no way to know how that major network is subnetted. Therefore, no subnets of a major network address can be advertised into another major network.

CHAPTER 6

1. IGRP does not use a UDP port. It is accessed directly from the network layer, as protocol number 9.

2. The maximum IGRP network diameter is 255 hops.

3. The default IGRP update period is 90 seconds.

4. IGRP specifies an autonomous system number so that multiple IGRP processes can be enabled within the same routing domain and even on the same router.

5. McCloy will advertise 192.168.1.0 to Acheson as a system route because the address is being advertised into another major network. Acheson will advertise 172.16.0.0 as a system route to McCloy, and as an interior route to Kennan.

6. The default IGRP holddown time is 280 seconds.

7. IGRP can use bandwidth, delay, load, and reliability to calculate its metric. By default, it uses only bandwidth and delay.

8. An IGRP update packet can carry up to 104 route entries.

CHAPTER 7

1. The Route Tag field, the Subnet Mask field, and the Next Hop field are RIPv2 extensions that do not exist in RIPv1 messages. The basic format of the RIP message remains unchanged between the two versions; version 2 merely uses fields that are unused in version 1.

2. In addition to the functions that use the new fields, RIPv2 supports authentication and multicast updates.

3. RIPv2 uses the multicast address 224.0.0.9. Multicasting of routing messages is better than broadcasting because hosts and non-RIPv2 routers will ignore the multicast messages.

4. When another routing protocol uses the RIPv2 domain as a transit domain, the protocol external to RIPv2 can use the Route Tag field to communicate information to its peers on the other side of the RIPv2 domain.

5. The Next Hop field is used to inform other routers of a next-hop address on the same multiaccess network that is metrically closer to the destination than the originating router.

6. RIPv2 uses the same UDP port number as RIPv1, port number 520.

7. A classless routing protocol does not consider the major network address in its route lookups, but just looks for the longest match.

8. To support VLSM, a routing protocol must be able to include the subnet mask of each destination address in its updates.

9. Cisco's implementation of RIPv2 supports clear-text authentication and MD5 authentication. Only clear-text authentication is defined in RFC 1723.

CHAPTER 8

1. EIGRP is a distance vector protocol.

2. By default, EIGRP uses no more than 50% of the link's bandwidth, based on the bandwidth configured on the router's interface. This percentage to be changed with the command **ip bandwidth-percent eigrp**.

3. EIGRP and IGRP use the same formula to calculate their composite metrics, but EIGRP scales the metric by a factor of 256.

4. The four basic components of EIGRP are:
   ◦ The Protocol Dependent Modules

   ◦ The Reliable Transport Protocol

   ◦ The Neighbor Discovery and Recovery Module

   ◦ The Diffusing Update Algorithm

5. Reliable delivery means EIGRP packets are guaranteed to be delivered, and they are delivered in order. RTP uses a reliable multicast, in which received packets are acknowledged, to guarantee delivery; sequence numbers are used to ensure that they are delivered in order.

6. Sequence numbers ensure that a router is receiving the most recent route entry.

7. EIGRP uses the multicast address 224.0.0.10.

8. The packet types used by EIGRP are:
   - Hellos
   - Acknowledgments
   - Updates
   - Queries
   - Replies

9. The default EIGRP Hello interval is 5 seconds, except on some slow-speed (T1 and below) interfaces, where the default is 60 seconds.

10. The EIGRP default hold time is three times the Hello interval.

11. The neighbor table stores information about EIGRP-speaking neighbors; the topology table lists all known routes that have feasible successors.

12. The feasible distance to a destination is a router's lowest calculated distance to the destination.

13. The feasibility condition is the rule by which feasible successors are chosen for a destination. The feasibility condition is satisfied if a neighbor's advertised distance to a destination is lower than the receiving router's feasible distance to the destination. In other words, a router's neighbor meets the feasibility condition if the

neighbor is metrically closer to the destination than the router. Another way to describe this is that the neighbor is "downstream" relative to the destination.

14. A feasible successor to a destination is a neighbor that satisfies the feasibility condition for that destination.

15. A successor to a destination is a feasible successor that is currently being used as the next hop to the destination.

16. A route is active on a particular router if the router has queried its neighbors for a feasible successor and has not yet received a reply from every queried neighbor. The route is passive when there are no outstanding queries.

17. A route becomes active when no feasible successor exists in its topology table.

18. An active route becomes passive when a reply has been received from every queried neighbor.

19. If a router does not receive a reply from a queried neighbor within the active time (3 minutes, by default), the route is declared stuck-in-active. A response with an infinite metric is entered on the neighbor's behalf to satisfy DUAL, and the neighbor is deleted from the neighbor table.

20. Subnetting is the practice of creating a group of subnet addresses from a single IP network address. Address aggregation is the practice of summarizing a group of network or subnet addresses with a single IP network address.

CHAPTER 9

1. From the perspective of an OSPF router, a neighbor is another OSPF router that is attached to one of the first router's directly connected links.

2. An OSPF adjacency is a conceptual link to a neighbor over which LSAs can be sent.

3. The five OSPF packet types, and their purposes, are:

    ○ Hellos, which are used to discover neighbors, and to establish and maintain adjacencies

    ○ Updates, which are used to send LSAs between neighbors

    ○ Database Description packets, which a router uses to describe its link state database to a neighbor during database synchronization

    ○ Link State Requests, which a router uses to request one or more LSAs from a neighbor's link state database

    ○ Link State Acknowledgments, used to ensure reliable delivery of LSAs

4. A router originates a link state advertisement to describe one or more destinations. An OSPF Update packet transports LSAs from one neighbor to another. Although LSAs are flooded throughout an area or OSPF domain, Update packets never leave a data link.

5. The most common LSA types and their purposes are:

    ○ Type 1 (Router LSAs) are originated by every router and describe the originating router, the router's directly connected links and their states, and the router's neighbors.

- Type 2 (Network LSAs) are originated by Designated Routers on multiaccess links and describe the link and all attached neighbors.

- Type 3 (Network Summary LSAs) are originated by Area Border Routers and describe inter-area destinations.

- Type 4 LSAs (ASBR Summary LSAs) are originated by Area Border Routers to describe Autonomous System Boundary Routers outside the area.

- Type 5 (AS External LSAs) are originated by Autonomous System Boundary Routers to describe destinations external to the OSPF domain.

- Type 7 (NSSA External LSAs) are originated by Autonomous System Boundary Routers within not-so-stubby areas.

6. The link state database is where a router stores all the OSPF LSAs it knows of, including its own. Database synchronization is the process of ensuring that all routers within an area have identical link state databases.

7. The default OSPF HelloInterval is 10 seconds.

8. The default RouterDeadInterval is four times the HelloInterval.

9. A Router ID is an address by which an OSPF router identifies itself. It is either the numerically highest IP address of all the router's loopback interfaces, or if no loopback interfaces are configured, it is the numerically highest IP address of all the router's LAN interfaces.

10. An area is an OSPF sub-domain, within which all routers have an identical link state database.

11. Area 0 is the backbone area. All other areas must send their inter-area traffic through the backbone.

12. MaxAge, 1 hour, is the age at which an LSA is considered to be obsolete.

13. The four OSPF router types are:

- Internal Routers, whose OSPF interfaces all belong to the same area

- Backbone Routers, which are Internal Routers in Area 0

- Area Border Routers, which have OSPF interfaces in more than one area

- Autonomous System Boundary Routers, which advertise external routes into the OSPF domain

14. The four OSPF path types are:

- Intra-area paths

- Inter-area paths

- Type 1 external paths

- Type 2 external paths

15. The five OSPF network types are:

- Point-to-point networks

- Broadcast networks

- Non-broadcast multi-access (NBMA) networks

- Point-to-multipoint networks

- Virtual links

16. A Designated Router is a router that represents a multi-access network, and the routers connected to the network, to the rest of the OSFP domain.

17. Cisco IOS calculates the outgoing cost of an interface as 10^8/BW, where BW is the configured bandwidth of the interface.

18. An area is partitioned if one or more of its routers cannot send a packet to the area's other routers without sending the packet out of the area.

19. A virtual link is a tunnel that extends an OSPF backbone connection through a non-backbone area.

20. A stub area is an area into which no type 5 LSAs are flooded. A totally stubby area is an area into which no type 3, 4, or 5 LSAs are flooded, with the exception of type 3 LSAs to advertise a default route. Not-so-stubby areas are areas through which external destinations are advertised into the OSPF domain, but into which no type 5 LSAs are sent by the ABR.

21. OSPF network entries are entries in the route table, describing IP destinations. OSPF router entries are entries in a separate route table that record only routes to ABRs and ASBRs.

22. Type 2 authentication uses MD5 encryption, whereas type 1 authentication uses clear-text passwords.

23. The three fields in the LSA header that distinguish different LSAs are the Type, Advertising Router, and the Link State ID fields. The three fields in the LSA header that distinguish different instances of the same LSA are the Sequence Number, Age, and Checksum fields.

CHAPTER 10

1. An Intermediate System is the ISO term for a router.

2. A Network Protocol Data Unit is the ISO term for a packet.

3. An L1 router has no direct connections to another area. An L2 router only routes inter-area traffic. An L1/L2 router routes both inter-area and intra-area traffic and acts as an inter-area gateway for L1 routers.

4. The borders of IS-IS areas are between routers, on links. The borders of OSPF areas are defined by the routers themselves.

5. The Network Entity Title is an address by which a router identifies both itself and the area in which it resides.

6. The NSAP Selector should be set to 0x00 in a NET.

7. The System ID uniquely identifies a router within an IS-IS domain.

8. The portion of the NET preceding the last seven octets is the area address.

9. IS-IS does not elect a BDR.

10. The Pseudonode ID is the last octet of a LAN ID. Its purpose is to distinguish LAN IDs which are originated by a single router which is the DR on multiple LANs.

11. The MaxAge of an IS-IS LSP is 1200 seconds (20 minutes).

12. OSPF increments the age up to MaxAge; IS-IS decrements the age down to 0. A new OSPF LSA has an age of 0, whereas a new IS-IS LSP has an age of MaxAge.

13. The refresh rate of an IS-IS router is 900 seconds (15 minutes).

14. A Complete Sequence Number Packet contains a full listing of all LSPs in a database. A CSNP is periodically sent by the Designated Router on a broadcast network to maintain database synchronization.

15. A Partial Sequence Number Packet contains a listing of one or more LSPs. It has two uses: On point-to-point networks, it is used to acknowledge the receipt of LSPs. On broadcast networks, it is used to request LSPs.

16. An IS-IS router uses the Overload bit to inform its neighbors that it is experiencing a memory overload and cannot store the entire link state database.

17. The Attached bit is used by L1/L2 routers to inform L1 routers that it is attached to the L2 backbone.

18. The ISO specifies four metrics: Default, Expense, Delay, and Error. Cisco supports only the Default metric.

19. The maximum value of any of the IS-IS metrics is 63.

20. The maximum metric value of an IS-IS route is 1023.

21. L1 IS-IS metrics apply to intra-area routes, and L2 IS-IS metrics apply to inter-area routes.

22. Internal metrics apply to routes to destinations within the IS-IS domain. External metrics apply to routes to destinations external to the IS-IS domain.

CHAPTER 11

1. Routes that are learned from another routing protocol, static routes, or a direct connection to the destination network can be redistributed into a routing domain.

2. In contrast to metrics, which are used to determine the best path among multiple routes to the same destination discovered by the same routing protocol, administrative distances are used to determine the best path among multiple routes to the same destination discovered by different routing protocols.

3. A route to a destination within a routing domain with a higher administrative distance can be redistributed into a routing domain with a lower administrative distance. If that route is redistributed back into the higher-distance domain, packets might be misrouted into the lower-distance domain.

4. Redistributing variably subnetted destination addresses from a classless domain into a classful domain can cause problems.

5. OSPF and IS-IS understand the default metric. RIP, IGRP, and EIGRP do not.

6. The **metric** command assigns a metric to specific redistribution statements. The **default-metric** command assigns a metric to all redistribution commands that do not include the **metric** command.

7. Without the **subnets** keyword, only major network addresses that are not directly connected to the router will be redistributed.

8. A router that originates a summary route should use the null interface as the next hop of the summary route. Any packets that match the summary route, but for which there is no more-specific route to the packet's destination address, will be dropped. This prevents the router from forwarding "lost" packets.

CHAPTER 12

1. The default route address is 0.0.0.0.

2. IGRP and EIGRP advertise a default address as an external address type.

3. Yes.

4. A stub router is a router with only a single link to another router. A stub network is a network with only one attached router.

5. Using a default route rather than a full routing table can conserve router memory by keeping the table small and can save router processing cycles by limiting the routing information that must be processed.

6. Using a full routing table rather than a default route can make routing more accurate.

7. ODR uses Cisco Discovery Protocol (CDP) to discover routes.

8. ODR is available in IOS 11.2 and later.

9. The medium over which ODR is to run must support SNAP.

CHAPTER 14

1. Route maps are similar to access lists in that they define match criteria and an action to take in the event of a match. Route maps are different from access lists in that they not only specify match criteria but also specify set criteria. The set action can modify a route or route a packet according to the parameters of the packet.

2. Policy routes are static routes that use route maps to determine which packets should be routed and where the packets should be routed.

3. Route tags are fields within routing information packets that allow external information to be carried through the routing domain.

4. Route tags have no effect on the routing protocols that carry them.

E

Solutions to Configuration Problems

CHAPTER 2

1. If the first four bits of a class D address are 1110, the lowest first octet is 11100000 and the highest first octet is 11101111. In decimal these two numbers are 224 and 239, respectively. Therefore, the first octet of a class D address will range from 224 to 239.

2. (a) Enough subnet bits n are needed so that $2^n - 2 >= 16,000$. There must be enough host bits h remaining so that $2^h - 2 >= 700$. A subnet mask of 255.255.252.0 provides 16,382 subnets of the class A address, and 1022 host addresses on each subnet. This mask is the only one that works. If one more bit is used for subnetting (255.255.254.0), there will not be enough host addresses. If one less bit is used for subnetting (255.255.248.0), there will not be enough subnets.

(b) Enough subnet bits n are needed so that $2^n - 2 >= 500$. Enough host bits h must remain so that $2^h - 2 >= 100$. A subnet mask of 255.255.255.128 provides 510 subnets of the class B address and 126 host addresses on each subnet. Again, this mask is the only one that works.

3. With six bits of subnetting, a class C address will have 2^6 – 2 = 62 subnets and 2^2 – 2 = 2 host addresses per subnet. With this subnetting scheme, a single class C address can be used for 62 point-to-point links. A point-to-point link requires only two host addresses—one for each end of the link.

4. A class C address with a 28-bit mask will have 14 subnets and 14 host addresses on each subnet. The subnets are derived first.

The subnets are:

```
11111111111111111111111111110000 = 255.255.255.240 (mask)
11000000101010001001001100010000 = 192.168.147.16
11000000101010001001001100100000 = 192.168.147.32
11000000101010001001001100110000 = 192.168.147.48
11000000101010001001001101000000 = 192.168.147.64
11000000101010001001001101010000 = 192.168.147.80
11000000101010001001001101100000 = 192.168.147.96
11000000101010001001001101110000 = 192.168.147.112
11000000101010001001001110000000 = 192.168.147.128
11000000101010001001001110010000 = 192.168.147.144
11000000101010001001001110100000 = 192.168.147.160
11000000101010001001001110110000 = 192.168.147.176
11000000101010001001001111000000 = 192.168.147.192
11000000101010001001001111010000 = 192.168.147.208
11000000101010001001001111100000 = 192.168.147.224
```

Next, the host addresses for each subnet are derived. The broadcast addresses for each subnet are also shown.

The host addresses for each subnet are:

```
11000000101010001001001100010000 = 192.168.147.16 (subnet)
11000000101010001001001100010001 = 192.168.147.17
11000000101010001001001100010010 = 192.168.147.18
11000000101010001001001100010011 = 192.168.147.19
11000000101010001001001100010100 = 192.168.147.20
11000000101010001001001100010101 = 192.168.147.21
11000000101010001001001100010110 = 192.168.147.22
11000000101010001001001100010111 = 192.168.147.23
11000000101010001001001100011000 = 192.168.147.24
11000000101010001001001100011001 = 192.168.147.25
11000000101010001001001100011010 = 192.168.147.26
11000000101010001001001100011011 = 192.168.147.27
```

```
110000001010100010010011000011100 = 192.168.147.28
110000001010100010010011000011101 = 192.168.147.29
110000001010100010010011000011110 = 192.168.147.30
110000001010100010010011000011111 = 192.168.147.31 (broadcast)
110000001010100010010011000100000 = 192.168.147.32 (subnet)
110000001010100010010011000100001 = 192.168.147.33
110000001010100010010011000100010 = 192.168.147.34
110000001010100010010011000100011 = 192.168.147.35
110000001010100010010011000100100 = 192.168.147.36
110000001010100010010011000100101 = 192.168.147.37
110000001010100010010011000100110 = 192.168.147.38
110000001010100010010011000100111 = 192.168.147.39
110000001010100010010011000101000 = 192.168.147.40
110000001010100010010011000101001 = 192.168.147.41
110000001010100010010011000101010 = 192.168.147.42
110000001010100010010011000101011 = 192.168.147.43
110000001010100010010011000101100 = 192.168.147.44
110000001010100010010011000101101 = 192.168.147.45
110000001010100010010011000101110 = 192.168.147.46
110000001010100010010011000101111 = 192.168.147.47 (broadcast)
110000001010100010010011000110000 = 192.168.147.48 (subnet)
110000001010100010010011000110001 = 192.168.147.49
110000001010100010010011000110010 = 192.168.147.50
110000001010100010010011000110011 = 192.168.147.51
110000001010100010010011000110100 = 192.168.147.52
110000001010100010010011000110101 = 192.168.147.53
110000001010100010010011000110110 = 192.168.147.54
110000001010100010010011000110111 = 192.168.147.55
110000001010100010010011000111000 = 192.168.147.56
110000001010100010010011000111001 = 192.168.147.57
110000001010100010010011000111010 = 192.168.147.58
110000001010100010010011000111011 = 192.168.147.59
110000001010100010010011000111100 = 192.168.147.60
110000001010100010010011000111101 = 192.168.147.61
110000001010100010010011000111110 = 192.168.147.62
110000001010100010010011000111111 = 192.168.147.63 (broadcast)
110000001010100010010011010000000 = 192.168.147.64 (subnet)
110000001010100010010011010000001 = 192.168.147.65
110000001010100010010011010000010 = 192.168.147.66
110000001010100010010011010000011 = 192.168.147.67
110000001010100010010011010000100 = 192.168.147.68
110000001010100010010011010000101 = 192.168.147.69
110000001010100010010011010000110 = 192.168.147.70
110000001010100010010011010000111 = 192.168.147.71
110000001010100010010011010001000 = 192.168.147.72
110000001010100010010011010001001 = 192.168.147.73
110000001010100010010011010001010 = 192.168.147.74
110000001010100010010011010001011 = 192.168.147.75
110000001010100010010011010001100 = 192.168.147.76
110000001010100010010011010001101 = 192.168.147.77
```

```
11000000101010000100100101001110 = 192.168.147.78
11000000101010000100100101001111 = 192.168.147.79 (broadcast)
11000000101010000100100101010000 = 192.168.147.80 (subnet)
11000000101010000100100101010001 = 192.168.147.81
11000000101010000100100101010010 = 192.168.147.82
11000000101010000100100101010011 = 192.168.147.83
11000000101010000100100101010100 = 192.168.147.84
11000000101010000100100101010101 = 192.168.147.85
11000000101010000100100101010110 = 192.168.147.86
11000000101010000100100101010111 = 192.168.147.87
11000000101010000100100101011000 = 192.168.147.88
11000000101010000100100101011001 = 192.168.147.89
11000000101010000100100101011010 = 192.168.147.90
11000000101010000100100101011011 = 192.168.147.91
11000000101010000100100101011100 = 192.168.147.92
11000000101010000100100101011101 = 192.168.147.93
11000000101010000100100101011110 = 192.168.147.94
11000000101010000100100101011111 = 192.168.147.95 (broadcast)
11000000101010000100100101100000 = 192.168.147.96 (subnet)
11000000101010000100100101100001 = 192.168.147.97
11000000101010000100100101100010 = 192.168.147.98
11000000101010000100100101100011 = 192.168.147.99
11000000101010000100100101100100 = 192.168.147.100
11000000101010000100100101100101 = 192.168.147.101
11000000101010000100100101100110 = 192.168.147.102
11000000101010000100100101100111 = 192.168.147.103
11000000101010000100100101101000 = 192.168.147.104
11000000101010000100100101101001 = 192.168.147.105
11000000101010000100100101101010 = 192.168.147.106
11000000101010000100100101101011 = 192.168.147.107
11000000101010000100100101101100 = 192.168.147.108
11000000101010000100100101101101 = 192.168.147.109
11000000101010000100100101101110 = 192.168.147.110
11000000101010000100100101101111 = 192.168.147.111 (broadcast)
11000000101010000100100101110000 = 192.168.147.112 (subnet)
11000000101010000100100101110001 = 192.168.147.113
11000000101010000100100101110010 = 192.168.147.114
11000000101010000100100101110011 = 192.168.147.115
11000000101010000100100101110100 = 192.168.147.116
11000000101010000100100101110101 = 192.168.147.117
11000000101010000100100101110110 = 192.168.147.118
11000000101010000100100101110111 = 192.168.147.119
11000000101010000100100101111000 = 192.168.147.120
11000000101010000100100101111001 = 192.168.147.121
11000000101010000100100101111010 = 192.168.147.122
11000000101010000100100101111011 = 192.168.147.123
11000000101010000100100101111100 = 192.168.147.124
11000000101010000100100101111101 = 192.168.147.125
11000000101010000100100101111110 = 192.168.147.126
```

```
110000001010100010010011011111111 = 192.168.147.127 (broadcast)
110000001010100010010011110000000 = 192.168.147.128 (subnet)
110000001010100010010011110000001 = 192.168.147.129
110000001010100010010011110000010 = 192.168.147.130
110000001010100010010011110000011 = 192.168.147.131
110000001010100010010011110000100 = 192.168.147.132
110000001010100010010011110000101 = 192.168.147.133
110000001010100010010011110000110 = 192.168.147.134
110000001010100010010011110000111 = 192.168.147.135
110000001010100010010011110001000 = 192.168.147.136
110000001010100010010011110001001 = 192.168.147.137
110000001010100010010011110001010 = 192.168.147.138
110000001010100010010011110001011 = 192.168.147.139
110000001010100010010011110001100 = 192.168.147.140
110000001010100010010011110001101 = 192.168.147.141
110000001010100010010011110001110 = 192.168.147.142
110000001010100010010011110001111 = 192.168.147.143 (broadcast)
110000001010100010010011110010000 = 192.168.147.144 (subnet)
110000001010100010010011110010001 = 192.168.147.145
110000001010100010010011110010010 = 192.168.147.146
110000001010100010010011110010011 = 192.168.147.147
110000001010100010010011110010100 = 192.168.147.148
110000001010100010010011110010101 = 192.168.147.149
110000001010100010010011110010110 = 192.168.147.150
110000001010100010010011110010111 = 192.168.147.151
110000001010100010010011110011000 = 192.168.147.152
110000001010100010010011110011001 = 192.168.147.153
110000001010100010010011110011010 = 192.168.147.154
110000001010100010010011110011011 = 192.168.147.155
110000001010100010010011110011100 = 192.168.147.156
110000001010100010010011110011101 = 192.168.147.157
110000001010100010010011110011110 = 192.168.147.158
110000001010100010010011110011111 = 192.168.147.159 (broadcast)
110000001010100010010011110100000 = 192.168.147.160 (subnet)
110000001010100010010011110100001 = 192.168.147.161
110000001010100010010011110100010 = 192.168.147.162
110000001010100010010011110100011 = 192.168.147.163
110000001010100010010011110100100 = 192.168.147.164
110000001010100010010011110100101 = 192.168.147.165
110000001010100010010011110100110 = 192.168.147.166
110000001010100010010011110100111 = 192.168.147.167
110000001010100010010011110101000 = 192.168.147.168
110000001010100010010011110101001 = 192.168.147.169
110000001010100010010011110101010 = 192.168.147.170
110000001010100010010011110101011 = 192.168.147.171
110000001010100010010011110101100 = 192.168.147.172
110000001010100010010011110101101 = 192.168.147.173
110000001010100010010011110101110 = 192.168.147.174
110000001010100010010011110101111 = 192.168.147.175 (broadcast)
110000001010100010010011110110000 = 192.168.147.176 (subnet)
```

```
11000000101010001001001110110001 = 192.168.147.177
11000000101010001001001110110010 = 192.168.147.178
11000000101010001001001110110011 = 192.168.147.179
11000000101010001001001110110100 = 192.168.147.180
11000000101010001001001110110101 = 192.168.147.181
11000000101010001001001110110110 = 192.168.147.182
11000000101010001001001110110111 = 192.168.147.183
11000000101010001001001110111000 = 192.168.147.184
11000000101010001001001110111001 = 192.168.147.185
11000000101010001001001110111010 = 192.168.147.186
11000000101010001001001110111011 = 192.168.147.187
11000000101010001001001110111100 = 192.168.147.188
11000000101010001001001110111101 = 192.168.147.189
11000000101010001001001110111110 = 192.168.147.190
11000000101010001001001110111111 = 192.168.147.191 (broadcast)
11000000101010001001001111000000 = 192.168.147.192 (subnet)
11000000101010001001001111000001 = 192.168.147.193
11000000101010001001001111000010 = 192.168.147.194
11000000101010001001001111000011 = 192.168.147.195
11000000101010001001001111000100 = 192.168.147.196
11000000101010001001001111000101 = 192.168.147.197
11000000101010001001001111000110 = 192.168.147.198
11000000101010001001001111000111 = 192.168.147.199
11000000101010001001001111001000 = 192.168.147.200
11000000101010001001001111001001 = 192.168.147.201
11000000101010001001001111001010 = 192.168.147.202
11000000101010001001001111001011 = 192.168.147.203
11000000101010001001001111001100 = 192.168.147.204
11000000101010001001001111001101 = 192.168.147.205
11000000101010001001001111001110 = 192.168.147.206
11000000101010001001001111001111 = 192.168.147.207 (broadcast)
11000000101010001001001111010000 = 192.168.147.208 (subnet)
11000000101010001001001111010001 = 192.168.147.209
11000000101010001001001111010010 = 192.168.147.210
11000000101010001001001111010011 = 192.168.147.211
11000000101010001001001111010100 = 192.168.147.212
11000000101010001001001111010101 = 192.168.147.213
11000000101010001001001111010110 = 192.168.147.214
11000000101010001001001111010111 = 192.168.147.215
11000000101010001001001111011000 = 192.168.147.216
11000000101010001001001111011001 = 192.168.147.217
11000000101010001001001111011010 = 192.168.147.218
11000000101010001001001111011011 = 192.168.147.219
11000000101010001001001111011100 = 192.168.147.220
11000000101010001001001111011101 = 192.168.147.221
11000000101010001001001111011110 = 192.168.147.222
11000000101010001001001111011111 = 192.168.147.223 (broadcast)
11000000101010001001001111100000 = 192.168.147.224 (subnet)
11000000101010001001001111100001 = 192.168.147.225
```

```
11000000101010001001001111100010 = 192.168.147.226
11000000101010001001001111100011 = 192.168.147.227
11000000101010001001001111100100 = 192.168.147.228
11000000101010001001001111100101 = 192.168.147.229
11000000101010001001001111100110 = 192.168.147.230
11000000101010001001001111100111 = 192.168.147.231
11000000101010001001001111101000 = 192.168.147.232
11000000101010001001001111101001 = 192.168.147.233
11000000101010001001001111101010 = 192.168.147.234
11000000101010001001001111101011 = 192.168.147.235
11000000101010001001001111101100 = 192.168.147.236
11000000101010001001001111101101 = 192.168.147.237
11000000101010001001001111101110 = 192.168.147.238
11000000101010001001001111101111 = 192.168.147.239(broadcast)
```

5. This solution shows a shorter technique than the last solution in which every host address of every subnet was written out.

A class C address with a 29-bit mask means that there will be 30 subnets and six host addresses on each subnet.

The subnets are:

```
11111111111111111111111111111000 = 255.255.255.248 (mask)
11000000101010001001001100001000 = 192.168.147.8
11000000101010001001001100010000 = 192.168.147.16
11000000101010001001001100011000 = 192.168.147.24
11000000101010001001001100100000 = 192.168.147.32
11000000101010001001001100101000 = 192.168.147.40
11000000101010001001001100110000 = 192.168.147.48
11000000101010001001001100111000 = 192.168.147.56
11000000101010001001001101000000 = 192.168.147.64
11000000101010001001001101001000 = 192.168.147.72
11000000101010001001001101010000 = 192.168.147.80
11000000101010001001001101011000 = 192.168.147.88
11000000101010001001001101100000 = 192.168.147.96
11000000101010001001001101101000 = 192.168.147.104
11000000101010001001001101110000 = 192.168.147.112
11000000101010001001001101111000 = 192.168.147.120
11000000101010001001001110000000 = 192.168.147.128
11000000101010001001001110001000 = 192.168.147.136
11000000101010001001001110010000 = 192.168.147.144
11000000101010001001001110011000 = 192.168.147.152
11000000101010001001001110100000 = 192.168.147.160
11000000101010001001001110101000 = 192.168.147.168
11000000101010001001001110110000 = 192.168.147.176
11000000101010001001001110111000 = 192.168.147.184
```

```
11000000101010000100100111000000 = 192.168.147.192
11000000101010000100100111001000 = 192.168.147.200
11000000101010000100100111010000 = 192.168.147.208
11000000101010000100100111011000 = 192.168.147.216
11000000101010000100100111100000 = 192.168.147.224
11000000101010000100100111101000 = 192.168.147.232
11000000101010000100100111110000 = 192.168.147.240
```

Next, the broadcast addresses of each subnet are derived by setting the host bits of each subnet to all ones.

The subnet broadcast addresses are:

```
11000000101010000100100100001111 = 192.168.147.15
11000000101010000100100100010111 = 192.168.147.23
11000000101010000100100100011111 = 192.168.147.31
11000000101010000100100100100111 = 192.168.147.39
11000000101010000100100100101111 = 192.168.147.47
11000000101010000100100100110111 = 192.168.147.55
11000000101010000100100100111111 = 192.168.147.63
11000000101010000100100101000111 = 192.168.147.71
11000000101010000100100101001111 = 192.168.147.79
11000000101010000100100101010111 = 192.168.147.87
11000000101010000100100101011111 = 192.168.147.95
11000000101010000100100101100111 = 192.168.147.103
11000000101010000100100101101111 = 192.168.147.111
11000000101010000100100101100111 = 192.168.147.119
11000000101010000100100101111111 = 192.168.147.127
11000000101010000100100110000111 = 192.168.147.135
11000000101010000100100110001111 = 192.168.147.143
11000000101010000100100110010111 = 192.168.147.151
11000000101010000100100110011111 = 192.168.147.159
11000000101010000100100110100111 = 192.168.147.167
11000000101010000100100110101111 = 192.168.147.175
11000000101010000100100110110111 = 192.168.147.183
11000000101010000100100110111111 = 192.168.147.191
11000000101010000100100111000111 = 192.168.147.199
11000000101010000100100111001111 = 192.168.147.207
11000000101010000100100111010111 = 192.168.147.215
11000000101010000100100111011111 = 192.168.147.223
11000000101010000100100111100111 = 192.168.147.231
11000000101010000100100111101111 = 192.168.147.239
11000000101010000100100111110111 = 192.168.147.247
```

Finally, the host addresses for each subnet are derived. They will be all addresses between the subnet addresses and the subnet broadcast addresses.

Subnet	Broadcast	Host Addresses
192.168.147.8	192.168.147.15	192.168.147.9 - 192.168.147.14
192.168.147.16	192.168.147.23	192.168.147.17 - 192.168.147.22
192.168.147.24	192.168.147.31	192.168.147.25 - 192.168.147.30
192.168.147.32	192.168.147.39	192.168.147.33 - 192.168.147.38
192.168.147.40	192.168.147.47	192.168.147.41 - 192.168.147.46
192.168.147.48	192.168.147.55	192.168.147.49 - 192.168.147.54
192.168.147.56	192.168.147.63	192.168.147.57 - 192.168.147.62
192.168.147.64	192.168.147.71	192.168.147.65 - 192.168.147.70
192.168.147.72	192.168.147.79	192.168.147.73 - 192.168.147.78
192.168.147.80	192.168.147.87	192.168.147.81 - 192.168.147.86
192.168.147.88	192.168.147.95	192.168.147.89 - 192.168.147.94
192.168.147.96	192.168.147.103	192.168.147.97 - 192.168.147.102
192.168.147.104	192.168.147.111	192.168.147.105 - 192.168.147.110
192.168.147.112	192.168.147.119	192.168.147.113 - 192.168.147.118
192.168.147.120	192.168.147.127	192.168.147.121 - 192.168.147.126
192.168.147.128	192.168.147.135	192.168.147.129 - 192.168.147.134
192.168.147.136	192.168.147.143	192.168.147.137 - 192.168.147.142
192.168.147.144	192.168.147.151	192.168.147.145 - 192.168.147.150
192.168.147.152	192.168.147.159	192.168.147.153 - 192.168.147.158
192.168.147.160	192.168.147.167	192.168.147.161 - 192.168.147.166
192.168.147.168	192.168.147.175	192.168.147.169 - 192.168.147.174
192.168.147.176	192.168.147.183	192.168.147.177 - 192.168.147.182
192.168.147.184	192.168.147.191	192.168.147.185 - 192.168.147.190
192.168.147.192	192.168.147.199	192.168.147.193 - 192.168.147.198
192.168.147.200	192.168.147.207	192.168.147.201 - 192.168.147.206
192.168.147.208	192.168.147.215	192.168.147.209 - 192.168.147.214

Subnet	Broadcast	Host Addresses
192.168.147.216	192.168.147.223	192.168.147.217 - 192.168.147.222
192.168.147.224	192.168.147.231	192.168.147.225 - 192.168.147.230
192.168.147.232	192.168.147.239	192.168.147.233 - 192.168.147.238
192.168.147.240	192.168.147.247	192.168.147.241 - 192.168.147.246

6. A class B address with a 20-bit mask will have 14 subnets and 4,094 host addresses on each subnet.

The subnets are:

```
11111111111111111111000000000000 = 255.255.240.0 (mask)
10101100000100000001000000000000 = 172.16.16.0
10101100000100000010000000000000 = 172.16.32.0
10101100000100000011000000000000 = 172.16.48.0
10101100000100000100000000000000 = 172.16.64.0
10101100000100000101000000000000 = 172.16.80.0
10101100000100000110000000000000 = 172.16.96.0
10101100000100000111000000000000 = 172.16.112.0
10101100000100001000000000000000 = 172.16.128.0
10101100000100001001000000000000 = 172.16.144.0
10101100000100001010000000000000 = 172.16.160.0
10101100000100001011000000000000 = 172.16.176.0
10101100000100001100000000000000 = 172.16.192.0
10101100000100001101000000000000 = 172.16.208.0
10101100000100001110000000000000 = 172.16.224.0
```

The subnet broadcast addresses are:

```
10101100000100000001111111111111 = 172.16.31.255
10101100000100000010111111111111 = 172.16.47.255
10101100000100000011111111111111 = 172.16.63.255
10101100000100000100111111111111 = 172.16.79.255
10101100000100000101111111111111 = 172.16.95.255
10101100000100000110111111111111 = 172.16.111.255
10101100000100000111111111111111 = 172.16.127.255
10101100000100001000111111111111 = 172.16.143.255
10101100000100001001111111111111 = 172.16.159.255
10101100000100001010111111111111 = 172.16.175.255
10101100000100001011111111111111 = 172.16.191.255
10101100000100001100111111111111 = 172.16.207.255
10101100000100001101111111111111 = 172.16.223.255
10101100000100001110111111111111 = 172.16.239.255
```

Using the derived subnet and broadcast addresses, the host addresses are:

Subnet	Broadcast	Host Addresses
172.16.16.0	172.16.31.255	172.16.16.1 - 172.16.31.254
172.16.32.0	172.16.47.255	172.16.32.1 - 172.16.47.254
172.16.48.0	172.16.63.255	172.16.48.1 - 172.16.63.254
172.16.64.0	172.16.79.255	172.16.64.1 - 172.16.79.254
172.16.80.0	172.16.95.255	172.16.80.1 - 172.16.95.254
172.16.96.0	172.16.111.255	172.16.96.1 - 172.16.111.254
172.16.112.0	172.16.127.255	172.16.112.1 - 172.16.127.254
172.16.128.0	172.16.143.255	172.16.128.1 - 172.16.143.254
172.16.144.0	172.16.159.255	172.16.144.1 - 172.16.159.254
172.16.160.0	172.16.175.255	172.16.160.1 - 172.16.175.254
172.16.176.0	172.16.191.255	172.16.176.1 - 172.16.191.254
172.16.192.0	172.16.207.255	172.16.192.1 - 172.16.207.254
172.16.208.0	172.16.223.255	172.16.208.1 - 172.16.223.254
172.16.224.0	172.16.239.255	172.224.16.1 - 172.16.239.254

CHAPTER 3

1. First determine the subnet addresses of each link and then write the static routes. Remember that the routers will already have entries in their route tables for any directly connected subnet. The static routes are:

RTA

```
ip route 192.168.2.64 255.255.255.224 192.168.2.131
ip route 192.168.2.160 255.255.255.224 192.168.2.131
ip route 192.168.1.128 255.255.255.240 192.168.2.131
ip route 192.168.1.16 255.255.255.240 192.168.2.131
ip route 192.168.2.32 255.255.255.224 192.168.2.131
```

```
ip route 192.168.1.160 255.255.255.240 192.168.2.131
ip route 10.1.1.0 255.255.255.0 192.168.2.131
ip route 10.1.3.0 255.255.255.0 192.168.2.131
ip route 10.1.2.0 255.255.255.0 192.168.2.131
```

RTB

```
ip route 10.1.4.0 255.255.255.0 192.168.2.132
ip route 192.168.1.128 255.255.255.240 192.168.2.174
ip route 192.168.1.16 255.255.255.240 192.168.2.174
ip route 192.168.2.32 255.255.255.224 192.168.2.174
ip route 192.168.1.160 255.255.255.240 192.168.2.174
ip route 10.1.1.0 255.255.255.0 192.168.2.174
ip route 10.1.3.0 255.255.255.0 192.168.2.174
ip route 10.1.2.0 255.255.255.0 192.168.2.174
```

RTC

```
ip route 10.1.4.0 255.255.255.0 192.168.2.185
ip route 192.168.2.128 255.255.255.224 192.168.2.185
ip route 192.168.2.64 255.255.255.224 192.168.2.185
ip route 192.168.2.32 255.255.255.224 192.168.1.20
ip route 10.1.1.0 255.255.255.0 192.168.1.173
ip route 10.1.3.0 255.255.255.0 192.168.1.173
ip route 10.1.2.0 255.255.255.0 192.168.1.173
```

RTD

```
ip route 10.1.4.0 255.255.255.0 192.168.1.29
ip route 192.168.2.128 255.255.255.224 192.168.1.29
ip route 192.168.2.64 255.255.255.224 192.168.1.29
ip route 192.168.2.160 255.255.255.224 192.168.1.29
ip route 192.168.1.128 255.255.255.240 192.168.1.29
ip route 192.168.1.160 255.255.255.240 192.168.1.29
ip route 10.1.1.0 255.255.255.0 192.168.1.29
ip route 10.1.1.3.0 255.255.255.0 192.168.1.29
ip route 10.1.2.0 255.255.255.0 192.168.1.29
```

RTE

```
ip route 10.1.4.0 255.255.255.0 192.168.1.163
ip route 192.168.2.128 255.255.255.224 192.168.1.163
ip route 192.168.2.64 255.255.255.224 192.168.1.163
ip route 192.168.2.160 255.255.255.224 192.168.1.163
ip route 192.168.1.128 255.255.255.240 192.168.1.163
ip route 192.168.1.16 255.255.255.240 192.168.1.163
ip route 192.168.2.32 255.255.255.224 192.168.1.163
ip route 10.1.2.0 255.255.255.0 10.1.3.2
```

RTF

```
ip route 10.1.4.0 255.255.255.0 10.1.3.1
ip route 192.168.2.128 255.255.255.224 10.1.3.1
ip route 192.168.2.64 255.255.255.224 10.1.3.1
ip route 192.168.2.160 255.255.255.224 10.1.3.1
ip route 192.168.1.128 255.255.255.240 10.1.3.1
ip route 192.168.1.16 255.255.255.240 10.1.3.1
ip route 192.168.2.32 255.255.255.224 10.1.3.1
ip route 192.168.1.160 255.255.255.240 10.1.3.1
ip route 10.1.1.0 255.255.255.0 10.1.3.1
```

2. The static routes are:

RTA

```
ip route 192.168.0.0 255.255..0.0 192.168.2.131
ip route 10.1.0.0 255.255.0.0 192.168.2.131
```

RTB

```
ip route 10.1.4.0 255.255.255.0 192.168.2.132
ip route 192.168.0.0 255.255.0.0 192.168.2.174
ip route 10.1.0.0 255.255.0.0 192.168.2.174
```

RTC

```
ip route 10.1.4.0 255.255.255.0 192.168.2.185
ip route 192.168.2.0 255.255.255.224 192.168.2.185
ip route 192.168.2.32 255.255.255.224 192.168.1.20
ip route 10.1.0.0 255.255.0.0 192.168.1.173
```

RTD

```
ip route 10.1.0.0 255.255.0.0 192.168.1.29
ip route 192.168.0.0 255.255.05.0 192.168.1.29
```

RTE

```
ip route 10.1.4.0 255.255.255.0 192.168.1.163
ip route 192.168.0.0 255.255.0.0 192.168.1.163
ip route 10.1.2.0 255.255.255.0 10.1.3.2
```

RTF

```
ip route 10.1.0.0 255.255.05.0 10.1.3.1
ip route 192.168.0.0 255.255.0.0 10.1.3.1
```

3. The static routes are:

RTA

```
ip route 172.16.7.0 255.255.255.0 172.16.2.2
ip route 172.16.7.0 255.255.255.0 172.16.4.2 50
ip route 172.16.6.0 255.255.255.0 172.16.2.2
ip route 172.16.6.0 255.255.255.0 172.16.4.2 50
ip route 172.16.8.0 255.255.255.0 172.16.4.2
ip route 172.16.8.0 255.255.255.0 172.16.2.2 50
ip route 172.16.5.0 255.255.255.0 172.16.4.2
ip route 172.16.5.0 255.255.255.0 172.16.2.2 50
ip route 172.16.9.0 255.255.255.0 172.16.2.2
ip route 172.16.9.0 255.255.255.0 172.16.4.2
```

RTB

```
ip route 172.16.1.0 255.255.255.0 172.16.2.1
ip route 172.16.1.0 255.255.255.0 172.16.6.1 50
ip route 172.16.4.0 255.255.255.0 172.16.2.1
ip route 172.16.4.0 255.255.255.0 172.16.6.1 50
ip route 172.16.9.0 255.255.255.0 172.16.6.1
ip route 172.16.9.0 255.255.255.0 172.16.2.1 50
ip route 172.16.5.0 255.255.255.0 172.16.6.1
ip route 172.16.5.0 255.255.255.0 172.16.2.1 50
ip route 172.16.8.0 255.255.255.0 172.16.6.1
ip route 172.16.8.0 255.255.255.0 172.16.2.1
```

RTC

```
ip route 172.16.1.0 255.255.255.0 172.16.6.2
ip route 172.16.1.0 255.255.255.0 172.16.5.1
ip route 172.16.4.0 255.255.255.0 172.16.5.1
ip route 172.16.4.0 255.255.255.0 172.16.6.2 50
ip route 172.16.2.0 255.255.255.0 172.16.6.2
ip route 172.16.2.0 255.255.255.0 172.16.5.1 50
ip route 172.16.7.0 255.255.255.0 172.16.6.2
ip route 172.16.7.0 255.255.255.0 172.16.5.1 50
ip route 172.16.8.0 255.255.255.0 172.16.5.1
ip route 172.16.8.0 255.255.255.0 172.16.6.2 50
```

RTD

```
ip route 172.16.1.0 255.255.255.0 172.16.4.1
ip route 172.16.1.0 255.255.255.0 172.16.5.2 50
ip route 172.16.2.0 255.255.255.0 172.16.4.1
ip route 172.16.2.0 255.255.255.0 172.16.5.2 50
ip route 172.16.9.0 255.255.255.0 172.16.5.2
ip route 172.16.9.0 255.255.255.0 172.16.4.1 50
ip route 172.16.6.0 255.255.255.0 172.16.5.2
ip route 172.16.6.0 255.255.255.0 172.16.4.1 50
ip route 172.16.7.0 255.255.255.0 172.16.5.2
ip route 172.16.7.0 255.255.255.0 172.16.4.1
```

CHAPTER 5

1. In addition to the RIP configurations shown here, a subnet of 192.168.5.0 must be configured between RTE and
   RTF, using secondary addresses. Otherwise, subnets
   192.168.5.192/27 and 192.168.5.96/27 are discontiguous. The RIP configurations are:

   RTA

   ```
   router rip
     network 192.168.2.0
   ```

   RTB

   ```
   router rip
     network 192.168.2.0
   ```

   RTC

   ```
   router rip
     network 192.168.2.0
     network 192.168.3.0
   ```

   RTD

   ```
   router rip
     network 192.168.3.0
     network 192.168.4.0
   ```

   RTE

   ```
   router rip
     network 192.168.4.0
     network 192.168.5.0
   ```

   RTF

   ```
   router rip
     network 192.168.4.0
     network 192.168.6.0
   ```

2. To unicast RIP updates between RTC and RTD, the configurations are:

   RTC

   ```
   router rip
     network 192.168.2.0
     neighbor 192.168.3.2
   ```

RTD

```
router rip
  network 192.168.3.0
  neighbor 192.168.3.1
```

3. The update time applies to the entire RIP process. If the update time is changed for the serial link, it will also be changed for the router's other links. That, in turn, means that the timers must be changed on the neighboring routers, which means those neighbors' neighbors must be changed, and so on. The cascade effect of changing the update timer on a single router means that the timers must be changed on every router in the RIP domain. The command to increase the RIP update period to 2 minutes, configured on every router, is:

```
timers basic 120 360 360 480
```

Because the update timer is changed, the invalid, holddown and flush timers must also be changed. Setting the invalid and holddown timers to six times the update period, as the default timers are, would make the conversion time of the internetwork extremely high. Therefore, the invalid and holddown timers are set to three times the update period. The flush timer must be longer than the hold-down timer, so it is set to 60 seconds longer.

4. Network 192.168.4.0 is 2 hops from RTA, so adding 14 to the metric will give the route an unreachable metric of 16. Remember that in Configuration Exercise 1 a subnet of 192.168.5.0 had to be configured on the same link as 192.168.4.0 using secondary addresses, so that the subnets of 192.168.5.0 are contiguous. Therefore, 192.168.5.0 is also 2 hops from RTB. Assuming the interfaces of RTA and RTB connected to RTC are E0 on both routers, the configurations are:

RTA

```
router rip
 offset-list 1 in 14 Ethernet0
 network 192.168.2.0
!
access-list 1 permit 192.168.4.0 0.0.0.0
```

RTB

```
router rip
 offset-list 1 in 14 Ethernet0
 network 192.168.2.0
!
access-list 1 permit 192.168.5.0 0.0.0.0
```

5. RTB, with its longer mask, can interpret all subnets correctly. The problem is at RTA. With a 27-bit mask, RTA interprets RTB's subnets 192.168.20.40/29 and 192.168.20.49/29 as 192.168.20.32/27—the same subnet as its directly connected link. Therefore, RTA does not have a correct "view" of the internetwork.

However, packets can still be routed if Proxy ARP is enabled. For example, suppose RTA has a packet to forward with a destination address of 192.168.20.50. RTA incorrectly interprets this address as a member of its subnet 192.168.20.32/27, and ARPs for the MAC identifier of 192.168.20.50 on that subnet. RTB hears the ARP; it correctly interprets 192.168.20.50 as being a member of its subnet 192.168.20.48/29 and responds with the MAC identifier of its interface on 192.168.20.32/29. RTA then forwards the packet to RTB, and RTB forwards the packet to the correct destination. If Proxy ARP is disabled, packets will not be delivered correctly from RTA to RTB.

CHAPTER 6

1. Using secondary IP addresses, a subnet of 192.168.5.0 must be added to the Ethernet interfaces of RTE and RTF to connect the noncontiguous subnets of those routers' Token Ring interfaces. The IGRP configurations are:

   RTA
   ```
   router igrp 50
     network 192.168.2.0
   ```

   RTB
   ```
   router igrp 50
     network 192.168.2.0
   ```

   RTC
   ```
   router igrp 50
     network 192.168.2.0
     network 192.168.3.0
   ```

   RTD
   ```
   router igrp 50
     network 192.168.3.0
     network 192.168.4.0
   ```

   RTE
   ```
   router igrp 50
     network 192.168.4.0
     network 192.168.5.0
   ```

   RTF
   ```
   router igrp 50
     network 192.168.4.0
     network 192.168.5.0
   ```

2. The minimum bandwidth of the route is that of RTD's Ethernet interface. The total metric is the sum of this bandwidth and the delays of each interface:

   1000 + 10 + 7 + 100 + 63 = 1180

3. The minimum bandwidth of the route is that of RTD's Ethernet interface. Because K5 is nonzero, the formula is

metric = [k1*BW$_{IGRP(min)}$ + (k2* BW$_{IGRP(min)}$)/(256-LOAD) + k3*DLY$_{IGRP(sum)}$] * [k5/(RELIABILITY+k4)]

K1 = K2 = K4 = K5 = 1, and K3 = 0, so:

metric = [1*1000 + (1*1000)/(256-1) + 0*DLY$_{IGRP(sum)}$] * [k5/(255+1)]

    = [1000 + 1000/255 + 0] * [1/256]

    = 3.922

Fractional portions of the metric are dropped, so the metric of the route from 192.168.2.96/27 to 192.168.5.96/27 is 3.

4. The lowest metric of the five paths between the two FDDI networks is 698, and the highest is 21541. 21541/698 = 30.86, so the commands that must be added to the IGRP configurations of the two routers are **maximum-paths 5** and **variance 31**.

CHAPTER 7

1. The statement **neighbor 172.25.150.206** can be added to Taos's RIP configuration, causing Taos to unicast RIP updates to that address. This approach works only if Pojoaque's RIPv1 process complies with the rule that the unused fields of RIP messages with version numbers higher than 1 will be ignored and the rest of the packet processed.

2. Begin by calculating the subnet(s) with the highest number of hosts. From the unused subnet bits, calculate the subnet(s) with the next-highest number of hosts, and so on. Remember that as a group of bits are used for a subnet, no subsequent subnet can begin with that same bit combination. For example, if the first subnet begins with

00, all subsequent subnets must begin with 01, 10, or 11. If the second subnet begins with 010, no subsequent subnet can begin with 010.

One solution (with the subnet bits shown in bold) is:

```
00000000 = 192.168.100.0/26    (62 hosts)
01000000 = 192.168.100.64/27   (30 hosts)
01100000 = 192.168.100.96/28   (14 hosts)
01110000 = 192.168.100.112/28  (14 hosts)
10000000 = 192.168.100.128/28  (14 hosts)
10010000 = 192.168.100.144/28  (14 hosts)
10100000 = 192.168.100.160/28  (14 hosts)
10110000 = 192.168.100.176/29  (8 hosts)
10111000 = 192.168.100.184/29  (8 hosts)
11000000 = 192.168.100.192/29  (8 hosts)
11001000 = 192.168.100.200/29  (8 hosts)
11010000 = 192.168.100.208/29  (8 hosts)
11011000 = 192.168.100.216/30  (2 hosts)
11011100 = 192.168.100.220/30  (2 hosts)
11100000 = 192.168.100.224/30  (2 hosts)
11100100 = 192.168.100.228/30  (2 hosts)
11101000 = 192.168.100.232/30  (2 hosts)
11101100 = 192.168.100.236/30  (2 hosts)
11110000 = 192.168.100.240/30  (2 hosts)
11110100 = 192.168.100.244/30  (2 hosts)
11111000 = 192.168.100.248/30  (2 hosts)
11111100 = 192.168.100.252/30  (2 hosts)
```

3. RTA, RTB, and RTD have the statement **version 2** in their RIP configurations. Additionally, the RIP configurations of RTA and RTB include the statement **no auto-summary**. The interfaces of RTA and RTB connected to subnet 192.168.2.64/28 have the statements **ip rip send version 1 2** and **ip rip receive version 1 2**. The interface of RTD connected to subnet 192.168.2.128/28 has the statements **ip rip send version 1** and **ip rip receive version 1**.

4. The following solution uses a key chain name of *CCIE* and a key string named *exercise4* on RTB and RTD. Assuming both routers' interfaces are S0, the configuration of both RTB and RTD is:

```
key chain CCIE
  key 1
    key-string exercise4
!
interface Serial0
  ip address 192.168.1.15X 255.255.255.252
  ip rip authentication mode md5
  ip rip authentication key-chain CCIE
```

5. The configuration here assumes that the authentication key in Configuration Exercise 4 was enabled on October 31, 1998, at midnight. The second key string used here is *exercise5a*, and the third key string is *exercise5b*.

```
key chain CCIE
  key 1
    key-string exercise4
    accept-lifetime 00:00:00 Oct 31 1998 00:00:00 Nov 3 1998
    send-lifetime 00:00:00 Oct 31 1998 00:30:00 Nov 3 1998
  key 2
    key-string exercise5a
    accept-lifetime 00:00:00 Nov 3 1998 duration 36000
    send-lifetime 00:00:00 Nov 3 1998 duration 36000
  key 3
    key-string exercise5b
    accept-lifetime 10:00:00 Nov 3 1998 infinite
    send-lifetime 10:00:00 Nov 3 1998 infinite
!
interface Serial0
  ip address 192.168.1.15X 255.255.255.252
  ip rip authentication mode md5
  ip rip authentication key-chain CCIE
```

CHAPTER 8

1. No further configuration is necessary, because automatic summarization is still enabled at Earhart.

2. The EIGRP configurations are:

RTA

```
router eigrp 5
  network 172.16.0.0
  network 172.18.0.0
```

RTB

```
router eigrp 5
  network 172.16.0.0
```

RTC

```
router eigrp 5
  network 172.16.0.0
  network 172.17.0.0
```

3. This solution uses a key chain named *CCIE* and key strings named *exercise3a* and *exercise3b*. Assuming today's date is November 30, 1998, and the first key begins being used at 8:30 AM, the configurations of the serial interfaces are:

```
key chain CCIE
 key 1
  key-string exercise3a
  accept-lifetime 08:30:00 Dec 2 1998 08:30:00 Jan 1 1999
  send-lifetime 08:30:00 Dec 2 1998 08:30:00 Jan 1 1999
 key 2
  key-string exercise3b
  accept-lifetime 08:30:00 Jan 1 1999 infinite
  send-lifetime 08:30:00 Jan 1 1999 infinite
!
interface Serial0
 ip address 172.16.3.19X 255.255.255.252
 ip authentication key-chain eigrp 5 CCIE
 ip authentication mode eigrp 5 md5
```

4. The EIGRP configuration of RTD is:

```
router eigrp 5
 network 172.16.0.0
 network 172.17.0.0
 no auto-summary
```

Auto summarization must also be turned off on RTB and RTA.

5. No changes are needed in the previous EIGRP configurations. The configuration of RTE is:

```
router igrp 5
 network 172.18.0.0
```

6. The EIGRP configuration of RTF is:

```
router eigrp 5
 network 172.16.0.0
 network 172.18.0.0
 no auto-summary
```

The statement **ip summary-address eigrp 5 172.18.10.192 255.255.255.224** is added to RTA's interface on subnet 172.18.10.96/27.

7. RTA can send a summary address of 172.16.3.128/25 to RTF and a summary address of 172.16.3.0/25 to RTB. All other summarization is performed automatically.

CHAPTER 9

1. The OSPF configurations are:

RTA

```
     router ospf 1
       network 10.0.0.0 0.0.255.255 area 0
```

RTB

```
     router ospf 1
       network 10.0.0.0 0.0.255.255 area 0
       network 10.5.0.0 0.0.255.255 area 5
       area 5 virtual-link 10.100.100.9
```

RTC

```
router ospf 1
  network 10.0.0.0 0.0.255.255 area 0
  network 10.10.0.0 0.0.255.255 area 10
  network 10.30.0.0 0.0.255.255 area 30
```

RTD

```
router ospf 1
  network 10.0.0.0 0.0.255.255 area 0
  network 10.20.0.0 0.0.255.255 area 20
```

RTE

```
router ospf 1
  network 10.0.0.0 0.0.255.255 area 0
  network 10.15.0.0 0.0.255.255 area 15
```

RTF

```
router ospf 1
  network 10.5.0.0 0.0.255.255 area 5
```

RTG

```
router ospf 1
  network 10.10.1.58 0.0.0.0 area 5
```

RTH

```
router ospf 1
  network 10.20.100.100 0.0.0.0 area 20
```

RTI

```
router ospf 1
  network 10.5.0.0 0.0.255.255 area 5
  network 10.35.0.0 0.0.255.255 area 35
  area 5 virtual-link 10.100.100.2
```

RTJ

```
router ospf 1
  network 10.15.0.0 0.0.255.255 area 15
```

RTK through RTN have Frame Relay interfaces. The four interfaces to the Frame Relay network are all on the same subnet, so the OSPF network type must be either broadcast or point-to-multipoint:

RTK

```
interface Serial0
  encapsulation frame-relay
  ip address 10.30.254.193 255.255.255.192
  ip ospf network point-to-multipoint
!
router ospf 1
  network 10.30.0.0 0.0.255.255 area 30
```

RTL

```
  encapsulation frame-relay
  ip address 10.30.254.194 255.255.255.192
  ip ospf network point-to-multipoint
!
router ospf 1
  network 10.30.0.0 0.0.255.255 area 30
```

RTM

```
  encapsulation frame-relay
  ip address 10.30.254.195 255.255.255.192
  ip ospf network point-to-multipoint
!
router ospf 1
  network 10.30.0.0 0.0.255.255 area 30
```

RTN

```
  encapsulation frame-relay
  ip address 10.30.254.196 255.255.255.192
  ip ospf network point-to-multipoint
!
router ospf 1
  network 10.30.0.0 0.0.255.255 area 30
```

2. The ABR configurations are:

RTB

```
router ospf 1
  network 10.0.0.0 0.0.255.255 area 0
  network 10.5.0.0 0.0.255.255 area 5
  area 5 virtual-link 10.100.100.9
  area 0 range 10.0.0.0 255.255.0.0
  area 5 range 10.5.0.0 255.255.0.0
```

RTC

```
router ospf 1
  network 10.0.0.0 0.0.255.255 area 0
  network 10.10.0.0 0.0.255.255 area 10
  network 10.30.0.0 0.0.255.255 area 30
  area 0 range 10.0.0.0 255.255.0.0
  area 10 range 10.10.0.0 255.255.0.0
  area 30 range 10.30.0.0 255.255.0.0
```

RTD

```
router ospf 1
  network 10.0.0.0 0.0.255.255 area 0
  network 10.20.0.0 0.0.255.255 area 20
  area 0 range 10.0.0.0 255.255.0.0
  are 20 range 10.20.0.0 255.255.0.0
```

RTE

```
router ospf 1
  network 10.0.0.0 0.0.255.255 area 0
  network 10.15.0.0 0.0.255.255 area 15
  area 0 range 10.0.0.0 255.255.0.0
  area 15 range 10.15.0.0 255.255.0.0
```

RTI

```
router ospf 1
  network 10.5.0.0 0.0.255.255 area 5
  network 10.35.0.0 0.0.255.255 area 35
  area 5 virtual-link 10.100.100.2
  area 0 range 10.0.0.0 255.255.0.0
  area 5 range 10.5.0.0 255.255.0.0
  area 35 range 10.35.0.0 255.255.0.0
```

3. The configurations are:

RTE

```
router ospf 1
  network 10.0.0.0 0.0.255.255 area 0
  network 10.15.0.0 0.0.255.255 area 15
  area 15 stub
```

RTJ

```
router ospf 1
  network 10.15.0.0 0.0.255.255 area 15
  area 15 stub
```

4. The configurations are:

RTC

```
router ospf 1
  network 10.0.0.0 0.0.255.255 area 0
  network 10.10.0.0 0.0.255.255 area 10
  network 10.30.0.0 0.0.255.255 area 30
  area 0 range 10.0.0.0 255.255.0.0
  area 10 range 10.10.0.0 255.255.0.0
  area 30 stub no-summary
  area 30 range 10.30.0.0 255.255.0.0
```

RTK

```
router ospf 1
  network 10.30.0.0 0.0.255.255 area 30
  area 30 stub
```

RTL

```
router ospf 1
  network 10.30.0.0 0.0.255.255 area 30
  area 30 stub
```

RTM

```
router ospf 1
  network 10.30.0.0 0.0.255.255 area 30
  area 30 stub
```

RTN

```
router ospf 1
  network 10.30.0.0 0.0.255.255 area 30
  area 30 stub
```

5. The configurations are:

RTD

```
router ospf 1
  network 10.0.0.0 0.0.255.255 area 0
  network 10.20.0.0 0.0.255.255 area 20
  area 20 nssa
```

RTH

```
router ospf 1
  network 10.20.100.100 0.0.0.0 area 20
  area 20 nssa
```

6. Only one end of a point-to-point circuit needs to be configured as a demand circuit. In this solution, RTC is chosen:

```
interface Serial0
  ip address 10.30.255.249 255.255.255.252
  ip ospf demand-circuit
!
router ospf 1
  network 10.0.0.0 0.0.255.255 area 0
  network 10.10.0.0 0.0.255.255 area 10
  network 10.30.0.0 0.0.255.255 area 30
  area 0 range 10.0.0.0 255.255.0.0
  area 10 range 10.10.0.0 255.255.0.0
  area 30 range 10.30.0.0 255.255.0.0
```

CHAPTER 10

1. This solution uses a System ID of 0000.1234.abcX, where X is a number that makes the router unique within the IS-IS domain. The System ID is six octets, which is required by Cisco IOS. The minimum NET length is eight octets, one of which is the SEL, so the area address is a one-octet number corresponding to the area number shown in Table 10.6. The configurations are:

RTA

```
interface Ethernet0
  ip address 192.168.1.17 255.255.255.240
  ip router isis
!
interface Ethernet1
  ip address 192.168.1.50 255.255.255.240
  ip router isis
  clns router isis
!
router isis
  net 00.0000.1234.abc1.00
  is-type level-1
```

RTB

```
interface Ethernet0
  ip address 192.168.1.33 255.255.255.240
  ip router isis
!
interface Ethernet1
  ip address 192.168.1.51 255.255.255.240
  ip router isis
  clns router isis
!
router isis
  net 00.0000.1234.abc2.00
  is-type level-1
```

RTC

```
interface Ethernet0
  ip address 192.168.1.49 255.255.255.240
  ip router isis
  clns router isis
!
interface Serial0
  ip address 192.168.1.133 255.255.255.252
  ip router isis
!
router isis
  net 00.0000.1234.abc3.00
```

RTD

```
interface Serial0
  ip address 192.168.1.134 255.255.255.252
  ip router isis
!
interface Serial1
  ip address 192.168.1.137 255.255.255.252
  ip router isis
!
router isis
  net 00.0000.1234.abc4.00
  is-type level-2-only
```

RTE

```
interface Serial0
  ip address 192.168.1.142 255.255.255.252
  ip router isis
!
interface Serial1
  ip address 192.168.1.145 255.255.255.252
  ip router isis
!
interface Serial2
  ip address 192.168.1.138 255.255.255.252
  ip router isis
!
router isis
  net 00.0000.1234.abc5.00
  is-type level-2-only
```

RTF

```
interface Serial0
  ip address 192.168.1.141 255.255.255.252
  ip router isis
!
interface Serial1
  ip address 192.168.1.158 255.255.255.252
  ip router isis
!
router isis
  net 00.0000.1234.abc6.00
  is-type level-2-only
```

RTG

```
interface Ethernet0
  ip address 192.168.1.111 255.255.255.224
  ip router isis
  ip router clns
!
interface Serial0
  ip address 192.168.1.157 255.255.255.252
  ip router isis
!
router isis
  net 00.0000.1234.abc7.00
```

RTH

```
interface Ethernet0
  ip address 192.168.1.73 255.255.255.224
  ip router isis
!
interface Ethernet1
  ip address 192.168.1.97 255.255.255.224
  ip router isis
  ip router clns
!
router isis
  net 00.0000.1234.abc8.00
  is-type level-1
```

RTI

```
interface Ethernet0
  ip address 192.168.1.225 255.255.255.248
  ip router isis
!
interface Ethernet1
  ip address 192.168.1.221 255.255.255.248
  ip router isis
  clns router isis
!
interface Serial0
  ip address 192.168.1.249 255.255.255.252
  ip router isis
  clns router isis
!
interface Serial1
  ip address 192.168.1.146 255.255.255.252
  ip router isis
!
router isis
  net 00.0000.1234.abc9.00
```

RTJ

```
interface Ethernet0
  ip address 192.168.1.201 255.255.255.248
  ip router isis
!
interface Ethernet1
  ip address 192.168.1.217 255.255.255.248
  ip router isis
  clns router isis
!
router isis
  net 00.0000.1234.abca.00
  is-type level-1
```

RTK

```
interface Ethernet0
  ip address 192.168.1.209 255.255.255.248
  ip router isis
!
interface Serial0
  ip address 192.168.1.250 255.255.255.252
  ip router isis
  clns router isis
!
  router isis
  net 00.0000.1234.abcb.00
is-type level-1
```

2. The configurations are:

RTD

```
interface Serial0
  ip address 192.168.1.134 255.255.255.252
  ip router isis
!
interface Serial1
  ip address 192.168.1.137 255.255.255.252
  ip router isis
  isis password Eiffel level-2
!
router isis
  net 00.0000.1234.abc4.00
  is-type level-2-only
```

RTE

```
interface Serial0
  ip address 192.168.1.142 255.255.255.252
  ip router isis
  isis password Tower level-2
!
interface Serial1
  ip address 192.168.1.145 255.255.255.252
  ip router isis
!
interface Serial2
  ip address 192.168.1.138 255.255.255.252
  ip router isis
  isis password Eiffel level-2
!
router isis
  net 00.0000.1234.abc5.00
  is-type level-2-only
```

RTF

```
interface Serial0
  ip address 192.168.1.141 255.255.255.252
  ip router isis
  isis password Tower level-2
!
interface Serial1
  ip address 192.168.1.158 255.255.255.252
  ip router isis
!
router isis
  net 00.0000.1234.abc6.00
  is-type level-2-only
```

3. The configurations are:

RTG

```
interface Ethernet0
  ip address 192.168.1.111 255.255.255.224
  ip router isis
  ip router clns
!
interface Serial0
  ip address 192.168.1.157 255.255.255.252
  ip router isis
!
router isis
  net 00.0000.1234.abc7.00
  area-password Scotland
```

RTH

```
interface Ethernet0
  ip address 192.168.1.73 255.255.255.224
  ip router isis
!
interface Ethernet1
  ip address 192.168.1.97 255.255.255.224
  ip router isis
  ip router clns
!
router isis
  net 00.0000.1234.abc8.00
  is-type level-1
  area-password Scotland
```

4. The configurations are:

RTC

```
interface Ethernet0
  ip address 192.168.1.49 255.255.255.240
  ip router isis
  clns router isis
!
interface Serial0
  ip address 192.168.1.133 255.255.255.252
  ip router isis
!
router isis
  net 00.0000.1234.abc3.00
  domain-password Vienna
```

RTD

```
interface Serial0
  ip address 192.168.1.134 255.255.255.252
  ip router isis
!
interface Serial1
  ip address 192.168.1.137 255.255.255.252
  ip router isis
  isis password Eiffel level-2
!
router isis
  net 00.0000.1234.abc4.00
  is-type level-2-only
  domain-password Vienna
```

RTE

```
interface Serial0
  ip address 192.168.1.142 255.255.255.252
  ip router isis
  isis password Tower level-2
!
interface Serial1
  ip address 192.168.1.145 255.255.255.252
  ip router isis
!
interface Serial2
  ip address 192.168.1.138 255.255.255.252
  ip router isis
  isis password Eiffel level-2
!
router isis
  net 00.0000.1234.abc5.00
  is-type level-2-only
  domain-password Vienna
```

RTF

```
interface Serial0.
  ip address 192.168.1.141 255.255.255.252
  ip router isis
  isis password Tower level-2
!
interface Serial1
  ip address 192.168.1.158 255.255.255.252
  ip router isis
!
router isis
  net 00.0000.1234.abc6.00
  is-type level-2-only
  domain-password Vienna
```

RTG

```
interface Ethernet0
  ip address 192.168.1.111 255.255.255.224
  ip router isis
  ip router clns
!
interface Serial0
  ip address 192.168.1.157 255.255.255.252
  ip router isis
!
router isis
  net 00.0000.1234.abc7.00
  area-password Scotland
  domain-password Vienna
```

RTI

```
interface Ethernet0
  ip address 192.168.1.225 255.255.255.248
  ip router isis
!
interface Ethernet1
  ip address 192.168.1.221 255.255.255.248
  ip router isis
  clns router isis
!
interface Serial0
  ip address 192.168.1.249 255.255.255.252
  ip router isis
  clns router isis
!
interface Serial1
  ip address 192.168.1.146 255.255.255.252
  ip router isis
!
router isis
  net 00.0000.1234.abc9.00
  domain-password Vienna
```

5. The configurations are:

RTC

```
interface Ethernet0
  ip address 192.168.1.49 255.255.255.240
  ip router isis
  clns router isis
!
interface Serial0
  ip address 192.168.1.133 255.255.255.252
  ip router isis
!
router isis
  net 00.0000.1234.abc3.00
  domain-password Vienna
  summary-address 192.168.1.0 255.255.255.192
```

RTG

```
interface Ethernet0
  ip address 192.168.1.111 255.255.255.224
  ip router isis
  ip router clns
!
interface Serial0
  ip address 192.168.1.157 255.255.255.252
  ip router isis
!
router isis
  net 00.0000.1234.abc7.00
  area-password Scotland
  domain-password Vienna
  summary-address 192.168.1.64 255.255.255.192
```

RTI

```
interface Ethernet0
  ip address 192.168.1.225 255.255.255.248
  ip router isis
!
interface Ethernet1
  ip address 192.168.1.221 255.255.255.248
  ip router isis
  clns router isis
!
interface Serial0
  ip address 192.168.1.249 255.255.255.252
  ip router isis
  clns router isis
!
interface Serial1
  ip address 192.168.1.146 255.255.255.252
  ip router isis
!
router isis
  net 00.0000.1234.abc9.00
  domain-password Vienna
  summary-address 192.168.1.192 255.255.255.192
```

CHAPTER 11

1. The difficulty with the internetwork of Figure 11.37, when running classful routing protocols on RTB, is that network 172.16.0.0 is variably subnetted. The solution is to use a 28-bit mask on RTB's E1 interface while RTC still uses a 27-bit mask for the same subnet. This solution works because 172.16.1.96 remains distinct in the internetwork of Figure 11.37, whether it is subnetted with a 27-bit mask or a 28-bit mask.

   RTB's configuration is:
   ```
   interface Ethernet0
     ip address 172.16.1.146 255.255.255.240
   !
   interface Ethernet1
     ip address 172.16.1.98 255.255.255.240
   !
   router rip
     redistribute igrp 1 metric 1
     passive-interface Ethernet0
     network 172.16.0.0
   !
   router igrp 1
     redistribute rip metric 10000 1000 255 1 1500
     passive-interface Ethernet1
     network 172.16.0.0
   ```

2. This configuration changes RTB's E1 mask back to a 27-bit mask. However, RIP does not advertise subnet 172.16.1.144/28. To remedy this problem, a static route is entered to that subnet but with a 27-bit mask. Because the mask references RTB's E0 interface, it is redistributed into RIP automatically.
   ```
   interface Ethernet0
     ip address 172.16.1.146 255.255.255.240
   !
   interface Ethernet1
     ip address 172.16.1.98 255.255.255.224
   !
   router ospf 1
     redistribute rip metric 50 subnets
     network 172.16.1.0 0.0.0.255 area 0
   ```

```
!
router rip
  redistribute ospf 1 metric 2
  passive-interface Ethernet0
  network 172.16.0.0
!
ip classless
ip route 172.16.1.128 255.255.255.224 Ethernet0
```

3. RTB's configuration is:

```
interface Ethernet0
  ip address 172.16.1.146 255.255.255.240
  ip summary-address eigrp 1 172.16.2.0 255.255.255.0
!
interface Ethernet1
  ip address 172.16.1.98 255.255.255.224
!
router eigrp 1
  redistribute isis level-2 metric 10000 1000 255 1 1500
  passive-interface Ethernet1
  network 172.16.0.0
!
router isis
  net 00.0000.1234.abc1.00
  summary-address 172.16.1.128 255.255.255.128
  redistribute eigrp 1 metric 20 metric-type external level-2
```

CHAPTER 13

1. RTA's configuration is:

```
router rip
  redistribute igrp 1 metric 3
  passive-interface Ethernet0
  passive-interface Ethernet1
  network 172.16.0.0
  distribute-list 1 in Ethernet3
!
router igrp 1
  redistribute rip metric 10000 1000 255 1 1500
  passive-interface Ethernet2
  passive-interface Ethernet3
  network 172.16.0.0
!
access-list 1 deny 172.16.12.0
access-list 1 permit any
```

2. RTA's configuration is:

```
router rip
  redistribute igrp 1 metric 3
  passive-interface Ethernet0
  passive-interface Ethernet1
  network 172.16.0.0
  distribute-list 2 out Ethernet2
!
router igrp 1
  redistribute rip metric 10000 1000 255 1 1500
  passive-interface Ethernet2
  passive-interface Ethernet3
  network 172.16.0.0
!
access-list 2 deny 172.16.10.0
access-list 2 permit any
```

3. RTA's configuration is:

```
router rip
  redistribute igrp 1 metric 3
  passive-interface Ethernet0
  passive-interface Ethernet1
  network 172.16.0.0
  distribute-list 3 out igrp 1
!
router igrp 1
  redistribute rip metric 10000 1000 255 1 1500
  passive-interface Ethernet2
  passive-interface Ethernet3
  network 172.16.0.0
!
access-list 3 permit 172.16.2.0
access-list 3 permit 172.16.8.0
access-list 3 permit 172.16.9.0
```

4. RTA's configuration is:

```
router rip
  redistribute igrp 1 metric 3
  passive-interface Ethernet0
  passive-interface Ethernet1
  network 172.16.0.0
!
router igrp 1
  redistribute rip metric 10000 1000 255 1 1500
  passive-interface Ethernet2
  passive-interface Ethernet3
  network 172.16.0.0
distribute-list 4 out Ethernet0
!
access-list 4 permit 172.16.1.0
access-list 4 permit 172.16.2.0
access-list 4 permit 172.16.3.0
access-list 4 permit 172.16.7.0
access-list 4 permit 172.16.8.0
access-list 4 permit 172.16.9.0
```

5. EIGRP assigns a higher distance (170) to external routes than to internal routes (90). If any destination within the EIGRP domain is advertised into EIGRP from IS-IS, it will be ignored unless the internal route to the destination fails. Therefore, the EIGRP distances do not have to be manipulated. The distance statements under the IS-IS configurations of RTC and RTD are:

RTC

```
distance 115
distance 170 192.168.10.254 0.0.0.0 1
!
access-list 1 permit any
```

RTD

```
distance 115
distance 170 192.168.10.249 0.0.0.0 1
distance 170 192.168.10.241 0.0.0.0 1
!
access-list 1 permit any
```

6. The **distance** statement under the IS-IS configuration of RTD is:

```
distance 115
distance 255 192.168.10.241 0.0.0.0 1
!
access-list 1 permit any
```

7. The **distance** statement under RTC's EIGRP configuration is:

```
distance eigrp 90 90
```

CHAPTER 14

1. RTA's configuration is:

```
interface Serial0
  ip address 172.16.14.6 255.255.255.252
  ip policy route-map Exercise1
!
interface Serial1
  ip address 172.16.14.10 255.255.255.252
  ip policy route-map Exercise1
!
access-list 1 permit 172.16.1.0 0.0.0.127
access-list 2 permit 172.16.1.128 0.0.0.127
!
route-map Exercise1 permit 10
  match ip address 1
  set ip next-hop 172.16.14.17
!
route-map Exercise1 permit 20
  match ip address 2
  set ip next-hop 172.16.14.13
```

2. RTA's configuration is:

```
interface Serial0
  ip address 172.16.14.6 255.255.255.252
  ip policy route-map Exercise2A
!
interface Serial1
  ip address 172.16.14.10 255.255.255.252
  ip policy route-map Exercise2B
!
access-list 1 permit 172.16.1.0 0.0.0.127
!
route-map Exercise2A permit 10
```

```
    match ip address 1
    set ip next-hop 172.16.14.13
  !
route-map Exercise2B permit 10
  match ip address 1
  set ip next-hop 172.16.14.17
```

3. RTA's configuration is:

```
interface Serial2
  ip address 172.16.14.18 255.255.255.252
  ip access-group 101 in
  ip policy route-map Exercise3
!
interface Serial3
  ip address 172.16.14.14 255.255.255.252
  ip access-group 101 in
  ip policy route-map Exercise3
!
access-list 101 permit udp any 172.168.1.0 0.0.0.255
access-list 101 permit tcp any eq smtp 172.16.1.0 0.0.0.255
access-list 102 permit tcp any eq smtp 172.16.1.0 0.0.0.255
access-list 103 permit udp any 172.168.1.0 0.0.0.255
!
route-map Exercise3 permit 10
  match ip address 102
  set ip next-hop 172.16.14.9
!
route-map Exercise3 permit 20
  match ip address 103
  set ip next-hop 172.16.14.5
```

4. The OSPF configuration is:

```
router ospf 1
  redistribute eigrp 1 route-map Exercise4
  network 192.168.1.0 0.0.0.255 area 16
!
access-list 1 deny 10.201.100.0
access-list 1 permit any
!
route-map Exercise4 permit 10
  match ip address 1
!
route-map Exercise4 permit 20
  match route-type internal
  set metric 10
  set metric-type type-1
!
route-map Exercise4 permit 30
  match route-type external
  set metric 50
  set metric-type type-2
```

5. The EIGRP configuration is:

```
router eigrp 1
  redistribute ospf 1 route-map Exercise5
  network 192.168.100.0
!
access-list 1 permit 192.168.1.0
access-list 1 permit 192.168.2.0
access-list 1 permit 192.168.3.0
!
route-map Exercise5 permit 10
  match ip address 1
!
route-map Exercise5 permit 20
  match route-type internal
  set metric 10000 100 255 1 1500
!
route-map Exercise5 permit 30
  match route-type external
  set metric 10000 10000 255 1 1500
```

Solutions to Troubleshooting Exercises

CHAPTER 2

1. Subnet: 10.14.64.0

Host Addresses: 10.14.64.1 - 10.14.95.254

Broadcast: 10.14.95.255

Subnet: 172.25.0.224

Host Addresses: 172.25.0.225 - 175.25.0.254

Broadcast: 172.25.0.255

Subnet: 172.25.16.0

Host Addresses: 172.25.16.1 - 172.25.16.126

Broadcast: 172.25.16.127

2. 192.168.13.175/28 is the broadcast address of subnet 192.168.13.160/28.

CHAPTER 3

1. Subnet 192.168.1.64/27 will no longer be reachable from Piglet. The subnets of 10.0.0.0 will still be reachable.
2. Mistakes occur in the following:
   ◦ RTA, the second entry

   ◦ RTB, the third entry

   ◦ RTC, the second entry

   ◦ RTC, the fifth entry
3. The mistakes are:
   ◦ RTC: The route to 10.5.8.0/24 points to the wrong next-hop address.

   ◦ RTC: The route to 10.1.1.0/24 should be 10.5.1.0/24.

   ◦ RTC: There is no route to 10.5.4.0/24.

   ◦ RTD: The route to 10.4.5.0/24 should be 10.5.4.0/24.

CHAPTER 5

1. The new access list causes two hops to be added to every route except 10.33.32.0.
2. RTB interprets all subnets of 172.16.0.0 according to its misconfigured masks. The consequences, as exhibited in each of the four entries in its route table, are
   ◦ Entry 1: This entry is correct because 172.16.24.0 can be masked with either 22 bits or 23 bits.

- Entry 2: Subnet 172.16.26.0 is advertised by RTC. Because the 23rd bit of this address is one and RTB is using a 22-bit mask, from RTB's perspective this one appears in the host address space. Therefore, RTB interprets the advertisement of 172.16.26.0 as a host route and marks it with a 32-bit mask in the route table.

- Entry 3: RTB interprets its interface address 172.16.22.5 as being a member of subnet 172.16.20.0/22, instead of 172.16.22.0/23. When RTB receives RTA's advertisement of subnet 172.16.20.0/23, RTB, thinking it has a directly connected link to that subnet, ignores the advertisement. Notice that subnet 172.16.22.0 is not in the route tables of RTA and RTC for the same reason: RTB is advertising it as 172.16.20.0.

- Entry 4: RTB interprets its interface address 172.16.18.4 as being a member of subnet 172.16.16.0/22 instead of 172.16.18.0/23.

3. The answer is in RTC's route table in Figure 5.24. Notice that the route to 172.16.26.0/23 has not been updated in 2 minutes, 42 seconds. RTC's invalid timer is expiring before it hears a new update from RTD, and it is declaring the route to 172.16.26.0/23 invalid. Because no routes from RTA or RTB are being invalidated, the problem is with RTD's update timer—the update period is too long. When RTD finally sends an update, it is re-entered in RTC's route table and remains until RTC's invalid timer again expires.

CHAPTER 6

1. RTB is receiving route updates for 192.168.3.0/24 from RTD, but is not including the subnet in its updates to RTA. Something is allowing the reception of this route at RTB, but is not allowing advertisement of the route. A misconfigured route filter, perhaps?

2. The answer is in Figure 6.40. RTC has been configured with **router igrp 51,** instead of with **router igrp 15.**

CHAPTER 7

1. RTA and RTB send and receive only RIPv2 messages. RTC receives both RIPv1 and RIPv2 but sends only RIPv1. Consequently, RTA and RTB do not have subnet 192.168.13.75/27 in their route tables. Although it receives the updates from RTA and RTB, RTC does not have subnets 192.168.13.90/28 and 192.168.13.86/29 in its route table because it interprets both of them as 192.168.13.64/27, which is directly connected to RTC's E0 interface.

2. Yes. Subnet 192.168.13.64/27 will be added to the route tables of RTA and RTB because they can now receive RIPv1 updates from RTC.

CHAPTER 8

1. The autonomous system numbers of the EIGRP and IGRP processes are not the same.

2. RTG is RTF's successor to subnet A.

3. RTC's feasible distance to subnet A is 309760.

4. RTG's feasible distance to subnet A is 2237184.

5. RTG's topology table shows RTD and RTE as feasible successors to subnet A.

6. RTA's feasible distance to subnet B is 2198016.

CHAPTER 9

1. Either the IP address or the mask is misconfigured on one of the neighboring interfaces.

2. One router is configured as a stub area router, and the other is not.

3. The receiving router is configured for MD5 (type 2) authentication, and the neighbor has no authentication configured (type 0).

4. The passwords configured on the two routers do not match.

5. The neighboring interfaces are not configured with the same area ID.

6. RTA's network statements are in the wrong order. The first statement matches IP address 192.168.50.242 and puts it in area 192.168.50.0.

7. Link ID 10.8.5.1 is the most likely suspect because its sequence number is substantially higher than the sequence numbers of the other links.

CHAPTER 10

1. Although IS-IS has formed an adjacency, the IP addresses are not on the same subnet and therefore the interfaces do not pass traffic.

2. The router sends only L1 Hellos, indicating that it is an L1 router. It receives only L2 Hellos from 0000.3090.c7df, indicating that it is an L2 router.

CHAPTER 11

1. Split horizon will prevent 192.168.10.0/24 from being advertised into the RIP domain from the IGRP domain.

2. No, because not all subnets of 10.0.0.0 are directly connected to Mantle on the RIP side.

3. The **network** statement under Robinson's EIGRP 1 configuration matches interface 192.168.3.32, even though no EIGRP Hellos are being forwarded out that interface. Therefore, the subnet is advertised as internal within the EIGRP 1 domain.

4. EIGRP automatically entered this summary route because subnets of 192.168.3.0 are being redistributed into EIGRP from OSPF.

5. 192.168.1.0/24 is in the OSPF domain, and OSPF is not being redistributed into EIGRP 2. Unlike OSPF, EIGRP uses split horizon. Therefore, although 192.168.1.0/24 is being advertised into EIGRP 1, it will not be redistributed from EIGRP 1 to EIGRP 2 through Robinson.

CHAPTER 13

1. The inverse mask of the first line of the access list is wrong. With this mask, all routes are matched. The line should be **access-list 1 deny 0.0.0.0 0.0.0.0**.

2. All routes not matched by the access lists are given a distance of 255 (unreachable). If a preferred route fails, Grimwig will not use an alternative path.

3. OSPF calculates its routes from the information learned from LSAs. The route filter has no effect on LSAs, and so the filter affects only the router on which it is configured.

4. The two route filters refer to the wrong interfaces. **distribute-list 1** should refer to E1, and **distribute-list 2** should refer to E0.

CHAPTER 14

1. Both errors are errors of sequence. First, the *telnet* keyword in access list 101 is associated with the destination port; the correct association is with the source port. Second, the route map statements are in the wrong order. Telnet packets from 192.168.10.5 match the first statement and are forwarded to 192.168.16.254.

Index